CHRISTIANITY AND
CLASSICAL CULTURE

CHRISTIANITY
AND
CLASSICAL CULTURE

A STUDY OF
THOUGHT AND ACTION FROM
AUGUSTUS TO AUGUSTINE

BY

CHARLES NORRIS COCHRANE

OXFORD UNIVERSITY PRESS
LONDON   OXFORD   NEW YORK

OXFORD UNIVERSITY PRESS

London   Oxford   New York
Glasgow   Toronto   Melbourne   Wellington
Cape Town   Ibadan   Nairobi   Dar es Salaam   Lusaka   Addis Ababa
Delhi   Bombay   Calcutta   Madras   Karachi   Lahore   Dacca
Kuala Lumpur   Singapore   Hong Kong   Tokyo

First published by the Clarendon Press, 1940
Reprinted, with the text revised and corrected, 1944
First issued as an Oxford University Press paperback, 1957

This reprint, 1974
Printed in the United States of America

PREFACE

THE theme of this work is the revolution in thought and action which came about through the impact of Christianity upon the Graeco-Roman world. This is a subject of profound importance, but it has not received the attention it deserves, especially perhaps from English-speaking scholars. The reason for this lies partly in the rather special character of the problems involved, partly, however, in the acceptance of a distinction between areas of investigation, which to my mind at least is wholly arbitrary and in no way warranted by the actual course of events. The result is that classical and Christian studies have become dissociated with consequences which are, perhaps, unfortunate for both.

In this work I have ventured to defy the accepted convention and to attempt a transition from the world of Augustus and Vergil to that of Theodosius and Augustine. I am fully aware of my temerity in embarking on such an enterprise. But I have been impelled to undertake it both because of its intrinsic interest and because of the light it throws on subsequent developments of European culture. And I have been emboldened to do so from a sense that, however difficult the religious and philosophic issues to be encountered, they cannot be neglected by the historian except at the cost of missing what is central to the events of the age.

In a subject so vast and intricate it has been necessary to make a somewhat rigid delimitation of the field. I have, therefore, taken as my starting-point the Augustan Empire, with its claim to 'eternity' as a final and definitive expression of classical order. This is not to suggest that the work of Augustus was in any deep sense novel. On the contrary, it was merely the culmination of an effort begun centuries before in Hellas, the effort to create a world which should be safe for civilization; and, from this standpoint, such originality as the emperor exhibited was merely one of method. In this sense, however, his settlement may well be accepted as the last and not least impressive undertaking of what we may venture to call 'creative politics'.

The history of Graeco-Roman Christianity resolves itself largely into a criticism of that undertaking and of the ideas upon which it rested; viz. that it was possible to attain a goal of permanent security, peace and freedom through political action, especially through submission to the 'virtue and fortune' of a political leader. This notion the Christians denounced with uniform vigour and consistency. To them the state, so far from being the supreme instrument of human emancipation and perfectibility, was a straight-jacket to be justified at best as 'a remedy for sin'. To think of it otherwise they considered the grossest of superstitions.

The Christians traced this superstition to the acceptance of a defective logic, the logic of classical 'naturalism', to which they ascribed the characteristic *vitia* of the classical world. In this connexion it is important to notice that their revolt was not from nature; it was from the picture of nature constructed by classical *scientia*, together with its implications for practical life. And what they demanded was a radical revision of first principles as the presupposition to an adequate cosmology and anthropology. The basis for such a revision they held to lie in the *logos* of Christ, conceived as a revelation, not of 'new' truth, but of truth which was as old as the hills and as everlasting. This they accepted as an answer to the promise of illumination and power extended to mankind and, thus, the basis for a new physics, a new ethic and, above all, a new logic, the logic of human progress. In Christ, therefore, they claimed to possess a principle of understanding superior to anything existing in the classical world. By this claim they were prepared to stand or fall.

It is none of my business as an historian to pronounce upon the ultimate validity of Christian claims as opposed to those of Classicism. My task is simply to record those claims as an essential part of the historical movement which I have attempted to describe. This I have done to the best of my ability by letting the protagonists on either side speak, so far as possible, for themselves. Still less appropriate would it be to hazard any application of issues debated in the first four centuries to the problems of our own distracted age. Nevertheless, to those who are looking for a solution to those problems, it may at least be suggested that the answer will not be found in any attempted revival of obsolete conceptions associated with the life of classical antiquity. This is not to disparage Graeco-Roman achievement, still less its close and attentive study. On the contrary, it is to see it in a perspective from which, I think, it gains immeasurably in value and significance. As the Christians (somewhat ungenerously) put it, the best approach to truth is through a study of error. And from this standpoint it cannot be denied that the great classics were one and all splendid sinners. Their work thus constitutes a 'possession for ever', if not quite in the sense they imagined, at any rate as an imperishable record of thought and aspiration in what must always be regarded as a chapter of unique importance in human experience.

The present work is one of interpretation. As such, it is based primarily on a study of the relevant material in ancient literature and citations from modern authors have been kept to a minimum. It is hardly possible to measure one's indebtedness to scholars whose labours have contributed to throw light on different aspects of the subject. I hope, however, that I have not failed to make a proper acknowledgement of my obligations in specific cases. In conclusion I wish to express my thanks to various members of my old university who have seen the MS. either in whole or part and whose criticisms have enabled me to avoid numerous errors both of style and content. I am particularly grateful for the help I have received from Professor R. G. Collingwood and Mr. R. Syme.

C. N. C.

OXFORD, *July* 1939.

CONTENTS

CHRISTIANITY AND
CLASSICAL CULTURE

PART I

RECONSTRUCTION

I

PAX AUGUSTA: THE RESTORED REPUBLIC

'MAY it be my privilege to establish the republic safe and sound on its foundations, gathering the fruit of my desire to be known as author of the ideal constitution, and taking with me to the grave the hope that the basis which I have laid will be permanent.'[1] In these words, which translate into the common language of human hope the formal professions of the *Monumentum Ancyranum*, the emperor Augustus is said to have expressed the ambition of his life and rested his claim to a place in history. It was his wish to be remembered as a second founder, the man who had restored and consolidated the republic, giving it a constitution adequate to its present and future needs. And so far were his ambitions fulfilled that his successors, one after the other, swore to administer their office *ex praescripto Augusti*, as they also assumed his name. Thus, if the younger Caesar fell short of greatness in the wider, he fully deserved it in the narrower sense. For he discovered what had eluded earlier statesmen, the formula by which the revolution was concluded and the empire launched upon the course it was to follow for at least two hundred years.

It is not surprising that the principate should have proved to be something of an enigma. Its creation was the personal achievement of a man whose signet-ring bore an image of the Sphinx and whose whole career involved, by his own admission, the deliberate assumption of a role. Originally an intrusion into the machinery of government, it was destined to be transformed, first into the naked military and bureaucratic absolutism of the pseudo-Antonines and later into the theocratic dynasticism of Diocletian and Constantine. It is not unnatural, therefore, to see these elements in the original system of Augustus. From this standpoint the 'destruction of citizenship as a meaningful concept' would coincide more or less definitely with the fall of

---

[1] Suetonius, *Aug.* 28: 'ita mihi salvam ac sospitem rem publicam sistere in sua sede liceat atque eius rei fructum percipere quem peto ut optimi status auctor dicar et moriens ut feram mecum spem, mansura in vestigio suo fundamenta rei publicae quae iecero.'

the republic, and thenceforth 'all that was new and significant in the political development of Rome' would be 'obscured by the process which reduced it to the form of those Oriental monarchies of which the world had already witnessed sufficient examples'.[1]

Such estimates are not confined to modern times. Already in the first century thoughtful men were divided regarding the true character of the principate, and discussion raged as to whether it should be accepted for what it professed to be or understood as a skilfully camouflaged scheme of personal domination.[2] Again, at the beginning of the third century, when the tide had set toward militarism and bureaucracy and a fresh Roman revolution was in the making, contemporary observers professed to find in the prerogatives of Augustus a precedent for those claimed by the Septimian house or, at least, they minimized the substantial differences between them;[3] just as the autocrats of the lower empire identified themselves in name with the Roman Caesars, although the real spiritual antecedents of Byzantinism lay in an indiscriminate mixture of Asiatic dynasticism and Hebraic divine right.

To maintain, however, that 'the aspects of Oriental absolutism, though veiled, were all present in the rule of Augustus' is to do something less than justice to his work. For this is to envisage it, not so much in terms of its actual character and purpose, as of the nemesis which was to overtake it two centuries later. Properly considered, the events which succeeded the fall of Commodus testify to the defeat, rather than to the fulfilment, of the Augustan hope, the failure of the idea to which, in the Pax Augusta, the emperor had laboured to give final and permanent expression. Evidence of that failure is everywhere apparent in the intellectual and moral phenomena of the age. In their apostasy from Augustan principles, men groped blindly for a new and commanding formula of life. The Pantheon was crowded to the point of suffocation by a host of extraneous deities. Powerful court circles listened with attention to the ravings of Asiatic theosophists. The vogue of astrology was such as to draw forth the condemnation of successive

---

[1] R. M. MacIver, *The Modern State*, p. 110.

[2] The arguments on either side are carefully marshalled by Tacitus (*Ann.* i. 9 and 10: 'multus hinc ipso de Augusto sermo', &c.).

[3] e.g. Dio Cassius, liii. 17, where he describes the principate as 'a pure monarchy'.

emperors, culminating in the fiery denunciation of Diocletian, 'the whole damnable art of the *mathematici* is forbidden' (*tota damnabilis ars mathematica interdicta est*). Short-lived war-lords, flung up sporadically on all frontiers, tried to evade their doom by drawing for support upon alien spiritual conceptions rooted in the life of the East. With oriental fanaticism, one prince, Heliogabalus, ventured to depose *Iuppiter Optimus Maximus* in favour of the Emesan Baal (*Sol Invictus Elagabal*). Another, Alexander Severus, with truly classical indifference, included Christ among the gods to be worshipped in his private chapel. Still another, Aurelian, sought to attract to himself something of the prestige of the revived Persian monarchy by assuming the diadem of the Invincible Sun. Diocletian and Maximian solemnly consecrated Mithra as chief tutelary deity of the empire, and represented themselves as his counterparts on earth. The crisis of the third century was thus a crisis of despair; disintegration resolved itself into chaos, and the bankruptcy of the Augustan system was finally exposed when the empire went into receivership at the hands of Constantine.

On the other hand, despite the perils and uncertainties to which it gave rise, the crisis which issued in the principate may be regarded as, on the whole, a crisis of adjustment, during which men never quite lost faith in the possibility of conserving the essential elements of the classical heritage. This, indeed, was precisely the aim of Augustus; his work marks a herculean effort to solve the problems of his age in terms consistent with the thought and aspiration of classical antiquity. From this standpoint, his problem was to associate the notion of power with that of service and thus, at one and the same time, to justify the ascendancy of Rome in the Mediterranean and that of the Caesars in Rome. To see it in this light is not merely to credit the founder with a sincere desire to reconcile the new demands of empire with the ancient claims of civic freedom; it is also to discover the possibilities of Classicism as a basis for the good life in what has been characteristically described as the happiest and most prosperous period in the history of the human race.[1]

Thus envisaged, the principate emerges as the outcome of more than a century of civil commotion, the origin of which

[1] Gibbon, *The Decline and Fall of the Roman Empire*, ed. Bury (1896), ch. iii, p. 78.

may be traced remotely to the wars of overseas conquest. So long as the activities of the Romans had been confined to Italy they had preserved the character of a peasant society, in which the impulses towards individual self-assertion, powerful though they were, were none the less held in leash by the collective egotism of the civic ideal. But, with the overthrow of Carthage and the kingdoms of the hellenized East, it presently became evident that the spirit which had served to create the empire contained no ingredient by which it might guard against its own excess. Intoxicated by the wine of victory, the Romans proceeded to exploit their position as lords of the world, but with consequences hardly less disastrous to themselves than to their victims. For while the empire, hitherto a model of justice and beneficence, was thus converted into an instrument of intolerable oppression, the constitution of Roman society was itself radically transformed.[1] In that transformation we may perceive the genesis of divisive forces which were destined to shatter the foundations of public concord and lay the republic in ruins. Those forces found their supreme embodiment in Julius Caesar.

From this standpoint the career of Caesar presents itself as the climax of that fierce struggle between Left and Right which constitutes the ultimate phase of republican history; he was, in the words of his biographer, the doom of the *optimates*.[2] For this he was marked out, not less by temperament and inclination, than by an hereditary affiliation with the family of Marius. With other survivors of the Sullan terror, he had as a young man withdrawn from Rome during the dictatorship. But, from the moment of his return to the city in 78 B.C., he set himself to revive and direct the forces of democracy. Thus, while holding aloof from premature and ill-considered ventures like that of the consul Lepidus, he lost no chance of advertising himself as the hope of the *populares*.[3] He seized the occasion of his aunt's funeral to recall the public services of Marius.[4] He supported the movement which led in 70 B.C. to the restoration of tribunician power.[5] The descendants of those proscribed by Sulla had been for ever deprived of property and civil rights; Caesar boldly agitated for their restoration. In order to establish the illegality of the so-called ultimate decree or declaration of martial

[1] Sallust, *Cat.* 10. 6: 'civitas immutata; imperium ex iustissimo atque optimo crudele intolerandumque factum.'
[2] Suet. *Jul.* 1.   [3] 3.   [4] 6.   [5] 5.

law by the senate, thereby vindicating the claim of the people to sole jurisdiction in capital cases, he instigated the prosecution of Rabirius, an obscure old man, who was supposed to have murdered the popular leader Saturninus in the disturbances of 100 B.C. At the same time he rendered himself notorious by the splendour of his life and, by the lavish distribution of personal favours, rapidly drew about him the elements of a Roman Tammany.[1] The success of his methods was conspicuously demonstrated in 64 B.C. when he was elected Pontifex Maximus in the face of powerful aristocratic opposition. This triumph was followed two years later by a praetorship with its concomitant, a military command in Spain;[2] to be succeeded in due course by the consulship, as the wits called it, of 'Julius and Caesar'.[3] In the historic debate of December 63 B.C. on the punishment of the Catilinarians, Caesar, as praetor-elect, had ventured to defend the conspirators before the senate and to urge upon that body a mitigation of the death-sentence which had been proposed against them. It was on this occasion that, according to Plutarch, the aristocracy 'missed the chance of exterminating the viper in its bosom'. The consequences of their failure were soon to be apparent. As consul in 59 B.C. Caesar, with a defiance of constitutional convention unprecedented in republican annals, forced through a programme of advanced social and economic legislation while, at the same time, he consummated his plans for the *societas potentiae*, the coalition with Crassus and Pompey, which was to yield him his 'extraordinary' command in Gaul, with its opportunities for profit and distinction.[4]

The next stage of Caesar's career embraced the conquest and annexation of the Gauls, the crossing of the Rhine, and the invasion of Britain. As proconsul, he startled the world by the tireless energy with which he planned and executed his military movements, as well as by the methods he adopted to develop the efficiency of his troops and to secure their devotion to himself.[5] The solid work of fighting and organization was accompanied by propaganda, in which Caesar represented himself as the man who had for ever disposed of the Gallic peril; together with preparations for a future, the nature of which could only be surmised. For, beginning with his second *quinquennium*, he

---

[1] Sall. *Cat.* 54.   [2] Suet. *Jul.* 18.   [3] Ibid. 19–20.
[4] Sall. *Cat.* 54. 4.   [5] Suet. *Jul.*, chs. 65–70.

embarked upon a wholesale corruption of the Roman world, the capital city, the Italian municipalities, and the more important allied states, not to speak of the client kingdoms beyond the frontiers.[1]

It is, perhaps, unnecessary to credit Caesar with any clear prevision of the enormous significance of his territorial acquisitions, any more than with the deliberate planning of the civil war. The ordinary practice of the day suggests that his object was merely to accumulate a fund of economic and political power sufficient to counterbalance that of Pompey. Nevertheless, his means became ends in themselves, the establishment of a firm bulwark on the Rhine against the restless tide of barbarism and, within the enlarged frontiers, the creation of a new Italy through the settlement of impoverished Italians on the undeveloped lands of Gaul and their fusion with the native Celts, in whom he saw potential material for a vast civilization of the Graeco-Roman type. But such ideas were in themselves enough to excite, in the hearts of his opponents, the utmost terror and apprehension. Accordingly, during the later and more critical years of fighting in Gaul, these men manœuvred persistently to destroy him, by setting up obstacles which would interfere with his election to a second consulship and by attempting to bring him to book for the irregularities of which he had been guilty since his first. The failure of their efforts provoked the senatorial stampede of 1 January 49 B.C., when the oligarchical diehards, supported by Pompey's legionaries, compelled a timid and reluctant majority to declare Caesar a public enemy, thereby precipitating the civil war.

Caesar was not slow to accept the challenge, which gave him the twofold opportunity of asserting his own political claims and of vindicating the majesty of the people, infringed in the persons of the tribunes who had vainly endeavoured to sustain them in the senate. In so doing, he treated the governing aristocracy merely as a 'faction', in no wise competent to speak for the sovereign people as a whole. Yet he entered upon armed conflict with reluctance; for he saw, as his adversaries failed to see, the consequence of intestinal strife, and especially the implications of an imposed rather than a negotiated settlement. Throughout the struggle he aimed consistently to prove that he was no Sulla, by maintaining a policy of studied moderation

[1] Suet. *Jul.* 26 foll.

(*clementia*) in the face of savage atrocities perpetrated by the senatorials and their barbarian allies. At the same time, he shook himself free from the more disreputable of his own followers; passing the famous bankruptcy law by which he sought to mediate between the claims of debtor and creditor in a fashion altogether new and refreshing in Roman history.

The victory of Caesar in the civil war made possible the fulfilment of his programme as a statesman. It is an exaggeration to describe that programme[1] as one of regeneration for his deeply decayed country. What Julius accomplished was rather a task of social and political reconstruction, and this was inspired by ideas, all of which fell within the ambit of Graeco–Roman thinking, which hardly contemplated, even in a metaphorical sense, the notion of rebirth. Thus, with regard to domestic problems, Caesar executed the testament of the great reformers from Gracchan times; just as, in the conquest of Gaul, he had fulfilled the dream of Marius and the new democratic imperialism. And, therein, he revealed himself as one of the greatest exponents of scientific statecraft in the history of antiquity. This was shown by measures which ranged all the way from a reform of the calendar to the reorganization of Italy on municipal lines and the extension of municipal rights to the Western provinces, especially Spain.[2]

There existed, however, insuperable barriers to the possibility of reform which were, as Caesar himself realized, the inevitable consequence of an imposed peace. It is unnecessary to dwell upon the circumstances which ultimately drove him towards complete military autocracy in the form of a perpetual dictatorship. These were not less the untrustworthy character of his own supporters than the behaviour of the conquered aristocracy, which oscillated from stubborn intransigency to disgusting subservience. Caesar laboured assiduously to dispel the impression that the basis of his régime was force and fear. Yet, despite all efforts to conciliate his opponents, he failed to obtain the co-operation needful to support his 'new concord'. Moreover, his own liberalism had inescapable limits: the cynics recalled the profession of loyalty to popular principles with which he had embarked upon the war, when he brushed aside the interference of the tribune Metellus in 49 B.C. and, still more, when

---

[1] With Mommsen, *History of Rome* (1894), vol. v, ch. xi, p. 308.
[2] Hardy, *Roman Laws and Charters* (*Lex Iulia Municipalis*).

he unceremoniously deposed Flavius and Marullus five years later. Finally, Caesar was acutely conscious of the difficulty in which he was placed by his assumption of personal control over the administration. 'How can I fail to be disliked', he observed, 'when men like Cicero must await my convenience for an interview?'

Such were the fruits of a conflict, the issues of which were presently to excite a storm of bitter controversy. The suicide of Cato at Utica had served, as nothing else could have done, to ennoble the cause for which he had perished; and, already during Caesar's lifetime, opposition to the dictatorship was to discover a focus in the memory of his traditional rival and anti-type.[1] In an effort to neutralize the force of this opposition, Caesar for once abandoned his professional clemency, and pursued Cato in the grave with a vehemence such as he had never exhibited towards him while he lived. But, as the opposition nevertheless continued to stiffen, he was finally compelled to resign all hope of conciliation or compromise. It was then that he determined upon the final subversion of republicanism, the structure of which had been crumbling with progressive rapidity since the outbreak of the civil war. 'The republic', he said, 'is merely a name, without form or substance.'[2] And, as though to signalize his contempt for republican institutions, he appointed Caninius consul for the last day of the year 45. 'He was', observes Cicero, 'a most vigilant magistrate, for during his term of office he never slept.' Then, too, he accepted what were felt to be 'excessive' honours; breaking 'all laws, human and divine', and scaling the heights of Olympus in a manner which represented a complete departure even from his own earlier pretensions, when he had merely sought for himself a place beside the ancient Roman kings. It might indeed be urged that, since those kings were the legitimate heads of a free people and the natural protectors of the commons, the *regium imperium* could properly be cited as a precedent for that which was to be claimed by Caesar. But no such argument was possible on behalf of a man who evidently aspired to associate himself with glories traditional to the line of Alexander. What Caesar at one time thought of Alexandrianism may be judged from his own scathing comments on the situation which he found to prevail in the

---

[1] The formal antithesis between the two is established in Sall. *Cat.* 54. For the rapid growth of the Catonian myth see Cic. *Ad Attic.* xii. 4. 2 and 21. 4.   [2] Suet. *Jul.* 77.

capital when he first invaded Egypt.[1] Yet the evidence leaves no doubt that in his last months he definitely embraced the scheme of Alexandrian monarchy, thus renouncing the visions and ideals of the classical commonwealth and plunging into the most degraded form of contemporary political obscurantism in the vain endeavour to find a basis for his régime. It was, indeed, beyond the capacity of Caesar, master of *Realpolitik* as he was, to discover the formula of transition between the old world and the new. And this he himself appears to have confessed when he remarked that 'by satisfying the claims of honour and glory' he had 'lived long enough'.[2]

In this significant pronouncement, we may perhaps see Caesar as he saw himself and as he appeared to the eyes of his contemporaries. Modern historical scholarship has discerned in him at once the greatest political architect and the greatest political destroyer of antiquity.[3] To antiquity itself he was both or neither; he was *par excellence* the gambler with fortune, and the stake for which he played was nothing less than mastery of the world. It was, on the other hand, equally evident that the destinies of the world were largely bound up with those of Caesar. Thus a contemporary publicist, in the second of two letters addressed to the dictator, hails him as the sole bulwark against perils which threaten the whole future of European civilization. 'Should this empire perish', he declares, 'either from disease or by fate, who can doubt that the result will be world-wide devastation, bloodshed, and strife?'[4] Such was the prevailing mood during Caesar's lifetime; and to it even Cicero appears to have subscribed at the moment when he wrote the *Pro Marcello*. 'Who', asks the orator, apostrophizing the dictator, 'who is so blind as not to realize that his personal safety is involved with yours; that on the life of Caesar depend the lives of his fellow countrymen. It falls to you alone to restore all that warfare has overthrown and destroyed, to re-establish the administration of justice, to recall confidence, to repress licence, to promote the growth of population, in short to bind together by strong legislation all that you see scattered and dispersed. The task of the day is to heal the wounds of conflict and no one but you can do it.'[5]

---

[1] *Bell. Civ.* iii *ad fin.*, esp. 110.   [2] Cic. *Pro Marc.* 8. 25.

[3] Mommsen, op. cit., vol. v, chs. x and xi; Ferrero, *The Greatness and Decline of Rome* (1909), vol. ii, ch. xvi, pp. 344-8.

[4] The pseudo-Sallust, Ep. ii ad Caes. *De ordinanda re publica*, widely accepted as a genuine work of the historian, composed in Africa during the summer of 46.   [5] §§22-3.

But for those like Suetonius and Plutarch, to whom the end
was a matter of record, the picture is somewhat differently
coloured; both observe, especially in Caesar's closing years,
evidences of *adrogantia* or ὕβρις which, by exciting divine displeasure, portends ultimate catastrophe. To Suetonius, as a
sceptic, the death of Caesar could mean nothing but extinction.
Nevertheless, he fails to escape from the impression created in
the public mind by that world-shaking event. Accordingly, he
notes, coincident with the death of the dictator, the appearance
of a new comet in the heavens, the *sidus Iulii* which, in Chal-
daean lore, marked his reception into heaven. 'Thus', he
concludes, 'Caesar was translated to the number of the gods,
not merely by the lips of those who so decreed, but also by
popular conviction.'[1] To the meteoric career of Caesar,
Plutarch finds an appropriate analogue in that of Alexander;
and for him it illustrates at once the glory and the nemesis of
power. 'That empire and ascendancy', he says, 'which Caesar,
had pursued with so much hazard throughout his career, he did
at last with much difficulty attain, only to reap from it nothing
but an empty name and invidious glory. But the great genius
which attended him in life remained after his death to avenge
his murder, pursuing through every sea and land all those who
were concerned therein, and permitting none to escape, but
overtaking all who were in any way either privy to the deed or
by their counsels in any way accessory to it.'[2]

In the light of these ancient concepts, Caesar emerges as a
figure at once fascinating and dangerous. For the spirit thus
depicted is one of sublime egotism; in which the *libido dominandi*
asserts itself to the exclusion of all possible alternatives and
crushes every obstacle in its path. We have spoken of Caesar
as a divisive force. That, indeed, he was: as Cato had put it,
'he was the only one of the revolutionaries to undertake, cold-
sober, the subversion of the republic'; finding support for his
designs with equal readiness among the rabble of the forum, in
uncivilized Gaul or in effete and decadent Egypt, and even
exploiting to his purpose the fierce religious nationalism of the
Jews. A force like this, however, does more than divide, it
destroys. Hostile to all claims of independence except its own,

---

[1] Suet. *Jul.* 88. Cf. Pliny, *N.H.* ii. 25. 94, who adds that for this reason a star was
placed on the head of the statue presently to be erected in the Forum. The date of
this consecration was 18 Aug., 29 B.C.   [2] Plut. *Caes.* 69.

it is wholly incompatible with that effective equality which is implied in the classical idea of the commonwealth. To admit it within the community is thus to nourish the lion, whose reply to the hares in the assembly of beasts was to ask: Where are your claws? The problem had long since appeared as one of the most baffling which confronted classical political science.[1] With Caesar, it finally emerged in Rome.

Thus envisaged, the career of the dictator presented itself rather as a warning than a model; and if it be true that his final solution was to 'sell out' in favour of Hellenistic autocracy, it is not surprising that he was in the end repudiated by many, even of his own former adherents. Loathed by the older republicans, such as Cicero, for having had the temerity to parade himself as a god, his name was associated, even in the minds of later Caesarians, with that of his great rival Pompey, as one who 'had hardened his heart to internecine strife and turned against its own vitals the might of the Fatherland'.[2] Accordingly, the deed of the 'liberators', puerile though it may have been in design and execution, was not wholly in vain. Despite the revulsion of popular feeling occasioned by Caesar's funeral, despite the spontaneous apotheosis of the dead leader, the assassination served to postpone the immediate orientalization of the empire. And, by demonstrating, however perversely, the tenacity of the native civic tradition, it helped to determine the settlement which was ultimately to be effected by Augustus.

In his last few months the dictator is said to have remarked that nothing but his life stood between the empire and chaos. And certainly the existence of Rome, with all that she meant to the world, never hung by a more tenuous thread than during the years of turmoil which succeeded the fatal Ides of March. The question might thus be asked: If Caesar, for all his talent and insight, had proved incapable of solving the Roman problem, who could now be expected to do so? The crisis was accentuated by the hopeless incapacity of the Regicides to control the situation created by their own act, and they soon discovered to their dismay the impossibility of appealing at once to the head and to the belly. Their failure was presently exposed by Marc Antony, whose subsequent career was, in fact, to constitute the most emphatic criticism of their deed. The latter, as sole surviving consul, brazenly abused his position in

[1] Arist. *Pol.* iii. 1284ª.   [2] Verg. *Aeneid*, vi. 832-3.

order to erect for himself a domination of the Caesarian type. Nor can there be much doubt that his schemes would have succeeded had it not been for the intervention of the young Octavian who, for the purpose of making good his claims as Caesar's heir, associated himself with the senate in its contest with Caesar's ape. Mutual suspicion and fear were soon to destroy this alliance, the incongruity of which became evident when, after Antony's reverse in Cisalpine Gaul, the senatorials endeavoured to break the sword of their self-appointed champion, as a preliminary to reversing the revolutionary measures of Caesar and re-establishing the domination of the oligarchy which for more than a century had lacerated the Roman world.

The result was a speedy recrudescence of Caesarism throughout the West. Octavian, betraying his betrayers, extended the olive branch to Antony, and on his part the humbled Antony revealed a willingness to effect a *rapprochement* with his hitherto despised opponent. One after another, provincial governors proclaimed the adhesion of their troops to the revived Caesarian cause, thus stripping the senate of all power of resistance, and it proved impossible for Cicero to enlist support for what was generally felt to be an empty and barren ideal. Finally, the conference of Bononia delivered the republic into the clutches of the three-headed monster (the triumvirate of Antony, Lepidus, and Octavian) which was destined to vindicate the name and fame of the dictator, to crush the remaining forces of the senate, and to end by destroying itself. Thus the events which succeeded the Ides of March demonstrated the truth of Cicero's lament that to kill the monarch was not to kill the monarchy.

This was but to confirm the verdict of Thapsus and Utica. Stoic idealism was, indeed, in later times to herald Cato as last of all the Romans. And Seneca, developing the Ciceronian thesis, *ab utroque dominatio quaesita*, was to declare: on the one side Pompey, on the other Caesar; between them Cato and the republic. It may well be admitted that the moral leadership of the so-called constitutional party belonged rather to Cato than to Pompey; for when, after his reverse at Pharsalus, the Roman Agamemnon, rather than face the accusing eyes of his partisans, slunk away to perish miserably on the sands of Egypt, Cato rallied the senatorial forces in a last desperate effort to ward off the menace of despotism. And, while it has been urged that a true leader has no business at the head of a forlorn hope, we should nevertheless remember that causes are sometimes more effectively advocated by the dead than by the living. Certainly, in the spasmodic outbreaks of terrorism which marred the régime of the Caesars, the victims of imperial despotism were to find in the martyrdom of Utica a precious example of inflexible pride and endurance; and, in this sense at least, the spirit of Cato was to find a place in the life of the future. Yet it remains true that Cato was strangely aloof from the realities of his age. As Cicero put it: he spoke as though he lived in *Platonopolis* rather than in this cesspool of Romulus. Native obstinacy, reinforced by the dogmas of Stoic excellence, might thus teach Cato how to die, but it could provide him with no real remedy for the social and political maladies of his time. The true issue, indeed, was not as between 'liberty' and 'monarchy', but rather the form which monarchy should assume.

Such was the problem as it had already presented itself to Cicero when he wrote the *De Re Publica* five years prior to the outbreak of civil war. As such, it emerged once more amidst the strife of factions which was renewed with increasing violence after Caesar's murder. The issue was for some time confused by the pretensions of rival leaders. Of the professed champions of republicanism, not even Brutus appears to have been wholly sincere; while, on the other hand, each of the representative exponents of the Caesarian tradition claimed in a sense to stand for a restoration of the republic. The situation, in some degree clarified as a result of Philippi, was further defined by the course of events within the period of the triumvirate, which left Antony and Octavian confronting each other and imposed upon contemporary opinion the necessity of judging between their respective claims.

There is nothing in the career of Antony to suggest that he possessed the faintest comprehension of or sympathy with the fading ideals of Roman republicanism. The evidence, such as it is, points to the fact that he was a typical child of the revolution, consumed with a lust for power endemic in his generation, but devoid of the qualities of mind and heart which might have made him in any real sense the spiritual heir of Julius, and capable only of burlesquing his ideas. As consul, he displayed himself as the typical demagogue, seeking to base his domination upon the proletariat and the army. He endeavoured to seduce the masses by advocating a right of popular appeal from the decisions of standing courts in cases of treason—a measure deprecated by Cicero as 'not so much law as the subversion of all law'—and he strove to capture the allegiance of the troops by proposing that a panel of centurions should be added to the juries, thus giving the army as such a significant place in the administration of justice. As triumvir, he rapidly moved to a position which constituted a flagrant outrage to Roman sentiment. Foremost in exacting a barbarous revenge from his enemies during the proscriptions, he probably fomented the abortive rebellion of his brother and wife at Perusia, the ostensible purpose of which was to 'restore the republic', though its real object was without doubt to embarrass his colleague in his effort to re-establish discharged veterans in civil life. He disgraced the arms of Rome in the East by his shameful defeat at the hands of Parthia, as well as by his treacherous capture of the Armenian king. His ultimate aims, however, became apparent only when, in order to distract attention from his anomalous position as Antonius-Dionysus, the Hellenistic 'divine-man', the bigamous consort of the Egyptian Cleopatra, he sought to lay the odium of tyranny upon Octavian by representing him to the public as the sole obstacle to a restoration of the constitution. Thus the man who, at the *Lupercalia* of 44 B.C. had offered a crown to Caesar, revealed his anxiety ten years later to procure one for himself.

On the other hand, the early career of Octavian was, to say the least, highly ambiguous, and criticism never succeeded in resolving anomalies which the future emperor himself was hardly able to conceal. Ambition was doubtless in the blood of the younger Caesar, as it was part of his inheritance; short of stultifying himself, there was no way of evading his destiny. Yet it is evident that, while he was thus drawn into the savage competition for place and power, seeking by devious and disreputable methods to vindicate his own claims and his father's memory, he was at the same time acquiring discretion in the harshest of all schools. While, therefore, Antony finally revealed himself as a renegade from native principles, Octavian gradually discovered his role as protagonist and defender of the Latin spirit, finding in this also the secret of his future ascendancy.

To suppose that the issue was deliberately manufactured is to forget the perils to which the less sophisticated European peoples had always felt themselves exposed through contact with the wealthy and powerful East. The Romans were familiar with the literature of Hellas and they could accept the interpretation which it had put upon the 'great deliverance' of Salamis. They could appreciate also the lesson of Alexander's conquests which, though nominally a triumph for Hellenism, involved in fact a fatal dilution of the Hellenic spirit.[1] Finally, they were conscious of the dangers to which their own Eastern conquests had given rise; for, if as yet the supremacy of Juppiter was not seriously threatened, nevertheless the Nile and the Orontes were already discharging their flood into the Tiber, and its waters were polluted.[2]

It is gratuitous to assume that Octavian himself was unaffected by the climate of contemporary opinion. But the question is not entirely one of his sincerity. He had mobilized his forces against Antony and Cleopatra by representing himself as champion of Latin civilization against a decadent and demoralized East. The shield of Aeneas[3] depicts the conflict of Actium as he wished his countrymen to see it: the assault of Antony, the shameless Egyptian woman by his side, his galleys crowded by a motley throng of barbarians levied from the conquered tribes of Asia and the Red Sea coast; opposed by Caesar, who marshalled the fathers and people, the armed might of Italy in defence of the fatherland. The issue was typified in the competing gods, the Latin deities of household and state pitted against the foul and obscene creatures of the perfervid Oriental imagination. While, therefore, yelping Anubis and the multitudinous and monstrous gods of Egypt, levelled their arms against Caesar, his triumph was assured by the help of Neptune, Venus, and Minerva, together with the patronage of Actian Apollo. In this sense Actium was felt to be of critical importance; in fact, the Roman Salamis, a victory for the classical idea of the commonwealth over the subversive forces of Orientalism. As such, it helped to fix the character of the Augustan settlement with its far-reaching consequences for Italy and the West. For,

[1] See below, Ch. III, pp. 89–90.
[2] The notion of an inevitable opposition between East and West had been a commonplace of popular Greek thinking, at least from the time of Herodotus. See Ch. XII, below, p. 460. It is, of course, nonsense since the entities in question are purely factitious. To accept it is, thus, 'to hypostasize the points of the compass' into historical forces. [3] Verg. *Aeneid*, viii. 675 foll.

by thus capitalizing the Latin political idea, Augustus had demonstrated its continuing vitality. Accordingly, by the very conditions of his victory, he was bound if possible to satisfy the expectations of those whose co-operation had made it possible. In other words, he was committed to a restoration of the Roman peace on fundamentally Roman lines. To this task he devoted the rest of his long and brilliant career.

Within the limitations thereby imposed upon him, there can be no doubt that the efforts of Augustus were successful. Thus Velleius, writing a generation after the inauguration of the new régime, but before the spell had been broken, records the impression made on the popular mind by the *Pax Augusta* in terms which fully admit the claims made by the emperor for himself:[1]

'There is nothing that man can desire from the gods, nothing that the gods can grant to man, nothing that wish can conceive or good fortune bring to pass, which Augustus, on his return to the city, did not bestow upon the commonwealth, the Roman people and the world. The civil wars ended . . . foreign wars suppressed, peace re-established, the frenzy of conflict everywhere lulled to rest, validity was restored to the law, authority to the courts, prestige to the senate; the power of the magistrates was reduced to its former limits, except that two were added to the eight existing praetors. The traditional form of the republic was revived. Agriculture returned to the fields, respect to religion, to mankind security of possession, old laws were carefully amended, new legislation enacted for the general good: the senatorial panel was rigorously, if not drastically, revised. Distinguished men who had held office and won triumphs were at the solicitation of the emperor induced to adorn the city with their presence . . . the dictatorship, which the people persisted in offering him, he as persistently refused.'

One may smile at the exuberance of this rhapsody on the part of a courtier, an officer of Tiberius Caesar who, like Tiberius himself, regarded the Augustan settlement as the last word in political wisdom. Velleius, indeed, writes like the retired colonel that he was. His observations must nevertheless be accepted as an authentic expression of the spirit of his time. They record the widespread sense of relief occasioned by the cessation of prolonged civil strife, and by the realization of security and well-being under the protection of a strong government. They are a reflection, in terms of the average limited intelligence, of

[1] Velleius, ii. 89.

sentiments which pervaded the literature and thought of the Augustan age.

These sentiments, so far from implying any subjection to alien ideals, register the apparent achievement of purposes inherent in the traditional idea of the commonwealth. They express, in fact, the almost universal belief in the final accomplishment of that new deal (*nova concordia*) towards which the aspirations of all but a few senatorial reactionaries had pointed ever since Gracchan times. Accordingly, they disclose Augustus as the ultimate heir and executor of the revolution whose gains he was now to consolidate. But this, in itself, does not exhaust the meaning of the Augustan settlement. For, in order to effect his purpose, Augustus alined himself with what was strongest in the conservative tradition which the elder Caesar had never understood. Moreover, he made heavy drafts on the Graeco-Roman social heritage which was common to Left and Right alike. In this sense, the *Pax Augusta* emerges as a final and definitive expression of the spirit of classical antiquity.

The character and aims of Roman radicalism, which gave rise to the tumultuous revolutionary activity of the first century B.C., may perhaps be illustrated by reference to the works of Sallust, the *Jugurtha*, the *Catiline*, and the fragmentary *Histories*, together with the two *Letters to Caesar* which, whether or not apocryphal, certainly embody stock ideas of the time. To judge from these works, the long period of senatorial ascendancy, dating from the wars of overseas conquest, constituted a usurpation which, notwithstanding the profit and glory it had brought to Rome, entailed the evils of monopoly. The genuine civic ideal, on the other hand, was enshrined in the forms of the primitive commonwealth, a society of peasants and soldiers from whose ranks were recruited the physical force (*vis*) necessary to protect the state, as well as the authority (*auctoritas*) and wisdom (*consilium*) by which it was directed and controlled. This society, by overcoming its economic problems (debt and land) through the conquest and federation of Italy, seemed to the author to have realized the fullest potentialities of the Roman order.

Accordingly, with Sallust, the Roman order is ultimately referred to a material principle. In this principle he discovered the secret both of its strength and of its weakness. For while it served to provide the impulse to overseas expansion, the process

of expansion sapped the foundations upon which it was thought
to rest. In other words, the acquisition of empire served to
introduce an era of unrestricted competition, transforming the
community of embattled farmers into a vast cosmopolitan
society in which a *bloc* of landed magnates and financiers confronted a submerged mass of proletarians, subjects, and slaves.
Thus, by the conquest of the world, the Romans had prepared
a virtual servitude for all but the few in whose hands lay the
means of exploitation, the control of economic and political
power.

To what extent the balance had been upset was revealed to
the new proletariat in the burning rhetoric of Gracchus: 'You
boast that you are Lords of the World, but you do not possess
a foot of land which you can call your own'. In the unforgettable
phrase already quoted,[1] Sallust records his sense of the evils
produced by this predatory imperialism at the same time as he
suggests its deeper implications. To him it not merely involves
a crime against the subject peoples; but, by undermining the
material basis of civic life, it overthrows the rights and liberties
of the commons. In so doing, it subverts the entire basis of the
Latin commonwealth.

In this context the revolution was conceived as a conservative
movement, a protest against the prostitution of a common good
(*res publica*) to the interests of a narrow and selfish plutocracy.
Hence its characteristic features; such, e.g., as the persistent
attempts made by reformers to break down senatorial control
over the executive and the judiciary as well as to restore the
material basis of freedom through a programme of land-
assignations in Italy and abroad, and to humble, if not to
destroy, the power of the speculator and money-lender. It was,
no doubt, as part of this scheme that the dole was introduced
and developed to the point where it became a scandal even to
revolutionaries. It could, however, be defended as a palliative,
which was at least less demoralizing than the bread-lines already
fashionable among great nobles as a means of exhibiting their
generosity and of acquiring political influence (*gratia*).

In such phenomena may be seen the blind but not wholly
ineffective revolt of the masses against tendencies which, as has
been suggested, involved the extinction of their civic personality.
These tendencies are clearly revealed in the speeches which

[1] p. 4, n. 1 above.

Sallust puts into the mouth of a Lepidus or a Catiline. They explain the utter inability of academic republicanism, such as that professed by a Cato or a Brutus, to cope with the situation. There was nothing in the armoury of their ideas by which they could appeal with conviction to men whose bellies were empty and whose spirits were soured by the glittering spectacle of aristocratic wealth and arrogance. They explain also the suspicion with which the masses received the advances of Cicero, whose liberalism hardly served to conceal his association with financial and political privilege and who, after the part he had played in suppressing the Catilinarians, was, by his own admission, the most unpopular individual in Rome.

For, as they implied a social rot of which Cicero, for all his generous ideas, was only dimly conscious, so also they required more drastic treatment than it was within the power of this self-styled saviour of society to provide. In other words, they called for a Caesar, as the only possible answer to an insistent demand for the subjection of power by power. But the spirit of Cicero was nevertheless seen in the terms and conditions by which that power was to be manifested in the Augustan principate.

The ascendancy of Augustus was signalized by the dramatic transfer of the republic from his own control to the authority of senate and people, and by the subsequent arrangements whereby, as prince, he accepted a delegated authority and a determinate commission. This undoubtedly involved an element of farce, the object of which was to conciliate the prejudices of an aristocracy to whom its rights and liberties were little less than a fetish. For, in thus paying his respects to the shades of Cato and Brutus, Augustus had no intention of putting back the hands of the clock, and this must have been evident to all but the purblind worshippers of an impossible past. Nevertheless, it is easy to underestimate the import of these arrangements, since to recognize the authority of the prince as derived was to assimilate it to the ancient *imperium legitimum*, thus stamping it as fundamentally magisterial in character. Such authority, coined so to speak in the mint of Roman law, differed *toto caelo* from the crude sovereignties which were the characteristic expression of Oriental mysticism.[1]

It is, therefore, significant of the role played by Augustus that he should have submitted to the necessity of formal election and

[1] See below, Chs. III and IV.

that, as occasion demanded, he should have asked for the concession of special powers analogous to his own for those who
were to be associated with him in the administration, choosing
this means, in particular, of designating his successor and of
introducing him to public life, while, at the same time, he gave
him a practical initiation in his duties. It is significant, also,
that the imperial prerogative should have developed as an
accumulation of extraordinary rights and duties in the main
detached from public office; so that the form and appearance
of the republic were preserved and, in some respects, the powers
of magistrates and senate substantially increased. For this
meant that, behind the façade of traditional republicanism, the
scattered elements of executive authority were drawn together.
On the one hand, the prince was clothed with rights of initiative,
control, and revision, sufficient to ensure to him the effective
direction of public policy. On the other, he himself assumed
responsibility for the conduct of certain departments, the most
important of which was that of foreign affairs and imperial
defence, involving command of the fighting forces by land and
sea, as well as the administration of unsettled frontier provinces.
The powers and duties thus assigned to the emperor were broad
and comprehensive. They were, moreover, rapidly enlarged as
functions traditionally attached to republican magistracies were
transferred one after another to the new executive, and executive action invaded fields which, under the former system, had
been consecrated to senatorial or popular control.[1] Finally, by
virtue of specific provisions, the substance of which is indicated
in the maxim *princeps legibus solutus*, the emperor was freed from
constitutional limitations which might have paralysed his freedom of action; while his personal protection was assured
through the grant of tribunician inviolability (*sacrosanctitas*) as
well as by the sanctions of the *Lex Maiestatis*. The prerogative was
thus built up by a series of concessions, made by the competent
authority of senate and people, no single one of which was in
theory unrepublican. Examined *en bloc*, they reveal the principate
as a wide and elastic commission, the terms of which were to be
embodied under Vespasian in the so-called *Lex Regia*, the instrument by which successive princes were invested with the *imperium*.[2]

[1] Tacitus, *Ann.* i. 2: 'munia senatus, magistratuum, legum in se trahere'; xi. 5
'cuncta legum et magistratuum munia in se trahens'.

[2] Bruns, *Fontes Iuris Romani Antiqui*, ed. 7 (1909), p. 202, no. 56: *S.C. de imperi
Vespasiani*.

Thus envisaged, the principate represented, of course, a radical departure from the ideals of the free republic. The essence of republicanism, as a political device, lay in the attempt to establish a system of checks and balances, based on the annual and collegiate principle and designed to neutralize the powers of the military *imperium*, thus securing to the subject a measure of freedom. This system, long since moribund, now became for practical purposes obsolete. Through his sole command of the legions and of the praetorian guard, the emperor possessed an effective reserve of power, contingent only upon his ability to 'hold the wolf by the ears'. Resistance was rebellion, and the only justification of rebellion was success. Political opposition was, if possible, still more futile. By virtue of his *maius imperium* and his *tribunicia potestas*, the emperor possessed the representative character of the magistracy and the anti-magistracy alike, wielding paramount authority over magistrates, senate, and people. All possibility of independent political action disappeared as the organs of republican expression slowly withered beneath the shadow of the imperial power. Thus the principate emerged as a *de facto* sovereignty, the implications of which were perhaps fully realized only after the death of the founder. For the crisis which marked the election of his successor made it evident that, extensive as were the prerogatives assigned to the prince, they could be neither discontinued nor divided; 'so completely had the long ascendancy of Augustus inured the Roman people to subservience'. A later and more acute crisis was to emphasize the truth that the principate was the only arrangement possible for a people 'capable neither of complete servitude nor of complete freedom'.[1] Thus the vitality of the institution enabled it to survive the manifold perversions to which it was liable and the fatal evils which they engendered, the tragic conflicts which blighted the life of the first century, constituting the theme of early imperial history and forming the grounds of Tacitus' famous indictment of the Caesars.

For, with all its inherent defects, the principate was dedicated to a re-establishment of the *res publica*, the common good implied in the Latin idea of the commonwealth. This fact determined the programme of the Caesars, and, despite their individual vagaries, imposed it decisively upon them as an inescapable condition of power. Thus, for example, it com-

---

[1] Tacitus, *Historiae*, i. 16.

pelled them to maintain a policy of peace, signalized by the closing of the temple of Janus and by the establishment of the *Ara Pacis Augustae*. New and strange to the race of conquerors, this policy was scarcely comprehended by the fighting aristocracy, who saw in it nothing but a jealous malignancy calculated to rob them of distinctions traditional to their class. It was felt as irksome, not to say anomalous, by the emperors themselves, who were forced to be content with petty laurels such as might be earned in purely defensive operations on the frontier. It even created difficulties for the historian. 'Nobis in arto et inglorius labor', says Tacitus,[1] since there was no longer anything spectacular to record. Nevertheless, with certain definite and perfectly intelligible exceptions such, for instance, as the conquest of Britain, the policy of refraining from territorial acquisition was consistently pursued as a logical presupposition to the task of social reconstruction by virtue of which the principate claimed to justify itself in the eyes of the world.

The first aspect of this task was the maintenance and extension of individual civic rights. This was to be effected by colonization and assimilation, in accordance with ideas which had been cherished within the revolutionary movement from its inception and which had been implemented on a vast scale by the dictator Caesar. In this respect, it was the policy of Augustus himself to hasten slowly, though the pace was to be accelerated by his successors. We may in this connexion recall the speech made by the emperor Claudius on a famous occasion when he intervened in the senate to support a motion for admitting the nobles of Gallia Comata to imperial honours (*ius honorum*); in the course of which he gave classic expression to what has been called 'the policy of liberal comprehension' with regard to citizenship;[2] a policy which, we may pause to note, was still viewed with suspicion and alarm by the more intransigent of the aristocrats. The significance of this programme was twofold. On the one hand, it aimed to rehabilitate the masses, to whom it offered a stake in the community, thereby providing an antidote to the parasitism of the later republic and widening the foundations of what may properly be described as 'civilized' life. On the other hand, it sought to strengthen the body politic by drawing upon fresh and uncontaminated sources for such

[1] *Ann.* iv. 32.
[2] xi. 23–4; cf. Furneaux, *The Annals of Tacitus*, vol. ii, Introd., p. 33.

elements as might enlarge its numbers and, in particular, supply
the man-power needed to maintain the armies in the field.

Beyond this, however, there was demanded a thorough purgation of society; the suppression of *gratia, tumor, voluptas* (Sallust),
luxus, ambitus, libido (Cicero), the *desidentes mores* to which Roman
moralists agreed in attributing the evils of revolutionary times;
together with the inculcation of a public spirit which would
enable the imperial people to reassert their place in the world.
The details of this programme, so far as they concern us, will be
reserved for future discussion. It is here sufficient to point out
that the task was conceived as political, to be accomplished by
means of the instruments which organized society affords.

Accordingly, while appropriating what was salutary in the
ideals of the revolution, the principate nevertheless managed to
avoid the imputation of decadence to which the Roman Left
was exposed, and which was destined to a belated triumph in
the bureaucratic socialism of the lower empire. This it did by
alining itself with what was best in the liberal-conservative
tradition of Cicero and Livy. In this way it came to embody a
principle which (in the words of Mommsen) made it at least as
different from the constitution of the lower empire as it was
from that of the free republic; at the same time entitling it to
rank as something more than a mere compromise between the
two and justifying the effort of the founder to discover a new
designation for what was in fact a novel manifestation of power.

Through this principle Augustus hoped to salvage what was
vital in the idea of the commonwealth, and thus commend his
work to the sober judgement of posterity. For it enabled him
to find a sanction for his authority and, at the same time, to
transform the state into a vehicle for the expression of what was
perhaps the most characteristic aspect of the Roman genius.
This was the rule of law; and, in this sense, law was to be the
gift of the Caesars to the world. For as there can be little doubt
that, even under the republic, the *imperium* rather than the
comitia had been the really creative source of law; so the rehabilitation of the *imperium* by the Caesars made it possible to un-
fetter law from the dominance of interest and make it the
expression of scientific and philosophic principle. This was
effected through a development of the legal prerogatives of the
prince, based on the imperial court of appeal which, though
constituted with strictly limited competence, found the scope

of its activities vastly enlarged as the popular courts disappeared in favour of magisterial *cognitiones*.[1]

Involving as it did the supersession of politics by law as the final expression of Roman genius in statecraft, the principate excluded much of the past. In particular, it left no room for the vivid life of senate-house and forum, the conflict between *optimates* and *populares* rendered familiar to students of the later republic in the pages of Sallust, Caesar, and Cicero. Yet, in compensation for this loss, it seemed to justify the ardent hope of contemporaries that the highest promise of Graeco-Roman civilization was at last to be fulfilled. For, if the claims of interest were not wholly eliminated (as the disputes between Sabinians and Proculeians show), those claims were nevertheless subordinated to principles of natural reason and equity, in the absence of which power was conceived as tyranny, and in terms of which it was 'justified'. In this way the City of Man was to be attuned to standards cherished within the heavenly city of Antonine philosophy. And if, as was inevitable, the goal was missed, this at least was achieved that, through the principles of classical jurisprudence, men were at last freed from the intolerable necessity of having to rule as the only alternative to being ruled—the exploitation of one another by contending factions which tore the mask of social harmony from the face of the Greek *polis*. For, public and private rights being henceforth conceived as mutually independent, the latter, so far from being impaired by the destruction of the former, were to attain under the Caesars their most perfect development and their fullest meaning.

Thus envisaged, the *Pax Augusta* gave fresh significance to the classical concept of the commonwealth. In the principate the Romans met the ultimate demand of the political idea and produced the *protector*, *rector*, *gubernator*, or *moderator rei publicae* of whom Cicero had dreamed, the agent through whom it was proposed to assert afresh the ideal of justice alike against the powerful forces of monopoly and the excesses of mob-rule. In this sense, the Caesars came not to destroy but to fulfil, and they restored the 'republic' not less in spirit than in form. This is not to suggest that they introduced any immediate millennium. Conservative in spirit and outlook, they attacked specific evils, which they aimed to restrain rather than to eradicate. Thus

[1] Greenidge, *Roman Public Life*, p. 381.

panis et circenses, the plague of the expiring republic, by-product of the fierce competition of great nobles for place and power, survived in a modified form under the new régime; and nothing more was attempted than to bring this deep-seated malady under a rigorous control. Under the Caesars, moreover, distant echoes were still to be heard of the exploitation of subjects and allies which had brought the republic down in ruins.[1] Finally, there was the Tantalean problem of combating venality and corruption within the administration, and the scandals of Claudian times were to show that the battle was a losing one. Nevertheless, with an extraordinary tenacity of purpose, the Caesars tried to overcome the forces of lawless impulse and passion, the excesses of the acquisitive spirit which had threatened the Roman system with disaster at a moment when its historic mission was still unfulfilled; looking for a corrective to those excesses in the sense of order which was so deeply rooted in the Roman temperament. They thus utilized the raw materials of human nature as they found it in order to realize the classical ideals of stability, prosperity, and leisure, the elements of what they conceived to be the 'good life'. In this sense, Cato in Hades 'delivering statutes' was to rank as a posthumous hero of the new régime.

For these reasons, the imperial system appeared to merit the consecration which it received in the apotheosis of Augustus and Rome. To grasp the full meaning of the imperial cult, it is necessary to consider the mental processes which led to its establishment. This we shall try to do at a later stage of the present work.[2] At this point, it is sufficient to observe that it constituted a public official recognition of 'surpassing qualities' of mind and heart thought to be embodied in the spirit (*genius*) of the city and its ruler. As such, it found expression in two modes, the veneration of the living and the deification of the dead emperor. In neither sense could it be regarded as wholly a novelty in Rome.[3] It has thus been noted that the veneration accorded to sovereigns throughout the Hellenistic world was extended to include Roman magistrates whose duties took them to the East. This began as early as the time of Flamininus

---

[1] Tac. *Ann.* iii. 40–6 and iv. 72–4.   [2] Ch. III, below.

[3] The origins of Caesar-worship have been studied by various writers, of whom we may mention W. Warde Fowler, *Roman Ideas of Deity in the Last Century of the Republic*; Toutain, *Les Cultes païens dans l'empire romain*; Lily Ross Taylor, *The Divinity of the Roman Emperor*; Lebreton, *Histoire du dogme de la Trinité*, i, p. 26 foll.

(196 B.C.), who was worshipped in Hellas in conjunction with Heracles and Apollo;[1] and it included others like the Scipios, Metellus Pius, Marius Gratidianus, and Sulla. Even Cicero was offered (and refused) divine honours during his proconsulate in Cilicia.[2] The triumph of Julius Caesar in the civil war was signalized by cults set up to him throughout the East;[3] while texts of Priene and Halicarnassus record the voting of similar honours to Augustus.[4] These cults served to mark the recipients as the source of beneficent activity issuing in some form of 'common good'. On the other hand, the consecration of deceased emperors had at least one precedent in Rome in that of the deified Julius, duly authorized by the senate in 42 B.C.[5] Following this precedent, it became the prime duty of a new prince, on succeeding to the imperial dignities, to nominate his predecessor to membership in the Pantheon. This was, on the one hand, a mark of *pietas* or loyalty; on the other, it was connected with the ratification of his *acta*, the executive measures which he had enforced during life by virtue of his *imperium*, and it had the effect of giving to them permanent validity. Applied in this way, it served also to register the verdict of what was equivalent to modern 'public opinion' with respect to the character and achievement of deceased princes. Thus, as the 'good' emperors were successively elevated to divine status, their spirits were thought to take a place alongside Juppiter, Juno, and Minerva as guardians and protectors of the Eternal City.

[1] Plut. *Flamin.* 16. 4.   [2] *Ad Attic.* v. 21. 7 and *Ad Quint. Fr.* i. 9. 26.
[3] Toutain, op. cit., vol i, bk. i, ch. i, p. 26 foll.
[4] Dittenberger, *Orientis Graeci Inscrip. Sel.* ii. 458, quoted by Lebreton, op. cit. i, p. 26; Brit. Mus. no. 894, quoted by Lebreton, p. 27.   [5] Dio, xlvii. 18–19.

II

ROMANITAS: EMPIRE AND COMMONWEALTH

THE Augustan settlement was hailed with almost universal enthusiasm as marking the successful termination of a crisis which threatened not merely the existence of the empire but the whole future of Western civilization. Defeatism and despair were succeeded by unbounded confidence and hope—confidence that the troubles which menaced the integrity of the state had been triumphantly surmounted, hope that, with the protection of the Roman gods and under the military presidency of the Julian race, nothing less than the golden age of Saturn would be restored.

That sentiments of this kind were widely entertained at the time needs no argument; for centuries, indeed, unique associations were to cling to the reign of Augustus as the dawn of a new and better epoch for humanity. To these the noblest expression was given by Vergil, who was at the same time largely responsible for their diffusion. Thus, despite the characteristic melancholy of the poet,

> Majestic in thy sadness
> At the doubtful doom of human kind,

Vergil constitutes a supreme embodiment of the optimism of his age. In him we may perceive the scope and character of those aspirations to fulfilment which were stirring in the contemporary world and which had come to a focus in the programme of the Caesars. But this, in itself, by no means exhausts the significance of his work. For, while revealing the substance of the Augustan hope, Vergil at the same time disclosed its essential basis, relating it to a vast background of human history and giving it, indeed, a cosmic setting. Viewed in the light of his imagination, the *Pax Augusta* emerged as the culmination of effort extending from the dawn of culture on the shores of the Mediterranean—the effort to erect a stable and enduring civilization upon the ruins of the discredited and discarded systems of the past. As thus envisaged, it constituted not merely a decisive stage in the life of the Roman people, but a significant point of departure in the evolution of mankind. It marked, indeed, the rededication of the imperial city to her secular task, the realization of those ideals of human emancipation towards

[1] Verg. *Aeneid*, vi. 789-800.

which the thought and aspiration of antiquity had pointed
hitherto in vain. From this standpoint, the institution of the
principate represented the final triumph of creative politics.
For, in solving her own problem, Rome had also solved the
problem of the classical commonwealth.

Accordingly, for Vergil, the events which succeeded the year
30 B.C. attained enormous significance. It was not merely that,
as he supposed with most of his contemporaries, the war to end
war had been fought and won at Actium. Nor yet that, as even
its enemies confessed, the principate offered a way of escape
from the violence, the political corruption, and the money-
power which, by paralysing the operation of law, had destroyed
all confidence in the authority of senate and people.[1] Deep and
powerful as were these sentiments, the hatred of war and the
distrust of republican liberty were mere negations. To Vergil,
however, the true significance of the Augustan settlement lay
in its positive character; he saw it, indeed, as the ultimate expression of the political idea. As such, it meant the assertion,
on a fresh and irrefragable basis and in terms suited to the
enlarged powers and responsibilities of the imperial city, of the
ancient ideal of civic peace. It meant the application of Roman
methods of pacification, as to Italy, so to the subject provinces.
And just as, in the one case, those methods had served, by
evoking the sense of Italian nationality, to heal the wounds from
which the peninsula had bled for centuries, so now they were
offered as a remedy for the chronic evils of a harried and
desperate world.

It is not surprising, therefore, that, notwithstanding the evident diffidence of the poet, the *Aeneid* was eagerly received by
Augustus as a revelation of the deeper implications of his work.
And, in thus bearing witness to the aims and methods of the
principate, Vergil provided inspiration and direction to the
imperial programme of reconstruction, thereby earning a position among the architects of empire hardly less significant than
that of the Caesars themselves. This, however, was but the
beginning of his influence. For, through the magnetic attraction
exercised by his works, he impressed indelibly upon posterity
his sense of the mission of Eternal Rome. By thus projecting

[1] Tac. *Ann.* i. 2. 2: 'suspecto senatus populique imperio ob certamina potentium
et avaritiam magistratuum invalido legum auxilio quae vi ambitu postremo
pecunia turbabantur.'

into the consciousness of mankind his vision of the common-wealth, he offered a basis for imperial solidarity throughout successive generations; a touchstone of thought and action which maintained its potency at least until the collapse of the great Antonine experiment. In so doing, he not merely pro-vided an ethical sanction for the system, but he gave final utterance to the spirit of classical paganism, the religion of culture which was later to be confronted by the culture of religion; and, by throwing down a defiant challenge to alterna-tive systems of life, he compelled them at least to formulate their principles with reference to those embodied in the imperial city.

Vergilianism marks the resolution of a problem with which the Romans had been confronted since the dawn of national self-consciousness in the days of Cato the Censor. With the conquest of the Mediterranean, this nation of intelligent peasants, sud-denly transformed into a great imperial power, was plunged into a state of unparalleled moral and intellectual confusion. Dimly conscious of the unique position into which chance or destiny had thrust them, but disconcerted by the novel character of the problems which they faced, their bewilderment found expression in the conflicting historical movements of the second century B.C. These movements came to a head in the revolution, the issue of which we have tried to describe. The outbreak of dis-order and bloodshed on the streets of the capital had been the signal that the *Pax Romana*, the traditional basis of social peace, was hopelessly destroyed;[1] and this fact imposed upon the Romans a problem of reconstruction, the solution of which became increasingly pressing as it slowly became evident that the alternative was collapse. Coincident, therefore, with the development of the crisis, there occurred in Rome a series of tentative efforts to formulate a new and more adequate basis of concord. It is no disparagement of these efforts to say that, coming as they did in a time of unprecedented economic, social, and political upheaval, none of them proved to be final. The Romans had, indeed, to wait until, with Vergil, they at last discovered the answer by which their doubts and perplexities were resolved; it was he, more than any other man, who charted the course of their imperial future. Nevertheless, the elements of the problem as he saw it were inherited from his predecessors, and for his solution he made heavy drafts upon them; so that,

[1] Appian, *Civil Wars*, i. 1 and 2.

directly or indirectly, they also contributed important ingredients to the common body of ideas which was to dominate the
life of imperial society.

The perils by which the ancient *Pax Romana* was threatened
were already evident in the days of the elder Cato, even if their
meaning was not yet fully understood. It was, indeed, Cato
himself who first sounded the note of alarm.[1] Viewing with
apprehension the rapid disintegration of the traditional morale,
he attributed it to a 'mixture of elements' brought about by the
wars of overseas conquest, which had exposed the state to the
influence of 'foreign customs and novel examples of living'. In
scathing terms he denounced the various forms of alienism
rampant within the empire, especially those which, derived in
the main from the degraded Hellenistic world, flaunted themselves in Rome under the distinguished patronage of the Scipios.
In these men Cato saw a personification of the sinister forces
which were invading and poisoning Roman life. From this
standpoint, their virtues themselves were hardly less abhorrent
than their vices, both alike being the reflection of a self-assertive
egotism which was as dangerous as it was novel. Conspicuous
for their public services during the Hannibalic crisis, exponents
of the new imperialism which followed the Second Punic
war, the Scipios claimed to be judged by standards other than
those which applied to ordinary men.[2] While, therefore, they
accorded an easy hospitality to relaxed modes of personal conduct, at the same time they asserted a right to special consideration and preferential treatment at the hands of their fellow
countrymen. By thus demanding exemption from the categories
of behaviour traditional to Roman citizens, they foreshadowed
the collapse of the established order and pointed the way to the
dangerously unrepublican theory of the superman.[3]

In his hostility to influences such as those represented by the
Scipios may be found the explanation of Cato's famous observation that the reception of Greek culture would mean ruin for
the Roman state. And therein he was right, in so far as Scipionic ideas of emancipation were drawn from the cosmopolitan
Hellenistic world, in which the deference paid to the divine
βασιλεύς was easily transferred to the republican *imperator*.

---

[1] See Livy, xxxiv. 2–4 (his speech on the repeal of the *Lex Oppia*) and xxxix.
40–4; cf. Plut. *Cato Major*, 4 foll.   [2] Livy, xxxviii. 42 and 51–60; xxxix. 6.
[3] See below, Ch. III, p. 113.

Already with Aristotle, despite the fact that his gaze was fixed upon the past, political philosophy had come to terms with this phenomenon of the future:

'but when a whole family, or some individual happens to be so pre-eminent in virtue as to surpass all others, then it is just that they should be the royal family and supreme over all, or that this one citizen should be king of the whole nation. . . . For it would not be right to kill or ostracize or exile such a person, or to require that he should take his turn in being governed. The whole is naturally superior to the part, and he who has this pre-eminence is in the relation of a whole to a part. But if so, the only alternative is that he should have the supreme power, and that mankind should obey him, not in turn, but always.'[1]

By thus endorsing doctrines which undermined the very being of the commonwealth, Aristotle revealed the inadequacy of philosophic naturalism to provide an effective sanction for the claims of civic freedom and equality. And if Aristotle thus played false to commonwealth ideals, what was to be said of Aristotle's successors in the Hellenistic cosmopolis? Cynics, Cyrenaics, Epicureans, as well as the earlier Stoics, whatever their internal differences, were nevertheless, historically speaking, the product of a time when, following the hint earlier thrown out in a moment of pessimism by Plato, men in general had abandoned the hope of political salvation. Addressing themselves to a world of *déracinés*, they preached a gospel of purely individual salvation or of salvation in 'society' regarded as distinct from and independent of political forms. It was these sects with whose activities the Romans were most familiar; and, dimly as they might apprehend their doctrines, they knew enough to realize that their purport was not merely to weaken, in general, the motive of communal action, but to threaten in particular the specifically Roman virtue of patriotism. In the contemporary world, the currency of these philosophies was paralleled by the widespread popularity of mystery cults, not the least subversive of which (that of Dionysus) had already in Cato's day raised its head in Rome itself.[2] And, if its appearance

---

[1] *Pol.* iii. 1288ª 15 foll. (Jowett's translation); Plato, *Politicus*, on the queen bee.
[2] Livy, xxxix. 8–18; xl. 19. Bruns, op. cit., p. 164. For details of the cult of Bacchus at Rome see the valuable analysis in Cumont, *Les Religions orientales dans le paganisme romain*, ed. 4, appendix, p. 195 foll., and notes, p. 303 foll. Also Tenney Frank, 'The Bacchanalian Cult of 186 B.C.', *Cl. Quart.* xxi (1927), p. 128 foll.

was the signal for bloody and brutal measures of repression, it was nevertheless a portent the significance of which could not fail to be understood. For this incident registered the profound change which, since the feverish years of conflict with Hannibal, had been creeping over the Italian temperament—a moral and spiritual lapse, especially of the younger generation, from the principles for which their ancestors had fought and died. Within the century the effects of this lapse were to be seen, not merely in widespread social unrest, but in the spectacle—unprecedented in Roman annals—of indiscipline and mutiny among Roman troops in the field.

In a gallant but unavailing effort to combat pernicious tendencies such as these, Cato undertook to lay the foundations of what was intended as a native approach to the problems of his day. Deeply suspicious of 'that nation of babblers', whose history had shown them incapable of preserving the idea which they had given to the world, he rejected the findings of Greek philosophy in order to fall back upon a shrewd peasant wisdom, the tenor of which is indicated by his many pithy observations on men and affairs. Stoutly empirical and pragmatic, his attitude may be illustrated by the famous remark on the state, quoted with approval by Cicero:[1]

'Cato used to say that the superiority of our city to others depended upon the fact that the latter almost always had their laws and institutions from a single legislator . . . whereas our republic was not created by the genius of any individual, nor in the lifetime of one man but through countless centuries and generations. For, as he observed, there never was a human being so perspicacious that nothing could escape him, nor have the combined talents of any single age been such that it could look forward and anticipate all possibilities without the lessons of time and experience.'

In this typical statement we may catch the spirit of a moral and political fundamentalism thenceforth to be associated with the name of Cato.

From this narrowly restricted point of view Cato discovered an adequate formula for conduct in the imitation of those representative figures who appeared to embody in their lives the traditional ideals of republican virtue as well as, by their careers, to exemplify the legitimate modes of republican self-expression. Of such men, Fabius Maximus and Manius Curius still survived

[1] *De Rep.*, ii. 1. 2.

to bear witness to a demoralized generation of the qualities which had served to create and maintain the state. Taking these men as his models, Cato schooled and disciplined himself in such a way that, if his name became proverbial for harshness, coarseness, and inhumanity, it stood also for endurance, temperance, industry, and self-control. These qualities he endeavoured, by both precept and example, to impress upon his son, whom he thus 'formed and fashioned to virtue' by giving him personal instruction in the arts, according to a 'simple, almost wholly technical and vocational scheme, embracing the study of oratory, agriculture, law, medicine, and war'; in this way taking his place at the head of the roster of Roman educationalists.[1] To this aspect of Catonism belongs also the famous treatise, De Re Rustica. First among the works of its kind to be produced in the native agrarian tradition, this essay shows that the author was fully alive to the possibilities of the newly established villa-system for the intensive exploitation of land and chattels, including the breeding and sale of slaves. But its chief significance is that, by exhibiting farming as a way of life, it illustrates the Catonian faith in work as supplying, if not a moral equivalent to, at any rate the moral counterpart of war.

Such was the mental equipment which Cato brought with him into a public life which, like that of Nestor, extended over three ordinary generations. Throughout that time he constituted himself a threat to evil-doers, making it his constant business to indict malefactors of rank and power.[2] But the highwater mark of his career was undoubtedly the censorship of 184 B.C., which he rendered notable, not merely by a vigorous execution of public contracts and by other measures calculated to restrain the activities of those who made free with the common property, but by extending the traditional functions of purgation connected with the censorial office, as, for example, by a steeply graduated luxury tax.[3] In imperial politics he placed himself in opposition to fresh conquests and commitments in the East; but, in view of the reviving menace of Carthage, this policy of 'limited liability' broke down in the West. While it

[1] Plut. Cato Major, 20.
[2] Plut. op. cit. 15; Livy, xxxix. 12–44.
[3] Catonian influence may also, perhaps, be detected in the S.C. of 161 B.C. whereby the praetor was authorized to expel all teachers of philosophy and rhetoric from the city. Suet. Rhet. i.

was probably for moral rather than for economic reasons that Cato raised the cry *delenda est Carthago*, nevertheless, in so doing, he disclosed the essential ambiguity of his attitude and played, so to speak, into the hands of the enemy. The fall of her ancient rival has rightly been taken to indicate a definite turn for the worse in the fortunes of the republic, marking the operation of those inexorable forces against which Cato and Catonism struggled in vain, and bringing the state one step nearer to revolution.

Accordingly, while the name of Cato might survive as of one who had sought 'to reclaim the commonwealth when it was declining into vice', nevertheless, in the society of his day, the man and his methods were equally anomalous. For mere republicanism could not save the republic. Thus, within little more than a decade after his death, the swift march of events delivered the state into the hands of his bitterest enemies. There can be little doubt that, with the Gracchi, Rome experienced the first shock of Scipionic ideas in action, just as, throughout subsequent years of trial and suffering, she was to experience other and still unsuspected aspects of the revolutionary spirit. It was, indeed, inevitable that the city should go through the fires of purgation in the process of adjustment to her imperial future. To state the principles of Catonism is thus to reveal its limitations. Nevertheless, it remains true that, as the Romans fumbled towards a new order, they still retained a memory of the salutary elements in Cato's teaching, and that reconstruction, when it did come, was based on principles not wholly alien from his life and thought.

The day of reconstruction, however, was still remote; and, with the steady progress of the revolutionary spirit, all the elements against which Cato had battled so vigorously came defiantly to the surface. Thus, in the society of Cato's great-grandson, the last shreds of traditional restraint had been contemptuously flung aside, and the dominant note was one of individual freedom and self-assertion. Inflamed by an insatiable thirst for novel forms of experience, members of the aristocracy let themselves go in a protracted orgy of extravagance and debauchery. The world was ransacked to provide the rarest and most exotic means for the satisfaction of the senses, and the last refinements of luxury and vice were introduced to titillate appetites already jaded by pleasure in its cruder forms. A

literature of lyric poetry grew up which reflected only too
vividly the prevailing atmosphere, and Catullus and others
survive to bear witness to the sophistication and decadence of
the imperial city during the revolutionary age. On the other
hand, history and satire, developing about the same time,
adopted a somewhat peevish and moralizing tone which, as it
presently became conventional, was to be imitated by writers
who, generations later, lashed at social evils which by their day
were largely obsolete.

Nor was the epidemic confined to the more exalted circles of
imperial society. Among the masses, bread and circuses on a
rapidly expanding scale afforded a counterpart to the Lucullan
banquets of the rich. At this time, also, the Roman tiger acquired his taste for blood, and political ambition was taxed to
discover means for the satisfaction of a voracious and depraved
appetite by the provision of increasingly elaborate and gory
spectacles. If, indeed, we may trust the sober and judicious
observation of Seneca, this was the climax of a materialism
which brought with it a speedy nemesis in the utter demoralization of Roman life. High and low alike, without distinction of
age, rank, or sex, the Romans indulged in a riot of sensationalism
and emotionalism which, while it promoted social disintegration, at the same time stimulated that fierce competition for
dominationes and *potentiae* which laid the political fabric in ruins.[1]

To this distracted world there came a message of salvation,
the gospel of Epicurus, naturalized by Lucretius in the *De Rerum
Natura* and advocated with all the persuasive and charming
eloquence of one who was not less artist than philosopher. It
is a wholly superficial view which sees in Lucretius nothing but
the rationalization of contemporary tendencies towards intellectual and moral anarchy. His object, indeed, was to show
how that anarchy might be overcome; and if, in a sense, he
speaks the language of revolt, it was with no intention of feeding
the devouring flames of revolutionary passion, but rather to
establish a new principle of understanding and control. That
principle was reason, which, as embodied in the teachings of
the master, represented for him the culmination of speculative
achievement. To it he looked for a revelation of the truth
which underlies phenomena, as the presupposition to a valid
theory of human life.

[1] See the description of contemporary society in Sall. *Cat.* 24. 3–4 and 25.

In so doing, Lucretius reflects one of the finest and most distinctive aspects of the classical spirit. It would, indeed, be hard to point to any classical author who is clearer in his perception or more emphatic in his denunciation of evils which vitiated the life of antiquity. These evils he ascribes to belief in the traditional gods of popular and poetic paganism. To this source he traces the multifarious impulsions and inhibitions which go by the name of *religio*, and which are evoked by a desire to win the favour or avert the wrath of beings supposed in some sense to control the destinies of mankind. And in it he sees the cause of evil and suffering such as no other force could possibly inspire.

From this analysis of the situation, the remedy follows as a matter of course. For the ills which thus afflict mankind are, as we should say, psychological; they are the product of 'unreasonable' hope or fear. As such, they depend upon a misconception regarding the character of ultimate reality. To remove this misconception, it is only necessary to destroy the foundation upon which it rests. This Epicurean science undertakes to do by propounding a view of nature which, as it discloses nothing but atoms moving in the void, stamps the claims of *religio* as sheer illusion. It thus offers to mankind emancipation from the terrors of the unseen and the impalpable; and, to replace the vast aspirations of pagan mysticism, it proposes a goal for life which, because it is independent of support from superhuman powers, is not doomed in advance to frustration. This goal is not to be attained by yielding to the savage urges of desire and passion. It is to be the outcome of a rational ordering of life in terms of the concrete satisfactions to be discovered in the normal human relationships, as measured by the criterion of individual pleasure and pain. What Lucretius thus advocates is, in a word, salvation through enlightenment. All that it involves is submission to the demands of mechanical law as revealed by the inspection of nature, *naturae species ratioque*, and, for this, nothing is required except the mere act of apprehension. Otherwise spontaneous and automatic, it depends, indeed, upon 'taking no thought for the morrow'. It thus deliberately cuts the nerve of effort:

> . . . nostro sine quaeque labore
> sponte sua multo fieri meliora videres . . .

Accordingly, the doctrine of Lucretius was administered, not as a stimulant, but as a sedative; as such, it was proffered as a specific for the disorders of imperial society.

The gulf between Cato and Lucretius is a measure of the distance which Rome had travelled in the intervening century. For both, indeed, the Roman problem was, in the last analysis, a psychological and moral problem. But the generation of Lucretius had embraced Hellenism as whole-heartedly as it had been rejected by Cato. While, therefore, Cato was disposed to see in native practice the real key to a solution, Lucretius had fallen back upon Greek science for a truer understanding of the meaning and purpose of human life. From this standpoint, he offered an analysis of the individual and of society in terms which would have stripped them both of mystery; rendering equally absurd the cult of the divine community and that of the divine man. But, in so doing, he set up a moral atomism which imposed no effective check upon the sway of individual caprice and provided no basis for political and social cohesion. It would, indeed, be false to describe Epicureanism as anarchic; since it recognized the state as the product of a compact intended to secure the *communia foedera pacis*.[1] Nevertheless, both because of its claims and because of the type of activity which it engendered, organized society, as it existed, lay under deep suspicion as the cause of dissatisfactions unknown to primitive man:[2]

> at non multa virum sub signis milia ducta
> una dies dabat exitio nec turbida ponti
> aequora lidebant navis ad saxa virosque . . .

While, therefore, prepared to accept the state as an economic expedient, Epicureanism explicitly rejected its pretension to be anything more, and pointed to distinctively non-political ends as the goal of human activity.[3] In so doing, it offered a complete negation to the classical idea of the commonwealth.

From this standpoint, Epicurean ἀταραξία or detachment implied both a repudiation of the Roman past and the denial of a specifically Roman future. Its vogue, therefore, such as it was, passed with the passing of the republic. With the rise of the principate it suffered an eclipse, so that while, in imperial times,

[1] *De Rerum Natura*, v. 1155.   [2] Ibid. 999, cf ii. 23–39; iii. 37–93; v. 1105–1135.
[3] C. Bailey, *Phases in the Religion of Ancient Rome*, pp. 225–7, argues that it offers the basis for a kind of morality in an imitation of the gods, conceived as ideals of tranquillity.

there were no doubt endless numbers who practised, few openly professed, the doctrines of Lucretius. This fact does not, however, mean that his teaching was without effect. For, in making the first systematic attempt to reach a solution of the Roman problem in terms of nature and reason, it raised the discussion from the level of prejudice to that of principle, thus serving as a challenge to alternative ways of thought. The challenge was accepted by Cicero, who undertook to answer Lucretius in similar terms.

The tendency of modern criticism has been to dismiss the work of Cicero as a compendium of platitudes; it is even suggested that, in the whole of his philosophical or semi-philosophical writings, there cannot be found a single original idea. This, however, does not in the least detract from his historical importance, which is out of all proportion to the intrinsic significance of his thought. No author has been more widely known or more intensively studied, and the range of his influence is indicated not merely by this fact but by the direct testimony of enthusiastic admirers. Velleius Paterculus, for example, credits him with establishing the autonomy of Latin letters and predicts for him a literary immortality as the one Roman with insight sufficient to comprehend the universe and power to elucidate its meaning.[1] Seneca, endorsing an opinion of Asinius Pollio, declares it superfluous to enlarge upon his talent and industry;[2] and, if we may believe the story told by Plutarch, the emperor Augustus himself pronounced him 'a great scholar and a great patriot'.[3] The almost unanimous verdict of early imperial times finds confirmation in Quintilian, who equates his name with eloquence itself and, in philosophy, couples it with that of Plato.[4]

The pre-eminence of Cicero both as thinker and writer was no less secure in the fourth and fifth centuries than it had been in the first. Speaking as a pagan, Ammianus Marcellinus delights in allusions to him and his teaching; and a famous passage in praise of philosophy[5] is no doubt meant to recall a similar passage of the *Pro Archia*.[6] On the other hand, as Cicero had done so much to create the moulds of *Romanitas*, so his spirit survived to influence, if not to dominate, the forms of Christian

[1] ii. 34 and 66.   [2] *Suasor*. 6. 24.
[3] Plut. *Cic*. 49.   [4] *Inst. Orat.* x. 1. 112 and 123.
[5] xxix. 2. 18: 'o praeclara informatio doctrinarum, munere caelesti indulta felicibus, quae vel vitiosas naturas saepe excoluisti!'
[6] 7. 15.

culture by which *Romanitas* was superseded. The *Institutes* of Lactantius are so evidently modelled on his work that Lactantius has often been described as the Christian Cicero. St. Ambrose, both in his *De Officiis* and in his Epistles, deliberately imitates Ciceronian diction and form. The well-known lament of Jerome, *Ciceronianus non Christianus sum*, testifies to the attraction of the orator for the translator of the Vulgate. But perhaps the highest tribute ever paid to Cicero was that of Augustine, who asserts that with him Latin speculation began and ended, and generously ascribes to him the inspiration of his own passion for philosophy.

These opinions, Christian as well as pagan, have been cited, not with a view to supporting Cicero's reputation, but simply to illustrate the extraordinary grip which he had upon the imagination of posterity. They bear witness to the fact that, so far as such a thing may be said of any individual, he was the medium for the propagation of those ideas which informed the law and institutions of the empire. From this standpoint, he was destined to a renaissance of his own in modern times. To Erasmus, the *Essay on Duties* was a vade-mecum which embraced all the principles necessary for a young man on the threshold of a public career; and, even to-day, Ferrero regards this work as 'embodying an important theory of the possibility of social and moral regeneration for Rome'.[1] Without entering upon a discussion of this question, we may agree that the essay provides a fairly comprehensive statement of doctrine to which Cicero did so much to give currency, the stock of 'commonplaces' cherished by unregenerate but high-minded pagans from his day to our own. And if modern liberalism, in its effort to combat the sinister and chaotic forces with which contemporary life is menaced, holds up the ideal of a world-society founded on justice, freedom, and humanity, calling for a united effort to release mankind from the obstacles which prevent a realization of that ideal, its purpose and methods must alike be understood, if not as a direct legacy from Cicero, at least as in close affinity with his way of thought.

Cicero was not less conscious than Lucretius of the malady which afflicted revolutionary Rome; the competition for domination and power which, in his own words, opened the door to 'theft, forgery, poisoning, assassination, the spoliation

[1] *Greatness and Decline of Rome*, iii, p. 108 foll.

of fellow citizens and allies, a thirst for ascendancy over free men', in short to every conceivable form of anti-social behaviour.[1] Like Lucretius, also, he traced these evils to a psychological cause; in his case, the emancipation from control of the so-called 'expansive' emotions (*affectiones animi*), notably those of desire, fear, anxiety or solicitude, and pleasure which, thus running riot, brought destruction not merely on individuals and families but on whole communities. On the other hand, he was equally anxious to discover an answer to the claims of self-assertive egotism, a principle whereby it might be possible to overcome the fatal antipathies which it excited, quenching the flame of passion and laying solid foundations for individual and social peace (*tranquillitas animi et securitas*). Finally, with Lucretius, he looked to philosophy to supply such a principle, regarding its findings as imperfect unless they pointed to conclusions which would be of practical service to mankind.

To Cicero, however, a cure for the contemporary fever was not to be found in Epicureanism, which was repugnant to him on both intellectual and moral grounds. Intellectually, he felt that the physics of scientific materialism were little better than a tissue of absurdities. 'It is astonishing', he says, 'that, when one soothsayer meets another, he does not smile; still more that, when you Epicureans come together, you can possibly refrain from laughter.'[2] But the real weakness of the system, as he saw it, lay in its implication for ethics. This weakness was twofold. In the first place, it raised in a particularly acute form the problem of human freedom and responsibility. Secondly, by identifying the good with emancipation from all obligation, it set up a cult of selfishness which left no place for the social virtues. By so doing, it subverted what were to Cicero the richest and truest values of life.

In undertaking to defend those values Cicero sought to avoid the imputation of obscurantism.[3] Himself a representative product of the Greek enlightenment, he was fully alive to the dangers of superstition which, with sturdy common sense, he tried to keep at arm's length. 'It is undeniable', he declares, 'that superstition, epidemic throughout the nations, has taken advantage of human weakness to lay its heavy hand upon

---

[1] *De Offic.* i. 20. 66–9.
[2] *De Nat. Deor.* i. 26. 71: the remark is put into the mouth of the Academic, Cotta.   [3] Op. cit. i; *De Fin.* i.

almost every one . . . could we but eradicate this evil, we should be doing ourselves and the world an immense service.'[1] But, at the same time, he was convinced that sentiments like loyalty and justice (*pietas et iustitia*), upon which the life of organized society depends, had their ultimate basis in religion and that they could survive only if this fact were recognized.[2] Accordingly, he rejected the facile identification which scientific materialism had made between religion and superstition, and maintained that the true alternative to superstition was a form of high religion, i.e. of religion purified and illumined by the knowledge of nature.[3]

The question thus presented itself : Was such knowledge possible? One of the strongest objections which Cicero had to Epicureanism was its intensely dogmatic character; its exponents, he says, delivered themselves with the self-assurance of men who had just descended from Epicurus' *intermundia* and whose one fear was that they might seem to have any doubts whatever.[4] The same objection applied with hardly less force to the rival system of the Stoics, whose rigid and inflexible tenets he subjected to ridicule in the *Pro Murena*. To Cicero himself nothing was more evident than the uncertainty of all speculation. This he ascribed in part to the extreme obscurity of the subject-matter, in part to the fallibility of the instrument, as indicated by the sharp differences of opinion which existed among conflicting schools of thought. Accordingly, he felt that the part of true wisdom was to follow the New Academy in admitting the principle of suspended judgement or philosophic doubt.[5] In the acceptance of such a principle he saw no reason for despair. On the contrary, it offered him ground for confidence that the intellectual and moral values established by antiquity (*vetustas*) could not be wholly false; to this extent, he alined himself with old Cato in the belief that truth was the daughter of time. But, with Cicero, respect for established values did not exclude a qualified faith in the judgements of the

---

[1] *De Divinat.* ii. 72. 148. For the exact connotation of the words *religio* (Lucretius) and *superstitio* (Cicero) see Mayor, *De Nat. Deor.* ii. 72 (vol. ii, p. 183).
[2] *De Nat. Deor.* i. 2. 4.
[3] *De Divinat.* loc. cit. Cf. *De Nat. Deor.* i. 42. 117: 'non modo superstitionem tollunt in qua inest timor inanis deorum, sed etiam religionem, quae deorum cultu pio continetur.'   [4] Ibid. i. 8. 18.
[5] 'Academicorum dubitatio'; 'suspensio assensionis'. For the spirit of Cicero's scepticism in general see *Acad. Prior.*, esp. ii. 17, 18, 32–6, 99, 103, and *Tusc. Disput.* v. 4. 11.

wise, i.e. in the power of reason and conjecture to yield a fund
of knowledge, the validity of which was attested by its service
in rescuing humanity from the grip of circumstance. Such
knowledge had been progressive and cumulative, at least from
the time of Thales, and every extension of it narrowed the
frontiers of blind hazard (*fortuna*) to which primitive life was
exposed.[1] Accordingly, to possess this knowledge was to vindicate one's claim to be civilized and, at the same time, to enter
into the spiritual inheritance of mankind.

From this standpoint, there was nothing in the universe
superior to reason; it constituted the link between man and
man, and between man and God.[2] This it did by revealing the
'divine' order of nature, the law of which was identical with that
of 'right reason'.[3] At this point, Cicero forgets both the objections raised by the incredulous and his own principle of philosophic doubt to assert in the most unequivocal terms his belief
in the existence of a real and fundamental distinction in nature
between truth and error, right and wrong. To make this assertion is to affirm that reason is not the servant of desire, except in
so far as it reaches out towards its affinity, viz. the truth. As
such, its function is not, as Lucretius had supposed, to minister
to the demands of utility. It is rather to legislate and to judge;
and this it does according to a standard which claims to be
'objective' and rooted in the very substance of things. As thus
conceived, the dictates of reason are mandatory and constitute,
so to speak, the law for man. That is to say, mankind is 'born
for justice', which thus exists not by 'convention' but by 'nature'.
In this natural justice is to be found the *ratio* or principle of
human association, the bond of community in human life.[4]
Accordingly, to the Lucretian gospel of freedom from the state,
Cicero replies with a message of freedom in the state, holding
out the vision of the *bene honesteque vivendi societas* as embodying
the highest values of civilized man. In so doing, he reasserts the
characteristic hope of classical antiquity.

[1] *De Divinat.* i. 49–50. 109–112 and ii. 6–7. 15–8.   [2] *De Legg.* i. 7. 23 foll.
[3] Loc. cit.; see also *De Rep.* i. 36. 56 and iii. 22. 33; also *De Nat. Deor.* ii. 22. 58:
'mens mundi . . . vel prudentia vel providentia appellari recte (potest)'. With
Seneca (*Nat. Quaest.* ii. 45. 1) it was destined to emerge as 'rector custosque
universi, animus ac spiritus mundi, operis huius dominus et artifex', i.e. as 'creator
and preserver of the cosmos'. From this standpoint, man, because of his participation in reason, is thought of as a microcosm.
[4] *De Offic.* i. 7. 20: 'ea ratio qua societas hominum inter ipsos et vitae quasi
communitas continetur.'

But if this was the hope of Cicero, it was mocked by the grim realities of life in revolutionary Rome. The recollections of his youth were those of a fatherland confronted by an imperial crisis of the first magnitude while, at the same time, it was torn by domestic schism and by a secessionist movement which threatened to destroy the unity of Italy. The horror of these experiences was never to be obliterated from his memory; and there was nothing he so much dreaded as a renewed outbreak of disturbances such as had characterized the time of Marius and Sulla. In this dread may be found the explanation of his solicitude regarding political movements of his later years; it accounts for the apparently tortuous and vacillating course of his policy, as he sought to mediate between the claims of opposing factions which he regarded as alike fatal to the republic. This is indicated by the comments which he has to make regarding the great figures of the revolution, beginning with the Gracchi.

Towards these men Cicero was not entirely hostile; he saw them as friends of the common people, and praised them for a restraint which was in decided contrast to the violence and cruelty exhibited by their successors.[1] Yet their programme marked a resurgence of the terrors commonly associated with Roman radicalism, and in their persons the ghosts of Sp. Maelius and Sp. Cassius rose from the tomb to menace the possessing classes with visions of the *tyrannis*. For the motives of the Gracchi, like those of these dim figures of tradition, were by no means unmixed. 'Tiberius Gracchus attempted to make himself king and, indeed, reigned as such for at least some months.'[2] By so doing he destroyed the liberty of his fellow citizens and thus, like his brother after him, met the fate he deserved. In the tragic death of Tiberius, Cicero saw the just doom of all aspirants to autocracy.[3]

But, salutary as was this example, it failed to check the progress of revolution, which moved spasmodically through alternate phases of action and reaction to a crisis in the Social and Civil Wars. With neither of the protagonists in these conflicts does Cicero whole-heartedly sympathize. Thus, while he eulogizes Sulla for his service in restoring the rule of law after the nightmare of a proletarian usurpation during which 'no one

[1] *De Leg. Agr.* ii. 12. 31.   [2] *De Amicit.* 12. 41.
[3] *De Offic.* i. 30. 109.

knew what he had or what he owed', nevertheless he was keenly alive to Sulla's limitations, which he describes as those of the typical faction-leader.[1] As such, his victory was 'oppressive and disorderly', and he was guilty of aiming at 'regal power'.[2] Sulla, moreover, was conspicuous for 'three pestiferous vices, luxury, avarice, and cruelty';[3] so that his very name became synonymous with ruthlessness and barbarity and as such was charged with evil omen for the future.[4] 'Better to live among wild beasts than in that atmosphere', thinks Cicero, concluding with the prayer: 'God save us from such another.'[5] Of Marius, his fellow towns-man, hero of the Jugurthan and Cimbric wars, Cicero's judge-ment is hardly less severe. On the one hand, he lauds him as 'a man of superhuman gifts, born for the salvation of this empire'.[6] On the other, he denounces him for a murderous cruelty which rivals that of his opponent; and from this point of view he would have agreed with Livy in wondering whether the state would not have been better off had this champion of democracy never lived.

It thus becomes evident that, for Cicero, there was little or nothing to choose between the extremists of the Right and those of the Left. In his eyes both alike are *furiosi* or madmen, con-sumed with a lust for power which obscures all sense of a good transcending their selfish interests; and he looks for nothing but evil from the triumph of either. Accordingly, to the preten-sions of contending factions he advances his own alternative, which is, in a very real sense of the term, the *front populaire*. This conception is, perhaps, best explained in his own words.

'Those', he says, 'who have aspired to play an active and dis-tinguished part in the public life of Rome have always been divided into two groups. Of these, the one has desired to be and to be known as popular, the other as optimate. Those who are anxious that their actions and words should please the masses are regarded as popular; those who so comport themselves as to win the approval of the best people, are optimate. What, then, is an optimate? Their numbers, if you must know, are infinite, for otherwise they could not possibly hold their own. They include the leaders of public policy and their followers, men of the highest standing, to whom the senate is open, together with Roman citizens of the municipalities and landed pro-

[1] *Pro Cluent.* 55. 151.
[2] *Pro Sulla*, 26. 72; *De Harusp. Resp.* 25. 54; *Ad Attic.* viii. 11. 2. [3] *De Fin.* iii. 22. 75.
[4] 'Sullaturio'; 'Sulla potuit, ego non potero?'—a remark attributed to Pompey.
[5] *In Verr.* iii. 35. 81. [6] *Pro Sestio*, 22. 50.

prietors in the country, business men as well as freedmen. Great, however, as are their number and variety, the group as a whole may accurately and summarily be defined as follows: All men are optimates who are inoffensive, of pure morals, not subject to passion or involved in debt. These are the safe and sane, the sound elements in the community; their ideal is that which appeals as finest and most eligible to persons of this character: it is social security (*otium cum dignitate*). All who cherish this ideal are optimates; those who work for it must be regarded as true men and genuine conservatives (*conservatores civitatis*). As for the foundations of this social security, to be defended even at the cost of life and limb, I may enumerate them as follows: the official religion of worship and divination, executive authority, senatorial influence, statute and customary law, the popular courts and magisterial jurisdiction, good faith, the provinces and allies, imperial prestige, military and financial strength.

'A state as large as ours includes multitudes who, from a consciousness of villainy and fear of punishment, are eager for revolutionary agitation and change or who, because of a kind of congenital madness, batten on civil discord and strife or who, since they are plunged in debt, prefer to see the community go up in flames rather than be themselves burned.'[1]

This declaration is not less illuminating than the formal treatises in which Cicero labours to expound and justify his political faith. Written shortly before the catastrophe which was to complete the ruin of his hopes, it reveals him, even more truly than Aristotle, as 'the first Whig'. As such, his creed finds appropriate expression in the twofold conception of order and freedom (*imperium et libertas*); and this he boldly identifies with the rights of property. It was indeed Cicero, rather than Locke, who first asserted that the purpose of organized society was to establish and maintain this principle.

'The primary concern of those responsible for the conduct of public affairs', he says, 'will be to make certain that every man is secure in his possessions, and that there is no invasion of private right on the part of government. . . . This, indeed, is the reason why states and republics have been created. For, though nature herself prompts men to congregate together, nevertheless it is in the hope of protecting what they have that they seek the protection of cities.'[2]

With all the fervour of a true Roman, Cicero believed that the mission of his country was to make the world safe for property. This he conceived not in any absolute sense but, in the termino-

---

[1] *Pro Sestio*, 45-6. 96-9. [2] *De Offic.* ii. 21. 73.

logy of jurisprudence, as an object (*res*) which exists only for a subject of legal right (*persona*); in other words, as an 'extension of personality'. As such, its function was to ensure independence, thus making possible either of the alternatives characteristic of a well-ordered society, inactivity without loss of standing and activity exempt from risk.[1] With these refinements, the Romans had arrived at a point of view which was foreign to the political thinking of the Greeks. For whereas the word *polis* had carried with it the suggestion of 'one big family' or an all-in partnership, the term *res publica* could hardly be used without an implied reference to its counterpart, the *res privata*. *Res privata*, although distinct from, was not in conflict with *res publica*, but rather its correlative, indissolubly linked to it by what may be called 'a principle of polarity' and, in a precisely analogous sense, the object of right. Thus envisaged, the 'republic' may be defined as 'that which belongs to the people', a people being 'no heterogeneous collection of human beings, but a society organized *iuris consensu et utilitatis communione*, i.e. on a basis of agreed rights and common interests'.[2] These rights and interests constitute citizenship and they exist, he adds, in order to make possible 'a better and happier life'. Accordingly, their origin may be traced not so much to human weakness as to the compulsions of nature, which have made mankind a gregarious and social rather than a solitary animal. But, in this respect, the role played by nature is that of stepmother (*natura noverca*); since, while she prompts men to associate, she leaves it to them to create the forms of association which will meet their needs.

The social thinking of Cicero, thus developed against the revolutionary background, is, so to speak, distilled into the *De Officiis*, a work which, composed for his son in the summer of 44 B.C., may well be described as his spiritual testament. The title[3] itself is significant of Cicero's attitude to life; he sees it as a complex of obligations to oneself and others, in the discharge of which a man realizes the fullest potentialities of his being. Of such obligations the most fundamental are those prescribed by the demands of rectitude, the absolute moral ideal (τὸ καλόν

---

[1] *De Orat.* i. 1. 1: 'qui in optima re publica . . . eum vitae cursum tenere potuerunt, ut vel in negotio sine periculo vel in otio cum dignitate esse possent.'

[2] *De Rep.* i. 25. 39.

[3] i. 3. 8: 'perfectum officium rectum, opinor, vocemus quoniam Graeci κατόρθωμα, hoc autem commune officium vocant.' The *De Officiis* is, thus, a text-book of 'civics'.

or *honestum*) as envisaged by Plato and those who shared his faith in the existence of a realm of truth independent of the material flux. A second group of obligations is that imposed by the requirements of expediency (*utile*); these being defined as 'duties which appertain to the embellishment of life, as well as to the provision of means and resources advantageous to mankind'.[1] Additional problems of obligation are thought to emerge (*a*) whenever the claims of expediency appear to conflict with those of rectitude, and (*b*) when it becomes necessary to institute a comparison of values, whether (i) from the standpoint of honour, or (ii) from that of utility. Cicero thus arrives at five topics or 'heads of deliberation', in terms of which he claims to comprehend the subject of obligations as a whole.

As for the specific duties which arise under these various categories, this question is, in Cicero's opinion, to be solved by reference to 'nature'. Accordingly, in language borrowed largely from the Stoics, he offers a conspectus of human nature designed to reveal the impulses and appetites fundamental to mankind. Of these, the first is the urge to self-preservation and reproduction common to all living beings. It is this which prompts a man to defend his existence, avoiding that which is harmful and pursuing that which is serviceable to this end. But, over and above these primary objects of desire, Cicero discerns certain appetites which he regards as distinctively human, since they depend upon the fact that mankind is endowed with reason, whereby he relates means to ends in an ordered scheme of life. The first of these is an inclination to social intercourse ('hominum coetus, orationis et vitae societas'). This causes him to identify his life with that of his fellows and to develop various forms of association with them. It thus becomes the chief motive for achievement ('quae cura exsuscitat animos et maiores ad rem gerendam facit'). The second is the pursuit and investigation of truth ('veri inquisitio atque investigatio, cognitionis et scientiae cupiditas'), which is excited with the liberation of the human being from the necessity of pursuing basic physical needs. It is with the satisfaction of this appetite that he comes to be most truly himself. The third is a passion for prominence or distinction ('adpetitio quaedam principatus'). This desire lies at the root of aspirations to knowledge and power. At the same time, it determines the limits of authority

---

[1] *De Offic.* ii. 1. 1.

and subordination among men, for deference may justly be
paid only to the claims of superior wisdom or of power which
is exercised for the common good. The fourth and last is a love
of order and sense of propriety, leading to moderation in word
and deed (τὸ πρέπον, or *decorum*). No animal shares in the sense
of beauty and harmony possessed by human beings and on the
satisfaction of which their conduct so largely depends.

Starting from this conspectus of human nature, Cicero undertakes to erect a scheme of ethics. Four possible ideals emerge,
corresponding to the four traditional cardinal virtues. These
are: (1) the life of wisdom or contemplation, (2) the life of justice
and beneficence, (3) courage or loftiness and strength of mind,
(4) temperance or moderation and propriety. These possibilities he considers in turn, but with a characteristically Roman
bias, as when he asserts that the pursuit of individual excellence
is in all cases to be subordinated to the paramount need of
maintaining the security and welfare of the organized community. Thus, for Cicero no less than for Vergil, salvation is
not individual, but marks the achievement of purposes which
are to be realized only in the corporate life.

With this preliminary warning, Cicero proceeds to discuss
wisdom or the life of contemplation. This he dismisses with a
brief reference to its besetting sins—hastiness of judgement and
the waste of time involved in aimless and unprofitable studies
which supersede activity—a kind of virtuosity by no means
extinct in modern times.[1]

Next comes justice, which, as the basis of human relationships
and, in a peculiar sense, the Roman virtue, receives a much
fuller treatment than the contemplative ideal.[2] Justice is described as the bond and principle of civil society. Its content is
indicated in two formulas:

To harm no one unless provoked by injury ('ne cui quis noceat
nisi lacessitus iniuria').

To employ common goods for communal ends, private goods for
one's own ('ut communibus pro communibus utatur, privatis
ut suis').

Thus civil society, considered as an embodiment of justice,
exists for the double purpose of redressing injuries and of
enforcing rights. Of these rights the most fundamental is that
of property. Tracing property to an origin in long-standing

[1] i. 6. 18–19.   [2] i. 7 foll. 20–60.

occupation, conquest, agreement, or allotment, Cicero asserts
that it constitutes a right, to interfere with which is to violate
the purpose which underlies human society. Justice includes
also the reciprocal exchange of mutual services ('communes
utilitates in medium adferre mutatione officiorum dando acci-
piendo'). As such, its basis lies in good faith, i.e. fidelity to
engagements. The mark of a just society will therefore be (a)
respect for the sanctity of contract, and (b) a determination to
see that every man receives his due ('tribuendo suum cuique et
rerum contractarum fide'). From these principles it is possible
to infer the character of injustice, the genesis of which may be
traced to selfishness, fear, or greed. It thus becomes evident
that there is a 'natural' limit to the pursuit of wealth, beyond
which it serves no useful purpose. To forget this limit is to open
the door to unrestricted competition (contentio) such as had
marked the economic and political imperialism of Crassus and
Caesar or to 'unsocial' money-making, the satisfaction of an
instinct for acquisition which reflects nothing but political
indifference or a miserly fear of incurring expense.

Justice involves a number of positive obligations; in describing which Cicero (notwithstanding his supposed lack of originality) attains a position radically different from that of Greek
idealism in its loftiest flights. For, while affirming that this
principle is the bond of men in states, Aristotle had accepted
the corollary that it is without application to members of
different communities, where there are 'no common magistracies to enforce engagements', thereby consigning inter-state
relationships to the sway of expediency or force. Cicero, however, with the long background of Roman history behind him,
propounds the view that, while the use of force is characteristic
of the beast, the method of settling differences appropriate to
men is that of debate or discussion ('vis proprium beluarum,
disceptatio proprium hominis'), and this rule he applies to the
relations of communities no less than individuals, making it the
basis for a theory of international law. From this standpoint,
he denied the legitimacy of war except for the purpose of exacting redress for injuries suffered (rebus repetitis), and then only
after a formal declaration. On the same principle, he denounced
all forms of national aggrandizement which were dictated merely
by the love of power and glory, thus transcending the Machiavel-
lism of classical antiquity and proclaiming the doctrine

that states as well as individuals are bound to keep faith.[1] Latin thinking, which recognized a difference between individual and community unfamiliar to the Greeks, gave rise to other no less significant conclusions. Thus, for example, Cicero accepted the distinction between 'combatants' and 'non-combatants' originally proposed by the elder Cato, and maintained that the obligations of individuals do not disappear by reason of the fact that the states of which they are members are at war.[2] But perhaps the most remarkable implication of Cicero's theory of justice had reference not to aliens or enemies but to slaves. The Stoic Chrysippus, according to Seneca,[3] had first enunciated the proposition that slaves are to be regarded as permanent hired employees. This Cicero accepted as a rationalization of existing Roman practice in the formula: 'ita uti ut mercenariis; opera exigenda, iusta praebenda.'

The third virtue to be dealt with is courage or fortitude.[4] This quality, though commonly regarded as more glorious than any of the other three, must nevertheless be associated with them if it is not to become a vice. For the spirit of fortitude is often accompanied by a love of power and by impatience of control, which give rise to acts of injustice such as those with which the society of Cicero's day was all too familiar. Emphasizing his distaste for militarism and imperialism, Cicero finds that true courage lies in the capacity for passive endurance with complete disregard for outward things, and for the active performance of great deeds attended with danger and difficulty. As such, it depends on (a) a correct appraisal of the good to be achieved, (b) freedom from all improper desires such as wealth, power, and glory. It thus presupposes a rigid subjection of the emotions to the imperatives of reason.

This is to socialize the notion of courage which, while it may dictate withdrawal from active life, on grounds, for instance, of poor health, will, in all but exceptional circumstances, call for the meticulous discharge of civic obligations. Normally, therefore, it will be exhibited in public relations and it will be apparent in the arts of peace no less than of war. When it is a question of vindicating the peace, courage requires that the citizen should take up arms, but the fighting qualities are the least significant element of this virtue, and the general at any rate will need a great understanding no less than a stout heart,

[1] § 38.   [2] §§ 37, 39.   [3] *De Beneficiis*, iii. 22. 1.   [4] *De Offic.* i. §§ 61–92.

if he is to avoid the behaviour which so often sullies the laurels of victory. Thus for Cicero courage is a moral and intellectual rather than a physical virtue; as such, it finds its supreme embodiment in the statesman who, without thought of private advantage, makes the good of the governed his sole aim, remembering that his office is a trust ('ut enim tutela, sic procuratio rei publicae'). Such a man will rise above partisan feeling and will speak his mind openly without hesitating to give offence; he will shun half-measures and equivocal courses; he will be lenient, affable, and courteous, strictly conscientious and exempt from passion when obliged to inflict punishment.

The fourth and last of the cardinal virtues is temperance.[1] Temperance prescribes a rule of decorum or propriety, which is characteristically defined as behaviour compatible with the inherent dignity of human nature. It thus implies that whatever a man says or does will be appropriate to the occasion. For nature herself has imposed on each and every one a role, which he must study to fulfil. In general, therefore, the duties ordained by propriety are: to follow nature's guidance, cultivating an earnest and thoughtful disposition, and keeping the emotions within bounds. Moreover, every person has two characters to support, viz. the one which he shares with all men as rational beings and the other which is peculiar to himself as an individual. While, therefore, he must take care always to act in accordance with reason, in so doing he will adopt a course which is consistent with his own disposition and aptitudes, thus avoiding the suggestion of incongruity or awkwardness. Accordingly, while developing the common graces of humanity, he will not do so at the cost of thwarting or perverting his own development.

Thus envisaged as a question of 'my station and its duties', the dictates of propriety become clear. Obligations of magistrate and subject, of citizen and alien, will depend upon and vary with their respective relations. The magistrate, for instance, will recognize that he acts in a representative capacity, 'carrying the person of the state'. His first obligation will therefore be to protect its dignity and prestige, and to maintain and expound its laws, remembering that these are the functions which have been entrusted to him. The private citizen, on the other hand, will seek to comport himself on a basis of equality

[1] i. §§ 93–151.

with his fellows, avoiding any excess of abasement and self-assertion, and desiring for the commonwealth justice and tranquillity. The alien, on his part, will confine his attention to his own affairs, eschewing impertinent interference with public business which is none of his concern.

Specific injunctions of propriety include modesty and decency in behaviour and speech, together with the maintenance of a suitable establishment. This last requirement involves a discussion of the occupations appropriate to a gentleman. 'Liberal' occupations are defined in general (according to a convention which is still maintained) as those which involve the exercise of more than ordinary sagacity and from which accrue results of more than ordinary utility. They therefore embrace agriculture, together with medicine, architecture, higher education, and commerce 'if on a large scale'.

Concluding with an effort to formulate a hierarchy of duties, Cicero reaffirms the superiority of justice to wisdom, and repeats that philosophy is without value unless it be applied to the practical purposes of life and to the advantage of mankind. Tracing the origin of civil society to social requirements rather than to necessity, he finds it to be inherently moral. This sets a limit to the claims of patriotism and disposes of any supposed obligation to defend the fatherland under all circumstances. The state, as an embodiment of the social consciousness, has no right to expect immoral conduct of its members. Accordingly, in the schematization of duties, the demands of religion come first, those of patriotism second, thirdly, domestic obligations, and, finally, the remaining obligations of civilized man.[1]

Having thus concluded his examination of rectitude, Cicero proceeds to discuss the question of 'utility' or, as we should say, of economic advantage as a motive in human life. That this was a factor of great importance he is fully aware; to the spokesman of financial interests in the Roman senate, it could hardly indeed have been otherwise. Accordingly, he pays to the economic motive a generous tribute as the source and inspiration of the arts to which social life owes its superiority over that of solitude, including among these the care of health, agriculture, navigation, export and import trade, the construction of buildings, roads, and aqueducts, together with enterprises such as irrigation and mining.[2] Nevertheless, as a humanist, he asserts

[1] §§ 152-60.   [2] ii. §§ 12-14.

his unequivocal opposition to the view that it is possible to dissociate the concept of utility from that of rectitude and to accept it as an independent principle; for him, its significance is and must be as the means to an end. From this standpoint, there cannot be any true utility which does not conform to the demands of the moral ideal (*nihil utile nisi quod honestum*).

On the other hand, it is possible to consider the elements of this world as ministering to our advantage; and, thus envisaged, they may be classified as inanimate, animate, and rational, i.e., as he says, 'gods and men'. Of these, the last are of the greatest moment, whether for good or evil;[1] to co-operation with one another, rather than to 'fortune' or 'circumstance', must be ascribed the most important achievements of mankind. Accordingly, to succeed in life, one must win the support of one's fellows, and for this purpose one must know the true grounds of honour and esteem among men.[2]

In this connexion, Cicero vehemently denies that the secret lies with persons like Crassus and Caesar, the contemporary exponents of power-philosophy to whom fear and interest were the sole motive-forces in human life.[3] Citing the fate of these men, he takes it to demonstrate the futility of their creed and to prove that goodwill provides the only sound basis for co-operative endeavour, a rule which he applies to the relations of societies no less than to those of individuals. From this point of view, the prestige of Rome in its best days was to be explained by the fact that it was in reality a *patrocinium* rather than an *imperium*, a big brother's movement and not a system of organized might.[4] On the other hand, Caesar and Crassus failed because they were guilty of a fundamental confusion of mind; with them, the lust for ascendancy (*libido dominandi*) had usurped the place of a thirst for distinction (*appetitio principatus*) which might have been satisfied without injury to their fellow men. For this reason, they missed the very glory on which they had set their hearts.

True glory depends upon affection, confidence, and admiration, sentiments which are to be evoked by acts of justice and beneficence. Of these, justice is the more important; on it rests the possibility of common action, and, in this respect, it is indispensable even to a gang of thieves.[5] Beneficence, however, is also a legitimate avenue to glory. As such, it takes the form

[1] § 16.   [2] 19.   [3] 22.   [4] 27.   [5] 40.

either of gifts or services.[1] In the one sense, it is seen in the provision of games, the erection of buildings, and the dispensation of hospitality, but it is never to be confused with extravagant and ill-considered bounty.[2] In the other, it manifests itself in various forms of personal activity such, for example, as pleading in the courts, and it may be rendered either to individuals or to the public as a whole.

With this consideration, Cicero arrives at the duties of public office, which he summarizes as follows:

(1) to maintain the rights of property;
(2) to abstain from burdensome taxation;
(3) to ensure to every one an abundance of the necessities of life;
(4) to be scrupulously clean-handed, above the suspicion of greed or corruption.

In the light of these maxims, he denounces as worthy of capital punishment statements like that of the tribune Philippus when he declared that, in all Rome, there were not above two thousand property-owners. In this he saw an attempt to inflame the passions of the mob and to promote an agitation for 'sharing the wealth' which would subvert the whole fabric of organized society. As such, it was typical of the levelling and confiscatory measures advocated by unscrupulous popular leaders in their efforts to win political influence (*gratia*). But, while setting his face against any attempt to enrich the debtor at his creditor's expense, Cicero offered no opposition to proposals which might help to relieve the crushing burden of indebtedness without doing violence to good faith, the basis of the commonwealth. And this, he felt, could survive only if the debtor was compelled to liquidate his obligations.[3] It was on this very issue, he says, that he resisted the Catilinarians. The conclusion was obvious: the first duty of government was to ensure through the machinery of law that every man should retain what he owned and that, while the poor and lowly should not be swindled out of their earnings, envy of the prosperous might not cause them to be robbed of their wealth. Such were the principles to which the ancient Romans had adhered and which had brought them influence and glory.[4]

---

[1] § 52.   [2] 54.
[3] 84: 'nec enim ulla res vehementius rem publicam continet quam fides, quae esse nulla potest, nisi erit necessaria solutio rerum creditarum'.   [4] 85.

With these general conclusions, Cicero arrives at the problem of conflict between the demands of rectitude and those of expediency, a problem which, to him, was more apparent than real. Recalling the principle *nihil utile nisi quod honestum*, he ventures the broad generalization that service is the law of life, and that to pursue one's own advantage to the detriment of another is to destroy the fellowship of mankind, just as the debilitation of any one of the bodily members involves the destruction of the organism as a whole. Nature, he affirms, denies to no man 'the right to live', but nature and the law of nations alike forbid him to harm others in the effort to do so, and this it is the purpose of law to prevent. It must thus be accepted as axiomatic that 'the good of each and every individual is the good of the whole' (*eadem utilitas uniuscuiusque et universorum*). To this law there can be no possible exception; it postulates the same consideration for fellow citizens as for kinsmen, and for aliens as for fellow citizens. To its elucidation and vindication he consecrates his third and final book.

The doctrine thus propounded admits of an interesting qualification which, as we may pause to note, Cicero accepts. This is that, strictly speaking, there can be no fellowship with 'tyrants', economic and political dynasts like Crassus and Caesar whom he describes as 'wild beasts in human form' (*ista in figura hominis feritas et inmanitas beluae*), and whose very existence he regards as incompatible with that of the commonwealth. With respect to such men, he boldly enunciates the proposition: killing no murder. 'This pestiferous and impious tribe must be expelled from the society of the free, as one cuts off a limb when it becomes moribund and threatens to poison the other parts of the body.'[1]

The good citizen, on the other hand, must resist with all his might the temptation of Gyges.[2] This temptation may arise from the supposed demands either of political expediency or of friendship.[3] In the one case, it results in acts such as the Roman destruction of Corinth, on which Cicero's comment is that nothing which is shameful can be truly expedient.[4] In the other, the only safe rule is that one should never serve a friend to the injury of the public or in violation of one's pledged word.[5] No reward, however great, is sufficient to justify crookedness, and the man who practises it is bound, in the end, to lose.[6]

[1] iii. § 32.   [2] 38.   [3] 43 and 44.   [4] 49.   [5] 43.   [6] 79-81.

The truth thus stated is vouched for and authenticated by nature herself. This fact is evident from the findings of jurisprudence in the light of which the hoary maxim *caveat emptor* is shown to be obsolete. For the true spirit of law, as revealed by the *Lex Aquilia de dolo malo*, is opposed to misrepresentation and fraud of any kind. This statute provides that, in selling an article, the vendor shall make known to the purchaser any defects of which he is cognizant; and, in confirmation of this, the jurists have held that it is an offence for him to remain silent when questioned. In so doing, it implies that the demands of good faith are paramount, binding even upon enemies so long as faith and honour may be postulated on both sides.[1] But, in its effort to realize the ideal of *bona fides*, moral philosophy goes farther than jurisprudence, which is concerned merely with objective fact. Accordingly, there arises a distinction between the civil law and the law of nature, and it constantly becomes necessary to invoke the latter in order to correct deficiencies in the former, according to the maxim of Scaevola: INTER BONOS BENE AGIER OPORTET ET SINE FRAUDATIONE EX BONA FIDE. This rule applies to all forms of contract—wardships, partnerships, trusts and commissions, purchases and sales, hirings and lettings —and rightly, because it is in accord with the highest demands of our nature, which is, at bottom, the real source of law; and it absolutely condemns sharp practice (*simulatio intellegentiae*) in all forms.[2] On it depends the obligation of keeping faith even in the crucial instance of pledges given to an enemy; for, in the last analysis, the oath has reference to the honour of the man who takes it rather than to any supposed vengeance of the gods. Regulus, therefore, was no fool in sacrificing himself to this principle.

We have already referred to the estimates placed upon the *De Officiis* by great modern authorities. In this essay the author gives final utterance to his conviction that the end for which nature has designed mankind is the achievement of what may be called empirical selfhood, and that the purpose of organized society is to promote its development by establishing and maintaining adequate social controls. In so doing, Cicero proclaims an ideal of excellence not unworthy of human beings. At the same time, he insists upon their capacity to realize that ideal through a self-imposed discipline in which the passions are

[1] § 61.   [2] 72.

subjected to the control of reason; and in this he sees a possibility of transcending the limitations of barbarism and of
'civilizing', without suppressing, the ego.

From this standpoint, there can be no question as to the
ultimate residence of sovereignty; it is and must remain with
the *populus* or organized community whose primacy is, thus,
theoretically secure and final. This community is the generative
source both of *imperium* and *dominium*, the former the principle
of public order, the latter that of private right. But, in contra-
distinction from *dominium*, *imperium* is non-hereditary and, so far
from conferring any title to ownership, it exists in order to protect
owners in their titles. Accordingly, to transform it into an
instrument of possession is to deny the fundamental idea of the
commonwealth and to confuse it with those forms of barbaric
kingship for which no such distinction exists. On this fact
depend the scope and character of magisterial power. The
magistrate is charged with the maintenance of public order and,
for that reason, armed with coercive authority. But that
authority is limited by the terms of his commission; to abuse it
is to create a right of resistance on the part of the sovereign
people whose 'majesty' is thus infringed (*laesa maiestas populi
Romani*). A situation like this is, however, pathological; it
develops only when terrorism (*vis et terror*) has replaced the true
basis of political cohesion, viz. consent (*voluntas*).

In this brief statement of republican doctrine there is nothing
especially novel; it merely reasserts, in terms of Roman legalism,
what may be called the paradox of the commonwealth, viz.
that, however conservative in spirit and intention, its roots are
nevertheless planted in the soil of revolution. Of this truth
democratic Athens had provided spectacular illustration in the
monument erected to the tyrannicides Harmodius and Aristo-
geiton. At Rome it found expression in traditions connected
with Brutus and other legendary champions of popular liberty.
But, as republicanism was now menaced by subversive forces
such as it had never before encountered, it was badly in need
of a fresh vindication, and this it was the mission of Cicero to
provide. Thus, despite the irresolution and inconsistency which
marked his behaviour on various critical occasions, he closed
his career as he had begun it, with a vigorous attack on despotism and an impassioned appeal for republican freedom and
justice. From this standpoint, there can be no doubt that he

made himself an accessory to the Regicide, and for this he was in due course to pay the penalty with his life. But, if he thus seemed to perish as the martyr to a lost cause, his eclipse was only for the moment. By reaffirming the eternal, though partial, truths of classical liberalism and by exhibiting their dependence upon idealistic foundations, he helped to check the progress of barbarization within the empire and to strengthen republican prejudices in such a way that they had to be reckoned with in the final accounting by Augustus Caesar. These prejudices were never quite to die out in the Western world; and they have emerged in curious places and unexpected forms in modern times. We may see them in the bitter denunciation of autocracy contained in Machiavelli's *Discourses*, and Jefferson restates them when he declares that, if the tree of liberty is to flourish, it must frequently be watered with the blood of its foes.

In his effort to give new life to the republic, Cicero appears to break new ground in at least one important particular. This is in what he has to say about public opinion as a factor of democratic control. It had been assumed in pre-revolutionary speculative circles that the problem was one merely of political mechanics and that its solution lay in a balance of opposing forces within the constitution. This, it was supposed, would neutralize possible excesses whether of the magistrate, the aristocracy, or the commons, thus preventing their respective 'perversions', tyranny, oligarchy, or mob-rule.[1] Furthermore, it was generally agreed that, by the establishment of such a balance, permanent equilibrium had actually been achieved at Rome. The disorders of revolutionary times were to expose the fallacy of this view and, doctrinaire though he was, Cicero was too acute not to perceive it. Thus, though he offered a nominal adherence to the theory of the mixed constitution, he recognized that this in itself was no adequate safeguard of freedom. What was needed, he urged, was an active and vigorous public opinion, such as was possible through the co-operation of men in all walks of life who believed in the preservation of republican ideals. This is what he meant by the *consensus* or *concordia ordinum*, a mobilization of sanity, as it seemed for a moment to have been realized at the time of his own consulship. In that case, however, the 'united front' was the result of a purely temporary panic; the question was how to give it permanence. This he

[1] Polyb. vi.

felt was, in the last analysis, a matter of initiative and direction. That is to say, it raised the problem of leadership in a free state.

At this point Cicero had arrived by 54 B.C., when he wrote the *De Re Publica*.

'I spend my whole time', he declares in an intimate letter, 'reflecting upon the character of the man whose lineaments, you will admit, I have drawn with sufficient accuracy in this work. Do you recall the standards by which we would have that guardian of the state measure all his acts? . . . Just as the pilot aims at successful navigation, the physician health, the general victory, so the object of this moderator of the commonwealth will be the happiness of his fellow citizens, that they may enjoy security of property, ample wealth, a full meed of glory, together with a life ennobled by virtue. And my desire is that he should be the means of fulfilling this, the greatest and most important task among men.'[1]

By thus indicating a need for leadership, Cicero gives utterance to what was without doubt a widespread and insistent demand of the time.[2] But for Cicero the requirements of such leadership were not met by any form of dictatorship, in which he saw merely the ultimate expression of the factious spirit he so deeply deplored. In his eyes, the true leader must have the qualities of a *moderator, gubernator, rector, protector rei publicae*, the prince or first citizen of a free society; and such a man was by no means easy to find. Thus, while at first disposed to cast Pompey for the role, he saw the vision fade, as the latter made himself the cat's-paw of reactionaries whose sole purpose was to translate the republic into the narrowest and most exclusive of dynastic monopolies. Then, after Pompey's miserable end, he turned with reluctance to Caesar, whose speedy fall he had earlier predicted, and gave to his régime a qualified endorsement while, at the same time, he urged upon him a programme of political action compatible with republican ideals.[3] When, finally, the *Nova Concordia* of Julius and, with it, the policy of reconciliation and appeasement gave place to his later schemes, Cicero hailed the murder of the dictator with a savage glee which indicates the depth of his resentment at pretensions that offended every instinct of order and decency in Roman life.[4]

---

[1] *Ad Attic.* viii. 11, 49 B.C.
[2] Cf. the address to Caesar, *De ordinanda re publica*, to which reference has already been made in Ch. I above, p. 9.   [3] *Pro Marcello*; *Ad Fam.* iv. 4. 4.
[4] *De Offic.* i. 8. 26: 'temeritas C. Caesaris qui omnia iura divina et humana pervertit'; cf. iii. 21. 82 and 83.

In Cicero's eyes, the failure of Pompey and Caesar was the result of a radical defect of character; 'both wanted power, their ambition was to be kings'. True leadership, on the other hand, was immune from temptations such as those to which Pompey and Caesar had succumbed. Superior to the vanities and deceits of material self-assertion, it was inspired by a thirst for honour and glory which found sufficient reward in ministering to the common good. In this way, it satisfied the demand of society for 'an element of monarchical distinction' (*quiddam praestans et reyale*) without doing violence to the most exacting standards of republican virtue. But, as such virtue was in his day conspicuous by its absence, Cicero discovered it, as he discovered the commonwealth of his dreams, in the past. In the idealized figure of the younger Scipio he saw precisely that combination of loyalty or devotion (*pietas*) with enlightened and refined perceptions of right (*iustitia*) which qualified him to be a true guardian or protector of the republic.

We need not pause to consider how far the portrait thus drawn corresponds with fact; certainly the Cato of history would have failed to recognize himself in the gentle and humane philosopher of the dialogue *De Senectute*, and in all probability the same may be said of Scipio Aemilianus. But, for the author, the question was not so much one of historicity as of artistic verisimilitude; and this is by no means accidental. He spoke as the exponent of Academic idealism, for which a genuine incarnation was both inconceivable and unnecessary. To this fact we may perhaps ascribe the deficiencies of Cicero the 'trimmer', the man whose professions were not seldom at variance with his practice, the *imperator* who was too proud to fight.

It is strictly in accord with this type of mind that, since it recognizes its inability to integrate thought and action in this world, it should look for a principle of integration in a world of the imagination. In this respect, also, Cicero runs true to type; for the only principle he can discover comes to him in the shape of a dream. The *Somnium Scipionis* represents the frail embodiment of his hope for a political salvation, and in it we may perceive the sanction for that hope. This depends, in part, upon traditional Roman beliefs regarding the stock; the faith that, while the individual was the creature of a day, the 'family' was immortal; the business of its members, while they live, being to 'carry the person' of the family, showing themselves worthy representatives of the ancestors whose names they bear. But, in the case of Cicero, these beliefs were reinforced by certain intimations of personal immortality, based on philosophic fancies derived from Pythagoras and Plato.[1]

We may thus conclude that, in his person, Cicero illustrates to perfection the strength and weakness of classical liberal idealism. From this standpoint, there can be no doubt that, so far from forecasting the concrete realities of the Augustan principate, he would have found them hardly less distasteful than, in fact, he found the monarchy of Julius. For, as the course of events was to demonstrate, a régime of justice and equity such as he desiderates was not to be realized even under the aegis of Augustus and Rome. It is none the less true that, if Cicero did not anticipate the work of Augustus, Augustus on his part did look back to Cicero, seeing in his doctrine a much-needed justification for his power. In this way, the spirit of the orator, tortured and frustrated throughout his life, came to enjoy a vicarious immortality in the household of his enemies.

It is a truism to say that ideas have no legs; by themselves they do not march. Something, therefore, in the nature of a dynamic was needed in order to impart to Ciceronianism the vitality which it lacked; something to win it acceptance and make it what it was destined to become—the common coin of posterity. This dynamic it was the function of Vergil to provide. In providing it, he supplied the final ingredient to the ideology of the Augustan age.

It is evident that the work of Vergil was written with conscious reference to his predecessors and that, to obtain the effects which he desired, the poet drew freely upon the whole classical heritage, Greek as well as Latin. The truth of this is amply illustrated by the commanding skill with which he appropriates to his use the language as well as the thought of antiquity. Nevertheless, in his attitude to questions which were of vital interest to his generation, he represents a sharp reversion from the Hellenic to the Italian point of view; and, just as the raw materials of his work are derived from native life and history, so also its matrix lies in *religio*, undoubtedly the most characteristic element of Italian experience. What we see in Vergil is thus a Catonism, but with its foundations widened and deepened, its character purified and ennobled, by the findings of Ciceronian

[1] Especially *Timaeus*, 41 D–42 E.

philosophy. The result is to produce such force and effectiveness that, in the refulgent light of the Vergilian revelation, the commonplaces of Cicero assume the proportion of cosmic truths. For it enables the poet to offer a consecration to the principles of classical humanism, which is thus revealed, not as a step to religion, but as religion itself; while, at the same time, he provides a justification of Roman methods for the realization of classical ideals. In this spirit, at a critical moment in the fortunes of Western civilization, Vergil puts forward his interpretation of the history and destiny of the Eternal City, defining and fixing the secular meaning of *Romanitas* in close relationship to and yet with proud and confident independence of the ideals of Hellas.

But, if he thus gave a final turn to Augustan philosophy, Vergil did so by having recourse to an expedient which makes it improper, in a strict sense, to speak of him as a philosopher. This was the adoption of poetic form and method—a kind of 'thinking with the blood'. Nevertheless, if he resorted to this device, it was with a sure instinct that his purpose was not to be achieved by any amount of argumentation, but only by the seductive power of art. This power depends to some extent on form, but its essence lies in method, the method of immediacy. In virtue of its pictorial and representative character, poetry achieves its effects, not by argument but by suggestion, stimulating the imagination and exciting the emotions in order to win an assent or produce a conviction of which philosophy, in the narrower sense, must remain for ever incapable. Thus, with Vergil, it becomes the inevitable medium of expression.

In adopting this vehicle Vergil was, no doubt, inspired to some extent by the example of Lucretius, who had followed a convention familiar to antiquity by expounding the elements of a speculative system in verse. But what was to Lucretius an accident was for Vergil essential to his purpose; and the difference between them is perhaps best illustrated by the fresh connotation which the latter gives to concepts which they held in common. Thus, while both unite in hailing Venus as *mater Aeneadum*, the Vergilian Venus is so specifically, that of Lucretius only incidentally and, as it were, by courtesy. To the disciple of Epicurus, Venus represents merely the principle of attraction within the physical universe, finding expression in the *foedera naturae* and therein triumphing over its opposite, the principle

of strife or repulsion typified in Mars. To Vergil, she exempli-
fies the working of an order which is neither mechanical nor
fortuitous but providential, her function being to convey the
decrees of fate through Aeneas to her chosen people, thus
inspiring and assisting them to realize their destiny. The difference is significant of the gulf between the two; and it involves
an entirely different interpretation of nature and of life. Rejecting the mechanical-materialist system of the atomists, Vergil
rejects with it the notion of an automatic or spontaneous good.
Aeneas suffers to achieve, discovering felicity in the accomplishment of ends which, while they depend upon a secure foundation
of material well-being and while they do not exclude the simple
gratifications of sense, point to a goal which transcends
both. This goal is the realization of an ideal order, represented
symbolically by the poet in the choir and furniture of heaven,
which thus for him constitute no mere apparatus of literary
convention but possess an objective existence rooted in the very
nature of things.

The work of Vergil, like that of Lucretius, is in a large sense
didactic; otherwise, the difference between them is as wide as
the difference between Greece and Rome. The one preaches
a gospel of salvation through knowledge; the other of salvation
through will. The one holds up an ideal of repose and refined
sensual enjoyment; the other one of restless effort and activity.
Lucretius urges upon men a recognition of the fact that they are
limited as the dust; that the pursuit of their aspirations is as
vain and futile as are the impulses of religion, pride, and ambition which ceaselessly urge them on. The purpose of Vergil is to
vindicate those obscure forces within the self by which mankind
is impelled to material achievement and inhibited from destroying the work of his own hands. While, therefore, he may address
his predecessor in the fine compliment,

> Felix qui potuit rerum cognoscere causas,

it is clear that, in his heart, he condemns the shallow hedonism
which the latter professes, as well as the conclusions to which it
leads, and summons Romans to renewed faith in the secular
meaning of what their ancestors had accomplished in the past,
and what they themselves might hope to accomplish in the
future. It is this difference which makes the distinction between
the melancholic resignation of Lucretius and the resigned

melancholy of Vergil; the one the creed of a man who accepts the intellectual assurance of futility, the other that of one who, despite all obstacles, labours to discover and formulate reasonable grounds for his hope. It is this difference that makes the distinction between the epic of civilized materialism and that of material civilization.

For, as Vergil sees it, civilization does not evolve of itself; it is not the ultimate but unforeseen result of a fortuitous collocation of atoms. It must be constructed, and Vergil envisages his countrymen above all else as builders. Properly to understand Aeneas, it is necessary to think of him in the role of immigrant and pioneer. Mankind against a background of nature which he seeks to subdue to his purpose; concentration of the powers of heart, head, and hand in the steady pursuit of an end kept in view to the exclusion of all subordinate aims; the will to work, the will to fight; boldness of innovation combined with an intense desire to preserve accumulated gains; that passionate affection for what has been achieved by blood and sweat, tears and misery, which men call patriotism, a sentiment even for us akin to religion, to the Romans religion itself—these are the elements of a picture unfolded by the poet in measures, the stately beauty of which accords precisely with the demands of the theme.

If, however, the *Aeneid* has in addition the character of a national epic, it is because Vergil perceives that to build a civilization requires something more than effort, and that is organization. The magnificent demonstration of disciplined obedience which, in all the greatest periods of her history, characterized the Roman state is reflected also in her greatest literary monument—leadership at once devoted and prudent (this, by the way, is the answer to Tertullian's charge that Aeneas had not the courage of a dog); authority and subordination based on that iron law of inequality which appears to mark the external relationships of men; co-operation, arising from the sense of a common purpose, shared alike by leader and led, in the task of constructing an impregnable fortress for the *Palladium*, the guarantee and pledge of the national fate.

Thus does Vergil seek to justify an urge to practical activity, the spirit of which we shall best understand if we think of the Romans as having achieved in the Old World precisely that to which men of European stock were to set their hands in the New. The state and empire of Rome depend fundamentally on will: virtue is not so much knowledge as character; and its fruits are seen in activity rather than in repose or contemplation. Aeneas is thus the pilgrim father of antiquity; his followers the *Mayflower* company of the Ancient World; while the organized society of the empire is the Graeco-Roman counterpart to the New England Kingdom of the Saints; subject, it may be added, to limitations and threatened by dangers which confront all societies in which consecrated egotism (*amor sui*) disguises itself as the love of God.

Accordingly, Vergil gives authentic expression not merely to the Roman temper but in considerable degree to that of Western civilization as a whole. In so doing, he touches a high-water mark of achievement in Latin letters; in him alone you see them all. For he discloses the real nature of the concord or agreement which underlies the Roman philosophy of the state—no shallow intellectual assent or compact but, as it had been defined by Cicero and as the word itself implies, 'a union of hearts'.[1]

The spirit and method of Vergil are evident even in his non-political works. The *Georgics* have been described as an epic of mother earth; they are not so much that as of 'wheat and woodland, tilth and vineyard, hive and horse and herd'; that is to say, a monument to the human effort which transforms the face of the earth and imparts to it, as has been said,[2] something of the warmth and life of an Italian landscape. What they suggest is not sentimental rapture but a call to work for the realization of moral values associated with the life of the farm, the qualities which enable Vergil thus to salute his native land:

> Salve, magna parens frugum, Saturnia tellus,
> magna virum . . .

as though the finest product of a country were the men she breeds.

Such ideas, already adumbrated in Vergil's earlier works, were to receive detailed treatment in the *Aeneid*. The epic is charged with a sense that, with the rise of Rome, fate has given birth to something novel in the evolution of peoples. And this, her last and greatest achievement, she has accomplished in the West. Thus did Vergil proclaim for the first time the autonomy

---

[1] Cic. *De Rep.* i. 32. 49 and ii. 42. 69.
[2] Wight Duff, *A Literary History of Rome*, p. 449, quoting *Georgics*, i. 99: 'exercetque frequens tellurem atque imperat arvis'; cf. Tenney Frank, *Vergil*, pp. 160–6.

of the Western spirit, the function of which was to resume and complete the work of emancipation which the Greeks had left unfinished.

This note, struck at the beginning of the *Aeneid*, is repeated with increasing insistence as the theme develops, above all in the terms of settlement with which the poem concludes:

'Let Latium be. Let Alban kings endure through ages, let Italian valour be potent in the race of Rome. . . . Ausonia shall keep her native speech and usage; and as her name is, so let it be. The Trojans shall sink mingling in her blood. I will add their sacred law and ritual, but make all Latins and of a single speech. Hence shall spring a race of tempered Ausonian blood, whom thou shalt see outdo men and gods in duty, nor shall any race so observe the worship of Juno.'[1]

The meaning of this is clear. Civilization was not to perish in the ashes of Troy, though the true significance of that disaster was to be apprehended only with the conclusion of Aeneas' quest of a new home for the spirit. It was the result of lessons learned by his failure in Thrace to found a second Ilium; of the enigmatic hint from Delian Apollo which was to send him wandering first to Crete, then on the long voyage past the new town of Helenus and Andromache, along the coast of Magna Graecia and Sicily, across to Africa and thence, finally, by way of Scylla and Charybdis, to his destined home on the Tiber.

Hic est Ausonia. This was the West of which the cryptic utterances of the immortal guide had given promise: 'the land Hesperia where prosperity awaits thee together with a kingdom and a king's daughter to wife'. Yet in the promise was involved a challenge.

'Here are no sons of Atreus nor glozing Ulysses. A race of hardy breed, we carry our new-born children to the streams and harden them in the bitter icy water. As boys, they spend wakeful nights in the chase, scouring the woodland; but in manhood, unwearied by toil and trained to poverty, they subdue the soil with mattocks and shake towns in war.'

Such was the human material which the Aeneadae were to subdue to their purpose, forging the elements of a new community, 'an Italy teeming with empire and loud with war, in which the servant of Fate was to transmit the blood of royal Teucer, through which he was to lay the whole world beneath his law'.

[1] This and the following quotations are from Mackail's translation.

But the merely physical dangers of the long and arduous pilgrimage were as nothing compared with the spiritual perils to be met and overcome. Of these, not the least serious was that of moral and spiritual contamination which would have made Ausonia subservient to a dominant culture of alien type. This danger presented itself in the contacts of the Aeneadae with the transplanted Orientalism of Carthage 'opulent and strong in war'; and it found expression in the Punic scheme of a common alliance against the nomads of the desert. 'The arms of Troy ranged with ours, what glory shall exalt the Punic stock!' In the tragic conclusion of the Dido episode Vergil prefigures not merely the issue of the Punic wars, but also, perhaps, emancipation from the pernicious legacy which Rome inherited from defeated Carthage, the economic and financial imperialism of the later republic. But, while rejecting the seductions of Dido, the Aeneadae were not exempt from temptations of a different order, viz. those of a hybrid and decadent Hellenism. For, despite the racial affinities between Greek and Trojan (Phrygians, Hellenes, and Latins were at bottom a single family), Hellenism was deeply corrupted; so that of all the Hellenes only Arcadian Evander, 'best of the Grecian race', was fit to be absorbed into the future Roman people.[1]

The basis of Western civilization was thus, in a sense, to be local and racial: its home Italy, its 'material' the pure and unspoiled Italian stock, full of drive and energy, and finding scope for the exercise of these qualities in the traditional pursuits of agriculture and war. But this by no means implied a throwback to primitivism, nor did it reveal any distrust of civilization such as was to mark the thought of Tacitus. To Vergil these were no more than raw materials in the hands of the political architect; in order to initiate progress, what was needed was just that capacity for direction and guidance which the Aeneadae were to infuse.

Thus, with the arrival in Latium of Aeneas and his followers, began the development of national progress, the advance by slow degrees and with infinite toil towards a goal to be realized only after a millennium of effort; a destiny to be accomplished through the unification and pacification of Italy. Therein lay mysteries which it was beyond the power of the poet to resolve:

[1] The feeling here is, perhaps, anti-Egyptian rather than anti-Greek. For Vergil, Cleopatra is the enemy.

'Was it well, O God, that nations destined to eternal peace should clash in so fierce a shock?' For, with the advent of the Aeneadae, Juno, their implacable foe, was to open wide the gates of the temple of Janus, that over Italy might brood the spirit of strife, diverting the children of Saturn from their warfare against nature to conflict with the immigrants and 'dispeopling the wide fields of husbandmen'. From this standpoint the losses imposed upon the natives were hardly less tragic than the sacrifices incurred by the Aeneadae themselves. The fall of a Mezentius, 'scorner of the gods', might indeed be understood and justified. But the fierce contention of Latin and Trojan involved more than this; it involved the death of a Turnus and of a Camilla. Turnus has been described as bad temper on two legs. It is truer to say that, in his proud and fiery soul, he embodied the elements of that *virtù* which was to be the backbone of Imperial Rome. The Achilles of the West, his only crime was that he was a barbarian. This circumstance drew down upon him a fate which involved also Camilla, who, except for the fact that she was uncivilized, typified all that was purest and best in Roman womanhood. On the other hand, the Aeneadae were not to achieve their purpose without paying a commensurate price. For, as they had made the Tiber only by leaving behind at Eryx 'the old, the feeble, all that were weak and fearful of peril', so now they were menaced in their new home with the prospect of losses before which the stoutest heart might quail; sustained by nothing except the hope of a reward which posterity alone would experience.

It thus becomes evident that, for Vergil, history is something more than a panorama, a glittering pageant which is yet without significance. To him it embodies a hidden meaning which, while it may be dimly forecast in the utterances of seers and prophets (Creusa, the Delian Apollo, the Cumaean Sibyl), is to be fully disclosed only with the culmination of secular process in the evolution of Eternal Rome. From this standpoint Vergilianism deserves, perhaps, in a peculiar sense to be called the religion of this world; as such, it gives rise to its own characteristic *Weltanschauung*.

The basis of Vergilian theology lies in a medley of ideas shared by the educated world of Cicero, Varro, and Ovid. Apart from the traditional farm and woodland spirits, the *di agrestes* to whom the poet paid such marked deference, its elements are drawn from the three great groups, according to the classification adopted by Varro from the pontiff Scaevola, viz. the gods of poetry, those of philosophy, and those of the state. In the work of Vergil, these are each made to fulfil the role to which convention assigned them. Subject as they are to a shifting connotation—the fate of all concepts—their exact meaning is more than often a matter of dispute; to a considerable extent they merely reflect the confusion of the pagan mind.[1] Yet out of this jumble there emerge certain fundamental notions in terms of which the poet seeks to communicate his sense of the process which gives rise to the imperial city. Throughout the poem the struggle of the Aeneadae to realize their destiny is typified in the conflict between Juno and Venus, the one the spirit of Carthage, the other that of Rome. Juno is 'unregenerate' or barbaric nature, manifesting itself in many different ways. Capable of bravery and generosity, she represents also implacable spite, vengeance, treachery, and stubborn pride, the strong temptations of vanity and delusion, a willingness to invoke the baser passions personified in Alecto, the minister of Hell—these and the weakness which would lay down the burden, as when Aeneas succumbs to the wiles of Dido or when, at Eryx, the women are moved to burn the fleet, crying: 'Here seek your Troy, here find your home . . .', until, in a violent revulsion, 'Juno was shaken out of their bosom'.[2] Throughout she is opposed to Venus, whose final triumph is, however, assured because she typifies in nature the spirit of rational order which is the ultimate law of its being. As such, she inspires and fosters the qualities of devotion and loyalty (*pietas*) as well as of a pity which is nevertheless tempered by the necessity of self-control. But her chief function is to prescribe such duties as are imposed by the larger utility, a sense of the common and permanent good to be achieved through the suppression of wayward and

[1] On the concepts of fate and fortune in Vergil there are some pertinent observations by Bailey, *Religion in Vergil*, p. 233: 'This is the supremely important point in Vergil's conception of fate. It is not a mechanical force, arising from the laws of nature, like the Greek ἀνάγκη, or an unmeaning caprice, as we find it sometimes in the Greek poets, but a deliberate purpose of the divine beings who are above the world and in the world.' On the other hand, *fortuna* means anything from fate (p. 237) to its very opposite (p. 212): 'a protest in favour of free will', 'marking the element of free will in the individual which by exceptional actions may thwart or modify the μοῖρα appointed by . . . fate'. (In other words, Vergil here oscillates between Stoicism and Platonism without being able to make up his mind between them.)

[2] Augustine, *De Civ. Dei*, x. 21: '(Iuno) a poetis inducitur inimica virtutibus.'

ephemeral impulses and desires. By this means she is enabled
in the end to redeem Juno herself, overcoming the conflict
within the members and bringing to pass the rule of reason
which is that of concord and peace. In this she is assisted by
Apollo, who, as the principle of light and leading, discloses occasional glimpses of the future, thus contributing to the fulfilment
of a destiny implicit in the will of Juppiter, Father omnipotent,
King of Gods and Men, and ultimately author of the Roman
fate.[1]

We may here observe that destiny, envisaged as a universal
law of reason, implies a certain freedom for humanity. It is
cosmic logic which men are at liberty to flout if they choose,
although, by so doing, they expose themselves to an inevitable
penalty. There was thus no fundamental obstacle to Aeneas'
remaining in the arms of Dido; and, indeed, he was strongly
tempted to do so. This, however, would have been to wrong
Ascanius, 'cheating him of his western kingdom and his destined
lands'; that is, it would have been to sin against oneself and
one's house. On the other hand, 'fortune must be borne to be
overborne, and, come what will, everything may be overcome
by endurance';[2] to subscribe to the dictates of Jove is to realize
the fullest possibilities of one's own nature, although, to win
through, one must possess the qualities of a Hercules. By thus
discerning, in the very order and constitution of nature, a
sanction for conduct, Vergil adds fresh meaning to the ancient
aphorism *faber suae quisque fortunae*, the pagan doctrine of justification by works. From this standpoint the undertaking of
Jove:[3]

> his ego nec metas rerum nec tempora pono:
> imperium sine fine dedi. . . .

constitutes at the same time a promise and a warning. For, as
it offers material rewards to virtue, so also it prescribes a
material penalty for vice.

This conception of cosmic justice governs the thought of the
poet as he paints his imaginative picture of Tartarus and the
Elysian fields.[4] It determines the list of capital vices and of
capital virtues for which men are to suffer or be rewarded in
the other world. It provides also a criterion of behaviour in

---

[1] For the development of Juppiter into a *numen praestantissimae mentis* see Warde
Fowler, *Roman Ideas of Deity* (1914), ch. ii.   [2] *Aen.* v. 709.   [3] *Aen.* i. 278.
[4] The Vergilian purgatory, *Aen.* vi. 733–51, recalls Plato, *Phaedrus* 249 A–B.

this, a basis for the appeal to Augustus; he will win unparalleled glory if he saves the empire and civilization. And, in a sense, the attitude of Vergil is endorsed by Augustine when he declares that, by devoting themselves to the things of this world, the Romans did not go without their reward.

The application to conduct of a standard by which it is appraised according to its social or anti-social character will serve to account for the sense of puritanism in Vergil; his stern desire to eradicate the *belli rabies et amor habendi*, the economic and political imperialism denounced uniformly by Roman thinkers as the source of demoralization. It helps to explain certain aspects of his work which are repugnant to the modern temperament, whether Christian or romantic, the 'pitilessness', for example, 'of the apostle of imperial autocracy'.[1] It is also, in all probability, the reason for certain maladjustments within the mind of the poet himself; the Vergilian humanity which rebels against the inhuman demands of his patriotism, the sharp conflict between the artistic and the missionary spirit which perhaps underlies the cryptic remark that he works in opposition to the muse (*invita Minerva*).

Thus envisaged, Vergil contains the elements of a philosophy of history such as was subsequently to find fuller and more adequate expression in the work of Augustine. In him we may perceive the spiritual foundations of the City of Man, over against which Augustine was to oppose its antitype in the shape of a city not built by human hands. At the same time, Vergil throws fresh light upon the process of the earthly city, which was to give birth to a doctrine of 'natural' rights destined likewise to be confronted by a code of rights based upon divine grace. These developments were, however, reserved for a future in which the cycle of the *civitas terrena* should have been completed and the classical doctrine, by working itself out, should have revealed its deficiencies. In the meanwhile, Vergilianism served as an inspiration to the liberalism of the classical empire. This liberalism was to be embodied in the social and political programme of the Caesars, especially the jurisprudence of the second and third centuries, which thus provides an authentic record of beliefs and sentiments cherished from the Augustan to the Antonine age.

In the light of this philosophy Vergil saw the history **and**

[1] Wight Duff, op. cit., p. 469.

destiny of Rome as something unique. As conceived by the poet, the empire was something radically different from any of the systems which it had supplanted—Carthaginian mercantilism, Hellenistic dynasticism, or Asiatic theocracy—and it was not for Rome to overthrow these rival systems simply to take their place, and go, in her turn, the same way. Ancient materialism had, indeed, worked out a 'pattern of empire', the *logos* of a process whereby nations successively achieved dominion only to have the sceptre torn from their grasp. This process had been explained to the Romans by Sallust.[1] To him it represented the working of a principle by virtue of which communities, one after the other, attained a Machiavellian 'concentration of *virtù*', i.e. of moral and intellectual qualities such as might enable them to satisfy the universal craving of mankind for power and glory by establishing their dominion over those among whom these qualities existed in lesser degree. But the same law which made possible this dominion also destroyed it, as, with the attainment of these ends, industry gave way to sloth, self-control and equity to lust, avarice, and pride. While thus explaining the history of other peoples, the Romans, however, found ground for believing that their own might prove an exception. Unique in its ideals, the Roman order was destined to a future also unique; for, as it embodied purposes which transcended the mere accumulation of wealth and power, so also it pointed to an eternity in sharp contrast to the ephemeral character of other systems. From the fate of such systems Rome was saved by the ends which *Romanitas* was to serve.

From this standpoint the permanence of *Romanitas* was ensured by the fact that it made possible a realization of what have been called 'the essential and indestructible elements of the private personality'.[2] In so doing, its success depended upon its method, which was that of building, so to speak, from the ground up; in other words, upon a recognition of the truth that 'in this earthly world the material seems grimly enough to be the basis from which men have to discover the sources of spiritual adequacy'. Of this impressive system, it may be observed, in the first place, that the dominant conception was novel. Amid the wreckage of empires founded on tyranny and

---

[1] *Cat.* 2. 4–5.
[2] Sohm, *The Institutes of Roman Law*, Eng. tr. (1907), Introd., p. 46.

exploitation it stood alone as the project of a world-community united by ties of the spirit. As such, it was genuinely *political*; it went beyond race, beyond colour, and, in all but a few exceptional instances, beyond religion as this was envisaged by antiquity. From this standpoint it might appear that *Romanitas* transcended all purely 'natural' bonds. This in fact it did, in so far as it denied the possibility of discovering any real basis for concord on the merely affective level of experience. But while transcending, it did not, however, repudiate the human affections, seeking rather to organize them in support of the imperial idea. Under the aegis of Eternal Rome, Greek and Latin, African, Gaul, and Spaniard remained free to lead their own lives and achieve their own destiny; as late as the end of the fourth century it was still possible for Augustine to speak (in his own words) 'as an African to Africans'. But, while local and racial differences continued to exist, citizens of the empire discovered a bond of community with one another on the plane of natural reason. It was on this account that the Roman order claimed a universality and a finality to which alternative systems of life could not pretend.

III

ROMA AETERNA: THE APOTHEOSIS OF POWER

THE Eternity of the Imperial City (*Aeternitas Populi Romani*) has popularly been identified with that of the Colosseum.

> quamdiu stabit Coliseus, stabit et Roma;
> quando cadet Coliseus, cadet et Roma;
> quando cadet Roma, cadet et mundus.

In reality it was that of an order which professed to satisfy the permanent and essential requirements of human nature, thereby fulfilling the secular hope of mankind. The order in question originated in response to a specific historical situation, i.e. to the material, moral, and intellectual problems created by the Roman revolution. Formally and substantially, it constituted the answer to those problems given by Augustus Caesar. But, in the solution he provided, the emperor claimed to have gone beyond the immediate needs of the occasion and to have laid the foundation for an enduring settlement. It was on this account that he demanded credit as the architect of what, as he supposed, was destined to prove the final form of organized society.[1]

The demand thus made was not gratuitous. On the contrary, it rested upon assumptions which were rooted in the thought and aspiration of classical antiquity. These assumptions were to become explicit in the Latin West with the reception of Greek culture. But, to appreciate their full significance, it is necessary to envisage them against the Hellenic background. We may begin by recalling the Aristotelian doctrine that man is an animal whose potentialities can be realized only in the *polis*.[2]

It is hardly necessary to point out that, in this pronouncement, Aristotle is stating a contention rather than enunciating a self-evident truth. This contention is a residue from centuries of experience during which the Greek peoples had struggled to raise themselves from the level of surrounding barbarism and to construct out of the available materials a world corresponding to what they conceived to be the true potential of humanity. In these circumstances it becomes almost impossible to do justice to the courage and ingenuity with which they attacked their problems, or to the wealth of their achievement in art and

[1] Chs. I and II. [2] *Pol.* i. 2. 1253ᵃ.

literature, science and philosophy.[1] Still less can we presume to identify the hidden forces which, throughout the vicissitudes of their long and painful history, impelled them to such manifold forms of endeavour.[2] But of one thing at any rate we can be reasonably certain: those forces were at bottom spiritual. What they thus signify is an urge to transcend the limitations of barbarism, the hazards of time and circumstance to which primitive life was exposed. And, from this standpoint, the vision of Hellas resolved itself into a vision of power.

In this vision we may distinguish two elements of paramount importance. The first was an ideal or pattern of what has been called 'strictly human' excellence, the excellence of man as man.[3] The second was a conviction which may with equal precision be called strictly human, viz. that this ideal was possible of realization by virtue of capacities inherent in human nature. It will, of course, be obvious that, even within the limits of this programme, there was room for considerable difference of opinion both as to ends and means. Greek literature reveals many varieties of excellence, and it points to many alternative ways in which it may find expression. In this it no doubt faithfully portrays one of the most remarkable aspects of Greek genius, the Faustian curiosity which helped to make their civilization progressive in fact, even if the Greeks themselves did not succeed in formulating an intelligible theory of progress. But, notwithstanding the diversity of its findings, Hellenism maintained throughout a consistent attitude in seeking to view its problem 'objectively' and looking to nature for the answer. And, from this standpoint, one ideal at least appeared to be excluded as beyond the reach of humanity; this was that of Cyclopean, i.e. of absolute individual self-sufficiency. Aristotle no doubt records the general verdict of Greek experience when he declares that he who can do without society is either a beast or a god.

[1] For a general estimate we may refer to Livingstone (ed.), *The Legacy of Greece*. Specific aspects have been studied by Murray, *Five Stages of Greek Religion*; Zimmern, *The Greek Commonwealth*; Heath, *The History of Greek Mathematics*, and many others.

[2] The problem has been examined, e.g., in connexion with the origin of Milesian philosophy by Burnet, *Early Greek Philosophy*, 3rd ed., pp. 39–50, who discusses the possibility that the Greek mind was fertilized through contact with the Orient. If so, it may at least be agreed that the seed did not fall on barren ground. Another theory is that Thales was himself a Semite who thus, so to speak, carried the virus of speculation 'in his blood'.

[3] Livingstone, *Greek Ideals and Modern Life*, on ἀρετή, *virtus* or 'manliness'.

But to reject the notion of Cyclopean independence is merely to settle one problem in order to raise others of hardly less magnitude and difficulty. For it at once provokes a question regarding the relation of the individual to the community of which he forms a part. And here Greek opinion appears to have divided into sharply opposing schools. On the one hand, it was argued that community is, or should be, a matter of pure εὔνοια, 'right mindedness' or, as we should say, 'goodwill'; on the other, that it is, in the last analysis, one merely of organized brute, i.e. physical, force. Aristotle himself, no doubt reflecting the common-sense desire for a *via media*, refuses to accept either of these mutually exclusive alternatives as final. Accordingly, he seeks to resolve the dilemma by referring both to a third concept in relation to which they are exhibited in a fresh and significant light.[1] This concept is 'justice', which is thus put forward as 'the bond of men in states', while 'the administration of justice, that is, the determination of what is just', is held to be the true 'principle of order in society'.[2]

In these terms Aristotle formulated his attitude towards what had long been recognized as a fundamental problem of Greek experience. As such, it is perhaps implicit in the Homeric picture of the Achaeans, whether assembled in council under their leaders to determine questions of common interest or, on the battle-field, marching in serried ranks against a horde of wild and polyglot barbarians. With Hesiod it has already come to a focus in consciousness, when the poet, revolting from the spectacle of powerful and unscrupulous nobles ruthlessly exploiting the weak, launches the project of a society ordered to the common good, wherein the 'worse form' of competition shall have been supplanted by a 'better'; at the same time pronouncing that society to be in accordance with the will of Zeus.[3] It was Solon, however, who first (apart from certain mythical lawgivers) actually undertook to implement this idea by prescribing for his countrymen a rule of law based on reason and humanity.[4] This was to give a profoundly significant turn to the spiritual history of Hellas: it was, in fact, to enunciate for the first time what we have ventured to call the classical idea of the commonwealth. It thus pointed to a future in which

[1] *Pol.* i. 1255ᵃ foll,   [2] *Pol* i. 1253ᵃ37; cf. *N.E.* v. 1129ᵇ25.   [3] *Works and Days.*
[4] See Aristotle, *Ath. Pol.*, esp. ch. 12, for quotations from the poems of Solon to illustrate his purpose and method.

Hellenism should devote its energies to exploring the manifold possibilities latent in that idea.

In saying this, we do not forget that, for two elements at least of Greek society, such possibilities were not likely to have much appeal. These we may designate as the 'rugged' and the 'soft' individualists respectively. The former included, on the one hand, eccentrics like the cynic Diogenes; on the other, Thrasymachean *supra-homines*, economic and moral dynasts who resented the pretensions of the organized state as arbitrary restrictions upon what they held to be a natural right of self-assertion. The latter consisted of Sybarites or hedonists who, with the lyric poets of Ionia, were prepared to dismiss the illusion of perfectibility and to abandon themselves to the seductions of mere sense. Manifestations of either kind were, no doubt, both frequent and dangerous, as indeed they proved to be in more than one celebrated case.[1] Yet their occurrence serves to emphasize the truth that, with the vast majority of men, allegiance was given to the *polis*, the development of which was thenceforth to become one of the chief preoccupations of the Greek mind. The result was a persistent effort of experimentation, as a consequence of which the Mediterranean coastland was strewn with the wreckage of working, if defective, models which, for one reason or another, failed to withstand the tests imposed upon them.[2] And, with a characteristic fertility of invention, Greek theory set itself to obviate the difficulties revealed in practice by devising an endless variety of ingenious and (more or less) instructive schemes.

It would be false, however, to suppose that all or, indeed, any considerable proportion of Hellenic polities were consecrated to a realization of human excellence ($\dot{a}\rho\epsilon\tau\dot{\eta}$), as this was apprehended by poets and philosophers. Plutarch, in fact, asserts that of the vast number which had flourished and passed away, one only, viz. Lycurgan Sparta, consciously and deliberately embraced such an ideal.[3] To the great majority of Greeks the *polis* must have commended itself, as it did to Pindar, as on the whole the most eligible 'state' for the man of middling circumstances. To such a man it offered the best prospect of obtaining

---

[1] e.g. that of Alcibiades. See Plut. *Alcib.* and Thuc. v–viii *passim*, esp. vi. 89–92, his speech at Sparta.

[2] In this connexion it will be remembered that Aristotle is supposed to have examined more than 150 such models in preparation for his *Politics*.

[3] *Lycurg.* 29–31.

what he really wanted—security from external danger and the promise of material well-being. Historically speaking, the *polis* was thus a middle-class solution to the problem of power, and, as an institution, its fortunes and misfortunes were bound up with those of the small landed proprietor.[1]

But it is precisely this fact which lends significance to the Aristotelian formula. Aristotle, like his master Plato, held that what was really wrong with these communities was the lack of a sound principle of organization. In default of such a principle they had succumbed to notions such as those popularized by the sophists, whereby power was resolved into a question of social mechanics and identified with the acquisition of specific techniques. In this connexion we may recall his criticism of Hippodamus, the 'town-planner', who professed an ability to lay out a society as he had laid out the Piraeus, according to a mathematical scheme; as well as of those contemporary statesmen who confined their attention exclusively to problems of economics or finance.[2] These criticisms have more than a merely antiquarian interest; they point, indeed, to what idealism conceived to be the essence of the problem.

For philosophical idealism the secret of power is 'order'; and order, if it is to be well founded, must be 'just', i.e. it must bear a definite and intelligible relation to a cosmic principle which lies deeper than all mere conventions of behaviour, whether of individual or communal life. Idealism is thus committed to the discovery of such a principle as the necessary basis for a valid science of 'nature' and of 'man'.

In this connexion we can afford to ignore the distinction between Platonic and Aristotelian science (ἐπιστήμη, *scientia*). For Plato the principle in question is strictly transcendental; for this reason it is 'hard to apprehend' and 'hard to communicate'. Nevertheless, it is (dogmatically) conceived as cosmic Mind or Intelligence (νοῦς), which thus presents itself as the 'beginning of motion' (ἀρχὴ κινήσεως) to which is ascribed the characteristic structure of the universe and all that it contains. As such, however, it does not operate *in vacuo*. On the contrary, it presupposes a substrate of uncreated primordial matter (ὕλη).

---

[1] See Thuc. viii. 97, on the government of the 5,000 in Athens. Also Arist. *Ath. Pol.* 33.
[2] *Pol.* ii. 1267ᵇ22 foll. and i. 11. 1259ᵃ36; cf. Aristotle's attitude to sophistic rhetoric, 'the Art', as expressed in his own work on the subject.

This substrate is variously described as Necessity (ἀνάγκη), blind chance (τύχη), the 'errant cause' (πλανωμένη αἰτία); it is an otherwise amorphous and insignificant flux, the sole function of which is to 'receive' the 'forms' or 'patterns' which Mind or Intelligence imposes upon it. Accordingly, ' the genesis of this universe may be ascribed to a combination of Intelligence with Necessity, the one influencing the other so as to bring what comes into being to the best possible issue.'[1] In this cosmology, it will be noted, on the one hand, that 'matter and motion' or rather the 'motion of matter', considered *in abstracto*, is neither bad nor good; strictly speaking, it is nothing or all-but-nothing apart from form. On the other hand, the forms or patterns which, by impressing themselves on matter, impart to it the nature of body, do not on that account lose anything of their formal character; they remain for ever timeless and immutable. These considerations will help us to understand what Plato means by *genesis*. In this process, as he sees it, the role of Mind or Intelligence is not so much creative as demiurgic; it may indeed be questioned whether its activity extends beyond the point of furnishing the 'archetypes' of being. Moreover, its operation is conditioned throughout by the difficulty of controlling the aberrant tendencies of matter-in-motion; and, from this stand-point, matter is recognized, if not as a positive source of evil (as the Manicheans of later times were to regard it), at any rate as a 'principle of limitation'. Accordingly, the world of 'body' is conceived as a world of 'becoming' which, however, never actually 'becomes'; since to do so would be to transcend its nature as body (γιγνόμενον μὲν ἀεί, ὂν δὲ οὐδέποτε). It thus remains a mere 'reflection' of the pattern or 'real' world.

Platonic cosmology leads to conclusions of the utmost importance with respect to human nature. To begin with, man is envisaged as a microcosm of the universe, a composite of 'body', 'soul', and 'mind'. In this composite the part designated 'mind' is, by a further act of dogmatism, identified with the cosmic principle and conceived as a 'scintilla' of the divine essence; that is why (under certain conditions) it is held to be capable of apprehending the archetypal forms. The composite, however, includes elements which are, *ex hypothesi*, 'external' to this principle, viz. those which go to constitute 'body' and 'soul'. We may here observe that the ambiguity attaching to

[1] *Timaeus*, 48 E; cf. 29 D, 30 B, 48 A, 69 B–D.

matter regarded as a 'principle of limitation' gives rise to grave problems which affect 'body', 'soul', and 'mind' itself. Is the material body, for instance, to be thought of merely as a tomb or prison-house (σῶμα σῆμα), as Pythagoras had suggested? If so, it would follow that the supreme problem of mankind must be one of escape. A hardly less serious difficulty is that which concerns the human essence, whether or not its character is archetypal. To see in matter merely a principle of limitation or division would appear to render some such conclusion inevitable. But this would be to raise in an acute form the question of individuality; to ask in effect whether Peter, Paul, and John are not essentially One; destined, as such, to self-realization only as they succeed in discarding that which 'separates' them as individuals in order to find their place in a comprehensive whole.[1] Finally, with regard to *Platonopolis* itself, to what world, it may be asked, does this belong? To locate it in the world of 'becoming' would be to destroy its character as a pattern or model city and to subject it to the sway of the temporal and contingent. To concede it a place in the world of 'being' would be to exempt it from mutability; but at the cost of converting it into a city of the dead. It is the merit of Plato that he saw these problems and that he endeavoured to meet them, devoting the later years of his life to the discovery of a logic that would be adequate to the task. And, if he did not succeed, he at least paved the way for the modified system of idealism which was to emerge from the hands of Aristotle.

Aristotle starts by envisaging the principle of order as immanent, i.e. as 'diffused' through individual objects in nature, which thus for him constitute the *prima substantia*. In so doing he was no doubt actuated by a desire to escape from the pitfalls of Platonic transcendentalism. But if this was the original impulse, it gained support from Aristotle's own studies, particularly in biology; for it made possible a fresh vision of nature whereby objects present themselves as specimens to be systematically classified according to their respective *genera* and *species*. This, in turn, suggested further questions, notably as regards the relation of physical endowment to the environment, together with problems of nurture, distribution of types, &c., as these were to be studied by Theophrastus.[2]

[1] This, as will be evident, points to what is popularly known as 'totalitarianism'.
[2] *On Plants.*

Our concern, however, is not with the Aristotelian system of universals in general, but merely with its application to *homo sapiens*, i.e. with its utility as the basis for a 'science' of human nature. And here we may note, to begin with, that Aristotle accepts without question the radical distinction between form and matter inherent in Platonic idealism. For him, therefore, development in nature is restricted to the formation of types and, thus, confined within limits imposed by the four operative causes (material, efficient, formal, and final). In this scheme the excellence (ἀρετή) of any given object is appraised in terms of its end (τέλος), and process acquires meaning and value only so far as it tends in the direction ordained by nature, i.e. towards a realization of the appropriate form. It is a tribute to the optimism of Aristotle that he regards this as a 'normal' outcome. To accept the Aristotelian scheme is to envisage human beings from the standpoint of their *entelecheia*, i.e. as impelled by the law of their nature (φύσει) towards a predetermined type. The type in question is unique: it is, as for Plato, a composite (σύνθετον) made up of body, soul, and mind, the last of which constitutes its differentia. Of such a creature the 'goods' must also be composite; for while its ultimate excellence may well be that of mind,[1] this mind has no residence apart from the 'body' and 'soul' in which it finds itself. This does not mean, however, that physical or psychical goods, as such, may be regarded as independent; they are, in fact, ordered hierarchically with a view to the supreme good, the good of that '*part*' which is distinctive and 'final' in human nature.

Despite superficial differences, the picture of human nature thus presented by Aristotle points to conclusions almost identical with those of Plato. In his famous simile of the charioteer driving the unruly steeds of passion, Plato had implied that a truly human order was one which involved the subjection to reason of all elements of irrationality; and this order he declared to be (so far as such a thing is possible here below) a replica or counterpart to the fixed and immutable order of the heavens. These cosmological analogies Aristotle dismisses as

[1] *N.E.* x. 7 foll. on contemplative activity (θεωρεῖν). Rohde, *Psyche*, 8th ed., Eng. tr., p. 409, n. 111, declares: 'The Aristotelian νοῦς is ἀπαθής, ἀμιγής, χωριστός. It is also devoid of all attributes of individuality (which reside entirely in the lower psychical powers) and thus appears as a common divine spirit. And yet it is said to be a μόριον τῆς ψυχῆς, present in the ψυχή, i.e. dwelling inside the body.'

somewhat fanciful, in order to focus attention upon the individual or *prima substantia*. Yet he fully agrees with Plato in supposing that the individual substance possesses significance only, so to speak, as the 'carrier' of a type; furthermore, that, while everything else in him belongs to the ephemeral world of γένεσις and φθορά, the 'typical' alone is permanent, essential, and intelligible (πᾶσα ἐπιστήμη τοῦ καθόλου); finally that for the realization of this permanent, essential, and intelligible 'part' of his being, what he requires is to live the life of the *polis*.

Thus envisaged, the *polis* constitutes a response to the specifically human demand for a specifically human order. In this sense it may properly be described as 'natural'. But its 'naturalness' is in no sense that of a spontaneous growth. On the contrary, it is that of an institution designed, within limits conditioned by the potentialities of the material, to secure mankind from 'accident' or 'spontaneity' (ταὐτόματον), thereby making possible the attainment of his proper τέλος. From this standpoint the order embodied in the *polis* is profoundly unhistorical. What it promises, indeed, is immunity from the 'flux' which is all that idealism discerns in mere movement. And this is the reason why, according to Aristotle, 'the man who first invented the state was the greatest of benefactors.'[1]

In this concept of the *polis* Aristotle finds a theoretical basis for classifying constitutions according to whether or not they minister to the end in view. It explains also his strictures on existing states, all of which, he declares, are either oligarchies or democracies, organized to promote the exclusive interests either of the 'rich few' or of the 'many poor'. In particular it accounts for his attitude to types such as those represented by Athens and Sparta, the one approximating to the libertarian, the other to the authoritarian ideal. With respect to Athens his criticism includes not merely the 'ultimate democracy' or ochlocracy which, by discarding all formal restrictions, publicly consecrates disorder as the norm of life.[2] It embraces also the earlier versions of democracy, with their roots in 'expansive emotion' as represented by the sea-faring rabble (ναυτικὸς ὄχλος). For Plato, the beginning of Athens' downfall dated from the overthrow of the Areopagus (461 B.C.) and the consequent elimination of religion (αἰδώς) as a force of restraint

[1] *Pol.* i. 2. 1253ª30.
[2] *Ath. Pol.* 41 for the abolition of the γραφὴ παρανόμων and its consequences.

upon the community.[1] Aristotle would agree, but he goes
further even than Plato, for he sees little good in anything
Athenian subsequent to the reforms of Solon.[2] So much for
the idealist attitude towards 'liberty' as a principle of political
cohesion, to the advocacy of which Pericles had addressed
himself with such eloquence in the Funeral Speech.[3] As for
Spartan authoritarianism, Aristotle's comments on it are hardly
less pungent. Sparta, he admits, does indeed stand for a
positive principle of social order and, in this sense, must be
regarded as superior to her rival. But the order in question
is not and cannot be enforced; its conventions are defied by
Spartan citizens whenever they find an opportunity. The
reason for this lies, not so much in human perversity, as in
defects inherent in the order itself. The Spartans have concentrated upon the promotion of an exclusively military *ethos*.
This, however, is but one aspect of excellence and to it they have
sacrificed other elements even more essential. On this account
their constitution falls short of what is demanded by true
political 'justice'.[4]

These criticisms do not in the least suggest any loss of faith
in the political idea. On the contrary, they serve to indicate
what idealism conceives to be the task of creative politics.
Translated into terms of practice, they point to an elaborate
and comprehensive scheme of social planning in which, with
the $\tau \epsilon \lambda o s$ of man constantly in view, 'function' shall be 'adjusted
to capacity' and 'instruments to both'.[5] In this connexion, we
may pause to note that the work of statecraft is complicated
by the fact that the elements with which it has to deal are more
or less inclined to resist manipulation. Hence, to begin with,
the necessity for a rigorous delimitation of the field. This
necessity finds expression in an ideal of communal self-sufficiency
($\alpha \dot{v} \tau \acute{a} \rho \kappa \epsilon \iota a$, 'autarky') which carries with it important implications in respect both to men and material. Thus, from the
standpoint of economy, it postulates a territory capable of producing everything needed for the secure and easy provision

---

[1] *Laws*, 698 B.   [2] *Pol.* ii. 12. 1274ᵃ.
[3] Thuc. ii. 37–46. It will be noted that Pericles employs a wholly fresh terminology to describe the relations of men within the new society, as he conceives it.
This, it would appear, is deliberate. It emphasizes his contention that Athens is a
$\pi a \rho \acute{a} \delta \epsilon \iota \gamma \mu a$ for the future; i.e. a real 'school for Hellas'.
[4] *Pol.* ii. 9. 1271ᵇ.
[5] For details see, *inter alia*, Barker, *The Political Thought of Plato and Aristotle*.

of daily wants (γῆ παντοφόρος . . . πρὸς ἀσφάλειαν καὶ πρὸς εὐπορίαν τῶν ἀναγκαίων¹), together with a supply of labour (σώματα οἰκετικά, ὄργανα ἔμψυχα) by which communal resources may be systematically exploited. We may here recall Aristotle's defence of slavery as 'natural', and his remark that nature tends to differentiate between the bodies and souls of freemen and slaves. It will also be remembered that he justifies predial slavery (i.e. of barbarians) as a 'form of hunting'.² But since, from the idealist standpoint, physical self-sufficiency is merely a basis for spiritual self-sufficiency, creative politics involves the recognition of still more vital functions; notably those of defence by means of an organized civic militia, the regulation through official priesthoods of religious thought and emotion, and the administration of justice 'retributive' and 'distributive' according to an accepted code of law. Again because, as Plato had observed, few people, if any, are spontaneously and naturally good,³ there devolves upon the *polis* as perhaps its supreme obligation a duty of education, conceived as the inculcation of a set of moral and intellectual virtues 'relative to the constitution' (ὀρθὴ δόξα). By such means it was hoped to impose an effective check upon the passions, especially those of 'avarice and ambition', and to achieve something of the moderation (σωφροσύνη) so assiduously preached by Delphian Apollo, pre-eminently the 'political' God. Finally this, as the true political order, was proclaimed to be the one avenue to 'self-realization'; i.e. to justice, peace, and freedom.

But however salutary such proposals, they fell largely upon deaf ears; and, while Plato and Aristotle prosecuted their campaign for social reconstruction on 'orthodox' lines, the condition of Hellas was undergoing a steady and progressive deterioration, until the final catastrophe at Chaeronea (338 B.C.). The situation, already in the fifth century full of peril, was greatly aggravated as a result of shocks sustained during the prolonged and disastrous Peloponnesian war (431–404 B.C.); which, as described by Thucydides, constitutes a terrifying record of human energy and resources dissipated to no profitable end. The conflict was one of confused and partially apprehended issues in which all concerned found themselves alike the victims to an (apparently) inevitable and remorseless

---

¹ *Pol.* vii. 5. 1326ᵇ27 and 6. 1327ᵃ19.   ² *Pol.* i. 7. 1255ᵇ37.
³ *Laws*, 642 C: ἄνευ ἀνάγκης αὐτοφυῶς, θείᾳ μοίρᾳ ἀληθῶς καὶ οὔτι πλαστῶς . . . ἀγαθοί.

necessity. On the side of Sparta it began as a struggle for 'autonomy' against the aggressions of the 'tyrant city'; and this shibboleth continued to be employed at least until the time of Brasidas' campaign in the north. On Athens' part it was heralded as a battle for 'liberty' through democracy and empire; a cry to be pathetically echoed in Sicily by Nicias when, calling upon his men for one last effort, he reminded them that they were fighting for the 'freest city in the world'. With the progress of the struggle there emerged various secondary issues, e.g. that of racialism as a factor in inter-state politics, when the slogan of Dorian *v.* Ionian was raised in the West. A Syracusan statesman promulgated the doctrine of regional isolation as the one salvation for Sicily, only to be met with the retort that this was simply a mask for Syracusan encroachment upon the independence of her neighbours in the island. Meanwhile class-conflict, breaking out at Corcyra, swept like an epidemic throughout Hellas, carrying with it not merely death and destruction, but the perversion of all conventions of honour and decency hitherto observed among civilized men.[1] At the same time, as the necessities of competitive politics became intensified, they served to produce a novel and sinister code of inter-state ethics, whereby the helpless and innocent were delivered over to the mercy of the strong; and this was proclaimed by Athenian generals before Melos to be the law of God and nature.[2] But the end came only when Sparta, desperate in her anxiety for victory, betrayed the cause of Hellenism by bartering to the national enemy the liberties of Asiatic Greece in exchange for Persian ships and gold.[3] From the consequences of this exhausting struggle Hellas was never to recover. The 'liberation' offered by Sparta was presently exposed as an inverted imperialism much more brutal and unenlightened than that of Periclean Athens; within a generation it crumbled to pieces in order to make way for the short-lived domination of fascist Thebes. A second Athenian confederacy, supported by the most ample guarantees of autonomy to the allied states, proved but a feeble instrument in defending Greek interests against the machinations of Philip of Macedon; while the city itself was torn by dissension between those who favoured and those who opposed a policy of appeasement with

[1] Thuc. iii. 82–4.   [2] Ibid. v. 98 foll.
[3] Ibid. viii. 18, 37, 58, the three treaties.

the king. Finally, fourth-century experiments in federalism were equally ineffective as a cure for the maladies of Hellas, serving merely to widen the area and complicate the issues in dispute. It is a curious and instructive commentary on human limitations that Aristotle should have been at such pains to vindicate the necessity of the *polis*, at the very moment when the *polis*, her historic mission concluded, was being relegated to the limbo of antiquities in order to make way for a fresh organization of power. This power was, of course, that of hellenized Macedonia.

Alexander the Great began his career as hereditary chieftain to a Macedonian tribe; he ended it as sovereign of the first empire which, by uniting East and West in one huge physical system, might justly claim to be universal. This achievement, made possible by force of arms, appeared to involve the promise of a radically new future for mankind. The question arises: What significance had that future for the history of politics?

So far as concerns contemporary opinion, the answer to this question must have been doubtful in the extreme. On the one hand, observers like Aristotle, however much they might admire Alexander as a man, could hardly have anticipated much good from his programme. For them the obliteration of the independent, self-sufficient *polis* must have implied the extinction of the political idea, in any sense in which it might be expected to minister to the demand for a truly human good. On the other hand, there can be no question that, to a very considerable number of Greeks, the Macedonian actually appeared as a deliverer. Hellenism had always envisaged two quite distinct types of human excellence, that of the 'hero' and that of the 'citizen'; the problem, indeed, was to reconcile the two.[1] During the brief hour of glory which followed the national wars of liberation the tendency had been to lay all possible stress upon 'civic excellence', and to attribute the victory of Hellas over Xerxes and his host to the disciplined valour and common patriotism of the co-operating Greek states.[2] Yet, even with respect to the *polis* as an institution, the Greeks always contemplated the necessity of occasional action, so to speak, from 'outside'. Its very origin, indeed, was commonly ascribed to the 'wisdom and strength' of hero-founders like Lycurgus and

---

[1] Arist. *Pol.* iii. 13. 1284ª.
[2] Thucydides (i. 69. 5) is sceptical of this interpretation.

Theseus.[1] Moreover, a crisis of political life was thought to justify the intervention of heroic virtue; such as occurred, for instance, during the late sixth and early fifth centuries where tyrannies or dictatorships everywhere seemed to be the need of the hour. In this connexion the example of Gelo, 'king' of Syracuse, provides an instructive comment on the technique of effective action.[2] Accordingly, with the progressive disintegration of the city-state after the Peloponnesian war, the Greek mind once more began to turn towards the idea of a hero-saviour. In the realm of pure theory Plato was calling for a 'dictatorship of intelligence', a model of which he offered in the 'philosopher-king'. But, as was perhaps suspected by the less guileless, qualities other than mere intelligence were also required of the successful leader; and Xenophon in his historico-philosophical romances[3] seeks to envisage the type from this more comprehensive point of view. From the moment of Isocrates' famous *Address to Philip*, the question, hitherto purely academic, entered upon a new phase. Thenceforth it became a problem of practical politics upon which Greeks of whatever shade of opinion were required to take sides. As such, it was to be decided (except for purposes of rhetoric) on the battle-field of Chaeronea.

Meanwhile, what of the man who was cast for the role of deliverer? Alexander, the son of Philip, fell heir to a kingdom which had been built up during a lifetime of skilful and unscrupulous intrigue, supported by ever-increasing military and economic power. He also inherited his father's passion for expansionist imperialism. But, over and above this, he had the benefit of what has been described as the best available education of his time, Aristotle himself having served as one of his tutors. Alexander could thus think of himself as a reincarnation of Achilles, a heroic spirit thirsting for glory and ready to endure anything for the satisfaction of his pride; or as a second Heracles, the man who, by labouring to benefit his fellow mortals, achieved a personal immortality, and whose descendant (as

---

[1] See Plut. *Lives*, and note especially the *Life of Theseus*, chs. 35–6, for the use made of the myth in relation to Cleisthenic democracy (marked by the translation of the bones of the hero to Athens under Cimon and by the formation of an official and popular cult).

[2] Hdt. vii. 153–65. See also Arist. *Pol.* v, on 'tyranny', where he anticipates almost every thing which was to be said on the subject by Machiavelli.

[3] e.g. the *Cyropaedia*.

we may remember) Alexander imagined himself to be. In the contemplation of Heracles and his destiny, it was possible to find justification for the vast enterprises to be undertaken by the new Achilles.

It has recently been argued[1] that the programme of Alexander involved a conscious and deliberate attempt to bring about 'a profound revolution' in human life; a revolution calculated to destroy for ever the idea of city-state self-sufficiency and to substitute for it nothing less than that of universal brotherhood, thereby offering to the world a prospect of 'something better than the menace of constant war'. Alexander is thus represented as striving, in the name of *homonoia*, 'likemindedness' or 'concord', to break down not merely the physical but also the ideological barriers which had hitherto separated Greek from barbarian, and to erect a new concept of human excellence, the excellence of the cosmopolitan or citizen of the world. It is further suggested that, in so doing, Alexander was inspired by a conviction that he was fulfilling a law of destiny; regarding himself, in Plutarch's words, as 'a common emissary sent from God to harmonize and reconcile the whole word (κοινὸς ἥκειν θεόθεν ἁρμοστὴς καὶ διαλλακτὴς τῶν ὅλων νομίζων), bringing to all men peace, concord, and community'.[2]

One may perhaps suspect that, in this passage, Plutarch is thinking not less of the 'good' Roman emperors of his own day than of the Macedonian king. Yet even so, it is an instructive lesson in the vitality of an idea that it should have been susceptible of such an amazing metamorphosis as it underwent with Alexander. For, whatever may have been Alexander's dreams, the significant point is that they were to be realized by methods which were essentially political. In saying this, we do not so much refer to his achievements as an exponent of scientific, i.e. 'civilized', warfare, although this in itself is a fact of indisputable importance, as is shown by the frequent allusions of Polybius and others to 'Alexandrian' strategy and tactics. What we have in mind is rather the policies whereby it was made possible for men to achieve a certain degree of practical 'likemindedness'. The mere fact of Macedonian ascendancy meant that the language of Homer came to be the lingua franca of the dominant classes from Egypt to the Caspian, and from

[1] W. W. Tarn, 'Alexander the Great and the Unity of Mankind', *Proc. Brit. Acad.* xix (1933), pp. 123–66.   [2] *De Alex. Fort. aut Virt.* i. 6 and 8.

the Danube to the Persian Gulf. Within this immense area, metropolitan centres were established at points of strategic and commercial importance along the great trunk-roads, and Greeks were encouraged to emigrate to these new *foci* of 'civilized' life. The king himself embraced and recommended to his followers a policy of racial assimilation through inter-marriage with natives of the East. But perhaps the most startling development was the institution of military schools in which Greeks and Iranians competed on equal terms for posts in the imperial service.

In this phase of political evolution a peculiar significance gathers about the idea of kingship. Beginning as a tribal chieftain, the original hold of Alexander upon his followers depended upon hereditary claims and personal prestige. In relation to the subjected city-states of Hellas, his position was that of 'captain-general', entrusted by common consent with a monopoly of military power. By right of conquest he became 'king of kings', heir to the vast dominions (*dominationes et potentiae*) formerly possessed by the line of Darius. Finally the oracle of Zeus Ammon hailed him as an authentic 'Son of Zeus'. But, over and above all this, Alexander professed to be a philosopher. It was, as such, that he is said to have dis-covered a formula of relationship with his subjects in the con-cept of philanthropy ($\phi\iota\lambda\alpha\nu\theta\rho\omega\pi\iota\alpha$), that love for the weak and helpless which inspires the man of divine attributes ($\theta\epsilon\hat{\iota}os$) to extend to them his protective care. In this sense the role of the sovereign was, so to speak, extra-political. Towards members of the cosmopolis he stood in the relation of Saviour and Benefactor ($\Sigma\omega\tau\dot{\eta}\rho$ $\kappa\alpha\dot{\iota}$ $E\dot{v}\epsilon\rho\gamma\dot{\epsilon}\tau\eta s$), a kind of 'intermediate being' occupying the somewhat vague borderland which divides God from men and, from that exalted station, discharging the function of an earthly providence.

Such a providence, however, lacks among other things the essential attribute of eternity. With the premature death of the philosophic monarch (upon whose shoulders the Herculean burden rested) the universal empire dissolved into the great Hellenistic succession states; and the world was in a position to consider how far he had made good his claims. There can be no question but that the Macedonian conquests had effected an immense transformation in the structure of society through-out the Near East, uprooting ancient and deep-seated ethnic and local traditions and sweeping even the Jews into the stream of a common life. Nor can there be much doubt that, through this transformation, there were opened up fresh and enlarged vistas for the human race. But if the Greeks who associated themselves with Alexander's programme entertained any hope that it would bring about a political millennium, they were soon to be undeceived. Doomed to the loss of all but a precarious independence, they found indeed a certain compensation in the opportunity which they now had of exploiting the barbarian world, and this they proceeded to do with a refined technique for which the crude Oriental systems of domination afforded no parallel. Yet by this very fact they risked the impairment of what had been finest in the older classical spirit, as they now devoted themselves to what were, after all, the mere *externalia* of human life. The result was a shocking deterioration in the quality of their intellectual output, such as is evident in the tone of Alexandrian philosophy and literature. Moreover, the Hellenistic cosmopolis never succeeded in overcoming its hybrid character. Alongside the advanced civic life of Alexander's numerous foundations there continued to exist the most primitive forms of rural economy; and many of the more remote sections of the empire lapsed slowly back into their original barbarism. Economically and socially the succession kingdoms exhibited even harsher contrasts and bitterer anomalies than those which had characterized the life of classical Greece, while they offered to their subjects a merely formal symbol of unity in the cult of the divine sovereign. Meanwhile the Antigonids, the Seleucids, and the Ptolemies, jealously watching one another's every movement, maintained an uneasy balance of power until, one after another, they finally succumbed to the growing might of Rome.[1]

But if the hopes aroused by Alexander's conquests thus gradually faded throughout the Hellenistic East, it was only to discover a new centre of fixation in the city on the Tiber. When, towards the close of the third century B.C., the mists which obscured the dawn of her history lifted to disclose the Latin republic, those of the Greeks who had continued to cherish classical ideals of excellence professed to discover in it a living model and exemplar of what they themselves had vainly striven to achieve. In this connexion there is no more important

[1] Polyb., *passim*.

witness than Polybius, who lived for many years as a hostage in intimate association with Scipio Aemilianus, one of the greatest contemporary exponents of Roman virtue[1] and one of the earliest of his countrymen to *hellenize*. Polybius was thus in a position to observe at first hand some of the most remarkable feats of Roman arms and diplomacy in the fifty years of uninterrupted triumph during which the sovereign people laid the whole Mediterranean at their feet. In particular, he was present with Scipio at the final siege and destruction of Carthage, the city which for centuries had successfully disputed with Hellas control of the West until, in an hour pregnant with fate, the Romans challenged and overthrew her monopoly of sea-power. Polybius' theme is the *imperium Romanum* in expansion, and on it he sets the seal of Greek approval when he declares it to be the result, not of chance, but of manifest destiny working through the agency of her chosen people;[2] adding, in characteristic fashion, that the success of the Romans is to be ascribed to the 'excellence of their constitution' which embodies all the advantages of the 'mixed form' at that time fashionable in Greek political philosophy.

It is doubtless, also, to the ingenuity of Greek writers that we owe the development of the Trojan myth in its application to the Eternal City. To have had ancestors who fought at Troy was, for the peoples of antiquity, a conventional badge of gentility and it was on this score that Procopius, sixteen hundred years after the fall of Ilium, was to recognize the right of the Goths to share in the Graeco-Roman heritage. The legend was employed in a precisely similar sense on behalf of the Roman people long before it was adopted to support the peculiar claims of the Julian house, and its effectiveness for the latter purpose attests its value for the former. In its accepted form, however, the Trojan myth involved the serious drawback of portraying the Romans as descendants of the 'national enemy'. It remained for a Greek of the Augustan age[3] by an ingenious manipulation of surviving 'evidence' to demonstrate that, however this might be, the constitution of Rome was thoroughly Greek; that, indeed, outside of Hellas she was the

[1] For its components see the *Elogia* on the tombs of the Scipios; Wordsworth, *Fragments and Specimens of Early Latin*, pp. 159–62.
[2] See below, ch. XII, p. 474.
[3] Dionysius of Halicarnassus, *Roman Antiquities*,

'most Hellenic of cities'. And it may be admitted that he was right in spirit if not in fact, so completely had the Romans by this time accepted the interpretation which Hellas placed upon their history.

The enthusiasm with which the Greeks originally welcomed their new champion was destined to evaporate under the protectorate; and it received an appalling shock when, with the destruction of Corinth in 146 B.C., they entered upon a fresh captivity, the bitterness of which was to be mitigated only by Roman contempt for their present wretched condition combined with an apparently genuine admiration for the glories of their past. But, notwithstanding the frictions inevitable in the political relationship, it is beyond question that there existed between the two peoples a real sense of spiritual affinity, based on a conviction that, in a world charged with alien and hostile influences, they stood for the realization of common purposes and common ideals. This feeling served to evoke, on the Roman side, that peculiar respect for Greek culture which moved the poet to proclaim the victory of the conquered over their fierce conqueror. Philhellenism was, no doubt, more generously and ungrudgingly expressed in the beginning when Flamininus, at the Isthmian games, solemnly liberated Hellas from the Macedonian yoke (196 B.C.). Nevertheless, it survived the centuries, and the last of Roman princes to profess loyalty to Classicism was proud to call himself a Hellenist.[1] The passion of the Romans for Hellenism may be illustrated from almost any page of their history; as for example when Julius Caesar, in pardoning the Athenians who had fought against him at Pharsalus, exclaimed with mingled tenderness and disgust: 'how long, miserable people, will the virtues of your ancestors save you!' And, while Caesar thus paid characteristic tribute to the home of civic freedom and the nursing-mother of thought, his preservation of the Massiliots—despite intense and repeated provocation—was inspired not so much by a sense of their past as by a hope he entertained of their future as a civilizing agency in the newly annexed provinces of Gaul. It may be added that, in thus forecasting the historic mission of Massilia, Caesar was not mistaken. Roman Massilia in the West, like Roman Athens in the East, survived as a university

[1] i.e. Julian the Apostate. See Ch. VII below. The emperor Hadrian was also, in his day, a notorious philhellene.

rather than a city; in that role both communities were destined to diffuse the light of civilization until the barbarian invasions destroyed the one, and Justinian, by closing the schools of the other, formally brought the period of Classicism to an end.

To Polybius the achievement of the Roman people was from two points of view unique. On the one hand, by overcoming the plague of internal dissension (στάσις or *factio*), the disease which constantly menaced the life of the *polis*, they had implemented to the full the promise of civic virtue in the concept of the *liber et legalis homo*. On the other hand the virtue of Roman citizens had proved equal to accomplishments rivalling those of Alexander himself; for it had enabled them, by an unparalleled combination of military pressure and political art, to impose a Roman peace upon the Mediterranean, thereby solving once and for all (as Polybius supposed) the vexed problem of external relationships. It thus appeared that, with Rome, two hitherto incompatible ideals of Hellas had finally been reconciled in the concept of the *imperiosa civitas*. That this judgement was premature will of course be only too evident. It was, indeed, uttered almost on the eve of the Gracchan insurrection, when the city was already bursting with explosive forces soon to pass beyond control. Yet if the high hopes entertained of the republic were to be dashed as she, in her turn, shuffled down the all too familiar pathway of revolution, they were to revive once more when, under the guidance of her new leader (*princeps*), she emerged from her long sickness with all the apparent vigour of renewed youth; thereby providing, as it would appear, fresh evidence that it was her manifest destiny to constitute the firm and immovable bulwark of civilization in the West. The question was: What chance had she to succeed where Hellas had failed?

Much, of course, depended upon the leadership to be provided by the prince, and it is hardly an exaggeration to say that, during the critical years of reconstruction, the fate of Europe was in his hands. This means that it was his sense of adequacy, of what was really needed, which was to be decisive for the future. In this connexion it is well to recognize[1] that the mentality of Augustus was that of a being *tout à fait politique*; for whom 'reason of state', as he saw it, constituted the *ultima ratio* of policy. In this judgement the emperor would have found

[1] With J. Buchan, *Augustus*.

a justification for that peculiar amalgam of opportunism and idealism which characterized his methods. The opportunism might almost be called a national characteristic; what it amounted to was an instinct to grapple with concrete issues according to the measure of their difficulty and without unnecessary scruple as to the means employed. As for the idealism, it was, if not precisely a national characteristic, at any rate a predominant fashion of the time. We have already shown how this idealism manifested itself in the work of Cicero and Vergil.[1] But should any doubt still exist upon the point, it may be settled by reference to still other documents of contemporary literature. Thus Horace, for example, while no doubt at heart always the Epicurean, publicly announced his conversion to the Augustan faith; and, in a series of political odes (iii. 1–6), proclaimed his allegiance to the ideals embraced by the emperor; while, in his *Carmen Saeculare*, he prophesied a renaissance of those ideals under his fostering care:[2]

> iam fides et pax et honos pudorque
> priscus et neglecta redire virtus
> audet, apparetque beata pleno
> copia cornu.

And if, in becoming a text-book, the poet suffered the fate which he most dreaded, this fact served merely to increase his currency as an agent of imperial propaganda. If, on the other hand, Ovid found himself an outcast and an exile, this was because, despite a not insignificant contribution to the official religious revival,[3] his work reflected a passion for self-indulgence which, like that of certain other poets of his generation, was out of harmony with the spirit and outlook of the Augustan age.

But, with the *imperiosa civitas*, the virtue of the leader was nothing apart from that of the sovereign people whom he claimed to lead; and, from this standpoint, the secret of Rome was her own. At some such truth the elder Cato had hinted when he remarked that the republic was the work of many hands and many generations.[4] Likewise, during the throes of the revolution, Sallust:

'We are bound', he declares,[5] 'to admire the versatility, quickness and subtlety of a mind like Cato's (the younger Cato). Such virtuosity is the fruit of Greek discipline. But manliness, energy, and

[1] Ch. II, above.   [2] ll. 57–60.   [3] In the *Fasti*.
[4] Ch. II, p. 32 above.   [5] *Ep. ad Caes.* ii, 9 3.

industry are non-existent among the Greeks. In fact, the sloth of that people has cost them their very freedom. Are we to suppose that, by following their precepts, we can hold this empire together?'

In these words the author proclaims his conviction that, despite contemporary degeneracy, Rome provides the best model for the reconstruction of Rome.

This, however, was merely to raise the question what was peculiar to the Roman genius. Of this Julius Caesar[1] had indicated at least one important aspect when he insisted that the Romans had never shrunk from adopting novel expedients in order to meet new facts and needs; and that they were ready to appropriate serviceable ideas alike from friend and foe. The record of the city was, indeed, one of persistent borrowings, the tradition of which goes back to her earliest contacts with her neighbours in prehistoric Italy. She had thus drawn upon the Etruscans for notions of industry, commerce, and building-construction, above all of religious practice, including the technique of divination (*haruspicina*). To the Greeks she ascribed the very framework of her constitution, together with elements of her fundamental law.[2] From the Samnites she boasted of having derived the legionary organization and equipment with which she had crushed the armies of Hannibal and Philip V; from the Carthaginians a model of the war-galley which served to win for her control of the sea in the First Punic war.

These examples will suffice to illustrate at least one significant element of the Roman character. What they reveal is a spirit bent on worldly success and capable of profiting by such gifts as fortune threw in the way, indeed of turning even the direst necessities to advantage. But, in this sense, they point to other and not less remarkable qualities of the imperial people. Our object is not to undertake an independent examination of those qualities, to which a vast amount of scholarly attention has been given.[3] We are merely concerned to discover, if possible,

---

[1] In Sall. *Cat.* 51. 37–8; cf. Polyb. vi. 25. 11.

[2] The Tarquins were supposed to be descendants of an immigrant Corinthian, Demaratus, Livy, i. 34. Parts of the XII Tables were based traditionally on Solon's legislation, in reality perhaps on that of Magna Graecia.

[3] For a general estimate see Grenier, *The Roman Spirit*; for specific aspects, various works on religion including Warde Fowler, *The Religious Experience of the Roman People* and *The Roman Festivals*; also C. Bailey, *Phases of the Religion of Ancient Rome*, Wissowa, *Religion und Kultus der Römer*. Other phases of Roman life are dealt with by Tenney Frank, *An Economic History of Rome*, as well as by numerous writers on ancient law and institutions.

how they were apprehended by contemporaries of Augustus. For this purpose we must consider, in addition to works like those of Vergil and Horace, the monumental effort of Livy to achieve a 'rationalization' of Roman life. His attitude will be apparent from what he has to say about 'history'.

'It is', declares Livy,[1] 'the peculiar value and profit of history that it provides you with evidence to illustrate in a striking manner every possible aspect of behaviour (*omnis . . . exempli documenta in inlustri posita monumento*). From these you may select both for yourself and for your country what is worthy of imitation; in them you may perceive these things—evil in inception and issue—which you must avoid.'

Envisaged in the light of this idea, the history of Rome assumes for the author a quite unique significance.

'Either I am blinded by love for my task, or there never was a state greater, purer, and richer in good examples; no community into which avarice and luxury penetrated so late; none where poverty and thrift were for so long held in such high esteem. The fewer our resources, the less there was of cupidity. It is but recently that an accumulation of wealth has stimulated avarice; the superabundance of material goods an itch on the part of men to indulge a passion which is ruinous to everything including themselves.'

This pronouncement conceals assumptions of the utmost importance for an understanding of the contemporary mind.[2] What they involve is a claim that it is both desirable and possible to erect a future upon the basis of an idealized past. Such a claim is, however, utterly unrealistic. In the first place it ignores the truth that history does not repeat itself; that ever-changing situations constitute a perpetual challenge to the ingenuity and endurance of mankind. In the second, it presupposes that men are in fact at liberty to choose between perfectly arbitrary and abstract alternatives of 'vice' and 'virtue'; in other words, that there is nothing to prevent them, should they so desire, from living the life of their own grand-

[1] *Praef.*, §§ 10-12.
[2] And, it may be added, for that of the classical Renaissance. The criticism of Livy which follows applies with equal force to his disciple, Machiavelli. The latter is commonly regarded as a hard-boiled 'realist'. He was, in fact, a romantic visionary, quite as much out of touch with the needs of his day as was Julian the Apostate with those of his. And for precisely the same reasons! In this connexion it is instructive to study the *Discourses on Livy* and the *History of Florence* alongside the *Prince*. See also the *Life of Castruccio Castracani* for use made of the classical concepts of *virtù* and *fortuna*.

fathers, the 'valiant men of old'. But this presupposition is wholly fallacious; since it implies that human beings stand in no essential or intrinsic relationship to social reality which, in point of fact, they themselves actually constitute. These defects are not accidental. On the contrary, they are the direct and inevitable outcome of a logic which, by ignoring this relationship, grossly misconceives the nature of the 'law' operative in human society. The logic in question is, of course, that of classical idealism.

The radical error of Classicism is to suppose that the history of mankind can properly be apprehended in terms applicable to the study of 'objects' in 'nature', i.e. in the light of the conventional concepts of form and matter.[1] In considering the difficulties which arise from any attempt to apply this scheme we may begin by observing that (as has been suggested, p. 81 above) it reduces the individual human being to the dimensions of a 'specimen' embodying a 'type'. But this is to abstract from all those features which give to him his specific character; in other words, to raise the question of Cleopatra's nose.[2] Furthermore, to envisage him in this light involves the assumption that he becomes fully 'intelligible' in terms of structure and function or, as Aristotle had put it, of 'what he was to be'. It thus raises the question of growth or development as this was conceived by idealism. To this question the answer must already be fairly evident. The type, *qua* type, does not and cannot possibly change; it merely renews itself incessantly in and through the individual; while the individual, on his part, achieves fulfilment (i.e. his end or τέλος) by virtue of this incessant renewal of himself in the type. In this highly formalized and schematized picture of life we may discern certain important implications for the idealist theory of human relationships. For it appears to suggest that the sole essential and intrinsic relation of the individual is with the 'type' to which he 'naturally' belongs. This is frankly admitted by at least one modern exponent of the idealist position when (speaking in his own name) he asserts that 'to idealize is to essentialize, to eliminate non-characteristic elements'.[3] But, in that case, what

---

[1] On the issues here discussed we may refer to a significant paper by R. G. Collingwood, 'Human Nature and Human History', *Proc. Brit. Acad.* xxii (1936), pp. 97–127.   [2] Examined by J. B. Bury, *Selected Essays*, 60; cf. *Introd.* xxiv–vii.

[3] Inge, *The Philosophy of Plotinus*, vol. i, p. 75, as though individual idiosyncrasies counted for nothing and the decanal essence could properly be identified with the universal or archetypal dean.

becomes of the relationships of individuals with one another? Are these (as the sophists had contended) to be relegated to the category of mere convention (νόμος) and thereby admitted to be 'unnatural'? Again, are they to be reduced to terms of mere animal gregariousness or explained as a community (κοινωνία) of interest in physical satisfactions like those which arise from the association of 'male and female' or of 'master and slave'?[1] To avoid this conclusion idealism casts about for a distinctive principle of integration, and this, as we have already noticed, it discovers in the ideal of justice which, as Aristotle rightly suggests, is the common property of all rational beings.[2] But since this ideal, as it stands, is wholly 'formal', it undertakes to give it content by identifying it with the 'justice' of the *polis*.

It is precisely at this point that the idealist commits the crime of Prometheus in seeking to appropriate what belongs to Zeus[3] or, like Adam in the garden, eats of the forbidden fruit in order to become 'like God'. In other words, what he does is to treat knowledge not as a means to 'wisdom' but as a source of 'power'. The power to which he thus aspires proves, however, to be quite illusory. For what he has in fact accomplished is to substitute his notion of order for the order which exists in the universe; the fictitious for the actual; the dead concept for the living reality. His problem is thus to give currency to this counterfeit of cosmic order by persuading or compelling men to accept it as genuine. The effort to do so constitutes the history of 'politics' in classical antiquity.

Not the least significant chapter of that history will be found in the work of Livy. With Livy we are far removed from the Thucydidean sense of history as a diligent and meticulous search for truth, conducted with due regard for the most exacting standards of evidence.[4] What Livy offers is rather an unabashed tract for the times; the Augustan version, in fact, of Plato's noble lie. And if this involves an element of artistic distortion, such distortion is to be justified in view of the purpose to be served, a purpose which excludes anything like an investigation of the facts in terms acceptable to (ancient or modern) critical

---

[1] Arist. *Pol.* i. 1. Note that for Aristotle these latter, although 'human', are conceived as infra-political and subsidiary to the genuinely 'political' relationship.

[2] *Pol.* i. 2. 1253ᵃ.

[3] It will be recalled that, for the Greeks, 'fire' has a twofold connotation; it is (1) literally, that which makes possible the arts of civilization, and (2) metaphorically, the cosmic equivalent of 'mind'.　　　　[4] Thuc. i. 22.

historiography. That purpose may be described, in the vernacular, as an effort to 'sell' the Augustan system. It is instructive to consider how the author sets about his task.

The method of Livy is essentially poetic: what he puts forward is a prose equivalent to what Vergil had offered in verse, i.e. an exposition of the elements of *Romanitas* designed to bring home the conviction of its essential greatness and goodness. These qualities he ascribes, in the conventional language of Classicism, to what has been called 'a unique combination of virtue and fortune'.[1] The question arises: What connotation is he to give these terms? We may begin by considering his treatment of the latter.

Like most contemporary humanists, Livy was fully aware of the dangers of obscurantism latent in the notion of fortune. That the Roman world possessed no immunity from those dangers is indicated by the existence of a popular and official cult rooted in the native tradition and going back to very early times, a cult which, if we may believe the authorities, was in itself relatively innocuous.[2] Yet the mere fact that such a cult existed is in itself significant; for it indicates that *Romanitas* was exposed to the peril of contamination from sources outside; and this peril became acute as ideas current in the Hellenistic world filtered into the West. Such ideas were to find expression with Sallust in a crass fortuitism, which, however, was not very tenaciously held.[3] Cicero, on the other hand, sought with might and main to neutralize the idea which, as he declares, is nothing but a word to cover up our ignorance of events and causes.[4] Yet he could not quite eliminate it, for it was inherent in the classical outlook upon life. With Classicism the concepts of 'virtue' and 'fortune' are complementary, linked together by what has been called a principle of polarity, and it is wholly

---

[1] The words are those of Gibbon, who thus faithfully reproduces the classical 'explanation'.

[2] See Wissowa, *Religion und Kultus der Römer*, 2nd ed., pp. 256–68, and Warde Fowler, *The Roman Festivals*, pp. 161–72.

[3] *Cat.* 8. 1: 'sed profecto fortuna in omni re dominatur; ea res cunctas ex lubidine magis quam ex vero celebrat obscuratque.' Compare, however, the formula in pseudo-Sall. *Ep. ad Caes* i. 1. 1–2, where he endorses the view of the poet that 'every man is the architect of his own fortune'. We may here perhaps note two remarks of Augustine on the subject, *De Civ. Dei*, vii. 3: 'Fortuna, . . . quam dicunt deam non rationabili dispositione, sed ut temere acciderit, sua cuique dona conferre' and, 'temeraria Fortunae potestas ... temerario iudicio'. It was this imputation which Cicero and other humanists sought to avoid.

[4] Cic. *Acad. Post.* i. 7. 29; cf. Lact. *Div. Inst.* iii. 29.

impossible to reject the latter without at the same time rejecting the former, i.e. to throw out the bath without the baby.
Conscious of this difficulty and eager to save virtue, classical
humanism resorts to the expedient of treating the two as
antithetic. They are thus opposed as 'art and industry' on the
one hand and, on the other, 'circumstance' or the material
environment. Cicero, for instance, speaking as a humanist,
declares:[1]

'no one can fail to see how much it depends on fortune or (as we
should say) "conditions" whether we are to experience prosperity or
adversity. Certain events are, indeed, due to natural causes beyond
human control. But in general . . . our misfortunes and failures . . .
and, likewise, our triumphs and successes . . . although they involve
an element of luck (*fortuita*), nevertheless presuppose active co-
operation with our fellows.'[2]

Livy fully shares what we may call the Ciceronian or humanistic prejudice. For him, therefore, the question of Roman
greatness resolves itself into a question of 'by what arts' the
Romans made themselves great.[3] These 'arts' he regards as
embodied in certain representative characters who thus, so to
speak, 'typify' various aspects of 'political' virtue; and these are
set over against others who likewise typify various aspects of
'political' vice. In this technique we may perceive an explanation of those curious Livian 'duplications' which have excited
the attention of critics. It has, for example, been pointed out
that there is no appreciable distinction between the portraits
of Appius Claudius censor and his namesake the decemvir;
though the two men are separated by the lapse of centuries,
similarly the tribune Apuleius who accuses Camillus is an
almost exact counterpart to his (hypothetical) descendant, the
Apuleius Saturninus of 100 B.C.; while the Gaius Flaminius of
the Second Punic war embodies the characteristic features
of the revolutionary demagogue in any age. The effect thereby achieved is not accidental; the figures depicted are man-
nequins rather than human beings, because for Livy, as an
idealist, the sole determinants of personality are 'form' and

---

[1] *De Offic.* ii. 6. 19.
[2] Cf. the significant passage from *Pro Marcello*, 2. 7: 'numquam enim temeritas
cum sapientia commiscetur, nec ad consilium casus admittitur', quoted by Warde
Fowler in *Cl. Rev.* xvii. 153, p. 75, article on *Fortuna*. Here again we may note the
implied antithesis.
[3] *Praef.*, § 9.

'matter', and of these the formal is the positive or active principle.

There could be no clearer or more instructive illustration of Livy's preoccupation with 'form' than in what he has to say about religion. Sallust had characterized his fellow country-men as *religiosissimi mortales*; and to judge from the tenor of Lucretius' polemic against Roman *religio*, he was probably not far wrong. But what is *religio* for Livy? This we may gather from his remarks about portents as indications of the divine will. Livy himself was no less sceptical than were most educated men of his day regarding the objectivity of such manifestations. Indeed, his own professed belief in the Stoic dogma of an immutable fate was in itself enough to exclude their very possi-bility.[1] Yet he does not hesitate to assert that, when confronted by these phenomena, 'his mind takes on as it were an antique tinge' and 'he is constrained to believe that they must have significance, seeing that the wisest of the ancients deemed them worthy of public attention'.[2] At the same time he denounces Epicureanism and Platonism because, as he rightly suspects, they tend to undermine popular faith in 'official' religion with-out providing any adequate substitute.

The attitude thus assumed by Livy must remain incompre-hensible until it is realized that for him, as for classical idealists generally, 'religion' resolves itself purely and simply into a matter of form. In this respect the cults authorized by the college of pontiffs (*religiones licitae*) correspond precisely to the demands of idealist thought. In origin and purpose, in the various techniques of propitiation and augury which they employ, in their ritual of purification and appeasement, their one and only object is to maintain the 'peace of the gods' (*pax deorum*). And for this literally anything will serve, so long as it is felt to be 'politically' expedient; even though, as with certain importations from the Orient, it may be found necessary to emasculate or quarantine the cult lest it should 'pollute' the native atmosphere.[3] But to say this is to suggest that the spirit of official religion was utterly pragmatic. Accord-ingly it becomes purely irrelevant to inquire into its substantial truth or falsehood; 'formally' speaking, a question of this kind

---

[1] xxv. 6: 'cuius lege immobilis rerum humanarum ordo seritur'.   [2] xliii. 13.
[3] See the discussions recorded by Livy in connexion with the Bacchanalian conspiracy of 186 B.C. Ch. II above, p. 31.

simply does not arise, though philosophers may well amuse themselves with such investigations, if they have the inclination to do so, provided that, in legal phraseology, they do nothing 'to upset the minds of the light-headed'.[1] We may perhaps add that the Romans, with the ingrained contempt of the 'man of action' for the intelligentsia, apprehended much more danger from the introduction of religious novelty than from the confused babble of the schools. Against this they stood firmly on guard, ready, in case of necessity, to crush it with the full force of the state. In this connexion Cicero quotes with approval a hoary provision of the XII Tables.[2] Under this legislation astrology or 'mathematics', together with other forms of 'illegitimate curiosity' had always been outlawed, and even Judaism, though tolerated as a *prava superstitio* appropriate to the Jewish race, was otherwise under a ban more or less strictly enforced. It is only by appreciating these facts that we can possibly understand how intelligent and high-minded citizens like Cicero or the emperor Augustus himself could have given any countenance to practices which, as they perfectly well knew, were sheer and unmitigated humbug, justifying themselves on the ground that these were material to the preservation of social order.

We may here observe that, according to the afore-mentioned principle of polarity, the counterpart to social order is social change. Change therefore constitutes both a fact to be recognized and a problem to be solved. This brings us to a crucial difficulty for classical idealism. We have already alluded to the (reported) views of a representative Roman like Julius Caesar on the subject. It may be added that Caesar, although notorious as an innovator, was by no means alone in perceiving that change was in some sense inevitable. Cicero, for example, in his argument for granting to Pompey an *imperium extraordinarium* in the East,[3] emphasized his belief that existing institutions must always be accommodated to evolving demands, and asked whether his fellow citizens had so far degenerated as to have lost the courage of a conviction so fundamental to their life as makers of history. The same point of view was to be forcibly

---

[1] Modest. in *Dig.* 48. 19. 30: 'si quis aliquid fecerit quo leves hominum animi ... terrentur'.

[2] *De Legg.* ii. 8. 19: 'separatim nemo habessit deos neve novos sive advenas nisi publice adscitos privatim colunto.' Cf. ii. 11. 27.

[3] *Pro Lege Manilia*, 20. 60.

expressed a century later by the emperor Claudius when, in urging upon the senate an extension of the *ius honorum* to nobles of Gallia Comata, he argued that the proposal now being justified by reference to precedent would itself be one day numbered among the precedents.[1] The problem, however, was to determine how precedents could be established without capitulation to the Great God *Whirl*, the terror of the 'political' mind. To this problem idealism made a characteristic contribution which we must now briefly discuss.

It will be evident that to interpret politics in terms of physics is to institute a parallelism between the 'legitimate' and the 'natural'. Conversely, it is to identify the (physically) unnatural with the (politically) illegitimate. But, in this context, the term 'legitimacy' means much more than mere legality conceived as the will of the sovereign regardless of its implied intention; as might appear to be suggested in the Hobbesian maxim *sit pro ratione voluntas* or the Austinian definition of law as a bare command of power. For, as Aristotle had insisted, if this command is to have validity, it must be recognized as just; otherwise, in his own somewhat heated words, 'by heaven it is not right'.[2] We are thus once more confronted with the question of justice as the bond of men in states; and therewith the idealist concept of what is just.

Here again the parallelism may be helpful. If, as idealism contends, justice in nature is the fulfilment by individuals of what 'they were to be', i.e. of the type, then its political counterpart must be a realization of the formal order of the state. This determines the scope and limits of political process, which thus bears the relation of 'evolving content' to idea; beyond that point process is 'illegitimate' and 'unnatural'. We may here note that, for classical idealism, the very possibility of growth is restricted to individuals; communal or social development in the sense envisaged by modern liberalism[3] is completely beyond its horizon. Thus, for example, it has been said of Livy[4] that

'while he vaguely feels that earlier centuries do not exactly resemble that of Augustus (as, e.g., *Ab Urbe Condita* i. 18. 1 and 57. 1), yet he never faces the question how they differ, but simply generalizes

---

[1] Ch. I above, p. 22.
[2] *Pol.* iii. 10. 1281ᵃ.
[3] See R. M. MacIver, *Community, The Modern State*.
[4] By H. Bornecque, *Tite-Live*, p. 88.

from what he sees about him. . . . It is clear that the adventurers camped with Romulus at the foot of the Palatine to pillage the commerce ascending the Tiber valley have nothing in common with the hard-working, thrifty, and disciplined peasants who were destined to triumph over Carthage and effect the conquest of the world, any more than these resemble the cultivated and somewhat effete Romans of Cicero's day. This difference escapes Livy or, if it does not wholly escape him, at least he makes no effort to indicate it explicitly in his work.' ·

It is hardly necessary to comment upon the intense conservatism implied in such a view of human life. It betrays an utter lack of faith in the goodness of any possible 'world to come' and invites men to conform to established models; forgetting that it is one thing to respect traditional folk-ways as a guide to conduct, but quite another to erect them into a principle of control, i.e. to extend to the dead a prescriptive right to govern the living. One result of this is to engender a fear and hatred of social change, regardless of its character and potentiality; and, with Livy, this manifests itself in a disposition to condemn as pernicious every tendency to innovation. Another is to inspire a profound distrust of the commons, to whose merely animal impulses are ascribed cataclysms, the equivalent in human life to what in nature are the blind and erratic thrusts of matter-in-motion. 'It is', declares Livy, 'the nature of the multitude that it either submits tamely to dictation or it strives openly for ascendancy. As for liberty, which is intermediate between the two, the masses are ignorant of how to achieve and how to maintain it in a temperate spirit'.[1] The conclusion must be obvious: what Leviathan needs is a head. To supply that head is the work of creative politics.

Thus envisaged, the problem of politics is to reconcile 'liberty' with 'authority'. We shall best understand the attitude of Livy towards this problem if we consider it against the background provided by Sallust. 'Romulus', declares Sallust, 'took over a population of rustics utterly devoid of law and authority. After they had come together within one fortification, notwithstanding differences of race, language, and custom, it is marvellous how quickly they coalesced. Thus, within a brief period, a loose and amorphous multitude was transformed into a civil

[1] xxiv. 25. 8.

society.'[1] It has been pointed out[2] that Sallust here inverts the
true historical order; the nucleus of Roman society (the *gentes*
out of which it was formed) must have possessed racial and
cultural affinities which the historian chooses arbitrarily to
ignore. The inversion is itself significant. It serves to emphasize
his conviction that states do not grow, they are designed and
manufactured; often, as was conspicuously the case with Rome,
out of such unpromising material as was assembled together in
the so-called 'asylum of Romulus'. But for this purpose what
is required is a catalyst, potent enough to transmute this
material into the elements of a body-politic. Accordingly it
presupposes a conscious and deliberate act of statecraft, an act
so stupendous in its nature and consequences as to be impossible
except for a being endowed with transcendent wisdom and
strength, in the words of Aristotle[3] 'of surpassing excellence,
goodness of a heroic or divine order'; or, as Cicero puts it,[4]
'a degree of right reason and constancy which must be deemed
superhuman and attributed to a god'. This act, which is
ascribed to a (mythical) hero-founder or lawgiver, consists of
imposing upon the assembled elements the characteristic forms
of the *polis* or *civitas*, i.e. of 'civilized' life. But, in the nature
of things, the original source of these forms must itself be
'formal', since otherwise it could not discharge its function.
Accordingly, it may be described (in the terminology of Sallust)
as *imperium legitimum*. To such a principle, as represented in the
prehistoric kings, the historian attributes 'the conservation of
freedom and the increase of public good'.[5]

As for the *modus operandi* of 'legitimate authority', we must
refer to Livy, from whom we may learn (as it is the business of
a genuine classic to teach us) the technique by which it undertakes to 'force men to be free'. In so doing we cannot afford to
linger over details. It is enough to remember that the founder
begins his work with a ritual act of unmistakable significance,
when, under the most favourable auspices possible, he traces

---

[1] *Cat.* 6. 2: 'hi (genus hominum agreste, sine legibus, sine imperio, liberum atque
solutum) postquam in una moenia convenere, dispari genere, dissimili lingua, alii
alio more viventes, incredibile memoratu est quam facile coaluerint; ita brevi multi-
tudo dispersa atque vaga concordia civitas facta erat.'
[2] Ihering, *Geist des römischen Rechts*, Ed. 7 & 8, i, p. 183 foll.
[3] *N.E.* vii. 1. 1145ª19.   [4] *De Nat. Deor.* ii. 13. 34.
[5] Sall. *Cat.* 6. 7: 'regium imperium (quod) initio conservandae libertatis atque
augendae rei publicae fuerat.'

the limits of the *pomoerium*, the sacred frontier across which it is death to trespass.[1] This task accomplished, he then proceeds to subject the rabble to a discipline which includes both the law of force and the force of law. But, over and above this, there is need for a fresh principle of integration, and this the second founder (Numa Pompilius) supplies by his 'constitution of religions', the myths of virtue whereby the people is to live.[2] The period of formation is, however, concluded only with the revolution of 509 B.C. and the struggle between the orders; and these the historian rationalizes in terms of his preconceived idea. Thus, for him, the expulsion of the 'tyrant' Tarquin serves to reaffirm the 'formal' distinction between public authority and private ownership (*imperium* and *dominium*). It initiates a process whereby the generality of law is realized,[3] while, at the same time, it attains its specific character. On the other hand, the social conflict between patricians and plebeians helps to promote the gradual evolution of the *populus*, 'a happy hierarchy of classes' as it has been called, in which privilege is equated with responsibility, and both are estimated in terms of a will and a capacity to serve. This development is marked by significant pieces of legislation such as the code of the XII Tables and the Valerio-Horatian laws of 449 B.C. The former is proclaimed to be the fountain of all right, public and private.[4] The latter, by restoring the traditional constitution under fresh and more effective sanctions, defines and fixes in perpetuity the Latin version of the commonwealth.[5]

We have already pointed out how, according to idealist theory, the work of creative politics is subject to limitations which arise from the recalcitrance of the material and which serve to impede, if not to frustrate, the effort of the statesman to impose upon it a perfect or absolute form. With Livy we have the conventional application of this theory to Rome. It is implied in his attitude to democracy as illustrated by the remarks already quoted.[6] Still more emphatically it governs his treatment of the popular or mass movements of early times. Thus, in describing the various 'secessions' of the plebs, the

---

[1] i. 7. 2.

[2] i. 19. 1: '(Numa) qui regno potitus urbem novam conditam vi et armis, iure eam legibusque ac moribus de integro condere parat.'   [3] ii. 3. 4.

[4] iii. 34. 6: 'decem tabularum leges . . . nunc quoque . . . fons omnis publici privatique iuris.'   [5] iii. 54–5.   [6] p. 104 above.

author admits, as indeed he must, the existence of substantial grievances on the part of the malcontents. Furthermore he recognizes that, so long as those grievances remain unadjusted, the community as a whole is exposed to the peril of imminent destruction at the hands of foreign enemies, to whom dissension among the Romans is a constant invitation to aggression. The problem is therefore to discover the means whereby conflicting elements within society may be persuaded or forced to cohere. This, of course, involves a certain degree of compromise and concession on all sides. But, as Livy urges, no settlement by mutual consent can be regarded as permanent unless all parties alike learn to understand and accept the places to which 'nature' has assigned them within the social system. And, so far as concerns the masses, this means that they must see themselves as members in relation to the organism as a whole. That is to say, their function, vital though it be to the life of the great beast, is nevertheless strictly subordinate; since it depends upon the nourishment which they receive from the belly. In this conviction we may perceive an explanation of the attitude of Livy towards demagogues who, for reasons of self-interest, are ready to exploit the passions of the multitude in a manner contrary to the public good. He thus presents us with a rogues' gallery, including Spurius Cassius, Spurius Maelius, and even Manlius Capitolinus, the former saviour of the Capitol, a man 'who would have been notable anywhere but in a free state'. These individuals, while certainly not devoid of admirable qualities, are none the less guilty of the one unpardonable offence: they have refused to accept the obligations of Roman citizenship, i.e. to conform to the political stereotype. Accordingly their fate is that of potential 'tyrants' with whose blood the tree of Roman liberty must be watered, if it is to flourish.

This brings us at last to the question of what has been called the moral intention of the writer. And here we must pause to make an observation of vital importance to our theme. In its revulsion from what may be designated the Livian pattern, modern historiography tends to take refuge in the notion of history without a moral. But the real difficulty does not appear to be that Livy introduces moral values into history; it lies rather in the nature of the values which he seeks to introduce. For this reason it is not enough to denounce him merely because he transforms history into an instrument of propaganda. Nor can we be satisfied simply with dismissing his standards of valuation as elementary or obsolete. Our problem is rather to discover, if possible, the process of thought by which he arrives at those standards. And, for this purpose, we must bear in mind the presuppositions which underlie his work.

We have already suggested that Livy's object is to recommend the principate as the one possible solution to the problems of his day. This conclusion follows as a logical consequence of his 'set up'. For, on his showing, it is evident that, when once the sovereign people have triumphed over their most formidable enemies, the elements of cohesion among them must *ipso facto* be weakened. This, however, means the release of forces which, as we have seen, are always present in the matter and which, since 'passion' is by nature unlimited, become more and more difficult to counteract and control, until they ultimately lead to disintegration. The consequence, as Livy sees it, is a progressive 'degeneration'; a process which by his day has gone so far that, to use his own words, 'our vices and their remedies have become equally intolerable'.[1] To say this, however, is to admit that the resources of government, in the ordinary sense, have been exhausted. It is to suggest that a situation has arisen which calls for nothing less than the intervention of a second founder. And, finally, it is to point to Augustus Caesar as the man.

In saying this we do not overlook the fact that the man thus hailed as a new Romulus and Numa had begun his career merely as a successful faction-leader. Nor do we forget that his actual power rested upon a conglomerate of elements which were in the last degree heterogeneous. King alike of the petty Alpine district of Noricum and of the vast and ancient realm of Cleopatra, he was from the beginning recognized by the hellenized Asiatics as 'autocrat' and 'basileus'. Meanwhile, to the barbarians of the Western provinces, he represented the head of the army which kept them in subjection; while in Rome and Italy he was, like his father before him, not so much 'rex' as 'Caesar'. In his struggle for ascendancy he had capitalized the deep-seated Latin sense of family right by asserting the claims due to an adoptive son of the deified Julius. At the same time he had appealed to the veterans at first through

---

[1] *Praef.*, § 9.

the magic of his father's name; subsequently, as *generalissimo*, he exploited to the full the methods devised by the dictator for securing the fidelity of his troops.[1] Through the *tribunicia potestas* he proclaimed himself champion of the *plebs urbana*, the 'forgotten man'. From all ranks of society, civil as well as military, he exacted a pledge of allegiance in the shape of a regular oath (*sacramentum*) taken publicly on his accession; while, for all alike, his office, if not his person, was bathed in the unearthly floodlight of the imperial cult. To such considerations the emperor doubtless owed the substance of his power. Their existence, however, served merely to throw into greater relief its 'formal' character.

In this connexion there are two points to be noted. In the first place, the emperor contends that his position is 'formally' correct—the ultimate manifestation, indeed, of *imperium legitimum* and so a genuine solution to the problem of leadership in a free state.[2] Secondly, his title to authority is held to depend upon the possession of certain specific qualities of excellence by reason of which he claims to embody the quintessence of Latin political virtue. We may here observe that the qualities to which the emperor lays claim are *virtus*, *clementia*, *justitia*, and *pietas*.[3] As it stands, this list represents an interesting modification of the conventional cardinal virtues which is evidently deliberate. For example, the use of *clementia* instead of *magnanimitas* is perhaps intended to constitute a link between the younger and the elder Caesar by associating him with what had been a prominent aspect of the Julian tradition. On the other hand, to substitute *pietas* for *prudentia* is to turn the spot-light upon a characteristic which, if not unique to Octavian, was at any rate of immense significance in his career.[4] This characteristic was now put forward as the fourth and ultimate pillar of Augustan political wisdom. What it suggests is that this wisdom

[1] It will be remembered that the troops looked directly to the emperor for pay and allowances, provision for which was made from the military treasury controlled by him and no longer depended upon *stipendia* voted by the senate. In addition, they might expect occasional donatives while on service and, with their discharge, grants of land similar to those made by the dictator in his 'Julian colonies'. The relationship thus approximated to that of patron and client, traditionally the closest and most intimate of bonds.

[2] *Res Gestae*, ed. Mommsen (1885), cap. 5. 31; 7. 43–6; 10. 21–5; and esp. 34. 13–23.

[3] See M. P. Charlesworth, *The Virtues of a Roman Emperor* (Raleigh Lecture, 1937), whose comments on the subject are very illuminating.

[4] See Tacitus on the subject, *Ann.* i. 10.

consists not so much in any capacity to foresee the future as in loyalty to the approved findings of the past. In this sense it recalls the spirit attributed by Vergil to *pius Aeneas*, the incarnation of just this quality. It also reflects a conservatism analogous to that which we have noticed in Livy. By so doing it points to what was to be a peculiar and distinctive feature of the *Pax Augusta*.

To recognize the Augustan peace as a direct outcome of Augustan excellence is to understand why the emperor should have been acclaimed on all hands as an earthly providence.[1] Nor is it possible to dismiss these apparently extravagant phrases as the idle compliments of court poets, unless indeed we choose to admit that the whole structure of *Romanitas* was erected upon a basis of fiction. They were, on the contrary, 'a genuine confession of devotion towards one who' was regarded as having 'wrought great things for the world and proclaimed a gospel of peace and glad tidings'; although it may be doubted whether they were in fact 'altogether wholesome' rather than the reverse, as the author appears to suggest.[2] But whatever view be taken of this question, it is at least clear that the sentiments thus expressed constitute a challenge to understanding. This challenge the historian must endeavour to meet, if he is to appreciate the full meaning of the Augustan system, and of the criticisms to be levelled against it by the Christians.

The cult of the Caesars is commonly regarded as a form of Orientalism transplanted into Italy from the Hellenistic world. But while this may well account for its derivation, it fails to explain why it should have been accepted in the new environment. Accordingly, in seeking to trace the genesis of the cult, we must begin by insisting that, so far from being foreign or exotic, it was rooted in theories of human nature more or less explicit in Classicism. From this standpoint it is much closer to the mentality of modern Europe than we should like to suppose.

We may begin by noting that popular Greek thought, starting from the concept of 'strictly human excellence', admits the occurrence, however sporadically and unevenly, of individuals who, for some mysterious reason, transcend the common

---

[1] 'praesens deus; deus nobis haec otia fecit; erit ille mihi semper deus.' See *Camb. Anc. Hist.* xi, ch. xviii, p. 583 foll.

[2] Warde Fowler, *Roman Ideas of Deity*, pp. 88 and 123.

measure of humanity. In the lyric poets[1] such individuals are conceived to enjoy capacities denied to the normal man; the ability to hit the mark ($\tau \upsilon \chi \epsilon \hat{\imath} \nu$), to apprehend and exploit situations, however difficult. At the same time they exhibit an inclination 'to live dangerously', defying the conventions which govern ordinary behaviour and achieving results to which the ordinary man would be mad to aspire. That is to say, they appear to possess a quite abnormal 'potential' of power. This power (as we have already had occasion to notice) is rationalized in terms of the familiar 'virtue and fortune' ($\dot{a} \rho \epsilon \tau \dot{\eta} \kappa a \dot{\imath} \tau \dot{\upsilon} \chi \eta$), complementary concepts which, as we should say, represent the 'subjective' and the 'objective' factors of success. Of these the former is commonly resolved into intelligence and endurance, for which the Romans were presently to discover suitable equivalents ($\sigma \dot{\upsilon} \nu \epsilon \sigma \iota \varsigma \kappa a \dot{\imath} \dot{a} \nu \delta \rho \epsilon \dot{\imath} a = sapientia$ et fortitudo). As for the latter, the meaning read into it varies in accordance with the outlook of those by whom it is employed.[2]

The type thus envisaged by popular thought is recognized by philosophy. Thus Plato[3] speaks of those who, having served their turn as guardians of the (ideal) city, depart to dwell in the islands of the blest; and for these he demands that shrines be erected and sacrifices publicly offered 'as to demons or at least to eudaemonic and divine men'. ($\mu \nu \eta \mu \epsilon \hat{\imath} a \delta' a \dot{\upsilon} \tau o \hat{\imath} \varsigma \kappa a \dot{\imath} \theta \upsilon \sigma \dot{\imath} a \varsigma \tau \dot{\eta} \nu \pi \dot{o} \lambda \iota \nu \delta \eta \mu o \sigma \dot{\imath} a \pi o \iota \epsilon \hat{\imath} \nu \ldots \dot{\omega} \varsigma \delta a \dot{\imath} \mu o \sigma \iota \nu, \epsilon \dot{\imath} \delta \dot{\epsilon} \mu \dot{\eta}, \dot{\omega} \varsigma \epsilon \dot{\upsilon} \delta a \dot{\imath} \mu o \sigma \dot{\imath} \tau \epsilon \kappa a \dot{\imath} \theta \epsilon \dot{\imath} o \iota \varsigma$.) Aristotle, on the other hand, contents himself with observing[4] that, in the hierarchy of nature, the human *psyche* normally ranks between that of gods and heroes on the one hand and, on the other, that of beasts; linked to the former by its intellect, to the latter by its affections; and he adds that, just as the affections of the sensible part are sometimes so corrupted as to produce the semblance of a beast, so also the rational part occasionally attains such a degree of perfection as to deserve the epithet 'divine'.

It has been suggested that, while, to begin with, such ideas

---

[1] See the *Anthology, passim.*

[2] See, e.g., the portrait of Nicias as given by Thucydides, v, vi, and vii, as compared with that of Plutarch's *Life of Nicias*. To the Athenian democracy Nicias was (subjectively) a competent and honest man; but (objectively) he was 'lucky' (*a*) because he 'had victory in his name', (*b*) because he was assiduous in propitiating the gods on every possible occasion. The *Life* constitutes a most instructive study in contemporary psychology.   [3] *Rep.* 540 B. Cf. *Laws* 951 B.

[4] *N.E.* vii. 1145ª15 foll.

were not indigenous to Italy, the soil was nevertheless favourable to their germination.[1] In this connexion the important point is that Latin ideology, despite or (perhaps) because of its very barrenness, presents no insuperable barrier to their acceptance. We thus find Cicero identifying the native *numen* of Juppiter with creative intelligence or the life-force as conceived by the Stoics (*numen praestantissimae mentis*) and going on to assert that man possesses within himself 'a certain spark of the divine mind'.[2] On this account he thinks it rational to deify mental and moral qualities.

'It is proper', he declares, 'to consecrate the intellect, loyalty, manliness, and good faith of humanity, to all of which temples have been publicly dedicated at Rome, in order that those who possess them—as all good men do—should feel that they have gods themselves dwelling within their own bosoms. For it is virtues, not vices that merit consecration.'

In this last observation we may perhaps detect a characteristically Roman prejudice. For the Greeks the 'power' of the daemonic man could, and frequently did, manifest itself in what we should call immoral or amoral ways.[3] But the strong social sense of the Romans revolted from the pretensions of a Salmoneus, 'the madman who paraded himself with the symbols of divinity and arrogated to himself the veneration of a god'. On the other hand, they were satisfied with the notion that, in and through the service of his fellows, a man might properly aspire to divinity. Accordingly, in the myth of Hercules, they discovered a form of the power-cult which appealed to them as elevating rather than degrading to the human spirit. 'Hercules', declares Cicero, 'has gone to join the gods; but he never would have done so, had he not paved the way for himself while he was still a man among men.'[4] Again,[5] 'the fact that the law commands us to worship certain of the human race who have been consecrated, like Hercules and others, indicates that, while, indeed, the minds of all men are immortal, those of the brave and good are intrinsically divine.' These, indeed, are 'the rulers and saviours of states', the 'patriots to whom the barriers of heaven are lowered'.[6] In these conclusions the Latin version of

---

[1] Warde Fowler, op. cit., p. 81.   [2] *De Nat. Deor.* ii. 2. 4; *De Rep.* iii. 1. 1.
[3] Rohde, op. cit., p. 138.   [4] *Tusc.* i. 14. 32.
[5] *De Legg.* ii. 11. 27, with which compare Tac. *Ann.* iv. 38. 5.
[6] *De Rep.* vi. 24. 26.

Classicism proclaims its inability to exorcize the cult of power. In so doing it paves the way for the recognition of Augustus Caesar as a political god.

We are now in a position to see the point to which the pursuit of 'strictly human excellence' by 'powers strictly human' has brought us; we have crossed the frontier of mere humanity and entered into the region of *supermen*.[1] In this region what has become of that substantial equality presupposed in political life and of the ideal of felicity to be realized by communal endeavour? They have simply disappeared. Henceforth, the hopes and expectations of mankind are fixed upon the 'august' being to whom they have now placed themselves in tutelage. In this connexion it may be pointed out that the deification of imperial virtue involves, as an inevitable corollary, the deification of imperial fortune. These considerations will help us to understand why the Christians, at least, looked with profound suspicion and disfavour upon 'the immense majesty of the Augustan peace'; why, indeed, despite the inestimable benefits of security and order which it embodied, a man like Tertullian felt himself justified in denouncing the realm of Caesar as the realm of the devil.

---

[1] The ugly word *superman*, so far from having been a product of 'nineteenth-century pseudo-philosophy', appears to have been coined by Pope Gregory the Great. This is pointed out by J. Maritain in *Theonas, Conversations of a Sage*, Lond. and N.Y. (1933), p. 189, who quotes Gregory's statement (*in Job*, xxviii. 21, *Moral. Lib.* xviii, cap. 54): 'More suo (Paulus) homines (vocat) omnes humana sapientes, quia qui divina sapiunt *videlicet supra-homines* sunt'; i.e. 'they are, so to speak (with apologies for the barbarism), supermen.' I owe the reference to a former pupil, Rev. L. C. Braceland, S.J.

The point which Gregory here seeks to make is of fundamental importance. Christianity, he urges, agrees with paganism in recognizing the phenomenon of superhumanity; from this standpoint the *divi Caesares* have an apparent analogy in the *divi* or *sancti* of the Church. It denies, however, that the attainment of sanctity is the result of intrinsic or inherent excellence (ἀρετή—*virtus*), since this would be contrary to the doctrine of original sin; and explains it as the fruit of *coelestis conversatio*, i.e. of cleaving to a good which is extrinsic to our merely human nature. As Augustine was to put it, the true *sapientia* which elevates men above the common level consists of 'sticking to God' (*adhaerere Deo*) not of 'self-realization'. Thus *verus philosophus amator Dei*.

true philosopher is lover of God

IV

REGNUM CAESARIS REGNUM DIABOLI

NEEDLESS to say, the claim of the Augustan order to finality was doomed to ultimate frustration. Yet the ideals symbolized in the splendid figure of the divinized emperor were to be implemented in large measure; and almost three centuries were to elapse before they were discarded in favour of those embodied in the likeness of a crucified Jew. During this period we may, perhaps, distinguish three phases of thought and action. The first was one of accommodation to the demands of the Augustan order; the second, the fulfilment of its promise when, as has been said, 'the Romans got their reward'; while the third was marked by various aspects of collapse and reconstruction, culminating in the formal adoption of a radically new principle of social integration, in the name of which the so-called Christian emperors were to undertake a renovation of *Romanitas*, the nature and scope of which we shall try to indicate in the second part of this work. The phases thus described correspond in general to the three successive centuries of the pagan empire. Accordingly, we may speak of the first century as roughly the century of adjustment, the second as that of fruition, the third as that of disintegration and decay; although it must be remembered that distinctions of this kind are largely arbitrary, since the web of history is seamless.[1]

[1] For a study of the period, Gibbon, *The Decline and Fall of the Roman Empire*, ed. Bury (1896), remains indispensable as a basis. The significance of this work is that it embodies such a faithful rendering of the ancient literary tradition. Modern historians have, of course, supplemented and corrected the picture by the aid of fresh sources of information, chiefly epigraphical and numismatic: the former assembled in the *Corpus Inscriptionum Latinarum* and subsequent publications; the latter in works such as that of Mattingly–Sydenham, *The Roman Imperial Coinage*, 5 vols. (1923–33). Results of recent critical investigation are reviewed in the *Cambridge Ancient History*, vols. x and xi, the latter carrying the narrative to A.D. 170. For the difficult period which follows, H. M. D. Parker, *A History of Rome from A.D. 138 to 337* (Hadrian to Constantine), will be found a clear and trustworthy guide. Specific aspects of the situation are discussed by Rostovtzeff, *The Social and Economic History of the Roman Empire*; Homo, *L'Empire romain* and *Les Institutions politiques romaines*; Chapot, *The Roman World*, and many other scholars. There are also monographs on a considerable number of individual emperors. Extensive bibliographies are contained in most of the standard works.

The prevailing fashion is to treat the period in a more or less impersonal way; attention no longer being focused, as it was for Gibbon, on the imperial palace and its occupants, but directed to economic and social phenomena which he to some extent overlooked. We may, however, doubt whether the need of the moment is

Humanly speaking, the problem of adjustment resolved itself into one of understanding and acceptance. As such, it pointed to a recognition of Caesarism, not merely as a rod for the back, but as a final and definitive embodiment of the *logos* of classical order; in other words, of imperial excellence as the ground and presupposition of imperial authority, by virtue of which the prince was qualified to discharge his commission.[1] As for the terms of that commission, they were to be stated in the words of the poet,

tu regere imperio populos, Romane, memento.

It thus involved a twofold undertaking: (*a*) to draw and hold together in one vast physical unity the heterogeneous elements of Mediterranean life, and (*b*) to subject those elements to the formal discipline of *Romanitas*. It is in the light of these purposes that we must seek to envisage the services provided by the Caesars. By comparison with what is expected of a modern state, those services were, in one sense, quite rudimentary. Yet, in another, they were much more comprehensive; since what they aimed at was to secure the possibility of 'felicity', the good life so far as this was deemed compatible with the inescapable conditions of existence here below. From this standpoint, organized social action may be regarded as falling into one or other of the three modes indicated by Sallust: viz. *vis*, *auctoritas*, and *consilium*. Our first task is thus to determine how these principles found expression within the 'immense majesty of the Augustan peace'.

And first as to *vis* or physical (military) force. To begin with, it will be recalled that the notion of indefinite expansion was repudiated by Augustus as part of the outmoded competition for *dominationes et potentiae* which had characterized the struggles of

not for a more adequate principle of discrimination than has so far been employed. With respect to certain of the recent imperial biographies in particular, it has rightly been said that the true answer to the tar-brush is not a coat of whitewash. We might also point to the danger of misunderstanding implicit in statements such as that of Alföldi [in *J.R.S.* xxvi–xxvii (1936–7), p. 256, reviewing Parker's work] when he speaks of '*great immanent forces that transcend individual emperors or movements of history*' (italics mine). To us this statement appears to involve a wholly false antithesis. The same criticism applies to a remark by F. B. Marsh [*The Reign of Tiberius*, p. 12]: 'the Romans had but a weak perception of economic or political causation in human affairs and turned naturally to the personality of the actors to explain the course of events.' The true desideratum is, surely, a more exact appreciation of the nature of economic and political action. This, however, is a question for philosophy, with which the 'pure' economist or historian, if indeed such a being exists, can hardly be expected to deal.   [1] Ch. III above, p. 109.

faction during the last decades of the expiring republic. Henceforth the problem was to 'protect' civilization. In this connexion it may be observed that the new policy was not in any sense the result of conscious weakness. For while the treachery of an Arminius might check the advance of the Eagles, the northern barbarians were as yet unprepared to challenge the Roman watch-on-Rhine; and, apart from the natural dismay occasioned by the annihilation of three veteran legions, the Teutoburg disaster served merely to emphasize the truth that the confines of the empire had been sufficiently enlarged and that the task of the future must be one of consolidation.[1] On the other hand, the success of Augustan methods in intimidating Parthia suggested that issues even of the most difficult and delicate character might be satisfactorily handled by diplomacy backed by an adequate show of strength. From this standpoint, the Vergilian *parcere subiectis et debellare superbos* was to constitute an accurate description of imperial foreign policy. What this entailed by way of fortifications, the construction of roads and bridges, not to speak of the recruiting, training, and disposition of armed forces by land and sea, we shall not presume to discuss.[2] For us the question is how far this part of the commission could be regarded as exclusive to the emperor. For, in this sphere of activity, it is evident that imperial virtue must have been largely that of the officers and men who fought under imperial auspices. Yet, if the army was to discharge its function as an instrument of public policy, it was essential that discipline should be maintained, and that striking power should not be squandered either in extravagant adventures beyond the frontiers or in debilitating civil strife. This, then, was the problem which confronted the emperor as commander-in-chief and commissar of foreign policy; and nothing less than the highest personal *auctoritas* (authority, prestige) on his part was needed in order, as Tiberius Caesar put it, to hold the wolf by the ears. We thus arrive at the question of imperial authority.

We have already referred[3] to the intimate relationship which subsisted between the *imperator* and his men and to the pledge of personal fidelity which they were required to give him. This pledge was reinforced by the traditional Roman powers of

---

[1] Tac. *Ann.* i. 11. 6 and 7 (Furneaux); Plut. *Moral.* 207 D.
[2] These problems have been studied by various scholars.
[3] Ch. III above, p. 109.

discipline, including the terrible right of decimation, which seems to have been invoked as late at least as the days of Julius Caesar. In all this there was nothing new; what were novel were the conditions of service which had been created by the revolution. These included two points of fundamental importance. The first was the professionalization of legionary service initiated by Marius and consummated by Augustus. The second was the loss of control by the senate over the armed forces of the state. These developments were of far-reaching importance. They transformed the army into a class apart: between it and the civil population the sole link was the prince-emperor. As Tiberius demanded of the trembling senate, when they ventured to suggest rewards to be given at the conclusion of a successful campaign: what have you to do with the troops? In these circumstances, it was vitally necessary that the emperor himself should possess both the will and the capacity to control the military machine in the interests of society at large. Nor was this by any means an easy task. For, even with the best intentions in the world, it was hardly possible to avoid compromising with the demands of strict economy by conceding the occasional donatives sanctioned by custom; while, on the other hand, it was difficult for a prince to grant such favours to the troops without awakening them to a sense of their power. The problem was to emerge in connexion with the accession of Tiberius, when the formations on the Rhine and Danube took advantage of the temporary dislocation of government to mutiny, demanding the redress of grievances and less onerous terms of service.[1] It was destined to become acute whenever weak or inexperienced princes assumed the purple. But, more even than the legionaries, it concerned the formidable praetorian guard who, stationed at the capital and enjoying every possible favour, may be said to have embodied in their persons at once the glory and the shame of the Augustan principate.

In its self-appointed task of 'bringing order out of chaos' or 'imposing order on anarchy', creative statesmanship required the support of substantial physical force (*vis*). The employment of such force could, however, be justified only as it served to promote the larger end. This was the realization of political justice, the *suum cuique reddere* of Cicero and the Roman *iurisprudentes*; through which alone it was thought possible to meet

[1] Tac. *Ann.* i. 16–45.

the demand for an order embodying 'good faith' and 'equity'. Accordingly, there devolved upon the prince in his capacity as chief magistrate extensive powers of regulation and control. We do not here refer so much to his multifarious executive functions, food supply (*cura annonae*), the highways commission (*cura viarum*), aqueducts (*cura aquarum*), the Tiber Conservancy (*cura alvei Tiberis*), essential though these undoubtedly were to the welfare of the urban populace. Nor are we thinking of the work of organization for which he was ultimately responsible in areas like that of imperial public finance. Our concern is rather with the role which he assumed in the administration of justice. And here we may note that his duties were twofold, corresponding to the broad distinction which emerged between *humiliores* and *honestiores*, the 'lower' and 'upper' classes respectively of the social hierarchy. The former, consisting of slaves, foreigners, and proletarians, although they probably made up a very large percentage of the total population, always remained a 'protected' class, subject to summary police jurisdiction and liable to the harshest measures of magisterial *coercitio*. With respect to these elements, it fell to the prince, through subordinates directly or indirectly responsible to him, to preserve order. As to the methods adopted for this purpose, we should have no illusions: in the words of Tacitus, 'the only way to keep such riff-raff under is by fear'.[1] This he says with particular reference to the slaves whose numbers had grown so huge in imperial Italy. But, apart from these, there were the various orders of society properly so called, senatorial, equestrian, and municipal as constituted or reconstituted by Augustus—the classes for whom the state theoretically existed and whose interests it was designed to serve. These interests were to find expression, over a period of centuries, in a growing volume of civil law. The actual content of that law must, of course, remain a subject for special and detailed study.[2] Our concern is merely to indicate the relation of the prince to the system; in other words, to ask what was gained and what lost with the loss of republican freedom. We may begin by noting certain changes which occurred in the field of criminal jurisdiction.[3]

[1] *Ann.* xiv. 44: 'conluviem istam non nisi metu coercueris.'
[2] Based, in the first instance, upon the texts, secondly, upon the ancient commentators and, finally, upon a host of modern works.
[3] On the subject in general, see Mommsen-Marquardt, vol. xviii, *Droit pénal*.

In primitive Rome, the notion of crime, in the modern sense, had been restricted to a very few offences, the most important of which was *perduellio* or treason. This included rebellion against the fatherland, the giving of aid or comfort to an enemy, and (subsequently) the murder of a fellow citizen. Acts such as theft or assault ranked simply as misdemeanours for which a penalty, commensurate with the gravity of the injury inflicted and with the social standing of the victim, was considered adequate. With respect both to crimes and misdemeanours, the duty of the magistrate (originally the king) was to see that satisfaction was rendered in accordance with the terms of civic peace; and to this end he was armed with power necessary to force his subjects to comply with his will. Legally speaking, one of the principal consequences of the revolution of 509 B.C. was to limit the application of magisterial *coercitio* by authorizing an appeal to the sovereign people *in comitiis*, whenever the *caput* of a citizen was involved; and this right, consecrated in the Valerian law of appeal, was thenceforth to constitute the palladium of civil liberty. Popular jurisdiction, thus initiated in 509 B.C., survived in theory for the remainder of Roman history. Actually, it was supplanted for all practical purposes towards the close of the republic by permanent jury courts (*quaestiones perpetuae*) instituted on the model of that set up for trying cases of maladministration by provincial governors under the *Lex Calpurnia de Rebus Repetundis* of 149 B.C. Seven such courts, consisting of a praetor as president and a group of approximately fifty jurymen empanelled from the upper ranks of society, were organized by the dictator Sulla to deal with various types of offence.[1] These courts operated under a system which has been described as only quasi-criminal and which admitted of almost endless opportunities for defeating the ends of justice.[2] They were, moreover, deeply involved in revolutionary politics, as control of their personnel became a subject of violent dispute between *optimates* and *populares* from the time of Gracchus. Accordingly, it is not surprising that they should in the end have perished with the republic.

The institution of the principate meant that criminal jurisdiction was improved and strengthened in various ways. A form of magisterial inquiry (*inquisitio*) took the place of the jury-session,

[1] Smith, *Dictionary of Greek and Roman Antiquities*, sub voc. *Leges Corneliae*.
[2] Strachan-Davidson, *Problems of the Roman Criminal Law*, vol. ii.

with its impassioned pleas by prosecution and defence conducted with hardly the slightest regard for what we should call
the rules of evidence. The reform of procedure made possible
the introduction of substantial refinements such, for example,
as the taking into account of intention in cases of homicide.
Punitive sanctions were, at the same time, reinforced; the
death penalty, virtually non-existent towards the close of the
republic, became once more a formidable reality. The salutary
effect of these changes was, however, somewhat neutralized as
delatio (the laying of information by professional informers)
made its appearance to blight the life of imperial society.[1] But
perhaps the chief evil of the new system developed in connexion
with prosecutions under the *Lex Laesae Maiestatis*, whereby a
statute originally designed to protect Roman freedom was converted into the instrument for its suppression.[2] The interpretation which, beginning with Tiberius Caesar, was put upon this
statute involved implications of the most subversive character.
In the first place, it identified the 'primacy' or majesty of the
people with that of the prince, thereby elevating him above the
laws whose minister in theory he was. In the second, it tended
to corrupt the administration of justice by assimilating all
offences to the gravest in the calendar, the one crime for which
torture, as a means of extracting evidence, was authorized in
the case of free men.

But if the reforms of criminal law and procedure in some sense
threatened the foundations of *Romanitas*, the exact reverse was
true of developments within the sphere of private law. During
the last years of the republic an intensification of domestic
faction combined with the growth of untrammelled executive
authority in the provinces had undermined *civilitas*, the natural
and proper attitude of one citizen toward his fellows, and ultimately brought dictatorship upon the city. Under the principate, the rights and obligations of *civilitas* were once more
recognized, and the state was in a position to enforce them
whenever necessary. The result was the elaboration of a
system of private relationships which has been described[3] as
a recognition of the creative mission of personality or, perhaps
less extravagantly, in words already quoted,[4] as an expression

---

[1] On this subject Tacitus is very bitter. See the *Annales, passim.*
[2] On this statute and its various amendments see Smith, op. cit., sub voc.
Maiestas.   [3] By Ihering, op. cit. ii, pt. i, 128; cf. p. 260.   [4] p. 72 above.

of 'the essential and indestructible elements of the private personality'.

In these developments the prince was destined to play a leading part.[1] The position which he attained is indicated in the famous text of Ulpian:[2] 'no one can doubt that the will of the prince has the force of law, inasmuch as by the *Lex Regia* the people have conferred upon him the sum-total of their own authority and power.' From this standpoint, the prince emerged as the ultimate mouthpiece of Roman right. This right he declared by means of *edicta, mandata, rescripta*, and *decreta* addressed through the magistrates to interested parties, in the framing of which he had the advice and assistance of professional jurists. At the same time, he gradually assumed a monopoly of legislation, which thenceforth took the form of imperial *constitutiones* promulgated in the senate through 'orations' read to and acclaimed by that body.

The competence of the prince as representative and exponent of the Roman order was marked by the attribution to him of censorial power, otherwise the 'supervision of laws and customs' (*cura legum et morum*), which thus constituted the final aspect of imperial *auctoritas*. This power, like others embodied in the principate, had its roots in primitive political life and seems to have been inherent in the Roman concept of magistracy. Originally it was no doubt connected, as the name suggests, with the quinquennial register of citizens for military and financial service to the state. As such, its character was, in the first instance, technically 'formal'. This fact did not, however, prevent its being utilized as an instrument of public policy; in which sense it permitted of the widest interference with what we should regard as the domain of private right.[3] It was thus invoked by the emperor Augustus to promote his schemes of social reconstruction, but only to be employed for well-understood purposes and with the invariable Augustan restraint and common sense. The more conservative of succeeding princes appear to have shrunk from the responsibilities which its possession imposed upon them.[4] On the other hand, those who (like Claudius or Domitian) were inclined to autocratic methods welcomed the possibilities of regimentation which it placed in

---

[1] See *Camb. Anc. Hist.* xi, ch. xxi, p. 806 foll., article by Buckland.
[2] *Instit.* i. 2. 6.
[3] See Plut. *Cato Major*, for characteristic examples.   [4] Tac. *Ann.* iii. 53–4.

their hands. To grasp the measure of these possibilities, we need only consult the text of the *Lex Regia*, where they are stated in the most comprehensive and unequivocal terms.[1]

So much for the formal competence of the prince. To what end it should be directed was, of course, a matter of *consilium*. That is to say, it raises the question of policy, the third and last phase of imperial activity, upon which the others were ultimately to depend. In this connexion, we have already examined the aims of the principate as laid down by the founder. Those aims may be summarized in the claim that he had solved the problem of *stasis* without resort either to the Hellenistic *basileia* or to the Latin dictatorship. As Dio Cassius, in the perspective of two centuries of subsequent history, was to put it:[2]

'he reconciled his authority with the sovereignty of the people, safeguarding their liberty while still preserving security and order; so that the Romans, exempt alike from the licence of mob-rule and the arrogance of despotism, experienced a sober liberty under the sway of one man but without terror, the subjects of a king but not slaves, the citizens of a democracy without dissension.'

Thus envisaged, the intention of the founder was nothing less than to translate into terms of universal application the classic principles of idealist philosophy. The question was how to impress those principles, not merely upon the present, but also upon the future.

Merely to state the plan of Augustus is to be sensible of the vast and complex problems which it involved. Those problems were, broadly speaking, twofold; they concerned at once the physical and the human material at his disposal, to be manipulated with a view to what Plato had described as 'the best possible result'. The manipulation of this material presented difficulties, not the least formidable of which concerned the physical or 'object' world. This difficulty may be briefly stated. We have seen how, according to idealist analysis, the world of objects was set over against that of subjects and opposed thereto as the area of fortune ($\tau \acute{v} \chi \eta$ or *fortuna*) on the one hand to that of 'art and industry' on the other. This area obviously came within the purview of the statesman, since it was the recognized source of what Aristotle had called the *choregia* necessary to the planned society. Yet, at the same time, it tended to elude apprehension;

---

[1] Bruns, op. cit., cap. v, no. 56, ll. 17–18.
[2] lvi. 43, § 4.

indeed, as the realm of the accidental or contingent, its control was in the long run a matter of sheer luck. This is the element of truth in the contention that a profit and loss account of the empire would expose the real reason for its ultimate collapse.

In these circumstances, it is not surprising that attention should have been concentrated upon the human material in an effort to circumvent the unknown and unknowable in nature. To this end, creative politics envisaged the possibility of a public discipline (*publica disciplina*) analogous to that which had obtained within the independent, self-sufficient *polis*. Such a discipline, embracing the field of economic as well as social life, would, ideally speaking, find expression in an economy based upon the maintenance of the middle class. The question was how to apply this ideal to the conditions of imperial society. This was to raise innumerable problems which we can only briefly indicate.

We may begin by noting that the question was one which primarily affected the imperial people. As for the provincials, at any rate under the early principate, their position was indicated in the grudging admission of Tacitus[1] 'that they had no objection to the existing state of affairs'. That is to say, they were now protected from the worst consequences of their fate as *praedia populi Romani*, victims of the ruthless struggle for dominion and power which had for so long convulsed imperial society. Apart from this, their status was as yet little more than that of passive spectators of a process, the course of which they were themselves, in some degree, to control in the future. But, if this was true of the provincials, the exact reverse must be said of the sovereign people; upon whose members the new régime imposed the necessity of radical modifications in what they had learned to regard as the ideal of life. This necessity may be summed up in the fact that, with the consolidation of the *Pax Augusta*, the era of predatory imperialism was brought to an immediate and conclusive end.

But while the resultant changes affected to some extent Romans of every degree, they were felt particularly by the dispossessed oligarchy, the economic and political dynasts of republican times. To the survivors of this oligarchy and their descendants they presented problems of adjustment which these men were ill-qualified, either by temperament or tradition,

[1] *Ann.* i. 2 and iv. 6.

to face; and these problems were, in the end, to be solved only by the liquidation of such of the great aristocratic families as failed to accommodate themselves to the new situation. What that situation involved for them is indicated in documents of early imperial literature. One aspect of it emerges with Petronius' portrait of the vulgar *nouveau riche*, the millionaire freedman Trimalchio;[1] others are vividly suggested in the picture of first-century society contained in the satires of Juvenal. To study these documents is to perceive that the difficulty was not less moral than material. As for the aristocracy, it was unable to see, much less to identify itself with, the fresh possibilities of life contained in the Augustan order. Hence the tragedy of a blind and stubborn opposition to that order which was to be concluded only with the virtual extinction of the ancient nobility of Rome.

Politically speaking, the conflict between old and new focused in the senate house, where it found expression in the so-called opposition under the Caesars. This opposition was to discover an ideological basis in the memory of Cato, in relation to which it betrayed a visionary romanticism not less extravagant than that of the 'martyr' himself. But, from the material standpoint, its main concern was with what we should call standards of living or, rather, the mode of life to which it was henceforth apparently condemned. And here the trouble was that it could not forget its past, the recollections of grandeur and magnificence associated with the bygone life of competitive imperialism. In this connexion its bitterness was no doubt accentuated by the display of wealth and power which emanated from the palace of the Caesars. To this may be added as a secondary but not less vital factor the intense consciousness of blood which dominated the minds of the *ci-devant* 'lords of the world'—a consciousness which, while it served to impel successive generations to achievement worthy of their progenitors, made it difficult for them to turn their faces to the future. This had its counterpart in a sense of inferiority evident among those whom the accident of birth had placed outside the charmed circle.[2] Accordingly, the aristocracy clung to its traditional habits of sumptuous and extravagant living until it finally ruined itself and, as Tacitus indicates, the accession of the rustic Vespasian

[1] Petronius, *Satyricon*.
[2] In this connexion the psychology of Domitian constitutes an interesting study.

ushered in the dawn of a more frugal and wholesome age,[1] but not without first having provided ample material for discussion on the subject of contemporary 'vice'. Into this debate we cannot go further than to point out that it was conducted within the accepted *cadres* of idealist philosophy. Thus, for example, it involved the old question of land-capitalism as the probable 'cause' of 'degeneracy'.[2] At the same time reformers persisted in denouncing 'luxury', and this they perversely identified with phenomena which the modern economist would normally take to indicate progress in living-conditions, e.g. the use of silk for articles of apparel.[3] Finally, in the absence of genuine insight, they were disposed to fall back upon the traditional expedient of calling for governmental intervention in sumptuary matters; in which connexion they were to encounter a marked hesitancy, especially on the part of intelligent conservatives like the emperor Tiberius. The sharp rebuke administered by the latter to senatorial busybodies introduced into the debate a note of practical common sense in refreshing contrast to the atmosphere of unreality which generally characterized discussions of this threadbare theme.[4]

The immediate and pressing need of the time was, of course, that of adaptation to the requirements of the Graeco-Roman cosmopolis. In relation to the aristocracy this meant collaboration on terms such as appear to have been envisaged by the founder in the so-called concept of dyarchy. For such collaboration there existed a philosophic basis in the relation between imperial virtue and the virtue of those from whose ranks the emperor had sprung; and it showed itself in what we cannot but regard as the sincere and deep sentiment of aristocratic solidarity manifested by conservative princes. The existence of this sentiment serves to account for the fact that, while the senate was no doubt condemned to a progressive decline under the empire, it was nevertheless so unconscionably long in dying. It explains also why, in the face of bitter disillusionment, successive emperors continued to invoke the co-operation of a body upon which, in the last analysis, the legitimacy of their own

[1] *Ann.* iii. 55: 'praecipuus adstricti moris auctor Vespasianus, antiquo ipse cultu victuque.' The chapter should be studied as a whole.

[2] Pliny, *N.H.* xviii. 6. 35: 'latifundia perdidere Italiam.'

[3] The real problem here was that of a foreign trade which is said to have drained the empire of specie at the rate of a pound of gold for a pound of silk.

[4] Tac. *Ann.* iii. 53–54 (A.D. 22), letter of Tiberius to the senate.

office was felt to depend; and this notwithstanding the circumstance that, with the new demand for specialized and technical
administrative proficiency, individual senators were increasingly
disqualified for the tasks of peace and war to be imposed upon
them; even if they could be trusted to discharge those tasks in
a spirit of fidelity, which was by no means always the case. As
for the senate in its corporate capacity, its surviving prestige
is illustrated by the fact that constitutionally minded rulers
accepted its verdict as equivalent to the judgement of history
even with respect to their own character and career; since it
rested with the senate to decree either the final apotheosis or the
damnatio memoriae of deceased emperors. But, to the general
possibility of collaboration under the new régime, there was one
condition attached: senators were obliged to sacrifice that ideal
of individual independence which lay at the heart of Roman
republicanism; loyalty to the prince demanded that they should
abandon the right (as Tacitus puts it) 'to think what you like
and say what you think'.[1] It was, indeed, upon this question
that the issue was joined between emperor and aristocracy.
Hence the sullen and suspicious attitude with which the latter
received the fairest professions of imperial *civilitas*. Hence also
the studied resistance, both active and passive, which they put
up against pleas for co-operation; until they found their status
and occupations gradually usurped by *parvenus*, while they
themselves were consigned to the abyss.[2]

But if the *Pax Augusta* spelt doom for the aristocracy, it was
not less fatal to the heirs of the founder himself; two successive
dynasties, indeed, were to go under before the process of adjustment was complete. With respect to the early Caesars, the
accounts given by ancient literary authorities are almost unani-
mously hostile. To accept them would be to suppose that,
beginning with Tiberius, a misanthrope had been succeeded by
a madman, himself in turn to be succeeded by a fool. On the

---

[1] *Hist.* i. 1. 4: 'sentire quae velis et quae sentias dicere.'

[2] For the activity of Augustus in enlisting the services of 'new men' in the years
A.D. 3–10 see Marsh, op. cit., p. 43. Claudius was to open a whole series of new
careers for the equestrian order. The elimination of the old houses came about
partly spontaneously as, e.g., with the Hortensii; partly, in consequence of a series
of 'terrors', the first of which occurred under Tiberius A.D. 31–7; the last under
Domitian A.D. 93–6. We may here, perhaps, recall the fact that at least one of the
ancient republican families survived until the middle of the third century, when
the last of the Calpurnii Pisones, 'twenty-eighth from Numa', perished as the result
of an unsuccessful conspiracy; Gibbon, op. cit., ch. x, p. 276.

other hand Nero, last of the Julio-Claudians, emerges as an incarnation of all the vices, guilty of extravagances which served not merely to pollute the already sophisticated atmosphere of the capital, but to threaten the life of the provinces as well. In the same context Vespasian is represented as having restored the Augustan order, but only that it should once more be compromised in the person of his sons, especially the younger, of whom nothing more invidious could be found to say than that he was a 'bald-pated Nero'. It is hardly necessary to point out that the portrait which has thus come down to us is grossly distorted; in some respects, indeed, little more than a parody of the truth. This is not to suggest that the Caesars are necessarily to be absolved from the charges of cruelty and lust which have been levelled against them. But it does indicate that, in the ancient literary tradition, we are confronted with a first-rate problem of historical interpretation. This problem concerns alike the 'goodness' of the 'good' and the 'badness' of the 'bad' emperors; what it raises, indeed, is the classical question 'of virtue and vice in states'.

In this connexion we must remember that a Roman emperor occupied a position quite unlike that of the modern constitutional sovereign; inasmuch as, to repeat the words of Cicero, 'he carried the person of the state'. In this sense he emerged as the supreme embodiment of Roman virtue, speaking and acting not merely *for* but also *as* the sovereign people whom he professed to 'represent'. In this respect Augustus himself had been eminently successful; he had exhibited himself as the *ne plus ultra* of the civilized ruler or citizen-prince. But the effort to do so presupposed qualities of self-restraint and endurance such as few men could be expected to possess; and it must have imposed a severe tax on the powers even of that most inscrutable of rulers.[1] This being so, it is not surprising that his successors should generally have found the task beyond them.

From this standpoint the history of the future was to a great extent implicit in that of Tiberius Caesar. The latter, after a strangely chequered career of military and political service, found himself at last elevated to the purple, according to Tacitus 'by a senile adoption and his mother's wiles'; in reality, as a

---

[1] For gossip regarding the behaviour of Augustus when 'off duty', see Suet. *Aug.* 67–78. To his enemies, of course, he was never anything but a whited sepulchre. It is, perhaps, more charitable to describe him as the original stuffed-shirt.

consequence of dynastic ambitions on the part of the founder which, however natural or expedient, were hardly compatible with the formal profession of republican principles. Despite obvious deficiencies of character and disposition, notably a diffidence (*haesitatio*) falsely identified by the historian with congenital pride (*insita Claudiae familiae superbia*), the new prince was doubtless the best available choice; since Agrippa Postumus, the one surviving male of Julian blood, lacked even the rudiments of imperial virtue.[1] At the same time Tiberius seems to have been conscious of personal limitations which quite definitely unfitted him for the office.[2] Accordingly, we need not question the sincerity of his repeatedly expressed desire to abdicate; it is wholly consistent with the fact that this intention was never to be carried out. He was thus impelled to cling to power, partly out of a sense of filial devotion (*pietas*); partly, no doubt, from fear of the almost certain consequences which would follow a restoration of the 'republic'. In the same spirit he endeavoured to discharge his duties, 'careless of popularity, provided that he might earn respect'. But his efforts to take an active part in the administration served merely to paralyse initiative in the senate house and courts. At the same time he was the object of persistent sabotage on the part of the aristocracy, against whose barely concealed malevolence he had to be constantly on guard. To the problem of a difficult relationship with his mother, the dowager empress to whose machinations he was said to have owed his position, was added that of a relationship not less difficult with Germanicus Caesar, his nephew and adoptive son who, so far from effacing himself as the situation demanded, courted publicity with an assiduity to be surpassed only by that of his ambitious and domineering wife. It was thus inevitable that the temper of the emperor, originally deficient in geniality, should have become increasingly sullen and morose. Meanwhile, beginning with the mysterious death of Germanicus, a succession of tragic events rocked the foundations of court and society; and, to escape from an atmosphere poisoned by suspicion and intrigue, Tiberius took the fatal step of withdrawing from the capital. By so doing he paved the way for the rise of Sejanus with its disastrous consequences to himself and his house. For, with the exposure of

---

[1] He was uneducated and uneducable, *rudis liberalium artium*.
[2] Tac. *Ann.* i. 11 and 12.

treachery on the part of the one man whom he seems to have fully trusted, the morale of the emperor finally broke down; the result was the Tiberian terror, the first of a series of political blood-baths which were to stain the history of the principate.[1]

But while circumstances thus conspired to promote the political *débâcle* of A.D. 31–7, they do not in themselves suffice to render it intelligible. To grasp its true significance we must see it as the outcome of anomalies inherent in the Augustan concept of *imperium*, in consequence of which the emperor was placed in an utterly false position, both with respect to himself and his contemporaries. It was, perhaps, an all-too-keen appreciation of those anomalies which prompted the emperor Tiberius to exclaim: After me the deluge. The tragedy of the Caesars has been the subject of persistent controversy since the days of the Caesars themselves. It was, in a word, the tragedy of men who, being required to play the part of gods, descended to that of beasts.[2] In saying this we do not for a moment subscribe to the *chronique scandaleuse* of the imperial palace, which may be dismissed as the expedient of writers who, having to say something, find themselves with nothing to say. Our concern is rather with a vicious ideology and with the disastrous consequences of its acceptance by those who were invested with the purple. This we have already tried to describe as the classical ideology of power.

We have observed how this ideology, erected upon the complementary concepts of virtue and fortune, had attained its apotheosis at Rome in the person of Augustus. Upon his successors it imposed a nemesis from which there could be no escape. We may thus see Tiberius begging the senate to remember that he was but a man, discharging the duties of a man and hoping for nothing but a reputation worthy of his ancestors; yet obliged to accept, in the name of himself and his mother, the veneration due to an earthly providence;[3] or Vespasian, with grim Italian wit, ridiculing the notion of apotheosis when, on his death-bed, he remarked: 'I suppose I'm becoming a god.' But, whatever its apparent flavour of absurdity, the idea was not one to be disposed of either by protests or jeers. Nor was it enough, as

---

[1] In this connexion we may question the assertion of Marsh (op. cit., p. 200), who declares that 'the whole picture of the Tiberian terror is a product of imaginative rhetoric quite unsupported by the evidence'.

[2] Ch. III above, p. 111.

[3] Tac. *Ann.* iv. 37–8.

Augustus appears to have imagined, to interpose merely territorial barriers against its reception in Italy; since this was to
admit that resistance to it rested, at bottom, on nothing more
than an obsolescent republican prejudice. For, already with
Gaius Caligula, the barriers were down, even if the prejudice
remained. In this fact we may, perhaps, discover the clue to his
brief and tragic career. A recent writer,[1] indeed, attempts to
explain it otherwise, but at the cost of dismissing rather too
abruptly the whole literary tradition. And nothing that he says
of Gaius' capacity for clear and logical thinking, or of his flashes
of sardonic wit, is inconsistent with the probability that he was
a paranoiac, the mad dog in fact of the Julio-Claudian house. As
such, 'his most individual characteristic', as the author admits,[2]
was ἀδιατρεψία, a 'shameless impudence'. That is to say, he was
audacious enough to act on assumptions that were everywhere
current about his literal 'God-head'. This was too much for
Roman stomachs at such an early date. But they were soon to
become accustomed to the idea. With Domitian, only forty
years later, it had become a convention of polite speech to hail
the emperor as *dominus et deus,* 'my Lord and God'. In the following century, even constitutionally minded princes like Trajan
had no hesitation in accepting these forms of address. In the
end it remained for a Christian, Tertullian, to protest against
their use. As for the successor of Gaius, Claudius, the 'soldiers'
emperor', he had been from youth rather more than a faintly
ridiculous figure—perhaps the severest handicap under which
one can labour who aspires to become a political god. Accordingly, on the throne, he constituted an excellent butt for contemporary wits who ventured even to prophesy his ultimate
'pumpkinification'. This fact, together with the circumstance
that his reign was marked by the domination of women and
freedmen,[3] has contributed to obscure the solid administrative
achievements of an emperor whose labours unquestionably
helped to preserve the principate from destruction in the crisis
which attended the enforced abdication and suicide of Nero.
That crisis was to reveal the truth that Neronian aestheticism
constituted no adequate substitute for character, especially on

---

[1] Balsdon, *The Emperor Gaius.*   [2] p. 214.
[3] Notably the so-called 'third triumvirate' of Pallas, Narcissus, and Callistus or
Polybius, jibes at whom reflect the hostility of the aristocracy towards the new
imperial secretariat created by Claudius, while, at the same time, they point to
reforms in its personnel to be effected later by Hadrian.

the part of a prince. It was also to expose 'the dangerous secret that emperors could (if necessary) be made elsewhere than at Rome'.[1] At the same time it emphasized the utility of the imperial office as the one guarantee of order and security, not merely in the city but also throughout the provinces.[2]

It was, no doubt, from a sense of its real importance that contemporary philosophy came forward with a fresh attempt to explain and justify the imperial power. To this effort belongs the essay of Seneca, *De Clementia*, in which the author exalts the majesty of the emperor, declaring that his will is limited only by his sense of mercy; that he is the bond by which the commonwealth is held together, the breath of life which is its very soul. In this extravagant language he was to be followed by the Greek sophists, Dio of Prusa *On Kingship*[3] and, somewhat later, Aelius Aristides who, in phrases with which we are all too familiar, hails the emperor as father and shepherd of his people, light of human happiness, excelling in virtues for which we cannot be sufficiently thankful.[4] And Pliny falls not far short of this in his panegyric on Trajan; although, with a characteristically Latin bias, he tries to protect himself by invoking the traditional principle of legitimacy in terms of which 'the prince does not stand above the laws, but the laws above the prince'.[5]

We cannot stop to consider the many social and political developments which were entailed in this conception of sovereignty. Such developments, which were already under way in the time of Augustus, embraced *inter alia* the evolution of a court (*aula*) with its characteristic phenomena hitherto confined to the hellenized Orient. These included the presence of rival factions, each aggressively pushing its particular interests, together with a brood of sycophants who were always ready, as the dying Tiberius bitterly expressed it, 'to turn from the setting in order to greet the rising sun'. They included also the recognition of a peculiar status to be accorded members of the imperial household, marked not less by the attribution of a title to the dowager empress Livia Augusta than by the special protection

---

[1] Tac. *Hist.* i. 4. 2.
[2] See, e.g., the speech of Cerialis recorded by Tacitus (ibid. iv. 73-4), where he warns his hearers not to be misled by the apparent greenness of distant fields, but to remember the solid advantages accruing from the institution.
[3] Under Trajan in the following century.
[4] xxxv, (Anonymi) εἰς βασιλέα, 22 and 38.   [5] *Paneg.*, 65.

provided for females of the dynasty beyond the *Lex Iulia de Adulteriis*.[1] Much the same consideration led to the establishment of a ritual of approach to the imperial presence, involving the search of visitors for concealed weapons formally introduced by Caligula. Such innovations, although relatively slight and simple to begin with, nevertheless forecast the situation of two centuries later when the cult of the *domus divina* was to be fully established and a Roman empress was to describe herself on public inscriptions as 'mater domini nostri sanctissimi imperatoris Severi Alexandri . . . et castrorum et senatus et patriae et universi generis humani'.[2]

These developments, however striking, serve merely to throw into greater relief the position of the emperor himself as representative and exemplar of the Augustan order. In this capacity there was imposed upon him as perhaps his chief obligation the duty of conformity to a type struck in the mint of the founder; and from this type even the slightest deviation was abhorrent. Accordingly, the last thing either expected or desired of a Roman emperor was that he should be himself. We need hardly comment on the immense psychological strain which this must have imposed on individual princes; nor is it astonishing to find that many of them looked more or less covertly for ways of escape. Thus Tiberius, if the tradition of his addiction to astrology may be taken as authentic, must be regarded as a secret renegade from the Augustan ideal. Caligula was, in one sense, in open rebellion against it; his 'shameless impudence' reflected, on its better side, an intense hatred of official sham. Something of the same quality may, perhaps, be credited to Nero as one of the few virtues in a character otherwise irredeemably vicious. But perhaps the most interesting illustration of what we mean is to be found in Titus. Elder son and destined heir to Vespasian, the restorer of Augustan principles, Titus was to be hailed by flatterers as 'the darling of the human race' (*amor et deliciae generis humani*). Yet, in view of the station to which he was marked out, his qualifications were dubious in the extreme. A sufficiently able soldier, as he had demonstrated by his work before Jerusalem, he had nevertheless embarked upon an association with an Oriental princess of Jewish extraction whom

---

[1] Tac. *Ann.* ii. 50.
[2] Dessau, *I.L.S.* 485. Cf. 429 and 439 for the use of the epithet *sanctissimus* by Roman emperors.

he proposed, in defiance of Roman sentiment, to make his wife. At the stern behest of his father he reluctantly abandoned the romance and presented himself in the city.[1] Yet if he did so, it was only to corrupt Flavian policy by exhibiting himself as an imperial boy scout; so that, in the caustic language of the historian, not the least element of his good fortune was the brevity of his reign.

Flavian dynasticism, thus imperilled by Titus, was to make utter shipwreck under Domitian, whose murder recalled the unhappy experience of the Julio-Claudian house. By so doing, it pointed to a recognition of the adoptive principle as a means of evading the conventional hazards of heredity and of selecting the best available man to fill the imperial office.[2] The acceptance of this device served to complete what we have called the process of accommodation. At the same time it provided the necessary perspective from which Tacitus, himself living into the 'period of rare good fortune' (rara temporum felicitas) when it was in vogue, was to survey the record of the early principate. From this standpoint, criticism of that record resolves itself largely into a criticism of its most important historian.

Tacitus begins his work with a vigorous profession of impartiality; he claims to write 'without enthusiasm and without hate' (sine ira et studio), the reasons for which 'have disappeared with the lapse of time'.[3] And we may concede that, on the purely factual level, he has amply justified this claim.[4] But the accuracy of his reporting serves merely to emphasize the savagery of his polemic against Tiberius; and the question arises: How can the animus of the historian be explained? This animus has been ascribed by some to the pangs of a spirit warped and perverted by personal suffering under the despotism of Domitian. By others it has been attributed to republican, otherwise 'aristocratic' prejudice. But if Tacitus was a republican, it was in a wholly academic sense of the word. He does, indeed, follow Livy in representing the primitive commonwealth as the embodi-

[1] Suet. Tit. 5 and 7.

[2] The hazards in question had been discussed by Aristotle, Pol. iii. 1286ᵇ22. The stock arguments were to be summarized by Tacitus in a speech put into the mouth of Galba, Hist. i. 15–16. We may, perhaps, note that princes who employed this method were uniformly without natural heirs. But this fact, also, could doubtless be attributed to the good fortune of the imperial people.

[3] Ann. i. 1.

[4] See his references to the administration of Tiberius, Ann. i. 72–5, ii. 48 and 50, iii. 69–70, iv. 6, vi. 7 and 51 (a final estimate).

ment of legal liberty; for him, the climax of Roman achievement coincides with the period of the XII Tables, subsequent
to which he sees nothing but a progressive development of
faction for which the principate offers the only possible cure.[1]
Tacitus is sufficiently remote from Polybian or Ciceronian ways
of thought to perceive that the 'mixed form of government'
constitutes no final solution to the problem of political power:
and he envisages no practicable alternative between a dictatorship of the masses and that of a single man. Of these, the latter
is the lesser of two evils; it is, therefore, to be endured, notwithstanding the vagaries of individual rulers and the terrible evils
of autocratic power. Accordingly, while lauding republican
integrity, he deplores as merely histrionic the deaths of those
who perished in the spirit of Cato. For, after all, the cultivation of 'virtue' is possible even under a bad prince. Tacitus,
therefore, preaches as the truest form of political wisdom a
realistic acceptance of the existing situation and, while unequi-
vocally condemning the grosser manifestations of Julio-Claudian
despotism,[2] he denounces with equal fervour any evidence of
subversive revolutionary activity.[3]

The dubious character of these political views points to something which goes much deeper than any mere republican or
aristocratic prejudice; it reflects a profound mental *stasis* on the
part of the historian; a *haesitatio iudicii* not unlike that which he
ascribes to the emperor Tiberius himself. This *haesitatio* is
evident in all his references to divination, which reveal a strange
medley of credulity and common sense;[4] the combination of an
unsteady necessitarianism with an equally unsteady libertarian-
ism in his treatment of *fortuna*; the stark realism which marks his
interpretation of later history by contrast with his idealized
picture of life in primitive times. Merciless in his strictures upon
the imperial aristocracy, he nevertheless displays nothing but
aristocratic contempt for the masses; the spirit of democracy, as
it had been apprehended, e.g., by Pericles, being totally beyond
his ken. But, most of all perhaps, the *haesitatio* of Tacitus finds
expression in his attitude toward what we should call 'progress'.
He has completely abandoned the Vergilian faith in a material
millennium to be realized under the Caesars. His writings are
'one long protest against degeneracy';[5] yet he has at his com-

---

[1] *Ann.* iii. 26–7.   [2] Ibid. i. 72.   [3] *Hist.* iv. 1. 3.   [4] *Ann.* vi. 21–2.
[5] Furneaux, *The Annals of Tacitus*, vol. i, Introd., ch. iv, pp. 23–37.

mand no weapon with which to attack the demon of degeneration. In this connexion we may recall the express doubts which
he raises regarding the ultimate value of the Roman order—
doubts which reveal him as the victim of a nostalgia common to
all ages of hyperculture, and finding an outlet in the creation of
dream-worlds as a means of escape from what appears to be the
intolerability of the present. With Tacitus this tendency manifests itself in an extravagant eulogy of primitive virtue. By
identifying this with the virtue of the Teutons, he starts the
myth of nordic superiority, which was thus manufactured not
in Germany but in Rome. At the same time, in his famous
prayer for a continuance of Germanic discord,[1] *maneat, quaeso,
duretque gentibus*, he almost anticipates the fate which was ultimately to overtake the city at the hands of the barbarians. By
thus denouncing without renouncing civilization, he betrays
the fundamental ambiguity of his outlook; while also exhibiting
a shocking declension from the spirit of Augustan Rome.[2]

We may thus conclude that the difficulty with Tacitus was, at
bottom, spiritual; he is caught in the meshes of an ideology from
which he can find no means of escape. To the defects of this
ideology may be ascribed the uncertain handling of the political
problem with which he undertakes to deal. The crux of that
problem may be said to have lain in the claim to divinity made
on behalf of the emperor. Against that claim, which he rightly
regards as a defiance both of experience and common sense, the
historian revolts with every fibre of his being. At the same time
he possesses no adequate intellectual defence against it; indeed,
he cannot refrain from a sneer at what he calls the 'lack of spirit'
evidenced by Tiberius in 'refusing to aspire to apotheosis on the
model of Romulus Quirinus and divus Augustus',[3] quite unconscious that the real victim of his sarcasm is none other than
himself. But Tacitean ideology embodies defects even more
radical than this; for, in the last analysis, it deprives him of the
power to understand either characters or events. Thus, with
regard to character, it yields the vision of Tiberius as a wolf in

[1] *Germ.* 33. 2.
[2] For a criticism of the *Germania* see *Camb. Anc. Hist.* xi, ch. ii, p. 68. The basis is
the conventional antithesis between civilization and barbarism, the literary tradition of which goes back at least to Herodotus. But with Tacitus the treatment is
modified by 'Rousseauistic or Stoic notions of the baleful influence of culture on
mankind'. To us this seems to enhance its significance as a social document.
[3] *Ann.* iv. 38.

sheep's clothing, whose inherent viciousness is disclosed only with the removal of the last external restraint.[1] The failure here is a failure to appreciate the significance of motivation; in other words, of the concrete situation as a vehicle for the expression of personality, in relation to which alone the actor becomes alive. And, in any such situation, the counterpart to the person is the event; the 'action' which, apart from the 'actor', must remain for ever unintelligible. Tacitus, failing in his characterization of personality, fails likewise to give an intelligible account of events. This unintelligibility he frankly concedes when, approaching the denouement of his theme, and confronted with the phenomenon of Sejanus, who was to be the emperor's evil genius, he undertakes to explain the rise and fall of this man by invoking the time-honoured but none the less barren concept of fortune. 'Fortune', he asserts, 'suddenly began to upset everything, to go mad herself or to lend strength to madness.'[2] Or, if not fortune, then the gods. 'It was not any cleverness on the part of Sejanus which enabled him to victimize Tiberius, but rather the wrath of heaven descending upon the Roman world, to which the rise and fall of this man were alike fatal.'[3] That is to say, he finds Sejanus simply inexplicable on any rational grounds.

It is easy to understand how, in view of these circumstances, the historian should have aspired to become an oracle of public opinion, as the one possible way of justifying his activity. 'Tacitus', observes his editor,[4] 'nowhere makes any formal profession of faith'; for the reason, we may add, that he has no faith to profess. With him what replaces faith is a lively interest in human beings which combines vague aspirations for personal immortality with a sense that men really survive in the memory of posterity. This determines his views regarding the function of the historian, inspiring him to record conspicuous examples both of the good and evil in life; history in this way to serve as a kind of conscience to mankind.[5] But, in this connexion, it should be remembered that his standards are those of classical virtue and vice, which were thus at last to come into their own in what was to go down in history as the golden age of the

[1] *Ann.* vi. 51.
[2] He is here, in fact, merely repeating Sallust, *Cat.* 10. 1. 'saevire fortuna ac miscere omnia coepit.'   [3] *Ann.* iv. 1 (A.D. 23).   [4] Furneaux, loc. cit.
[5] *Ann.* iii. 65: 'ne virtutes sileantur utque pravis dictis factisque ex posteritate et infamia metus sit'.

Antonines—a period when, the stress and strain of adjustment having finally been concluded, providence in the person of the 'five good emperors' settled down to her secular task.

Or so, at any rate, it seemed. For, under Nerva and his successors, the empire had attained its zenith. The battles of the nations were ended and the whole Mediterranean acknowledged the sway of the imperial city. Within frontiers scientifically defined and protected by trained and disciplined armies, vast areas were opened for exploitation and settlement. Throughout the Roman world emerged that galaxy of autonomous *civitates*, each with its community centre and its attributed territory which, to the ancient observer, constituted the essence of the universal commonwealth. Historic differences of race, language, and religion rapidly disappeared, and so far advanced was the process of assimilation that the provinces of Spain and Gaul were already giving emperors to Rome; while the Roman aristocracy itself was almost wholly reconstituted upon an imperial basis, and the new nobility had apparently learned the lesson that its function was not to command but to serve. The time, indeed, was rapidly approaching when the rights of citizenship, once the jealously guarded privilege of the sovereign people, should be extended to every free inhabitant of the Roman world; whether this was to mark a fulfilment of the secular mission of Rome, or the *reductio ad absurdum* of the Roman order.

Threats or protests against the established system were relatively insignificant, at least until the troubled reign of Marcus Aurelius. On the northern frontier there was the normal garrison warfare, punctuated by occasional punitive expeditions. Defences were steadily consolidated, as for example by the erection of the British walls under Hadrian and Antoninus, and by the construction of the *limites*, an elaborate system of fortifications to shorten the Rhine–Danube re-entrant. On the Danube the menace of Decebalus and his romanized military monarchy was eliminated by Trajan in two vigorous wars (A.D. 101–2 and 105–6); the result of which was to add to the empire the mineral resources and agricultural lands of Dacia. The success of Trajan was marked by the construction of a forum and column in the capital, and precautions were taken to prevent the occurrence of similar dangers in the future. An absolute embargo was placed upon the exportation of arms across the boundary, and drill-instructors were forbidden on pain of death to lend their services to the barbarian. In the East the prestige of Rome was sufficient not merely for expansion but, more impressive still, for withdrawal; and Trajan's grandiose schemes of acquisition were abandoned by his successor.

From within the empire there was no element either capable or desirous of offering an effective challenge to the imperial system. Intransigent republicans had long since followed Cato to the grave, thus compensating by the manner of their death for the ignominy of their lives under Julio-Claudian and Flavian tyranny. Now[1] even the Stoics, despite an uneasy suspicion of dynasticism, had found a way of reconciling their traditional republicanism with existing practice, in the theory that sovereignty inheres 'naturally' in the 'best' man. The troops indeed ventured on occasion to try their old game of making or breaking emperors; but incipient sedition against Nerva was hastily circumvented by the adoption of Trajan and, in the same year (97), a mutiny of the praetorians was easily suppressed. Failure of a senatorial conspiracy to prevent the election of Hadrian was marked by the (unconstitutional) execution of four consulars. The revolt of Avidius Cassius (175) against Marcus was the one serious case of legionary unrest, and it was not fully backed even by the Eastern troops.

The social peace was well maintained. Of the two great elements in society, the *honestiores* had nothing to complain of; and of the *humiliores* little was to be heard. In 96 it was Nerva's duty to suppress disturbances among slaves and freedmen who had been encouraged to inform against their masters during the 'terror' of Domitian.[2] Yet the days of Spartacus and the Sicilian slave wars were over. With the conclusion of the period of conquest, great slave-markets like Delos were deserted, and labour had become more valuable. Moreover, the wide diffusion of humanitarian sentiment gave to the servile classes a protection for which they had reason to be grateful, and the most vital of their privileges, the contract for freedom, was fully secured by the law.[3] Throughout the Antonine period the only widespread and serious revolts which occurred were those of the Jews, whose fierce religious nationalism had not been sup-

---

[1] As Rostovtzeff points out, *The Social and Economic History of the Roman Empire,* p. 108 foll.
[2] Dio, lxviii. 1.   [3] Bruns, op. cit., ch. v, p. 204, no. 58: *S.C. Rubrianum.*

pressed even by the destruction of Jerusalem, and who were now thought to be in league with their compatriots beyond the Euphrates in threatening the peace of the Eastern frontier. There were two concerted Jewish rebellions, one against Trajan in 115, another sixteen years later against Hadrian, provoked by the rebuilding of the Holy City as *Aelia Capitolina* and the consecration of a temple to Juppiter Optimus Maximus on the site of the temple of Jehovah. But Antoninus Pius, while forbidding any attempt on the part of Jews to proselytize, allowed them to practise circumcision, thus initiating a modified policy of appeasement. To the general spirit of acquiescence existing within the empire there remained then but one exception. The Christians, their numbers silently recruited from all ranks of society, constituted a focus for all who were in spiritual revolt against what they regarded as the barrenness and superficiality of dominant ideals.[1] In the West, however, their voice was hardly articulate, at least until the close of the Antonine age.

Meanwhile the five 'good' emperors devoted themselves to implementing the soundest features of Augustan policy. These princes were noteworthy for the profession and (with occasional lapses) the practice of constitutionalism. The long and sordid record of indictments for *lèse-majesté* was terminated by Nerva, who likewise suppressed the plague of delation. Reverting to the policy of Tiberius, which had been abandoned by Claudius, the same emperor forbade imperial procurators to arrogate to themselves judicial functions by hearing the claims of the fisc. Nerva also regularized the practice by which, through the form of adoption, the reigning prince co-opted his successor, or rather 'recommended' him to senate and people as the man best qualified to inherit his powers.

The goal of these emperors may be described as that of a planned society; but, while this involved a certain degree of bureaucracy, regulation had not as yet degenerated into regimentation, and the authorities were satisfied with a measure of vigorous government control. Trajan thoroughly overhauled the military machinery of the empire. He also fostered the development of licensed workers' guilds. The chief concern of Hadrian was with 'civil discipline', in the interest of which he conducted a ceaseless round of imperial tours. By his consolidation of the edict he helped to rationalize the principles and

[1] Ch. VI below, p. 221.

practice of the law. In keeping with this reform was the institution of four travelling justices (*IVviri iuridici*) for Italy. Through extensive grants of the Latin right, the stepping-stone to citizenship, he paved the way for the application of Roman law to vastly increased numbers in the provinces. He also instituted a more effective control over imperial and municipal finance, the former by a development of the central imperial fisc, the latter by his introduction of *curatores* or *correctores* (comptrollers) into the *civitates*.

Within the limits of their vision, the Antonines embarked upon an energetic programme of social and economic reform. With this we may connect the agrarian legislation which began with Nerva, as well as the construction of roads, aqueducts, and public buildings throughout the empire. But of this effort of amelioration, undoubtedly the most remarkable feature was the alimentary system which, inaugurated by Nerva and developed by his successors, was to survive until the collapse of credit in the following century. This undertaking involved the provision through judicious investments in land of generous endowments for the support of orphan children, male and female, in the municipalities of Italy. It was thus at once a form of education for citizenship and an advanced scheme of social service, by which the wastage of the system was 'economically' and 'scientifically' combated. As such, it may perhaps be taken to illustrate the quintessence of the Antonine spirit.

Devoted to the cult of service, the Antonine emperors advertised their measures by means of slogans for which ancient history affords no parallel; and these slogans, like the cries of modern politicians, were to be parroted on coins and inscriptions long after they had ceased to have any meaning. Thus in his *iustitia Augusta, libertas publica* Nerva proclaimed the reconciliation of liberty and authority through the return to constitutionalism, as well as a renaissance of Rome (*Roma renascens*) to be brought about through the *alimentaria Italica*, the *restitutio Italiae*, his *virtus et felicitas, concordia, pax* and, last but not least, the *adoptio* by which he marked out his successor. Trajan, whose watchword was the happiness of the age (*felicitas temporum*), exhibited on his coins the imperial cornucopia pouring the concrete blessings of corn, oil, and wine upon a grateful world. He is said to have contemplated state-intervention to prevent abuses of marital authority such as that arising from the traditional right of a Roman husband to discipline a bibulous wife.[1] Hadrian's favourite mottoes were *liberalitas* (relating to the cancellation of unpaid taxes), *disciplina*, and *stabilitas*.[2] Pius, though because of his penchant for economy vulgarly known as the cheeseparer (κυμινοπρίστης), proclaimed his *liberalitas*, the *munificentia Augusta* which was responsible for the prosperity (*felicitas*) and happiness (*laetitia*) of the age. On his coins he featured the type of Hercules, the divine servant of mankind, and it was commonly asserted that 'fortune' was his obedient servant. But the essence of his policy is perhaps best indicated in the word *aequanimitas* which is said to have been on his lips when he died. Marcus, the philosopher-king, whose reign was to close the period, added as his quota *felicitas Augusta*, *salus Augusta*, and, significantly enough, *securitas publica*, the 'safety' in defence of which he was to spend the best years of his life, toiling and fighting on the Danube.[3]

Despite superficial analogies, the Antonine system does not present itself as, in any significant sense, an anticipation of modern 'capitalism'. For the spirit which animated its economic, social, and political life was not so much that of expansion as of stability. As such, it found expression in policies characteristic of classical conservatism. In this connexion, we may observe that the process was now complete by which the Roman world was adjusted to the demands of a genuinely imperial economy, a fact which was noticed by contemporary observers like Tacitus.[4] This economy was in general one of production and distribution rather than of exploitation; and, if it left room for any kind of social parasitism, it was that of the *rentier* rather than of the speculator. Large-scale 'manipulation', such as had characterized the activities of powerful financial groups in the last decades of senatorial ascendancy, was, to all but a very limited extent, a thing of the past. The basis of life was, as it had been ideally conceived by Plato and Aristotle, the land; but with the development of an imperial system of food-control for the capital, and with the extension of civil rights throughout the provinces, there was no place left for the methods rendered odious by a Verres. Gambling in food-products was

---

[1] Pliny, *N.H.* xiv. 13. 89–91: Val. Max. ii. 1. 5 and vi. 3. 9.

[2] Yet his own temper was sufficiently 'unstable' to cause uneasiness and he is said to have 'died hated of all': Parker, op. cit., Introd., p. xi.

[3] Mattingly–Sydenham, op. cit., vols. ii and iii.

[4] *Ann.* iii. 54. 6 and 7. Cf. *Camb. Anc. Hist.*, vol. xi, ch. xiii.

not again to attain considerable proportions until the hey-day of economic demoralization which preceded the accession of Diocletian.[1] Meanwhile, we may guess how elaborate must have been the agricultural system from the evidence of Diocletian's edict on prices, which exhibits merely its wreckage. The unit of production was the *latifundium* which, following the great wars of overseas conquest, supplanted peasant farming; and, at least until the end of the Julio-Claudian period, there was probably a tendency towards the accumulation of estates in fewer hands, to which the only effective check was confiscation. This may be inferred from the familiar statement that, among them, six landlords possessed almost the half of Africa till Nero had them executed. Thus the imperial estates (*res privata*) grew till they became an important department of government. And, if we may accept the evidence of republican times, certain municipalities also possessed extensive areas of valuable provincial land. As early as the days of Cicero, Arpinum was the owner of a colonate in Cisalpine Gaul, sufficient (if the rents were paid) to ensure the upkeep of all public buildings and services in the town.[2] So far as mineral wealth was concerned, it was largely a monopoly of the state; the mines being worked either directly by convict-labour or through contractors (*publicani*) who, in consideration of the privilege, were obliged to subscribe to imperial charters governing the life of mining communities.[3] With regard to trade and transportation, the largest companies were those which operated by sea. Trimalchio, the hero of Petronius' satire on the *nouveaux riches*, boasted of having made three fortunes out of his mercantile ventures; but the most important element of Mediterranean traffic—the grain-trade from Africa and Egypt to the capital— was no doubt subject to vigilant governmental supervision, as it was favoured by exemption from harbour-dues. Handicrafts, as has been pointed out,[4] tended to be decentralized throughout the provinces, though, if it is possible to judge from Diocletian's edict, the cities of Egypt and Syria continued to dominate certain special industries like that of weaving. As for labour, it had now become a commodity of considerable value; but the

[1] See below, p. 175.
[2] On the question of municipal revenues in general, see Winspear, *Augustus and the Reconstruction of Roman Society*, p. 226 foll.
[3] Bruns, op. cit., p. 289, no. 112: *Lex metalli Vipascensis*.
[4] By Rostovtzeff, op. cit., p. 150.

elaborate 'racketeering' which in the bad old days had been the chief occupation of Cilician pirates and Roman noblemen was no more. Thus, in many ways, the activities of the irresponsible financial pirate were rendered difficult, even if they were not entirely suppressed.

Maintenance of the imperial economy was made possible by the employment of such techniques as were appropriate to it. These were in the main inherited from the distant past; it has been remarked that no significant innovations[1] were made during the historic Graeco-Roman period. The paramount claims of stability would, indeed, have served to render scientific invention and its application to industry of more than doubtful benefit. The very word 'invention' was, indeed, limited to the discovery of verbal conceits in literature. In this connexion, the conventional attitude may perhaps be illustrated by the story told of a man who, in the days of Tiberius Caesar, discovered a flexible or shatter-proof glass, of which he offered a spectacular demonstration before the emperor. The latter, having first assured himself that the secret of the inventor would perish with him, had him summarily beheaded on the ground that, if such glass came on the market, nothing could prevent the collapse of all existing values in gold.[2] Yet to suppose, on this account, that the Romans were wholly unsympathetic towards economic 'progress' is to overlook the fact that, e.g. in the adoption of techniques appropriate to their needs, they created precedents even for the modern world, such, for example, as a method of dry-farming for the inadequately watered grass-lands of northern Africa.

But within the sphere of economic life the greatest victory for stability was perhaps in relation to the currency. Under the republic, monetary standards had exhibited a more or less constant tendency to depreciate, a tendency most evident during critical periods such as that of the Hannibalic war. Fixed by Augustus, who in virtue of his *imperium* possessed the right of controlling issues of gold and silver, units of exchange were maintained at virtually the same level until the time of Marcus Aurelius.[3] The latter, in order to finance his Danubian wars,

[1] Toutain, *The Economic Life of the Ancient World*, Introd., p. xxvi.
[2] Dio Cassius, lvii. 21; Petronius, *Satyricon*, 51; Pliny, *N. H.* xxxvi. 26. 66.
[3] Nero, however, adulterated the silver denarius with copper, and, under Trajan, the percentage of copper amounted to 15 per cent.: Mattingly–Sydenham, op. cit. i, p. 28; ii, pp. 6 and 242.

initiated a policy of inflation which was to culminate in the collapse of credit during the third century.

Thus it was that the Antonine age came to merit the encomium of Gibbon as 'the happiest and most prosperous period in the history of the human race'. By contrast, at least, with the disorders which were to follow, this period attained a level of material well-being which, in the eyes of posterity, gave it the character of a veritable age of gold. Nevertheless, it would be a mistake to dismiss it on this account as nothing but a triumph of materialism. For this material well-being was significant, not in itself, but as the *sine qua non* of what till then had been the still-unrealized dream of the classical commonwealth. It thus pointed to a fulfilment of the spiritual aspects of the Augustan hope, the 'good life', as this was conceived by the idealists of Graeco-Roman antiquity.

Translated into terms of concrete fact, this meant that the Antonines had succeeded in constructing a world which was adequate to the demands of civilized man. The empire of the second century constituted a community in which Aristotle might at last have found a spiritual home, but on a scale which would have astonished the philosopher of the Greek *polis*. This it achieved by promoting the growth of civic life in semi-sovereign *civitates* which embodied, for all general purposes, the classical principle of autarky or self-sufficiency. These *civitates* were, indeed, uniformly deprived of the dangerous right of making war and peace, and there still existed among them a ladder of graduated privilege descending from that of the *colonia civium Romanorum* to that of the ordinary *civitas stipendiaria*. Subject to these qualifications, however, the states were free to minister to the spiritual no less than to the material needs of their members, whose ambitions they satisfied whether through the *decurionatus* or, in the case of wealthy freedmen (the leading representatives of the labouring class), through the *Augustalitas* or priesthood of Augustus. Over and above the municipalities stood the imperial aristocracy of property and office, with its vast estates scattered throughout the provinces but holding, as required by a law of Trajan, at least one-third of its capital invested in Italian land.[1] There was, also, as compared with the situation in republican times, an increasing tendency towards the stratification of life. Yet, each in its own way and to the limit of its powers,

[1] Pliny, *Epp.* vi. 19, 4.

local and imperial aristocracies aimed to secure for their members the fullest possible measure of satisfaction. Both accepted the classical theory which subordinates 'production' to 'activity' and, as the traditional activities of the *polis* continued to be pursued in the *municipium*, so those of imperial society were to find expression in occupations such, e.g., as those of the two Plinys, the one a *savant* destined to perish as a victim of scientific curiosity in the eruption of Vesuvius; the other a cultivated country-gentleman, conscientious and diligent public servant, and accomplished man of letters.[1]

The triumph of classical idealism is in no way better illustrated than by the general acceptance of a public discipline such as had been called for on all hands during the revolution and was now to be embodied in the imperial system of education for citizenship.[2] In elaborating this system the Romans were to raise a monument to their genius hardly less significant than that of classical jurisprudence; together with which it was, indeed, to survive the empire itself, in order to provide a legacy of 'commonplaces' to form the core of subsequent European culture. Organized to promote the inculcation and diffusion of classical ideals, it effected its purpose, firstly, by serving as a reagent to dissolve all forms of particularism; secondly, by erecting 'universal' standards of judgement and taste.

The principles of such a public discipline already existed when Augustus began his work, and it remained only to apply them to the conditions of imperial society. It was, perhaps, Cato who had first laid down the outlines of an educational curriculum;[3] but, with the evolution of the humanistic ideal in the last century of the republic, it had assumed a character quite remote from his simple, almost wholly technical and vocational scheme. In so doing it emerged as the system of *bonae* or *liberales artes* which was destined to take such root in the life of the empire and, with necessary modifications, to constitute the basis of training during the Middle Ages. In this transformation we may once more perceive the hand of Cicero.[4]

[1] See *Camb. Anc. Hist.*, vol. xi, p. 853, for a characterization of the spirit of the age.
[2] See Gwynn, *Roman Education from Cicero to Quintilian*, and Haarhoff, *The Schools of Gaul*, for a general discussion of this topic.   [3] Ch. II, p. 33.
[4] See Gwynn, op. cit., p. 82, and Cicero, *De Rep.* iii. 3, where he urges the value of the liberal arts as a means of 'maintaining the prosperity and virtue of the commonwealth.

Cicero had exhorted his son to follow his own example in basing his studies on the two classical languages. At the same time he had insisted upon the advantage of combining literature (grammar and rhetoric) with philosophy; and, in this connexion, he recommended the reading of his own works along with those of the Academics, Peripatetics, and Stoics.[1] For the resultant discipline he claimed a sovereign merit; asserting that it fulfilled the double purpose of ensuring right conduct and correct expression.[2] In other words, it satisfied the demands of thought and action implied by life in society. In this programme Cicero claims that the combination of literature and philosophy is peculiarly Roman, i.e. his own contribution to educational theory.[3] Whether or not this was the case, the deliberate substitution of literature for mathematics in what had been the characteristically Platonic combination marks a distinct departure from the spirit and purpose of the Academic discipline, and its historical significance can hardly be exaggerated. For, by imparting to Classicism precisely that 'literary and aesthetic bias' which Plato had so earnestly deprecated, it modified the whole complexion of Western culture, giving to it a rhetorical cast from which it was hardly to free itself even under the powerful stimulus of modern mathematical and physical science.

In seeking to appraise the results of this Latin discipline we can afford to touch lightly upon the more obvious. It served, for example, a useful economic purpose in the training of speakers and writers, the importance of which should not be underestimated, even though the avenues of expression were drastically curtailed with the disappearance of political freedom. In this connexion perhaps the most significant development was an exaggeration of the characteristic weaknesses of rhetoric —its preoccupation with form, resulting in rule-ridden traditionalism and the tiresome 'echoing' of Cicero and Vergil, its emphasis upon aesthetic effort, which issued in the manufacture of 'verbal honey-balls', crammed with false sentiment and exhibiting every form of dexterity possible to authors who aspired to virtuosity without any particular regard for truth.

[1] *De Offic.* i. 1, and the argument of the *De Oratore* as a whole.
[2] *De Orat.* iii. 15. 57: 'illa doctrina . . . et recte faciendi et bene dicendi magistra.'
[3] Ibid. i. 8. 33: 'hic humanus cultus civilisque.' Gwynn, on the other hand, traces the combination to Isocrates and distinguishes it as 'cultivation' (παιδεία) from philosophy or reflection (φιλοσοφία): op. cit. iv, p. 46 foll.

These weaknesses reached their climax with the panegyrists, the worthlessness of whose efforts was in direct proportion to their proficiency in fulsome and nauseating adulation.

Already in the first century Seneca had put his finger on what was to be a typical criticism of the literary discipline, when he said: *non vitae sed scholae discimus*.[1] This accusation was to be repeated by Petronius.[2] In other words, what these critics deplored was the fact that it did not constitute a 'preparation for life'. From the narrowly practical standpoint this has remained a common objection to the kind of training provided and, in view of the characteristic failings of classical scholarship, it is not altogether beside the point. The charge, however, lies against the extravagances of the system rather than the system itself and, as regards pedantry and remoteness from reality, other disciplines have proved to be at least equal sinners with the classics. Moreover, if the peculiar demands of imperial society be taken into account, Seneca's accusation turns out to be anything but valid. For centuries, indeed, the classical discipline was to play an essential part in a scheme of assimilation which, operating through colonization, through the graduated scheme of *municipia* erected in the provinces, through the training of legionary and auxiliary troops and their intermarriage with barbarian women, as well as through the influences of trade and communication, culminated on the plane of higher education.[3] Thus, in a society constituted in the last analysis upon the basis of a common body of ideas, this education became a passport to the rights and privileges of the community. And, if this was to erect somewhat artificial barriers against admission, such barriers were necessary in view of what membership entailed.

The ultimate answer to Seneca's criticism, however, is that it ignores or misconceives the central idea of the Ciceronian scheme. This was, as we have shown, to provide a moral and spiritual no less than an intellectual discipline, and, in order to be effective, it was essential that all vocationalism should be subordinated to the general cultural end. Thus we are brought face to face with the vital question: What did the

[1] *Epp. ad Lucilium*, 106. 12.
[2] *Satyricon*, 1. 3: 'et ideo ego adulescentulos existimo in scholis stultissimos fieri, quia nihil ex his quae in usu habemus aut audiunt aut vident.'
[3] For the empire as a melting-pot or, as he calls it, 'mixing-bowl', see Plut. *De Alex. Mag. Fort. aut Virt*. i, 6.

humanist mean by philosophy? This question hardly presented itself to Seneca, so uncritically did he himself accept the presuppositions of the system which he undertook to criticize. Yet it is a question which must be faced, if the strength and limitations of classical humanism are to be rightly estimated.

There can be little doubt that the term 'philosophy' was apprehended in a singularly narrow and attenuated sense. Already, by virtue of the Socratic tradition, limited to the study of mankind, its connotation was further restricted through the unqualified acceptance by Cicero of the attitude and outlook of the Greek idealists. Thus, while it claimed to be 'scientific', it differed so radically from modern science, that it should perhaps be designated as SCIENTIA.[1] It is easiest to see what this implies by showing what it excludes.

To begin with, it excludes the study of physics as this had been understood among the earlier Greeks. To the assiduous questioning with which the Hellenic intellect had plied her, nature had returned but equivocal answers, so that the impulse to further investigation was already failing when the Romans established contact with Hellas. Moreover, among the Romans, the spirit of inquiry was never very strong. Even Lucretius was concerned with knowledge mainly as a basis for action and, as we have seen, Cicero was deeply suspicious of the investigation of truth for its own sake. Thus, with the triumph of humanism, Roman science evaporated into aimless and erratic exercises such as that of Pliny,[2] whose *Natural History* remains a museum-piece of undigested book-learning and superstition quaintly interlarded with vigorous and acute personal observation, but totally devoid of recognizable method.[3] In this sense only did the Romans study nature; and science, in the modern sense, obtained no foothold in the schools. Thus, to those who declare that science would have saved *Romanitas*, it may be answered that, in order to purchase this salvation, *Romanitas* should have ceased to be itself.

If natural science was thus excluded, the same may be said of the human sciences or rather of the modern scientific approach to human problems. For, while the Romans undoubtedly studied psychology, it was on the basis of vast assumptions which

---

[1] See below, p. 414 foll.   [2] In this he was preceded by many Alexandrians.
[3] The younger Pliny, *Epp.* iii. 5. 6, describes his uncle's work as 'opus diffusum, eruditum nec minus varium quam ipsa natura'.

were never seriously questioned or tested by any objective standard. The tone of Seneca's *Moral Essays* and *Letters*, for instance, suggests that human nature contains no unsuspected potentialities and that there is nothing radically new to be discovered about it. As for economics, inquiry in this field was of course possible on 'classical' lines; but its technical character made it unsuitable except for specialists, and accordingly it was relegated by Cicero to the exclusive attention of bankers and business men.[1]

As for history, the situation was, if possible, still more deplorable. In the *De Legibus*[2] Cicero had distinguished history from poetry on the ground that it aimed at truth rather than pleasure; and in the *De Oratore* he had boldly declared that the prime duty of the historian was to eschew all falsehood and to shrink from no truth; avoiding the appearance either of fear or favour.[3] Elsewhere, in the same work, history is described as a 'storehouse containing all the countless lessons of the past'. As such, it is apostrophized[4] as 'witness of the ages, light of truth, life of tradition, teacher of life, messenger of antiquity'.

Nevertheless, in a letter to Lucceius,[5] asking him to prepare and publish an account of his consulship, Cicero invites the biographer to exercise a bold and skilful shamelessness in embroidering the evidence, on grounds to be explained in the *Brutus*.[6] He then goes on to express the opinion that history is a kind of prose poem, the object of which is to delight the reader by exciting the tragic emotions, which are in no way more acutely stimulated than by a lively account of changing circumstances and the vicissitudes of human fortune.[7] This conception of history as an art, and an art inferior to poetry, could have nothing but fatal results.[8] Thus, in the humanistic discipline,

---

[1] *De Offic.* ii. 24. 87: 'sed toto hoc de genere, de quaerenda, de collocanda pecunia, vellem etiam de utenda, commodius a quibusdam optimis viris ad Ianum medium sedentibus quam ab ullis philosophis ulla in schola disputatur.'   [2] i. 1. 5.

[3] *De Orat.* ii. 15. 62: 'quis nescit primam esse historiae legem ne quid falsi dicere audeat? deinde ne quid veri non audeat? ne quae suspicio gratiae sit in scribendo, ne quae simultatis?'   [4] *Ibid.* ii. 9. 36.   [5] *Ad Fam.* v. 12. 4.

[6] *Brutus*, 11. 42: 'concessum est rhetoribus ementiri in historiis, ut aliquid dicere possint argutius.'

[7] *Ad Fam.* v. 12. 5: 'viri excellentis ancipites variique casus habent admirationem, exspectationem, laetitiam, molestiam, spem, timorem; si vero exitu notabili concluduntur, expletur animus iucundissima lectionis voluptate.'

[8] Seneca, *Epp.* 88. 3: 'grammaticus circa curam sermonis versatur et, si latius evagari vult, circa historias, iam ut longissime fines suos proferat, circa carmina' (i.e. metres, versification, &c.).

history came to be regarded as a bond-servant to literature rather than as the matrix from which literature, like all other forms of human expression, derives its character and content; and this humble status it was to occupy until the rise of modern science.

But, if Classicism thus excluded many of the subjects of most concern to the modern mind, or if it approached them in an entirely inadequate manner, it nevertheless raised jurisprudence to a plane never before attained. And while of course this was to remain a professional study, its general interest gave it a unique significance in the educational scheme. Jurisprudence, defined as the *scientia rerum humanarum et divinarum*, was conceived as, *par excellence*, the science of human relations, and the spirit of humanism was just what was needed to free it from traditional formalism and promote its development along rational lines. In this connexion it invoked the concept of a 'natural law' (*ius naturale*), applicable to all men, in all places, and at all times. The problem was to relate this law to that based on *ius gentium*, the so-called 'law of nations' which was, in reality, nothing but equitable practice as seen through the eyes of the Roman praetor. For Gaius, perhaps the earliest of the great classical jurists, the two were at bottom identical. By distinguishing them his successor Ulpian exhibited a keener appreciation of the true character of historical and political justice. The problem was to assume an acute form in relation to the crucial question of slavery; and Ulpian's attitude serves to emphasize the cruel discrepancy between the facts of imperial life and the theories which characterized the heavenly city of Antonine philosophy. In this sense it was premonitory of troubles to come.

It is hardly possible to overstate the strength and tenacity of this great classical tradition operating within the Graeco-Roman world. In the fifth century Augustine was to see it as the ultimate manifestation of the *pax terrena*.[1] As such it was, of course, subject to limitations both physical and moral. To begin with, its application was necessarily on a selective basis. Among the barbarians the general principle was that stated by Tacitus, *principum filios liberalibus artibus erudire*.[2] Within the

---

[1] *De Civ. Dei*, xviii. 22: '. . . condita est civitas Roma . . . per quam Deo placuit orbem debellare terrarum et in unam societatem rei publicae legumque perductum longe lateque pacare. . . .'   [2] *Agric.* 21; cf. *Ann.* iii. 40 and xi. 23–4.

community proper higher education must with few exceptions have been confined to members of the imperial and municipal aristocracies, if only on grounds of expense.[1] Apart from this, if the system involved any limitation, it was that of closed minds rather than closed books. Wholly devoid of originality, it sought to teach men how to 'act' rather than to 'produce' or 'construct'. To this end it supplied them with standards of 'action' which claimed the finality of Eternal Rome herself. By so doing it played its part in blinding them to the significance of change; and thereby helped to prepare the crisis of the third century.

Of the magnitude of that crisis there can be little doubt. It was, indeed, a prelude to the long agony of the decline and fall; and, though the Roman world, by a heroic effort of reconstruction, was to survive the disasters of the time, it was to do so only by submitting to revolutionary changes as a result of which the principles of Graeco-Roman polity were hopelessly defaced and mutilated, if not utterly destroyed. Complete collapse of the imperial fabric was averted only by the services of the fighting Illyrian emperors, the last of whom, with some show of right, merited the title of *restitutor orbis*. But in salvaging the poor remains of *Romanitas*, Diocletian transformed it almost beyond recognition. Under the bureaucratic and militarized régime which he established, the empire experienced the ultimate nemesis of the political idea. In order to meet the insatiable demands of the fisc, this so-called 'Camillus of the lower empire' introduced a harsh and brutal regimentation of social life which reduced the subject to a condition of virtual peonage. The taxpayer, his ranks thinned by constant defection, staggered under an intolerable financial burden, while sovereignty, now finally transferred from camp to palace as it had earlier been transferred from senate-house to camp, claimed adoration in the person of the imperial *dominus et deus*. Such was the economically and morally bankrupt system which, in the dynastic troubles succeeding the abdication of Diocletian, was to pass into the hands of Constantine. With frantic energy this prince and his successors devoted themselves to the task of injecting new life into the moribund body of *Romanitas*. That their efforts were not wholly fruitless is proved by the fresh outburst of intellectual activity which marked the declining centuries of

[1] Pliny, *Epp.* iv. 13, on the situation in his day in northern Italy.

the empire, Christian vying with pagan writers in paying tribute to the venerable mother of civilization and law. But the object of the Constantinian and Theodosian houses was not so much restoration as renovation; they aimed to bring in a new world to redress the balance of the old. This was to effect a complete reorientation of imperial policy, the chief preoccupation of which was thenceforth to be with problems arising out of the novel relationship of Church and State. Thus, while accepting the fatal legacy of a crushing administrative and fiscal system, Constantine involved the empire in fresh controversies, in which the languages of Cicero and Demosthenes were used to debate issues that would have been incomprehensible to either; and the dwindling spiritual energies of Romans were consumed by incessant strife between pagan and Christian, orthodox and heretic. Accordingly, when the barbarians once more descended like vultures upon the empire, it was to pluck out the eyes of a corpse. The crisis of the third century was, thus, in a peculiarly significant sense, a point of departure in human history. It marked, if not (in Gibbon's famous phrase) the defeat of civilization by 'superstition and barbarism', at any rate an eclipse of the strictly classical ideal of virtue or excellence. In this sense it heralded the end of the great spiritual adventure of Graeco-Roman antiquity.

The great depression of the third century dated from the usurpation in A.D. 235 of the ferocious and brutal peasant-soldier Maximin, self-styled 'friend and advocate of the military order', to the final triumph of that order in 284 with the accession of Diocletian. Within this period we may distinguish three phases, the first, 235–52 (Maximin to Decius), marked by progressive disintegration; the second, 253–69, the age of Valerian and Gallienus when, the dikes having burst, acute anarchy and widespread demoralization prevailed; the third, 270–84, fifteen years of slow and precarious recovery initiated by Aurelian.[1]

This *débâcle*, which has recently been interpreted as the conscious and deliberate revolt of a proletariat consisting of semi-civilized peasants and soldiers against the dominant municipal *bourgeoisie*,[2] was formerly, and perhaps more simply, understood

---

[1] For the general history of the period see (besides Gibbon) Parker, op. cit., and Th. Schultz, *Vom Prinzipat zum Dominat* (1919).

[2] Rostovtzeff, op. cit., ch. x.

as the consequence of a duel between the two functions of administration and defence. But, whatever its ultimate significance, it certainly began with an indecisive struggle between sword and toga which was prolonged through the reigns of the Gordians and of Philip the Arabian. Coincident with this internal trouble, there occurred a vast accession to barbarian strength; due, on the one hand, to the consolidation of a new Achaemenid empire in 227 by Ardashir (Artaxerxes) of Persia; on the other, to the development of federalism among the Germans on a novel military and feudal basis. And, as pressure was thus intensified upon the empire, it presently gave rise to the familiar phenomena of general and chronic *stasis*.

The breakdown affected every aspect of Roman life. Politically, the situation may be judged from the fact that, of twenty-six reigning emperors, only one escaped violent death. In every section of the Roman world emerged war-lords (the so-called 'thirty tyrants'); their rise and fall depending upon the caprice of the troops. The destruction of private quickly followed that of public law. Government by *pronunciamiento* became the rule, and terrorism, punctuated by acute phases, the normal principle of administration. Thus, while the empire was flooded with secret agents, citizens were threatened in turn with spoliation, forced labour, and the sword. Meanwhile barbarian hordes flung themselves across the almost undefended frontiers to carry their raids into Achaea and Asia or westward towards the Pyrenees, harrying town and country and departing, laden with prisoners and spoils; while beyond the Euphrates loomed the menacing figure of Sapor, son and successor to Ardashir, threatening to undo at a stroke the whole Roman settlement of the East.[1]

Political anarchy was accompanied by acute economic and social distress. Plague and famine swept mercilessly across the provinces, depopulating vast areas. The inflation and flight of currency undermined the basis of municipal economy and shook the very foundations of the social system.[2] In various parts of the empire there broke out terrible peasant revolts, culminating in that of the Gallic *Bagaudae* in 282. With the disruption of

[1] He invaded Syria and menaced Antioch as early as A.D. 242: *Hist. Aug. (Gord.)* 26, §§ 5 and 6.

[2] The 'flight' began as early as 208; see Homo, *L'Empire romain*, p. 343 (the Decree of Mylasa attempting to check speculation in money). For the situation at the height of the crisis, see ibid., pp. 346–50.

economic and social life emerged once more the profiteer, whose sinister activity in buying, selling, and withholding from market essential consumers' goods was to be bitterly stigmatized by Diocletian.[1] The climax was reached under Gallienus when particularism, reflecting incipient nationalist sentiment and the natural economic divisions of the Roman world, triumphed conspicuously over the principle of centralized control in the form of Palmyran autonomy and the semi-independent 'empire of the Gauls'.

The results were not less disastrous in the realm of spiritual and intellectual life. All efforts to maintain a *cordon sanitaire* about Italy finally collapsed; Orientalism in its grosser forms broke in wave after wave upon the capital, and there now began in earnest that process of dilution whereby occidental values were to be overwhelmed.[2] Meanwhile, the voice of Greek and Latin literature, which had been heard without interruption for centuries, was almost stilled; and the very silence testifies with eloquence to the wretchedness of the time. Such miserable records as survive point to an intensification of anxiety as the empire plunged into more and more hopeless confusion; and men began to anticipate the actual end of the world.

In the absence of reputable evidence from pagan sources, we may recall the appalling picture of conditions given by St. Cyprian. 'Behold', he says in his so-called letter to Donatus, 'the roads closed by brigands, the sea blocked by pirates, the bloodshed and horror of universal strife. The world drips with mutual slaughter, and homicide, considered a crime when perpetrated by individuals, is regarded as virtuous when committed publicly.'[3] Seven years later, in the treatise to Demetrianus, he affirms his conviction that the end of the *saeculum* is at hand:

'This truth, even if we remain silent and do not adduce the prophecies of Holy Writ, the world herself attests, proclaiming by the evidence of universal decay her imminent collapse. No longer is there sufficient rain in winter to nourish the crops, or heat in summer to bring them to maturity. Spring no longer makes provision for the sowing, nor autumn for her fruits. Less and less are blocks of marble wrested from the exhausted hills; less and less the worn-out mines

---

[1] Edict on Prices. See p. 175 below.
[2] For the light it throws on this process, scholarship owes an immense debt to studies such as that of Cumont, *Les Religions orientales dans le paganisme romain*, 4th ed. (1929). [3] *Epp.* i, ch. 6.

yield their stores of gold and silver; daily the impoverished veins become shorter until they fail. The field lacks labourers, the sea mariners, the camp soldiers. Innocence departs from the forum, justice from the court, concord from friendship, skill from art, discipline from conduct.'[1]

To this theme he recurs in still another passage, written while a deadly plague was ravaging the empire and concluding with a no less positive assertion of the imminence of the end.[2] Discounting the elements both of classical rhetoric and of Christian millennialism, we may perceive in these words the utterances of a man without illusions and without hope.

The shock of the catastrophe was intensified by the fact that it was almost totally unexpected. There was, indeed, evidence of increasing distress in certain sections of the empire;[3] and the sophists prattled vaguely about the exhaustion of virtue in a world growing old. But even a man like Tertullian, detached and critical though he was, was far from anticipating what lay immediately ahead. To him, indeed, the peaceful and prosperous state of the empire under Septimius, Caracalla, and Geta seemed to warrant the belief that it was favoured by divine providence and that it would endure till the end of time.

'What reforms', he declares,[4] 'has this age not witnessed! Think of the cities which the threefold virtue of our present sovereignty has built, augmented, or restored, God bestowing his blessing on so many Augusti as on one! The censuses they have taken! The peoples they have driven back! The classes of society they have honoured! The barbarians they have kept in check! In very truth, this empire has become the garden of the world!'

Yet these words were written almost on the brink of the abyss.

The malady of *Romanitas*, in many ways still the most impressive secular system ever constructed by human hands, has inevitably excited much attention and, since the days of Cyprian himself, students of society have been concerned to diagnose its cause. To trace the history of their efforts would provide a fascinating comment on the development of social science, and even to catalogue the various explanations proposed is not

---

[1] *Ad Demetr. Apol.*, ch. 3.

[2] *De Mortalitate* (A.D. 253–4), ch. 25: 'corruente iam mundo et malorum infestantium turbinibus obsesso . . . mundus ecce nutat et labitur et ruinam sui non iam senectute rerum sed fine testatur.'

[3] Parker, op. cit., pp. 120–1, discusses the situation in Egypt. See also the *Decree of Mylasa*, referred to above, p. 153.   [4] *De Pallio*, ii. 8–9.

without interest. There is, for example, the classical theory that the empire was suffering from the incurable disease of old age (*mundus senescens*)—a notion which, so far from having been invented by Gibbon, was part of the stock-in-trade of Graeco-Roman rhetoricians. A modern variant of this hypothesis is that empires, by the necessity of their constitution, expand until they burst; when, with the dissipation of the wealth which forms the basis of centralized power, they break up like a compound into its original elements, the agricultural village and the small local mart. Such explanations have their roots in the classical doctrine of cyclical evolution. For this reason they were already to come in for severe criticism at the hands of Christian apologists. And this criticism (whether the metaphor be chemical or biological) appears to be justified. For the validity of the latter depends upon the dubious assumption that societies, like individuals, fulfil the life-history of an organism; while the former is made plausible only by a Procrustean distortion of the material evidence.

Contemporary distrust of *a priori* reasoning has prompted historians, in general, to cast about for theories of a positive character. Thus, for example, the decline of Graeco-Roman culture has recently been connected with what is called the 'water-cycle of antiquity',[1] according to which the grain-growers during the early centuries of our era were engaged in a losing battle with the Scythian nomads; though they were ignorant of this fact until, with the progressive desiccation of the Asiatic heartland, its inhabitants were forced outwards, thereby propelling the Germans in irresistible numbers upon the frontiers.

To those who prefer to look for an explanation within society itself rather than in any environmental condition such as drought, malaria, or the exhaustion of natural resources, a host of possibilities present themselves. Of these, one of the most obvious is dysgenic selection, the consequence of warfare and of social evils (like celibacy and vice) which bring about the extermination of the best;[2] although, if this be taken to imply that certain stocks are 'bearers of culture', then to one mystery is simply added another. A second possibility is that of slavery, regarded as part and parcel of a fundamentally wasteful eco-

[1] E. Huntington, *Civilization and Climate*; J. Huxley, 'Climate and History' (in *Saturday Review*, July 1930).
[2] Seeck, *Geschichte des Untergangs der antiken Welt*, vol. i, ch. iii, p. 269 foll.

nomy which, by distributing wealth in an arbitrary and illogical fashion, condemns the masses to perpetual subjection, hardship, and want. Or again, if to the purely economic be added a moral factor, it may be argued that 'Christianity, by preaching the gospel to the poor, unhinged the ancient world'.[1] Finally, there remains the political explanation, Caesarism, with all its obvious weaknesses, including a failure to solve the problem of the succession. This theory has recently been restated by an eminent authority,[2] and it will always carry weight with those who think in terms of political liberalism.

The *débâcle*, however, was not merely economic or social or political, or rather it was all of these because it was something more. For what here confronts us is, in the last analysis, a moral and intellectual failure, a failure of the Graeco-Roman mind. From this standpoint, we are not concerned to enter into a dispute as to the relative importance of the various theories proposed, but may freely admit that they all have a place within the complex tissue of material fact. If, however, the Romans themselves proved unable to come to grips with that fact, the reason must surely be supposed to lie in some radical defect of their thinking. In this defect we may find the ultimate explanation of the nemesis which was operating to bring about the decline and fall of ancient civilization.

Nor is it unreasonable to suggest that the defect in question was intimately connected with the classical *logos* of power. Classicism, as we have seen, resolved the concept of power into a subjective and an objective factor; the former, character (art and industry); the latter, circumstance (fate and fortune or the gods); tracing its genesis to a combination or, at least, a coincidence of the two. But, as must be evident, this solution was no solution at all. For, in this combination, no intelligible relationship could be established between the two component elements. That is to say, it involved a degree of obscurantism which classical reason strove in vain to eliminate, and, though reason did succeed in clearing a limited area into which the sunlight might penetrate, the forest remained in the background, ready and waiting to creep forward and resume its control. Accordingly, the doom which awaited *Romanitas* was that of a civilization which failed to understand itself and was, in conse-

---

[1] Lange, *The History of Materialism*, Eng. tr. (1892) i, p. 170.
[2] Ferrero, *La Ruine de l'Empire romain*.

quence, dominated by a haunting fear of the unknown. The fear in question could by no possibility be exorcized; since it was a consequence of weaknesses which were, so to speak, built into the very foundations of the system. In this sense, however, it was not peculiar to *Romanitas*; it was merely the last and most spectacular illustration of the fate which, sooner or later, was to overtake the ideologists of classical antiquity.[1]

In this fear we may see an explanation of many of the most characteristic phenomena of classical and post-classical times. To begin with, it serves to account for the steady and persistent growth of a belief in 'luck'. 'Throughout the whole world', declares Pliny,[2] 'in every place, at all times, Fortune alone is named and invoked by the voices of all; she alone is accused and put in the dock, she is the sole object of our thought, our praise, and our abuse.' This belief Juvenal was to single out as one of the most significant aspects of contemporary 'vice'; and he denounced it in various satires, notably the fifteenth. But, in his attack on superstition, the satirist had no recourse other than to fall back on the prejudices of Ciceronian and Livian humanism, which he thus reaffirmed in the well-known lines:[3]

> nullum numen habes si sit prudentia, nos te
> nos facimus, Fortuna, deam caeloque locamus.

A still more sinister development, if possible, was that of a belief in astrological and solar determinism, a faith which invaded the empire with the Chaldaeans or *mathematici*. For an account of this faith, we may refer to the summary statement of Censorinus:[4]

'The Chaldaeans', he says, 'hold first and foremost that what happens to us in life is determined by the planets in conjunction with the fixed stars. It is the varied and complicated course of these bodies which governs the human race; but their own motion and arrangement are frequently modified by the sun; and, while the rising and setting of different constellations serve to affect us with their distinctive "temperature", this occurs through the power of the sun. Accordingly, it is the sun to whom we ultimately owe the spirit which controls us, since he moves the actual stars by which we are moved and, therefore, has the greatest influence over our existence and destiny.'

The evil of this superstition was, of course, that it utterly denied

---

[1] See, e.g., Ch. XII below.   [2] *N.H.* ii. 7. 22.   [3] x. 365–6.
[4] *De Die Natali*, ch. 8 (*circa* A.D. 238), quoted by Cumont, *La Théologie Solaire*, p. 27, n. 4, who thinks that it is borrowed, in the first instance, from Varro and, ultimately, from Posidonius.

the reality of human freedom and responsibility, reducing men to the status of mere automata. The poem of Manilius indicates that it was already enjoying a considerable vogue in the early empire.

The acceptance of such beliefs involved a picture of nature in terms either of sheer fortuity or (alternatively) of inexorable fate. By so doing, it helped to provoke an increasingly frantic passion for some means of escape. This passion was to find expression in various types of supernaturalism, in which East and West joined hands to produce the most grotesque cosmologies as a basis for ethical systems not less grotesque. Of such mani-festations, none was more characteristic than Gnosticism, 'the barbarous and orientalized Platonism'[1] which resulted from an indiscriminate conflation of elements derived from Greek ideal-ism with the metaphysical dualism of the Orient.[2] Gnosticism began by identifying evil with the world of matter ($\H{\upsilon}\lambda\eta$). It then proceeded to assert an absolute antithesis between matter and spirit. Human beings, it declared, are in the material world, the evil of which thus enters into their constitution. But, as spirits, they are not of that world and their one problem is to escape from it. This, it supposed, was to be effected through the communication of celestial revelation ($\gamma\nu\hat{\omega}\sigma\iota\varsigma$). Such gnosis, conceived as 'illumination' rather than 'knowledge', laid empha-sis upon outlandish and esoteric modes of apprehension. As such, it was thought to mark the culmination of an advance upon successive planes of experience in which the pilgrim made his way through a universe peopled by demons and hobgoblins, including the seven devils of Babylonian mythology. From this standpoint, Gnosticism admitted of the widest oscillations between exaltation and abasement, and it combined the most rigid asceticism with outbursts of unbridled libertinism. Thus, ethically, it stood at the opposite pole from the classical ideal of *sophrosyne*; just as, in its contempt for objective science, it regis-tered the suicide of classical reason.

It does not lessen the tragic character of these developments that they were a logical outcome of moral and intellectual

[1] Inge, op. cit. i, p. 103.
[2] The history of pagan *gnosis* is discussed by Lebreton, op. cit., bk. ii, ch. i, p. 83 foll., where it is described as a 'great religious movement anterior to Christianity and, in its tendencies, profoundly contradictory to it. In the first centuries of our era it invaded the whole Graeco-Roman world and attacked the Hellenic and Jewish religions before it attacked Christianity.'

shortcomings inherent in the classical world. The effort of Classicism was, as we have seen,[1] an effort to rescue mankind from the life and mentality of the jungle, and to secure for him the possibility of a good life. That is to say it was envisaged as a struggle for civilization against barbarism and superstition. In this secular conflict with the powers of darkness Augustus imagined himself to have scored a decisive victory. But, as events were to show, the Augustan system possessed no real immunity from disorders such as had threatened previous political experiments. On the contrary they were enshrined at the heart of the system itself in the worship of the divinized sovereign. In this sense the destiny of the empire was implicit in that of the Caesars.

We have tried to show how, according to Classicism, the power deemed necessary to protect civilization was supposed to depend upon a fortunate coincidence of character and circumstance, a coincidence thought to have been finally realized in the person of Augustus. From this standpoint the future of Rome appeared to be bound up with the cult of Augustan excellence which, together with *fortuna omnipotens et ineluctabile fatum*,[2] was to constitute the guarantee and pledge of her eternity. But, if this was the Augustan hope, it was destined to disappointment. For, notwithstanding its pretension to finality, its basis in fact was merely pragmatic; and, though the emperor might seek to account for his success in terms of his 'virtues', there could be no certainty regarding the part which 'luck' had played in bringing it about. This meant in practice that those who accepted the system at its face-value found themselves committed to a hopeless battle against the forces of change—a battle in which 'order' was opposed to 'process' and identified with the maintenance of conventions established by the founder as norms for all time to come. The defect of this analysis was its failure to do justice to the sense of substantial growth or development. As a consequence it served to produce a sharp division between conservatives and innovationists, in which both sides were, no doubt, partially at fault. The tendency of the conservative was to regard all change as *ipso facto* evil or, at the very least, suspect as a dangerous leap in the dark. He was thus disposed to resist it, forcing everything into existing moulds of thought with the

---

[1] Ch. III above.
[2] Verg. *Aeneid*, viii. 334.

result that the moulds were ultimately bound to crack. On the other hand the weakness of the innovationist as such was that he lacked any adequate notion of direction. For this reason he was inclined to meet the demands of 'novelty' simply by letting himself go with the tide; and, by so doing, he exposed himself to the conventional charge of barbarism. The conflict had the effect of dividing the emperors into two opposing camps. It tended also to produce a 'heresy' of individual emperors, so to speak, against themselves, a heresy which may be detected even within the formal and superficial unity of what has been called the Hadrianic synthesis. In this way it prepared the ground for what was to materialize as the moral and intellectual crisis of the third century.

The heresy, which thus manifested itself in the realm of politics, was but one phase of a wider and deeper cleavage within the ranks of imperial society. Horace had prophesied that the greatness of Rome would continue so long as Juppiter and the Capitol remained unshaken, thereby advocating the conservation of strictly national ideals; and Vergil, while perhaps more generous and cosmopolitan in his outlook, was not less keenly alive to the perils of an indiscriminate internationalism. But now, under the nominal presidency of Jove, the Pantheon was steadily enlarged; and the national deities fraternized with a heterogeneous mob composed of all the Mediterranean gods except those which, like the Carthaginian Baal, were distinctly below civilization or those which, like the Jewish Jehovah, were above it. It thus became evident that, after all, the victory of Venus and Apollo over the forces of darkness had been incomplete.

The expansion of the Roman pantheon, which has been taken to indicate a spirit of toleration, testifies in reality to the absence of anything like a genuine principle of discrimination within *Romanitas*. The imperial *pax deorum* concealed a mass of moral and intellectual incongruities; it was not a hierarchy but a hotchpotch, symbolizing, as has been said, the amazing congeries of races, customs, and traditions, not to speak of the profound economic and social distinctions which subsisted within the body-politic. The empire, indeed, was not so much a 'body without a soul' as an example of multiple personality. As such, it offers a grim comment on the Plutarchian doctrine of the 'mixing-bowl'. For, to begin with, the masses remained relatively untouched by culture, their role within the system being one of mere acquiescence. The widening divergence between the literary language and the vernacular is a measure of the gulf which separated the refined citizen of the *municipium* from the rough peasant or soldier of the township and the frontier. Moreover, while cultivation was thus restricted to the dominant classes, those to whom letters were accessible found themselves confronted by the claims of rival schools of opinion which, however well equipped as 'sects' to dispute control of the human mind, could provide no real basis for spiritual unity. Quite the contrary, they actually promoted tendencies towards disintegration which could be held in leash only by physical force. Vespasian, with shrewd peasant wit, had declared of the ideologues: 'I do not strike the dog that barks at me.' Nevertheless individuals vaguely designated 'philosophers' were, in general, suspect within the *regnum Caesaris* and, on more than one occasion, the government undertook to purge society of subversive influences by expelling them from the capital.

The activities of such men serve to illustrate the truth of the maxim that societies die at the top. Or, in the vigorous language of Tertullian:[1] 'they come into the open and destroy your gods, attacking your superstitions amidst your applause. Some of them even dare with your support to snap and bark at your princes.' It is thus apparent that, through the very discipline she provided, *Romanitas* equipped her traducers with a weapon to dig her grave. The empire could, indeed, afford to ignore the yelpings of a Commodian, which reflected merely the half-articulate hatred of the under-dog, buoyed up by some dim Messianic hope and giving vent to a Christian cynicism not unlike that of Diogenes himself. But the diffusion in intellectual circles of doctrines such as we have indicated helped to prepare for a revolt against civilization, by inculcating a widespread sense of failure and frustration, in striking contrast with the unshakable faith of Vergil in the mission of Eternal Rome.

Against these tendencies there was little, if any, effective protest. As late, indeed, as the time of Nero, a Seneca might be found to come to the defence of the age, clothing in scintillating phrases the commonplaces of a shallow optimism, the beautiful day-dream of human perfectibility and brotherhood under the Caesars. But the brilliance of Seneca's rhetoric fails to conceal

[1] *Apol.* 46.

the inherent anomalies of his position. Seneca proclaimed the doctrines of liberty, equality, and fraternity while himself acting as prime minister to the last and worst of Julio-Claudian 'tyrants'. He attacked 'superstition' but recommended the worship of the political gods both as 'a matter of form' and as expedient 'for binding the masses to civil society'; thereby, it has been said, exhibiting himself as 'more hypocritical than any actor'.[1] Finally, while steadily keeping his eye on the main chance, he argued volubly that the business of philosophy is to teach men 'to despise life'. The inconsistencies of Seneca are such as to indicate a radical breach between theory and practice. As Augustine was to put it: 'the freedom manifested in his writings was totally absent from his life.'

But if Seneca thus wore the mask of an accomplished actor, it was not that he was deliberately perverse or insincere. On the contrary, all the evidence goes to show that, notwithstanding notorious weaknesses of character, he was a high-minded and well-intentioned man. This, indeed, was precisely the source of his difficulty; for it rendered him the victim of a 'heresy' which, with his intellectual equipment, he was powerless to overcome. The heresy which, with Seneca, found expression in a forced and strident optimism, manifested itself among other contemporary writers in a different but not less characteristic way. In this connexion, we need say nothing of Lucan with his vain regrets for the republic, further than to point out that they betray an utter lack of accord between the writer and the world in which he lived. With Juvenal, a similar incapacity for adjustment takes the form of a stinging criticism of conventional 'vice'; as though the lash of sarcasm and invective could be expected to do anything except to exacerbate the sore. Much the same thing may be said of Lucian's 'exposure' of philosophic humbugs in the contemporary Hellenic world.

The heresies of imperial literature had their roots in those of imperial philosophy. The immense material changes which culminated in the establishment of the Augustan empire had brought with them no fresh stimulus to human thought. Philosophy was thus condemned to live upon the inspiration of a receding past, with the result that it achieved nothing beyond certain minor modifications of the traditional formulae. For its

---

[1] Aug. *De Civ. Dei*, vi. 10 and iv. 32.

spirit and method, we have the evidence of Diogenes Laertius.[1] Diogenes, in his introduction to the *Lives of the Philosophers*, points out that speculative activity, beginning with the Ionian Greeks, developed both chronologically and logically according to the following scheme:

(1) Physics (theoretical science, including theology, mathematics, the natural sciences, psychology).

(2) Ethics (practical science—ethics, aesthetics, economics, politics).

(3) Logic (critical examination of the instrument of knowledge and of its *modus operandi* by way of demonstration, induction or generalization, eristic or argumentation).

It will be noted that what comes first in this scheme is physics or 'cosmology', i.e. the 'story' which the observer tells himself in order to 'account for' the phenomena of nature or, as the Greeks put it, 'to save the appearances'. This account is fundamental; it is the 'hypothesis' or basis which underlies what he has to say about 'ethics', the motto of which thus becomes (for all the schools, not merely for the Stoics) 'to follow nature'; whatever the specific connotation to be given to the term.

This scheme once established was to determine the pattern of all subsequent thought. This it did by giving rise to various schools of opinion which divided according to their respective 'preferences', and each of these preferences constituted what Diogenes calls a 'sect' or 'heresy'. The history of these heresies is the history of the philosophic succession or *diadoché*; one of the most significant aspects of which (as he notes) is the tendency towards a cleavage between those who were inclined to affirm and those who were inclined to deny; i.e. between dogmatists and sceptics. In imperial times the sceptical position was maintained mainly by the Academics, who, starting from the logical principle of suspended judgement, carried this principle so far as to question even the common-sense assurance of selfhood, thereby largely stultifying themselves. Dogmatism, on the other hand, was represented by at least two important groups of opinion. These groups were at one in accepting a picture or representation of the cosmos in terms of 'form' and 'matter'. Where they differed was on the question which of these two principles was to be regarded as the ultimate determi-

---

[1] His dates are uncertain, but he probably flourished at the beginning of the third century.

nant of cosmic order. Hence the historical distinction between 'idealists' and 'materialists', and a dispute which was destined to prove interminable for the simple reason that each of the proposed alternatives was, in fact, equally arbitrary. The issue, which thus defied solution on its merits, was to divide Stoics and Epicureans throughout imperial times until, in the end, Augustine dismissed the claims of both sectaries alike with the abrupt comment: *Only their ashes survive.*

But, though this was to be the ultimate fate of Stoicism, it should not blind us to the significance of its role as, perhaps, the dominant type of idealism in the first two centuries of the empire. This position it attained as one of the last, if not one of the greatest, attempts of classical *scientia* to meet the legitimate demand of thinking men for a just and reasonable world; and, in this sense, it claimed the merit of a system which was 'reverent without superstition' ($\theta\epsilon o\sigma\epsilon\beta\dot{\eta}s$ $\mathring{a}\nu\epsilon\upsilon$ $\delta\epsilon\iota\sigma\iota\delta\alpha\iota\mu o\nu\dot{\iota}\alpha s$). It thus began with an attempt to get behind the merely formal definition of superstition as that which stands over and above the cults authorized by the state, and to discriminate between popular and vulgar belief on the one hand, and true religion on the other, on the basis of a cosmology erected upon the concept of 'fate', the $\epsilon\dot{\iota}\mu\alpha\rho\mu\dot{\epsilon}\nu\eta$ or *ordo, series causarum* of 'nature'. It then proceeded to assert, as the supreme command of ethics, the precept: Follow nature. The significance of such a command must, however, remain questionable in this particular context; since, if nature is in fact fate or destiny, it is not clear how far any one is at liberty to defy her ordinances, as is perhaps indicated in the famous verse from the hymn of Cleanthes: *ducunt volentem fata nolentem trahunt.* The difficulty thus raised constituted the main problem of Stoic logic, which evaded rather than solved it by resorting to a number of wholly arbitrary identifications, the result of which was merely to emphasize its dogmatic character. These identifications had to do with the Stoic *logos* conceived impersonally as an 'immanent cosmic reason'. Thus envisaged, it was equated subjectively with 'mind', objectively with the 'fiery fire' ($\pi\hat{\upsilon}\rho$ or $\pi\hat{\upsilon}\rho$ $\pi\upsilon\rho\hat{\omega}\delta\epsilon s$, *spiritus* in the language of Seneca) which, diffused throughout nature, activated the great animal while, at the same time, it constituted the basis for a universal 'sympathy' among its various components.

However dubious such identifications, they were nevertheless held to warrant the inference that 'to follow nature' was 'to follow reason'. In this way, they served to provide a sanction for the ideal of Stoic wisdom or *sapientia*. With Seneca, this *sapientia* was to find expression in a series of propositions in which he uses terminology so startlingly like that employed by the Christians as to have given rise to the myth that he was in secret correspondence with St. Paul. The terminology includes phrases like the 'City of God', the 'fatherhood of God and the brotherhood of man', the 'law of charity or benevolence', and the list could be lengthened almost indefinitely. Such apparent analogies should occasion no surprise; since all they mean is that the Stoics agreed with the Christians in dreaming of a better world. The real point, however, is what ground of assurance they had for so doing. In this connexion, the weakness of Stoic *sapientia* was that it failed to build a bridge between 'order' and 'process'; one result being that whatever did not fit in with the preconceptions of its ideal order was denied or dismissed as 'unreal'.[1]

We may thus perceive Seneca, in his determination to maintain the Stoic ideal of the *immota, inconcussa mens*, withdrawing from the *turbulenti motus* of actual life to a private world of his own creation where, at any rate, the milk of human kindness might be thought to flow freely. But for Marcus, the philosophic emperor, last of Seneca's successors in the Stoic *diadoché*, no such solution could be regarded as admissible. Accordingly, we find him dwelling with a pathetic insistence upon the right to believe in an orderly world, despite an accumulation of evidence which seemed to belie his faith.

'If', he declares,[2] 'the intellectual part of us is common to all, so also is the reason which gives us our status as human beings. Grant this and the (practical) reason which bids us do or not do must also be common. Hence it may be concluded that there is but one law; and, if the law be one, we are all fellow-citizens and members of one body-politic; that is to say, the universe is a species of state. For what other conceivable community can there be of which it may be said that the whole human race are citizens? And from this universal state must proceed those very faculties of intellect and reason, together with our concept of (natural) right.'

The religion of reason thus professed by Marcus has been hailed

---

[1] Hence the Stoic paradoxes, such e.g. as that the wise man is happy even on the rack. [2] *Med.* iv. 4; cf. vii. 9.

as 'the absolute religion, that which issues from the simple fact
of a high moral sense face to face with the universe'. This
religion has been declared 'independent of race and country'.
'No revolution, no progress, no discovery could possibly upset
it.'[1] In point of fact, it constitutes an audacious anthropomorphism, a kind of sky-writing which projects upon the cosmos
a merely human rationality and translates it into an account of
nature and of God.

To the difficulties created by the Stoic dogma of divine
immanence, classical *scientia* offered but one possible alternative;
apart, of course, from the scepticism which always remained
available as an anaesthetic for those who were wearied of
thought. This alternative was to be found in the doctrine
of transcendence originally derived from Plato. One purpose of
this doctrine was to do justice to the sense of human freedom
and responsibility which, as we have suggested, was largely
obscured in Stoic ideology. To effect this object, it shifted the
stage in such a way as to separate the *logos* or principle of cosmic
order from the matter or ὕλη in which, according to Stoicism, it
was immersed. The result was to vindicate the possibility of
freedom, but at the cost of rehabilitating 'chance' or 'necessity'
which thus once more emerged as a function of the (more or less)
independent matter. By so doing, it restored the traditional
Platonic ethic in which a human insight (*prudentia*) confronting
the flux was envisaged as the (subjective) counterpart to an
(objective) order in which an analogous role was assigned to
'divine providence'. Thus opposed to material disorder, the
providence of the *logos* was, in turn, supposed to depend upon
a still more remote and inaccessible principle from which it was
thought to derive its 'character' and 'energy'; and the vision of
this latter principle, presently to be personified as the 'supreme'
or 'most high' God, was reserved for a future in which mankind
should have disembarrassed himself of the physical body, the
muddy vesture of decay.

In early imperial times the principal exponent of these ideas
was Plutarch of Chaeronea (*circa* A.D. 40–120). They are set
forth, for example, in the essay on fate (*Moralia*, περὶ εἱμαρμένης
or *De Fato*), in which the author institutes a criticism of Stoic
doctrine on the basis of notions propounded in the *Timaeus* and
elsewhere. The essay begins with a somewhat scholastic dis-

[1] Renan, *Marc-Aurèle*, ch. xvi, p. 272.

tinction between fate conceived (*a*) as activity (ἐνέργεια), and (*b*) as substance (οὐσία); the former being identified with what we may call the *operatio Dei*, the latter with its outcome, the *opus operatum* or nature.[1] Envisaged as 'activity', fate is declared to embrace within its orbit 'all things which change from infinite to infinite', including 'the total revolution of the universe and the whole course of time'. As such, however, it cannot itself be infinite but must be finite in character (πεπερασμένη). How, then, does it fulfil its task?[2] To answer this question, says Plutarch, we may invoke the analogy of civil law which speaks in general terms (πολιτικὴ νομοθεσία καθόλου); thus determining the character of individual things (τὰ καθ' ἕκαστα) only so far as this is implied in the *ratio* of their being.[3] From this standpoint, it becomes possible to assert that 'fate comprehends all things' without subscribing to the proposition that 'everything occurs by fate', i.e. while still leaving room for a measure of contingency. Or, as he puts it, a ship, in order to be a ship, must fulfil definite specifications but it need not necessarily be 500 feet long. Thus to restrict the function of divine providence was to exempt it from responsibility for 'error' on account of 'material' deficiencies in its work.

To this picture of creative activity in nature, Plutarch finds a counterpart among men in the work of mind or intelligence. It is this intelligence, he thinks, which supplies to mankind the prudence and wisdom (πρόνοια, εὐβουλία) without which he would be 'more unlucky than the beasts'.[4] With this 'set-up', we are back once more to the traditional antithesis between 'character' and 'circumstance', 'virtue' and 'fortune'; in which virtue, identified with insight and foresight, is opposed to the environmental world and encouraged to face and overcome it in the conviction that 'measurement leaves no room for chance'.[5] We cannot follow Plutarch in his pursuit of this idea through all its various ramifications. It is presupposed in his theory of education defined as the 'perfection of virtue' through the discipline of 'nature', 'reason', and 'habit'; this disciplined virtue being pronounced invulnerable to the buffets of time and circumstance.[6] In this sense, it is utilized as a basis for interpretation; for example in the two essays on the *Virtue or Fortune of Alexander the Great*, where the conclusion is reached

---

[1] Ch. 1.   [2] Ch. 3.   [3] Ch. 4.   [4] περὶ τύχης or *De Fortuna*, 3.
[5] Ch. 4.   [6] *De Educat. Puer.*

that 'the more you praise the fortune of the King, the more you extol the virtues which made him worthy of it'.[1] The point is reiterated in the *De Fortuna Romanorum*, the story of a people among whom, as he declares, Fortune entered 'to take off her sandals and remain forever'.[2] But more clearly, perhaps, than anywhere else, it comes out in the familiar *Parallel Lives*. To examine the technique of these biographies is to see that they are each and all constructed in terms of precisely the same concepts. Plutarch thus selects various 'typical' figures of Greek and Roman history in order to depict them as examples of classical character and achievement. The figures depicted are truly representative; but they attain that quality only because the excellences they enshrine belong to an ideal order which is, *ex hypothesi*, independent of the flux. The *Lives* thus serve to illustrate, both on its strong and weak sides, the value of Plutarchian idealism as a principle of understanding; and, in that sense, they constitute a permanent and distinctive contribution to the classical religion of humanity.

In his search for a *Weltanschauung* which might serve to explain and vindicate his conclusions, Plutarch deserts the outworn myths of Greek and Roman theology in order to fasten his attention upon that of Egypt. This latter, finding expression in the theory and practice (τὰ δεικνύμενα καὶ δρώμενα) of the Isiac priests, he puts forward as 'no mere spiders'-web growing of itself and without foundation', but as an accurate description of events within the physical universe; although, of course, presented in 'symbolical' form.[3] In this theology, the supreme or ultimate principle (τὸ θεῖον) is hidden behind a veil of inaccessibility, but this does not mean that it exerts no influence upon the visible and tangible world. On the contrary, it manifests its power through the agency of secondary forces which, personified as 'demons', are thought to embody 'differences of virtue and vice' precisely analogous to those which manifest themselves among men.[4] Of such demonic forces, two are distinguished as paramount: the former, Osiris, the principle of moisture and so of 'orderly growth' in nature;[5] the latter, Typho, the fiery element, the drought which, while it consumes and kills, is

---

[1] Op. cit. ii. 8. [2] Op. cit. 4. [3] *De Isid. et Osir.* xx and lxxvi.
[4] xxv γίνονται γὰρ ὡς ἐν ἀνθρώποις καὶ δαίμοσιν ἀρετῆς διαφοραὶ καὶ κακίας.
[5] xxxv, thus identified with Dionysus or Bacchus, 'laetitiae dator, qui gratis frugibus arbores fecundat'.

nevertheless essential to perfection.[1] Osiris, conceived as the principle of orderly growth in the object world, is further identified with *mens* and *ratio* in the subject, and thereby hailed as 'lord and master of all good things'; while Typho, who in nature emerges as disease, tempest, earthquake, the 'failure' of sun or moon, indeed, as any 'unseasonable' occurrence, is equated with that 'part of the human soul which is devoid of reason, subject to a variety of emotions, tumultuous and brutal';[2] that is to say, it is the 'power of disruption, clinging to those things which are susceptible of affection and mutation'.[3] To a 'mixture of these opposites' are attributed the 'genesis and composition of the cosmos' in which, however, they manifest themselves with 'unequal strength', since 'supremacy is always with the better'.[4] Accordingly, what we behold in nature may be described (in theological language) as an endless conflict between Osiris and Typho for possession of Isis, 'mother earth', envisaged not as a fortuitous concourse of atoms but as 'that which has an urge to be informed'; in other words, as a *receptaculum*, the negative or female principle which, apart from Osiris, must remain for ever barren.[5] On the other hand, the *coitio* of Osiris with Isis, taking place despite Typho, serves to generate Horus, 'the sensible image of the intelligible world'.[6] We need not recount the story of Typho's malicious effort to destroy Osiris and to make away with his offspring or, at least, to brand him as a 'contamination' of incongruous elements and therefore 'illegitimate'. The effort is destined to ultimate frustration, since the father is by nature 'eternal and indestructible',[7] while the son 'born in matter is the image of his father's essence and an imitation of his being'.[8] The apparent, though temporary, success of this effort is commemorated in the 'sad and gloomy sacrifices' of the late winter season; its defeat in the annual spring festival of awakening life.[9]

What this hoary myth may have signified for the native Egyptians must remain a question. Our concern is merely to indicate what it meant when seen in the light of Greek and Roman philosophy.[10] From this standpoint, it was put forward as a gospel for all men,[11] i.e. a 'rationalization' of truths for which

---

[1] xxxix. [2] xlix and l. [3] lv. [4] xlix.
[5] liii τὸ τῆς φύσεως θῆλυ καὶ δεκτικὸν ἁπάσης γενέσεως: cf. lviii. [6] liv.
[7] liv ἀΐδιος καὶ ἄφθαρτος.
[8] liii εἰκὼν οὐσίας ἐν ὕλῃ γένεσις καὶ μίμημα τοῦ ὄντος τὸ γιγνόμενον.
[9] lxix. [10] lxviii λόγος ἐκ φιλοσοφίας. [11] lxvi.

the human mind has been groping since the beginning. It was thus, declares Plutarch, implied in the 'riddles of Homer and Thales';[1] especially, perhaps, in the Homeric picture of men 'made in the likeness of and on an equality with the gods';[2] and it fitted in with speculations of Xenocrates, Empedocles, and Plato regarding the nature and activity of demons.[3] As such, it pointed to two conclusions of practical importance to mankind. The first of these concerned his future while 'in the body'. Here all that could be anticipated was an endless struggle for the supremacy of mind over matter, with the prospect of seasonal fluctuations but no substantial change. Beyond this, however, there was extended the hope of an ultimate release for mind from 'all that is susceptible of death and destruction' and of its translation, under the conduct of Osiris, 'king and leader of the dead', to a realm pure and undefiled by material things; where, at last, it should enjoy the beatific vision and receive, at the hands of Isis, 'fulfilment of all that is beautiful and good'.[4]

Plutarchian transcendentalism begins by widening the gap between God and the universe, the 'intelligible' and the 'sensible' worlds; and then seeks to bridge it by evoking the notion of demons as 'intermediaries' between the two. By so doing it suggests two dangerous possibilities, both of which were to be fully exploited by Plutarch's successors in the Platonic tradition. The first was that of a further investigation into demonology; the second that of perfecting a technique for 'working the demons'. The result was to give rise to a series of theosophies and theurgies; these together constituting the theoretical and practical aspects of what professed to be a science of spiritual dynamics. We cannot pause to characterize these developments further than to say that they included various forms of mesmerism,[5] hypnotism, and auto-suggestion;[6] table-rapping;[7] clairvoyance or second sight;[8] and necromancy, or evocation of the spirits of the dead. Such tendencies were to be not merely endorsed, but actually promoted by Apuleius, Porphyry, and others during the second and third centuries. We have no wish to build up a case against Classicism by dwelling unnecessarily upon these weaker and darker manifestations of the classical

---

[1] xxxiv.   [2] xxvi θεοειδέας καὶ ἀντιθέους.   [3] Ibid.

[4] lxxviii τὸ μὴ φατὸν μηδὲ ῥητὸν ἀνθρώποις κάλλος . . . ἀναπιμπλάναι τὰ ἐνταῦθα πάντων καλῶν καὶ ἀγαθῶν.   [5] Tert. Apol. 22–3.

[6] Aug. De Civ. Dei, xiv, ch. 24: the case of the priest Restitutus.

[7] Amm. xxix. 1. 29.   [8] Philost. Vit. Apollon. Tyan.

spirit. Accordingly, we shall content ourselves with observing that, to the generally deplorable character of intellectual leadership during this period, there was at least one brilliant exception. That exception is to be found in the work of Plotinus.

The work of Plotinus represents the final effort of classical reason to attain to a correct picture of the universe and of man's place in it. It takes the form of a restatement of Platonic doctrine in terms such as would be intelligible to contemporaries. Marked by a studied reverence for the authority of the master, it embodies a solid core of Platonic thought. Nevertheless, as it is constructed in conscious reaction to current tendencies, it includes also such Academic, Stoic, and Neopythagorean elements as might be accepted on the philosophic level; and its animus is directed, on the one hand, against surviving forms of materialism; on the other, against the supernaturalism of the pagan and Christian gnostics. With Plotinus, the centre of gravity is shifted from the objective and positive to the intuitive and mystical aspects of Platonism; and, from this standpoint, many hitherto unexplored areas of human experience are brought to light. In this way, Neoplatonism came to be immensely important as a factor in the *praeparatio Evangelii*; and large elements of it were to find their way into Augustinianism, as Augustine himself generously acknowledged.[1] Nevertheless, with Plotinus, the central deficiency of classical *scientia* remains; and the philosopher is at last driven to take shelter behind the wall. Stubbornly clinging to the notion of salvation for the sage, a salvation to be achieved through 'the intensive cultivation of the speculative faculty', Plotinus carries it to the point where it yields an ecstatic vision of the One which lies beyond reason and beyond existence. From this exalted level, the moral and social virtues recede into the background. 'The wise man', declares Plotinus, 'will attach no importance to the loss of his position or even to the ruin of his fatherland.'[2] Thus, as the scaffolding of the *polis* falls away, the individual devotee is revealed in solitary communion with his God. In these circumstances, it is not surprising that, as a modern writer puts it,[3] Plotinus 'ignored the chaos which surrounded his peaceful lecture room'. To read him, one would never suspect that he was a contemporary of Valerian and Gallienus. Yet this fact in

---

[1] What these elements were we shall try to indicate in the concluding part of the present work.   [2] *Enn.* i. 4. 7.   [3] Inge, op. cit. i. 27.

itself is enough to indicate that, with him, classical philosophy had reached the end of the road. By contrast with Plato's vision of a renewed and invigorated commonwealth, the *Platonopolis* of his disciple was nothing but a monastic retreat from the grim realities of life during the crisis of the third century.

The economic, social, and political developments which contributed to bring about that crisis must remain a matter for critical investigation; though, in view of the scanty evidence available, it is not easy to see how any very exact conclusions can be reached on the subject. Several possibilities have already been proposed.[1] To these may, perhaps, be added the suggestion that the problem of the empire was at bottom military and fiscal.[2] But, in a situation otherwise difficult and obscure, one fact emerges as clear beyond question. Whatever may have been the realities of that situation, it was actually conceived as a question of classical 'virtue' and 'vice'. This, at least, may safely be deduced from the evidence of that mysterious compilation, the *Augustan History*, the alleged 'biographies' of emperors from Hadrian to the accession of Diocletian.[3] In this sense the crisis may be envisaged as, in the last analysis, a crisis of the human spirit; the issue being whether the values of 'civilization' which had been consecrated in the Augustan and Antonine empires were any longer to prevail.

From this standpoint, it is difficult to detect the truth which lies behind the hysterical denunciation of 'degenerate' emperors from Commodus to Gallienus; although, no doubt, the animus of the biographers serves to conceal (at least in certain cases) facts of social and political experimentation on a vast and comprehensive scale.[4] This does not imply that the innovations sponsored by these princes were necessarily in the right direction; and the historian, as such, cannot concern himself with mere possibilities such as those involved in the scheme of decentralization apparently contemplated by Gallienus. On the

[1] pp. 155–7 above. [2] Homo, *Essai sur le Règne de l'empereur Aurélien*.
[3] The controversy with regard to these documents has been ably reviewed by N. H. Baynes, *The Historia Augusta* (1926). The author is certainly right in identifying them as 'undisguised (reactionary) propaganda'. Whether this propaganda can with equal assurance be connected with the movement launched by Julian the Apostate (361–3) is, perhaps, not so certain; since the concepts of 'virtue' and 'vice' employed throughout are, *ex hypothesi*, timeless and immutable. Accordingly, they have just as much (or just as little) relevance to the actual circumstances of the third as they have to the fourth or, indeed, any other century.
[4] See, e.g., Keyes, *The Rise of the Equites in the Third Century*.

other hand, it is evident that the methods adopted for dealing with a situation depend upon the way it is apprehended. In this connexion, it is surely significant that the task of the hour was, in general, conceived to be one of restoration; the dream of the third century was to 'recover', if possible, the prosperity of the second. This is suggested by the literary tradition of what has been called the 'great moral and republican reaction' associated with the so-called censorship of Valerian. And here the literary tradition is supported by a body of numismatic evidence which indicates that a long succession of princes claimed the title of 'restorer', *restitutor orbis*, *restitutor totius orbis*, *pacator et restitutor orbis*.[1] Philosophy, however, having abjured her secular task, the duty of restoration was left to the rough men of the camp. It is hardly accurate to dismiss the fighting emperors merely as 'foci of irresponsible force'; for, one and all, they worked with the sword of Damocles over their heads. What they represent, in fact, was the instinctive effort of a crumbling society to protect itself from dissolution by any and every means in its power. At the same time, they sought to justify strong-arm methods by recalling the time-honoured imperial principles, *pax*, *aequitas*; *aeternitas*, *laetitia*, *virtus*, *providentia Augusta*; *felicitas saeculi*, *felicitas temporum*; *Fortuna Redux*; and these ancient ideals were to be combined with a note of pacifism probably unique in antiquity when, as he mobilized his troops for a final effort on the Danube, the emperor Probus assured them that 'the day was at hand when soldiers would no longer be needed'. The task of restoration, thus undertaken by the Illyrian princes, involved two features. The first was the application of ever-increasing pressure upon recalcitrant elements; the second, a certain degree of concession to evolving facts and needs. As such, it may be said to have culminated with the work of Diocletian.

Diocletian is often regarded as the founder of a new order; but it is more accurate to describe him as the last great exponent of the old. The elements of his policy, already foreshadowed by previous princes, were drawn in the main from the experience of the third century. It thus included the Sacred College, the new capitals, administration by rescript addressed directly to the civil and military hierarchies without even the formality of endorsement by the imperial senate. It included also an elabo-

[1] See the list made by Homo, op. cit., pp. 126–7 and his note.

rate organization which made the empire, in all perhaps but its techniques, the prototype of the fully-fledged modern corporative state. Under this imperial drill-sergeant, the empire as a whole was treated as a vast armed camp, the civilian population as camp-followers. The spirit of the administration is perhaps best illustrated by the language used in the preamble to the edict on prices. In rambling and diffuse sentences, the emperor launches into a violent attack upon the rascality and greed of profiteers and, repudiating the optimistic doctrine of a self-regulating imperial economy, he proposes coercion as the only effective means of equating supply with demand. This he advocates on the ground of a 'common good' to be identified with the claims of the military and the necessities of the poor. He concludes by imposing a scale of maximum prices upon an immense list of goods and of services ranging from that of scavenger to that of schoolmaster; the schedule to be applicable without qualification in all provinces and the penalty for infringement, whether by buying, selling, or withholding from market the commodities named, being death. Thus freedom of contract was displaced in favour of another freedom, viz. the freedom of the poor to live. In this way, as well as by measures of taxation contrived to support the official hierarchies (*maior numerus accipientium quam dantium*), the former paradise of the *bourgeoisie* was converted into a veritable hell on earth. As Lactantius graphically put it, it was equally expensive to live and die.[1]

In his search for a new formula wherewith to consecrate the imperial power, Diocletian also developed to their logical consequence policies which made the extermination of the Christians inevitable.[2] He thus concluded his second *decennium* by initiating the most thoroughgoing and ruthless persecution of the century.

Nevertheless the emperor lived to see the inefficacy of his methods conclusively demonstrated. For, with his abdication in 305, the Sacred College, which was the crown and apex of his administrative system, dissolved into discordant and warring factions; and, six years later, the edicts of persecution were suddenly revoked. Making a virtue of necessity, various

[1] *De Mortibus Persecutorum*, 23; for the *Edictum de pretiis rerum venalium*, *C.I.L.* iii, pp. 801–41 and supplements or Dessau, *I.L.S.* 642.

[2] i.e. in the sanctification of the monarchy under the patronage of Jove and Hercules. For the dates of the three edicts of persecution and their content, see Parker, loc. cit. p. 177 below.

emperors and aspirants to the purple embarked upon a competition in which they sought to outbid one another for Christian support. The Edict of Milan does not stand alone; it represents the conclusion of a series of manifestoes, each of which offered better terms to the despised and persecuted 'slaves of Christ'.[1] But it is none the less unique in its significance. For, while his rivals promised various degrees of toleration, Constantine definitely and finally threw the gods overboard and, by a curious anticipation of nineteenth-century liberalism, laid down in principle the absolute religious neutrality of the state while, at the same time, he sued humbly for the prayers of the faithful on behalf of the new régime. By so doing, he defied the whole authority of Graeco-Roman antiquity, abjuring, in its very essence, the classical idea of the commonwealth.

[1] The first of these issued April, 311, by Galerius. Lact. *De Mort. Persec.* 34; Euseb. *H.E.* viii. 17.

PART II
RENOVATION
V
THE NEW REPUBLIC: CONSTANTINE AND THE TRIUMPH OF THE CROSS

THE year 313 has rightly been taken to mark a turning-point in European history. During the first three centuries the tendency of events had been, on the whole, to accentuate the elements of opposition between the Church and the world.[1] It is, indeed, true that Christianity never preached or advocated the forcible overthrow of the Roman order. None the less, it regarded that order as doomed to extinction by reason of its inherent deficiencies, and it confidently anticipated the period of its dissolution as a prelude to the establishment of the earthly sovereignty of Christ. Accordingly, it viewed with detachment the nemesis which, in the years of anarchy and confusion, appeared to have overtaken *Romanitas*; while, at the same time, it provided, within the Church, a refuge from the cares and sorrows of a disintegrating world. In this spirit, too, it offered a triumphant resistance to the persecutions of various emperors,[2] culminating in a final trial of strength with the Sacred College. The three edicts promulgated in the spring of 303 represented the crowning effort of the reforming zeal of Diocletian and Maximian.[3] Inspired by what has been called a 'conservative devotion' to official paganism, these edicts formed the basis of a systematic and concerted effort to exterminate the faith. Their subsequent revocation was, therefore, deeply significant. By admitting the victory of Christianity over the secular order, it brought to a sudden and unexpected end the phase of opposition between the two; and by demonstrating, as nothing else could have done, the utter bankruptcy of the ancient religio-

[1] For an extreme statement of the opposition in question, see Tert. *Apol.* 38: 'nobis nulla magis res aliena quam publica'; *De Pallio*, 5: 'secessi de populo'; *De Idol.* 19: 'non potest una anima duobus deberi'; cf. *De Spect.* 28-9; *De Corona*, 14; *Ad Martyres*, 3; *De Praescript.* 7: 'quid Athenis et Hierosolymis? quid Academiae et Ecclesiae?'   [2] Notably those of Decius 249-50 and Valerian 257.

[3] Euseb. *H.E.* viii. 2-16; Lact. *De Mort. Persec.* 13 and 15, by whom the persecution is attributed to pressure from a fanatically anti-Christian party led by the Caesar Galerius. For the development of Diocletian's religious policy, see Parker, op. cit., part v, ch. 1, § 4.

political idea, it pointed the way to a development of fresh
relationships between the empire and the Church. These
relationships were to find expression in the so-called Edict
of Milan.[1]

The Edict of Milan had, of course, a specific purpose; its
object was to secure for Christianity the privileges of a 'licensed
cult' (*religio licita*). With this in view, it made a number of sweeping provisions in favour of the Christians. In the first place, it
guaranteed the right of all to profess the faith, and removed
any legal disabilities which they might suffer in consequence.
By so doing, it restored the status of those who had been expelled from the imperial services on religious grounds, as well
as of those who, because of a conscientious objection to sacrificing
in the pagan courts, had been denied the privilege of legal
action under the Sacred College. In the second place, it
asserted that no man should be prevented from discharging the
obligations of his religion. It thus ensured to believers the right
to subscribe, as individuals, to the 'Christian law' and, at the
same time, established their claim to perfect freedom of assembly
and worship. Thirdly, it made effective provision for the restitution of lands and buildings confiscated during the persecutions,
including those which had been disposed of by sale or grant to
private parties, at the same time undertaking to indemnify
those who were prepared to resign them without objection.
Finally, it recognized the Church as a corporation by authorizing it to hold property.[2]

In thus according recognition to Christianity, however, Constantine and Licinius went far beyond the terms required for
the licensing of a new cult, and enunciated certain principles
of broad and far-reaching significance. For the liberty thereby
guaranteed to the faithful was likewise extended to adherents
of all religions.[3] '. . . ut daremus et Christianis et omnibus liberam
potestatem sequendi religionem quam quisque voluisset . . . ut
nulli omnino facultatem abnegandam putaremus qui vel ob-
servationi Christianorum vel ei religioni mentem suam dederet
quam ipse sibi aptissimam esse sentiret. . . .' Henceforth a man

---

[1] Duchesne, op. cit. ii,[4] p. 56 foll. For a critical review of the problems relating to
this subject, see N. H. Baynes, 'Constantine the Great and the Christian Church',
Proc. Brit. Acad. xv (1929), pp. 409–12, n. 42. We may repeat Baynes' conclusion
that 'though the Edict of Milan may be a fiction, the fact for which the term stood
remains unaltered' (p. 349).   [2] Lact. op. cit. 48; Euseb. op. cit. x. 5.
[3] Lact. loc. cit. (quoting the Edict).

was free to entertain whatever beliefs he deemed most suitable to himself. This represented, on the part of the state, a formal and explicit abandonment of any attempt to control the spiritual life, which was thus proclaimed to be autonomous. Toleration, or rather complete religious neutrality, was embraced, not merely as a political expedient, but as a fundamental principle of public law; so to remain[1] until the accession of Theodosius in 378 and, as such, to be reaffirmed by successive emperors from standpoints as diverse as those of Julian and Valentinian.

Thus envisaged, the Edict of Milan constitutes a milestone in the history of human relationships. It marks a decisive repudiation of recent attempts to reconstruct the Roman order by the aid of notions derived from the pagan East—so far, at least, as these affected the theory and practice of the imperial power. In this regard, the mission of Diocletian and his colleagues had been to revive and carry to a logical conclusion policies initiated by Aurelian but interrupted by the reaction which followed the assassination of that emperor. Those policies had issued in the *forma regiae consuetudinis*[2]—a kind of 'totalitarianism' which, by reason of the absolute, exclusive, and uncompromising nature of its claims, represented the final stultification of *Romanitas*.

But if Constantine thus in effect rejected the pretensions of the Oriental sacred monarchy, it was not with any intention of returning to the moribund humanism of the Graeco-Roman past, the classical *polis* in which the cult of certain official deities was recognized as a necessary function of organized society. From this standpoint, his proclamation of spiritual freedom represents a genuine departure from anything to be found in the experience of antiquity. The formal segregation from political control of a whole area of human life reduced the *res publica* to relative insignificance, giving effect to claims long since voiced by Christianity in the famous text, 'render unto Caesar' (*reddite Caesaris Caesari*). It thus appeared to make possible an accord with the faithful to whom, at the same time, it offered a challenge to develop and apply the elements of a specifically Christian social philosophy. In this way, it pointed to an utterly novel idea—the project of a Christian commonwealth. Through this idea, the tendency of centuries was to be reversed, and *Romanitas* was to secure a fresh lease of life under

[1] Mommsen–Marquardt, op. cit. xviii, *Droit Pénal*, ii, § 2, p. 303 foll.
[2] Eutrop. ix. 26.

the aegis of the Church. The Edict of Milan may thus be described the great charter of the *New Republic*.

To say this is not necessarily to credit the emperor with any clear anticipation of what was implied in his momentous act when he raised the *Labarum* and proclaimed himself a soldier of the Cross. On the contrary, it is highly probable that his motives were ambiguous, and that he did not look beyond the immediate situation with which he was confronted. Constantine was a warrior-statesman, in every way typical of the age in which he lived. At the same time, he was one of the *epigoni*, by far the shrewdest and ablest of those who were struggling for the mantle of Diocletian. Originally hailed Augustus by the troops at York, after the premature death of his father, the emperor Constantius Chlorus, he had been reluctantly accepted as a Caesar by Galerius, the then senior member of the second tetrarchy (July 306). Some months later, he entered upon a dynastic connexion by marrying the daughter of Diocletian's original colleague Maximian, who had perforce abdicated in conjunction with his partner on 1 March 305, continuing, at any rate from 307, to describe himself as Augustus, although Galerius had meanwhile invested Licinius with the diadem in the West (Nov. 308). In the year 310, when Maximian ventured upon his ill-starred attempt to regain the purple, Constantine caused him to be arrested and put to death. Thereafter, he asserted an independent hereditary right, through Constantius Chlorus and Claudius Gothicus, as *divi Claudi nepos, divi Constanti filius*.[1] The death of Galerius at Nicomedia in the year following provoked a dynastic crisis which led to an uneasy *entente* between the former rivals, Constantine and Licinius. In 312, Constantine, crossing the Alps, overthrew the usurper Maxentius (son of Maximian) at the famous engagement of the Milvian Bridge, and entered the ancient capital, while Licinius undertook to suppress Maximinus Daia, another of the nominees of Galerius who, after his decease, had as senior Augustus occupied the East. By these steps Constantine and Licinius emerged as joint masters of the Roman world, their connexion cemented by a marriage alliance and by the fact that they had jointly committed themselves to the terms of the protocol framed at Milan.

Such, in barest outline, was the issue of a struggle for power

[1] Dessau, *I.L.S.* 699, 702.

which, following the retirement of Diocletian, exposed the futility of his scheme to ensure political stability by means of an automatically self-recruiting tetrarchy. Personal ambition, reinforced by dynastic associations and hereditary claims, had intervened to bring about a series of civil wars which recalled the worst memories of the previous century; the situation being complicated by the fact that, within their respective jurisdictions, the several *epigoni* adopted radically different attitudes towards principles of policy which the Sacred College was supposed to hold in common.

What these men had inherited was, indeed, an evil legacy. Under the Sacred College, justice was no longer conceived as the expression either of popular will or of universal reason, and it was not of right but of grace. Accordingly, altars were set up in the law-courts and, in order to plead, litigants were required to sacrifice to the imperial majesty, addressing his ministers as agents of the 'divine' will. Moreover, since the new theory of sovereignty involved a confusion between magisterial and dominical right, it admitted no limit to the powers claimed by the state as against the subject. Thus, in the imposition of a general assessment, fiscal officials are said to have invaded the provinces in the spirit of armed conquerors.[1] By the liberal application of lash and rack, Italians and provincials alike were forced to disclose the last detail of taxable wealth; and the *annonae* or subsidies thus levied were collected with no less ruthlessness than they had been imposed. Civil rights received as little consideration as those of property. Torture, which under the principate had been confined (except in the solitary instance of treason) to slaves, was now inflicted not merely upon freemen but upon members of the municipal aristocracy, and that in civil as well as criminal cases. To the *honestiores*, the horrors of the death-penalty were intensified by the adoption of servile and degrading forms of execution such as crucifixion; while for culprits of the lower class was reserved the exquisite torment of being burned alive in slow flames.[2] The introduction of such methods has been attributed more particularly to Maximian, but the preamble to Diocletian's

[1] For these assessments, the dreaded indictions instituted by Diocletian, see Parker, op. cit., pp. 283–5. They included (*a*) the *iugum* or land-tax, and (*b*) the *capitatio* or poll-tax. Lactantius' words reflect the opposition encountered by the government when it sought to impose these taxes, especially in Italy, which had been exempt from direct taxation since 167 B.C.   [2] Lact. op. cit. 21–3.

edict on prices reveals a spirit no less arbitrary and autocratic. Between them, they indicate an utter extinction of the reign of law.

The absolutism which thus demanded the suppression of political, was not less hostile to religious, freedom. Within a system claiming such finality there could, indeed, be no security for the Church; and, from remarks of Lactantius, it is possible to see how, in the contemporary mind, the two issues had become confused. For, vital as had appeared the earlier differences between Christianity and Classicism, both were agreed in asserting, in some sense, the indefeasible rights of personality. Accordingly, in their common opposition to the new despotism, the Church and what was left of the older republicanism discovered at last the basis of a possible *rapprochement*. And in Constantine they found a champion who was prepared to exploit their hostility thereto. The daring and originality of the emperor lie in the fact that he saw his chance and took it.

From this standpoint the role of Constantine was in some measure determined by his antecedents; tradition is clear that the pro-*bourgeois* and pro-Christian sympathies of Constantius Chlorus foreshadowed those of his more famous son. Thus Eutropius, after describing Constantius as an exceptional man, noteworthy for his sense of civic obligation,[1] goes on to add that he was studious in maintaining the prosperity of provincials and reluctant to press the demands of the fisc, deeming it better that wealth should be diffused through private hands than concentrated in a single purse. And Eusebius of Caesarea stresses his friendliness towards the Christians who, within the sphere of his jurisdiction, were everywhere raised to the highest offices of state and maintained therein despite the general edicts of persecution emanating from Nicomedia;[2] while he elsewhere remarks on the pure and wholesome atmosphere prevalent within his household and reflecting, no doubt, his devotion to the *supremus deus*, the 'most high god' of Platonic solar monotheism.[3]

But whatever may be thought of the character and motives of Constantine, there can be no question regarding the immense significance of his work. Profoundly religious or (it may be) superstitious in temperament, his recorded utterances are full

---

[1] x. 1: 'vir egregius et praestantissimae civilitatis.'　　[2] *Vita Const.* i. 13–16.
[3] Ibid., chs. 16 and 17. On this cult, see Baynes, op. cit., p. 345, together with his references to Toutain, Cumont, Wissowa, and others. See also Ch. VI, below.

of allusions to the 'deity' (*divinitas*) to which, like his father, he
gave unqualified allegiance; until, with the lapse of time, that
vague concept slowly assumed the lineaments of Jehovah.
Instinctu divinitatis, mentis magnitudine, the inscription engraved
upon his arch at Rome, seems to portray him as the inspired
hero or man of destiny.[1] It was as such that he made his appearance during the Italian campaign when, according to Christian
tradition, he experienced a vision of the Cross and received the
watchword, *hoc signo vince* or τούτῳ νίκα.[2] The invasion of Italy
(312) thus marked a crisis in the life of Constantine and committed him to a future from which there could be no escape.
Emerging as a champion of spiritual liberty, he was, in the
course of years, gradually to be transformed from protector to
proselyte of the Church.[3] At the same time, the conversion of
the emperor served to initiate a fresh cycle of historical development by suggesting the project of a Christian empire.

Once more, as in the far-off days of Augustus Caesar, the
Roman world was stirred by a sense of fresh hopes and fresh
beginnings. Unlike Augustus, Constantine had no poet to
hymn his praises; but, in default thereof, he naïvely recalled the
Messianic utterances of Vergil, together with elements of Sibyl-
line prophecy, and applied them, with superstitious veneration,
to himself; in much the same spirit as he appropriated material
from Trajan's arch to decorate the monument by which he
sought to blazon the glories of his own régime. His eulogists, as
though conscious of a need for moderation in view of the vast
amount of evil still to be expunged, were content to speak of
the age as gilded and refrained from describing it as a veritable
age of gold.

But if Constantine lacked a Vergil to proclaim his virtues, he
at least had his Eusebius. Eusebius of Caesarea ranks as the
first of a long succession of ecclesiastical politicians to pass across
the European stage. In view of his position as one who 'lived
in close communication with the emperor and knew much of
the inner working of his policy', as the man who sat to the right
of the imperial throne during the sessions of the Nicene Council

---

[1] The words *divinus instinctus* are used in precisely this sense by Plutarch, *De
Alex. Mag.Virt. aut Fort.* i. 9, with reference to Alexander the Great, διὰ τὸν ἐπὶ τοῖς
καλοῖς ἐνθουσιασμόν, so also ii. 10. Alexander, like Heracles, confronts fortune and
overcomes her by virtue of his μέγα φρόνημα (*magnitudo animi*).

[2] See again Baynes, op. cit., pp. 401 and 402, n. 33.

[3] Gibbon, op. cit., ch. xx, p. 289.

and exercised a decisive influence in framing the creed and discipline of the universal church,[1] it is not too much to see in his most extravagant utterances an authentic voice of the time.

To Eusebius the glorious and unexpected triumph of the Church constituted decisive evidence of the *operatio Dei*, the hand of God in human history. At the same time, by an easy and natural confusion of thought, it suggested the dangerous error that Christianity was a success-philosophy. Eusebius quotes with approval the emperor's own profession of faith, made after the defeat of Licinius had delivered him from his last formidable enemy:[2]

'. . . it appears that those who faithfully discharge God's holy laws and shrink from the transgression of His commandments are rewarded with abundant blessings and endued with well-grounded hope as well as ample power for the accomplishment of their undertakings. On the other hand, those who have cherished impiety have experienced consequences in keeping with their evil choice. . . . I myself was the agent whose services God deemed suitable for the accomplishment of His will. Accordingly . . . with the aid of divine power, I banished and destroyed every form of evil which prevailed, in the hope that the human race, enlightened through my instrumentality, might be recalled to a due observance of God's holy laws and, at the same time, our most blessed faith might prosper under the guidance of the almighty hand. . . .'

Our concern is not so much with the truth or falsehood of these sentiments as with the consequence of their acceptance. From this standpoint, Constantine is portrayed as the champion delegated by the Most High to be the minister of His vengeance upon the persecutors,[3] whose fate is described in terms which recall the fulminations of Hebrew prophecy. Elsewhere[4] the emperor emerges as the destroyer of those God-defying Titans who madly raised their impious arms against Him, the supreme king of all. Hence[5] God rewarded Constantine by making him sovereign, granting him success in such measure that he alone, unsubdued and invincible, pursued an uninterrupted career of victory, and became a ruler greater than any which history and tradition record. In these phrases we may discern the *victoriosissimus et maximus, maximus piissimus felicissimus Augustus* of the inscriptions, the prince on whose behalf the troops were taught to pray, *Deus, incolumem et victorem serves imperatorem.*[6]

---

[1] F. J. Foakes-Jackson, *Eusebius Pamphyli*, p. 3.   [2] *Vita*, ii. 24 and 28.
[3] *Paneg.* 7, 623 B–624.   [4] *Vita*, i. 5.   [5] 6.   [6] iv. 20.

The triumphs, which everywhere attended the standard of the cross,[1] gave promise of a day when the Christian sovereign should hold dominion from sea to sea, and from the river to the ends of the earth. Thenceforth peace, the happy nurse of youth, should extend her sway throughout the world, and, with abundance of peace, righteousness. 'They shall beat their swords into ploughshares and their spears into sickles, and nation shall not take up arms against nation, neither shall they learn to war any more.' These ancient pledges, made to the Hebrews in days gone by, were now to receive a visible fulfilment in the New Republic.[2]

It thus appears that what Eusebius looked for in the age of Constantine was nothing less than a realization of the secular hope of men, the dream of universal and perpetual peace which classical Rome had made her own, but of which the *Pax Romana* was merely a faint and imperfect anticipation; and it is important to note the grounds of his conviction. These lie in the fact that Christianity provides a basis, hitherto lacking, for human solidarity. With something less than justice to the syncretistic movements of the Hellenistic and Graeco-Roman world, Eusebius ascribes the persistence of competition among peoples to their belief in the existence of national and local deities which serve as focal points for particularist ideals. But, through the revelation in Christ of the one true God, creator and preserver of all mankind, the many deities of paganism are overthrown and the supremacy of Jehovah is proclaimed to all, both rude and civilized, to the ends of the habitable earth.[3]

Under God, the emperor. One type at least of Christian thinking (that derived from St. Paul) had conceded the fullest measure of legitimacy to temporal authority. For Eusebius, such authority, when exercised by a Christian prince, itself approximates to the divine.

'He frames his earthly government according to the pattern of the divine original, feeling strength in its conformity with the monarchy of God . . . for surely monarchy far transcends every other constitution and form of government, since its opposite, democratic equality of power, may rather be described as anarchy and disorder.'[4]

'Our emperor derives the source of his authority from above, and is strong in the power of his sacred title. Bringing those whom he

[1] *Vita*, ii. 7.   [2] *Paneg.* 16.   [3] 9.
[4] 3: κατὰ τὴν ἀρχέτυπον ἰδέαν τοὺς κάτω διακυβερνῶν.

rules on earth to the only-begotten Word or Saviour, he renders them fit subjects for His kingdom. . . . He subdues and chastens the adversaries of the truth according to the usages of war. . . .'[1]

Constantine was therefore Emperor by divine right.

'The God of all, the supreme governor of the whole universe, by His own will appointed Constantine, the descendant of so renowned a parent, to be prince and sovereign; so that, while others have been raised to this distinction by the choice of their fellows, he is unique as the one man to whose elevation no mortal may boast of having contributed.'[2]

These sentiments are echoed by the Christian Lactantius.

'The providence of the supreme deity has elevated you to the dignity of prince, enabling you with true devotion to reverse the evil policies of others, to repair their errors and, in a spirit of fatherly mildness, to take measures for the safety of men, removing from the commonwealth the malefactors whom the Lord has delivered into your hands, in order that the nature of genuine sovereignty may be manifest to all. . . . By an inborn sanctity of character and with a recognition of truth and God, in everything you consummate the works of justice. It was fitting, therefore, that, in the task of ordering human affairs, divine power should have employed you as its agent and minister.'[3]

It thus appears that Constantine gained rather than lost by his willingness to exchange the style and title of a god for that of God's vice-gerent. Utterances such as those of Eusebius and Lactantius suggest, indeed, that, while bitter experience may have taught the Christians to appreciate the dangers of hostility and persecution, they had still to discover those to be apprehended from the Greeks bearing gifts. As those dangers materialized, it became evident that there was need to qualify, in some sense, the pretensions of the new *imperium*, so far, at least, as to guard against political interference in the internal affairs of the Church. In this respect, Constantine himself exhibited throughout an attitude of studied restraint, contenting himself with the designation 'overseer of those outside'

---

[1] *Paneg.* 2.   [2] *Vita*, i. 24.

[3] Lact. *Divin. Instit.* vii. 26. (Migne); possibly an interpolation. In C.S.E.L. xix. i. p. 668 (Vienna, 1897) it is printed as a footnote to ch. 27. So also Mayor-Souter (Camb. 1917). Monceaux, *Histoire Littéraire de l'Afrique chrétienne* (1905) iii, pp. 301–3, suspects it. Pichon, *Lactance* (1901), p. 6 foll. accepts it as genuine. See discussion in Bardenhewer, *Geschichte der altkirchlichen Literatur* (1914), ii, p. 535.

(ἐπίσκοπος τῶν ἐκτός).[1] This moderation he illustrated by his deferential conduct during the Arian controversy. For while he himself described the question as nothing but a 'trifling and foolish dispute about words', which should in no wise be allowed to interfere with the paramount need for ecclesiastical unity,[2] nevertheless, by submitting it to a representative gathering of bishops convoked at Nicaea, he confessed that the decision of such an issue was beyond his competence. His son Constantius, however, exercised no such forbearance. Boldly thrusting himself into theological controversy, in his desire to impose upon the ecclesiastical authorities a modification of the Nicene formula, he argued that, as the divine repository of imperial power, his authority was paramount in Church as well as state; and, in the declaration, 'my will must be considered binding' (ὅπερ ἐγὼ βούλομαι, τοῦτο κανὼν νομιζέσθω), he assumed a more than papal infallibility.

In view of such developments, it is not surprising that efforts should presently have been made to introduce some kind of limitation into the theory of the prerogative. This limitation could not, of course, be constitutional in character; *imperium legitimum* was an obsolete conception, meaningless except as a part of the outworn classical idea of the commonwealth. The fourth-century opponents of Caesaropapism were therefore driven to a new expedient. They argued that the emperor was a member of the *ecclesia* and not its head; subject, like every one else, to the Christian law and, in consequence, to the discipline of the Church divinely appointed to be its custodian. The introduction of such ideas imparts a peculiar flavour to the Christian empire, and serves to distinguish it from the forms of Oriental monarchy with which it is sometimes confused. Their effectiveness was to be tested during the century, first in the successful resistance offered by Athanasius to political pressure at the hands of Constantius and, subsequently, in the submission of Theodosius to the stern demands of Ambrose of Milan. These heroic combats illustrate the result of committing what, from a strictly political point of view, may be accounted 'dangerous authority' to the 'priestly guardian of the emperor's conscience',[3]

---

[1] Euseb. *Vita*, iv. 24. For this interpretation of the phrase, see Baynes, op. cit., footnote 70. Baynes takes it to be a Christian rendering of the pagan title *pontifex maximus*. So also Parker, op. cit., p. 301.   [2] *Vita*, ii. 71.

[3] Gibbon, op. cit., ch. xxvii, pp. 175–6.

as they also foreshadow the famous conflicts between popes and princes in medieval times. They are, in fact, landmarks in the growth of ecclesiastical imperialism.

Such developments however, were still, in the future. So far as concerns the immediate situation, the fact of prime significance was that contemporary Christian thinking seemed to provide a fresh vindication of imperial authority, assimilating it, if anything, to the theory of Hebrew kingship, although more than a century was still to pass before a ruler was to accept his crown at the hands of a priest.[1] Accordingly, the emperor was delivered of limitations from which none of his predecessors had been able to shake themselves free. Sovereign by the grace of God, he could without hesitation develop a dynastic policy which satisfied at once his personal ambition and the inclination of the troops who demanded for their rulers 'the sons of Constantine and no others'. At the same time, he secured fresh warrant for the idea of political action, especially as regards the use of law for purposes of reform; his reign, indeed, was to introduce a period of unparalleled legislative activity. These two notions provide the clue necessary to an understanding of movements within the Christian empire; political absolutism, social and moral renovation, these were the key-notes of the era initiated by Constantine.

Thus, for example, the Christian monarch experienced no sense of impropriety in appropriating to himself the regal observances which, under the Sacred College, had supplanted the forms of 'republican' liberty. Accordingly, he took over the recently elaborated court ceremonial, including such humiliating practices as that of prostration in the 'sacred' presence, together with the forms of adoration by which *divalia praecepta*, as imperial missives came to be described, were received by local dignitaries to the extremities of the empire. Such innovations, the product of Diocletian's aim to impart an odour of sanctity to imperial power, had registered the high-water mark of what is popularly described as Orientalism within the Roman world. Under the Christian empire they were accepted in a qualified but still somewhat ambiguous sense; as may be seen, e.g., from the laboured efforts of the Code to discriminate between divine worship and veneration of the imperial portraits.[2] Thus, while adopting the diadem and jewelled robes instituted by his im-

---

[1] Bury, *Selected Essays*, p. 104.   [2] *Cod. Theod.* xv. 4. 1. (425).

mediate predecessors, Constantine also assumed the titles—
pius, felix, invictus[1]—conventional to them, albeit such epithets
were more becoming to pagans than to an adherent of Christ.

Still other features survived, like débris, within the Lower
Empire, to mark the level reached by Orientalism at its height
and to impart to Byzantine majesty its specific character as
the intermediary between East and West. Of this, illustration
may be found in the elaboration of palace life, with its throngs
of barbers, cooks, grooms, and eunuchs whose numbers were
to reach scandalous proportions under Constantius II.[2] It may
be seen also in the unabashed dynasticism which, upon the
accession of the sons of Constantine, was to occasion a blood-
bath unprecedented in Roman annals—the wholesale liquidation of potential rivals from which but two youths of the blood
royal escaped alive. This dynasticism was presently to assume
bizarre forms, as when, in the presence of the troops, Valentinian I solemnly conferred the purple upon his son Gratian, at
that time a child of eight; thereby setting an example for the
action of Theodosius in entrusting the welfare of the empire to
the nominal charge of two adolescents, the one a sluggard, the
other a half-wit. It was signalized, also, by the use of marriage
connexions for the purpose of consolidating imperial claims
when, for instance, Gratian espoused the granddaughter of
Constantine in order to acquire rights hereditary to the Second
Flavian house. The system was finally to place the effective
administration of the empire in the hands of females; the later
history of the Theodosian dynasty revolves largely about the
lives of Placidia and Pulcheria, the first actual empresses of
Rome.

Notwithstanding such innovations, however, *Romanitas* did
not wholly lose its ancient character. Thus, in the intervals
when dynasticism failed, the time-honoured expedients of
military election and co-optation were invoked to supply its
deficiencies; and the Church, regardless of the merely natural
circumstances which elevated men to the purple, gave its blessing to a Valentinian or a Theodosius, as it had already done
to a Constantine. Moreover, fourth-century law, which continued to evolve as a legacy from the past, was, to a very considerable degree, stamped with the impress of the traditional
vetus ius. Apart from such survivals may be noted a fresh and

[1] Dessau, *I.L.S.* 702.   [2] Amm. xxii. 4. 1–5.

decidedly significant development, viz. the control exercised over imperial policy by the Christian Church. This showed itself in two ways: (1) through the action of ecclesiastical councils which, in a sense, functioned as parliaments embodying the philosophic, if not the political, wisdom of the empire, (2) through the mobilization of enlightened opinion in support of Christian principles by individual leaders such as Athanasius and Ambrose. The signed, public protest against Constantius, addressed to him by the Catholic community of Alexandria 'for the salvation of his immortal soul',[1] is a document unique in the history of antiquity. These considerations suggest that, despite all accretions, the Roman empire was now, as always, like nothing so much as itself.

Consolidation of sovereign power in the hands of Constantine enabled him to proceed with a further organization of public life along lines determined by recent experience and, to a considerable extent, embodied in the scheme of Diocletian; and, whether or not these emperors were conscious of the fact, their efforts resulted in an articulation of functions within the body politic, strongly suggestive of Platonic ideals of order and discipline (classical εὐνομία). Thus, for the purposes of civil administration, Constantine accepted the morselization of provinces devised by his predecessor, and erected therein a hierarchy of offices culminating in the four great praetorian prefectures or vice-royalties with final jurisdiction, a process which could hardly have been completed until after the fall of Licinius in the year 324; while he recognized the exceptional position of the two imperial capitals (Old and New Rome) by segregating them under the jurisdiction of the two urban prefects. Besides this, he took over and perfected the existing headquarters' system, civil and military, with its immense bureaux or departments.[2] He made his contribution, also, to the formidable array of titles which served at once to identify and distinguish various grades within the imperial *militia*, by the invention of the new patriciate.[3] Thus provided with a full equipment of public services, controlled and directed by leadership which, if we may accept its repeated professions, was

[1] Athanasius, *Hist. Arian.* 81.
[2] *Cod. Theod.* xi. 30. 16; cf. i. 5. 1–3 and 16. 1–6.
[3] The details are carefully summarized by Parker, op. cit., part v, ch. iv, p. 262 foll.

inspired with the one object of furthering Christian ideals, the Constantinian system presents an impressive spectacle. The question arises: What promise did it offer of a genuine renaissance?

To answer this question it is necessary to consult the work of contemporary representatives of Christian thought. In this connexion we have already had occasion to refer to the hopes and expectations cherished by Eusebius of Caesarea. Turning to the West, we are confronted in the first instance with the figure of Arnobius Afer.[1] In Arnobius, however, we shall find but little that is useful for our purpose. His preoccupation with narrowly theological issues stamps him as belonging to the earlier secessionist tradition. The feebleness with which he handles those issues testifies to what we have elsewhere[2] noted as the intellectual weakness of secessionist thought. The case is different, however, with Arnobius' fellow-countryman, Lucius Caecilius Firmianus Lactantius. The leading contemporary exponent of Latin letters, tutor to Crispus, the emperor's eldest son, Lactantius deserves, in much more than a purely verbal sense, to be called 'the Christian Cicero'. And, in his *Divine Institutes*, his object was precisely analogous to that of Cicero in his generation; the work was intended to serve as a *De Officiis* for the New Republic. From this standpoint, it merits the close attention of those who desire a clue to the spirit of the Constantinian age.

Dedicated to the emperor himself, the *Institutes* begin with an attempt to vindicate belief in divine providence, proofs of which are drawn from the two sources of reason and authority. On the side of reason, the argument consists largely of commonplaces lifted from Cicero and the Stoics; they serve merely to indicate the affiliations between Christianity and classical idealism as against the materialism of Epicurus and Lucretius. With respect to authority, it may be noted that Lactantius, in a spirit not unlike that of Constantine himself, cites indiscriminately texts from Holy Writ and from pagan seers, poets, and philosophers; utterances of Orpheus, the Sibyl, Hermes Trismegistus, Vergil and Ovid, Thales, Aristotle and Cicero being quoted alongside passages from the Hebrew Scriptures in support of the belief.

[1] Author of seven books *Adversus Gentes*: Migne, *Patr. Lat.* vol. v.
[2] See pp. 230–1 below.

Passing over his account of sin and error, the origin of which he ascribes to the insidious wiles of the devil suborning the fallen angels to his will,[1] we may pause to examine the attitude of Lactantius to classical philosophy. This he denounces on the double ground that it possesses no insight into divine truth, and that it is without power to reform character (*non abscindit vitia, sed abscondit*). Accordingly, it has become involved in the vain search for a purely human justice, exhausting itself in elaborate schemes of social reconstruction which serve only to provoke violent repercussions from outraged nature. The author thus assails Platonic communism, and maintains that genuine equality depends upon the suppression of selfish pride and arrogance rather than any mechanical rearrangement of material goods. It is therefore to be realized, he argues, only with the diffusion of a new sense of values inspired by true religion.[2] In the same spirit he decries as madness the remark of Zeno that pity is a disease; it is, in fact, a manifestation of *humanitas* or fraternity, the sentiment which alone makes possible co-operation among men. What Lactantius thus discovers in Classicism is a dread of the instinctive affections; which, in consequence, it tends to thwart or pervert. This he traces to an initial error, the 'separation of reason from faith'. The fruits of that error he sees in 'philosophy fumbling towards a false or imperfect religion, rather than true religion giving rise to its own characteristic philosophy'.

The vanity of philosophy, declares Lactantius, is proved by the fact that its history has been one of perpetual disagreement. But the opposite may be said of a wisdom which grows out of religion, a wisdom which alone discloses the truth regarding human nature. To apprehend this truth is to see at once that men are 'social and communal animals', intended, as such, to live in peace and amity with one another.[3] From this standpoint the

[1] *Divin. Instit.* ii. 9 and 15 and *Epit.* 27–8. Cumont, *R. O*[4]., p. 283, n. 71, points out the approximation of this doctrine of evil to Mithraic and Manichean dualism.

[2] *Divin. Instit.* iii. 22: 'non rerum fragilium sed mentium debet esse communitas.'

[3] *Epit.* 34: '(homo) animal sociale atque commune. ferae ad saevitiam gignuntur; aliter enim nequeunt quam praeda et sanguine victitare . . .; nihilominus generis sui animalibus parcunt. . . . quanto magis hominem, qui cum homine et commercio linguae et communione sensus copulatus est, parcere homini oportet, eumque diligere!' This looks like a deliberate modification of the Aristotelian formula ἄνθρωπος πολιτικὸν ζῷον. (The *Epitome* is thought to have been made by Lactantius himself, Duchesne, op. cit. ii,[4] p. 53.)

author scornfully dismisses the theories of association proposed by Classicism, whether along materialistic or along idealistic lines.[1] It is, he thinks, quite unworthy of human intelligence to suppose that the vast network of human relationships could ever have been created by the mere pressure of physical necessity; on the other hand, the notion of a contract is gratuitous, since this presupposes that the elements of which society is constituted are originally discrete. Whereas, in point of fact, all men are sons of God, and this is the only conceivable basis for the conclusion that they are all brothers. On the acceptance of this truth depends the possibility of realizing a genuinely co-operative commonwealth, a society of mutual aid (*congregatio hominum humanitatis causa*). To the question how this possibility may be realized, Lactantius addresses himself in his three concluding books.

Of these books, not the least significant is that on *Justice* (Bk. v). For Lactantius, true or 'human' justice resolves itself into philanthropy or love of one's fellow men. As such, it contains two elements which, though inseparable, may be distinguished as *pietas* and *aequitas*. *Pietas* he defines as devotion to God; its function is to supply a universal basis for what may be called the collectivist attitude of mind. The latter is the sense which, by prompting men to accept their neighbours as 'equals', brings human relations within the scope of the golden rule.[2] Historically speaking, the inability of Classicism to achieve true justice had been the result of a failure to appreciate the real character of these principles. Thus Rome, for example, had misconstrued the nature of *pietas* by identifying it with the economico-political idea. *Pius est qui patrem dilexit*, she declared; thereby setting up a complex of merely secular loyalties as a substitute for loyalty to the one true God. Accordingly, while devoting herself to the inculcation of the so-called civic virtues, she lost sight of the supreme virtue apart from which the others are, in the last analysis, negligible. In this respect, her failure, he argues, is the failure of Classicism generally. Indeed, without God, there can be no sound basis for idealism of any kind, and it is quite impossible to overthrow the argument of Carneades. *Honores, purpurae, fasces*, the various objects of secular ambition

---

[1] *Divin. Inst.* vi. 10.
[2] Ibid. v. 15; *Epit.* 60: 'omne fundamentum aequitatis est illud, ut ne facias ulli quod pati nolis, sed alterius animum de tuo metiaris.'

are, despite Plato, the reward not of justice but of injustice in this world.

Lactantius then goes on to enunciate certain interesting conclusions. In the first place he condemns the power- or class-state, based on *inaequalitas*, for a failure to bring to mankind the 'liberation' which it promises. He traces the genesis of the political order to a hypertrophy of the acquisitive instinct which, he asserts, transforms the natural collectivism of primitive or Saturnian society into the economic individualism typical of the reign of Jove. This economic individualism gives rise to conflict within 'political' society, for Jove is a tyrant and so are his followers. Secondly, he denounces the process of competitive imperialism which results from the ambition of power-states to achieve their ends at the expense of their neighbours. What, he asks, is the advantage of my country but the disadvantage of yours? To pursue such advantage is to shatter the bond of fraternity (*vinculum humanitatis*) and to disrupt the unity of the human race (*discidium aut diremptio generis humani*). Finally, as an alternative to this suicidal activity, he outlines the elements of a programme of reconstruction in which emphasis is laid on the family as the focal point of associational life. Thus conceived, however, the family is no longer that of pagan Rome, a creature of the state, deriving its constitution from law and reflecting the paramount demands of the economico-political order. It is pre-eminently a natural association, based on consanguinity and devotion to common ideals, rather than on property—the real seed-bed of the social virtues, the most powerful instrument available for the sublimation of the passions, which it thus seeks, not to eradicate, but to subordinate to the true end of life. With Lactantius we are far removed from the sense of terror with which Tertullian envisaged woman as the 'gateway to perdition', while the monastic ideal of celibacy lies still largely in the future.

Thus to revise and, at the same time, to enhance the role of the family is to lay foundations for what, to the author, is a society corresponding to the true demands of human nature, 'natura hominum solitudines fugiens et communionis et societatis appetens'. In this society men will discover themselves in the peaceful exchange of reciprocal services as determined by reciprocal needs. These needs, moreover, are primarily spiritual; the only criterion of 'duties' in the New Republic is that which helps to save the soul (*omne officium solius animae con-servatione metimur*).

In this ideal there is embodied the vision of life as a continuous process of self-development which presupposes, in all external relationships, a respect for humanity such as had been but imperfectly realized in the classical commonwealth. This, thinks Lactantius, is the *ratio mundi*, the law of nature which he identifies with the law of God—the principle to which man must subscribe if he is to achieve felicity and to realize his ultimate destiny as a *caeleste ac divinum animal*. For that, in the last analysis, is precisely what he is.

To accept these propositions is to see the *polis* and political machinery in a fresh light. In the New Republic the primary object will be to secure, to all alike, liberty to profess Christianity and to live the Christian life. This postulates freedom for the Church, a freedom which will be extended to non-believers, since by its very nature religion is something which cannot be imposed upon the mind by force (*religio cogi non potest*). At the same time men will be at liberty to practise, without impediment, such characteristically Christian virtues as hospitality, the redemption of captives, defence of widows, care of the sick, burial of strangers and paupers. But, in view of the continued prevalence of vice and ignorance, there will still be need for the intervention of positive law, and this will constitute a reason for the survival of the state. In the new order, however, *Romanitas* will find justification only as it ministers to the superior demands of *humanitas*. And, as the principles of *humanitas* gradually win acceptance, the state may be expected to fade into a classless, non-coercive society governed solely by the law of love.

The faith of Lactantius has been described as 'of a moral rather than a mysterious cast';[1] and in this fact we may perhaps discover the explanation of his shortcomings as an exponent of Christian social theory. What is utterly missing from his teaching is any sense of what was implied in the doctrine of original sin. We thus find him asserting with Cicero and the Stoics the essential virtue of the natural man.[2] As a consequence he is driven to assume that the ἁμαρτία of mankind lies in 'vice'; and this he identifies with an abnormal development of the passions,

---

[1] By Gibbon, op. cit., ch. xx, p. 307, n. 57; see below, p. 219.
[2] *Divin. Inst.* v. 5, 6, and 7.

especially cupidity (the root of all evil), which have entrenched themselves in civil society. Salvation thus resolves itself simply into a question of releasing the fundamentally sound affections; and this is to be effected by a restoration to the emotions and sentiments of the primacy which Classicism had conceded to the mind—a transfer of authority, so to speak, from the practical reason of Aristotle to the 'love and pity' of Christ. In this doctrine nothing in reality is added to the classical concept of nature, nor are any of its characteristic difficulties resolved. Moreover, the emancipation proposed is in all respects analogous to that offered by Classicism itself, although the direction indicated is precisely the reverse. To Lactantius, however, this is the sum and substance of the Evangel; and it exhausts the meaning of the Christian revolution.

Accordingly it is evident that the author fails to rise to the height of his argument. The brand of Christianity which he expounds is relatively innocuous in itself and hardly likely to prejudice the existing economic and political structure. For, while he pays lip-service to 'Christian ideals', he sees in them merely a 'better way' of life, which will become a reality as men's eyes are gradually opened to the fatal limitations of their narrowly prudential (economico-political) outlook. From this point of view, the 'viciousness' of human nature lies simply in a kind of intellectual myopia; and the purpose of the Evangel is fulfilled if it serves merely to enlighten and inspire. Superficial even by classical standards, this gospel points to nothing but a progressive amelioration of conditions not unlike the Utopia prophesied centuries before by Vergil, a new era of softer manners in which the lion is to lie down with the lamb. At the same time, it subtly defers to an indefinite future its promise of an earthly millennium, resting its real hopes meanwhile upon the state. And, by thus delivering the future of Christianity into the hands of the new Machiavelli, it clearly forecasts that era of 'godly and righteous' legislation, of generous but not excessive reform, which was to be the net contribution of Constantinianism to the Kingdom of God. Under this dispensation, the empire was presently to experience an application of that peculiar mixture of pagan humanitarianism and Christian sentiment which goes by the name of Christian socialism, a compound in which the real virtues of either element are largely neutralized by the other. From the fate which overtook this liberal-social-democratic programme, it is possible to forecast the probable outcome of analogous movements in modern times.

To Constantine himself is credited the observation that a changed religion involves a changed social order;[1] and the Roman world, whether for the moment dazzled by the prestige of the imperial physician or, perhaps, because of its sickness ready for the most desperate expedient, appears to have accepted his ministrations without much visible indication of the scepticism which they deserved. Those ministrations consisted of carefully regulated doses of the highly volatile compound just described—a mixture dangerous if prescribed in quantity but otherwise calculated to rejuvenate the body politic by 'humanizing' (in the Lactantian sense) the relations of men and women. This purpose is indicated in various features of the imperial reform programme, a study of which reveals a striking correspondence between the notions of Christianity entertained by emperor and sophist. Needless to say, the existence of such a correspondence does not imply any necessary dependence of the one upon the other, although it does most emphatically suggest that both were representative products of the mentality prevalent in court circles at the time.

Considerations of space make it impossible to examine in detail the whole of Constantine's legislative and political activity; and we must be satisfied merely with an attempt to illustrate its general spirit and purpose. If this be done, it will become evident that the pledge of official neutrality contained in the Edict of Milan must not be taken to imply any kind of indifference, on the part of administration, towards questions of religion. As a matter of fact the Constantinian policy embraced two parallel but distinct objects, undertaken tentatively at first but pursued with increasing energy and assurance towards the end, especially after the fall of Licinius had removed the last serious obstacle from the path. These objects may be described as follows:

(1) to create a world fit for Christians to live in;
(2) to make the world safe for Christianity.

The former represents the attitude of the emperor to individual believers; it finds expression in an extensive scheme of moral and social reform designed to satisfy their demands and to pro-

[1] Euseb. *Vita*, ii. 65.

mote their interests. The latter reflects his views regarding the Church as an institution, and it manifests itself in the project of a Christian establishment conceived more or less along the lines of existing pagan state-cults.

The social legislation of Constantine has been described as a 'mitigation of the savage traditions of Roman law'. This, to put it mildly, is a very questionable statement, for the temper at least of classical jurisprudence was anything but savage; granted the spiritual limitations of its authors, it was essentially equitable and humane. But, as it gradually attained those qualities, it continued to exhibit a masculinity in sharp contrast with the emotionalism and sentimentality which distinguished the legislation of the New Republic and which, under Arcadius and Honorius, was to culminate in a kind of hysteria, almost the direct antithesis of the Antonine spirit. With Constantine, however, such manifestations were kept in strict subordination to the dominant political motive. Thus, if there was any single thing to which Christian social theory pointed, it was to a complete reconstitution of the *familia* or household as conceived by Roman pagan law—an institution the very existence of which was rooted in notions of property and, despite ameliorations introduced by successive pagan emperors, still bound in strict subjection to the almost despotic sway of the *paterfamilias*, armed with his traditional powers of domestic discipline. One result of this was to condemn the female of imperial society to the vain pursuits of personal adornment and to deny her access to any serious or worth-while form of activity.[1]

Constantine's reforms were, however, limited to a certain tenderness towards dependants, women, children, and slaves. Women, for example, were no longer to be compelled to undergo trial in the public courts,[2] widows and orphans were to have special consideration at the hands of the judiciary and not to be forced to travel long distances for hearings. The hardships of slavery were mitigated by a law which forbade the separation by sale of man and wife;[3] and the practice of manumission was encouraged, especially if it took place in church.[4] On the other hand, any one finding an exposed infant was permitted to retain it to the exclusion of all claims on the part of

---

[1] Val. Max. ix. 1. 3: '⟨feminas⟩ imbecillitas mentis et graviorum operum negata affectatio omne studium ad curiosiorem sui cultum hortatur conferre.'
[2] *Cod. Theod.* i. 22. 1. [3] ii. 25. 1. [4] iv. 7. 1.

those who had abandoned it;[1] although a somewhat earlier statute[2] had enacted that individuals buying or rearing such infants whom they found were to enjoy *dominica potestas* over them, provided always that the original owner might recover possession, should he so desire, by defraying the cost of their upbringing or by handing over for them a slave of equal value. Constantine also enacted[3] that the subsequent marriage of parents rendered legitimate offspring born to them out of wedlock. An early measure[4] repudiates as abhorrent to the spirit of the age the practice of destroying or selling into slavery or prostitution superfluous and unwanted children, and seeks to prevent this by a revival of the Antonine *alimentaria*, in the form of food and clothing to be drawn by indigent parents from the public stores. In other respects, also, the emperor tried to maintain the cohesion of the family, especially by prohibiting divorce except on statutory grounds; in the case of a wife, adultery, poisoning, or procuring, in that of a husband, assassination, poisoning, and grave-robbing; to the specific exclusion of 'frivolous pretexts' such as drunkenness, gambling, and infidelity. In this we may perceive the merely tendentious character of Constantine's legislation; since, although he concedes to a wife as well as a husband the right of entering suit, he still preserves a double standard of morality; and, for any repudiation on other than statutory grounds, he penalizes the woman by deportation and the loss of dower rights, while merely condemning the man to a total restitution of dowry and forbidding him to remarry.[5]

The introduction of such measures undoubtedly helped to impart what may be called a new complexion to the Roman family. By that very fact, however, it serves to emphasize the much more fundamental truth that, in his general legislation, Constantine neither aimed at nor achieved any radical alteration in the traditional constitution of imperial society. Originating out of the primitive peasant community and rising to full stature upon its ruins, that society was already by Cicero's time assuming the characteristic forms of a cosmopolitan class-state; and, as such, it had been consolidated under the principate of

[1] v. 9. 1 (331). [2] v. 10. 1 (329).
[3] *Cod. Iust.* v. 27. 5; cf. *Cod. Theod.* iv. 6. 3; with, however, characteristic qualifications, such as that the concubine must be of free birth.
[4] *Cod. Theod.* xi. 27. 1 (315) and 2 (322).
[5] iii. 16. 1.

Augustus. To the last centuries of the republic may thus be traced the beginnings of a scheme of ceremonious etiquette to govern social relationships which was to be so elaborated during the lower empire and which is often ascribed to the orientalism of the Sacred Monarchy. In the evolution of imperial society, the drift throughout the third century had been towards a strongly marked division of functions, based upon occupational lines; and, by fixing and consecrating these changes, Diocletian had succeeded in giving to this society something of the character of a system of castes, revealing in this, as in other respects, the nemesis of the classical *polis*.

From this system the only possible escape, humanly speaking, lay in a revolutionary programme of emancipation of which neither the thought nor inclination of Constantine was in the slightest degree capable. We have already noted how the Constantinian family tradition looked back to a more flexible, though still strictly *bourgeois*, type of society; and how, at the earliest stage of his public career, the emperor had somehow managed to confuse this Ciceronian paradise with the real demands of the City of God. Once in power, however, he seems to have abandoned any such notion; for he maintained in all its rigour the legal framework of the class-society. This is indicated by his attitude both to persons and to property; as the following illustrations will perhaps serve to demonstrate.

It has just been explained how, in his attitude to the Roman household, the sentimentalism of Constantine dictated a certain tenderness towards the hapless victims of paternal despotism. This tenderness, however, did not prevent him from forbidding, under the most stringent penalties, voluntary connexions between free women and slaves;[1] while a subsequent enactment[2] prohibits the secret cohabitation of a free woman with her own slave under pain of capital punishment and loss of testability; her servants in any such case being encouraged to inform against their mistress with the promise of freedom if they prove the charge. At the same time Constantine reasserted the classical principle that the offspring of slave women by free men should follow the maternal condition.[3] With similar inconsistency he revoked the Augustan laws which laid disabilities on the celibate and the childless, while exempting their estates from the special death-duties previously levied upon them. He also made such

---

[1] *Cod. Theod.* iv. 12. 1 (314).   [2] ix. 9. 1 (326).   [3] iv. 8. 4 and 7; xii. 1. 6.

persons capable of receiving legacies on the same terms as others.[1]
This measure can hardly be explained except as the result of a
desire to promote the worldly interests of the clergy.

In his attitude to property rights Constantine did not hesitate
to sanction the contesting of wills by brothers-german of the
testator if the beneficiaries were prostitutes, bastards, or stage-
players.[2] On the other hand, he displayed the highest respect
for such rights even when they conflicted with what might well
be regarded as the rights of common humanity. Thus runaway
slaves, if apprehended, were once more to be reduced to a
servile condition.[3] Corporal punishment of slaves by their
owners, although brought under government regulation, was
still permitted. Thus[4] a master was authorized to flog, stone, or
imprison a slave for purposes of correction; in the event of the
slave's death from such treatment, the master might be charged
with homicide only if it could be shown that he had deliberately
taken the life of his victim. At the same time it was enacted that
freedmen who displayed an attitude of pride or haughtiness
might be haled back to servitude by their former masters.[5]

The Christian fathers denounced with almost uniform consistency and no little vigour the evils of usury. Ambrose in
particular is loud in his protests against the instinct of acquisition, 'the love of money which sinks in and dries up every kindly
impulse'.[6] Constantine merely fixed the annual rate of interest
at 12 per cent, the ancient limit provided by the XII Tables.[7]
Under Augustus Caesar good times and security had done
better, for the rate at that time had fallen to the unprecedented
level of 4 per cent.

These examples must suffice to illustrate the attitude of Constantine to the social system, the future of which he helped to
fix by the long series of *constitutiones* recorded especially in books
xii and xiii of the *Codex Theodosianus*. By these measures he promoted the tendency towards social evolution upon an occupational basis; in each and every case seeking to attach to the
legal person fixed obligations commensurate with the privileges
to which his status in the community entitled him; and, at
the same time, scattering immunities and exemptions with
a generous hand among favoured groups whose services he

---

[1] viii. 16. 1 (320).   [2] ii. 19. 1.   [3] v. 17. 1.
[4] ix. 12. 1 and 2 (319 and 326).   [5] iv. 10. 1.
[6] Amb. *De Offic.* i, ch. 49; iii, chs. 8 and 9.   [7] *Cod. Theod.* ii. 33. 1.

regarded as peculiarly valuable to the régime.[1] In these circumstances it is not surprising that 'Dii te nobis servent: vestra salus nostra salus' should have been the cry of his officers and veterans (A.D. 320). But, under the Constantinian system, no element within the community was to receive more detailed or more invidious attention than the wretched *bourgeoisie* which, in happier days, had been described as the bone and sinew of the republic. If Constantine ever really sympathized with their cause, he was now shamelessly to betray it in favour of the new orders whose interests had since become paramount with him. For, while officials of the imperial service (military, civil, and ecclesiastical) were accorded one privilege after another, the various devices contrived by recent tyranny were applied in wholesale fashion in order to extract revenue from the one great source available, viz. the land. Accordingly, the dreaded indictions of Diocletian and Maximian were continued, without appreciable change either of spirit or method.

In this programme of systematic and unremitting oppression, the decurions or local aristocracies were marked out as chief victims. Over and above their individual burdens, these men were saddled with a collective responsibility for any default within their corporations and actually compelled to assume the fiscal obligations attached to abandoned or worn-out land while, at the same time, they were prohibited under increasingly savage penalties from any attempt to evade their fate by escaping into the ranks of the army or the Church.[2] In this sense Constantine made himself a contributing agent to the fiscal grief (*tributaria sollicitudo*) which, by paralysing energy and initiative and by quenching the flickering embers of hope, helped to extinguish the last sparks of patriotic feeling among Roman citizens throughout, at least, the western provinces of the empire. At the same time it should be pointed out that this emperor, if not his successors, was still dimly conscious of rights possessed by the delinquent taxpayer; for, in a lengthy edict addressed directly to the people,[3] he insisted that imprisonment, chains, and the leaded lash were punishments properly reserved for convicts, and that judges, whether from perversity or in

[1] *Cod. Theod.* vi. 35. 3 (the *palatini*, or imperial military police); vii. 20. 1–5 (veterans); xiii. 3. 1–3 (physicians, teachers, and professors); xii. 5. 2 (pagan priests); xvi. 2. 1–7 (the clergy), 8. 2–4 (rabbis). vii. 21. 1 indicates how he tried to safeguard privileges accorded to the military from the fraudulent pretensions of civilians.　　　[2] xii. 1. 1–22; xvi. 2. 3, &c.　　　[3] xi. 7. 3 (320).

anger, must not resort to such measures in order to exact sums due from fiscal debtors, against whom it was sufficient to distrain on the property and, in the event of a persistent refusal to pay, to sell it for taxes due.[1]

In his frantic pursuit of revenue Constantine did not confine his attention to the land, but instituted other forms of taxation such, for example, as the general sales tax (*lustratio* or *auri lustralis collatio*) imposed on business,[2] the tax on personal income extracted from imperial senators, the many forms of service attached to occupations such as transportation by land or sea, baking and milling, &c.; the mere existence of which goes to show that the government was deeply committed to the maintenance of the existing social structure, if only for the sake of revenue to be derived therefrom. Any deliberate changes must therefore be ascribed to social and religious rather than to economic considerations, as, for example, the illogical privileges extended to Catholics as opposed to Jews, pagans, and heretics, whose condition was to become progressively worse with the lapse of time.[3]

It is, perhaps, within the field of criminal law and procedure that the distinctive characteristics of the new régime most clearly emerge. In criminal jurisdiction the most remarkable features are the frequency of capital punishment, often of a peculiarly brutal character, the abolition of traditional offences and penalties and the introduction of new ones, the use of legislation to improve moral and social conditions, with its inevitable concomitant, a growing confusion between the notions of sin and crime. Among the more significant innovations were[4] an ineffective prohibition of gladiatorial exhibitions and the abolition of crucifixion as a form of punishment, no doubt out of respect for the memory of Christ (315). With this tasteless expression of Christian sentiment may be compared the enactment which forbade the branding of human beings on the face 'because the face is made in the image of God', while slaves, criminals, and even conscripts continued to be branded on other parts of the body.[5] And, although bloody spectacles were denounced as out of keeping with the spirit of the times, it was provided, as an alternative, that convicts might be consigned

[1] xi. 7. 4 (327).
[2] Zosimus, ii. 38; *Cod. Theod.* xiii. 1. 1, as renewed under Constantius in 356.
[3] xvi. 8. 1–9.   [4] xv. 12. 1 (325).   [5] ix. 40. 2.

to the living death of the mines 'in order to work off their penalties without loss of blood'.[1] Adultery on the part of an *uxor tabernarii* was visited with severe punishment no less as an offence against the contractual rights of the husband than as a sin against the Christian concept of the family;[2] just as an attempt was made to enforce the discharge of filial obligations, the ancient Roman *pietas* no longer being adequate to sustain them.[3] In a similar spirit, elopement was included within the number of statutory offences and classified as rape.[4] With respect to blasphemy, the common-sense republicanism of Tiberius Caesar had prompted the sentiment *deorum iniuriae dis curae*. Constantine, however, undertook to support the prestige of deity by a law which forbade blasphemous utterances under pain of a fine of one-half one's goods. But his obvious lack of any sense of the limitations of law is most of all apparent when, so to speak, he enters the pulpit, to fulminate in terms strange and foreign to classical jurisprudence against evidences of bad faith in buying or selling,[5] against the abuse of power and money to buy acquittals from the courts, against the increase of official corruption and rascality.[6] In view of these considerations one ceases to be surprised at the preference manifested in favour of the newly established episcopal courts in which, if contemporary evidence may be trusted, the litigant might reasonably expect to receive cheap, swift, and even-handed justice.[7]

In seeking to explain why the new religion failed to check the process of social decay which was demoralizing and degrading the middle classes while, at the same time, it transformed the free peasant into a serf, a jurist[8] declares that, though Christianity came to proclaim the gospel to the masses, it arrived too late to effect any decisive reform in existing economic conditions. But, quite apart from the assumption that Christianity embodies a ready-made system of enlightened economics, this statement appears to lay altogether too heavy a burden upon the *Zeitgeist*. It thus tends to exonerate Constantine and his associates from their share of responsibility for evils which developed with such progressive rapidity during the reign. As we have tried to show, there was hardly an element in the thinking of these

---

[1] xv. 12. 1.   [2] ix. 7. 1.   [3] ii. 19. 2.   [4] ix. 24. 1.   [5] iii. 1. 1.

[6] i. 16. 7: 'cessent iam nunc rapaces officialium manus, cessent, inquam; nam nisi moniti cessaverint, gladiis praecidentur.'

[7] i. 27. 1 (318); cf. *Constitutiones Sirmondianae* (333).

[8] Sohm, op. cit., introd., p. 45.

men which pointed to a genuine amelioration of conditions; while, on the other hand, there were many which tended to aggravate those very conditions, and thus to accelerate the process of decay.

To say this is not to forget the existence of that pro-*bourgeois* sentiment with which the emperor had started but which, apart from the fact that it may still have possessed a certain vitality in the Gallic provinces, was otherwise a mere survival from an obsolete and discredited past. In the career of Constantine the function of that sentiment was to provide an initial impulse. As a part of the opposition which he mobilized against the tyranny of the Sacred College, it helped to provide him with the support he needed to carry him to victory in the struggle for domination and power which culminated in 313, the year of his conversion. Thereafter it was gradually to be discarded in favour of other and politically more valuable elements of the Constantinian programme.

What those elements were, the Roman world was presently to discover. The indemnification of Christian communities for material losses suffered during the persecutions was, no doubt, implied in the terms of the Edict of Milan; this, however, could hardly be said of measures by which the Christian clergy were exempted from all civil and personal obligations.[1] Repeal of the Augustan laws against celibacy, and the concession to ecclesiastics of normal inheritance rights, were succeeded by an enactment in virtue of which the Church, as a corporation, was permitted to accept gifts and legacies.[2] By such measures the emperor and the clergy acquired a common benefit and achieved a common interest. This, however, was not to be shared by the unhappy decurions who, already in 320, were sternly forbidden to aspire to holy orders and informed, in so many words, that their role within the new society was to provide the sinews of war.[3] To the militarized bureaucracy which he had inherited from Diocletian, Constantine thus added the powerful ecclesiastical interest as a second dominant partner in the new régime.

The hopes entertained of this combination were, however, somewhat beclouded through the outbreak in Africa of the

[1] *Cod. Theod.* xvi. 2. 2 (319); cf. Euseb. *H.E.* x. 7.
[2] *Cod. Theod.* xvi. 2. 4 (321).
[3] xvi. 2. 3: 'decurionem . . . instructum idoneis facultatibus atque obeundis publicis muneribus opportunum . . . civilibus obsequiis inservire.'

so-called Donatist schism (A.D. 313). The immediate cause of this schism was, of course, the question whether those who had been branded as 'traitors' during the persecutions should be eligible for reinstatement in the sacerdotal office. And, in the doubts expressed as to the validity of sacraments administered by such persons, there was an unmistakable echo of the 'spiritualism' of Tertullian; as, in the cry against imperial interference, there was also an echo of his question: What has the emperor to do with the Church? (*quid est imperatori cum ecclesia?*). The failure of an African synod to reach a settlement led to an appeal to the emperor, as a consequence of which the issue was brought to trial before ecclesiastical boards successively convoked at Rome and Arles and, finally, before Constantine himself at Rome (316). Whereupon the emperor, no doubt as the self-appointed 'overseer of those outside', undertook to implement the verdict of the courts. Imperial commissioners, variously described as 'servants of God' and 'two wild beasts', were dispatched to Africa. These men rashly undertook first to bribe, then to coerce the dissentients. The former policy involved the state in the heavy expense of endowing the Catholic Church in Africa, Numidia, and Mauretania;[1] the latter had a still more sinister outcome, for it was the occasion of a prolonged and disastrous civil and class war.

In this conflict the antagonists were, on the one side, the Catholic community backed by the imperial troops; on the other, what has been described as the 'strength and scandal' of the Donatist faction—a left wing made up of communist-anarchist-millennialist fanatics known as the *Circumcelliones* or Vagabonds. Gathering in irregular bands on the barren uplands, and equipping themselves with heavy clubs called *Israelites*, they descended under the so-called *Captains of the Saints* upon the peaceful and industrious country-side; and their war-cry, *Laus Deo*, served to initiate a novel kind of revolt for which the traditional Roman peasant or servile wars afforded no precedent. More than six years of truceless fighting was insufficient to subdue their spirit and, in 320, Constantine admitted defeat by conceding liberty of conscience to the Donatists, who were destined to survive as an independent communion in Africa until the days of Augustine.

By these and similar developments, such as the enactment of

[1] Euseb. *H.E.* x. 6.

a Lord's Day Act (321),[1] it became apparent that the emperor was becoming deeply involved in a line of policy which was in flagrant contradiction to the spirit of official neutrality embodied in the Edict of Milan. This policy was presently to give rise to the second great crisis of his career, the break with Licinius and the subsequent destruction of Crispus, his eldest son. For, despite the evidence (contained on coins and inscriptions) of a desire to reassure his pagan subjects, despite his retention of pagan titles and of the traditional hocus-pocus of public divination, it was increasingly evident that the divorce between religion and politics contemplated in the Edict could hardly be maintained. In other words, Constantine's personal religion was rapidly becoming the religion of state. If this fact, in itself, were insufficient to explain the apostasy of Licinius, it would only be necessary to add the jealousy of a rival who saw his glory eclipsed, his equality undermined by Constantine's skilful manipulation of the growing ecclesiastical interest. Accordingly, in 323, Licinius, 'expelling the Christians from the palace', committed his future to the issue of war.[2] The last recruit had become the first renegade from the Constantinian new deal. The easy defeat of Licinius was followed, within two years, by the destruction of Crispus, the man who, in forcing the Dardanelles, had made that defeat possible. Absence of any real evidence connected with the trial and execution of the young prince, coupled with vague hints thrown out by the ecclesiastical historians of a sordid palace intrigue in which the Empress Fausta (Crispus' stepmother) was cast for the role of Potiphar's wife, lends support to the suggestion that the true motive of the murder was political. For such an act the Roman annals afforded a precedent in the myth of Brutus, who had slain his offspring for the good of the republic; but it is probable that Constantine, whose point of view was becoming more and more Hebraic, conceived of himself rather as an Abraham, prepared to sacrifice his first-born to the glory of the Lord.

Whatever the truth concealed in this obscure transaction, it is none the less apparent that, by triumphantly surmounting the crisis of 323–5, Constantine made possible the full development of a programme which was presently to give rise to the novel phenomenon of Caesaropapism. The pagan emperors had been traditionally devoted to self-advertisement, but it

---

[1] *Cod. Iust.* iii. 12. 2.　　　[2] Euseb. *H.E.* x. 8; *Vita*, i. 49–56 and ii. 1–18.

remained for the first Christian sovereign to discover a more
effective instrument of propaganda than any hitherto devised.
As the emperor himself became more and more the tool of
designing churchmen, the pulpits of the empire resounded with
fulsome adulation of the political saint whom it was not considered impious to designate as 'equal to the Apostles'. Even
Eusebius, who normally leads the chorus of praise, feels bound
at one point to sound a somewhat apologetic note. 'The most
conspicuous quality of Constantine', he declares, 'was that of
benevolence. On this account he was frequently imposed upon
by the violence of rapacious and unprincipled men who preyed
upon all classes of society alike, and by the scandalous hypocrisy
of those who wormed their way into the Church, assuming the
name, without the character, of Christians.'[1] It would be hard
to describe in more precise terms the characteristic features of
this last phase of Constantine's career.

Throughout this period the evidence points to a widespread
patronage of the Church, coupled with a subtle glorification of
the Church's patron.[2] An edict forbidding the discharge of
pagan sacrificial rites by imperial officials had the effect of
packing the administrative services, from the great praetorian
prefectures down to the government of the meanest province,
with nominal Christians. Wherever the plea of public interest
afforded ground for intervention, pagan cults were vigorously
suppressed; as, e.g., that of Aesculapius at Aegae for superstitious quackery, that of Venus (Astarte) at Heliopolis in
Phoenicia for temple prostitution and other vices.[3] In some
cases pagan temples were reconsecrated as Christian churches,
and new Christian foundations were set up with funds diverted
from the public account, especially to mark the site of martyr-
doms. On the occasion of Constantine's twentieth anniversary
the magnificent Church of the Holy Sepulchre was dedicated
at Jerusalem with elaborate pomp and ceremony; at the same
time, Jews who tried to rebuild the Temple had their ears cut
off and were flogged to death by the public executioner. In
order to maintain themselves and to raise money for charitable
purposes, the clergy had traditionally conducted small business

---

[1] *Vita*, iv. 54; cf. Zosimus, ii. 38.
[2] *Vita*, ii. 44–50 and iii. 1; details in part substantiated by surviving enactments in *Cod. Theod.*
[3] In this he appears to have done a good job. See Cumont, *R.O.*[4], p. 110, on
revolting features of the cult.

enterprises; but now, owing to the immense expansion of their revenues, they had evidently begun to invest on a considerable scale, and a canon of the Nicene Council [no. 17] threatened to unfrock any ecclesiastic found guilty of usury. The *Vicennalia* of Constantine, celebrated in 326, was marked by splendid donations everywhere to the churches. But the climax of his achievement was undoubtedly the building of New Rome, on a site long since marked out by nature but now, for the first time, fully exploited under the hand of the imperial magician (dedicated 11 May, 330). The new capital was adorned with venerable objects of art, such as the Delphian tripod, which were torn from the feeble communities of Greece; it was provided with a system of *annonae* similar to that which, since the days of the Gracchi, had made Old Rome the parasite of the world; in one respect only was it unique, for it was to be the wholly Christian capital of a prince devoted to the faith.[1]

Such measures, if completely successful, could have had but one result and that the utter sterilization of the Church which, under this régime, was obviously expected to confine itself to the preaching of innocuous 'Christian ideals', while it committed its destiny and that of the Roman world to the hands of its generous and powerful benefactor. The number and scope of his constitutions indicate only too clearly how far the emperor felt himself free to go within the ambit of official neutrality. For it should be remembered that, throughout, Christianity was merely Constantine's personal religion, as the *Labarum* was his personal standard. Nevertheless, with a characteristic disregard for the logic of the situation, he undertook the functions of a Christian *Pontifex Maximus*, a pagan title which he anomalously continued to hold—the part, in fact, which he had endeavoured to play in relation to the Donatist schism. With the rise of the Arian controversy, however, he was to be apprised of specific features in Christianity which distinguished it from any pagan cult, at the same time giving to it a peculiarly intractable character. These developments were to occur in connexion with the Council of Nicaea, the deliberations of which served to indicate that, in the organized Church, the empire was confronted not merely with a 'corporation', a creature of the state, but with a co-ordinate, if not superior, spiritual power.

[1] *Vita*, iii. 48 and 54; iv. 58–60.

Full realization of this truth was, no doubt, reserved for his successors; as for Constantine himself, when he heard of the issue raised by the Alexandrian presbyter, 'he fulminated like a powerful herald of God against intestine strife within the Church as more dangerous than any kind of war or conflict';[1] and, in pursuance of his settled policy, he convoked a representative ecclesiastical assembly to decide a question, the real meaning of which, according to his biographer, he only dimly apprehended. The general council thus assembled (A.D.325) was made up of no less than 318 bishops, and the emperor was heartened by the sight, not merely of representatives from all sections of the empire, but of delegates from Armenia and Scythia as well.[2] Thus, apart from the hypothetical primitive Council of Jerusalem, the Universal Church was now for the first time given a voice. In discussions lasting over three months, it laid down various canons to govern morals and discipline and, with but two or three dissenting votes, it carried the great doctrinal formulation to be known in history as the Nicene Creed, the fundamental law and charter of Trinitarian Christianity.[3]

This formulation was at once accepted by Constantine as a basis for spiritual unity within the empire. It was followed[4] by a characteristic *pronunciamiento* in which dissentients were denounced as evil and impious men, enemies of the truth, whose works were to be collected and destroyed. Thus began the burning of the books, especially those of Arius and his followers, a measure undertaken 'not merely that his depraved teaching might be utterly destroyed, but that not a single record of it should be left to posterity'; and the penalty for any one discovered in possession of a work written by Arius and refusing to burn it was that he should suffer death.

But, from the standpoint of Constantine, the establishment of ecclesiastical unity contained the promise of even more spectacular achievement, in the shape of an empire bigger and better than that of Augustus Caesar himself. For, in the evangelization of Germans and Orientals, the emperor discerned the beginning of a new and significant phase of inter-

---

[1] Euseb. *Vita*, ii. 61 foll.; iii. 12 and 21.
[2] For a contemporary description see *Vita*, iii. 7–22; other references in Athan. *De Decretis Nicaenis*.   [3] Details in Duchesne, ii⁴, pp. 144–53.
[4] Euseb. *Vita*, iii. 17–20, 63–6; Socr. *Hist. Eccles.* 1. 9.

national relationships, at one and the same time a justification of his notorious philo-Gothism and the basis for a fresh cosmopolitanism, to bear fruit in solidarity with barbarians everywhere beyond the ancient confines of *Romanitas*. He thus addressed a letter to King Sapor, proclaiming himself defender of the faithful, the enemy of tyrants and persecutors. 'I learn with satisfaction', he declares, 'that the best parts of Persia are full of Christians. These I commend to your humanity. Treat them kindly. For so you will do yourself and us an immense service.' In such communications the emperor envisaged himself as the sword of the Lord, assured of victory by the presence, within his lines, of the awe-inspiring *Labarum*, and of the famous *tabernaculum* or prayer-tent, the efficacy of which had been tested in the critical struggle with Licinius.[2] So far from implying any triumph for pacifism, they suggest the spirit of 'Christianity and 6 per cent', supposed to have characterized English imperialism during the nineteenth century. Nevertheless, they are significant as marking the origin of a new outlook which was presently to subvert the ancient classical ideal of political self-sufficiency.

It is a necessary task to expose the weaknesses of Constantinianism, weaknesses due in part to personal deficiencies of the emperor (such as the lust for power), in part, however, to a mental attitude which he shared with many of his contemporaries. The professed object of Constantine was to legislate the millennium in a generation: merely to state this is to be sensible of the insuperable difficulties involved; were it not for extravagant claims which he himself made and which others made on his behalf, it would be much easier to sympathize with the imperfections of his compromise. His very errors were, however, necessary in order that the Christians should be compelled to undertake a fuller and more adequate statement of the social and political implications of their faith.

It is perfectly obvious that Constantine did not consciously or deliberately weave a spider's web for Christianity; if, indeed, he wove one at all, it was destined, by destroying his successors, to ruin his own dynastic hopes. Author of one of the greatest revolutions in human history, architect (to a very great extent) of the Middle Ages, the real tragedy of his life was that he knew not what he did. As for the immediate fruits of his policy, he

[1] *Vita*, iv. 5–14.   [2] ii. 7–12.

did not survive long enough to taste their bitterness; of all men, it might be said that he was fortunate in the moment of his death.

If it is, in any sense, appropriate to describe Diocletian as the Camillus of the Lower Empire, then Constantine deserves to be called its Scipio Aemilianus. Like Scipio, he was endowed with an acute sense of the practical which found expression in a continuous series of triumphs both in politics and in war; like him, also, he was distinguished by a dreamy mysticism, claiming an intimate communion with powerful supernatural forces beyond the ken of ordinary men; just as his favourite motto, *instinctu divinitatis, mentis magnitudine*[1] links him with his spiritual forebears, the divine-men of the Hellenistic world who, by virtue of conspicuous talent and fortune, were peculiarly qualified to usher in a time of change. And it was in fact his destiny, as it had been that of Scipio, to guide his countrymen into new and untrodden paths.

Throughout his life Constantine both professed and practised a religion of success; his biographer offers the assurance that his enterprises were invariably attended by good fortune, until at last, his glory still undimmed by the slightest reverse, the emperor, not unlike an eponymous Greek hero-founder, was borne to rest at New Rome in the Church of the Twelve Apostles. Canny to the end, and aware of the cruel necessities which from time to time confront the politician, he had delayed the ceremony of baptism until the eleventh hour. He died as a neophyte, clad in the white robe of innocence; conscious, not so much of his sins, as of the immense services which, in the course of a long and spectacular career, he had been privileged to render to God and to his fellow men. His age possesses all the ambiguities of a period of violent transition. Those ambiguities were dramatically epitomized in the person of the emperor himself. He is perhaps unique as the one human being to have enjoyed the distinction of being deified as a pagan god, while, at the same time, he was popularly venerated as a Christian saint.

[1] Dessau, *I.L.S.* 694.

VI

QUID ATHENAE HIEROSOLYMIS? THE IMPASSE OF CONSTANTINIANISM

THE acceptance of Christianity by a Roman emperor served to introduce a period of great interest and importance for the Church. Less than a century before, when the struggle with the empire was approaching its climax, Tertullian had pronounced the notion of a Christian Caesar to be a contradiction in terms.[1] 'The fact that Christ rejected an earthly kingdom', he declares, 'should be enough to convince you that all secular powers and dignities are not merely alien from, but hostile to, God.' Accordingly, 'there can be no reconciliation between the oath of allegiance taken to God and that taken to man, between the standard of Christ and that of the devil, between the camp of light and that of darkness. *Non potest una anima duobus deberi*: it is impossible to serve two masters, God and Caesar.'[2]

In this spirit the author had proclaimed the secession of Christians from the Roman order. 'For us', he asserts, 'nothing is more foreign than the commonwealth. We recognize but one universal commonwealth, viz. the world.'[3] His apostasy from *Romanitas* is complete. 'I owe no obligation to forum, campus, or senate. I stay awake for no public function, I make no effort to monopolize the platform, I pay no heed to any administrative duty, I shun the voters' booth, the juryman's bench. . . . I serve neither as magistrate nor soldier, I have withdrawn from the life of secular society (*secessi de populo*). . . . My only concern is for myself, careful of nothing except that I should have no care. . . . No man is born for another who is destined to die for himself.'[4] There could thus be no bond of sympathy whatever between the believer and his environment. 'Society will rejoice, you will be sad. Let us therefore mourn when the heathen are happy and, when they begin to mourn, let us be glad lest, if we now rejoice together, we may hereafter lament together. . . . What greater pleasure than contempt for pleasure, than scorn for the activities of the world!'[5] Such an

---

[1] *Apol.* 21: 'sed et Caesares credidissent super Christo, si aut Caesares non essent saeculo necessarii, aut si et Christiani potuissent esse Caesares.'
[2] *De Idol.* 18 and 19.
[3] *Apol.* 38.   [4] *De Pallio*, 5.   [5] *De Spect.* 28-9.

attitude was fitting since, though an outcast from secular society, the Christian was a citizen of the New Jerusalem, and, from this standpoint, nothing in this world mattered except that he should leave it as speedily as possible.[1] Accordingly, he looked forward with eagerness to the moment of his release. 'For, if we think of the world itself as a prison, we realize that to enter Caesar's prison is to become free. . . . To you, who are outside society, it is of no consequence what you are in society.'[2]

In considering these sentiments two points should be borne in mind. To begin with, they are the utterances of a man whose personal tendencies towards eccentricity were in the end to be reinforced by the extravagances of Montanism. Then, too, they are the product of a time of crisis, when the dispute between Church and empire had entered upon its last and most acute phase. They do not so much reflect the normal attitude of the believer as the spirit with which he resisted imperial persecution. But, even so, they are not without significance, for they point to elements of opposition between Christianity and Classicism which were not to be ignored. They thus indicate the magnitude of the step taken by Constantine when he abandoned the official gods of *Romanitas* in order to pledge his allegiance to Christ. In so doing, they provoke two questions both of vital importance to an understanding of the fourth century. The first concerns the motive of the emperor in breaking thus emphatically with tradition. The second is much less easy to dispose of, since the issues it involves are fundamental. That is to say, it raises, in a fresh and significant context, the problem of the Gospel proclaimed three centuries before on the stony hills of Palestine, and of its value as a doctrine of salvation for what was to be described, in the words of Augustine, as a 'rotting and disintegrating world' (*doctrina saluberrima tabescenti et labenti mundo*).

As to the former question, there can be little occasion for dispute: the concluding sentence of the Edict of Milan embodies a candid statement of the Constantinian hope. That hope, as the emperor himself expressed it, was that 'the divine favour, which he had experienced at this critical juncture of his life, should continue for ever to rain benefits upon his successors, at the same time ensuring the happiness of the commonwealth'

[1] *De Coron.* 13–15; *Apol.* 41.   [2] *Ad Martyr.* 2.

('fiet ut . . . divinus iuxta nos favor, quem in tantis sumus rebus experti, per omne tempus prospere successoribus nostris cum beatitudine . . . publica perseveret'). In this aspiration we may perceive something more than a desire for mere appeasement such as might, perhaps, have been attained by an agreement to live and let live. The object of Constantine was to lay hold of a fresh principle of political integration. In this there was nothing to be surprised at; it was quite in accord with the politics of restoration which, as we have seen, had been pursued by successive princes since the middle of the third century. What was, however, astonishing in its novelty was his evident notion that such a principle might be derived from Christianity.

From this standpoint it is not difficult to estimate the significance of the settlement projected by the emperor. What he saw in Christianity was simply a talisman by virtue of which *Romanitas* would be assured of material prosperity such as official paganism had failed to give it; and, as an uninterrupted series of successes appeared to vindicate this hope, he came more and more to identify the promise of the Evangel with that of the empire and of his own house. It was, indeed, in keeping with the pragmatic spirit of his faith that he should have retained on his coins, at least until middle age, the figures and emblems of the traditional pagan gods and that, while forbidding divination in general, he should at the same time have specifically sanctioned it 'in the public interest'.[1] Meanwhile, however, he girt himself, so to speak, with the armour of righteousness. In the critical struggle with his colleague Licinius, prayer was opposed to sacrifice, the *tabernaculum* to the temple; while, at the head of his forces, guarded by a special *corps d'élite*, moved the dreaded *Labarum* which, with 'its divine and mysterious potency', received from pagan and Christian alike something of the superstitious veneration accorded by the ancient Hebrews to the Ark of the Covenant.[2] These considerations, in themselves, constitute no valid reason for impugning the sincerity of the emperor. But they do most emphatically suggest that his apprehension of Christianity was imperfect. They thus indicate that, whatever his errors, they were merely those of a man who, in the transition to a new

---

[1] *Cod. Theod.* xvi. 10. 1 (321).
[2] Euseb. *Vita*, ii. 4–16.

world, carried with him a heavy burden of prejudice from the old.[1]

The mistake of Constantine was to identify the substance with the form of Christianity; i.e. it was the characteristic error of classical idealism. His real problem, however, was to dissociate himself from classical ways of thought. In this he was not wholly successful as will be evident, for example, from the application to himself of the famous *instinctu divinitatis, mentis magnitudine*.[2] This, as we have elsewhere noted, is merely the Latin translation of a phrase used by Plutarch with reference to Alexander the Great, and it points to a kind of 'co-operation' with God appropriate to the Hellenistic superman. Other survivals of pagan mentality may, perhaps, be found in the em-

---

[1] The purpose and methods of Constantine have provided material for controversy both in ancient and modern times. Current opinion has been subjected to critical examination by Professor N. H. Baynes in his challenging essay, 'Constantine the Great and the Christian Church' (*Proceedings of the British Academy*, xv, 1929). We may agree with the author in rejecting the view that the emperor was either a conscious and deliberate hypocrite or, on the other hand, a 'political saint'. But it is difficult to accept the conclusion (pp. 367–8) that he was 'no mere philosophic monotheist', and that 'he identified himself definitely with Christianity, with the Christian Church and with the Christian creed'. The real question here is the *quality* of Constantine's faith. To the discussion we can add nothing except to point out that, in the opinion of at least one competent and almost contemporary observer, this was not of a very high order. See Augustine, *De Civ. Dei*, v. 24, 'Quae sit Christianorum imperatorum et quam vera felicitas' (the so-called 'Mirror of Princes'): Christian emperors are not to be regarded as happy because they have reigned a comparatively long time and have died quietly, leaving their sons to succeed them, or because they have subdued the enemies of the state and have been able either to prevent or suppress risings of unfriendly citizens against them. These and other consolations or rewards of this troublesome life even worshippers of demons have been privileged to receive although, unlike Christian princes, they do not belong to the Kingdom of God, and this has come about through God's mercy, lest those who believe in Him should put too high a value on such benefits. 'But we call them happy if they rule justly, if they are not carried away by the flattery of courtiers and the obsequiousness of subjects, but remember that they are mortal; if they place their power at the service of God in order to propagate His worship; if they fear, love, and honour God, preferring that Kingdom wherein they do not fear to have associates; if they are slow to punish and quick to pardon,' &c. Specific application of these ideas to Constantine is made in chapter 25, where it is argued that God guarantees no special temporal advantage to rulers merely because they are or profess to be Christians. Perhaps the justest estimate of Constantine remains that of Cumont, *R.O.*[4], pp. 302–3: 'Le déisme vague de Constantin s'ingénia à concilier les contradictions de l'héliolâtrie et du Christianisme.' It is thus 'un curieux produit d'un dilettantisme théologique, construit sur un fondement essentiellement panthéiste avec l'aide d'un petit nombre de termes chrétiens et de moins encore, peut-être, d'idées chrétiennes'.

[2] Discussed by Baynes, op. cit., footnote 36, pp. 404–5.

peror's apparent belief in the efficacy of a mechanical discharge of religious rites,[1] together with the fear of divine punishment as an incentive to good conduct,[2] suggestive of the *modus operandi* attributed to God in the semi-pagan *De Mortibus Persecutorum*. These beliefs are based on the notion of a contractual relationship (ἀμοιβή) between God and man which has much more in common with official paganism than with mature Christian thinking.

The errors of the emperor, if natural, were not on that account the less serious. For, though he perhaps succeeded in creating a temporary and largely illusory sense of public betterment, it cannot be said that he effected any permanent solution of the traditional problems of Rome. On her northern and eastern frontiers the empire was still confronted with the barbarian peril—a peril with which the new faith rendered her in various respects less competent to deal. For, while Christianity contributed to extinguish the already flickering civic virtues, at the same time it suggested a wholly fresh point of contact with the barbarian in the shape of a common religion disseminated on either side of the boundary; thus tending to stimulate the process of fusion, especially with the Germans, but on a basis utterly different from that of the cultural assimilation required within the pagan empire. From this standpoint the notorious philo-barbarism of the first Christian emperor was to constitute not the least of his offences in the eyes of his reactionary nephew.[3] Meanwhile, as has already been suggested,[4] the social and economic forces which were grinding the life out of the provincials continued to operate remorselessly; a century and a half of *tributaria sollicitudo* (fiscal distress) was sufficient to demonstrate the tragedy of a situation which it seemed impossible either to cure or to endure. Such were the more remote fruits of the Constantinian settlement, the net result of which was thus to confirm, but in a fashion quite the reverse of what was intended, the ultimate fate of the city.

Nor were the immediate dynastic hopes of the emperor destined to a future any less ironic. To his successors the legacy of Constantinianism was one of confused ideas in which pagan and Christian elements were inextricably mingled. It was by

---

[1] Ibid., p. 348.   [2] Ibid., pp. 351–4.
[3] Amm. xxi. 10. 8: 'eum aperte incusans ⟨ Iulianus⟩ quod barbaros omnium primus ad usque fasces auxerat et trabeas consulares.'   [4] Ch. V above.

no accident, nor in any mere conventional sense, that Constantius II spoke of himself as 'divi Constantini optimi maximique principis ⟨filius⟩, divorum Maximiani et Constanti nepos, divi Claudi pronepos'.[1] Last survivor in the direct male line of the Second Flavians, the purpose of this emperor was to implement, so far as possible, the policies initiated by his father; and, throughout his reign of twenty-five years, renovation upon those lines proceeded without abatement. But the coexistence within the scheme of elements so hopelessly incongruous served to create tensions unparalleled in any purely pagan system and, in the end, those tensions proved to be intolerable. Accordingly, the way was paved for a deliberate and thoroughgoing reaction under Julian the Apostate who, in his person, embodied the nemesis of the Second Flavian house.

The ambiguities of Constantinian Christianity may be ascribed, not to any deliberate wickedness on the part of the emperor, but to the enormous difficulty of breaking away from what Augustine was to call the 'pernicious habit' (*pessima consuetudo*) of classical life and thought. Confusion of thought was, indeed, an inevitable consequence of the effort to pour new wine into old bottles, without causing the bottles to break. It is hardly possible to exaggerate the difficulties encountered by the Christians in avoiding the pitfalls involved in Classicism, with its still surviving prestige as the most significant impulse towards a scientific apprehension of the world and a rational ordering of human life thus far undertaken by mankind. In this respect, the deficiencies of the emperor were those of the teachers with whom he was most closely in contact. It has thus been observed with respect to Eusebius that 'his mentality was, at bottom, that of Arius. But whereas the latter was clear and precise in his formulations, the bishop of Caesarea excelled in enveloping his ideas in a cloud of words and in saying much in order to say nothing.'[2] On the other hand, an ancient critic has pointed in no uncertain terms to the shortcomings of Lactantius. 'Would that he had stated our position', laments St. Jerome, 'as effectively as he demolished that of our opponents!'[3] This weakness of the 'Christian Cicero' was to be explained as the result of inadequate grounding in Christian principles. Gibbon, for example, cites a papal bull in defence of the Nicene Creed to the effect that he 'was almost entirely ignorant

[1] Dessau, *I.L.S.* 732.   [2] Duchesne, op. cit. ii, p. 133.   [3] *Epp.* lviii. 10.

of Christian teaching and much better versed in rhetoric than in theology' ('erat paene rudis disciplinae Christianae et in rhetorica melius quam in theologia versatus'); and characteristically adds that his faith was 'of a moral rather than of a mysterious cast'.[1] From this standpoint the affiliations of Lactantius with Cicero and the Stoics are no accident; as we have already noticed, he embodies much in common with the findings of high-minded paganism. Indeed, his thinking appears to have been dominated by concepts derived from divergent and, in some degree, incompatible elements from within the classical tradition. The *De Opificio Dei* and the *De Mortibus Persecutorum* betray an historical materialism not unlike that which is to be found, for example, in Tertullian, with God as *deus ex machina* in full operation. The *Christian Institutes*, on the other hand (if, indeed, this work is by the same author), exhibit a thinly disguised idealism of the classical type—an idealism which, while no doubt softened and sentimentalized, nevertheless betrays a faith in creative politics similar to that of the officially discarded past. These considerations make it important to determine, if possible, what the Church as such really stood for, its sense of a mission in the world. For this purpose we may begin by recalling something of the spirit and purpose of Christianity as it found expression in the Roman world during the first three centuries.

In the course of this period the Church had gradually attained the character of an invisible empire, in the words of an apologist, a *latebrosa et lucifugax natio*.[2] The members of that empire were recruited not merely from every Roman municipality but from beyond the confines of *Romanitas*, and they were united by the tie of a common allegiance not less strict than that which bound his subjects to Caesar. For the forms of their organization the Christian communities had made heavy drafts upon contemporary secular society. In the *civitas*, for instance, they had discovered a model for the *ecclesia*, its *ordo* (clergy) and *plebs* (laity) corresponding respectively to the *curia* and *populus* of the municipality. They likewise had their officers or overseers similar to those of the *municipium*; but whereas, with the decay of civic spirit, the commons had relinquished control over the election of the magistrate, who thus became a kind of *podestà* appointed by the *curia* or senate, democracy survived among

---

[1] Ch. V above, p. 195.   [2] Minuc. Felix, *Octav.* 8. 4.

the Christians in the popular acclamation which generally preceded the formal ordination of a bishop by his fellows, as well as in a sense that he ought normally to be selected from among the clerics of his own neighbourhood. The Church thus appears to have combined a characteristically Graeco-Roman feeling regarding the choice of its leaders with the notion of a consecrated priesthood derived originally, no doubt, from Israel. Similarly, for her ecclesiastical buildings, she had appropriated the conventional forms of secular architecture while certain aspects at least of her ritual exhibited extraordinary parallels with those of the Hellenistic mystery cults. In other respects, also, the *ecclesia* had emerged as an antitype to the *civitas*. It embodied, for instance, an elaborate scheme of organized relief which was, however, dispensed, not like the dole or *alimentaria* within the Roman order, but uneconomically according to the Christian law of charity, and was on this account to be stigmatized by the emperor Julian as one of the principal snares for the poor and weak. Moreover, the jurisdiction of secular society had its counterpart within the Church. To ordinary civil procedure there corresponded a system of episcopal arbitration, the outcome of a reluctance on the part of believers to 'go to law'; the equivalent to penal justice was a penitential discipline which included, in some congregations at least, the duty of public confession;[1] while excommunication, as the ultimate weapon of a purely spiritual association, provided the Christian alternative to public and criminal law. Finally, just as the life of the *civitas* focused about an elaborate system of local and imperial cults, so also the *ecclesia* discovered its animating principle in religion.[2]

These numerous analogies, far from revealing any tendency towards contamination, serve merely to emphasize the cleavage between the Christians and organized secular society. To both alike, the sense of such a cleavage was evident. On the side of the pagans this found expression, not merely in spasmodic outbreaks of mob-violence against those who embraced the new religion, but also in the attitude of the government, which invoked the ban against unlicensed associations in order to

[1] Tertullian, *De Pudic.* 18.
[2] This comparison was originally made by Origen, *Contra Celsum*, iii. 29 and 30. It has been elaborated by various modern writers. For a more detailed study consult Duchesne, op. cit. i, ch. xxv, 'Les Mœurs chrétiens', and ch. xxvi, 'La Société chrétienne'.

subject them to a more or less continuous persecution, a mere
'confession of the name' being accepted as tantamount to
treason. The popular animus was to some extent reflected in
literature. In this connexion we may perhaps ignore the earlier
references, which reveal nothing but misunderstanding and dislike for a cult which was still confused with 'Jewish atheism' and
vaguely felt to be subversive.[1] One of the first clear statements
on the subject is that of Pliny in his report to Trajan on the
Bithynian Christians.[2] This throws light on the salient features
of Christianity as they appeared to an intelligent and not unsympathetic observer, and it indicates something of the problem
which its diffusion presented to the Roman administration. On
the other hand, for an idea of contemporary Christian feeling,
we may refer to the *Apology* addressed by Justin Martyr to the
emperor Pius, about the middle of the second century.[3]

'Before we became Christians', he declares, 'we took pleasure in
debauchery, now we rejoice in purity of life; we used to practise
magic and sorcery, now we are dedicated to the good, unbegotten
God; we used to value above all else money and possessions, now
we bring together all that we have and share it with those who are
in need. Formerly, we hated and killed one another and, because
of a difference in nationality or custom, we refused to admit strangers
within our gates. Now since the coming of Christ we all live in
peace. We pray for our enemies and seek to win over those who hate
us unjustly in order that, by living according to the noble precepts
of Christ, they may partake with us in the same joyful hope of obtaining our reward from God, the Lord of all.'

In this brief summary the author attempts to record his sense
of the moral and intellectual change to be experienced through
an acceptance of the faith. The chief note struck is one of
emancipation; the convert has found release, not merely from
the routine cares and preoccupations of secular society, but
from certain of its more sinister activities. At the same time he
has achieved something of the 'more abundant life' promised
by the Gospel. In this connexion nothing is said of the special
graces ($\chi\alpha\rho\acute{\iota}\sigma\mu\alpha\tau\alpha$), the gifts of 'illumination' and 'power' which
were frequently claimed by members of the primitive Church,
and attributed to the working of the Spirit. What is emphasized
is the fact that he has entered into a world governed not by fear

---

[1] Tacitus, *Ann.* xv. 44 and *Hist.* fr. 2; Suetonius, *Claud.* 25; *Nero*, 16; *Domit.* 12.
[2] *Epp.* x. 96.   [3] *Apol.* i. 14.

or distrust but by love—a world from which the divisions and
oppositions of secular society have vanished and there is neither
Jew nor Greek, bond nor free. The consequence is a new
sense of community which finds expression in mutual service.
Furthermore, the values to which the neophyte has dedicated
himself are felt to be ultimate. They thus provide an irrefragable sanction for pure and upright living. And finally, since
there is no inherent reason why the Gospel should not be universally accepted, there is an overmastering passion to communicate its benefits to all men.

This pronouncement may be taken as a faithful reflection of
apostolic and sub-apostolic teaching; and it loses nothing of its
significance when we remember that, according to tradition,
Justin Martyr was himself a former Platonist, converted about
the year 133.[1] For this means that he had discovered in
Christianity what philosophy had failed to give him, namely,
the basis for a radically fresh and original attitude towards
experience, in the light of which the wisdom of the *saeculum*
appeared, in the words of St. Paul, to be mere foolishness. That
interpretation rested, not on the guesses of human sagacity, but
on a revelation in the Master of the 'good, unbegotten God',
and from this standpoint everything depended upon belief in
Christ as the 'rock' upon which the edifice was to be erected.
The statement of Justin thus serves to introduce what has sometimes been described as the issue between 'science' and 'faith'.

In their efforts to formulate this issue certain of the Christians
indulged in such extravagant language as to leave the impression that their opposition to 'science' was an opposition to reason
itself. Thus Tertullian, in a familiar outburst, was to ask:

'What has Athens to do with Jerusalem, the Academy with the
Church? . . . We have no need for curiosity since Jesus Christ, nor
for inquiry since the Evangel.'

'Tell me', he adds, 'what is the sense of this itch for idle speculation? What does it prove, this useless affectation of a fastidious
curiosity, notwithstanding the strong confidence of its assertions? It
was highly appropriate that Thales, while his eyes were roaming the
heavens in astronomical observation, should have tumbled into a
well. This mishap may well serve to illustrate the fate of all who
occupy themselves with the stupidities of philosophy.'

He then proceeds to outline the reason for his attitude:

[1] Duchesne, op. cit. i, p. 205.

'This is the substance of secular wisdom that it rashly undertakes to explain the nature and dispensation of God. . . . Heretics and philosophers deal with similar material, and their arguments are largely the same. It is the Platonic ideas which have supplied the Gnostics with their aeons, the Marcionite deity (the ideal of tranquillity) comes from the Stoics, the identification of God with matter is a doctrine of Zeno, with fire of Heraclitus, . . . the Epicureans supply the notion of annihilation of the soul; and all alike are agreed in denying any possibility of regeneration for the flesh. . . . Unhappy Aristotle, who supplies them with a logic evasive in its propositions, far-fetched in its conclusions, disputatious in its arguments, burdensome even to itself, settling everything in order to settle nothing.'[1]

Hence, as he elsewhere demands,

'What is there in common between the philosopher and the Christian, the pupil of Hellas and the pupil of Heaven, the worker for reputation and for salvation, the manufacturer of words and of deeds, the builder and the destroyer, the interpolator of error and the artificer of truth, the thief of truth and its custodian?'[2]

The conclusion follows: 'To know nothing against the rule of faith is to know everything.'[3]

The appeal of Tertullian thus resolves itself into an appeal to 'simple faith'.

'It is not to thee that I address myself, the soul which, formed in the schools, trained in the libraries, belches forth a fund of academic wisdom, but thee, the simple and uncultivated soul, such as they have who have nothing else, whose whole experience has been gleaned on street-corners and cross-roads and in the industrial plant. I need thine inexperience since in thy little store of experience nobody believes. . . . It is the "secret deposit of congenital and inborn knowledge" which contains the truth, and this is not a product of secular discipline. The soul comes before letters, words before books, and man himself before the philosopher and the poet.'[4]

In these words he sums up his notion of the *anima naturaliter Christiana.*

The hostility of Tertullian to classical discipline prompts him to state the doctrine of the incarnation in a most provocative way. 'The Son of God was born, I am not ashamed of it because it is shameful; the Son of God died, it is credible for the very reason that it is silly; and, having been buried, He rose again, it is certain because it is impossible.'[5] This is the notorious

[1] *De Praescript.* 7.　　　[2] *Apol.* 46.　　　[3] *De Praescript.* 7.
[4] *De Testimonio Animae,* chs. 1 and 5.　　　[5] *De Carne Christi,* 5.

credo quia absurdum which, by asserting the shameful, the silly, and the impossible as against the evidences of good taste, probability, and reason itself, hurls a defiant challenge in the face of the classical world.

These sentiments are not, perhaps, quite typical; they are inspired by a passionate fear of the dangers to be apprehended from contemporary movements both outside and inside the Church: on the one hand, the seductive religious liberalism professed by certain members of the Septimian dynasty; on the other, the development of speculative activity among theologians in a way which seemed to obscure, if not to undermine, the foundations of the faith. Nevertheless, they may be accepted as an overstatement[1] rather than a misstatement of the Christian position. For if there was any single thing to which Christian teaching pointed, it was to a recognition of the authority of the Master as the one avenue to truth. This authority was conceived as absolute and exclusive. As such, it involved consequences of the most far-reaching character, the full significance of which was certainly not apparent, at any rate during the ante-Nicene period. But this much, at least, was evident, that it meant a departure from what, as we have elsewhere tried to show, was the conventional classical approach to the problems of human life, that is, through 'nature and reason'. At the same time it suggested a new ideal and a new method of thought to be achieved through 'dependence' on Christ. And, from this standpoint, the duty and privilege of the Christian were not so much to investigate as to apprehend.

Accordingly, the primary obligation of believers was to determine their convictions with respect to the Master. And here the appeal was, in the first instance, to history, i.e. to the recognition of Jesus of Nazareth as an actual human being who 'ate, drank, and suffered' under Tiberius Caesar.[2] This was fundamental, for on it depended the distinction between Christianity and the pagan mystery cults whose objects were, in general, 'mythical'; i.e. figments of the imagination.[3] The second question was one of greater delicacy: it was to formulate their sense of the meaning of Jesus' life in terms which should record

[1] Better, perhaps, a partial or *ex parte* statement.
[2] Ignatius, *Ad Trall.* 9. 1; *Ad Smyrn.* 2.
[3] The point has been emphasized by Lebreton, *Histoire du dogme de la Trinité*, i, p. 181.

with strict fidelity the sense of Scripture and, at the same time, be comprehensible to the contemporary mind. In so doing, the Church was governed by texts such as that which concludes the Gospel of St. John: 'This has been written in order that you may believe that Jesus is the Christ, the Son of God, and that, so believing, you may have life in His name.'[1] Thus epitomized, the fundamentals of Christian doctrine found expression in the so-called rule of faith (*regula fidei*) to be professed by believers at baptism. This formulation, which is thought to embody apostolic teaching, was already traditional in Rome in the third century, and types analogous to it were current among the Churches of Egypt, Palestine, and Asia Minor.[2]

The rule of faith contained two propositions of vital importance. To begin with, it affirmed that the historical Christ was the 'only Son' of the Father and so, quite literally, the God to end gods. It thus underlay what was commonly regarded as 'Christian atheism'. For to accept this thesis was to reject as fraudulent the multifarious deities of secularism and, in particular, the claim to divinity put forward on behalf of the 'virtue' and 'fortune' of Caesar. At the same time it was to dissociate oneself from the hopes and fears embodied in the Augustan empire. It thus accounts for that sense of alienation which led the Christian to describe himself as a pilgrim or foreigner in imperial society, and for his absolute refusal to participate in many of its most significant activities. It also explains why he found himself denied the easy toleration which was normally accorded to 'unlicensed cults'.

The second element of the Christian *credo* was no less important than the first. This was the prospect of 'eternal life' extended to the faithful. That prospect was based, not on the common pagan aspiration to transcendence, but on a new sense of the relationship between 'body' and 'spirit' as revealed in the life of the Master, and therewith of the potentialities of human nature to be realized through a 'redemption' of the flesh. The problem was to grasp the meaning of this revelation, especially in relation to ideas of apotheosis prevalent in the contemporary pagan world. In this connexion, perhaps the chief difficulty was to overcome the tendency to think in terms of 'form' and 'matter'; i.e. of concepts which were a legacy from

---

[1] xx. 31; cf. 2 Pet. i.
[2] Hastings, *Encyclopedia of Religion and Ethics*, sub voc. 'Creeds'.

the effort of classical *scientia* to construct for itself a picture of the cosmos. We have already noted certain of the developments to which this led in imperial philosophy.[1] In the religious consciousness the counterpart to these developments was the rise of various systems of 'gnosis'. These systems had little in common except the desire to escape from what was felt to be the 'contamination' of body, and the claim to have discovered an effective technique for so doing. In this crisis the Church found a champion in Irenaeus, who vigorously opposed the Gnostics in the name of the Incarnated Word.[2]

The error of the Gnostics was to have misconceived the significance of matter and motion which they regarded as inherently 'evil'. In this they were not unique, for a precisely similar tendency was presently to manifest itself among an important group of churchmen, the Christian idealists of Alexandria. It has, for instance, been noted that Clement puts forward a theory of Christian gnosis which is hardly to be distinguished from that professed by contemporary pagan mystics, whereby the *logos* serves to guide the neophyte through successive stages of illumination. At the same time he advocates a scheme of Christian propaedeutics which is obviously based on Neopythagorean-Platonic practice. With Origen the admission of pagan ideology is hardly less apparent. He has thus been convicted of a wholesale adoption of Aristotelian terminology and definitions.[3] And, in his great work on First Principles ($\pi\epsilon\rho\grave{\iota}\ \dot{\alpha}\rho\chi\hat{\omega}\nu$), he envisages his problem in terms of the concepts traditional to pagan science. The starting-point is the conventional opposition of the 'One' and the 'Many', contact between which is established by means of a hypothetical *logos*, envisaged as a 'second god' and so a 'creature' ($\kappa\tau\acute{\iota}\sigma\mu\alpha$) who is thought to contain within himself the archetypes or forms of the spiritual world. These, in turn, are 'imprisoned' in bodies, angelic, demonic, and human, as a 'punishment'. The cosmos is without beginning and without end, but an escape from the world of body is offered through belief in Christ conceived as 'pure' spirit.[4] So far was Origen from appreciating the significance of Christianity as an 'historical' religion based on

[1] Ch. IV, p. 164 foll.
[2] For his services in this connexion, see Lebreton, op. cit. ii, p. 395 foll.; cf. E. Brunner, *Der Mittler* (*passim*).   [3] G. Bardy in *Mélanges Glotz*, i, pp. 75–83.
[4] Duchesne, op. cit. i, p. 340 foll.

the sense of an organic relation between soul and body and promising immortality through a regeneration of the flesh.

To Tertullian the errors of the heretics served to illustrate the dangers of 'speculation'. Accordingly, his answer to them was to reassert in the most vigorous and emphatic terms the breach between 'science' and 'faith'. For him this breach was absolute, and it involved an irreconcilable opposition between the claims of Christ and those of the world. It thus pointed to a criticism of secular values which included every possible aspect of secularism.[1] In particular, it suggested an attack on the Roman order as the ultimate repository of these values. This attack was directed against the idealization of Roman achievement, which was a legacy from Cicero and Vergil,[2] and the author invoked all the rich resources of Latin rhetoric in order to give it point and emphasis. Thus, he contends, there is nothing unique or distinctive in the empire. 'Unless I am mistaken all kingdoms and empires owe their existence to the sword, their expansion to success on the battlefield.' Accordingly, the history of Rome is prefigured in Babylon, the very type of imperial magnificence; corpses rather than laurel-wreaths are the true symbols of her secular progress and, so far from having grown great by subduing the proud, she herself waxes proud by the slaughter of the saints.[3] The Romans imagined that their achievement had been due to their intense religious consciousness, but this, in fact, was to invert the true logic of the situation. 'It was not their religion that made them great, but their greatness that made them religious.'[4] Accordingly the Capitol, sanctified by tradition as the heart and centre of the official religion, is described as a 'temple of all the devils'.[5] So much for the claims put forward by exponents of *Romanitas* on behalf of the Eternal City as the climax and goal of all human endeavour.

What Tertullian here objects to is the attempt to consecrate a set of purely secular values in the name of Augustus and Rome. This objection takes the form of a protest against the divinity of Caesar.

'I refuse to call the Emperor a god. If he is human, it behoves him as such to bow the knee to God. Augustus, the founder of the

[1] References *passim*; esp. *Apol.* 4 (law); *De Spect.* 21; *De Pudic.* (ethics); *De Idol.* 10 (literature); &c.   [2] Ch. II above.
[3] *De Coron.* 12; *Ad Nat.* i. 17; *Adv. Iud.* 9 (*sanctorum debellatrix*); *Adv. Marc.* iii. 13.
[4] *Apol.* 25; *Ad Nat.* ii. 17.   [5] *De Spect.* 12.

Empire, was reluctant to be addressed even as Lord (*dominus*), and
this, indeed, is an appellation of God. I am willing to call the
Emperor Lord but only in the conventional sense, never in the sense
in which I accord that title to the Omnipotent and Eternal who is
his Lord as well as mine.'[1]

What he thus demands is the complete secularization, as we
should say, of the political order. The essence of true religion,
he significantly adds, is its voluntary acceptance.[2] Or, in a
famous aphorism, 'non religionis est cogere religionem, quae
sponte suscipi debeat, non vi'.[3]

In the requirements of religious freedom Tertullian finds a
limit to political obligation. Thus, in discussing the words
'render unto Caesar', he asks: What then belongs to Caesar?
The answer is instructive.

'We have, for Caesar,' he declares, 'the image of Caesar which is
impressed on the coin, for God, the image of God which is impressed
on human beings. Give Caesar his money; give yourself to God. . . .
Accordingly we follow the apostolic injunction to submit to magistracies, principalities, and powers, but only within the limits of discipline; that is, so long as we keep ourselves clear of idolatry.'[4]

In other words, political obedience can involve no obligation
to commit sin. This for Tertullian includes military service.
'Will the son of peace,' he demands, 'to whom even litigation is
improper, settle his differences by the sword? And will he, who
is bound not to avenge even his own injuries, resort to the instruments of imprisonment, torture, and death?'[5] All that the
state can legitimately demand of the Christian is that he should
support it by his taxes and his prayers.[6] This service, however,
is not less essential than any other. For, as the fall of the empire
is to be attended by its dismemberment among ten sovereigns,
and this, in turn, is to be followed by the reign of Antichrist,
the Christian is hardly less interested than the pagan in the
postponement of the end.[7]

The attitude thus indicated represents the sharpest possible
revulsion from conventions which had, with minor exceptions
such as were to be found among Cynics and Cyrenaics, dominated the life and thought of classical antiquity. Its strength is

---

[1] *Apol.* 33–4.   [2] Ibid. 24, 28.   [3] *Ad Scap.* 2.
[4] *De Idol.* 15.   [5] Ibid. 19; *De Coron.* 12–13.
[6] *Apol.* 30, 42, 43, 44; *Scorp.* 14; *Ad Scap.*; &c.
[7] *Apol.* 32; *De Resur. Carnis*, 24; &c.

that it marks a fresh sense of the value and significance of the individual as the 'vessel of the Spirit' and so heir to the promise of a more abundant life; its weakness that, if pressed to the ultimate limit, it tends to undermine all institutional authority, that of the organized church no less than the organized state. From this consequence Tertullian does not shrink. 'I hear', he says, 'that an order has gone forth to be obeyed without question. Our *Pontifex Maximus*, forsooth, by whom I mean the Bishop of Bishops, thus proclaims: "to those who have discharged the required penance, I remit the sins of fornication and adultery". What an edict! We cannot possibly endorse it with a "well done!".' Proceeding, he argues that, since the spiritual power is committed not merely to Peter but to the Church as a whole, its true and only sovereign must be spiritual, the Trinity of Father, Son, and Holy Ghost. The Church will, indeed, forgive, but only the Church of the Spirit through a spiritual man and not the Church regarded as a number of bishops. 'Power and authority belong to the master, not to the servant; to God and not the priest.'[1] Elsewhere[2] he argues that the clergy and the laity are on precisely the same level and enjoy precisely the same powers. Thus every man becomes his own priest and, 'where two or three are gathered together, even though they are laics, there is the Church. . . . Moreover, since the individual has in himself this priestly power, so also he ought to have, where it is needful, the priestly function of discipline.' This was to carry to the extremes of protestant evangelicalism the doctrine of the 'inner light'.

Such were the conclusions to which Tertullian was led by his desire to establish an absolute antithesis between 'science' and 'faith', between the 'psychic' or physical and the 'pneumatic' or spiritual man. But it involved further and not less serious consequences for the author himself, since it helped to blind him to the true issue between Classicism and Christianity and, indeed, to expose him to the very contamination which he denounced in others. In his effort to combat the fallacies of Docetism current among the Gnostics, Tertullian jumped to the conclusion that idealism was the enemy.

'Plato', he declares, 'asks us to believe that there are certain substances invisible, incorporeal, supermundane, divine and everlasting,

---

[1] *De Pudic.* 1; 21.   [2] *De Exhort. Cast.* 7.

which he designates as Ideas, Forms, or Exemplars; that these are the causes of those natural manifestations which are rooted in sense, and that the Ideas are the truths, the latter merely reflections of them. . . . Cannot you now discern the seeds of Gnostic and Valentinian heresy, the source from which they derive the distinction between animal or bodily senses and spiritual or intellectual powers?'[1]

We may here pause to note that Tertullian was not unique in his suspicion of idealism with its radical distinction between the two worlds of thought and sense (κόσμος νοητός . . . αἰσθητός): already, because of his discovery of the immanent *logos*, Justin Martyr had called Heraclitus 'a Christian before Christ'.[2] But Tertullian, in his hostility to idealism, falls into the error of accepting a crass materialism which translated God Himself into terms of body.[3] This materialism finds expression in many passages, but nowhere more explicitly than in the long and elaborate essay on psychology, *De Anima*. Despite its interest, we cannot afford to linger over this work, but its general tone is illustrated in the aphorism, 'everything is bitter to those who secrete too much bile'[4] and, in it, thought is reduced to the proportions of a function of sense.[5] This helps to explain the element of millennialism to be found in Tertullian, together with his evident belief in a material hell, a vision of the disordered imagination without parallel except, perhaps, among his spiritual descendants, the New England Puritans.[6]

The weaknesses thus exhibited by men like Origen and Tertullian served to produce a vigorous reaction in the contemporary Church. Thus Cyprian, while cherishing the memory of Tertullian and following him in insisting upon the perils of worldliness, at the same time preached an authoritarianism and a traditionalism which were quite the reverse of what Tertullian had taught. In this spirit the African bishop urged the need for implicit obedience to constituted authority and, as though to forecast the rise of the great councils and of conciliar action during the following century, he stressed the representative character of the episcopal office. In the same way he fell back

---

[1] *De Anima*, 18.
[2] A point noted by Lebreton, op. cit. i, p. 55.
[3] *De Carne Christi*, 11: 'omne quod est corpus est sui generis. nihil est incorporale nisi quod non est'; *Adv. Prax.* 7: 'quis enim negabit deum corpus esse, etsi deus spiritus est? spiritus enim corpus sui generis in sua effigie.'
[4] Ch. 17: 'qui redundantia fellis auruginant, amara sunt omnia.'
[5] Ch. 18.   [6] *De Spect.* 30.

upon tradition for the interpretation of scriptural texts as, for example, in the matter of St. Paul's observations on marriage and their relation to problems of his own day. While thus taking refuge in a kind of theoretical conservatism, he emerged as a strong practical leader who carried his flock through successive crises of persecution under Decius and Valerian.

It is none the less evident that the real problem of the Church was to work out the elements of a philosophy in keeping with its own distinctive first principles; that is, it was a problem of understanding and application. And, from this standpoint, the third-century fathers deserve the consideration of pioneers who, by their very errors, made the discovery of new worlds possible. For the lack of just such a philosophy, that century marked a turning-point in the history of the Church. Morally bold and vigorous, it was still intellectually timid or weak; and, victorious as a way of life, it was still philosophically deficient. Accordingly, it suffered hardly more from the malice of its enemies than from the ineptitude of its friends and, impotent to overcome its own intellectual difficulties, it was obviously without the heavy artillery needed to beat down paganism. Hence paganism was to survive in the more exalted circles of imperial society, in order to make a final bid for ascendancy under Julian the Apostate.

The evolution of a specifically Christian philosophy was to some extent promoted by theoretical attacks against the faith such as those levelled by Celsus and Porphyry in the third, and by Julian and his circle in the fourth, century. It was stimulated also by events in the world of action, such as the persecutions from Decius to Diocletian and, subsequently, the Caesaro-papism of the New Monarchy. It was, indeed, this latter which gave point and significance to the theological controversies which intervened between the adoption of the Nicene Creed in 325 and its confirmation, fifty years later, at Constantinople. And it was not until she had undergone these experiences that the Church was in a position to 'spoil the Egyptians'; that is to say, until she could construct out of the dismantled fragments of *Romanitas* a system of thought designed to supplement and reinforce the appeal of naïve Christianity, and thus secure its final victory. But in this respect her shortcomings were in 313 still painfully apparent. Accordingly the day was yet remote when a Christian could write: 'Can paganism, I ask you,

produce anything equal to ours, the one true philosophy?'[1] Yet
this was the moment when the emperor Constantine made his
astonishing gamble with fortune by calling upon the Christians
to provide an immediate and specific remedy for the ills of an
expiring world.

The problems of Christianity were not lessened but increased
through the political revolution by which it was drawn into the
full current of imperial life. To begin with, there was the
powerful attraction of the Constantinian court, with its strongly
marked secular interests, including an evident desire to transform the Church into an instrument of public policy. Then,
too, there was a natural desire on the part of churchmen to
compromise, so far as possible, with the wishes of their powerful
patron. And finally, there was still the vitally important question,
of understanding and application. In this connexion, discussion
centred on the meaning to be attached to the life and personality
of Christ. Thus, for example, Eusebius of Caesarea notes the
revival in his day by Paul of Samosata of the so-called heresy of
Artemon.

'This heresy,' he says, 'which claims that the Saviour was a mere
man (ψιλὸς ἄνθρωπος), has been criticized[2] as a recent innovation,
which its authors have sought to make respectable by ascribing to
it an origin in antiquity (195 B). . . They have brazenly corrupted
Holy Scripture, they have set aside the traditional rule of faith, they
have ignored Christ; not searching for what the Scriptures have to
say but sedulously considering what kind of reasoned argument may
be devised to support their atheism. . . . If any one confronts them
with a text of Holy Writ, they discuss whether it can be put in the
form of a conjunctive or disjunctive syllogism. . . . Repudiating the
sacred writings, they apply themselves to geometry. . . . Of the earth
earthy, they speak as it were from below and reject Him who comes
to us from on high. They study and admire Euclid, Aristotle, and
Theophrastus; some of them, no doubt, bow down and worship
Galen' (197 A, B).

The suggestion that the Redeemer was a 'mere man' had
horrified Eusebius; but the question arose, if this was not the
case, what then was He? To this question Arius, presbyter of
Alexandria, was now to attempt an answer.[3] The object of Arius

---

[1] Augustine, *Contra Iulianum*, iv. 14. 72: 'obsecro te, non sit honestior philosophia
gentium quam nostra Christiana, quae una est vera philosophia.'
[2] *H.E.* v. 28, quoting an unknown author of the period.
[3] For the personal history and background of Arius, including his connexion

was to rebut a contention recently put forward by Sabellius that the 'Son' was a mere 'power' or 'function' (ἐνέργεια) of the Father; in other words, that there were no substantial distinctions within the Godhead; the three so-called 'persons' (πρόσωπα) of the Trinity being simply three different modes of divine action.[1] This theory, technically known as modalist monarchianism, was intended to exclude the possibility of tritheism, but it was exposed to precisely the same objection, namely, that it was an attempt to comprehend the divine nature in terms of arithmetic. That is to say, it was merely a reflection of the ancient philosophical problem of unity in plurality. In answer to Sabellius, Arius invoked the notion of an ultimate principle, in itself simple but all-inclusive, the 'Monad' which, in the language of Neoplatonism, was 'beyond knowledge and beyond existence'. To this principle he ascribed the genesis of all creatures, including that of the *logos*, who was thus described as 'of another substance' from the Father and of whom it could be said that 'there was a time when he did not exist' (ἦν ποτὲ ὅτε οὐκ ἦν). It was further argued that the *logos* owed his origin, not to any inherent necessity, but to a free and voluntary act on the part of the Father whose creature he was (ποίημα, γέννημα, κτίσμα τοῦ πατρός; ἐξ οὐκ ὄντων γέγονεν ὁ λόγος). As a creature in time the *logos* was theoretically subject to change (τρεπτός, ἀλλοιωτός). His divinity, therefore, was not substantial (οὐσιῶδες) but acquired by merit (ἀρετή) and, if he possessed the wisdom (σοφία) and power (δύναμις) of the Father, it was simply by 'participation' in them (μετοχῇ). In other words he was the typical 'intermediate being' of Neoplatonic theology, neither 'very God' nor 'very man' but, through the Spirit which he in turn was believed to engender, a 'link' between the two.

Arianism has been described as a common-sense heresy, and it has been suggested that the real trouble with the heresiarch was that 'he could not understand a metaphor'.[2] This is doubtless true, but the difficulty goes even further. Arius appears to have supposed that his problem was one of 'composition'; that is to say, he started with the notion of two worlds which it was

---

with the school of Antioch, see Duchesne, ii, ch. iv, pp. 128 foll., who points out that the immediate source of his ideas was not Paul but Lucian of Antioch.

[1] His formula was τρεῖς ὀνομασίαι ἐν μιᾷ ὑποστάσει or μία ὑπόστασις καὶ τρεῖς ἐνέργειαι.

[2] H. M. Gwatkin in *Cambridge Mediaeval History*, vol. i, p. 119.

his duty to bring together. This he attempted to do in the orthodox scientific fashion by inventing a hypothetical connexion between them in the shape of the *logos*. But the solution was not wholly successful. For the *logos*, conceived as a link between the temporal and the eternal, was nevertheless regarded as subject to time, which was thus conceded a status independent of the 'second' or 'demiurgic' god. This was to deny all finality to the revelation of the Word in the historic Christ. As Arius himself put it: Many words hath God spoken, which of these are we to call the only-begotten Son? As a consequence, the door was once more opened to polytheism with its myriads of 'intermediate beings', gods, demigods, demons, and demonic men.

It is a commonplace that the intellectual affiliations of Arius were with Philo, Origen, and the Neoplatonists. That this was evident to contemporaries is clear from the fact that Constantine, in an edict published immediately after the Nicene Council and no doubt reflecting its findings, ordered that Arius' followers should thenceforth be known as *Porphyriani*.[1] Accordingly, the question raised by Arianism was whether the substance of paganism was to survive under Christian forms. That question became acute as the movement developed markedly propagandist tendencies; and so serious was the storm created that the emperor deemed it advisable to convoke the general council which met at Nicaea under his own presidency in 325.

It is instructive to consider how the fathers undertook to deal with the issues raised by Arius. As has already been suggested, Arius thought of his problem as one of 'composition', it was to show how God, the eternal and immutable, could enter into combination with nature, the world of 'flux', without suffering degradation in respect of His essential attributes. This problem he attempted to solve on characteristically classical lines. It may here be recalled that Aristotle, when faced with the same question, had argued that, while nature was everywhere in motion, God, not being in space and time, was therefore not in motion. From this he had drawn the logical inference that God could not be the author of nature as a whole, but only of the orderliness in nature, and that simply because nature 'loved' order, not *vice versa*. Arius, on the other hand, following the Neoplatonists, had produced in his *logos* a derivative deity

[1] For this edict, see Baynes, op. cit., p. 367, n. 75.

which however, since it was subject to time, could only be described as *deus in fieri*. That is, he protected the substance of the Father but at the expense of that of the Son.

In opposition to these conclusions, the action of the fathers was to reaffirm the sense of a substantial or essential union of the divine and the human in the historical Jesus, as this had found expression in the literature and tradition of the ante-Nicene Church. This belief rested ultimately on the text: 'the Word became flesh and dwelt amongst us'.[1] It embodied a conviction that the Master was in no sense a 'creature', 'naturally' subject to time or necessity, 'morally' alterable, $\theta\epsilon\hat{\iota}os$ rather than $\theta\epsilon\acute{os}$, that is, God as 'participating' in the attributes of divinity, or God not 'essentially' but 'accidentally' and 'of grace'.[2] This conviction was formulated in the most unequivocal terms, and it was reinforced by an anathema directed against any one who should presume to suggest otherwise. The doctrine, thus promulgated at Nicaea, was to be refined and emphasized in subsequent pronouncements, which asserted the absolute co-existence or hypostatic union ($\kappa\alpha\tau\grave{a}$ $\acute{\upsilon}\pi\acute{o}\sigma\tau\alpha\sigma\iota\nu$) of the two natures, divine and human, in the person of the Saviour. Thus, on the one hand, it was maintained that Christ was 'perfect man', qualified as such by every possible attribute except sin. By this was meant, not merely that He was ethically flawless, but that He was equipped with all the capacities appropriate to a human being, including reason and sense.[3] On the other hand, it was contended with equal assurance that He was 'perfect God', the 'only begotten of the Father', 'born of the substance of the Father', and thus to be identified with the Word which was 'in the beginning'. Authority for these statements was found in texts such as John x. 30: 'I and the Father are one' and xiv. 9: 'He who hath seen Me hath seen the Father'. What this pointed to was no mere 'compound' of the divine *logos* with what may be called 'brute' flesh, but rather a genuine 'assumption' of the flesh, that is, of the full humanity (reason and sense) of the man Jesus by the *logos* as its 'leading

[1] John, i. 14.

[2] $\kappa\alpha\tau\grave{a}$ $\chi\acute{a}\rho\iota\nu$. The same conviction was otherwise expressed in the tradition of human maternity and a divine paternity. The problem here is to grasp the meaning which it was sought to convey. To apprehend this is to apprehend the reality of the alleged 'miracle'.

[3] $\psi\upsilon\chi\grave{\eta}$ $\lambda o\gamma\iota\kappa\grave{\eta}$ $\nu o\epsilon\rho\acute{a}$, $\sigma\grave{a}\rho\xi$ $\acute{\epsilon}\mu\psi\upsilon\chi os$ $\lambda o\gamma\iota\kappa\acute{\eta}$, in the words of contemporary controversialists.

principle' (τὸ ἡγεμονικόν). Stripped of the somewhat formidable phraseology of contemporary thinking, this amounts to
a denial that there existed any such hiatus as the pagans had
supposed between being and becoming, God and nature. On
the contrary, the two were immediately related, and the
relationship between them had actually been demonstrated
(however illogical this might appear) in the life of the Saviour.
The fathers thus exhausted every resource of vocabulary to
reiterate not merely that Christ *had* the truth but that He *was*
the Truth (*quod deus habet, id est*);[1] i.e. precisely the same conviction as the Evangelists, particularly St. John, had sought
to convey in narrative form. Accordingly, they held, access
to the world of eternal truth did in fact exist for men. It
was made possible through Christ who thus gave them power,
by apprehending it, to be 'deified' and made 'sons of God'.[2]
From this standpoint, the revelation of Christ was accepted as
specifically a revelation of the Godhead.

According to this revelation, as it was understood and propounded by the council, the Godhead presented itself as a
Trinity,[3] the first element or 'person' of which, God the Father,
the great I AM of the Hebrew Scriptures, emerged specifically
as substance or being. We may here note, to begin with, that
to acknowledge the Father, the ἀρχὴ ἄναρχος, as the ultimate
foundation and source of all being in the universe was to deny
the reality of any opposing principle such as had been imagined
by the Manicheans; in other words, to bar the door to metaphysical dualism. Furthermore, the being thus ascribed to the
Father was not the abstract being of philosophy; that is to say,
it was in no sense exclusive of becoming like τὸ ὄν to τὸ γιγνόμενον in Greek thought. On the contrary, it was held to comprehend the sum of all perfections, including those of order and
motion which were thus recognized as complementary to each
other and, at the same time, inherently related to substance.
Accordingly, the second person of the Trinity, the Son or Word,
was described as 'of the substance of the Father', the term *nasci*
as applied to Him being taken to indicate unity and parity of

---

[1] Aug. *De Civ. Dei*, xi. 10.
[2] John, i. 12.
[3] Authority for this doctrine was found in various references, the most explicit
being that of Matt. xxviii. 16–20, which has been called the great Trinitarian text
of the New Testament.

nature. On the other hand, as embodying the intellectual determinations of the Father, He appeared specifically as the *ratio*, the principle of order and discrimination in the cosmos. Similarly with the third person, the Holy Spirit, the principle of energy or movement, which was said to 'reveal the substance of the Father which is in the Son', therein discharging a dual function as the source both of life and perfectibility in the creature. Thus constituted, the Godhead might be described either as 'trinity in unity' or 'unity in trinity'. To envisage it as a trinity was to see its elements as in some sense 'opposed' to one another; being was not to be identified with order, nor order with process, nor yet were all three to be resolved into terms of an undifferentiated, all-inclusive one. It was, moreover, to recognize that the oppositions in question were substantial; i.e. that they possessed the real existence of 'persons' and were not mere logical distinctions subsisting only in the human mind. On the other hand, to envisage it as a unity was to acknowledge that these oppositions, far from being ultimate, were simply those of necessary relations on what was essentially the same plane of reality.

We may here observe that there was no attempt whatever to demonstrate the truth of these assertions in terms acceptable to classical science. On the contrary, they were propounded as strictly *de fide*, a matter of faith, beginning and ending as affirmations of the religious consciousness. As such, their validity was felt to depend ultimately upon the sense of scripture, and disputes which arose, for example, as to the propriety of using the word 'consubstantial' to indicate the relation of persons within the Trinity, turned on the question of whether this adjective had adequate scriptural authority. But they were not on that account put forward, in the defiant spirit of Tertullian, as inconsistent with nature and reason. Rather, they were offered as the clue to an understanding of problems by which the natural reason had hitherto been baffled. They did, however, suggest a fresh attitude to these problems, the approach no longer being, as for Classicism, through nature to God, but rather through God to nature.

The doctrine of the Trinity provided the basis for a radically new and unclassical account of the structure and content of experience. The assumption of Classicism, or at least of Platonism, had been that there was, in nature, an exact equivalence between 'being' and 'knowledge'. Its effort had therefore been directed to the attainment of a 'pure' knowledge as the means of apprehending 'pure' reality. Behind this assumption there lurked the heresy of two worlds, the one that of the intelligibles (κόσμος νοητός) accessible to the scientific understanding (ἐπιστήμη), the other the sensible world (κόσμος αἰσθητός) of which no genuine science was possible but only opinion (δόξα) or belief (πίστις). Christianity denied the original assumption and, therewith, the implied heresy. For it there was but one world of experience and that common to all human beings on precisely the same terms. It thus dismissed as a vain illusion the Platonic dream of an ἀρχὴ ἀνυπόθετος to be apprehended through the disciplined mind, together with its corollaries, the Platonic dictatorship of intelligence and Platonic 'orthodoxy'. As against these notions, it asserted that the true starting-point for thought and action must remain for ever invisible to the eye of the flesh.[1] This was to alter the entire perspective and to maintain that, for all men without exception, the question of primary importance was not so much their capacity for thinking as the presuppositions which governed their thought. And, from this standpoint, faith in the God of revelation was proposed as indispensable to full understanding. To accept this faith was to believe that, however obscure this might appear to the scientific intelligence, the *esse* of the Father embraced within itself the elements of order and movement and that these were not less integral than substance to the divine nature. It was, moreover, to hold that on these essential constituents of the Deity depended the structure and process of the universe. Thus envisaged, however, the Deity presented itself, not as an object of, but as the basis for, experience, the God 'in whom we live and move and are'.

This vision of the *operatio Dei* shed fresh light on certain of the traditional problems which had haunted the classical mind. The first of these had to do with the question of cosmology. Thus, for example, the classical materialists, beginning with the concept of an independent, self-moving matter, had found themselves in the position of explaining the universe, including that of thought, in terms either of 'chance' or 'necessity' or, if it was to contain any element of freedom, an arbitrary com-

---

[1] Col. i. 15 τοῦ θεοῦ τοῦ ἀοράτου.

bination of the two.[1] The idealists, on the other hand, had rejected the notion of spontaneous or mechanical generation, but only to find themselves confronted with difficulties hardly less serious. In this connexion we may dismiss those types of 'pure' and largely post-classical idealism which represented the cosmos as a necessary mode of divine self-fulfilment, thereby involving themselves in the difficulties of pantheism. Of much more significance were the qualified idealisms which saw it as a product of opposing forces; that is, of 'forms' imposing themselves upon a substratum of primordial and more or less reluctant 'matter'. We have already examined some of the theoretical and practical conclusions which resulted from this way of thought. They are summarized in the fact that it gives rise to a cosmos which is doomed to irremediable imperfection or evil.

By the Christians, the radical defect in classical accounts of *genesis* was ascribed to the inadequacy of the starting-point furnished by the 'scientific' imagination. On the other hand, they themselves professed to discover in the God of revelation a principle by virtue of which it became possible to construct an adequate picture of nature or the physical world. In the light of that principle, the cosmos presented itself as a world of real, concrete, individual substances, each and every one of which found a 'natural' expression in orderly but unimpeded development leading to its appropriate end. Thus conceived, however, the world of nature was neither self-generating nor self-fulfilling, but depended absolutely upon the intelligent and beneficent support of God as its creator and preserver.[2] The word 'creation', defined as 'productio ex nihilo, ab omni necessitate libera', was intended to indicate this sense of direct and immediate divine activity, free from all compulsion or limitation, whether internal or external. In such a world there was to be found no essential imperfection or evil; to look upon it was to see that it was good.

In subsequent chapters[3] it will be possible to develop in some detail the consequences which followed from this reorientation of attitude, as these were to emerge from the historic debates of

---

[1] See, for example, the Epicurean cosmology as worked out by Lucretius, *De Rerum Natura*.

[2] In the words of the Nicene Creed, 'unus deus . . . creator omnium visibilium et invisibilium', cf. texts like Col. i. 17: τὰ πάντα ἐν αὐτῷ συνέστηκεν and 1 Cor. xii. 6: ὁ δὲ αὐτὸς θεὸς ὁ ἐνεργῶν τὰ πάντα ἐν πᾶσιν.

[3] Part III below.

the fourth century. At this point, we need only say that it put an end to 'the search for causes' as this had been understood and practised by the philosophers of classical antiquity. Likewise, it disposed of all the multifarious theosophies which had been devised by human ingenuity during classical and post-classical times. But it did so, only to raise fresh problems of understanding, such as were to constitute the theme of discussion from Athanasius to Augustine. This discussion was largely concerned with man and with his status in the hierarchy of nature.

We may here note, to begin with, that to envisage man as a creature in nature was to think of him as a being whose structure and functions, like those of other creatures, were completely dependent upon 'the will of God'. But, on the other hand, his *esse* contained elements of *nosse* and *posse*, which served to distinguish him from other beings whether animate or inanimate by making it possible for him to know himself. In this sense, he was said to have been made 'in the image of the Trinity', naturally (not potentially or hypothetically) immortal and 'marked out' for 'divine sonship'.[1] Paradoxical as this may sound, it nevertheless underlay the whole of Christian teaching with regard to the constitution and history of mankind. For, they insisted, it was by virtue of this gift of self-consciousness that man was enabled to recognize his powers and limitations and, thereby, to 'co-operate' with the Creator in accomplishing his destiny.

But, if the destiny of man was eternal life, how then was it possible to account for the notorious fact that he was everywhere subject to death? To this question there could be but one answer, sin. To say this was to offer a new interpretation of what had long since engaged the attention of Classicism as the ἁμαρτία or *vitium* of human life. This defect, as the Christians saw it, could not possibly be one of nature; that is to say, it was not inherent in the substance of his being. Nor yet was it a defect of habit, to be ascribed ultimately to the material conditions under which he lived. This is not to suggest that the Christians were oblivious to physical or social evil; quite the contrary. But it does indicate that they considered this evil to be the by-product of an evil which was much more fundamental, namely, the refusal of man to acknowledge his privi-

[1] See below, p. 448, n. 7.

leges and responsibilities in the economy of nature, the vain
dream that he could usurp the place of the Creator and be
another God. To indulge this dream was not, of course, to
alter in the slightest the laws which governed that economy; it
was merely to incur the penalty inevitable to their violation.
And, from this standpoint, the failure of man was a matter of
record; his history, indeed, was one of continuous and persistent
self-abuse. This self-abuse began with Adam when, according
to the legend, he consciously and deliberately defied the precept
of probation. By this act he was said to have lost the 'gift of
integrity', that is, of perfect adjustment to the demands of his
nature, and to have started the warfare of the members—a conflict between flesh and spirit the inevitable issue of which was
physical death. It was thus 'through one man', as the Apostle
had expressed it, 'that sin came into the world'.¹ This sin persisted in all the sons and daughters of Adam not as 'actual' or
positive wrongdoing, but as a state, tendency, or predisposition
to repeat his error, and from this none was exempt, if only
because it was a potential of human freedom and the human
capacity for choice. It was thus described as *una cum origine* or
original, and said to have been 'propagated by generation' from
the seed of Adam. We are well aware of the curious and shocking interpretations that have been placed upon this doctrine
which, indeed, constitutes one of the supreme problems of
Christian thought. As Augustine was to put it: 'there is nothing
more notorious and yet more difficult to grasp'.² In considering
what it really means, it is well to remember that 'original sin'
was specifically distinguished by post-Nicene theologians from
'ancestral sin', a kind of hereditary biological or social taint
such as had been envisaged by the Greek tragedians, and that
it was diagnosed as strictly individual, *peccatum personale*, or, as we
should say, a problem of personality. In this connexion it will
be recalled that Adam was an individual and, at the same time,
he is everyman. We may thus conclude that, in a very real
sense, the original sin is being a man.

Paradoxical though it may seem, the Christians discovered in
this doctrine reason for comfort rather than despair. To apprehend it was to grasp what St. Paul had called the law of life or
law of the Spirit which was thus put forward as the one means of

¹ Rom. v. 12: δι' ἑνὸς ἀνθρώπου ἡ ἁμαρτία εἰς τὸν κόσμον εἰσῆλθεν.
² Augustine, *De Mor. Eccl.* i. 22.

redeeming men from the 'law of sin and death'.[1] For it enabled them to perceive that the only creature of whom eternal life could properly be predicated was the individual human being, because he alone was the real unit of conscious and deliberate activity. From this it followed that, just as sin and error were matters of individual aberration, so also salvation depended in the last analysis upon the individual, and this was merely a question of getting him to recognize the truth. This was to set up a wholly new ideal and a wholly new technique of human perfectibility (Christian τελείωσις), namely, the recovery of the natural *donum integritatis* to be achieved through the 'rebirth' of the 'carnal' as a 'spiritual' man.

To examine in detail the various controversies to which this doctrine gave rise would be to anticipate discussions which have been reserved for a more appropriate place in this work.[2] Here we need only observe that regeneration, in the sense just indicated, was felt to be contingent on divine grace. This was no more than to acknowledge that, ultimately, the remedy for the ills of life must come from the same source and on the same terms as life itself; in other words, that it was not to be achieved by kicking against the pricks. But in asking the question 'Hath not the potter power over the clay?' the Apostle had not meant to suggest any programme of mere passivity or resignation, but merely to stipulate as the *sine qua non* of effective action a willing acceptance of the conditions under which it becomes possible to act effectively. And, of these conditions, the first and foremost was that the individual should cease to regard himself as an accident of cosmic process, whether that of aimless self-moving matter or that of self-existent forms, patterns, or types in whose hypothetical reality he vaguely 'participated'. This was to insist that human experience was not to be comprehended 'objectively' in terms applicable to the study of phenomena in nature, but only in terms of the movement of the Spirit, that is, of what is in the minds and hearts of men. To think of it otherwise was to miss its essential significance. It was, indeed, precisely this error which, they held, had vitiated human life and transformed it, in the words of Augustine, into a 'race towards death'. To eliminate it was, therefore, the

---

[1] Rom. viii. 2: ὁ νόμος τοῦ Πνεύματος τῆς ζωῆς ἐν Χριστῷ Ἰησοῦ ἠλευθέρωσέν σε ἀπὸ τοῦ νόμου τῆς ἁμαρτίας καὶ τοῦ θανάτου.

[2] Part III below.

necessary preliminary to any real understanding of the nature and conditions of progress.

Of all elements in Christian teaching, there was none more remarkable than the notion of progress and none more incongruous with the thought and practice of classical antiquity. As originally put forward in the apocalyptic literature, it took shape as the vision of a millennium, the character of which was depicted in language so charged with metaphor and allusion as to give rise to strange misapprehensions on the part of Christian and pagan alike. It thus presented a formidable problem of interpretation which had, nevertheless, to be solved, for it was in a very real sense the *ultima ratio* of the whole Christian attitude to life.

In approaching the problem, the first thing necessary is to distinguish between progress as a fact and progress as an idea. The fact of progress is indisputable; it is, as Aristotle had observed in the *Politics*,[1] bound up with the notion of conscious and deliberate activity; 'all men', as he puts it, 'aim at some good'. But so also, we may add, is the fact of retrogression; for the activity of men is often such as to destroy the good at which they aim. The question, then, resolves itself into one of meaning: what is the ultimate good and how is it to be achieved? And here the greatest difficulties arise both as to ends and means. The history of Classicism provides ample evidence of both.

And first as to ends. For Classicism, two general possibilities had presented themselves: the good, it asserted, consists either in the life of thought or the life of action, or some combination of the two. With respect to the former, we may remember how Sophocles, in a famous chorus of the *Antigone*,[2] had proclaimed the conquest of nature by the 'versatile mind of man', or rather the conquest of everything in nature except death, which was thus conceded to be an inescapable law of life. By this admission he provoked a question which could not long remain unanswered without inspiring the gravest doubt as to the ultimate value of classical *curiositas* or the 'life of science'. Vergil, on the other hand, was an apostle of action which, as we have seen,[3] he sought with all his immense gifts to explain and justify. And, while profoundly sensitive to the transitory and painful character of individual experience, he discovered a compensation for

---

[1] i. 1.   [2] ll. 332-75   [3] Ch. II above.

this in the welfare and 'eternity' of the whole. For this ideal of corporative immortality he invited his countrymen to work and die while, at the same time, reserving a heaven of individual apotheosis for those exceptional spirits who, as he agreed with Cicero, could properly be described as saviours of the state. In so doing, he pronounced the *passo romano* to be for all time the march-step of humanity. This also, as we may well suspect, was not enough. Like the ideal of science, it fell short of the justice which was demanded by the reason and conscience of mankind.

The Christians broke with these interpretations in order to assert that the good for man is eternal life and that this consists in the knowledge and love of God as the principle of his own being. In this connexion, it is important to notice that the good thus proposed was strictly a 'personal', not a 'corporative' or 'collective' good. As such, it claimed to be real, not problematical or imaginary, both because its subject was real, the concrete individual, and because it was the object of his immediate experience. But to say this was to raise the question of direction and process.

And here, so the Christians claimed, the error of Classicism had been to look 'outside' for the creative and moving principle. This, they insisted, was to expose oneself to the danger of idolatry, that is, of identifying reality with the picture or representation of it framed by the conceptualizing imagination. It was also to create an insoluble problem of intelligibility, thus permitting the materialist or idealist magician to produce any rabbit he liked out of the philosophic hat. Finally, it was to give rise to false antitheses in flat contradiction to the findings of experience, such as that between formless matter and motionless form; and then attempt to construct out of these nonentities an authentic description of the universe.

To these difficulties of Classicism the answer of the Christians was a demand that it should acknowledge the Trinity as the creative and moving principle. To do so, they urged, was to perceive that the difficulties in question, however serious, were difficulties not in the structure of reality but merely in the effort to apprehend it. It was to recognize that what, in fact, constitutes the nature of any substance is the order and movement which are in it, and that these are not to be thought of as in any sense external to that substance, dependent either on self-existent 'types' or on a substratum of anarchic 'matter'. It was thus to see in the world of natural objects not God, indeed, nor any part of God but, as they put it, the *vestigia* or traces of divine activity. As for the human being, the knowing subject, what they claimed for him was the unique satisfaction of access to this eternal truth through the Word and the Spirit.[1] And, from this standpoint, the only barrier to his progress towards full perfection was that which he imposed upon himself by his blind and stubborn refusal to see it.

Such, if we are not mistaken, were the nature and basis of the Christian theory of progress. Considering its remoteness from the common sense of antiquity, we need not wonder that it proved to be a difficult notion to communicate to the classical mind. Nor is it surprising that the Christians themselves should have experienced some perplexity in formulating it in intelligible terms. For what it pointed to was a way of thought utterly different from that in which they had been brought up. We thus find Origen, for instance, protesting vigorously against the Platonic theory of cycles—the notion, as he says, that 'in another Athens another Socrates will be born who will marry another Xanthippe and will be accused by another Anytus and another Meletus'.[2] But it is one thing to deny with him the possibility of such repetitions and quite another to discover how to break away from 'the wheel'. Tertullian, on the other hand, was much more sensitive than Origen to the fact and necessity of change. This is illustrated by his attack on convention and especially the conventions of *Romanitas*. 'The truth', he declares, 'appears to be instinctively hated.'[3] Nevertheless, things do move, even in a society ridden by traditional standards.

'In your clothing, your food, your habits, your feelings, finally even in your language, you have repudiated your ancestors. You are always praising antiquity, but you renew your life from day to day.'[4]

'Consider whether the general accusation which you bring against us, namely, that we have discarded ancestral custom, may not be levelled equally against yourselves. To me it appears that, in every aspect of your life and discipline, the practice of antiquity has been corrupted and destroyed . . . your own authority overrides the whole authority of the past.'[5]

---

[1] John xvi. 13: ὅταν δὲ ἔλθῃ ἐκεῖνος, τὸ Πνεῦμα τῆς ἀληθείας, ὁδηγήσει ὑμᾶς εἰς τὴν ἀλήθειαν πᾶσαν.

[2] *Contra Celsum*, iv. 68.　　[3] *Apol.* 14.　　[4] 6.　　[5] *Ad Nat.* i. 10.

This change he is inclined to identify with progress.

'If you look at the world as a whole, you cannot doubt that it has grown progressively more cultivated and populated (*cultior de die et instructior pristino*) Every territory is now accessible, every territory explored, every territory opened to commerce. The most delightful farmsteads have obliterated areas formerly waste, plough-land has subdued the woods, domestic cattle have put to flight the wild beast, barren sands have become fertile, rocks are reduced to soil, swamps are drained, the number of cities to-day exceeds the number of isolated huts in former times, islands no longer inspire fear nor crags terror: everywhere people, everywhere organized communities, everywhere human life. Most convincing as evidence of populousness, we men have actually become a burden to the earth, the fruits of nature hardly suffice to sustain us, there is a general pressure of scarcity giving rise to complaints, since the earth can no longer support us. Need we be astonished that plague and famine, warfare and earthquake come to be regarded as remedies, serving as it were to trim and prune the superfluity of population?'[1]

But, when Tertullian undertakes to prove the reality of progress, what he does is actually to fall back for evidence, in a genuinely classical manner, upon external nature (τὰ ἔξω; τὰ ἔξωθεν), the only difference being that, whereas Classicism had seen in nature order or rather a tendency towards order, Tertullian sees in it nothing but change or mutation. This law, he declares, manifests itself in the regular movement of celestial bodies (*naturae totius solemne munus*), the solar year, the monthly phases of the moon, the rising and setting of the constellations (*siderum distincta confusio*), day and night, sunshine and cloud, storm and calm. The earth as a whole has changed; at one time it was entirely submerged in water. Sea-shells are to be found even on the mountain-tops, as though to vindicate the contention of Plato that the very highlands were once flooded, and even to-day earthquakes occasionally produce changes of the kind.[2] This law of physical mutation, he thinks, applies also to animals and men; these since primeval times having extended their habitat over the greater part of an empty world.[3] Although, he significantly adds, this cannot in all respects be considered an improvement.[4]

It will be evident from these statements that Tertullian has utterly missed the point of the Christian position as we have

---

[1] *De Anima*, 30; no apologies to Malthus!
[2] *De Pallio*, 2.   [3] 3.   [4] 4.

tried to put it. He has failed to realize that the law of progress is a law for man, and that no coherent and intelligible theory thereof can be erected on speculation regarding the structure and process of external nature. 'Heaven and Earth shall pass away but my Words shall not pass away.' As a consequence of this mistake, Tertullian emerges not as an exponent of the Christian theory of progress but as the first apostle of modern relativism. This comes out especially in his idea of progressive truth. Thus, in the *De Virginibus Velandis*, a treatise of his Montanist period, he argues that no prescription whatever can be imposed upon truth. Nothing, he declares, has power to do so.

'Our Lord Jesus Christ described Himself as truth and not as custom. . . . Apart, therefore, from the one immutable and irrefutable principle, the rule of faith, all other truths whatsoever of theory and practice admit of modification, since presumably the grace of God continues to operate and to produce results till the very end of time. . . . The Lord has sent His spirit, the Paraclete. . . . I have much still to say to you, He declares, but not until you have power to receive it. . . . When the Spirit of truth shall have come, It will guide you into the way of all truth and will proclaim to you what is still to come. . . . What, then, is the service of the Spirit except to make possible the direction of training, the revelation of Scripture, the reform of understanding, the achievement of better things? . . . *Nihil sine aetate et omnia tempus exspectant*; there is nothing which has not its season and all things await their time.'[1]

But it is one thing to admit that there is much truth still to be discovered, and quite another to suggest that the discovery of this truth is contingent upon the working of an erratic and wholly incalculable force, the Montanist Paraclete.

The difficulties of Tertullian have been traced to what has been called the 'unexpunged remnant of classical materialism', which was embedded in his thought. This finds expression in interesting and often startling ways. It comes out, for instance, in his attempt to visualize the soul as a sort of astral or ghost body.[2] Then too, it underlies his notion of a material millennium as an event which is, so to speak, fatally determined, quite regardless of whatever efforts human beings put forward to bring it about. In other words, it is involved in 'the movement of matter' and thus, in the last analysis, quite unin-

---

[1] op. cit. 1.   [2] *De Anima*, 7–9 and 53; cf. *De Resur. Carnis.*

telligible. But the supreme example of Tertullian's materialism is to be found in his notion of Hell as a kind of unearthly Colosseum in which, by way of compensation for their former sufferings, the saints and martyrs of the Church are provided with ring-side seats in order that they may taste the peculiar physical satisfaction of watching the physical torment of the damned.[1] This sort of thing, it should be noted, was deeply rooted in the ideology of the early Church and it was by no means easy to dispose of. We may thus find it emerging as late as Augustine, when he seriously discusses, *inter alia*, the prospect of a Gehenna of fire and brimstone, though such a possibility is clearly inconsistent with his own best level of eschatological thought.[2]

The effect of the Nicene formulation was largely to exclude errors such as had marred the thinking of Origen and Tertullian, and to lay the foundation for a new and distinctively Christian *Weltanschauung*, to accept which was to enter into an area of experience utterly different from that of secular society. The problem arises: What was the relation between this world and the vast structure of secular values which had been erected under the auspices of the pagan empire? The question resolves itself entirely into one of meaning. And, in this connexion, we may agree that for vast numbers who were content not to think but simply to follow the leadership of the emperor, it was merely a matter of substituting Christ for Juppiter, the Eucharist for the sacrifice, baptism for the *taurobolium*, and pretending to themselves that otherwise everything was the same.[3] But for those who could not be satisfied to live a life of flagrant inconsistency, no such solution was possible. What, then, did the change imply for them? We have seen how, with men like Tertullian, it resulted in a rash and hasty repudiation of all natural values, including even the simplest satisfactions of normal life. Christians, he declared, should practise the most rigid asceticism; second marriages (especially for widows) are tantamount to bigamy, and to be fat is merely to provide good food for the lions.

But what application had such doctrine to a period when the lions had ceased to roar for Christians, when the empire had not only desisted from persecution but had actually taken them

---

[1] *De Spect.* 30.
[2] *De Civ. Dei*, xxi. 9 and 10.   [3] See Duchesne, op. cit. iii, p. 159.

to its bosom? Merely to formulate the question is to realize that it must have involved the greatest confusion and perplexity, especially as it first presented itself toward the beginning of the fourth century. But certain considerations were soon to become evident. One was that Christianity subverted the ancient interpretation of life in terms of the concepts virtue and fortune, or rather that virtue and fortune were thenceforth to lose their status as independent principles. And, therewith, it subverted the notion of felicity (the *summum bonum*) to be realized through security and independence, otherwise control of the environment (τὰ ἔξωθεν) or the monopolization of physical and economic power. That is to say, it subverted the central idea of creative politics as this had been pursued throughout classical antiquity. But if the state thus ceased to be regarded as final, what then was to replace it? And what was to be the relation of the New Republic to any fresh institution which might arise, with claims to finality not less insistent than those of the now discredited *polis*?

Such questions are much easier to ask than to answer. But of one thing, at least, we may be sure, and this was that the state did not propose to yield the substance of its traditional prerogatives without a struggle. We thus find Constantine already in 335 (only ten years after Nicaea) looking for a way of escape from the implications of the Nicene formula, and seeking to have it neutralized in the direction of Arianism. He began by condoning Arian attacks on Athanasius at Tyre. Shortly afterwards he banished the stubborn ecclesiastic to the remoteness of Trèves, and formally demanded of a metropolitan synod the readmission of Arius to communion. Finally, he indicated his own personal feeling by accepting baptism at the hands of the Arian Bishop of Nicomedia, thus dying in the odour of Arian sanctity and leaving a legacy of trouble to his sons.

The Christological controversies which immediately broke out and which were to continue for the better part of the fourth century may, perhaps, be dismissed as 'meaningless and unedifying wrangles' by those who perversely regard thought as a function of matter. But for those who believe that what men do has a direct relationship to what they think and what they want, it is impossible to avoid the issues raised at that time. And, from this standpoint, those issues concern the historian no less directly than they do the theologian; he cannot, therefore, neglect them except at the cost of missing what was really central to the economic, social, and political movements of the age. This will serve to justify the attempt, however inadequate it may have been, to expose the essential elements of the Christian position, as they were apprehended in the period subsequent to Nicaea.

Accession of the sons of Constantine initiated a period of violent oscillation, of action and reaction which clearly portended the destruction of his hopes. The period was marked by a series of intrigues between the heirs, as well as by anti-dynastic and 'republican' (i.e. pagan) military movements in Gaul and Pannonia.[1] Sedition at Antioch and a Jewish revolt put down with savage cruelty by the Caesar Gallus point to the existence of dangerous unrest in Syria and Palestine. In opposing the usurper Magnentius, Constantius had invited the Franks and Alemanni across the Rhine; but his barbarous allies proceeded to overrun and harry the Gauls in a fashion reminiscent of the worst horrors of the previous century. The peace which Constantine seems to have imposed on Persia expired with his death; and, on the usual pretext of Roman interference in Armenia, Sapor invaded the trans-Euphrates provinces, besieging Nisibis in 338 and again in 346, while the Romans, on their side, claimed a great victory at Singara (348). Trouble with the Quadi and Sarmati on the Danube culminated in a fierce campaign (355) which required the personal attention of the emperor; and so serious had become the pressure along the Rhine–Danube frontier that, in the following year, Constantius found it necessary to elevate his hated cousin Julian to the purple, and to commission him as Caesar in Gaul.

Meanwhile, within the empire, there is evidence of increasing governmental regulation designed at once to maintain the semblance of justice and to check the multiplication of abuses within the official hierarchy. Thus, with regard to the administration of law,[2] we may note an edict whereby provincial justices were threatened with fines if they ignored or postponed

---

[1] Evidence on coins of Magnentius *renobatio urbis, liberator reipublicae, restitutor libertatis*, Eckhel, *Doct. Num.* viii, p. 122; cf. *Cod. Theod.* xvi. 10. 5 (353): 'aboleantur sacrificia nocturna Magnentio auctore permissa.' Any pagan reaction had, of course. to be more or less covert.   [2] *Cod. Theod.*, bk. i.

the enforcement of rescripts,[1] as they had earlier been enjoined
not to block appeals by delay.[2] On the other hand, diocesan
vicars were ordered to transmit forthwith to imperial head-
quarters questions referred to them by provincial governors and
fiscal officials,[3] all such questions to be submitted through the
vicars.[4] An enactment of 349 provided that no one should be
granted a public salary except by special instruction from the
emperor.[5] The disposition of officials to grasp at perquisites of
various kinds prompted a regulation which confined the right
of authorizing such grants to the praetorian prefects.[6] Subsequent measures provided that requisitions were to be made
only upon the diocese of the official in question and then only
when personally endorsed by the emperor.[7] Another edict
contains detailed regulations governing the organization and
discipline of the imperial courier service, the *agentes in rebus*
under the Master of the Offices.[8]

A feature of the time appears to have been the tendency of
officialdom to impose unusual and unjust demands upon the
civilian population while, at the same time, it usurped a quasi-
judicial coercive power over its victims. An edict of 344,[9] applicable to Africa, forbade imperial functionaries to abuse their
position in this way. Thirteen years later it became necessary
to provide relief for shippers, who found themselves subjected
to special burdens over and above their normal legal obligations in the transport of public grain.[10] An enactment of 361
records the organization of a *defensio senatorum* for the protection
of imperial senators against similar impositions.[11] Meanwhile,
the tenants of imperial estates were declared amenable to jurisdiction at the hands of regular provincial courts, on the same
terms as provincials themselves;[12] while the same courts were
authorized to deal also with cases involving the imperial
couriers. Two laws (*De Dignitatibus*) relate to the *curiosi*,
stationarii, and *curagendarii*, members of the imperial ministry of
transport. The first[13] prohibits them from exercising summary
jurisdiction (including the right of imprisonment) upon provincials who were liable to obligations connected with the
public transport service, ordering them to submit all complaints

---

[1] i. 2. 7 (356).   [2] i. 5. 4 (342).   [3] i. 15. 2 (348).   [4] i. 15. 3 (353).
[5] xii. 2. 1.   [6] i. 5. 5 (355).   [7] i. 5. 6 and 7 (358).
[8] i. 9. 1 (359).   [9] viii. 10. 2.   [10] xiii. 5. 9.   [11] i. 28. 1.
[12] ii. 1. 1 (349).   [13] vi. 29. 1 (355).

to the provincial authorities and to support them by valid evidence; the second[1] forbids them to grant free passes to any one other than the imperial couriers, as well as the use of excessive equipment.

While thus seeking to check the growth of official laxness and corruption, as well as of official encroachment upon the rights of civilians, the government at the same time endeavoured to prevent the escape of any one from what were regarded as his original obligations, i.e. the duties imposed upon him by virtue of his birth and status; and, in so doing, it was mainly concerned to enforce the obligations of the unhappy members of municipal corporations whom we have earlier described as the chief victims of the Constantinian system. That these local aristocracies numbered among them many who were in no position to meet heavy fiscal demands is indicated by the law[2] which states that the holding of twenty-five *iugera* of private land or even less renders the possessor liable to curial duty, even though he tries to escape by pleading the privilege of a *colonus* on the imperial estates.

In order to prevent evasion by these *curiales* of their *obsequia*, it was provided by the same law that individuals seeking to decrease their assessments by means of fictitious sales were liable to have the properties thus sold confiscated to the treasury. Landowners disposing of pieces of property were likewise forbidden to retain *coloni* or land-workers, whose services were attached thereto, by transferring them to remaining portions of their estates.[3] The purchase of imperial honours was discountenanced under heavy fines,[4] and a period of not less than twenty years' service as imperial agent was prescribed as a condition of exemption from 'original' curial duties, the same rule applying also to service in the imperial record office, chancery, treasury, or estates' department. Meanwhile, any one trying to evade his responsibilities under colour of superior rank was made liable, on conviction, to a fine of 30 lb. silver;[5] *ex-comites* (former ministers of executive departments), *ex-praesides* (former provincial governors), and *ex-rationales* (former revenue officials), in short all *ex-perfectissimi* (if their status was honorary) being subject to this rule;[6] although the enforcement of curial obligations against persons in possession of *honorarii*

[1] vi. 29. 2 (357).   [2] xii. 1. 33 (342).   [3] xiii. 10. 3 (357).
[4] vi. 22. 2 (338).   [5] xii. 1. 24 (338).   [6] xii. 1. 26 (338).

codicilli was not to involve them in the loss of their status.[1] By a regulation of 344, *curiales* by origin were made liable to their fiscal duties, no matter how long employed in the imperial civil service;[2] ten years later it was ordered that all such persons should be released from their oaths and dismissed to their original municipalities.[3] In 361 the same regulation was applied to individuals who had worked their way into the imperial senate.[4] Even the ranks of the army afforded an imperfect refuge from curial obligations. Members of the *palatini* (imperial military police), who lacked the credit of five years' service, were to be relegated forthwith to their communities of origin,[5] and the ranks of the *domestici* and *protectores* (head-quarters' troops) were to be combed for delinquents.[6] Recruits for the army were not to be accepted unless, in the presence of the local decurions, their origin and their freedom from curial liability were publicly attested.[7] Meanwhile, the government tried to supplement the dwindling ranks of *curiales* from outside. Sons of soldiers, who were ordinarily liable to the same obligations as their fathers, if after sixteen years found unfit to bear arms, were to be posted to curial duty.[8] All veterans must carry regular discharge certificates, and any one found descending to brigandage was threatened with capital punishment if he did not at once betake himself either to agriculture or industry.[9]

Similar heavy-handed enactments were promulgated with the object of maintaining essential social services as milch-cows for the state. The rule enforcing liability to their obligations upon *curiales*, no matter how long employed in the imperial *militia*, was applied also to corporations or guilds outside the *curia*, such as those of lime-burners, armourers, and silversmiths.[10] All traders (*negotiatores*) were subjected to the *lustratio* or business tax, exemption being accorded only to ecclesiastics, veterans, and farmers retailing the produce of their own land.[11] In the municipality of Rome, any one contracting a marriage with the daughter of a member of the bakers' guild, which was charged with the responsibility of preparing bread to be issued as part of the public dole, rendered himself liable to the *obsequia* of that guild.[12] Provincial governors were forbidden to confer immunity

---

[1] xii. 1. 41 (353).　　[2] xii. 1. 37.　　[3] xii. 1. 42.　　[4] xii. 1. 48.
[5] xii. 1. 31 (341).　　　[6] xii. 1. 38 (346).　　　[7] vii. 13. 1 (353).
[8] xii. 1. 35 (343).　　　[9] vii. 20. 7 (353).　　　[10] xii. 1. 37 (344).
[11] xiii. 1. 1–3 (356–61).　　　　　[12] xiv. 3. 2 (355).

from any obligations relating to the maintenance of roads, bridges, and other public works throughout the empire.[1]

In criminal law and procedure we may perceive a continuation of tendencies observed during the reign of Constantine. In this connexion, certain enactments are of special interest as designed to protect the currency of the New Republic. Counterfeiters of the standard gold *solidus* were to be burnt alive, and a reward was offered for information leading to their conviction.[2] Persons found guilty of melting down coins or of transporting them abroad for sale were liable to capital punishment.[3] No one was to buy or hoard money 'as the currency in circulation is not itself a commodity but rather a means of exchanging commodities'. Any one detected in possession of minted coins other than those in regular circulation was liable to have them confiscated. Merchants and shippers were permitted to carry only the amount of cash requisite for their business. Such measures indicate a determination to prevent the recurrence of conditions such as had prevailed during the anarchy of the third century.

The strength of the indictment against Constantinianism lies in the accumulation of detail contained within this wearisome record; and this must serve as an excuse for piling up evidence to illustrate the inefficiency and corruption of the imperial bureaucracy, as well as the evident distress of its victims. But, with this brief review of social and economic conditions, we must now turn to what was the main concern of Constantius, viz. the religious question. And here we may suggest that it was the fate of the son to ignore all that was best and to promote all that was worst in his father's policy. For, if the spirit of Lactantius be taken to characterize the age of Constantine, that of Firmicus Maternus must be regarded as no less typical of the reign of his successor. And, as has been pointed out,[4] the work of this man, especially the *De Errore Profanarum Religionum*, addressed to the sons of Constantine, is a veritable handbook of intolerance. In pronouncing 'the sentence of God' upon paganism, it pointed the way to a persecution of adherents of the old faiths in a fashion analogous to that whereby the old faiths had formerly persecuted the new, but in an even fiercer spirit ('nec filio iubet parci, nec fratri, sed per amatam coniugem gladium

[1] xv. 1. 5 (338). [2] ix. 21. 5 (343).
[3] ix. 22. 1 (343) and 23. 1 (356). [4] Boissier, *La Fin du paganisme*, i. 68.

vindicem ducit'). By thus exciting a spirit of religious fanaticism and strife, by fomenting discord within the empire, it helped to seal the doom of Constantinianism and to make inevitable the coming reaction under Julian.

Throughout this period the watchword and motto was *cesset superstitio, sacrificiorum aboleatur insania.*[1] Under this caption, paganism was now to experience the nemesis of its own earlier offences. By an edict of 346, dated from Constantinople and repeated, in substance, ten years later at Milan, all temples whatsoever were to be closed, except as museums of art, access to the altars being specifically forbidden; the death-penalty, together with confiscation of goods, was to be inflicted upon persons found guilty of participating in sacrifices, and magistrates were threatened with fines for any failure to enforce the law.[2] The animus against pagans was reflected also in an increasingly restrictive and ungenerous attitude to the Jews. Any Jew purchasing a slave of Gentile stock was liable to have him summarily confiscated; for the purchase of slaves known to be Christians, he was to suffer the total confiscation of all his servants; if he presumed to have such slaves circumcised, the penalty was death.[3] As for the association by Jews in their rites of Christian women operatives in the *gynaecea* or state textile works, this crime also was to be visited with capital punishment.[4] Shortly afterwards the conversion of free men to Judaism was discountenanced by the threat of total confiscation of goods.[5] Meanwhile, under the criminal law (bk. ix), it was made a capital offence for any one to consult a *haruspex*, a *hariolus*, or a *mathematicus*; *sileat omnibus perpetuo divinandi curiositas*, ran the edict.[6] And, despite the immunity from this punishment normally accorded to members of the imperial service, *magi* and diviners caught in its ranks were declared liable to torture.[7]

But, while thus implementing against pagans the sentence of God upon paganism, Constantius undertook at the same time to promote and foster the interests of Christianity, and the spirit of his missionary effort may be judged from a series of

---

[1] *Cod. Theod.* xvi. 10. 2 (341). In connexion with this and other enactments we may recall the salutary warning of Toutain, *Economic Life of the Ancient World*, p. 327: 'The mere fact that so many were issued shows how ineffective they were.' All that can safely be inferred from them is the spirit and direction of governmental policy.

[2] xvi. 10. 3, 4, and 6.   [3] xvi. 9. 2 (339).   [4] xvi. 8. 6 (339).
[5] xvi. 8. 7 (357).   [6] ix. 16. 4 (357).   [7] ix. 16. 6 (358).

edicts issued in his name. Thus, in a manifesto addressed to the clergy,[1] he declared that they and their slaves were exempt from all new and special levies, as well as from liability to the onerous obligation of quartering imperial officials (*hospitalitas*); they were likewise authorized to conduct business enterprises for purposes of subsistence, free from the *lustratio* or business tax. In 349 all clerics were pronounced exempt from curial and other obligations, their children, unless liable by origin to curial duties, to be classified as ecclesiastics;[2] four years later they and their children were specifically exempted from personal burdens (*sordida et corporalia onera*) and from the business tax (*lustratio*) on account of profits from shelters and workhouses, on the ground that these institutions were helpful to the poor. This indulgence to sweated labour was extended also to the wives, children, and slaves, male or female, of the clerics in question, and repeated in substance after a further interval of four years.[3] About the same time Constantius conceded to bishops accused of criminal offences the right to be heard only before their peers, thus giving a dangerous complexion to the Constantinian ecclesiastical courts.[4] The concession of such special immunities and privileges was only too eagerly accepted; and the appetite apparently grew by what it fed on. Towards the close of the reign (359 or 360), the emperor was confronted with a brazen demand put forward by the ecclesiastical synod of Ariminum, viz. that *iuga* or taxable land-units belonging to ecclesiastics should be exempt from public obligations. This impudent suggestion he had the courage to refuse; but he confirmed the immunity of small businesses undertaken by clerics for maintenance, ordering all others to be put on the *matricula* or business assessment roll. The general spirit of his policy was expressed in a final edict (361), which exempted from public obligations all those who devoted themselves to the 'Christian law', i.e. the monks.[5]

But while Constantius thus professed to see in prayer rather than work the bone and sinew of the New Republic, his critics preferred to interpret his policy as a deliberate attempt to prostitute the Church to his own sordid purposes. Thus, in a

[1] xvi. 2. 8 (343).   [2] xvi. 2. 9.
[3] xvi. 2. 10 (353) and 14 (357).   [4] xvi. 2. 12 (355).
[5] xvi. 2. 16: 'gaudere enim et gloriari ex fide semper volumus, scientes magis religionibus quam officiis et labore corporis vel sudore nostram rem publicam contineri.'

famous passage,[1] the sturdy and sensible pagan, Ammianus Marcellinus, declares that the emperor confounded the Christian religion, simple and clear by nature, with womanish superstition; and the text may be accepted as referring to the legislation reviewed above, as well as to the specifically ecclesiastical policy. For, as a means of reducing the Church to a condition of subservience, Constantius added to this gross and demoralizing patronage an attempt to complicate the 'clear and simple truths' aforesaid with subtleties propounded no doubt mainly by Valens, the Arian bishop of Mursa who, having helped by his prayers to win the battle against Magnentius, had been accepted by the emperor as his confidential spiritual adviser. These subtleties Constantius endeavoured to impose upon the Church; and, as he merely succeeded in stirring up discord, he convoked synod after synod in an effort to have them ratified, so that the imperial transport service almost broke down under the strain of carrying ecclesiastics dashing hither and thither at the behest of the emperor.

In these synods Constantius assumed the impossible position of Bishop of Bishops and, as has earlier been suggested,[2] boldly asserted the principle later to be known as that of divine right. In order to make good his claims, he harried his opponents within the episcopacy and, in particular, put intolerable pressure upon the aged Liberius, bishop of Rome; altogether his efforts might well have succeeded, had it not been for the lion in his path.[3]

The spectacle of *Athanasius contra mundum* has excited the generous admiration of Gibbon, who describes in detail the resistance which this gallant soldier of the Church put up against imperial interference, in the face of obloquy and persecution during which he suffered no less than five different periods of exile under three successive monarchs of the Constantinian house. The strength of Athanasius was the strength of the man with but one idea; the defence of orthodoxy was the inspiration of his life's work. And, if it be true that Nicaea put teeth into Christianity, it is equally fair to say that, with Athanasius, the Church showed how she could bite the hand that fed her. For while Arian and Catholic bishops, as individuals, were per-

---

[1] xxi. 16. 18.   [2] Ch. V, p. 187 above.
[3] Athanasius, elected bishop of Alexandria in succession to Alexander, who died 18 April 328.

haps equally capable of compliance or intransigency, according to whether their interests were promoted or threatened, nevertheless it cannot well be denied that there was an element of hardness in the orthodox position, as represented by Athanasius, which was lacking on the other side. And, as the spirit of persecution invoked by Constantius against paganism was presently applied to the 'healing' of schism within the Church itself, Nicene orthodoxy was now to experience treatment such as it had not yet learned to expect at the hands of a nominally Christian emperor. As Athanasius himself put it, 'persecution was peculiarly the disgrace of the new heresy'.[1]

Among those who supported the effort of Constantius to subvert the Trinitarian position, orthodoxy discovered two allied and partially co-operating groups. The first was composed of the so-called Anomoeans or extreme Arians who declared that the Son was of quite another essence than the Father; the second of the semi-Arian *Homoiousians*, whose position differed from the orthodox or *Homoousian* faction 'merely by an iota'. But, in that iota, as Athanasius saw it, lay all the difference between the claim of the Evangel to finality and a Platonic theory of 'participation' which, by leaving open the question of 'how much' the Son resembled the Father, was exposed to the possibility of numberless other 'revelations', past, present, and to come.

The special contribution made by Athanasius towards an elucidation of the theological and philosophical issues involved must be reserved for its appropriate place in this work.[2] At present we are concerned with him merely as a man of action who, in defence of what he conceived to be spiritual truth, stubbornly opposed the pretensions of the Arianizing court.[3] With this purpose in mind he was ready in practice to adopt any one of four different kinds of action. In the first place, he never tired of recalling the plenipotentiary authority of the oecumenical council as the original author of the Nicene formula. Secondly, he made it his business to mobilize whatever episcopal support could be mustered in defence of that formula, especially at Rome and throughout the West during his exile at Trèves. Thirdly, he developed the use of direct popular propaganda as, for example, when he caused a letter of public protest to be drafted and circulated for signature at Alexandria, begging the emperor to desist from his anti-

---

[1] *Hist. Arian.* 67 foll.   [2] Ch. X below.   [3] Athan. *Hist. Arian.*

Trinitarian programme 'for the sake of his immortal soul'. Finally, he showed himself willing to submit to personal indignity, as attested by various humiliations which he suffered on account of his refusal to accede to the emperor's demands. In helping to frame a theory of ecclesiastical independence, the work of Athanasius was no less important. He repeatedly asserted the impropriety of imperial intervention in the internal affairs of the Church. 'When', he demands,[1] 'has an ecclesiastical judgement ever received its validity from the emperor? Or rather, when has his decree ever been recognized by the Church?' Moreover, he protested against the assumption by imperial power of any control over ecclesiastical organization and discipline, and denounced the episcopal appointments of Constantius as the work of Antichrist.[2] In this it would appear that he was fully justified, if the elevation of the notorious George of Cappadocia to the see of Alexandria may be regarded as, in any sense, typical.[3] In these various respects he laid the foundation of a specifically Christian political theory.

Space forbids us to trace in detail the progress of a struggle during which the emperor, in his endeavour to escape from the net which was closing about him, resorted to the most amazing expedients. It is sufficient to observe that, by his actions, he laid the material for a crisis in the relations of Church and state. On all sides there was increasing evidence of venality in ecclesiastical high places. Meanwhile the widespread corruption of the imperial civil service, already referred to, was being traced by observant critics to the scandal of the palace, from which the eunuchs, a specifically Byzantine importation from the Orient, now for the first time in Roman history dictated the policy of the empire.

Constantius' policy was one of recession from the difficulties of the Constantinian system. There was no formal repudiation of Christianity; quite the contrary, as is shown by evidence from the Code. Nevertheless, the 'supreme God' who, under the father, had slowly assumed the lineaments of Jehovah, was under the son imperceptibly metamorphosed once more into his original self. But the fact that Constantius remained a nominal Christian added a certain piquancy to Athanasius' denunciation of the pious emperor as Antichrist; and thus gave

[1] Op. cit. 52.   [2] Op. cit. 74–5.
[3] See below, Ch. VII, p. 271, on this extraordinary character.

point and sting to his attack on the régime. At the same time, it suggested very clearly the vanity of any attempt on the part of the emperor to escape from the implications of Constantinianism within the formal limits of Christianity. Accordingly, the crisis provoked by Constantius turned out to be at once ecclesiastical and political; or, to put the issue otherwise, just as Constantinianism had involved a *mariage de convenance* between state and Church, so the way of escape from its anomalies seemed to lie in a divorce between the two. Thus, at the very moment when Athanasius in his conflict with the emperor had reached a position equivalent to that of stalemate, he was at last to find a champion both able and willing to vindicate his cause. But the avenger was not to arise from the tents of Israel. It was as a renegade from the faith that Julian, assuming the diadem in Paris, executed his Napoleonic thrust across the continent at Constantinople; only to find, on his arrival, that his enemy was already broken and dead, while the Christian capital prepared to accord a royal welcome to the avowed enemy of Christianity.

VII

APOSTASY AND REACTION

WITH the entry of Julian into Constantinople (December 361), philosophy, for the second time in Roman history, assumed the imperial purple.[1] A son of Julius Constantius brother of Constantine the Great, the new emperor had been born in the capital just thirty years before. As a child of six he had suffered a terrible shock through the extermination of his kinsmen in the massacre of potential rivals which marked the accession of the sons of Constantine, Julian himself and his elder brother Gallus having alone escaped from the slaughter. At the age of thirteen he had been relegated, along with Gallus, to the remote and inaccessible fortress of Macellum in Cappadocia, there to spend the next seven years in close confinement, 'cut off from every liberal study and from all free intercourse'.[2] But the dynasticism, which had thus seared his childhood and adolescence, was later to bring about a strange reversal of his fortunes. On the death of Constantine, Constantine II, his eldest son, had inherited the Gauls, Spain, and Britain, while the youngest, Constans, received Italy, Illyricum, and Africa as his portion of the empire. Within three years Constans had overthrown Constantine and seized his dominions to make himself sole Augustus in the West (340). Ten years later Constans himself was murdered by Magnentius, his Master of the Horse. The usurpation of the purple by Magnentius, co-incident with the revolt of Vetranio in Pannonia, made it necessary for Constantius, now sole survivor of the brothers and himself without an heir, to invoke the aid of his cousins, if the dynasty was to be preserved. Thus Gallus, by his appointment as Caesar, was suddenly translated from the prison to the throne (351); while Julian, then a youth of twenty, was removed to the capital in order to receive the status, if not the consideration, of a prince of the blood. Gallus, however, was soon deposed and executed by Constantius (354), partly because the overthrow of Magnentius had rendered him superfluous, partly also by reason of temperamental vices which made him a

[1] Dessau, *I.L.S.* 751: d. n. Fl. Cl. Iulianus dominus totius orbis filosofiae magister venerandus princeps piissimus imperator victoriosissimus Augustus. ὁ ἐκ φιλοσοφίας βασιλεύων. . . . Φλ. Κλαυδ. Ιουλιανὸς ὁ μέγιστος καὶ θειότατος αὐτοκράτωρ.

[2] Julian, 271 c (except where otherwise stated, references are to the Teubner text, ed. Hertlein, 1875).

liability, rather than an asset, to the Flavian house. Meanwhile, since the emperor was then in the West, Julian was ordered to Milan and kept under strict surveillance at the court. There, however, the friendship of the empress Eusebia won him a brief interlude of freedom and happiness; as a result of her entreaties, the young man was permitted to withdraw for study to Athens and Bithynia.[1] But the depredations of the Germans soon put an end to his leisure and, in the year following (355), he was dragged from his retirement in order that, as Caesar, he might represent the family interest in the Gauls.[2] In that capacity, Julian was evidently expected merely to serve as a mask for the corrupt and inefficient administration of Constantius' praetorian prefect; but, stimulated by an ideal of public service out of all proportion to the resources at his command,[3] the shy and diffident scholar emerged as a man of action, whose skill and enterprise in clearing the West of barbarians were equalled only by his solicitude for the harried and overtaxed provincials within his jurisdiction. The position of colleague and understudy, at all times difficult, could in no case have been more so than with Julian in Gaul; and it is not surprising that an attempt on the part of his cousin to weaken him by withdrawing all but a fragment of his veteran formations should have provoked the mutiny which led to his assumption of the diadem. In declaring himself emperor, the action of Julian was more than a protest of bitter personal resentment against domestic tyranny; for it placed him at the forefront of a major revolutionary movement, the most significant since the rise of Constantine himself. But, unlike the movement headed by Constantine, that of Julian was one of reaction, the watchword of which was to be, *from Christ to Plato*.

Julian's undertaking was in a peculiar sense a personal enterprise, and it can be understood only if this fact is borne in mind. In this connexion we may note that the Apostate was endowed with not a little of the genius hereditary to the second Flavians. As Caesar in Gaul, he had developed qualities of statesmanship which served vividly to recall the memory and achievements of his grandfather, Constantius Chlorus, while his work as a soldier was not unworthy of Constantine himself. The boldness

---

[1] Julian, *Oratio*, iii. 118 c. [2] Amm. xv. 8. 1 foll.
[3] Julian, 277 D and frag. ζ'. He had been furnished with just 360 soldiers, 'who only knew how to pray!'

and initiative shown throughout the German campaigns and
in the march on Constantinople were, indeed, to manifest themselves during the invasion of Mesopotamia as fatal rashness and
folly. But therein Julian merely paid the penalty for a failure
such as his uncle had never experienced: as a gambler with
fortune, it had been the distinction of Constantine that his luck
held to the end. We may add that, in his passion for reform and
regimentation, not to speak of his strong interest in theological
and speculative issues, Julian curiously resembled his uncle;
and, if the cause to which he devoted himself was the reversal
of the latter's work, he nevertheless displayed the same zeal as
an imperial missionary. On the other hand, there can be no
question that he was the victim of an obsession, the result, no
doubt, of sufferings experienced under Constantius. These
sufferings served to kindle in him a blind hatred, not merely
for his cousin, but for the uncle to whom he attributed the woes
of the empire and the dynasty. The perils to which he was
exposed compelled Julian to hide his real feelings towards his
family with the greatest care.[1] Driven within himself, he
grasped eagerly at the delights of literary and philosophic study
provided by his tutors, and this experience helped to excite in
him a spirit of romantic, one might almost say Quixotic, anti-
quarianism. That spirit was to find expression in a fervent,
though distinctly academic, devotion to Classicism, together
with a passion to measure up to the highest standard of excellence provided by the classical world. From this standpoint,
personal and private grievances came to be mingled with considerations of public welfare, and Julian envisaged himself in a
dual role, first as the predestined restorer of *Romanitas*, second
as the alumnus of King Helios, by whose agency the household
of his forefathers should be cleansed from pollution, the Orestes,
so to speak, in the tragedy of the Christian Agamemnon.[2]

The views which Julian entertained of Christianity were
largely coloured by his impression of Constantine. How he
managed to confuse the two will be evident from what he has to
say of the latter in the *Caesars*. In this essay he stigmatizes

---

[1] Amm. xxi. 2, esp. § 5.
[2] For Julian's mystical fatalism see *Epigrams*, 6 (Bidez and Cumont, 170):
ὡς ἐθέλει τὸ φέρον σε φέρειν, φέρου· ἢν δ' ἀπιθήσῃς,
καὶ σαυτὸν βλάψεις, καὶ τὸ φέρον σε φέρει.
For the thought of himself as an instrument of divine vengeance, 234 c (*Orat.* vii):
τὴν προγονικὴν οἰκίαν αἰδοῖ τῶν προγόνων ἀποκαθῆραι.

Christianity as a typical escape-religion, the attraction of which
was that it offered a means of evading 'the iron law of retributive justice'. A competition having been held among the deified
emperors (including Alexander and Caesar) for the prize of
excellence, the award is made to Marcus, the philosopher-king.
The contestants are ordered to depart and live in future, each
under the tutelage of his appropriate deity. This they proceed
to do. As for Constantine, failing to discover among the gods
a pattern of himself, he at last catches sight of *Luxury* (Τρυφή) and
sits down beside her. Luxury receives him with tender affection
and, having adorned him with embroidered raiment, presents
him to *Incontinence* ('Ασωτία). At this moment, the emperor discerns Jesus, pacing to and fro and shouting aloud: 'He that is a
seducer, he that is a murderer, he that is stained with the
corruption of sacrilege, let him approach fearlessly. With this
water I shall wash him and at once make him clean.' 'And,
though he be guilty again of the same offence, I shall permit
him to be cleansed, if only he will smite his head and beat his
breast.' 'To him', adds Julian, 'Constantine joyfully attached
himself.' 'Nevertheless', he concludes, 'the avenging deities
punished both the Emperor and his sons, by exacting from them
requital for shedding their kinsmen's blood, until Zeus in his
mercy granted them a respite for the sake of Claudius Gothicus
and Constantius Chlorus.'[1] It would be grossly unjust to accept
this statement as evidence of the spirit in which Constantine
had, in fact, embraced Christianity, but it does indicate quite
clearly what Julian thought about it. To him Constantine was a
renegade, the Marc Antony of his age, ready to sell out to barbarism in order to gratify his own barbarous instincts; and for
this he found the necessary sanction in a gospel which put forward ideals of pity, love, and forgiveness in lieu of justice, the basis
of the classical commonwealth. But, in accepting this gospel,
he had planted a mere 'garden of Adonis' which was soon to
wither away, because its roots were not in the soil of reality.[2]

From this standpoint, the advent of Christianity, so far from
heralding a new dawn for mankind, represented[3] merely the

---

[1] 336 A and B. [2] 329 C and D.

[3] The text of Julian's formal attack on Christianity, the *In Galilaeos*, is lost, but
a reconstruction has been made by Neumann from fragments embedded in the
refutation by Cyril of Alexandria. This is reprinted in the Loeb edition of
Julian's works. On the following pages references to the *In Galilaeos*, as distinguished from Julian's extant works, are indicated by an asterisk.

latest phase in the endless conflict between civilization and barbarism. In this sense, the faith had a natural history which could be traced to the laws of Moses, the *fons et origo* of Hebrew life.[1] But while Julian, like Machiavelli, thus cites the legislative activity of Moses as the point of departure for Judaism, he is at pains to demonstrate the inferiority of the Mosaic order to those set up by Lycurgus, Solon, and Romulus, the great lawgivers of classical Greece and Rome. Accordingly, he everywhere opposes characteristic examples of Jewish wisdom to their Graeco-Roman counterparts and asserts that, by comparison with the immense achievements of *Romanitas*, the record of the Hebrews is contemptible.[2] If history proves anything, it is that the Jews are a god-forsaken race and not, as they imagine, the special favourites of the Deity. They have shown themselves deficient in general enlightenment, and their story has been one of successive captivities.[3]

To Julian, however, this 'Galilean superstition'[4] could not claim to represent even the better side of Judaism. For, of the two strains within the Jewish tradition, the 'Law' and the 'Prophets', its affiliations were with the latter, i.e. with those who would innovate upon rather than with those who would conserve the Mosaic Code. Thus, as he says, 'the Galileans, like leeches, have sucked the worst blood from that source and left the purer'.[5] 'They have deliberately followed men who have transgressed their own law and who have paid an appropriate penalty for having chosen to live in defiance of the law and to proclaim a strange and novel gospel.'[6]

In this spirit, Julian draws up a more or less comprehensive indictment of the Christian faith. He begins by denying the divinity of the Master as a fable which appeals only to that part of the soul which is childish, silly, and credulous.[7] For him Jesus of Nazareth, so far from embodying a full and final expression of the Word, is nothing but an illiterate peasant whose teachings, while devoid of truth and beauty, are at the same time weak, impractical, and socially subversive.[8] In this connexion, he

---

[1] *43 A; 253 B.   [2] *168; 171–94; 200 foll., esp. 209–18; 235 B and C.

[3] *209 D and E; 213 A; 218 B; 221 E.

[4] 380 D; δεισιδαιμονία.   [5] *202 A.

[6] 432 D, ζῆν παρανόμως; various illustrations, e.g. *351 (circumcision abandoned), *354 (use of unleavened bread), &c.

[7] *39 A and B; cf. Ep. 79 (Bidez and Cumont, no. 90).

[8] *191 D.

denounces the precept 'Sell all thou hast' as a piece of advice which, if put into effect, would result in the immediate destruction of every state, every community, and every family on earth. Along with the claims of Christ to divinity go those of His pretended revelation which Julian proceeds to brand as false and blasphemous.[1] Reason, he asserts, enables us to attain a knowledge of the divine essence quite independently of any disclosures on the part of Moses, Jesus, or Paul.[2] Such knowledge depends ultimately upon the providence of the Supreme God but, through the beneficent activity of King Helios, the Intellectual Sun, who by one and the same creative act makes possible vision and visibility (ὄψιν καὶ ὁρατόν), it is brought within the comprehension of mankind.[3]

In the light of this knowledge, the fallacies of Hebrew-Christian wisdom become apparent. The most serious of these concerns the Godhead. This has a background in the Mosaic conception of Jehovah, short-sighted, jealous, resentful, capricious, sectional or particularist, essentially the deity of a primitive and uncivilized folk.[4] But while Julian follows Marcion in emphasizing the inconsistencies between the God of the Old Testament and that of the New, he concludes none the less that they are one and the same, for inconsistency is precisely what characterizes a being who thus manifests Himself as *Will* rather than as *Reason*. Closely connected with these errors were those which concern matter and the origin of evil. To the Christian, as we have seen,[5] the universe, as the expression of divine purpose unlimited by any kind of necessity, is essentially good. If, then, evil exists, it must be due, not to any inherent imperfection of the cosmos, but to some perversion of the human mind and heart.[6] But this, argues Julian, is either to impute a lack of prescience to God or it is to saddle Him with responsibility for sin and suffering. Accordingly, he confronts his opponents with the choice between ascribing impotence or malignancy to the Creator.

We need not linger over these criticisms which, as will be evident, are merely those of classical common sense. As such, their genealogy may be traced to Celsus, the gist of

---

[1] *49 A foll.; 94 A. [2] *52 B. [3] 133 foll. (*Orat.* iv).
[4] *86 A; 93 E; 94 A; 106 D; 148 B and C; 155 C and D; 168 B.
[5] Ch. VI above. [6] *49 A; 75 B; 86 A.

whose argument has been summarized by a modern writer as follows:[1]

'Celsus considered Christianity as a doctrine which endowed a figure, unworthy of the honour, with the ancient and outworn myth of deification. He affirms that the idea of a redemption taking place at a certain period of history does not harmonize with divine love or justice, which could not be restricted to such a limited result. To the theory of salvation, he opposes the immutable and eternal laws of nature, in which evil and sin inherent in matter have their necessary place and man is by no means the *raison d'être* of the world. In this negation of the anthropocentric position of man and of the anthropomorphic essence of the divinity, Celsus is almost a precursor of modern thought.'

To quote Celsus himself:

'God is in the universe and Providence has never abandoned it, and the universe has never become worse. God, through all time, has never retired within himself, and is never irritated because of men, as he is never irritated by monkeys or flies. And he never threatens beings, the fate of each one having been specifically determined.'

We have said enough to indicate the nature and source of Julian's opinion regarding Christian doctrine. The next problem is to determine what he thought of the so-called Christian life. In this connexion it will be remembered that Christianity had itself proposed a challenge to Classicism in the text: *by their fruits ye shall know them*. That challenge Julian accepts.

'You yourselves', he declares, 'must realize the difference to the intelligence which results from a study of our writings as compared with yours. From yours no one could hope to attain to excellence, or even to ordinary goodness; from ours any person could improve himself, even if he were largely devoid of natural endowment. But he who is well endowed by nature, and acquires besides an education in our literature, becomes in fact a gift of the gods to men, either by kindling some spark of learning, or by inventing some kind of polity, or by routing vast numbers of enemies on the battlefield, or by extensive travels over land and sea, thus exhibiting himself as a man of heroic mould.[2] . . . Consider, therefore, whether we are not your superiors in every respect: knowledge of the arts, wisdom and intelligence.'[3]

To Julian it appeared that the Christians, by repudiating

[1] Negri, *Julian the Apostate* (Eng. tr.), vol. i, p. 293.
[2] *229 D and E. [3] *235 C.

the heritage of Classicism, had thrown away inestimable advantages to embrace a life of self-sacrifice, self-abnegation, and mortification of the flesh—the ideal of a barbarous and servile mentality which, in his eyes, was fittingly symbolized in the worship of its 'bleeding and dying god'. And, as the appeal of the 'crucified Jew' was presently extended to include an ever-widening circle of followers, the Christians had added as objects of adoration 'to the original corpse a host of other corpses newly dead'.[1] It remained, indeed, for the sophist Eunapius, friend and contemporary of the emperor, to utter what was perhaps the bitterest of all pagan comments upon the devotion of Christians to the saints and martyrs of the faith. 'Pickled heads and mouldy bones,' he declares, 'these have become the new gods of the Roman people.'[2] But if the remark was his, the sentiment was that of Julian; for it was with mingled pain and disgust that he saw his countrymen turn aside from the brilliant Olympians to venerate what he regarded as a heterogeneous mob of arch-criminals and renegades, the ringleaders of Christian 'atheism'. The same objection to what he considers degrading superstition comes out in the jibe that 'the sum and substance of their theology boils down to these two things: whistling to keep away the demons and making the sign of the cross upon their foreheads'.[3]

Among contemporary manifestations of the Christian life, none perhaps excited greater attention than that of monasticism. This movement, which had already begun in the later third century, was to attain enormous proportions during the fourth, its growth having no doubt been stimulated by the desire of earnest men to escape from the projected Caesaro-papism of the New Republic. Inspired by a passion for Christian perfection, monasticism took the form of a flight from the world, a renunciation of its conventions and obligations no less than its seductions and its snares, the devotees either retiring to the fastnesses of the Egyptian or Syrian deserts in order to embrace the life of hermits, or entering into communities whose members submitted themselves to a régime of strict discipline according to the 'Christian law'.[4]

The development of monasticism inevitably gave rise to

---

[1] *335 B. To this charge Augustine among others was to undertake an answer. *De Civ. Dei*, viii. 26 and 27 (on hagiolatry).

[2] Eunapius, *Vita Aedesii*, quoted by Gibbon, ch. xxviii, p. 208.

[3] *Ep.* 78 (Bidez and Cumont, no. 79), no paging.

[4] See below, pp. 338–44.

extravagances which were mainly the result of an exaggerated desire to display exemplary conduct. Chief among these was perhaps a tendency to exhibitionism, of which the behaviour of Simeon Stylites remains the classical example, although it may be remarked that Simeon belongs to the pathology of the movement, and his conceit can hardly be regarded as typical. Others took to the road with staff and cloak and, exploiting the sanctity conferred upon them as exponents of the 'Christian law', assumed the character of sturdy beggars, to prey upon the soft-hearted and the sentimental when they were not engaged in more sinister activities; for it soon became notorious that, in any lawless assault upon Jews or pagans, leadership was provided by the haggard and wild-eyed monks. Other characteristics of the profession, if not so perverse, were hardly less offensive. In Theodosius' time, for example, there was said to be a colony established on Capraria which, like the animal from which the island takes its name, could be smelt from afar. But while such manifestations contributed no doubt to throw discredit on the movement, its real danger was that it denied the claims of organized secular society. A formal statement of the emperors Valentinian and Valens specifically accuses the monks of bad citizenship while, at the same time, it imputes to them at least the suspicion of hypocrisy.[1] In this sense, monasticism may be taken to embody the fourth-century version of the traditional Christian animus against the *polis*; and even Theodosius, good Christian though he was, confessed to the difficulties which their existence presented when he pathetically demanded of Ambrose: What am I to do with these fanatical monks?

Accordingly, it is not surprising that Julian should have regarded monasticism with the greatest distaste and that, in administering a rebuke to the degenerate Cynics of his day, he should have compared them with these professional exponents of the 'Christian law'.

'Long ago', he declares, 'I hit on a way to describe you, but now, I think, I shall write it down. To certain sectaries (solitaries and heretics) the impious Galileans apply the word. Of these the majority are men who, at little personal sacrifice, have accumulated much or rather everything from all sources, in addition to which

---

[1] *Cod. Theod.* xii. 1. 63 (370? or 373): 'quidam ignaviae sectatores, desertis civitatum muneribus, captant solitudines ac secreta et specie religionis cum coetibus monazonton congregantur.'

they secure for themselves honour, attention and flattery. . . . Like them, you have abandoned your fatherland, to wander as vaga-bonds about the world . . . troublesome and insolent.'[1]

To monks and Cynics alike, the emperor suggests that there is no short-cut to excellence, least of all by seizing a staff, letting the hair grow long, and defying social convention. To both he holds up the ancient classical ideal of καλοκάγαθία. 'The be-ginning of true wisdom lies in self-knowledge, its end is an approximation to the ideal.'[2]

Notwithstanding its vogue in the fourth century, monasticism remained a somewhat unusual manifestation of the Christian life. Largely spontaneous in origin and character, the move-ment appealed mainly to persons of acute sensibility and peculiar temper; and, although favourably regarded by church-men like Athanasius, it was still largely beyond the control of ecclesiastical authority. In this sense there was some truth in Julian's charge that the monks were the Cynics of the Christian world. Nevertheless, there was one characteristic shared alike by monks and ordinary Christians who, without any aspira-tion to perfection, submitted themselves to the teaching and discipline of the Church. This was their common repudiation of 'reason', of knowledge of the world as the means to self-knowledge, the hard intellectual core which had given charac-ter and consistency to classical life. And, to Julian, the rejection of reason meant the rejection of all objective standards for a life based upon the purely subjective forces of impulse, emotion, and sentiment. With individuals like Constantine this was taken to imply, as we have seen, devotion to luxury and vice. With communities, as for instance the specifically Christian city of Antioch, it meant the rejection of classical justice in favour of licence, an ideal of 'go as you please'.[3] In either case, it repre-sented the subversion of civilization by barbarism.

From this standpoint, the Church, the embodiment of such principles or lack of principle, was to Julian a mixture of organized iniquity and fraud. It was fraudulent in the sense that it battened upon the folly of the puerile and weak, to whose superstitions it ministered by its degrading and demoralizing rites. It was iniquitous, inasmuch as its leaders, most of whom were by this time educated men, could not but have been con-scious of deceit and hypocrisy. Of the wolves in sheep's clothing

[1] Julian,224 A and B: *ad Heraclium.*   [2] 225 D.   [3] 355: *Misopogon.*

who disgraced the Constantinian Church, the most notorious was beyond doubt George of Cappadocia, Arian bishop of Alexandria, whom Julian knew, both as 'an impious creature guilty of inexpiable crimes' and as a bibliophile who had accumulated one of the most valuable private libraries at that time in existence. George was a man who systematically exploited his position for selfish and worldly ends. Finally, in the name of Christ, he introduced an army into Alexandria, seized the shrine of the national god Sarapis, and stripped it of its treasures and objects of art; whercupon he was assaulted and lynched by an exasperated pagan mob.[1] Julian rebuked the Alexandrians in such mild terms as to give the impression that he condoned their lawless act. At the same time, he made every effort to secure George's collection for the imperial library.

The animus of Julian was not, however, confined to men like George; it included churchmen like Athanasius, whose stubborn factiousness was even more obnoxious to him than were the luxury and vice of his Arian rival. Speaking of Athanasius, Ammianus Marcellinus describes him as 'a haughty prelate, who was reputed to have cultivated the arts of soothsaying and augury, as well as to have indulged in other illicit practices'.[2] To Julian, the bishop of Alexandria embodied all that was objectionable in Christianity, and, in various allusions to him, the emperor almost exhausts the Greek vocabulary of vituperation.[3] Julian's attitude was dictated by a sense that, if unreason was the mark of Christianity, Athanasius in his person represented the very spirit of unreasonableness. In a well-known passage Ammianus describes the emperor as censuring the Christians for their quarrelsome disposition; at the same time, he hints that Julian's edict of universal toleration was inspired by a Machiavellian hope that, in order to destroy Christianity, it was necessary only to give the brethren freedom, 'knowing by experience as he did that there are no wild beasts so hostile to mankind as are the Christians to one another'.[4]

---

[1] For an account of the circumstances see Bidez, *L'Empereur Julien*, p. 234.

[2] Amm. xv. 7. 7 foll.: 'Athanasium episcopum eo tempore apud Alexandriam ultra professionem altius se efferentem. . . . Dicebatur enim fatidicarum sortium fidem quaeve augurales portenderent alites scientissime callens aliquotiens praedixisse futura.' He must certainly have been a mystery to the pagans.

[3] 376 B and C: ὁ θεοῖς ἐχθρός, μιαρός; 398 D: τολμηρότατος, ἐπαρθεὶς θράσους; 435 B and C: πανοῦργος, πολυπράγμων, ἡ τοῦ δυσσεβοῦς αὐτοῦ διδασκαλείου μοχθηρία.

[4] Amm. xxii. 5. 3–4; cf. xxvii. 9. 9: 'Christianorum iurgia.'

The pagans ascribed Christian disputatiousness partly to an *odium theologicum* such as is apparent in Tertullian, partly to the struggle for place and power within a world-wide organization which had by this time the richest of earthly prizes in its gift. The Constantinian age provided ample evidence of both. We have already referred to the controversies which shook the Roman world in the fifty years succeeding the Nicene Council.[1] Ammianus took these controversies to illustrate the passion of ecclesiastics to force everything into conformity with their own notions.[2] As for the growth of avarice and ambition within the Church, the same author mentions it repeatedly, and contrasts the behaviour of metropolitan bishops with that of the provincials, who had not forgotten their vows of poverty and humility.[3] With these developments Julian was sufficiently familiar, even if he did not live to witness the scandal of the century, the open bloodshed which marked the contest between Damasus and Ursinus for election to the see of Peter.[4] It was this incident which provoked the famous *bon mot* of Praetextatus, the urban prefect: Make me bishop of Rome and I will at once become a Christian.

But while, with the growth of monasticism and ecclesiasticism, a vast amount of energy was being diverted to anti-political or, at least, non-political ends, the efforts of the government showed that Christianity, at any rate in its orthodox form, was hardly to be pressed into the service of the state. Julian describes the attempt of his cousin to impose a formal Arianism upon the Church.[5] 'Many were imprisoned, persecuted and driven into exile. Whole troops of those who were styled heretics suffered death. . . . In Paphlagonia, Bithynia, Galatia and many other provinces, towns and villages were utterly destroyed.' Facts such as these were enough to convince Julian that, in Christianity, the empire had taken to its bosom a vampire which, if not immediately extirpated, would soon drain its life-blood. This conviction determined the spirit and purpose of the reaction of which he made himself the head.

With the return to Hellenism under Julian, the wheel of destiny came full circle. Starting from the Platonic solar mono-

---

[1] Ch. VI, p. 232 foll.
[2] xxi. 16. 18: 'ritum omnem ad suum trahere . . . arbitrium.'
[3] xxvii. 3. 14–15.
[4] xxvii. 3. 12 foll. (367). For the facts, see Duchesne, ii, pp. 455–8.   [5] 436 A.

theism of his ancestors,[1] Constantine had identified himself with Christianity, only to realize in his last years that in the Church he had, so to speak ,caught a Tartar. Under his successors, both Constantius and Julian, as the logic of the situation became apparent, there was an increasingly desperate effort to escape from the implications of Constantine's settlement, an effort in which the son and the nephew both shared. But whereas, with the former, this had developed as a gradual recession from the system, with the latter it assumed the character of an abrupt and violent revolt against it. Under Constantius, without any specific disavowal of Christian forms, there was a persistent endeavour to emasculate the Nicene formula, accompanied by a vigorous attempt to build up an Arian state church. As has been seen,[2] this programme, by creating intolerable tensions within the body politic, defeated itself, thus paving the way for Julian. With the Apostate came the open and avowed repudiation of Constantinianism as the only possible means of ridding the empire of moral and social ambiguities created by the recognition of Christianity, together with a formal restoration of paganism as the basis for a rehabilitated *polis*, in which the sentiment of 'religion' would find a natural expression as a function of organized political life. The movement was, in general, from 'revelation' to 'reason'. That is to say, it marked a return to the spirit and method of classical *scientia* which we have elsewhere tried to describe.[3] What it thus presupposed as the condition of wisdom was not a rebirth in the Spirit but rather sharpened perceptions making possible a knowledge of 'nature' or the physical world. Over and above this, however, it contained elements which were distinctively Platonic. We have seen how, within the classical tradition, there were many who were agnostic in their 'physics' or who, from a critical examination of the instrument of knowledge, had come to distrust the validity of its findings. As a consequence, such persons had either fallen into complete scepticism or they had stopped short with a humanism like that of Cicero.[4] Julian, however, accepted without reserve the claims of Platonism and discovered in the Ideas the veritable objectivity and universality for which

---

[1] 'Platonic', as Cumont points out (*Théologie Solaire*), because it had substituted the notion of divine transcendence for that of immanence. The doctrine of immanence which characterized earlier forms of solar theology was derived originally from the Stoics.   [2] Ch. VI above.
[3] Ch. IV above.   [4] Ch. II above, p. 41.

men crave. To him the problem was merely to apprehend these Ideas as the clue to a true and final science of nature and of man. Undeterred, moreover, by the failure of so many who had gone before him, he undertook to apply this science in one last heroic effort to cure the sickness of society, assuming the task of social physician to which, as the typical philosopher-king, he felt himself appointed, in order to bring about a new and better dawn for *Romanitas*.

It may be conceded that the work of Julian adds little or nothing to our knowledge of Platonic thought. With him, the interest lies wholly in the attempt to relate it to the problems of his day. We shall not follow the emperor in his tedious and painful endeavour to fit the gods of popular Mediterranean polytheism into his scheme, although this, as will be seen, had its own importance as a basis for the possible moral and political syncretism which he contemplated. It will be sufficient to note that the central position is occupied by King Helios, Lord of the Ideal Order, and thus the primary agent of physical creation, with whom are identified Zeus, Mithras, and Horus. Under Helios, as his minister, comes the Mater Deorum, with whom is associated Athene Pronoia or Prometheia, the source of practical intelligence and the creative arts, especially that which underlies political association (ἡ πολιτικὴ κοινωνία) and, as such, the daughter of Zeus-Helios, sprung from him 'whole from whole'.[1] Apollo, the author of illumination, together with Dionysus-Osiris-Sarapis, the principle of division and individuation, are his sons. In the same way, operating with King Helios as a 'secondary cause' in the endless generation of living creatures (ἡ ἀειγενεσία τῶν ζῴων) is Aphrodite; while, as their preserver, Asclepius finds an appropriate place within the pantheon.[2] Thus Julian develops the elements of a new Hesiodic theogony, a hierarchy of divine beings 'derived' by emanation from the supreme God, as a means of bringing together the intelligible and the sensible world—the emergence from a self-existent principle of unity (αὐθυπόστατος) of the multiple phenomenal world, the individual entities of which acquire reality and significance as they are comprehended by the pre-existing and intelligible One.[3]

[1] 149 B: ὅλη ἐξ ὅλου.
[2] See esp. *Oratio*, iv, 'To King Helios', and *Oratio*, v, 'To the Mater Deorum'.
[3] 139 B: ἐν παντελῶς τὸ νοητὸν ἀεὶ προϋπάρχον, τὰ δὲ πάντα ὁμοῦ συνειληφὸς ἐν τῷ ἑνί.

From this confession of faith, two fundamental facts become
apparent. In the first place, the Idea is hypostatized, i.e. invested with the character of being; in the second, it is envisaged
as a cause. 'We assert', he declares, 'the existence of matter as
well as of form embodied in matter or material form. But if no
prior cause be assigned to these, we should unconsciously be
thinking in terms of Epicureanism. For, if there be nothing
higher than these two principles, then spontaneous motion and
chance must have brought them together.'[1] Julian thus offers
the usual idealistic objection to the theory of mechanical or
automatic generation. Envisaging the world of bodies ($\sigma\acute{\omega}\mu\alpha\tau\alpha$)
as 'compounds' of form and matter, he assumes that matter is
the negative or passive, form the active or dynamic principle.
From this assumption he argues that, since there must be
reasons and causes ($\lambda\acute{o}\gamma o\iota$ $\kappa\alpha\grave{\iota}$ $\alpha\emph{i}\tau\acute{\iota}\alpha\iota$) for the material forms,
and since these reasons and causes must themselves be material
($\emph{\'e}\nu\nu\lambda o\iota$ $\alpha\emph{i}\tau\acute{\iota}\alpha\iota$), so also for the material causes there must exist
causes which are immaterial ($\alpha\emph{i}\tau\acute{\iota}\alpha\iota$ $\emph{\'a}\emph{\"u}\lambda o\iota$) until, in ascending
order, he arrives at the third creator who is described as a
'wholly immaterial cause' ($\alpha\emph{i}\tau\iota o\varsigma$ $\pi\alpha\nu\tau\epsilon\lambda\hat{\omega}\varsigma$ $\emph{\'a}\emph{\"u}\lambda o\varsigma$). In other words,
he asks his reader to accept the existence of a hierarchy of sub-
stances and forces culminating in Helios, the Intellectual Sun,
who, as the ultimate in nature ($\emph{\`\eta}$ $\tau\epsilon\lambda\epsilon\upsilon\tau\alpha\acute{\iota}\alpha$ $\phi\acute{\upsilon}\sigma\iota\varsigma$), contains
within himself the various patterns of the 'material forms' as
well as the 'connected chain of causation' and, through his
superabundance of generative power, descends through the
starry empyrean as far as earth on his creative mission.[2]

This notion of form as essence and cause is, of course, a
commonplace of Platonic idealism. As applied by Julian to the
science of man and society, it yields conclusions of considerable
interest. In this connexion we may note what he has to say of
human nature. 'Why', he asks, 'are there so many kinds of
creatures? Whence arise male and female? Whence the differentiation of things in types according to their species, unless
there are pre-existing and pre-established forms existing beforehand to serve as patterns and causes?'[3] In this doctrine he finds
the secret of racial character and genius.[4] 'Tell me,' he
demands, raising again the question to which the physician
Hippocrates had originally attempted an answer seven cen-

---

[1] 162 A: *Mater Deorum.*   [2] 161 D.
[3] 162 D, 163.   [4] *134 D foll.: *In Galileos.*

turies before, 'why is it that Celts and Germans are fierce, but Greeks and Romans, generally speaking, disposed to a civilized and humane life, while at the same time firm and warlike? Why are the Egyptians more intelligent and proficient in technical ability, the Syrians unwarlike and luxurious, combining high intelligence and quick perception with a hot temper and vanity? If any one discerns no reason for these racial differences (ἡ ἐν τοῖς ἔθνεσι διαφορά), and asserts that everything happens of its own accord, how can he still believe that the universe is subject to providential administration? . . . As for human laws, it is evident that these have been determined by human nature in accordance with its demands. As a general rule, the laws are civilized and humane (πολιτικοὶ καὶ φιλάνθρωποι) wherever the spirit of humanity (φιλανθρωπία) has been cultivated. Otherwise they are savage and brutal. And lawgivers have added but little through discipline to the native aptitudes of men.'[1] 'How utterly different', he adds, 'are the bodies of Germans and Scythians from those of Libyans and Ethiopians! Surely this difference is not to be ascribed to an empty *fiat*, but climate and country operate jointly with the gods to determine even colour.'[2] This, if true, would appear to set a limit to the possibility of assimilation in the imperial 'mixing-bowl'. 'With very few exceptions', he says, 'you will not find members of the Western races inclined to philosophy, mathematics and similar pursuits, despite the fact that the Roman Empire has long been dominant among them.'[3]

The presumed existence of 'racial types' suggests to Julian truths of far-reaching significance, to which he thinks experience bears witness, regarding the nature and activity of God.[4] For while, as he says, the creator or demiurge is the common father and king of all, specific functions have been assigned by him to various subordinate deities, each of whom operates in accordance with his specific character. Thus, since in the Father all things are perfect and all are one, while his subordinates are distinguished by different characteristics, it may be said that Ares dominates the fighting peoples, Athene those who are prudent as well as warlike, Hermes those who are intelligent rather than bellicose; in short, that the leading characteristics of any people are those of the god or gods by whom they are

[1] *116 A and B; 131 B and C.   [2] *143 D.   [3] *131 C.   [4] *115 E.

determined.[1] This explanation serves also to account for the persistence of racial characteristics. 'For, just as the qualities of any plant are normally transmitted for a long time, and each successive generation resembles the one preceding, so also among human beings descendants will ordinarily bear a close resemblance to their ancestors.'[2] With Julian this thought is pressed to its logical conclusion. 'Can we suppose', he asks, 'that there is not some mark or symbol indelibly stamped upon the souls of men, which will accurately indicate their descent and vindicate it as legitimate?'[3] 'When a man has virtuous progenitors and is himself like them, he may with confidence be described as nobly born.'[4]

In this theory of human nature Julian finds the basis for an ethic wherein felicity or the *summum bonum* is identified with the realization of 'that which is best and noblest in us, viz., the life of reason'.[5] This he considers to be the only way of escape from the sub-human life of sense which mankind shares with the animal. He does, indeed, pay tribute to the traditional virtues of antiquity and, in a long list of these, he includes freedom, independence, justice, temperance, as well as the disposition to do nothing at random.[6] To these he adds practical judgement (φρόνησις), the quality which prompts one either to withstand, submit to or co-operate with circumstance.[7] In this connexion he quotes Plato's *Laws* to the effect that 'God governs all things and, with God, chance and opportunity (τύχη καὶ καιρὸς) govern human affairs, but there is a less harsh view that art needs to go with them and be their associate'.[8] For Julian, however, the perfection of virtue cannot stop at this point but must include as its ultimate objective a knowledge of the divine nature. And since, in the last analysis, this is a question of insight or intuition, it is accessible only to the pure in heart. This serves to emphasize the importance of asceticism, and life resolves itself into a continuous effort of purgation. Accordingly, while σωφροσύνη, the classical principle of self-control, still remains, it yields primacy in the hierarchy of virtues to piety or holiness (εὐλάβεια, εὐσέβεια), a quality closely akin to the Christian sense of dependence on God. One result of this is to enhance the desire for personal chastity as a precondition of fulfilment.[9]

[1] *115 D and E; 143 B. [2] 348 B and C. [3] 81 D. [4] 83 A and B.
[5] 194 D. [6] 202 A. [7] 255 A. [8] 257 D. [9] 293 A.

The foundation for individual is, at the same time, a foundation for social ethics. For, since the 'incorporeal reason'[1] is by its very nature common, there can arise no conflict between the demands of an individual and of a social good. In other words, man *qua* man is a communal and political animal.[2] As such, his obligations are summed up in the word 'philanthropy' (φιλανθρωπία) and, in the light of philanthropy, 'Every beggar in the street becomes an insult to the gods.'[3] The 'incorporeal reason,', which is thus put forward as a basis for communal and political solidarity, serves also to yield a basis for the solidarity of mankind. For, just as the national or group spirit finds expression within the *polis*, so also the spirit of humanity as a whole is embodied in the imperial system, the 'form' of which exhibits a relatively higher degree of universality. In the celestial hierarchy, national and political (local) gods, while representing the group-life of autonomous communities, will, at the same time, find a place as functional, departmental deities in the imperial pantheon, presided over by King Helios, divine sovereign of the universal empire. Thus, in solar monotheism, Julian discovers the basis for a grandiose syncretism which is to include even Jehovah, if only Jehovah will make up his mind to come in.

In this moral and political 'set-up' the achievement of even a moderate degree of excellence calls for the exercise of all the faculties; as for the perfection of virtue, the task is veritably Herculean. Yet the prize of success is correspondingly worth while, nothing less, in fact, than a Herculean or conditional apotheosis. Julian is obsessed with the problems and obligations of leadership. From this standpoint, his essay on the *Caesars* is to be taken, not as a mere *jeu d'esprit*, but rather as a synopsis and criticism of various possible ideals of imperial virtue. Considered as such, it is not surprising that, among the kings of men, Alexander and Caesar, Octavian, Trajan, and Constantine, all fall short of the ideal, Marcus alone measuring up to the requirements, because in his private and public conduct he alone makes it his object 'to imitate the gods'.[4] The obligation to do so lies most heavily upon those who presume to the right of governing their fellows. 'Even though the prince be by nature human, he must resolve to become divine and a demigod,

---

[1] 182 D: ἀσώματος λόγος.   [2] 201 C: κοινωνικὸν καὶ πολιτικὸν ζῷον.
[3] 289, 291, 292.   [4] 333 C.

banishing from his soul all that is mortal and brutish, except what is requisite to minister to his bodily needs.'[1]

This, the pattern of Platonic monarchy, constitutes both a model and a warning for kings.[2] In the second of two ostensible panegyrics on Constantius, Julian deals with the physical, moral, and intellectual qualities demanded of a ruler, hardly troubling to make more than a conventional application of his ideas to the nominal subject of his address.[3] He paraphrases Plato to the effect that the man, particularly the king, best-equipped for life, is he who depends on God for all that relates to happiness, without relying upon other men whose actions, whether good or bad, are likely to divert him from his purpose.

'But when Plato says "depends on himself", most assuredly he does not refer to his physique, his resources, his birth or his ancestry. These things, indeed, belong to him, but they are not the man himself. His real self is his mind and intelligence, that is to say, the God within.'[4]

'It is this initial (divinely implanted) virtue which enables him to exhibit those qualities by which the true sovereign is distinguished from the vulgar tyrant, making him the saviour and protector of the state, stout guardian of the existing laws, superior as a political architect, capable of suppressing civil dissension, vicious morals, luxury and vice. He will select and train an aristocracy to assist in the administration. With respect to the commons, he will reward the peasantry suitably for their services and, while ministering to the physical needs of the urban proletariat, he will at the same time check their impudence and idleness.'[5]

It was fortunate for the youthful panegyrist that, under Constantius, the conventions of the genre rendered it a suitable medium for the expression of a secret and forbidden paganism. For it was in a thoroughly pagan spirit that, in the *First Panegyric*, Julian dealt with the question of education for kingship and, omitting the slightest reference to the emperor's Christian training, portrayed him as a model of secular virtue, produced through a combination of good breeding with a discipline imposed according to the approved formula of idealist science.

---

[1] *Ad Themist. Philos.* 259 A–B.   [2] *Oratio,* ii. 49–50.
[3] Bidez, *L'Empereur Julien*, p. 175, shrewdly remarks: 'La royauté philosophe que le César décrit avec tant d'enthousiasme n'est autre que l'idéal de gouvernement qu'il se proposera un jour de réaliser lui-même.'
[4] 68 c and D.   [5] 88 foll., 91–2.

Bearing in mind the results of this analysis, it becomes possible
to appreciate more exactly the spirit of Julian's apostasy, as
well as to assess his projects of purgation and reform. Advertised as a return to the liberalism of Constantius Chlorus, the
programme of Julian was in fact revolutionary in so far as it
embodied a deliberate attempt to platonize the state. From
this standpoint, we may estimate at their proper valuation certain polite gestures of the emperor to the older republicanism;
such, for example, as his contemplated rejection of the diadem
along with the title of *dominus*,[1] or his rebuke to the consuls who
rushed to offer him the conventional New Year's salutation, by
the affectation of a pose of *civilitas* which, in the circumstances,
was little less than inane.[2] Of still slighter moment, if possible,
was the appeal to public opinion with which Julian inaugurated
his régime in a series of manifestoes addressed to historic communities whose approval was as devoid of significance as was
their political position in the fourth century. For, as has been
seen, Julian was no liberal. And all his pedantry does not serve
to conceal the truth that he no more dreamed of restoring
Augustan 'liberty' than the Ciceronian humanism which was its
basis. But, if he disbelieved in the ancient freedoms, still less
can it be said that he gave his adherence to the new. It must
not, therefore, be supposed that, in reviving the edict of toleration, Julian had any more intention of enforcing an effective
separation of Church and state than had Constantine himself
when he originally introduced it. With Julian, as with Constantine, this was but a necessary step towards securing the
predominance of his own religious principles.[3] It was in this
spirit, certainly, that he legislated to prevent any interference
with pagan rites and ceremonies, as well as to provide endowments for a state-supported pagan priesthood. Thus, also, he
suppressed tumults at Alexandria, provoked through resentment of the Athanasian faction at the appointment of George of
Cappadocia, by methods analogous to those which Constantine
had employed against the African *circumcelliones*, thereby involving himself in what might easily have developed into the
horrors of a religious war.[4] Finally, it has been suggested that
his projected restoration of the Temple at Jerusalem was intended
as a counterblast to Constantine's erection of the Church of the

---

[1] 343 c and d.   [2] Amm. xxii. 7. 1–2.
[3] Ibid. 5. 2.   [4] Ibid. 11.11; cf. Julian, *Ep.* 10.

Holy Sepulchre, and conceived in precisely the same spirit.[1] Indeed, it might almost be said that the policy of Julian was modelled upon that of his predecessor, whose actions he endeavoured, in a spirit of slavish imitation, to reverse.

To assert this without qualification, however, would be to ignore certain positive and salutary elements of the *Pax Iuliana*. Of these, perhaps the most significant was a return to 'republican' justice. Needless to say, this did not embrace the elimination of the imperial bureaucracy—a project excluded not less by the logic of events since Diocletian and Constantine than by that of Platonism itself. As a good Platonist, Julian must have believed in a specialization of functions within the body politic. Accordingly, his efforts were directed to a rationalization of the existing system and, in particular, the destruction of parasitism within it. With this end in view he invoked the heavy sanctions conventional to his age and authorized, so to speak, by Plato himself. Thus, while he simplified judicial procedure by permitting provincial governors to depute cases of minor importance to subordinates,[2] at the same time he tried to facilitate the rapid decision of suits by prohibiting the dilatory methods of litigants and lawyers.[3] On the other hand he authorized the infliction of torture upon tax-assessors convicted of fraud;[4] and, to check abuses in the transport service, he withdrew from provincial presidents and vicars the privilege of issuing passes, limiting this right to viceroys (*praefecti praetorio*) on whom, at the same time, he imposed rigid restrictions as to its use.[5] He also forbade the employment of public wagons for the conveyance of private goods, in certain areas prohibiting entirely the requisitioning of transport from the *plebs rustica* by public officials.[6]

The checking of corrupt practices on the part of the bureaucracy was, however, but one aspect of a wider programme which aimed at the rehabilitation of municipal life. For, little as the depressed *curiales* of the lower empire might be supposed to resemble their prototypes of the ideal republic, nevertheless for Julian they were still the mainstay of *Romanitas*. Accordingly, he sought to improve their lot, principally by equalizing and

[1] Amm. xxiii. 1. 2: 'imperii sui memoriam magnitudine operum gestiens propagare.' [2] *Cod. Theod.* i. 16. 8 (362).
[3] ii. 5. 2 (362): 'studio protrahendae disceptationis'.
[4] viii. 1. 6 (362). [5] viii. 5. 12 and 13 (362).
[6] viii. 5. 15 and 16 (363).

moderating the fiscal burdens under which they staggered. No fresh imposts were to be levied upon them without his specific approval.[1] The rich were to be forced to pay their fair share of taxes. Connivance between them and imperial tax-collectors was forbidden; and all persons were declared liable to public obligations on account of lands in their possession, bargains involving the alienation of property on a tax-free basis being pronounced illegal.[2] On the other hand, an attempt was made to protect the smaller holders from undue exactions.[3] We have noted the growth under the earlier Flavians of a widespread system of privilege, principally in favour of the Christians. So far from abolishing this vicious principle, Julian proceeded to confer in substance upon the pagan priesthood all that he had withdrawn from the Christian.[4] In the imperial head-quarters services he limited the numbers of *domestici* and *protectores* entitled to receive grants from the public purse;[5] but he modified the conditions under which imperial agents and members of the secretariat might obtain exemption from hereditary curial obligations;[6] while, as an encouragement to philoprogeneity among the *municipales*, he quaintly conceded an 'honourable release' from curial duty to fathers of thirteen children.[7] The immunities granted to teachers and professors of literature were extended to include physicians.[8] Thus, for one favoured class within the community, Julian merely substituted others. Yet he tried his best to secure justice for the provincials and, so far as possible, he eased the intolerable burden of taxation.[9] In so doing, however, he maintained and even extended the protective principle, therein revealing himself as at once a disciple of Plato and a child of his age.[10] Accordingly, it is vain to look for any sign of increased freedom or flexibility in social relations as a consequence of his activity.

With Julian, as with his immediate predecessors, the question of chief importance was not so much economic and social as ecclesiastical policy. As a good Platonist, it was his firm conviction that the sheet-anchor of 'political' life was religion; and he attributed to the acceptance of Christianity the false ideal

---

[1] xi. 16. 10 (362).   [2] xi. 3. 3 (363).
[3] xii. 1. 50; xiii. 1. 4 (362).
[4] Julian, 430 c; cf. *Cod. Theod.* xii. 1. 50.   [5] *Cod. Theod.* vi. 24. 1 (362).
[6] vi. 26. 1 (362) and 27. 2 (363).
[7] xii. 1. 55 (363).   [8] xiii. 3. 4 (362).   [9] Eutrop. x. 16.
[10] *Cod. Theod.* iii. 1. 3 (362); 13. 2; xiv. 4. 3 (363).

of human relationships which prevailed within the Constantinian empire. 'Innovation', he declares, 'I abominate above
all things, especially as concerns the gods, and I hold that we
ought to maintain intact the laws which we have inherited from
the past, since it is evident that they are god-given.'¹ In this
spirit he undertook to disestablish and, if possible, to destroy the
Constantinian Church. But, in his dealings alike with individual Christians and with the Church as a body, it is not too
much to say that, by repudiating as barbarous the harsh and
indiscriminate methods of his cousin, he introduced a new
phase of the secular conflict between Christianity and Classicism. In this phase the main assault was directed, not so much
against individual believers as against the ecclesiastical corporation, regarded as the chief instrument of intellectual and
moral corruption, the chief obstacle to a reassertion of social
justice and social peace.

The problem being conceived as 'political', it was to be solved
by essentially political methods. This involved, of course, the
immediate cancellation of immunities and exemptions lavished
by previous emperors upon the Church, together with a restoration to municipalities of public property (temples, &c.) which,
'in the recent troubles, had passed into private hands, such
property to be leased out at a just valuation'.² It involved, also,
the general edict of toleration, whether or not this was actually
inspired by the hope that 'as freedom served to foment their
dissensions, the government should no longer have to fear the
unanimity of the Christian populace'. These measures were
subsidiary to the enforcement among the sectaries of a *Pax
Iuliana* which, while it guaranteed them freedom from molestation at the hands of their enemies, undertook also to mitigate
the violence and disorder (ἀκοσμία) prevalent among themselves.

'By heaven,' declares Julian, 'I want no Galileans killed, scourged
or otherwise injured contrary to law.'³

'It is by reason that we ought to persuade and instruct men, not
by blows, insults or physical violence. I therefore reiterate my
injunction upon all true believers to do no wrong to the Galilean
communities, neither to raise hands nor direct insults against them.
Those who err in matters of the gravest import deserve pity, not
hatred; for, as religion is indeed the greatest of all goods, so is

---

¹ 453 B.   ² *Cod. Theod.* x. 3. 1 (362).   ³ 376 C.

irreligion the worst of evils. This is the situation with those who have turned aside from the gods to worship corpses and relics.'[1]

On the other hand, Julian punished the wealthy Arian congregation of Edessa for having attacked the Valentinians, by confiscating their property 'in order that poverty might teach them to behave themselves and that they might not be deprived of the heavenly kingdom promised to the poor'.[2]

In this policy Ammianus sees an attempt of the emperor to keep 'religion' as such out of politics,[3] an effort to tread the strict path of equity which, in his opinion, constituted the chief glory of the administration.[4] As such, it stood in refreshing contrast with treatment recently experienced under Constantius. Yet, for Julian, toleration offered no sanction for subversive political activity. It was thus as a disruptive element that he justified his attitude to Athanasius. It was because of Christian ἀκοσμία that he undertook the suppression of mob-action on the part of recalcitrants who, in his own words, 'go mad because they are not allowed to tyrannize'.[5] But while any disturbance of the peace might and did provide occasion for forcible intervention, nevertheless for ordinary purposes Julian found it enough to act on the principle that the protection of the law should be withdrawn from the lawless. This meant that, in general, there were to be 'no killings'; punishment was limited to the cancellation of private rights, especially those of entering legal actions and of testability, the giving and receiving of legacies (δικάζειν, γράφειν διαθήκας). In adopting this policy Julian not merely reflected credit upon himself as a civilized ruler but, to some extent, set a precedent for analogous political action during the Theodosian age.

Like Constantine, Julian found the principle of toleration compatible with the extension of privileges and favours to those who shared his belief. 'Godly men I desire to be encouraged and frankly say they ought. This Galilean folly has turned almost everything topsy-turvy, and nothing but the mercy of heaven has saved us. We ought therefore to honour the gods

[1] 438 B and c. [2] 424 D.
[3] Amm. xxii. 10. 2: 'et quamquam in disceptando aliquotiens erat intempestivus, quid quisque iurgantium coleret tempore alieno interrogans, tamen nulla eius definitio litis a vero dissonans reperitur, nec argui unquam potuit ob religionem vel quodcunque aliud ab aequitatis recto tramite deviasse.'
[4] Julian himself claims it as an expression of his philanthropy: 436 A; cf. 424 C, πράως καὶ φιλανθρώπως. [5] 436 B.

and godly men and cities.'[1] Such 'encouragement' took the form of squeezing conscientious Christians out of the imperial services by associating with them the traditional religious ceremonial of *Romanitas*. This was especially true of the army, wherein once more pagan emblems replaced the *Labarum*, while every military movement was preceded by elaborate rites of divination and sacrifice, personally conducted by the emperor. In this we may perceive what St. Jerome describes as a 'blanda persecutio illiciens magis quam impellens ad sacrificandum'.[2]

It has been suggested that 'in the idea of grafting a fruitful Church life upon the stock of paganism' is to be found 'Julian's best claim to originality, if not to greatness', and furthermore that the notion was 'borrowed from Christianity'.[3] We may agree that Julian shared with Constantine a sense of the need for a state religion, without for a moment admitting that he had to go to Constantine for the idea. By the time of Aurelian such notions were already in the air and, under the second tetrarchy, they had become practical politics.[4] But the project had a genealogy much more ancient and honourable even than this. For, among the numerous seminal ideas thrown out by Plato himself, there is none more remarkable than his scheme of public institutional religion.[5]

Accordingly, as between Julian and Constantine, the question was: If a state religion, why not Hellenism, the religion of good citizenship rather than of bad?[6] The problem was to present Platonic solar monotheism as the foundation for a cult of civilization, capable of unifying and vitalizing *Romanitas* while, at the same time, offering a fresh sanction to local and national loyalties within the larger whole. Doomed though it was to failure, the scheme is interesting from many points of view. It involved, among other features, a general restoration of the temples and images, the material representations through which Julian saw a popular way of access to the Most High

---

[1] 376 c and D.   [2] *Trans. Euseb. Chron.* ii (anno 366).

[3] Rendall, *The Emperor Julian*, p. 144; cf. Duchesne, ii, p. 328: 'Julien . . . cherchait à insinuer l'esprit chrétien dans le cadavre exhumé du paganisme.'

[4] Lact. *De Mort. Persec.* 36: 'sacerdotes maximos per singulas civitates singulos ex primoribus ⟨Maximinus Daia⟩ fecit': cf. Euseb. *H.E.* viii. 14. 9 foll. and ix. 4. 2.

[5] *Laws*, x.

[6] Bidez, op. cit., p. 261, sees a 'deterioration' of Julian's policy in the attempt to transform Hellenism into theocracy. This he ascribes to the influence of theurgists and dates from the spring of 362.

God.[1] With this went a revival of the splendid and impressive ritual of pagan sacrifice, in which the smoke of hecatombs rose to heaven from the altars. To support the system Julian himself undertook the selection and training of a professional priesthood on a basis of fitness for office. As *Pontifex Maximus*, he drew upon the ancient Roman legacy for authority to organize and direct the imperial cult, as well as to admonish or rebuke its ministers.[2]

Along with the rehabilitation of religion, Julian planned to rehabilitate the study of the classics. We have already noted the intimate relation which subsisted in the empire between literature and life. This relationship had been acknowledged even by Christian princes like Constantius who, although himself a renegade from official paganism, still regarded the *liberales artes* as an indispensable qualification for promotion within the civil service.[3] But, for Julian, a study of the classics involved much more than any mere question of utility; it was essential to the formation of classical ideology. As such, it counted second only to warfare among the activities of the state.[4] It is not surprising, therefore, that he should have embarked upon a significant experiment in the history of Roman education by asserting public control over the educational machinery of the empire. The setting up of private schools was prohibited; all teachers were thenceforth to be licensed by their municipalities, subject to the personal approval of the emperor.[5]

In a lengthy rescript,[6] Julian explains, at the same time as he seeks to justify, the elements of this programme. The argument, which is not without interest for modern times, raises the general question of academic freedom and, specifically, it throws down a challenge to the Christians:

'We consider that a proper education consists not in the ability to use words with precision and force but in the acquisition of a

---

[1] Amm. xxii. 5.　　　　　　　　　　　　　　　[2] Julian, 288–305.

[3] *Cod. Theod.* xiv. 1. 1 (357): 'ne autem litteraturae quae omnium virtutum maxima est praemia denegentur, eum qui studiis et eloquio dignus primo loco videbitur, honestiorem faciet nostra provisio. . . .'

[4] vi. 26. 1 (362).

[5] xiii. 3. 5 (362): 'magistros studiorum doctoresque excellere oportet moribus primum, deinde facundia. sed quia singulis civitatibus adesse ipse non possum, iubeo, quisque docere vult, non repente nec temere prosiliat ad hoc munus, sed iudicio ordinis probatus decretum curialium mereatur optimorum conspirante consensu. hoc enim decretum ad me tractandum referetur, ut altiore quodam honore nostro iudicio studiis civitatum accedant.'　　　[6] Julian, 422–4.

healthy attitude of mind and of sound opinions concerning good and evil, propriety and impropriety. Any person, therefore, who, while thinking one thing, teaches another, is as remote from knowledge as he is from righteousness. And, though the discrepancy between his statements and his beliefs be trifling, even so he is blameworthy, though the measure of his crime is not great. But, when he entertains certain opinions in matters of vital importance, and puts forward the reverse, this is assuredly the conduct of a huckster and a villain, since he teaches the very thing he considers wrong. . . .

'All those who undertake to be instructors ought, therefore, to be of sound moral character, and to introduce no opinions which are novel and at variance with accepted belief. This applies especially to those who train the young in ancient literature, whether as rhetoricians, grammarians or (most of all) philosophers, who profess to be masters not merely of language but of customs and ideas and to provide instruction in the conduct of public affairs. Whether or not their claim is justified is a question which, for the moment, I leave open. I honour those who pursue studies of such outstanding importance; I should praise them still more if they did not deceive and stultify themselves by thinking one thing and teaching another. Homer, Hesiod, Demosthenes, Herodotus, Thucydides, Isocrates and Lysias regarded the gods as authors and inspirers of their wisdom. Did not certain of them consider that they were dedicated to Hermes, others to the muses? It is therefore absurd that persons who expound their work should pour contempt on the religion in which they believed. Because I hold this to be absurd, I do not, however, on that account order them to change their opinions for the sake of a livelihood. But I do insist that they ought to refrain from teaching what they do not believe to be true. If, however, they prefer to teach, let them begin by instructing their pupils that . . . none of those authors whom they have condemned for impiety, folly and theological error, is guilty of what they have said. Otherwise, by accepting a living and deriving emolument from their works, they write themselves down as greedy and sordid mercenaries. . . .

'Until the present, many circumstances have prevented them from embracing the true religion; the universal terror has served as a pretext why correct opinion regarding religion should not be expressed. Now, however, since by the favour and mercy of heaven we have obtained freedom, it seems to me absurd that men should teach what they do not regard as true. But, if they think there is any wisdom in what they teach and interpret, let them try above all things to imitate the piety of those authors. If, however, they are convinced that the authors in question are mistaken in their view of the holy gods, let them enter the Galilean churches and there study Matthew and Luke. . . .

'The following regulation is laid down to govern the conduct of professors and teachers: that any student wishing to attend is to be admitted to the schools. It would be equally unreasonable to exclude from the best path boys who are still too ignorant to know which way to turn, and to frighten them against their will into the beliefs of their ancestors. Though, indeed, there is something to be said for treating them, even against their will, as one treats the insane; but for the fact that we ought to have sympathy with those who are thus afflicted. And we ought, I think, to instruct, rather than to punish, the demented. . . .'[1]

By thus 'calling up' the schools, Julian raised the question whether literature was to be regarded as a pillar of the existing order or as the common heritage of mankind—the chief instrument of a functional society, designed to equip a ruling class for its duties, by ensuring to it a degree of inner or spiritual conformity, rather than a medium of enlightenment accessible to all. And it is noteworthy that, in this conception of education, the emperor failed to carry with him the support even of high-minded pagans. 'We ought to pass over in perpetual silence', declares Ammianus, 'the harsh decree by which he tried to prevent adherents of the Christian Church from teaching as grammarians and rhetoricians.'[2] The issue was one of fundamental importance for liberal paganism. While, therefore, it is possible to make much of Julian's republicanism, the fact cannot be ignored that, in seeking to monopolize culture, he aimed to impose upon his subjects a servitude not less pernicious than that from which he professed to set them free. In this, as in other respects, the policy of Julian marks a steady drift towards totalitarianism within the fourth-century empire. As for the Christians, they were not slow to perceive the fatal consequences which would have resulted from any prohibition of liberal studies. They saw, in the imperial policy, a move which would presently have rendered the faith in fact what Julian persistently asserted it to be: the mere continuation of a semi-barbarous cult bounded by the narrow confines of Galilee; in this way destroying the significance of the Evangel as the culmination of a *praeparatio* which embraced the total spiritual

[1] For Christian opinion on the issue see Aug. *De Civ. Dei*, xviii. 52.
[2] xxii. 10. 7; cf. xxv. 4. 20.

experience of mankind. Accordingly, they joined issue with the Apostate in a fiercely contested battle of the books which was to be concluded only with his death.

It was perhaps fortunate for his enemies that the logic of Julian's position was, within a measurable time, to bring about that consummation of their hopes. As we have noted, it was an essential part of Julian's repudiation of Constantinianism that he should have rejected the philo-barbarian policy of his uncle. On the northern frontier this meant a cessation of those humiliating subsidies which, while they drained the resources of the municipalities, served merely to inflate the pride and rapacity of the recipients. In the East it meant a revival of the traditional military glories of *Romanitas* through the chastisement of the Persian king.[1] But the project which was thus designed to restore the republic proved in the end to be its ruin. Speaking of the recent battle of Mursa, in which Constantius had overthrown Magnentius, Eutropius declares that it had consumed a vast amount of military strength, which might otherwise have served to protect the security and glory of the empire in any number of foreign wars.[2] That strength had with difficulty been recreated, largely through Julian's own efforts in the West. But now, in order to build up an expeditionary force, the emperor stripped Gaul of its frontier defences and united them with the troops which he had inherited from his cousin to form what (by ancient standards) was a highly mechanized and articulated field army of 65,000 men. This force, together with his own life, he was destined to throw away on the sandy wastes of Mesopotamia. In so doing he contributed to the military paralysis which marked the last decades of the empire.

The reactionary programme of Julian has deserved a full and sympathetic consideration as the final effort of Graeco-Roman paganism, sailing under its own flag. Hence also the significance of his death-bed utterance—a confession of faith which, not less by its studied and deliberate artifice than by the evidence of a lofty and generous spirit which it reveals, discloses Julian as the last-surviving spiritual heir of Cato and of Socrates. In this final statement of classical ideals the Apostate begins by recalling the traditional philosophic view of death as the inexorable law of life; and he indicates his willingness to

[1] Amm., xxii. 12 and xxiv. 1.   [2] Eutrop. x. 12.

discharge a debt, the payment of which will exempt him from the hazards of a world in which fortune and circumstance share with the gods control of human fate. But such perils, while they destroy the weak, serve merely to try the mettle of the strong who, confronting them in a manly spirit, give value and significance to their lives. By this standard Julian professes himself ready to die, as he had lived, in the full consciousness of having done his duty both as subject and as ruler. Preserving unspotted the trust which devolved upon him by reason of his affinity with the divine, he had repudiated 'the corrupt maxims of despotism' and had shown himself obedient to the imperious voice of the commonwealth by consulting, alike in peace and war, the demands of reason and utility. To the ever-living God he gave thanks for having preserved him from death by treachery, lingering disease, or the end of a criminal, as well as for taking him from the world while he was still at the height of his prosperity and fame; and, as a loyal son of the republic, he expressed the hope that she might find a good prince to succeed him.[1]

Julian thus died, as he had lived, a martyr to Platonic science. A fragment preserved from a contemporary source contains evidence of the sense of loss occasioned among his followers by his tragic end.

'Even the vulgar felt that they would soon find another leader; but such another leader as Julian they would never find, even though a πλαστὸς θεός, a god in human form. Julian, who had a mind equal to the deity, triumphed over the evil propensities of human nature . . . he held commerce with immaterial beings while still in the material body . . . and condescended to rule because a ruler was necessary to the welfare of mankind.'[2]

To the verdict of his followers Prudentius also subscribes in the famous verses:[3]

> . . . ductor fortissimus armis
> conditor et legum, celeberrimus ore manuque,
> consultor patriae . . .
> perfidus ille Deo, quamvis non perfidus orbi . . .

If, then, the movement to which Julian devoted himself was doomed to failure, this failure cannot be ascribed to any lack of intelligence or endurance on his part. In words which recall the Thucydidean verdict upon Nicias, Ammianus does, indeed,

[1] Amm. xxv. 3. 15–20. In this paragraph I have followed the paraphrase in Gibbon, ch. xxiv, p. 515.
[2] Eunapius, *frag.*, quoted by Gibbon. [3] *Apotheosis*, 450 foll.

censure the emperor for 'an excessive interest in the knowledge of portents (*praesagiorum sciscitatio*) which carried him beyond the bounds of legitimate divination into gross superstition'.[1] Among the numerous instances of this superstition may be cited the fact that he desisted from rebuilding the Temple when 'terrific balls of fire, bursting with frequent explosions from the foundations, rendered the place inaccessible to the workmen'. These explosions, the true cause of which was probably the release of imprisoned subterranean gas, were ascribed by the emperor to supernatural agency.[2] But this is to point to deficiencies, not so much in the character of Julian as in the system of thought which he professed.

In this connexion we may perhaps recall the observation of Gibbon that the 'genius and power of the emperor were unequal to the enterprise of restoring a religion which was destitute of theological principles, of moral precepts, and of ecclesiastical discipline'. That is to say, he put forward in King Helios a sun without heat, and thus incapable of resolving ambiguities which were inherent in the idealist approach to experience. And, from this standpoint, even the frivolity of contemporary materialism must be regarded as a rebuke to his misguided zeal. His failure, however, cannot be ascribed merely to the fact that the materialists were deaf to his message. For it contained no real appeal to old-fashioned humanists such as Ammianus; and, among the Christians, there were few serious thinkers whom he could hope to seduce from the faith. Accordingly, he was driven for support to the narrow band of Neoplatonic intellectuals, 'the sophists', whose academic advice and assistance proved, indeed, to be in the nature of a boomerang. Otherwise the emperor ploughed a lonely furrow. To his profound dismay he presently discovered that, as his mission produced not the slightest conviction, so it evoked not the least spark of enthusiasm in the minds of men. Misunderstanding himself, he could not, indeed, hope to comprehend the minds and hearts of others. Accordingly, the result of his effort was merely to confirm the verdict of the third century. But, in his failure, Julian assumes the proportions, if not of a heroic, at least of a tragic figure, like Cato in his generation throwing away his energies and his opportunities for a lost cause.

[1] Amm. xxv. 4. 17.   [2] xxiii. 1. 3.

VIII

STATE AND CHURCH IN THE NEW REPUBLIC

WITH the accession of Valentinian, *Romanitas* entered upon the penultimate stage of its existence as an organized system of life. During this period the storms of religious and philosophic controversy which, under the sovereigns of the Constantinian dynasty, had blown with unremitting violence, at last subsided; and, in view of the increasing perils which encompassed the empire, the question arose whether, in their efforts to achieve a new world, the Romans were not in danger of losing all that was best of the old. In this atmosphere the native genius once more asserted itself in a characteristic effort of consolidation. Protected by nominal conformity to the demands of a Christian order, the ancient culture dug itself in; and, as the forms of secular life were fixed and hardened, the Roman world prepared for the last phase under Theodosius.

The defeat of Julian had been dramatically emphasized, not merely by his death on the plains of Mesopotamia but in the election of his successor. Attended though it was by the conventional pagan rites,[1] the choice of the troops fell on a man who, by reason of his notorious adherence to the faith, was to be known in history as *Christianissimus Imperator*. An obscure and undistinguished figure, Jovian, for the greater part of his brief reign, appears to have governed in the name of his predecessor. Few as they were, however, his official acts suffice to indicate a sharp reaction from the principles and policy of Julian. As the readiest means of extricating the remains of the Roman grand army from a difficult, if not impossible situation, Jovian procured a safe retreat by ceding to the hereditary enemy the five provinces beyond the Tigris annexed in 297 by Diocletian together with eastern Mesopotamia, including the great fortresses of Nisibis and Singara, while, at the same time, he renounced the traditional Roman claim to a protectorate over Armenia. The judgement 'ignominious but inevitable', pronounced by Christian historians upon the hastily negotiated peace of Dura, was perhaps inspired by religious bias rather than by any serious consideration of the political and military factors involved. The verdict is nevertheless supported by the fact that

---

[1] Amm. xxv. 6. 1: 'hostiis pro Ioviano extisque inspectis.'

Jovian's successors honoured the treaty, conscious though they must have been of the dangers which it presented to the Asiatic empire of Rome. While thus cutting the losses of Julian abroad, Jovian at the same time reversed his internal policy, by restoring to the Christian Church the status and privileges of which it had been deprived by the Apostate. In so doing he signalized the definite and final repudiation of official paganism.

The failure of reaction, by exploding for ever the hope of reconstruction upon a strictly 'political' basis, clarified to that extent the issues of the century. Following the time of Julian, the old religion showed little or no fight and, within less than a generation, it was to accept its death sentence with hardly an effort of resistance. On the other hand, the attempt of Julian to destroy Christianity had served, by a curious irony, to invigorate the faith. Deprived of imperial favour the Church was purged of many of the scandals of Constantinian times, while it also recovered something of the spirit with which it had resisted third-century persecution. At the same time, in the face of a common danger, contending factions drew together, Catholics and semi-Arians discovering at last a formula ($\mu\iota\alpha$ $o\upsilon\sigma\iota\alpha$ $\epsilon\nu$ $\tau\rho\iota\sigma\iota\nu$ $\upsilon\pi\sigma\sigma\tau\alpha\sigma\epsilon\sigma\iota\nu$) whereby their mutual animosities were overcome and a wide measure of agreement achieved. In consequence of these developments the Roman world was once more committed to evolution upon Christian or nominally Christian lines.

From this standpoint, however, the role of 'his most Christian majesty' was simply to point the way to the future; the actual course of events was to be charted by other hands. With the Apostate, devotion to the empire had involved treason to God. With his successor, devotion to God seemed to imply treason to the empire. And, while Rome might accept the restoration of Christianity, the defeatism of the Christian emperor was more than it could endure. Thus, when Jovian suddenly died, leaving the purple to his infant son, the army, ignoring the recent investiture, discharged its historic role by once more electing a soldier as its *imperator*. Conscious of the urgency of his problems,[1] the new Augustus lost no time in co-opting a trustworthy colleague; and, for eleven years, Valentinian and Valens, proclaiming a fraternal unity of purpose,[2] together supported the burden of administration.

[1] Amm. xxvi. 4. 3: 'magnitudine urgentium negotiorum.'
[2] Dessau, *I.L.S.* 762: 'fratres concordissimi.'

The 'divine brothers', like Jovian, both professed orthodoxy, although Valens was to be accused of a lapse toward Arianism at the close of his reign. But the re-establishment, in their persons, of a strong and efficient Christian régime excited no revival of the grandiose expectations of Constantinian times. The basis of Constantinianism had been the semi-pagan promise of an earthly millennium, to be attained through the amalgamation of principles which third-century apologists had loudly declared to be incompatible. But, as the vision of universal peace, of an empire united in the bonds of confraternity with its neighbours, had long since been dismissed to the limbo of illusion, so also had vanished the dream of a society which, while cherishing the elements of its imperial heritage, was nevertheless to be rejuvenated through the acceptance of 'Christian ideals'. Half a century of bitter controversy and strife, culminating in the crisis of reaction under Julian, had sufficed to dissipate the hopes of the first Christian Caesar and to reveal the truth that, so far from repairing the inner deficiencies of *Romanitas*, the new faith had brought with it not peace but a sword.

The change of atmosphere was marked by a reversion, on the part of the new administration, to the position originally assumed by Constantine and Licinius in 313. In language which recalls the terms of the Edict of Milan, Valentinian once more proclaimed the principle of toleration as fundamental to the New Republic:[1] 'testes sunt leges a me in exordio imperii mei datae, quibus unicuique quod animo inbibisset colendi libera facultas tributa est.' In this declaration we may perceive at once a sharp revulsion from the spirit and methods of Constantinian Christianity and, at the same time, a fresh attempt to come to terms with the forces stirring in the contemporary world. Theoretically it embodied a declaration of neutrality towards the claims of conflicting religions, thus foreshadowing the nineteenth-century ideal of a free Church in a free state. In practice it pointed to a deliberate and sustained effort to satisfy the reasonable aspirations of pagan and Christian alike, thus disposing of a question which had confused the issues of the last fifty years.

This intention is apparent in the measures whereby Valentinian sought to implement the principle of toleration. Thus,

[1] *Cod. Theod.* ix. 16. 9 (371)

while confirming Christian exemptions and immunities,[1] he
intervened in the name of the state to prevent the abuse of
ecclesiastical privilege. To persons entering the lower ranks of
the clergy, provided they did so at the request of the people
and with the consent of the municipal authorities, the emperor
Constantius had accorded the right of retaining their possessions, the revenues from which thus ceased to benefit the public.
Withdrawing this privilege, Valentinian ordered that the estates
of such persons should either be conveyed to their nearest
relative or surrendered to the *curia* from which they proposed
to withdraw; and that individuals convicted of any attempt to
evade these rules should be relegated by force to the service of
their *patria*.[2] In so doing the emperor associated himself, in a
modified way, with the principle laid down by Julian, 'decuriones qui ut Christiani declinant munia revocentur'.[3] Similarly he forbade the assumption of ecclesiastical status by
members of the imperial millers' corporation as a means of
escaping the obligations attached thereto.[4] Furthermore, in
nullifying bequests by widows and wards to their spiritual
advisers, Valentinian struck a blow at the latest and most disreputable phase of ancient parasitism—a measure the necessity
of which is indicated by the remark of St. Jerome, that he does
not so much resent the law as deplore the conditions which
prompted its enactment.[5] Finally, by an edict promulgated in
376, the year following Valentinian's death, but reflecting his
surviving influence, the competence of ecclesiastical courts was
reasserted, but this was specifically limited to the decision of
civil suits, the *actio criminalis* being retained in its own hands by
the state.[6]

In a similar spirit Valentinian, though tolerating paganism,
extended indulgence only to the traditional Graeco-Roman
cults. Thus, while nocturnal sacrifices and magical rites were
in general forbidden on pain of capital punishment, a pointed
exception was made of the Hellenic mysteries.[7] Divination,
also, was proscribed in all but the native Latin form[8] while, in
the edict, *cesset mathematicorum tractatus*, astrology was once more
pronounced a capital offence.[9] Finally, Manichean assemblies

[1] xvi. 1. 1 (365) and 2. 18 and 19 (370).   [2] xii. 1. 59 (364).
[3] xiii. 1. 4 (362).   [4] xiv. 3. 11 (365).
[5] xvi. 2. 20 (370); Gibbon, op. cit., ch. xxv, p. 29, n. 80.
[6] *Cod. Theod.* xvi. 2. 23.   [7] ix. 16. 7 (364); cf. Zosim. iv. iv. 3.
[8] ix. 16. 9 (371): 'haruspicina.'   [9] ix. 16. 8 (370/3).

were prohibited; teachers of the *profana institutio* were stigmatized as infamous; lands and buildings devoted to the cult were declared liable to confiscation. A subsequent enactment threatened with fines all magistrates who failed to enforce the law.[1]

In these measures may be found an index to the spirit and purpose of Valentinian. By contrast with the missionary enterprise displayed under Constantine and his successors, they embody a policy of studied moderation towards the diverse religions current within the empire—a policy which, on the testimony of Ammianus Marcellinus, constituted the chief glory of the reign.[2] Thus far, they mark the acceptance by Valentinian of the Constantinian revolution and, at the same time, his determination to avoid the errors of the Constantinian house. But, while dissolving the alliance between religion and politics which had transformed emperors into bishops and bishops into politicians, he did not thereby admit the autonomy of the 'inner' or 'higher' life. For, however generous and liberal in spirit, his measures were dictated throughout by concern for the public order and, in defence of that order, they presumed a right to regulate the forms not merely of action but of belief. By thus undertaking to determine questions of faith and morals from the standpoint of political expediency, Valentinian reaffirmed in substance the ancient claim of the classical commonwealth. Moreover, both in his hostility to foreign or subversive influences and in his tenderness to the traditional Graeco-Roman cults, he betrayed the fact that, despite a nominal adherence to Christianity, his spiritual affiliations were in reality with the Roman past rather than with the future promised by the Church.

From this standpoint, the first concern of the emperor was the defence of the community against military dangers the like of which had not been experienced since the terrible years of the third century. For, with her field armies shattered in consequence of Julian's misadventure, with fallen prestige and diminished resources, Rome was suddenly confronted by an unprecedented movement among the barbarian peoples, a

[1] xvi. 5. 3 (372) and 5. 4 (376).
[2] Amm. xxx. 9. 5: 'hoc moderamine principatus inclaruit quod inter religionum diversitates medius stetit nec quemquam inquietavit nec ut hoc coleretur imperavit aut illud; nec interdictis minacibus subiectorum cervicem ad id quod ipse coluit inclinabat, sed intemeratas reliquit has partes ut repperit.'

movement in which the names of new and hitherto unknown
assailants appeared alongside those who for centuries had
troubled the peace of the northern frontier. In Britain, Picts
and Scots emerged to fling themselves across the wall or upon
the western coast; while pirates, operating from the German
Ocean, began their devastating raids upon what was already
known as the Saxon shore. On the Continent pressure was no
less acute. The Alemanni, a federation of Teutonic tribes
organized for military purposes, crossed the Rhine, plundering
the city of Moguntiacum and threatening the Roman hold upon
Upper Germany. Meanwhile the Goths, ejected from their
Scythian homes by hordes of Huns and Alans pushing outward
from the heart of Asia, were already swarming along the
Danube, in an effort to penetrate the weakened frontier defences
and to gain the security of the right bank.

In these circumstances the accession of a fighting emperor
served to introduce a brief but significant interlude in the
fortunes of *Romanitas*. His task being to save the empire, Valentinian, with tireless energy, undertook the defence of the West.[1]
Last of his countrymen to cross the Rhine, in the years 366 and
368, he routed the Alemanni; two years later a section of this
people, the Burgundians, were conquered and settled as *coloni*
upon the vacant agricultural lands of the Po valley. The work
of subjugation was accompanied by a renewed fortification of
the frontier; and by 375, the year of his death, it could fairly be
said that the emperor had re-established the Roman watch on
the Rhine. Meanwhile his colleague divided his time between
Antioch and Sirmium, as the exigencies of the situation demanded; and, after suppressing a pagan reaction under Procopius, he was preparing to challenge the settlement of Dura
when, the Gothic menace having become acute, he was forced
to concentrate his attention upon the Danube.

The strain thus involved was, however, terrific and, from this
moment, it is no exaggeration to say that conditions within the
exhausted empire approximated to those of a permanent state
of siege. This being so, everything was subordinated to the
paramount necessity of defence. The Code bears eloquent
testimony to the effort required to reconstruct the Roman
armies, by the mobilization of fighting men and the raising of
money and supplies needed to keep them in the field. Thus,

[1] Amm. xxvi. 5. 9–14.

while wasteful expenditure was everywhere curtailed, taxation was put upon a war basis, and the unhappy *curiales*, as local agents of collection, were subjected to the most rigorous demands. The ruthlessness of these men in exacting the sums required served, no doubt, to fix the evil reputation which they bore as a class (*quot curiales, tot tyranni*). Meanwhile, the last resources of man-power were pressed into service. We have already noticed the enactment whereby Valentinian sought to recall to civil and military duty all able-bodied monks.[1] In order to supply recruits for the army, children of soldiers were required to follow their father's profession except for reasons of physical incapacity; in which case they were drafted into other forms of public service.[2] Conscription for active service in fighting units was applied to able-bodied freemen who tried to shelter themselves behind the lines as camp-followers.[3] The standard height for recruits was fixed at five feet seven inches Roman measure.[4] An edict of 367 revived the provision of Constantine whereby persons mutilating themselves to evade service should be consigned to menial duties with the forces; a second edict prescribed the penalty of *concrematio* (burning alive) for this type of offence, and, at the same time, threatened with heavy punishment landlords whose dependants were convicted thereof.[5] Moreover, the heavy hand of the law descended upon individuals found guilty of harbouring deserters; the offender, if a plebeian, was made liable to penal servitude in the mines, if an *honoratus*, to the confiscation of half his property.[6] Subsequent efforts to entice deserters back to the colours under promise of immunity[7] may be taken to illustrate at once the inadequacy of coercive measures and the urgent need for men.

Following the general tendency of the fourth century, the provision of recruits was regarded as an obligation attaching to property ('tironum praebitio in patrimoniorum viribus potius quam in personarum muneribus conlocetur'). On this basis landlords were obliged, in a fashion resembling that of Imperial Russia, to furnish from their estates a specified number of bodies (*corpora*) for enlistment according to a carefully regulated scheme of rotation from which there was to be no evasion, while, when money instead of recruits was required, they were

---

[1] Ch. VII, p. 269 above.   [2] *Cod. Theod.* vii. 1. 5 (364).   [3] vii. 1. 10 (367).
[4] vii. 13. 3 (367).   [5] vii. 13. 4 and 5.
[6] vii. 18. 1 (365).   [7] Amm. xxvii. 8. 10 (368).

one and all liable, *pro modo capitationis suae.*[1] By legislation of
Gratian, Valentinian Junior, and Theodosius, in the years immediately following, no one was permitted to submit for active
service a slave or prostitute, a baker or miller, any one whose
deformity rendered him incapable of service or any one from
the workhouse.[2] Two mutilated individuals were prescribed as
the equivalent of one physically sound recruit.[3]

To the measures of coercion thus adopted were added special
inducements calculated to enhance the attractiveness of the
military career. Two early enactments confirmed the right of
veterans to engage in commerce without liability to *portoria* or
customs dues, and granted immunity even from hereditary
curial obligation to men who could prove five years' efficient
service in the ranks, which was thus held to be equivalent to
twenty-five years in other branches of the imperial service.[4]
By a law of 320, veterans had been relieved of all personal and
civic obligations to which they might be hereditarily liable, and
were authorized to occupy and cultivate vacant lands free of
taxation, as well as to draw from the public treasury fixed sums
with which to equip and stock them.[5] A fresh provision now
entitled them, upon conclusion of their period of service, to
settle in whatever part of the empire they desired. This was
in sharp contrast with the prevailing disposition to attach
civilians by the strictest of ties to their place of origin.[6]

In his military enterprises, as well as in the methods adopted
to ensure their success, Valentinian exploited to the full the
traditional resources of the *imperium*. As a basis for his high
statesmanship, the emperor Julian had invoked the authority of
Plato. To Valentinian as a professing Christian, such a course
was impossible. But, while affirming his personal belief in the
Evangel, he nevertheless made no effort to exploit it, as his
predecessors had done, in order to give theoretical justification
to his régime; still less to win for it the active support of the
organized Church. On the contrary he was satisfied, as lord of
this world,[7] to assert an independent right to pursue secular
objects by methods essentially secular. In the case of a simple
and realistic man of action such as Valentinian, it would be
vain to look for any positive statement of his views regarding the

---

[1] *Cod. Theod.* vii. 13. 7 (375).   [2] vii. 13. 8 (380).   [3] vii. 13. 10 (381).
[4] vii. 20. 9 (366) and 1. 6 (368).
[5] vii. 20. 3.   [6] vii. 20. 8 (364).   [7] Amm. xxix. 5. 46.

source and nature of the imperial power. But, quite apart from the use to which he put it, his sense of the prerogative is evident in the terminology officially employed. Valentinian and Valens 'the divine and most concordant brothers' were *domini orbis*, 'lords of the world', *perpetui* and *perennes Augusti, victoriosissimi* and *invictissimi principes, aeterni imperatores*.[1] It is evident also in the enactment by virtue of which the private manufacture of gold- and silk-embroidered garments, the habiliments of sovereignty, was for the first time formally prohibited.[2] And it also finds expression in the dynasticism which elevated first a brother, then two sons in succession, to the purple.[3]

The imperial power being thus conceived as independent and self-sufficient, it is natural that the legislation of Valentinian should exhibit little or no trace of the positive influences commonly associated with Constantinian Christianity. Infanticide was, indeed, once more pronounced a capital offence, and that on grounds which suggest the operation of a religious rather than an economic motive.[4] Constantine's law of rape was, however, qualified by the provision that indictments under this category must be made within five years of the alleged offence.[5] And, while rejecting the claim of the Church to share in the administration of criminal justice, Valentinian and his brother manifested their conservatism by reasserting, although in an attenuated form, the ancient right of family discipline, subject, however, in the case of major offences, to the intervention of public authority.[6]

While thus abandoning any attempt to read Christian principles into the law, the new administration continued the reform programme initiated by Julian, by enunciating a series of sane and equitable principles for the administration of justice, in keeping with the best traditions of Roman jurisprudence. Thus all cases, both civil and criminal, were to be tried in open court, magistrates being forbidden to make secret arrangements with the litigants, 'ut neminem lateat quid secundum legum vel veritatis ordinem fuerit iudicatum'.[7] They were, moreover, instructed to reject any representations submitted by either party out of court.[8] A series of measures regulated the procedure to

---

[1] Dessau, *I.L.S.* 5910, 5535, 5555, &c.
[2] *Cod. Theod.* x. 21. 1 (369).   [3] Amm. xxvii. 6.
[4] *Cod. Theod.* ix. 14. 1 (374): 'si quis necandi infantis piaculum adgressus adgressave sit, erit capitale istud malum.'   [5] ix. 24. 3 (374).
[6] ix. 13. 1 (365 and 373).   [7] i. 16. 9 (364).   [8] i. 16. 10 (365).

be adopted in criminal cases. Charges were to be tried only in the province where the alleged crime had been committed.[1] The accuser was to complete the necessary formalities in writing and thus undertake to support his case, and no one was to be committed to custody until this was done.[2] Confessions involving other parties were not to be accepted except from those who had previously proved their own innocence.[3] Provincial governors were authorized to arrest and detain suspected criminals of whatever dignity, and were to refer their cases to the emperor personally or (failing time) to the *praefectus praetorio* or (should the suspect be a soldier) the *magister militiae*.[4] In trying senators on capital charges, the *praefectus urbi* was to associate with him as assessors five men of 'reputable character', chosen by lot.[5]

A similar spirit is evident in the attempts of Valentinian and Valens to improve upon the existing administrative system. The effort of rationalization, undertaken by Julian, was continued in successive edicts, by virtue of which refinements were introduced into the office of vicar, as the intermediary between provincial magistrates and the praetorian prefecture.[6] In the same way additional regulations were made to govern the use of public transport.[7] But, in this connexion, perhaps the most significant development was an elaboration of machinery designed to check abuses characteristic of bureaucracy. This is illustrated in the so-called *defensio civitatum* or *defensio plebis*, a fourth-century counterpart to the primitive tribunate of the plebs. The origin of this institution lay in the *defensio senatus* established by Constantius II, a device whereby imperial senators were granted the right of selecting in each province one or two of their number 'to defend the patrimonies of all' against unwarranted exactions on the part of revenue officials. Accepting this arrangement, Valentinian and Valens extended it to the municipalities in a form designed to serve the interests of the commons.[8] But, while priding themselves on this innovation, the emperors soon found it necessary to frame additional regulations in order to check bribery and corruption in the choice of patrons or *defensores*, who had evidently discovered in their office simply a means of graft and

---

[1] ix. 1. 10 (373).   [2] ix. 3. 4 (365).
[3] ix. 1. 12 (374).   [4] ix. 2. 2 (365).   [5] ix. 1. 13 (376).
[6] i. 15. 5 (365); 6 (372); 7 (377); 8 (377).
[7] vii. 4. 10–17 (364–77).
[8] i. 29. 1 (364).

oppression.[1] The institution, nevertheless, survived to clog the administrative system and, by so doing, to provide a curious and ironic commentary on the text, *quis custodiet ipsos custodes?* Measures of Theodosius, a generation later, directed against malfeasance on the part of *defensores*, indicate the nature of their offences and the steps necessary to prevent them.[2]

Significant as they were, the military activities of Valentinian, his judicial and administrative reforms, are seen in their true perspective only as part of the Herculean effort of consolidation characteristic of the reign. In this connexion, perhaps the most striking developments were those which governed the evolution of corporative life. With these developments the evolution of state-control which, originating in the troubled times of Gallienus and Aurelian, had gathered impetus during the fourth century, was finally completed; and the corporations, *corpora* or *collegia*, into which the working and professional classes were organized, emerged as creatures and instruments of the state.

Of these corporations the most important were those concerned with the discharge of essential public services, such, for example, as provisioning the capitals, and these were subject to stringent regulation and control. The spirit of this regulation may be illustrated by reference to contemporary legislation governing the *consortium* or *corpus pistorum*, the millers' and bakers' corporation, obligated to the duty of supplying bread for the dole. This obligation was hereditary, and was attached to property held by *pistores*, so that in all cases it devolved upon their heirs.[3] Thus no imperial senator or member of the official hierarchy was permitted to buy such property.[4] On the other hand, should a baker become a senator, he must arrange for a substitute to take over his hereditary duties;[5] and the corporation as a whole was required to assume the obligations of members who were under the age of twenty.[6] In the case of this, as of other corporations, new members were to be recruited as they were needed from the ranks of *libertini* or freedmen who

---

[1] i. 29. 3, 4, and 5 (368 foll.).

[2] i. 29. 7 (392): 'defensores nihil sibi insolenter, nihil indebitum vindicantes nominis sui tantum fungantur officio: nullas infligant multas, nullas exerceant quaestiones. plebem tantum vel decuriones ab omni improborum insolentia et temeritate tueantur, ut id tantum quod esse dicuntur, esse non desinant'; i. 29. 8 (392): 'removeantur patrocinia quae favorem reis et auxilium scelerosis impertiendo maturari scelera fecerunt.'

[3] xiv. 3. 3 (364): 'paneficii necessitatem suscipere successionis iure coguntur.'

[4] loc. cit.   [5] xiv. 3. 4 (364).   [6] xiv. 3. 5 (364).

possessed the necessary property qualification.[1] A general law provided that no one might evade the obligations of the *pistrinum* even by entering the Church, and individuals who attempted to do so were liable to be relegated to their hereditary status.[2]

Analogous regulations governed the *corpus naviculariorum*, the imperial shipping corporation which was bound to the transportation of grain, wood, and other commodities required by the state. An edict of the year 369, addressed to the prefect of Rome, instructs him to recruit the personnel of the Roman corps to the number of sixty, by conscribing suitable persons to fill existing vacancies.[3] Two years later the prefect of the Orient was ordered to reconstruct in the same way the corps of the eastern provinces.[4] For this purpose the original materials for shipbuilding were to be requisitioned from all the provincials, while the *navicularii* themselves were to bear the annual cost of repairs and renewals out of an immunity accorded to their land. Membership of the corps was to be constituted of *honorati* (except those engaged in service within the imperial palace), of *curiales*, and, with their own consent, of imperial senators, together with such of the existing group of *navicularii* as were available; and the list of members, old and new, was to be submitted (in duplicate!) to the imperial record office. As thus reorganized, the Oriental corps was to enjoy the same status and rights as that of Africa.

The *navicularia functio*, like that of the millers and bakers, depended upon property, and individuals purchasing the assets of shippers (*naviculariae facultates*) found themselves liable *pro modo portionis comparatae* to obligations attaching thereto.[5] Elaborate rules were framed to prevent fraud on the part of those engaged in overseas transport. Shippers were permitted to leave port only after obtaining clearance papers from the provincial authorities; they were required to carry with them on board ship a government inspector and, upon discharging their cargoes, they were bound to account before a harbour commission for every item taken on board. Those claiming to have suffered loss or damage by sea were obliged to apply to the nearest provincial governor for a court of inquiry, at the same time producing 'a reasonable number' of the crew for examination under torture ('quo eorum tormentis plenior veritas possit

---

[1] xiv. 3. 9 and 10 (368).   [2] xiv. 3. 11 (365).
[3] xiii. 5. 13.   [4] xiii. 5. 14.   [5] xiii. 6. 4–7 (367 and 375).

inquiri'). The findings of this court were to be reported without
delay to the praetorian prefecture; and no claims were to be
entertained unless presented within one or, in the case of longer
voyages, two years from the date of the alleged loss.[1]

Such were the contributions of Valentinian towards a system
of state-control typical of the fourth century—a system which,
in at least one instance, was presently to make the corporation,
as such, criminally responsible for defalcations on the part of
its members, in flat defiance of principles consecrated in the
classical jurisprudence.[2]

The spirit of regulation, which thus pervaded the great
imperial services, found expression also in codes governing the
activity of minor corporations. Such codes, elaborated by successive administrations throughout the century, were imposed
under Valentinian upon the *catabolenses*, the carriers' union
apparently attached to the bakers' guild;[3] the *suarii, pecuarii*, and
vini susceptores, purveyors of pork, beef, and wine to the market
of the capital, who operated under a scale of prices fixed by
Julian,[4] bath-attendants and dealers in firewood,[5] builders
and outfitters,[6] the lime-burners of Rome and Constantinople,[7]
individuals navigating cargo-boats on the Tiber,[8] and the Ostian
longshoremen's guild, to which was accorded a monopoly of
handling goods entering the harbour.[9]

State-control, thus enforced upon the workers, was extended
by Valentinian to include also the professional classes. In a
significant enactment the emperor authorized the appointment
of one chief physician for each of the fourteen regions of the
capital, to be selected (subject to imperial approval) from
among the leading members of the craft and, in consideration
of a public salary, to undertake the care of indigent sick within
his district. With this development, fourth-century Rome
achieved a kind of state medicine, the theory of which is indicated in the text.[10] In a similar spirit Valentinian set up a guild
of licensed painters, *picturae professores*, members of which, if
freemen, were to enjoy the immunities accorded to other professions, including exemption from the dreaded obligation of

[1] xiii. 9. 1 and 2 (372).
[2] xiv. 3. 16 (380): 'quidquid ex horreis plectibili usurpatione praesumptum sit,
id per pistores, in quos totius criminis confertur invidia, matura exactione red-
datur.'   [3] xiv. 3.   [4] xiv. 4.   [5] xiv. 5.   [6] xiv. 8.   [7] xiv. 6.   [8] xiv. 21.   [9] xiv. 22.
[10] xiii. 3. 8 (370): '... qui, scientes annonaria sibi commoda a populi commodis
ministrari, honeste obsequi tenuioribus malint quam turpiter servire divitibus.'

official hospitality, together with rent-free offices in the municipal squares. These painters were not to be required by local magistrates to decorate public buildings or to execute the imperial portraits (*sacros vultus efficiendos*) without adequate payment. Municipal authorities were obliged, on pain of sacrilege, to recognize the privileges extended to them.[1]

With these developments Valentinian completed the outlines of the functional society which, substantially in the form he gave it, was to be his legacy to the Theodosian age. The principle governing this society was that of service: 'nemo aliquid immune possideat.'[2] As this idea became dominant, a rich and varied terminology was devised to indicate the manifold obligations imposed by the state on its members. The language used is profoundly suggestive, obligations being variously designated as *munera, onera, ministeria, servitia, nexus, necessitates,* otherwise *functionum obsequia, obsequia publicorum munerum,* or *solemnitates civilium munerum.* Individuals or corporate groups obligated to such duties were described as *obnoxii functioni,* and, so far as the state was concerned, their business was to discharge an unending round of services prescribed by supreme authority (*functiones tolerare, implere militiam*). Thus, in the last phase of its history, *Romanitas* resolved itself into a community in which theoretically every one was a worker but no one could be said to work for himself. And, for all but active members of the imperial services, such work was purely fiscal, taking the form of contributions to their support.

In the assessment of these contributions[3] the principle was that of service according to capacity.[4] They thus included labour as well as money and goods. As such, they were classified as either 'personal' or 'civil'. *Munera personalia,* otherwise *corporalia* or *sordida,* embraced the various forms of physical toil imposed upon the poor. *Civilia munera,* on the other hand, represented obligations attaching to property and varied with the status of the possessor, according to the principle *sollicitudo ac honor,* the fourth-century counterpart of *noblesse oblige.* There were, indeed, certain indispensable functions to which all property-holders were theoretically liable, such, for example, as the maintenance of public roads;[5] and, to these functions, even

---

[1] xiii. 4. 4 (374).   [2] xiii. 10. 8.   [3] i. 28. 3: 'dispositio fiscalium functionum.'   [4] xii. 1. 109: 'functio pro qualitate generis.'   [5] xv. 3. 3: 'a viarum munitione nullus habeatur immunis.'

the imperial domains were ultimately made liable.[1] Otherwise the incidence of burdens was arranged to correspond with a presumed ability to discharge them; and the imposition of a specific burden carried with it in every case commensurate privileges and immunities.

Considerations of space make it impossible to enlarge upon the application of these principles, which are illustrated by the most minute prescriptions scattered throughout the Code. Certain implications of the system may, however, be noted. In a society governed by the principle *functio pro qualitate generis*, the motive of individual enterprise was, indeed, largely eliminated, but property (or even the lack of it) nevertheless remained the 'immovable foundation of human relationships', the basis of rights and duties, public and private. And, both as a natural extension to the idea of property, and as the readiest means of enforcing the obligations attaching thereto, emerged the hereditary principle, by virtue of which services were normally designated as *patriae functiones* or *originalia vincula*. With regard to the bureaucracy, Constantine had already in 331 asserted the principle of 'original obligation'.[2] Evidence already submitted shows how under Valentinian the *corporati* or *collegiati* were subjected to the same rule. By Valens it was applied to the children of senators, male and female.[3] An edict of Theodosius was presently to affirm the principle as binding also upon members of the municipal aristocracies.[4]

In the functional society the notion of property was thus entirely dissociated from that of freedom of contract. Restrictions imposed upon the buying and selling of lands belonging to members of the bakers' and shippers' corporations have already been noticed. Similar restrictions were soon to be attached to those of decurions. By a law of 386 decurions were forbidden to dispose of real property or chattels except when absolutely necessary and then only by permission of competent authority.[5] As a sanction for this measure, it was presently to

[1] xv. 3. 4.
[2] vii. 22. 3: 'ii, qui ex officialibus quorumcumque officiorum geniti sunt sive eorundem parentes adhuc sacramento tenentur sive iam dimissi erunt, in parentum locum procedant.'   [3] vi. 2. 12.
[4] xii. 1. 101 (383): 'exemplo senatorii ordinis patris originem municeps unusquisque sequatur.'
[5] xii. 3. 1 (386): 'denique nihil erit postmodum, quo venditor vel circumventum se insidiis vel obpressum potentia comparatoris queri debeat.'

be enacted that any one venturing to purchase the land of decurions without government approval should forfeit the purchase price as well as the land in question.[1]

Such was the nemesis which, in the last stage of his history, overtook the Roman man of property. It is a grim comment upon the process of *Romanitas* that the state which, according to Cicero, had originated for the protection of property-right, should finally have transformed it into the basis of a system of servitudes unparalleled in the annals of civilized man.

As such theories triumphed within imperial society, the process of secular evolution was concluded, and the Eternal City which, in the course of her long and varied history, had offered in succession the model of a vigorous and aggressive peasant community, then of the imperializing, colonizing, and assimilative world-power, finally presented to the world a picture of immobility, the immobility of a fully matured civilization. To the pioneer or democratic mind the social system of the fourth century is a foreign and unnatural thing, and it becomes comprehensible only from a detailed study of the Theodosian Code. We may, however, observe that this system involved a rigid stratification of the various orders in a nicely articulated scheme, the status of each being meticulously defined according to its 'economic' importance; i.e. the role which it played within the social organization as a whole. In this scheme, members of each and every group possessed their *codicilli* or patents, by virtue of which they could, when necessary, authenticate their claims; and the names even of humbler members of society were inscribed upon the *matricula* or roll of their group.[2] Classes were distinguished also by differences of dress and insignia; and dress order within the city was carefully prescribed, its enforcement being committed to the *censuale officium*.[3] The established order was subjected to continuous refinement in a series of prescriptions which extended throughout the Theodosian age. Thus, by an edict of 397, the wearing of breeches was prohibited within the city under threat of perpetual exile together with the confiscation of all property.[4] Some years later it was forbidden to appear in public with long hair, and the use of skins, even by slaves, was banned in the capital and its environs.[5]

To the various groups and classes within society were accorded

[1] xii. 3. 2 (423).   [2] e.g. xvi. 2. 15: 'negotiatorum matricula'.
[3] xiv. 10. 1 (382).   [4] xiv. 10. 2.   [5] xiv. 10. 4 (416).

honorific titles, ranging from the *illustres, spectabiles*, and *claris-simi*, the three grades within the imperial aristocracy, to the *egregiatus* or *perfectissimatus* which satisfied the ambitions of civil servants or *municipales* who had lived to fulfil certain specified duties; and the scheme included fresh distinctions such as that of count, as well as the historical *senatoria dignitas*. Within this latter, the honour of the new patriciate instituted by Constantine, combined with that of the ancient dignity of consul, constituted a distinction which raised the possessor to a social equality with holders of the great vice-royalties or prefectures. Such titles were eagerly coveted, if not for their intrinsic value, at least for the privileges and immunities which their tenure conferred. The importance of status was further emphasized in an elaborate order of precedence, the general principle of which was to be laid down by legislation of Theodosius[1] and defined by his successors. It was emphasized also in a ceremonious code of etiquette which included the specification of forms of access and address (*ius adeundi, ius osculandi*, &c.) to be employed in relation to various grades of the civil and military hierarchy.

Such was the system which, evolving out of that erected by Augustus and the Antonines, and developed by successive administrations during the third and fourth centuries, was finally to be projected into the Theodosian age. To each of these administrations it owed something, if only by way of accretion; and of such accretions, certain ones like that of prostration, may undoubtedly be traced to influence from the Orient. Nevertheless, the elements of this order were still Roman and, as such, they might have been understood by Augustus or by Hadrian. In the words of Gibbon,[2] 'the forms, the pomp and the expense of the civil administration contributed to restrain the irregular license of the soldiers; and, although the laws were violated by power or perverted by subtlety, the sage principles of Roman jurisprudence preserved a sense of order and equity, unknown to the despotic governments of the East'. That is to say, despite the efforts of various emperors to give it a fresh complexion, *Romanitas* still embodied at heart the classical ideal of εὐνομία or good order. From this standpoint, it should be remembered that the role of individuals and groups within the system was to adjust themselves to the demands of an architectonic whole,

[1] vi. 22. 7 (383).   [2] Op. cit., ch. xvii, p. 200.

and mere 'liberty' was hardly at any time more than an excrescence.

In making possible this adjustment, no function of society was more essential than that of education. We have already discussed the place of education in the economy of *Romanitas*, and have noted the rise of a scheme of public instruction, beginning with Cato and Cicero and developing on lines laid down by the latter throughout early imperial times.[1] As state-control developed within the empire, the theory and practice of education became not less but more important; and to it Valentinian made a contribution of supreme significance.

It has elsewhere been observed that Julian, in his effort to consolidate the forces of reaction, had attempted to monopolize the machinery of instruction and transform it into an instrument of political control. By asserting a right of nomination to all teaching appointments, he had excited the bitter opposition of Christians and provoked the *Kulturkampf* which was to mark the conclusion of his reign. But here, as elsewhere, what Julian had vainly endeavoured to achieve by the authority of Plato, Valentinian was able to accomplish in the name of Christ. Under the latter, state-control of education began with the suppression of the independent, private teacher, the 'philosophic missionary' whose spiritual history ascended to the days of Periclean Athens and whose activities had formed such a conspicuous feature of life in the Antonine world.[2] An edict of 369 required that wandering sophists, 'riff-raff' discovered to have assumed the philosophic habit without authority, should be rounded up and relegated to their places of origin, there to discharge their hereditary duties.[3] By a subsequent edict, promulgated in 376, provision was made for the establishment of an elaborate system of state education throughout the various dioceses of Gaul. In each of the larger towns, authorities were instructed to appoint grammarians and rhetoricians (both Greek and Latin) at a generous salary, fixed by statute, to be defrayed from the municipal chest. Metropolitan cities were to have a choice of the best-qualified instructors, and these were to be paid on a more liberal scale in keeping with their superior abilities and with the status of the cities concerned.[4] In this way the teaching profession was transformed into a closed caste.

---

[1] Ch. IV above.   [2] Dill, *Roman Society from Nero to Marcus Aurelius*, pp.334–83.
[3] *Cod. Theod.* xiii. 3. 7: 'haec conluvies'.   [4] xiii. 3. 11.

Contemporary tendencies towards a state monopoly of education found expression also in the establishment of imperial universities both in Old and New Rome.[1] By the constitution of these universities the urban prefect was invested with proctorial power; and students applying for admission were required to present a certificate from the authorities of their place of origin, accrediting them as fit and proper persons to attend. They were required also to outline a proposed course of study, for the approval of the prefect. The *censuale officium* was to keep a record of their place of residence in the city. It was to warn students of the dangers of unseasonable and excessive indulgence, especially by way of too frequent attendance at the spectacles; and, in the case of offenders, it was to inflict the punishment of public flogging and rustication. Diligent and well-behaved students, on the other hand, were permitted to continue their work till the age of twenty; and the names of successful students were to be reported annually to the imperial record office as potential recruits for the civil service. Coincident with the foundation of these state universities went the rehabilitation of the national libraries, through the appointment of a permanent commission to repair and replace books.[2]

As the crown and apex of a national system of education, the imperial universities, thus established by Valentinian, were to survive, like so many of his institutions, into Theodosian times. An enactment of the younger Theodosius completed their constitution by adding to the existing chairs in grammar and rhetoric (Greek and Latin), one in philosophy and two in law. At the same time it reasserted the state monopoly by forbidding unauthorized persons to offer public instruction and by denying them the immunities accorded to the Capitoline staff.[3] Thus the Capitol, in ancient times the seat of Juppiter, Juno, and Minerva, branded by Tertullian as 'temple of all the devils', the place where once the sacred geese had cackled, now echoed to the voices of professors expatiating on the language, literature, and institutions of classical Greece and Rome.

The programme of Valentinian provides ample evidence of what has been described as the heroic effort of consolidation characteristic of the reign. At the same time it emphasizes the truth that this effort was directed towards maintaining, at all costs, the existing structure of secular society. For this purpose

[1] xiv. 9. 1 (370).   [2] xiv. 9. 2 (372).   [3] xiv. 9. 3 (425).

the emperor was ready, as occasion demanded, to resort to the most drastic expedients. If further illustration were needed of this truth, it could be found in legislation such as that which forbade the imposition of curial status, with its attendant obligations, upon any man as a punishment,[1] or in the subsequent enactment whereby, while confirming the privileges of decurions, the administration threatened with the death penalty any magistrate who inflicted torture upon them for offences other than treason or sacrilege.[2] At the same time, the leading members of the *curia* were specifically exempt from applications of the 'leaded lash'. But the most striking evidence of this intention is unquestionably to be found in an edict which prohibited, as a capital offence, the intermarriage of Roman provincials and barbarians, men or women, of whatever rank or locality.[3] Significant of the effort of *Romanitas* to maintain itself against the rising tide of barbarism, the full import of this measure can be appreciated only by contrast with revolutionary changes which were to occur within the next generation, when, upon the revival of fusionism under Theodosius, two princes, the one united to a woman of Frankish, the other to one of Vandal blood, were to occupy the imperial throne, while their sister, a daughter and mother of emperors, was for some years to be the consort of a barbarian king.

In setting himself to preserve the essential constituents of the Roman order, Valentinian gave expression to an attitude common to at least two classes within the community. The first consisted of traditionalist or philosophic pagans who, though they had manifested little or no enthusiasm for the reactionary programme of Julian, nevertheless rejected the alternative proposed by Christianity. The second was composed of an increasing number who, while professing adherence to the new faith, saw it in reality through pagan eyes.

Of the former, Ammianus Marcellinus may be taken as representative. We have already cited the testimony of Ammianus in favour of the religious policy of Valentinian. Elsewhere he comments with appreciation upon the fact that, under this régime, all persons received the protection due to their

---

[1] xii. 1. 66 (365).   [2] ix. 35. 2 (376).
[3] iii. 14. 1 (370): 'quod si quae inter provinciales atque gentiles adfinitates **ex** huiusmodi nubtiis extiterunt, quod in his suspectum vel noxium detegitur, capitaliter expietur.'

rank and station, except in the solitary case of treason ('in qua sola omnibus aequa conditio est'). In so doing, he endorses the claims made by the administration on its own behalf.[1] And, in general, he bears witness to the excellence of the government, pronouncing Valentinian weak only in his attitude to powerful army-officers and Valens both stern and honest.[2] The sentiments thus expressed were to be repeated in the years immediately following when, the clouds of Christian persecution having gathered round their heads, devoted adherents of the ancient culture recalled the measures of Valentinian as the pledge and guarantee of a freedom which by their day had ceased to exist.[3]

Ammianus, however, as his works show, lived in the past. His spiritual equipment was derived from the theologians and sophists of classical antiquity, whose names he revered and whose speculations in physics, ethics, and logic he made the basis of a personal philosophy of life. In this philosophy there is no appreciable advance upon views current among educated men in the days of Cicero and Livy. The same effort is made to rationalize the notions implicit in popular mythology; the gods are depersonalized and reduced to qualities of things. Things, however, take their revenge inasmuch as, by this process, they acquire a positive character and exercise a positive influence upon mankind, constituting the conditions or controls which are imposed upon human activity, 'ea quae accidunt nobis non per nos sed aliunde et vires eae quae extra nos sunt'. For these conditions the collective name is *Fortuna*, which thus once more emerges as the correlative to *Virtus*, and in the interaction of *Virtus* and *Fortuna* is to be found the *lex naturalis*, *fatalis ordo*, or destiny of man.[4]

As a robust survival from the days of Cicero and Livy, the thought of Ammianus may, perhaps, be regarded as not quite in tune with the spirit of his age. A much more significant and, at the same time, sinister phenomenon is to be found in the mentality of those representative fourth-century figures who, while offering a nominal allegiance to Christianity, betrayed by their attitude and outlook an utter failure to understand it. In this connexion a difficulty arises from the impossibility of deter-

---

[1] Amm. xxviii. 1; *Cod. Theod.* ix. 35. 1 (369).   [2] Amm. xxvii. 9. 4; xxxi. 14. 2 foll.
[3] St. Ambrose, *Epist.* cl. 1. 17; *Relatio Symmachi* 3: 'repetimus igitur religionum statum qui rei publicae diu profuit.'   [4] See Chs. III and IV above.

mining what elements of their thought are to be attributed merely to convention and what, on the other hand, represents a genuine 'hang over' from the officially pagan past. This difficulty emerges with the panegyrists who, as we have noticed in speaking of the efforts of the youthful Julian, were in the habit of reiterating the threadbare pagan compliments hallowed by continuous usage since the time of Pliny. The same problem arises in connexion with the poets who, Christian no less than pagan, regularly employed the ideological apparatus traditional to classical art. Such as it is, however, the ambiguity may fairly be said to disappear with Ausonius, than whom there could hardly be a character more typical of his age. Lawyer and rhetorician of Bordeaux, Ausonius was summoned to court by Valentinian to act as tutor to Gratian and, in generous recognition of his services, Gratian was later to elevate him to the consulship. In his well-known *Easter Hymn*[1] Ausonius, after speaking of the Trinity, *Pater, Natus, Spiritus*, thus concludes:

> tale et terrenis specimen spectatur in oris
> Augustus genitor, geminum sator Augustorum,
> qui fratrem natumque pio complexus utrumque
> numine partitur regnum neque dividit unum,
> omnia solus habens atque omnia dilargitus.
> hos igitur nobis trina pietate vigentes,
> rectores terrae placidos caelique ministros,
> Christe, apud aeternum placabilis adsere patrem.

The difficulty involved in elaborating this simile is by no means inconsiderable; in order that it may in all respects be precise, Valentinian, the senior Augustus, must be represented as 'father' to Valens as well as to Gratian, and thus the 'first person' of that triune majesty which, through its several members, controls the destinies of the one and indivisible empire. Apart from this discrepancy, however, the poet, in a flight comparable with anything achieved by his pagan predecessors, has succeeded in translating the central dogma of Christian orthodoxy into a piece of characteristic mythological fancy; while, at the same time, he transmutes the imperial power into a kind of earthly providence. By so doing he aptly illustrates, if not the nature of the Trinity, at any rate the triumph of pagan over Christian ways of thought. And, in thus bearing witness to a victory for

[1] *Opusc.* iii. 2, ll. 24-31.

the old way of thought over the new, he associates himself, in effect, with what still survived of the sentiments and aspirations consecrated in the secular system of Rome.

In these circumstances it becomes instructive to consider the estimate which contemporary secularism placed upon the position and prospects of the empire. For this purpose we may advert once more to the authority who, of all that survive, was perhaps best equipped to undertake an analysis and interpretation of the existing scene. At once a man of letters and of affairs, Ammianus combined in his person the qualities which antiquity demanded of the ideal historian. As a soldier he had served under Constantius and his successors; he had witnessed something of Julian's fatal Persian expedition and its aftermath, and he had participated, with Valens, in the fighting on the northeast frontier. He was, moreover, conversant with the workings of the imperial administrative system and thus in a position to discern both its strength and weaknesses. Finally, his experience included a first-hand acquaintance with the society, not merely of the provinces, but also of Rome and Italy. To his work as an historian Ammianus brought an independence of judgement which was the result both of temperament and training; in particular, he was deeply suspicious of the methods adopted by the second Flavians to bring about a new heaven and a new earth. But, while detached and critical in his attitude towards the project of a Christian social order, he was nevertheless far from being a reactionary, and his conservatism was satisfied with the arrangement whereby Valentinian attempted to polarize the relations of Church and state. In this respect he revealed himself decisively as a man of his age. As such, his observations carry with them the authority of one who saw the existing system, so to speak, from within.

With regard to this system, Ammianus has but two general comments to offer, and, of these, the first concerns the Roman aristocracy. In a number of striking passages, which have been used by Gibbon as the basis for a brilliant portrayal of contemporary imperial society, Ammianus lets himself go in a scathing indictment of this class.[1] With Juvenalian scorn he stigmatizes the aimless frivolity of lives made possible only through swollen incomes derived from the exploitation of the provincials and consecrated to no purpose worthier than the ostentatious dis-

[1] xiv. 6; xxviii. 4; Gibbon, op. cit., ch. xxxi, p. 295 foll.

play of wealth and pride. He describes the incessant round of amusements, bathing, driving, hunting, yachting, and the exchange of hospitality, whereby the worthless aristocrats of his day sought to conceal from themselves the futility of their existence. He points with disgust to their moral and spiritual shortcomings, their cowardice and effeminacy, their avarice and wastefulness, their quickness to borrow, their slowness to repay; above all to the childish superstition which prompts them to resort, on the slightest pretext, to diviners and soothsayers who prey upon their fears. This superstition he attributes to the lack of any serious principles of conduct, a defect for which they have themselves to blame, inasmuch as they have turned from the cultivation of the mind, rejecting the heritage of philosophy through which alone such principles may be attained, in order to immerse themselves in mere sensationalism. Accordingly, among their retainers, the crooner has replaced the philosopher, the teacher of histrionics that of oratory; they seal their libraries like tombs, but construct for themselves hydraulic organs.[1]

By thus resigning themselves to the cult of futility, the Roman aristocrats no doubt exposed themselves to criticism such as has always been levelled against the idle rich. Yet, in view of the conditions which governed ancient life, the influence of their follies and extravagances must have been relatively circumscribed and, in order to see and appreciate their worthlessness, it was necessary to visit the imperial playground which had once been Italy. Whatever importance they had was, therefore, mainly symbolic: it pointed to a callous indifference on the part of the possessing classes to the hardship and suffering rampant throughout the provinces. Otherwise, their lives possessed not the slightest social significance.

A second and much more incisive criticism was one which applied, not to any limited class within the community, but to imperial society as a whole and which, so far as it could be substantiated, indicated a failure on the part of the Roman order to make good its essential claim. It had been generally accepted, since the time of Vergil, that the Eternal City had realized an ideal of social justice through the establishment and maintenance of a rule of law; and that, in thus discharging her

[1] Amm. xiv. 6. 18: 'denique pro philosopho cantor et, in locum oratoris, doctor artium ludicrarum accitur et, bibliothecis sepulchrorum ritu in perpetuum clausis, organa fabricantur hydraulica . . .'

secular mission, *Romanitas* had found justification in the eyes of the world. But, as Ammianus points out, the subject, to whom this priceless boon was offered, accepted it only to find himself enmeshed in one of the most elaborate legal systems ever devised, and hence a potential victim to the machinations of lawyers by whose sinister activities the ideal of justice was systematically warped and perverted. This danger had become increasingly great with the evolution of bureaucracy and socialism during the fourth century; for, under these conditions, imperial society had become more than ever before a society of lawyers. Lawyers crowded the ranks of the civil hierarchy, importing into it their characteristic point of view. They were active in the courts of justice throughout the provinces. Thus what had once been a flourishing, honoured, and useful profession had become one of the chief plagues of contemporary society. To Ammianus, as a simple and rugged soldier, lawyers are a violent and rapacious crew, dashing from town to town, besieging the door-steps of the rich and, like thoroughbred hounds, sniffing even at bedroom doors for cases. They capitalize domestic differences in order to build up an edifice of hate and, by undertaking to unearth obsolete laws for a sufficient price, they guarantee to secure the acquittal of a man, even if he has murdered his mother. Once in their clutches, the victim is sucked to the marrow without a hope of getting away.[1]

The criticisms thus launched by Ammianus, however acute, are obviously lacking in depth and penetration. He carps at the abuse of privilege; but he does not appear to realize that privilege was a value built into the very structure of Graeco-Roman life. He assails the perversion of law, without for a moment considering whether the classical ideal of justice might not itself be imperfect. Yet in the very superficiality of his opinions lies their historical significance; it testifies in the clearest possible way to limitations in the ideology of Graeco-Roman secularism. These limitations are emphasized in what he has to say about the empire. He has no sense of the deeper perils confronting the Roman order, and he fails completely to appreciate the force of the indictment levelled by Christianity against it. For him, as for those to whom he owed his ideas, the greatness of Rome had been the result of a 'unique and almost incredible combination of *virtue* and *fortune*'. What threatened that great-

---

[1] Amm. xxx. 4. 8 foll.

ness was *vice* on the part of fortune's favourites, as a consequence of which her gifts were thrown away. Thus envisaged, the problem admitted of no solution other than that which had proved effective in the past. In an earlier crisis of her fate, the principate had arisen to save *Romanitas* and, by overcoming contemporary tendencies towards degeneracy, had offered the empire the promise of renewed life. The poets might hail this as the intervention of an earthly providence; but for Ammianus, as for Livy four centuries earlier, the *modus operandi* of that providence was evident: the remedy for the evils of government could be nothing but more government.

If it be just to assume that the limitations of the critic were those also of the statesman whose work he endorsed, this fact may help us to estimate the meaning of what we may describe as the experiment of Valentinian. Valentinian stands between two worlds, to neither of which he wholly belongs. In his repudiation of official paganism he identifies himself with the forces making for a new order. But, by his resolute independence of the Church and by his exclusive reliance upon the weapons of secularism, he reveals his fundamental dependence upon the old. In a very real and significant sense the last of all the Romans, Valentinian devoted himself to the maintenance of a system which had outlived the impulses to which it owed its being; and, as the last exponent of traditional methods, he elaborated the machinery of administration to a point where it began to stultify itself. By thus exhausting the resources of government, he made it apparent that, if *Romanitas* was to be saved, it must somehow manage to draw fresh vitality from an outside source. In so doing he paved the way for the revolutionary changes which were to mark the age of Theodosius.

IX

THEODOSIUS AND THE RELIGION OF STATE

THE programme of renovation, originally undertaken by Constantine, was consummated by Theodosius. With the hope of imparting fresh vitality to the Roman order, Constantine had invoked the aid of Christianity, thereby creating the issues of the fourth century. Theodosius resolved those issues but, in so doing, he shattered the foundations of *Romanitas* and crossed the divide which separates the ancient from the medieval world. These considerations lend a peculiar interest and significance to the Theodosian experiment, whether regarded as a last, desperate effort to save society, or as an attempt to promote, along lines hitherto unexplored, the project of a Christian commonwealth.

The accession of Theodosius was the result of a crisis which developed in the empire following the death of Valentinian. As senior Augustus in succession to his brother, Valens had initiated the dangerous policy by which the Goths were admitted as *foederati* within the frontier. For the disastrous issue of that policy, responsibility must be shared between him and his ministers.[1] The revolt of the Gothic refugees precipitated an emergency for which the united strength of the Romans was hardly adequate; but, in view of the danger of withdrawing his garrisons from Gaul, Gratian, the new colleague of Valens in the West, made but a feeble attempt to render assistance. For this reason, or because he sought the glory of a victory single-handed, Valens advanced alone to his defeat and death at the fatal battle of Adrianople, the Cannae of the lower empire (9 Aug. 378). As a consequence of this disaster, the East was for almost a year without a ruler, a helpless prey to the victorious barbarians who ranged the Balkan peninsula, carrying destruction to the very gates of Constantinople. Meanwhile the youthful Gratian, now senior in the college of emperors, wrestled in vain with problems of state, until he discovered a competent colleague in the person of Theodosius.

It was the mission of Theodosius to vindicate, for the last time, the integrity of the empire. This he effected by a judicious

---

[1] Amm. xxxi. 4. 9 and 10: Lupicinus . . . et Maximus . . . quorum insidiatrix aviditas materia malorum omnium fuit . . .

admixture of diplomacy and force. Menaced by successive waves of invasion from Lombards, Franks, and other barbarians, while still confronted with the problem of a hostile nation in arms within his boundaries, the first task of the emperor was to deal with the Goths. Upon these he was able to impose an uncertain peace through the cession of extensive areas for settlement, in return for the promise of military assistance. With the aid of his new allies he then succeeded in repulsing Lombards and Franks, while the Grothingi were subdued and settled as *coloni* in Roumania. At the same time his growing prestige enabled him to bring about a renewal of the Persian peace; and, with this achievement, the more pressing of his external difficulties were solved.

The problem of defence was complicated throughout by the necessity of supporting the administration of ineffective colleagues. In the year 383 Maximus, proclaimed Augustus by the legions in Britain, overran the territories of Gratian, who was murdered near Lugdunum by his own troops. To the claims of the usurper, *reparatio, restitutio, felicitas rei publicae*, which ominously recalled the *stasis* of earlier times, Theodosius replied by associating his son, Arcadius, in the purple. More than this he could not for the moment do and, for four years, Maximus boasted of a *concordia imperatorum* which did not exist. When, however, Maximus invaded the Po valley to dethrone Valentinian II, Theodosius overthrew the tyrant and reversed his acts, at the same time restoring the young prince to his throne at Milan (388). The subsequent murder of Valentinian and the assumption of the purple by Eugenius, as stool-pigeon for Arbogastes, his barbarian *magister militum*, necessitated a second expedition to Italy, in consequence of which a second son of Theodosius was invested with sovereignty in the West. To Arcadius and Honorius, as his heirs and successors, Theodosius was able to effect a peaceful transfer of the empire (395).

But if Theodosius thus succeeded in restoring the Roman order, he did so at the cost of regimentation on a scale unparalleled in its history. As a means of satisfying his military requirements, the emperor continued to legislate in the spirit of Valentinian and Valens, his measures becoming progressively harsher and more brutal with the increasing urgency of his need. By a decree of 379, operators of farms on which were discovered either persons of alien origin (*alienigenae*) or evaders of military service were threatened, no longer with fines or penal servitude, but with death by flames.[1] An enactment of 380 confirmed the provisions of earlier legislation and, as an incentive to the betrayal of deserters, promised liberty to slaves, to freemen immunity from taxation.[2] Successive edicts, promulgated in the decade following, repeated, at the same time as they refined upon, the measures already on the statute book.[3] Recruits, moreover, as they were drafted into the ranks, were branded like slaves or convicts, that none might escape. A law of 398 (Arcadius and Honorius) was to extend this practice to the *fabricenses* or imperial armourers' corps, members of which thenceforth bore on their arms the public mark, 'ad imitationem tironum . . . ut hoc modo saltem possint latitantes agnosci'.[4]

In the crisis which threatened *Romanitas*, money and services were hardly less essential than fighting power itself. Accordingly, hand in hand with the conscription of men went that of wealth and even, it might be said, of poverty. Thus, while the empire was scoured for recruits, these were nevertheless required to submit full information regarding their place of origin and social standing, that 'no one might evade the *curia*'; even the front line was no longer to serve as a refuge to the harassed taxpayer.[5] An earlier enactment had already recalled all *curiales* to their hereditary functions, whether they had succeeded in 'passing' into the ranks of the senate or those of the bureaucracy.[6] This order was to be reiterated on successive occasions during the following years.[7] In 383 the exemptions formerly accorded to Jewish rabbis were rescinded; and persons desiring to enter the Christian ministry were permitted to do so only if they found a substitute to take over their fiscal obligations.[8] Subsequent edicts cancelled the right of decurions to transfer their obligations to substitutes, and decreed that the ranks of army and civil service should be combed for fugitives.[9] By a law of 387, decurions found guilty of fraud in connexion with the assessment or collection of revenues were rendered liable to flogging at the hands, not merely of the praetorian prefect, but

---

[1] *Cod. Theod.* vii. 18. 2.   [2] vii. 18. 4.
[3] vii. 18. 5, 6, 7, 8, &c. (381–91).   [4] x. 22. 4.   [5] vii. 2. 1 (383).
[6] xii. 1. 82 (380): 'omnes ad curiam praecipimus revocari qui ad munera subeunda originalibus vinculis occupati officia conantur exhibere maiora, sive se splendidissimo senatui tradiderunt sive, per officia militantes, obsequia patriae denegarunt . . .'   [7] xii. 1. 93 (382), 94 (383), and 95 (383).
[8] xii. 1. 99 (383) and 104 (383).   [9] xii. 1. 111, 113, 114 (386).

of ordinary magistrates.[1] In 392 the public debtor was denied the rights of sanctuary, and clerics who sheltered him were threatened with trial in his stead.[2] In 395, heavy fines were instituted to check the concealing of delinquents 'under the shadow of the powerful'.[3] Such were the expedients to which Theodosius resorted in order to ensure the collection of revenue. Not satisfied, however, with preventing the landowner from escaping his obligations, the emperor made a vigorous effort to abolish tax-exemptions and to subject even the imperial domains to such obligations as fell upon the land.[4] Nevertheless, the pressure of unremitting warfare made it necessary to devise fresh forms of taxation, taxation so burdensome as to provoke a formidable rebellion at Antioch.[5] The demands of the fisc culminated, towards the end of the reign, in a fresh general survey of the empire, preparatory to a further morselization of provinces and to a consequent elaboration of the administrative hierarchies, military and civil.

It thus appears that, in accepting the purple, Theodosius accepted, along with the task of defending the frontiers, the whole apparatus of bureaucratic despotism as he had inherited it from his predecessors. At the same time he accepted the theory and practice of the sacred monarchy, the pretensions of which were, indeed, under this sovereign and his descendants, to attain their climacteric. Sanctity of the imperial person was implied in the constant use of titles such as *sacratissimus princeps, numen nostrum, nostra perennitas.* The dwelling of the emperor was the *sacrum palatium,* and even Rome, the nominal capital, became the *urbs sacratissima,* while state banquets were officially described as *divinae epulae,* 'feasts of the gods'.[6] Successive enactments restricted to a privileged few the right of 'touching the purple' and of 'adoring his serenity'.[7] As for the masses, to whom the imperial person was inaccessible, they had to be content with prostrating themselves before the 'sacred portraits'.

The legal consequences of this conception of sovereignty were hardly less significant than the moral. For, since the sanctity of the emperor involved that of his acts, imperial constitutions became *caelestia* or *divalia statuta,*[8] as emanating from 'the

---

[1] xii. 1. 117: 'plumbatarum ictibus'.   [2] ix. 45. 1.   [3] xii. 1. 146.
[4] xiii. 10. 8 (383).   [5] Cedrenus, *Hist.* 320 A–B (386).
[6] *Cod. Theod.* vi. 13. 1 (413).
[7] vi. 24. 3 (364); vi. 24. 4 (387): 'sacram purpuram adorare; contingere nostram purpuram'; vi. 23. 1 (415): 'in adoranda nostra serenitate'.   [8] i. 15. 11.

authority of the imperial oracle' and 'consecrated in his most
sacred name'. As such, they were received with solemn 'adoration' by local dignitaries to whom they were addressed. Law
observance was thus prescribed as a divine admonition,[1] ignorance or neglect of which was treated as sacrilege. For this
offence the penalty ranged from condemnation to the beasts or
burning alive to penal servitude in the mines or simple banish-
ment.[2] These sanctions applied to the most ordinary operations
of government, such, e.g., as the assessment:[3] 'If any one with
sacrilegious knife cuts down a vine, or in any way limits the
productivity of fruit-trees, with the object of cheating the
assessors and of cunningly devising false evidences of poverty,
upon detection, he shall be subject to capital punishment and
his property shall be confiscated to the fisc.' In this edict the
word 'sacrilegious' is no idle metaphor; it is a grim reminder of
the claim that to defraud the emperor was to defraud the earthly
vicegerent of God.

The sanctity of the sovereign being taken to imply that also
of his ministers, this fact served to place the whole administration above criticism. An edict of 385 forbade discussion regarding the merits of any one chosen by the emperor to serve him,
pronouncing it the equivalent of sacrilege to question the
imperial judgement.[4] Entrance to public office thus became a
kind of ordination; to leave it was to lay down a sacred trust.[5]
With the establishment of these principles the imperial service
assumed a veritably hieratical character.

The sanctions employed to protect the administration were
invoked also to maintain the existing structure of society and,
while ensuring to every one a status corresponding to his birth
and origin, to prevent irregular movements from one class to
another: 'Valentinian of blessed memory,' runs an edict of
Gratian, Valentinian II and Theodosius, 'the father of our
divinity, has laid down for each and every order and dignity a
certain deserved place. If any one, therefore, thrusts himself
into a position to which he is not entitled, let him not defend
himself by the plea of ignorance, but let him be tried for sacrilege, as one who has neglected the divine precepts of the

---

[1] xvi. 5. 7: 'divina monitio.'   [2] Dig. 48. 13. 7 and 11.
[3] Cod. Theod. xiii. 11. 1 (381).
[4] i. 6. 9: 'disputari de principali iudicio non oportet: sacrilegii enim instar est
dubitare an is dignus sit quem elegerit princeps. . . .'
[5] i. 29. 1: 'ordinati'; vi. 13. 1: 'depositum sacramentum.'

emperor.'[1] Thus, with the final obliteration of republican distinctions, *ambitus*, formerly a crime or misdemeanour, came to
be regarded as a sin. At the same time, the apotheosis of the
state was revealed as the apotheosis of immobility itself.

The principles thus enunciated led to the most extravagant
consequences, the full extent of which was to be revealed only
under the sons of Theodosius. On the one hand, malfeasance
on the part of civil servants was defined as sacrilege, to be
visited with appropriate penalties.[2] On the other hand, conspiracy with soldiers, civilians, or barbarians to compass the
death of prefects, generals, senators, or higher officials was
declared tantamount to actual murder and, as a further deterrent to subversive activity, the law struck savagely at the dependants and friends of any one found guilty of this offence. Thus,
while allowed their bare lives as of grace, the sons of a convicted conspirator were denied the right of inheritance and
branded for ever with the odium of their fathers' crime ('ut
infamia eos paterna semper comitetur, ad nullos unquam
honores, nulla prorsus sacramenta perveniant . . . perpetuo
egentes et pauperes'). Equally severe penalties were laid down
for his wife, daughters, and associates, who were presumed, in the
absence of evidence to the contrary, to have a guilty knowledge
of his intention.[3] This legislation, which has been stigmatized
'as violating every principle of humanity and justice',[4] is
ascribed to the sinister influence of the eunuch Eutropius and,
it should be added, was reversed two years later upon the fall
of the minister.[5] Short-lived though it was, it serves none the
less to throw a vivid light upon tendencies inherent in the sacred
state.

The novelty of Theodosianism, however, lies not so much in
the attribution of sanctity to the state as in the methods whereby
it sought to merit sanctification. In this respect the policy of
the emperor was, no doubt, governed to some extent by recent
historical experience. We have seen how, by a natural revulsion from Constantinianism, Valentinian had emphatically

---

[1] vi. 5. 2 (384).
[2] vi. 29. 9 (412): 'haud dubie sacrilegii crimine obligantur.'
[3] ix. 14. 3 (397).   [4] Gibbon, op. cit., ch. xxxii, p. 365.
[5] *Cod. Theod.* ix. 40. 18 (399): 'sancimus ibi esse poenam ubi et noxa est. pro-
pinquos notos familiares procul a calumnia submovemus, quos reos sceleris
societas non facit. . . . peccata igitur suos teneant auctores nec ulterius progrediatur
metus quam repperitur delictum.'

reasserted the dualism of powers and functions which the second Flavians had sedulously endeavoured to conceal. But the state, which was thus declared independent of the Church, found itself in a peculiarly difficult position; for, while rejecting the support of organized Christianity, it could not claim the sanction of a frankly pagan system such as that proposed by the Apostate. Accordingly, its existence depended wholly upon its own limited store of vital energy; and, since this was consumed by the very effort of self-preservation, the 'statism' of Valentinian hardly survived the life of its author. The increasing moral and physical debility of the system was apparent, even before the battle of Adrianople, in the tentative advances of Valens and Gratian, the one towards Arianism, the other towards orthodoxy. The shock of that catastrophe sealed its doom. But, while political conditions were now desperate, even by comparison with those of seventy-five years before, the Church, despite her internal dissensions, despite also her immersion in the muddy waters of secularism, had steadily grown in strength and cohesion of purpose since the beginning of the century; so that the attitude of patronage, which had been adopted by Constantine towards the new religion, was no longer even thinkable. Important as were these considerations, they would not, however, be sufficient to account for the position assumed by Theodosius, apart from his own personal inclinations. The immediate predecessors of the emperor had been Catholic by environment, upbringing, and perhaps by policy. Theodosius, on the other hand, was a Catholic by conviction, baptized as such in 380, the third year of his reign, and his behaviour throughout indicates the sincerity of his profession. As the real prototype in history of 'the Christian Prince',[1] he was profoundly concerned to work out the logic of his position; and it is this fact, more than anything else, which determined the scope and character of his effort to bring about a radical readjustment of existing relationships between the temporal and the spiritual powers.

Indications of such a readjustment were, indeed, already apparent in the abandonment by Gratian of the title *pontifex maximus*, which had been borne by pagan and Christian emperors alike since the days of Augustus Caesar. They were evident, also, in the resumption by him of 'godly and righteous legisla-

---

[1] Aug. *De Civ. Dei*, v. 26: 'de fide ac pietate Theodosii Augusti.'

tion' such as that with which the world had become familiar in Constantinian times. This legislation was to continue in ever-increasing volume throughout the Theodosian age and it took the form, either of conceding special privileges to the Church or of revising the law in the light of presumably Christian principles.

With respect to ecclesiastical privilege, two characteristic developments of the period may be noted. The first was the application of fresh and more rigorous sanctions to protect the position of the clergy. Thus, while confirming their fiscal immunities, the law now threatened with the penalty of sacrilege any one who sought to impose upon them obligations from which they were legally exempt.[1] The same sanction was likewise invoked against those who ventured to break into Catholic churches, to assault Catholic priests, or otherwise to disturb the cult.[2] The second development was no less significant. By a law of 412, ministers of the Catholic religion, from bishops to subdeacons, were accorded immunity from trial except in ecclesiastical courts, while, at the same time, the accuser was declared liable to the loss of his rank and status, unless he proved his charge.[3] The concession of such a privilege appears to have excited an outburst of anti-clericalism, a novel phenomenon, destined to culminate in the usurpation of Johannes at Ravenna. It was nevertheless reiterated, in still more emphatic terms when, after the fall of the tyrant, his acts were reversed.[4]

The attempt to read Christian principles into the law found expression in a series of measures demonstrating the respect of the government for the new religion of state. Thus, there were to be no criminal trials during Lent.[5] On the other hand, following a precedent set by Constantine, all convicts, except those guilty of treason, murder, rape, incest, poisoning, and certain forms of sacrilege, were to be released from prison on the occasion of the Easter festival.[6] Moreover, death sentences imposed by imperial authority were not to be executed until after the lapse of thirty days.[7] This measure, designed to prevent hasty and ill-considered action on the part of the administration, has been attributed to the influence of Ambrose over Theodosius,

---

[1] *Cod. Theod.* xvi. 2. 26 (381) and 40 (412).   [2] xvi. 2. 31 (398).
[3] xvi. 2. 41: 'clericos non nisi aput episcopos accusari convenit.'
[4] xvi. 2. 47 (425): 'fas enim non est ut divini muneris ministri temporalium potestatum subdantur arbitrio.'   [5] ix. 35. 4 (380).
[6] ix. 38. 6 (381); 8 (385): 'Paschalis laetitiae dies.'   [7] ix. 40. 13 (382).

and connected with the massacre of Thessalonica. In an effort to prevent the exploitation of religious sentiment for commercial purposes, retail trade in the bones and relics of martyrs was forbidden.[1] Sunday-observance laws dating from the time of Constantine were revived and amplified; on the Lord's day there were to be no theatres, horse-races, or amusements unless it marked the occasion of an imperial birthday or anniversary, an exception presently to be removed.[2] At the same time, measures were taken to prevent desecration of the day by the pursuit of ordinary secular activities, public or private.[3]

In this connexion, unquestionably the most significant development was the disintegration, under Christian influence, of classical conceptions of the family and of family right. Evidence of this may be found in legislation protecting the succession of children even to mothers dying intestate against claims by male relatives.[4] It may be seen also in the final disappearance of the *ius liberorum* which, after 410, could no longer be invoked as a means of settling disputed claims to inheritance.[5] The ancient *patria* or *dominica potestas* was, at the same time, further impaired by an enactment that individuals convicted of prostituting their daughters or female slaves should forfeit their legal rights over them.[6] Contemporary developments of the criminal law pointed in the same direction. In 388 the ancient practice of maintaining private prisons was finally suppressed as treasonable.[7] In 420 an emendation to the law of rape assimilated it to an ordinary public crime in case nuns were the victims, all persons being authorized to prosecute.[8] Christian influence showed itself also in the revision of existing legislation relating to marriage. Constantius had branded as incestuous the union of a man with his niece, threatening the guilty party with burning alive and confiscation of goods.[9] In 396 these savage penalties were revoked, but such unions were declared illegitimate, the offspring being totally excluded from the right of in-

[1] ix. 17. 6 (381) and 7 (386): 'nemo martyrem distrahat, nemo mercetur.'
[2] ii. 8. 20 (392), 23 (399), 25 (409); xv. 5. 2 (386).
[3] xi. 7. 13 (386): 'solis die, quem dominicum rite dixere maiores, omnium litium et negotiorum quiescat intentio; debitum publicum privatumque nullus efflagitet; ne aput ipsos quidem arbitros vel e iudiciis flagitatos vel sponte delectos ulla sit agnitio iurgiorum. et non modo notabilis, verum etiam sacrilegus iudicetur, qui a sanctae religionis instinctu rituve deflexerit.'
[4] v. 1. 3 (383); cf. viii. 17. 2 (410).
[5] viii. 17. 3.   [6] xv. 8. 2 (428).
[7] ix. 11. 1.   [8] ix. 25. 3.   [9] iii. 12. 1 (342).

heritance.[1] In 415 unions between a man and his deceased wife's sister, or between a woman and her deceased husband's brother, were placed in the same category.[2] In these enactments it is noteworthy that the provisions of the law applied to men and women alike. We have elsewhere referred to Constantine's divorce law, with its double standard of morality for the sexes. In 421 this law was subjected to various amendments which, among other provisions, compelled a man who had repudiated his wife merely on grounds of incompatibility (*dissensio animorum*) to surrender to her his own marriage gifts as well as her dower, at the same time forbidding him ever to remarry, while the woman in question was permitted to take another husband after the lapse of a year.[3]

Such developments have, no doubt, a certain interest, as indicating the trend of social and economic change, stimulated by Christian and humanitarian influence, during the Theodosian period. But, for the student of fourth-century history, they contain little that is either novel or surprising. That which gives to Theodosianism its distinctive character, making it, indeed, a significant point of departure in world history, was the new religious policy initiated by the emperor himself in an edict promulgated from Thessalonica, 27 February 380:

'We desire that all peoples who fall beneath the sway of our imperial clemency should profess the faith which we believe to have been communicated by the Apostle Peter to the Romans and maintained in its traditional form to the present day, the faith which is observed likewise by the pontiff Damasus and by Peter of Alexandria, a man of apostolic sanctity; to wit, that, according to apostolic discipline and evangelical teaching, we should believe in one deity, the sacred Trinity of Father, Son and Holy Spirit, to be worshipped in equal majesty. And we require that those who follow this rule of faith should embrace the name of Catholic Christians, adjudging all others madmen and ordering them to be designated as heretics ... condemned as such, in the first instance, to suffer divine punishment, and, therewith, the vengeance of that power which we, by celestial authority, have assumed.'[4]

[1] iii. 12. 3.   [2] iii. 12. 4.   [3] iii. 16. 2 (421).

[4] *Cod. Theod.* xvi. 1. 2: 'cunctos populos quos clementiae nostrae regit temperamentum in tali volumus religione versari quam divinum Petrum apostolum tradidisse Romanis religio usque ad nunc ab ipso insinuata declarat quamque pontificem Damasum sequi claret et Petrum Alexandriae episcopum, virum apostolicae sanctitatis, hoc est, ut secundum apostolicam disciplinam evangelicamque doctrinam patris et filii et spiritus sancti unam deitatem sub parili maiestate et sub

This pronouncement marks the net result of fourth-century efforts to discover a fresh basis for the Roman order. By the manifesto of Constantine and Licinius there had been substituted for the classical idea of the commonwealth the notion of two more or less distinct orders, the one political, the other ecclesiastical. With that of Theodosius, the relationship between these orders was finally determined by the complete subordination of the temporal to the spiritual power. Thus, in the transition from Graeco-Roman antiquity, the Edict of Thessalonica marks a stage not less significant than that recorded by the Edict of Milan; for, if the one served to inaugurate the New Republic, the other heralded the process by which the New Republic was to be transformed into the Orthodox Empire.

By contrast with earlier forms of polity, the Orthodox Empire was characterized by two developments of fundamental importance. The first was the explicit acceptance of Nicene Christianity as embodying the substance of the Catholic faith; the second, the deliberate adoption of that faith as a principle of social integration. In accepting Catholicism, the state finally abandoned pretensions which, originally put forward by pagan authorities on behalf of the Augustan empire, had nevertheless been maintained in an ambiguous sense by Christian sovereigns from Constantine to Valentinian. In this connexion it is no mere coincidence that the doctrinal formulations, first made by the Council of Nicaea, should have been reaffirmed, almost contemporaneously, at the Council of Constantinople, the Church thus vindicating to itself prerogatives which, since the time of Vergil, had been claimed by the Eternal City. But, while primacy thus passed from the secular to the spiritual power, at the same time the recognition in Catholicism of a principle of universal validity and application suggested the possibility of its adoption as the basis for a new social order, in which the state should find justification for its existence in 'defending the peace of the Church'. In this idea may be seen the spirit and purpose of Theodosianism, and it found expression in a thoroughgoing effort to realize, within the framework of the Roman system, the forms of a Catholic state. With this con-

pia trinitate credamus. hanc legem sequentes Christianorum Catholicorum nomen iubemus amplecti, reliquos vero dementes vesanosque iudicantes haeretici dogmatis infamiam sustinere . . . divina primum vindicta, post etiam motus nostri, quem ex caelesti arbitrio sumpserimus, ultione plectendos.'

summation, the ambiguities, which had characterized the inter-val from Constantine to Theodosius and which were perhaps inevitable in an age of transition, finally disappeared; and there ensued a period of energetic imperial house-cleaning, in which the last energies of government were invoked to enforce the theory and practice of orthodoxy.

The formal liquidation of paganism under Theodosius and his successors has been characterized as 'perhaps the only example of the total extirpation of any ancient and popular superstition' and thus deserving of consideration as 'a singular event in the history of the human mind'.[1] For this the ground had been prepared by earlier emperors, especially Constantius II, to whose efforts in this direction we have elsewhere referred.[2] Nor had the pretended religious neutrality of Valentinian I prevented him from once more claiming for the fisc vast sums which, in the reaction under Julian, had been diverted to the re-endowment of pagan shrines.[3] But, with Theodosius, the administration embarked upon a systematic effort to abolish the various surviving forms of paganism through the disestab-lishment, disendowment, and proscription of surviving cults. This intention was implemented in a series of revolutionary measures, by virtue of which the accumulated debris of cen-turies was contemptuously swept away.

Legislative activity against paganism began with the edict of 381, branding it as sacrilegious to participate in forbidden rites either by day or night with the object of divination, or to use for such purpose any existing shrine or altar.[4] The year follow-ing witnessed the nationalization of the temples and of their treasures (including the statues of the gods) which were thrown open to the public as monuments of art, access to the altars alone being prohibited.[5] In 385 the campaign against divina-tion was extended to include the prohibition of *auspicia* even by native rites.[6] These and similar measures were followed in 392 by what has been called a final and comprehensive enactment against paganism:[7]

'No one of whatever rank, position or dignity, high or low, rich or poor, in any place whatsoever in any city, shall sacrifice an innocent victim to senseless images; nor, in the more intimate efforts of pro-

[1] Gibbon, op. cit., ch. xxviii, p. 188.
[2] Ch. VI above, p. 254. [3] *Cod. Theod.* x. 1. 8 (364).
[4] xvi. 10. 7. [5] xvi. 10. 8. [6] xvi. 10. 9. [7] xvi. 10. 12.

pitiation, shall he worship the *lar* with fire, the *genius* with wine, the *penates* with savour, by lighting flames, laying on incense or suspending garlands. . . .

'Individuals presuming to sacrifice victims or to consult their entrails shall be assimilated to the position of those charged with treason, all persons being authorized to lay an accusation against them and, upon conviction, they shall suffer the penalties provided by law, even though they have made no inquiries contrary or relative to the safety of the prince. It is enough to convict them that they should have desired to break the laws of nature itself, by prying into and unfolding forbidden mysteries. . . .

'Any one who worships an image constructed by human hands and thus foolishly reveals his fears of that which he has himself made, who decorates trees with fillets or erects altars of cut turf, shall be punished by the confiscation of the property upon which he is shown to have indulged in such superstition.

'Any one who attempts, either in public temples or shrines or on private properties other than his own, to perform any act of pagan sacrifice . . . shall be liable to a fine of twenty pounds, gold.'

The prohibition of pagan worship was followed, in 396, by a final cancellation of privileges and immunities accorded by ancient law to the priests and ministers of pagan cults, whose profession was now officially outlawed.[1]

Along with the abolition of pagan cults went the abolition of the pagan calendar. By Theodosian times this calendar had come to be a veritable hotch-potch embodying layer upon layer of religious sentiment and recording the moral and spiritual developments realized during a millennium of history during which the gods had been conceived as active forces guiding and civilizing the world. It thus included a vast number of festivals ranging all the way from those of the primitive domestic and agricultural religion to those of the latest cults authorized by the state; and it was punctuated at intervals by days, lucky or unlucky, marking the anniversary of historic victories or defeats. Furthermore, many *civitates* both of Italy and the provinces still possessed local *fasti*, which enshrined the record of their own political and social life. To Theodosius the European world owes the existence of a uniform calendar corresponding to the needs of a universal society and based upon the Christian year. The legislation instituting such a calendar is to be found in book ii of the Code.[2] It will be remembered that Constantine

[1] xvi. 10. 14.   [2] *De Feriis.*

had declared Sunday to be a legal holiday, except for emancipations and manumissions.[1] In 386 Theodosius reaffirmed this measure with the significant addition: 'et non modo notabilis, verum etiam sacrilegus iudicetur, qui a sanctae religionis instinctu rituque deflexerit.'[2] In this characteristic addendum he invoked the strongest possible sanctions against those who desecrated the Lord's day. In 389 Valentinian II, Theodosius, and Arcadius, in an edict addressed to the prefect of the city, pronounced all days to be juridical, with the following exceptions:[3]

(a) the long vacation (24 June to 15 October) on account of the summer heat and the necessities of the autumn harvest;

(b) 1 January (concluding the customary holiday week);

(c) the anniversaries of Rome and Constantinople;

(d) the Easter holiday of two weeks, including seven days preceding and seven days following Easter Sunday;

(e) Sundays (dominici dies);

(f) anniversaries of the birth and accession of reigning emperors.

In the year 400 Christmas Day and the Epiphany were also consecrated, thus completing the 'Christian Year'.[4] In 412, by an interesting and significant concession to the Jews, it was provided that the courts should not sit on Saturdays (the Sabbath).[5] The enforcement of the new calendar was ensured by the suppression of the old.[6] By expunging pagan festivals from the list of public holidays, the empire cut one of the most familiar links binding her to her historic past.

These measures will serve to illustrate the methods employed by Theodosius in stamping out the vestiges of paganism. They reveal the official Graeco-Roman religion as a victim of weapons which it had itself invoked against Christianity in the days of its ascendancy. In legislating the gods out of existence, the role of the state was purely formal and, formally, the victory appears to have been pathetically easy and swift. Opposition developed chiefly among the nobility of the ancient capital; where the successive removals and reinstatements of the famous statue of Victory in the Senate House may be taken to illustrate fluctuations in the strife between the conservative aristocracy on the

[1] Cod. Theod. ii. 8. 1 (321).   [2] ii. 8. 18.   [3] ii. 8. 19.
[4] ii. 8. 24.   [5] ii. 8. 26.   [6] ii. 8. 22 (395).

one hand and, on the other, the government supported and encouraged by the insistence of Ambrose of Milan.[1] This opposition was marked by a last resurgence of traditional *religio*, which vented itself in premonitions of imminent disaster, if Rome thus abandoned the symbol and embodiment of her historic mission. And, by a curious coincidence, these premonitions were soon to be fulfilled when, for the first time since the raid of Brennus exactly eight hundred years before, Alaric and his Gothic host marched triumphant through the streets of the sacred capital. Otherwise the administration encountered serious resistance only among the volatile masses of great Eastern cities such as Alexandria, where the conflict between pagan and Christian was bitter and prolonged. The issue, however, was never really doubtful since the failure of Julian to rehabilitate the Olympians; and, on the whole, it may be said that the gods of Classicism were deservedly buried amid the ruins of the civilization they had failed to save.

The suppression of official paganism was but one aspect of a sweeping programme, the object of which was to establish a more or less exact coincidence between Catholicism and citizenship; and, for the realization of this programme, it was necessary to destroy the various forms of heresy current within the empire. From this point of view, the attitude of the government was already indicated in the edict of 379, which decreed the permanent extinction of all heresies forbidden 'by divine and imperial law'.[2] Two years later the Photinian, Arian, and Eunomian heresies were proscribed by name; and, in order that 'the name of the one supreme God should everywhere be celebrated', and that 'there should be afforded no opportunity for the recusant to indulge his madness', it was provided that all church-buildings should forthwith be surrendered to bishops who professed the Catholic faith.[3] These measures were supplemented by others which laid the adherents of different heresies under disabilities varying with the presumed degree of their 'guilt' in deviating from the norm provided by the Nicene Creed. Thus, for example, with respect to the Manicheans, the government claimed the right to treat them as guilty of sacrilege (*veluti sacrilegii reos tenemus*); but, as its object was remedial

---

[1] Boissier, *La Fin du Paganisme*, ii. vi, ch. 1.
[2] *Cod. Theod.* xvi. 5. 5: 'omnes vetitae legibus et divinis et imperialibus haereses perpetuo conquiescant.'   [3] xvi. 5. 6.

rather than punitive, it was satisfied to impose upon them a kind of civil excommunication, by virtue of which they were denied 'all right of making wills and living according to Roman law' ('testandi ac vivendi iure Romano omnem protinus eripimus facultatem'). To prevent evasion of this penalty, it was enacted that properties conveyed by Manicheans even to their natural heirs should be liable to confiscation and, as a further precaution, the law was made retroactive, exemption being extended only 'to those of their children who, though brought up as Manicheans, have had the good sense and respect for their own interest to dissociate themselves from that "confession" '.[1] By another edict of the same year, Eunomians, Arians, and Aetians were forbidden to erect churches either in town or country, under penalty of confiscation.[2] In 382 the intestability of Manicheans was confirmed while, at the same time, certain other types of heretic were declared liable to the death penalty.[3] By two edicts of 383, Eunomians, Arians, Macedonians, Pneumatomachi, Manicheans, and others were denied the right of assembly, and forbidden to hold ordinations; while their properties were confiscated, their priests and ministers relegated to their place of origin, magistrates being subject to a fine in the event of failure to enforce this rule.[4] Five years later these orders were repeated and applied as well to the Apollinarists, who appear to have been consigned to a kind of ghetto and refused all rights of access and petition to the imperial courts.[5] The moral and perhaps physical isolation of those deemed guilty of infectious heresy is implied also in legislation of 389 relative to the *Eunomiani spadones*, whose name suggests the opprobrious character of their cult; but it was applied also to Manicheans in the same year.[6]

The heresy-hunt thus initiated by Theodosius was, like other aspects of his policy, pursued with exaggerated zeal under his sons. In this connexion may be noted certain statements of principle, contained in legislation of the year 407. By this legislation, which finds its counterpart in the code of Justinian,[7] it is laid down that heresy is a public crime, 'because any offence which is committed against divine religion involves an injury

[1] xvi. 5. 7 (381).　　[2] xvi. 5. 8.　　[3] xvi. 5. 9.　　[4] xvi. 5. 11 and 12.
[5] xvi. 5. 14: 'adeant loca, quae eos potissimum quasi vallo quodam ab humana communione secludant.'
[6] xvi. 5. 17: 'nihil ad summum habeant commune cum reliquis'; and 18: 'nihil ad summum his sit commune cum mundo.'　　[7] *C.J.* i. 5. 4.

to all'.[1] In justifying the confiscation of properties belonging to convicted heretics, the same edict assimilated their offence to that of *maiestas* and declared their testaments null and void. It also accorded legal protection to slaves of heretics who deserted their masters and submitted themselves to the service of the Catholic Church. Another edict, promulgated after the fall of Stilicho, whose Arianism had rendered him suspect, provided that no enemy of the Catholic faith should hold office in the imperial service, ('ut nullus nobis sit aliqua ratione coniunctus, qui a nobis fide et religione discordat').[2] This principle was reasserted in the year 410.[3]

The measures thus taken to enforce uniformity of belief could hardly in the nature of things be applied to Jews, whose religion was regarded as in some sense a reflection of national and racial peculiarities which rendered them permanently incapable of assimilation within the Orthodox Empire. While, therefore, the measures against heretics were, as has been said, remedial, varying with the supposed perniciousness of their offence and with the moral or social dangers to be apprehended therefrom, the Jewish question was felt to require somewhat different treatment. As a consequence Jews were assigned a unique status in the Theodosian system. Thus, by an edict of 393, their religion was recognized as legal.[4] This meant that they were guaranteed the right of assembly and protected in person and property from molestation at the hands of Christian mobs. This principle was reaffirmed in 412.[5] On the other hand, steps were taken to ensure, so far as possible, the social isolation of an element tainted with *nefanda superstitio*. To this end it was laid down that no Jew should presume to purchase a Christian slave or, having done so, to proselytize him, under penalty of forfeiting all his slaves.[6] The harshness of this law was subsequently mitigated by the provision that, while allowed to possess Christian slaves, Jewish owners should grant them complete freedom to observe the requirements of their own religion.[7] But, in order that the practice might so far as possible be curtailed, they were forbidden to purchase Christians or to accept them as gifts; and those found guilty of any attempt to proselytize them were

[1] xvi. 5. 40: 'ac primum quidem volumus esse publicum crimen, quia quod in religionem divinam committitur, in omnium fertur iniuriam.'
[2] xvi. 5. 42 (408).   [3] xvi. 5. 48.
[4] xvi. 8. 9: 'Iudaeorum sectam nulla lege prohibitam satis constat.'
[5] xvi. 8. 20.   [6] iii. 1. 5 (384).   [7] xvi. 9. 3 (415).

declared liable to capital punishment.[1] Furthermore, the inter-marriage of Jews and Christians was classified as adultery, thus falling under the savage penalties imposed by Constantine for this offence, with the added provision that, in the event of such a marriage, any person was competent to lay the charge.[2] Finally, that the expansion of Judaism might be checked, Jews were denied the right of building new synagogues;[3] and their social inferiority was emphasized by the fact that they were not allowed to aspire to the imperial service.[4] As might be antici-pated, these last measures are to be associated with the reign, not of Theodosius, but of his sons.

The steps thus taken against pagans, heretics, and Jews served to implement, in the fullest possible manner, what may be regarded as the underlying principle of the Theodosian order. This principle, as laid down in an edict of 380, was that 'any one is guilty of sacrilege who either confounds the sanctity of the divine law by ignorance or violates it by negligence'.[5] Application of this principle depended to some extent upon political considerations. It has, for example, been suggested that, in 386, the empress Justina intervened from Milan to procure for those who had supported the Arianism of Con-stantius a limited right of assembly. This concession was, how-ever, subject to the qualification that, if they employed it in order to create any agitation against the official ecclesiastical policy, they should be liable to the death penalty as 'authors of sedition and disturbers of the peace of the Church'.[6] A sub-sequent edict, forbidding the public discussion of religious issues, may be taken as indicating the government's fixed determina-tion to prevent any criticism or question of its settled policy.[7] This determination is further emphasized by its attitude towards apostasy, which it regarded as a lapse towards moral and spiritual particularism. Reversion to paganism was penalized by intestability, the sons and brothers german of the guilty party (if Catholic) being allowed to inherit.[8] These disabilities were likewise imposed upon renegades to Judaism or Mani-cheism.[9] In 391, apostates of whatever rank were shorn of their

---

[1] xvi. 9. 4 (417). [2] iii. 7. 2; ix. 7. 5 (388). [3] xvi. 8. 25 (423).
[4] xvi. 8. 16 (404) and 24 (418).
[5] xvi. 2. 25: 'qui divinae legis sanctitatem aut nesciendo confundunt aut negli-gendo violant et offendunt, sacrilegium committunt.'
[6] xvi. 4. 1 (386). [7] xvi. 4. 2 (388).
[8] xvi. 7. 1 (381) and 2 (383). [9] xvi. 7. 3 (383).

privileges and immunities, branded with perpetual infamy, and classified with the humblest members of the populace.[1]

The new religious policy was, no doubt, inspired by a deepening conviction that the state, deprived by the action of Constantine of its traditional sanctions, could hope to survive only if it established itself firmly upon new ones. But, in the effort to create such sanctions, Theodosius went beyond anything contemplated by his predecessor. As has already been suggested, Constantine had thought of Christianity as a tonic, to be administered in carefully regulated doses to the debilitated body-politic. What Theodosius proposed was not so much a tonic as a blood-transfusion, as the only possible means of restoring to the *polis* something of the vitality which, in the interval since Constantine, had passed from it to the *ecclesia*. And therein he was sustained by a firm belief that in Orthodox or Trinitarian Christianity was to be found a principle of political cohesion, acceptance of which would ensure to the empire a finality in keeping with her secular claims. From this point of view, the Theodosian order, closed though it was to pagans, heretics, and Jews, was nevertheless 'open' to all those who were prepared to recognize their birthright as sons of the Church.

Thus apprehended, however, Theodosianism betrays a fatal confusion of ideas. For to envisage the faith as a political principle was not so much to christianize civilization as to 'civilize' Christianity; it was not to consecrate human institutions to the service of God but rather to identify God with the maintenance of human institutions, i.e. with that of the *pax terrena*. And, in this case, the *pax terrena* was represented by the tawdry and meretricious empire, a system which, originating in the pursuit of human and terrestrial aims, had so far degenerated as to deny to men the very values which had given it birth; and was now held together only by sheer and unmitigated force. By so doing, it rendered the principle purely formal while, at the same time, it suggested the application of conventional 'political' methods for its realization. While, therefore, under governmental pressure, the empire rapidly shed the trappings of secularism to assume those of Christianity, it remained at

---

[1] xvi. 7. 5 (391): 'de loco suo statuque deiecti perpetua urantur infamia ac ne in extrema quidem vulgi ignobilis parte numerentur . . . quid enim his cum hominibus potest esse commune, qui infandis et feralibus mentibus gratiam communionis exosi ab hominibus recesserunt?'

heart profoundly pagan and was, to that extent, transformed merely into a whited sepulchre. The net result of the Theodosian revolution was thus not to herald the passing of politics in the ancient sense, but simply to change the issues for which the state contended. That is to say, it transformed the clash between civilization and barbarism into a conflict of religions, in which recusants of every description discovered a programme for common action in opposing the pretensions of the imperial power, finding therein also grounds for affiliation with the hereditary enemies of the empire, notably the Goths who had been evangelized by the Arian bishop Ulfilas. Theodosianism thus points in two directions. In one sense, it was destined to survive in Byzantium where, in the name of orthodoxy, a close alliance of religious politics and political religion was to conserve for another millennium all that was left of the classical heritage. Otherwise, so far from rejuvenating *Romanitas*, the attempted substitution of religion for culture as a principle of cohesion served merely to add a final and decisive element to the forces making for the dissolution of the Roman order.

From this point of view, it becomes possible to estimate the true significance of the role played by Theodosius in imperial history. Gibbon has declared that the genius of Rome expired with Theodosius. And we may agree that, in the face of overwhelming difficulties, he overcame the crisis provoked by the defeat of Valens and for the last time 'restored the empire'. It is equally evident that, in his effort to do so, he drained it of the last reserves of moral and physical energy which it possessed. Thus, with him, the 'tragedy of bureaucratic despotism' became fully apparent, a tragedy

'in which, by an inexorable fate, the claims of fancied omnipotence ended in a humiliating paralysis of administration; in which determined efforts to remedy social evils only aggravated them until they became unendurable; in which the best intentions of the central power . . . were mocked and defeated alike by the irresistible laws of human nature and by hopeless perfidy and corruption in the servants of government'.[1]

To expect of any ruler, however wise and just, a cure or even a substantial mitigation of such evils would perhaps, in the circumstances, be unreasonable. But the man who, seeing them, imagined that a remedy was to be found in the introduction of

[1] Dill, *Roman Society in the Last Century of the Western Empire*, p. 234.

a new and highly controversial issue can hardly be acquitted of
egregious error. Such a man was Theodosius, whose effort to
consecrate the decaying empire by forcing it into a mould of
politicized Catholicism thus ranks as the final and most desperate attempt of the century to achieve a new world without
sacrificing any essential element of the old. It is not surprising,
therefore, that, regarded as a measure of consolidation, the new
religious policy was condemned to irretrievable disaster. But,
although from this standpoint barren, it was none the less profoundly significant by reason of its indirect and incidental consequences. To assert this may be to detract from the intrinsic
greatness of Theodosius, but it serves to emphasize his historical
importance. Seeking, like Julius Caesar in his day, to ride
the whirlwind, like Julius he failed to achieve anything beyond
a merely negative result. His true distinction is thus not as a
conservator but as a destroyer. Yet, with both Caesar and Theodosius, the work of destruction was a necessary prelude to the
work of reconstruction which was to follow. And as, in the first
case, out of the ruins of the republic had arisen the Augustan
and Antonine empire, so, in the second, that empire was finally
dismantled in order to make way for the nation-states of
modern Europe.

This consummation was, however, reserved for a time when
Theodosianism should have done its work; and our concern is
not so much with that as with the immediate consequences of
Theodosian policy. Needless to say, the effect of that policy was
simply to enforce a formal and external conformity upon the
empire. Yet the mere profession of a nominal Catholicism imposed upon the government a distinctly novel attitude towards
the faith, with the result that it was no longer in a position to
oppose or even to restrict religious developments of the utmost
consequence.

Of such developments, not the least significant was that of
monasticism. We have already alluded to this movement which,
in the course of the century, had assumed menacing proportions
as, in their anxiety to embrace the 'Christian law', thousands
upon thousands of citizens repudiated the claims of family and
of state to betake themselves either to the desert or to the open
road. From this standpoint, it becomes possible to understand
the attitude of Julian, who, in fulminating against the monks,
reflected the animus of organized society against those who

refused to share its burdens. It will also be recalled that, Catholic though he was, Valentinian resisted to the utmost the efforts of monks to escape conscription. Not unnaturally, the attitude of Julian and of Valentinian finds an echo in modern times. Thus the monks have been stigmatized as individuals who, 'inspired by a savage enthusiasm which represents man as a criminal and God as a tyrant . . . embraced a life of misery as the price of eternal happiness'.[1] The 'epidemic' of monasticism has otherwise been described as follows:

'There is, perhaps, no phase in the moral history of mankind of a deeper or more painful interest than this ascetic movement . . . A hideous, sordid and emaciated maniac, without knowledge, without patriotism, without natural affection, passing his life in a long routine of useless and atrocious self-torture, and quailing before the ghastly phantoms of his delirious brain, had become the ideal of the nations which had known the writings of Plato and Cicero and the lives of Socrates and Cato.'[2]

Such observations may serve to characterize the excesses of a movement to which, none the less, saints and geniuses as well as rogues and madmen were irresistibly attracted; and this could hardly have been so had it not contained at least some elements of genuine spiritual value. What those elements were may, perhaps, be inferred from the *Life of St. Anthony*, a work which, attributed to Athanasius,[3] reveals not merely a profound sympathy for monasticism but also a vivid appreciation of its significance. As such, it exercised no little influence in shaping monastic ideals and recommending them to the contemporary mind.[4]

With respect to those ideals it may be observed, to begin with, that their 'political' value was precisely nothing. Accordingly, monasticism contained no message for the man who, while impressed by the salutary character of Christian teaching, sought in any way to reconcile it with the battered ideals of Classicism. On the contrary, what it proposed was an utter and final renunciation of the world, as the necessary presupposition of a life consecrated to strictly individual salvation. In so doing, it pointed to a literal acceptance of evangelical precepts, such as

---

[1] Gibbon, op. cit., ch. xxxvii, p. 57.
[2] Lecky, *History of European Morals* (ed. 7), ii. 107.
[3] It is accepted as authentic by Duchesne, ii⁴, p. 488, n. 3.
[4] Augustine, *Conf.* VIII. vi. 15.

that which had so excited the ire of the emperor Julian: *sell all
thou hast . . .*[1] And, while in its initial impulse wholly voluntary
and spontaneous, it pointed also to deference towards ecclesiastical authority, as a manifestation of humility, the supreme
Christian virtue.[2] Such were the foundations of a life characterized by self-discipline, the rigour of which was determined
by the paramount necessity of subjugating the flesh.[3] In the
case of Anthony this involved trials which were no less bitter
than prolonged. For twenty years he endured the existence of
a solitary amid the ruins of an abandoned fortress by the Nile;
to avoid temptation he withdrew farther and farther into the
wilderness, but even so he was not secure. His indefatigable
persistence was, however, rewarded by successive triumphs over
the enemy; as when, for example, he fled at top speed from the
sight of visible gold exposed among the rocks at his feet.[4] And
his final triumph over the powers of darkness was attested by the
fact that he lived to attain a ripe and serene old age.[5]

From the standpoint of the author, the life of Anthony was
chiefly significant because it illustrated the moral value of the
monastic *ascesis*, by virtue of which the saint was enabled to
offer various proofs of what was conceived to be the working of
the Spirit. Among such manifestations he records numerous
instances of faith-healing which were, he is at pains to note, in
every case 'accomplished through Christ alone by prayer'.[6] Of
equal importance was the fact that, as occasion demanded,
Anthony issued from his desert retreat to bear witness to
Christian principles in Alexandria. On the first of these occasions he descended upon the city during a critical period of
persecution, not, as was alleged, with the object of courting
martyrdom, but in order that he might render moral support
to the harassed 'confessors', which he did with conspicuous
success.[7] The second occasion was during the heat of the Arian
controversy, when the monk, though quite devoid of formal
education, confuted the heretics merely by the power of inspiration.[8] In a similar spirit he overcame the pagan philosophers,
not by argument, but by healing certain persons who were vexed
with demons, thus demonstrating the superiority of faith over
science and the life of action over that of thought.[9] Finally, as

---

[1] *Vita Antonii*, 2 and 3.   [2] 67 and 68.
[3] 5 and 6.   [4] 12 and 13.   [5] 89, 90.
[6] 48, 57, 63, 64, 70, 71, 83, 84.   [7] 46.   [8] 69.   [9] 80.

the reward of assiduous and unremitting effort, Anthony ultimately attained a gift of insight which enabled him to prophesy.[1]

The spirit of monasticism was marked not less by dependence on God than by independence of man. And therein may be found the secret of Christian democracy, such as was illustrated by Anthony when, in answer to letters addressed to him by the emperor Constantine and his sons, he wrote commending them for the fact that they worshipped Christ, at the same time exhorting them not to think too much of the present, but to remember the coming judgement and to recognize the Saviour alone as the true and everlasting king.[2] Therein, also, may be found the source of his strength and influence as 'God's physician to Egypt', as a result of which 'many soldiers and men of property laid aside the burdens of life and became monks for the rest of their days'.[3]

Without attempting to follow the growth of monasticism from its beginnings with Anthony and Pachomius, we may pause to note certain significant developments which took place within the movement during the fourth century. These developments were associated largely with the life and work of St. Basil.[4] The contribution of Basil was twofold: (1) as theologian, (2) as νομοθέτης or lawgiver. As theologian, he helped to 'rationalize' the movement on a scriptural and doctrinal basis, thus, in effect, working out the elements of a specifically Christian *moralia*. As lawgiver, he drafted a scheme of communal organization designed to provide the appropriate means for its realization—an organization embodying principles which made it a model, not so much of, as for, the *polis*. The first of these principles may be described as that of inner control, to be achieved through common faith, regular and frequent communion, and the practice of daily contemplation, self-examination, and confession. The second was that of economic and moral interdependence, including the equality of the sexes. These principles offered a basis for communal self-sufficiency, which found expression in organized labour, agriculture, industry, arts and crafts as well as in the study of Christian literature—activities both manual and intellectual in which every one participated to the limit

---

[1] 82 and 86.   [2] 81.   [3] 87.
[4] *Cambridge Mediaeval History*, i, ch. xviii: 'Monasticism'; Clarke, *St. Basil the Great*.

of his capacity. They offered a basis, also, for Christian social service; since, production being for use rather than profit, the surplus was available for purposes of hospitality, especially the rearing and education of children. And, as these varied forms of activity became possible only by co-operative endeavour, it may be said that, with Basil, Christian communism triumphed completely over the eremitical way of life.

A third phase of monasticism may be illustrated from the *De Moribus Ecclesiae* of St. Augustine,[1] which reveals both its penetration into the West and the modifications to which, under Western influence, it was subjected. In this third phase it will be seen that the original purpose of the movement, individual salvation, was not forgotten. The work is written in sharp opposition to Manichean dualism and to the ethic based upon it, which found expression in various forms of superstitious abstinence and in 'unspeakable mysteries'. As against these manifestations, the product of Manichean 'science', Augustine invokes the principle of authority to be found in the Scriptures.[2] In the light of this authority he asserts that, just as there is no 'nature' which is essentially and inherently evil, so there is no essential or inherent evil in the life of sense. The problem of salvation is thus not to destroy or to suppress the affections; it is rather that they should be reoriented with a view to the supreme good. That good lies in God, the search for whom (*secutio*) may thus be described as the *appetitus beatitudinis*,[3] of which love constitutes the dynamic.[4] From this point of view, love subsumes the four cardinal virtues of Classicism which, at the same time, it irradiates with fresh significance.[5] In this way the self-same principle which, when directed to the pursuit of mundane ends, gives rise to moral confusion and ruin, is conceived by Augustine to yield the motive power necessary to a realization of creative peace, the Kingdom of God within.

In making possible such peace, love at the same time makes possible a social good to be achieved by treating other men as

---

[1] *Circa* 390.   [2] i. 3.   [3] i. 13.

[4] i. 17. 31: 'amore petitur, amore quaeritur, amore pulsatur, amore revelatur; amore denique in eo quod revelatum fuerit permanetur.'

[5] i. 15. 25: *temperantia*—'amore integrum se praebens ei quod amatur'; *fortitudo*— 'amor facile tolerans omnia propter quod amatur'; *iustitia*—'amor soli amato serviens et propterea recte dominans'; *prudentia*—'amor ea quibus adiuvatur ab eis quibus impeditur sagaciter seligens'.

ends rather than as means.[1] It thereby supplies the basis for a specifically Christian 'order' which, founded on *mutua caritas* or *fraternitas*, manifests itself in the duties of charity (*officia caritatis erga proximum*). From this point of view, the life of the anchorite continues, no doubt, to exhibit value, as indicating that he has achieved a 'pinnacle of sanctity' (*fastigium sanctitatis*) surpassing the endurance of ordinary men.[2] But the law of mutual love points not so much to this ideal as to that of communal living in societies wherein the normal rules of competition are discarded and from which exploitation and parasitism, the twin evils of *Romanitas*, disappear.[3] The basis of such societies will normally lie in manual labour, since this allows most easily for the provision of physical necessities without alienating the mind from God. In them men will eat to live rather than live to eat; and, while entertaining no foul superstitions regarding food and drink, they will so far abstain from flesh and wine as to keep in subjection the lusts of the flesh (*pro sufficientia domandarum libidinum*), thus imposing a rational limit upon their asceticism. As surpluses accrue, they will be distributed through the deacons to the poor in the outside world. Meanwhile the members, under the guidance of their superior or father, will devote themselves to the cultivation of moral and spiritual values, in all their necessary relations with one another exercising authority without pride and practising obedience without servility. Such societies, organized in groups of about 3,000 for men, have their counterpart in similar groups for women; and those both of men and women illustrate, to perfection, the economy of the Christian life.[4]

As thus conceived, monasticism represents, in some sense, a throw-back to the spirit of the pre-Constantinian era. Yet, since its development occurred mainly in the fourth century, it must be understood as a protest against conditions in the New Republic. Accordingly, it serves to emphasize, in the most emphatic manner, the failure of emperors from Constantine to Theodosius to effect any real amalgamation between ideals so incongruous as those cherished respectively by the Church and by the state.

[1] i. 30. 62: 'Christianis haec data est forma vivendi, ut diligamus dominum nostrum ex toto corde et ex tota anima et ex tota mente, deinde proximum nostrum tanquam nosmetipsos.'   [2] i. 31. 66 and 67.

[3] i. 31. 67: 'nemo quidquam possidet proprium, nemo cuiquam onerosus est.'

[4] i. 35. 79.

That failure is further attested by reference to another and no less arresting phenomenon of the age. This was the withdrawal of so many men, pre-eminent for character and ability, from the ranks of secular society, in order that they might devote their undivided energies to the service of the Church. These included, among others, Jerome, who was destined from his retreat at Bethlehem to lay the foundations of a specifically Christian scholarship; Ambrose and Augustine, the former presently to become famous as an exponent of ecclesiastical statesmanship, the latter as one of the leading philosophers of Western Christianity. Such transfers of allegiance cannot properly be taken as evidence for what has been called 'a social triumph' on the part of the Church. On the contrary, they point to its moral triumph over the claims of this world. As such, they may be ascribed to a growing disgust for the ends embodied in the secular order, what Augustine calls 'the drudgery of earthly things'. And it should be remembered that this disgust was shared by pagans such as Ammianus, little as Ammianus shared the faith of Christians in the value of their alternative. At the same time they reveal an increasing sense of the inefficacy of political methods for the treatment of the characteristic maladies of *Romanitas*. These transfers of allegiance did not, of course, imply any secession from the world such as that involved in monasticism, for, among the clergy, the pastoral function remained dominant.[1] Nevertheless, in every case, they meant a direct loss to the public service.

Such losses, added to the steady attrition of man-power and material, were, politically speaking, irreparable; and they were to be made good, if at all, only by drawing on resources from beyond the frontiers. This involved a revival of what has earlier been described as Constantinian philo-barbarism. And, under the dynasty of Theodosius, this is precisely what occurred. It has been asserted that 'a natural partiality for good material (for the army and civil service) turned Constantine and Theodosius into the deliberate partisans of the newer races', and furthermore that 'this was the logical corollary of the whole imperial idea'. So far as concerns the earlier empire, this statement overlooks the fact that some degree of cultural assimilation was regularly demanded of those who aspired to admission into anything but the lowest grades of imperial society. From this

---

[1] i. 32. 69: 'non enim sanatis magis quam sanandis hominibus praesunt.'

standpoint, nothing in the radicalism of Julius Caesar had excited deeper animosity than his admission of long-haired and betrousered Gauls into the Roman senate. In this connexion it should be noted that the problem was not so much one of 'race' as of 'culture'. This is shown by the fact that, in the reign of Claudius, descendants of those self-same Gauls were freely accorded the highest honours of the state. As for Constantine, his original predilection for the Goths originated, no doubt, from the hereditary connexion existing between them and the second Flavians, a connexion which dated, perhaps, from the time of Claudius Gothicus. Yet, with him, the traditional relationship of patronage and clientship was transformed into one of moral and social equality. For this revolutionary change of attitude there can be but one explanation.[1] The conversion of the emperor involved a radical modification of outlook, as a result of which cultural divergence ceased to be the decisive factor governing the relations between citizen and foreigner. It thus cut straight across traditional lines of cleavage and, to a very considerable extent, rendered them meaningless. From this standpoint, the philo-barbarism of Constantine was part and parcel of the renegadism which excited the antipathy of his nephew. But the antithesis between Roman and barbarian, reasserted by Julian on its conventional basis, depended upon the success of the pagan revival; and, as this proved abortive, it was among those elements of a dying society which his successors found it impossible to preserve.

The reign of Theodosius marks the final abandonment of all attempts to withstand dilution; in his treatment of barbarians, as in other aspects of his policy, the emperor was responsible for innovations of the most far-reaching character. Theodosian philo-barbarism manifested itself in two distinct, though not mutually exclusive ways. The first of these was through federation. Federation (*foederatio*) represented a radical departure from conventional practice, inasmuch as it involved the recognition of autonomous nations within the empire. As has been said, 'they acknowledged the sovereignty of the emperor without submitting to the inferior jurisdiction of the laws and magistrates'. From this point of view, its true significance became apparent when the Goths, repudiating their old king and electing a new one, embarked on their long struggle for 'better

[1] Euseb. *H.E.* iv. 7, esp. § 11 foll.

terms'.[1] Its function was thus to conceal the process by which, through a succession of treaties or agreements, the empire was gradually to divest itself of effective sovereignty over the West. Nevertheless, barbarian kings, ruling over territories which contained a population of Romans mixed with their own nationals, legitimatized their position by concessions from the emperor and, in the exercise of their rights, were content to appear as deputies and agents of the imperial power. Thus 'contractualism', a typically Roman idea, was employed by Theodosius and his successors to facilitate the transition from centralized empire to nation-state and, in this sense, it was to be among the last gifts of *Romanitas* to the world. In serving this purpose it was supplemented and reinforced by a no less striking feature of Theodosian policy, viz. that of fusion between Roman and barbarian. Theodosian fusionism found expression in a policy which committed the defence of the empire, together with the custody of dynastic interests, to the care of great barbarian chieftains like Stilicho, men of dubious or divided loyalty, whose anomalous position was epitomized in the fact that they served as consuls and dukes of the empire while, at the same time, they remained kings of their own people. It found expression, also, in a series of alliances by which those chieftains were united in marriage to members of the imperial house. It will be recalled that Valentinian, as the last active protagonist of *Romanitas*, had forbidden the intermarriage of Romans and barbarians on pain of death. Nothing could more effectively illustrate the collapse of his policy than the fact that, within the space of a single generation, this law had fallen into desuetude, and the reigning dynasty had, so to speak, cast in its lot with the barbarian.

There can be no doubt that, in their efforts to implement the ideal of the Catholic state, the sovereigns of the Theodosian house hoped to merit the approval and support of the Church. This being so, it becomes important to consider how far the Church, on its side, subscribed to the programme and methods of the empire. To this question an answer may be found in the career of a man who, by virtue of his noble personal qualities, his position of eminence in the hierarchy, and his unique relations with various representatives of secular authority, may

[1] Isid. *Chron.* 712 (*anno* 382): 'Gothi, patrocinium Romani foederis recusantes, Alaricum regem sibi constituerunt.'

properly be regarded as the leading contemporary exponent of ecclesiastical statesmanship. This man was Ambrose, bishop of Milan.[1]

From the moment of his elevation to the episcopate in 374, Ambrose devoted himself with vigour and determination to the service of the Church and, as against both heretics and pagans, he asserted the claims of Catholicism in a spirit worthy of Athanasius himself. His attitude towards heresy is revealed *inter alia* by his refusal to hand over his church to emissaries of the Arian empress Justina, when the bishop, surrounded by a loyal and devoted congregation, stubbornly resisted expulsion from the basilica, prepared to die rather than to surrender.[2] Towards paganism he was no less intransigent. In a sermon preached on the death of the young prince Valentinian II he boldly denounced Arbogast for the murder; as he later administered a stinging rebuke to the usurper Eugenius because of his attempts to relax the imperial laws against heathenism.[3]

These incidents will serve to illustrate the concern of Ambrose to vindicate the autonomy of the Church. That autonomy he conceived to embrace (*a*) its right as a corporate body to self-determination, (*b*) the freedom of its ministers in their representative capacity to speak and act as they thought fit. He thus denied the claim of the temporal power to interfere in matters such as the appointment of bishops. 'We, by the law of Jesus Christ, are dead to that law which sanctions such decrees.'[4] At the same time, he maintained that, 'just as it is improper for the state to deny freedom of expression, so also it is incumbent upon the priest to express what he feels'; since, in virtue of his sacred office, 'the priest is a messenger proclaiming the kingdom of Christ and Eternal Life'.[5] And, in order to protect the autonomy of the Church and its ministers, he repudiated the equivocal advantage of public endowments, the official bounty which, by reducing Christianity to a *religio mendicans*, placed it on a level with the pagan cults. 'The wealth of the Church', he declared, 'is what it spends upon the poor.'[6]

The rights thus asserted on behalf of the Church were based on a sense of its fundamental importance in the economy of human life and they implied a corresponding limitation in the claims of secular society. From this point of view, the institutions

[1] For a full study of him see Dudden, *The Life and Times of St. Ambrose*, 2 vols.
[2] Amb. *Ep*. i. 20; Aug. *Conf.* ix. vii. 15. [3] *Ep*. i. 57. [4] i. 21. [5] i. 40. [6] i. 18. 16.

of civilized man were envisaged as a 'remedy for sin', their origin being traced to the necessity of devising some means for satisfying and, at the same time, moderating the passionate desires of fallen man. Thus 'nature', as such, affords no warrant for the existence of private property, the genesis of which is attributed to the growth of social convention, while its maintenance as an institution depends on the use to which it is put.[1] As with property, so also with the state, which attains its highest development as it gives rise to norms of common utility to which the sovereign power itself subscribes.[2]

Thus envisaged, human institutions are subject to a relativity from which escape becomes possible only as they are made to conform to the demands of a principle which is always and everywhere valid; and such a principle cannot be discovered elsewhere than in the absolute authority of Christ and the Scriptures.[3] From this standpoint, Ambrose offers a fresh derivation of political power which, as it is traced to the ordinance of God, is justified when it is employed for the fulfilment of God's purposes.[4] Hence, for him, right no longer depends on might, but receives its mandate from divine authority. Recognition of this truth he regards as the condition of social, no less than individual, welfare.[5] As 'political justice' assumes this fresh complexion, the obligation to Christian service becomes binding upon the sovereign no less than on the subject, since the emperor, like the humblest plebeian, is a 'son of the Church'. 'Do not exalt yourself; if you wish to maintain your authority, you must submit yourself to God.'[6]

With Ambrose, by an easy and natural extension of this idea, submission to Christian principles is identified with submission to the will of the priest. From this standpoint, the temporal power remains autonomous, but it ceases to be 'independent'.[7] Ambrose thus arrives at the so-called 'indirect power'—the claim to a right of intervention in secular affairs (ratio peccati) which, regarded as an inalienable right of the spiritual, approximates

---

[1] De Offic. i. 28. 132: 'natura ius commune generavit, usurpatio ius fecit privatum.'
[2] Ep. i. 21. 9: 'quod praescripsisti aliis, praescripsisti et tibi.'   [3] De Fide.
[4] Exposit. Ev. S. Lucae, iv. 29: 'a Deo ordinatio potestatis, ut Dei minister sit qui bene utitur potestate.'
[5] Ep. i. 17. 1: 'aliter enim salus tuta non poterit, nisi unusquisque Deum verum, hoc est Deum Christianorum, a quo cuncta reguntur, veraciter colat.'
[6] i. 20. 19.
[7] i. 21. 4: 'in causa fidei episcopos solere de imperatoribus Christianis iudicare.'

to concrete sovereignty. According to him such intervention is required whenever the action of government threatens the rights of personality, and it calls for the subordination of economico-political motives to moral and spiritual ends. The theory, as thus derived from Ambrose, was to find its way into modern Catholic political thought.[1] By Ambrose himself it was invoked on more than one occasion as a means of ensuring 'ecclesiastical guidance for divine ends'. Such guidance was either admonitory or disciplinary; and it included, in at least one famous instance, the excommunication of Theodosius himself.[2]

The excommunication of Theodosius as the result of his responsibility for the so-called massacre of Thessalonica may be taken to indicate some degree of personal moral guilt. But Ambrose claimed a right of intervention more extensive even than this. For him there could be no real neutrality in organized society as between sin and righteousness, error and truth. Thus, when the pagan party of the senate, led by the urban prefect Symmachus, petitioned Valentinian II to restore to its place in the *curia* the venerable statue of Victory, Ambrose entered the lists with threats of divine and ecclesiastical displeasure if the young prince yielded to their solicitations. *Causa religionis est, episcopus convenio*: 'it is a case involving religion, I as a bishop enter my suit.'[3] In the historic discussion which followed,[4] the classical and Christian philosophies at last met face to face; and there can be little doubt to which side the honours of debate must be accorded. To the plea of the pagans for the easy toleration of Valentinian's time Ambrose replies by a stern demand for the enforcement of the law of Gratian. When they ascribe the recent famine to the malignancy of the offended gods, he answers that the laws of nature are not subject to the control of demonic forces. They suggest that 'Victory' may desert the Roman arms if her statue is thus disgraced; he retorts that their historic triumphs have been due to the strength of their warriors rather than to entrails of animals or senseless images. 'Victory is not a power but a gift.' They appeal on pragmatic grounds for the retention of cults which have proved efficacious in the past: 'what difference does it make how a man searches for truth; surely there must be more than one avenue of

---

[1] See, e.g., J. Maritain, *The Things that are not Caesar's*, p. 12.
[2] *Ep.* i. 51.   [3] i. 17. 13.   [4] i. 17 and 18.

approach to a secret so vast'. He answers dogmatically that the material, moral, and intellectual progress of mankind is to be ascribed to the providence of the one true God. In this progress the mission of Christ marks a fresh point of departure and, by constituting a full and final revelation of the divine nature, it pronounces a sentence of death upon paganism.

Such were the views of Ambrose, and they were asserted as stoutly as they were tenaciously held. It is not unjust, therefore, to see in him the master mind behind the programme of religious reform associated with the name of Theodosius. From his standpoint, indeed, there could be no hope of salvation for the empire unless it dissociated itself from the errors of paganism, Judaism, and heresy.[1] And if, in its efforts to do so, the empire invoked the weapons of coercion, Ambrose was ready to endorse even this. Athanasius had declared persecution to be the weapon of the devil; but Ambrose was prepared to use the devil's weapons as a means of realizing the kingdom of God. Accordingly, it becomes true to say of him that he maintained the cause of humanity and that of persecution with equal energy and with equal success, thus to some extent obscuring the glory of his nobler achievements. It is, for example, impossible to sympathize with his attitude when, by threats of excommunication, he forced the reluctant Theodosius to desist from his intention of exacting restitution from a Christian mob for the destruction of a Jewish synagogue or when, in promising prayers to the emperor Gratian for success against the Goths, he encouraged him to believe that a war against Arians was a holy war.[2] In so doing, Ambrose perhaps revealed a tendency to confuse the two realms, thereby betraying a mistaken notion regarding the true role of Christianity in the historic process. If so, the error may be ascribed to the fact that, like so many of his contemporaries, he carried with him into the Church a weight of prejudice acquired during a lifetime of experience in the civil administration. And, certainly, even in his defence of freedom, there is to be detected a note of authoritarianism which is peculiarly Roman. For the freedom which he bespeaks is freedom only for the priest: toward the *plebs* his attitude is wholly protective. In Ambrose's position, therefore, the danger was of setting up, in the Church, merely an alternative institutionalism to that of the

---

[1] *Ep.* i. 17. 2.

[2] *Ep.* i. 40; *De Fide,* i. 16; see Gibbon, op. cit., ch. xxvii, p. 176.

state. And, in proposing an incipient theocracy as a substitute for the dying republicanism, he pointed not so much to a regenerated *Romanitas* as to the ecclesiastical polity of medieval times.

The ultimate consequence of Theodosianism was, of course, to lay the foundation for a new European order. Its immediate result, however, was to precipitate the final destruction of the old. The period following Theodosius may be characterized in general as one of twilight government by twilight men, whose puny and distracted efforts proved utterly inadequate to forfend the approaching doom. That doom was signalized in the destruction of cities, the devastation of the country-side, and the disruption of communications. Already in 396, the first year of Arcadius and Honorius, the situation, as portrayed by a contemporary observer, was little better than hopeless.

'The mind shudders', declares St. Jerome,[1] 'to contemplate the ruin of our time. For the last twenty years, the blood of Romans has drenched the lands between Constantinople and the Julian Alps, where innumerable and ferocious tribes spread devastation and death. . . . The bodies of the free and noble, of matrons and virgins have become the prey of lust. Bishops are imprisoned; churches plundered; horses have been stabled at the altars of Christ; the bones of martyrs flung out of their coffins. . . . Everywhere grief, everywhere lamentation, everywhere the shadow of death!'

Ten years more, and the same story was to be repeated in Gaul. The few remaining legions having been concentrated for the defence of Italy, on New Year's Eve 406, a mixed host of Vandals, Sueves, and Alans crossed the ice of the undefended Rhine, to occupy permanently and without resistance the provinces of the West. This memorable incident 'may be considered as the fall of the Roman empire in the countries beyond the Alps; the barriers which for so long had separated the savage and the civilized nations . . . were from that fatal moment levelled to the ground'.[2] The climax was reached, four years later, in the rape of the Eternal City itself. Otherwise insignificant, this event, because of its spectacular character, shook the Roman world to its foundations. 'The city which has captured the whole world is herself taken captive'; 'the bright light of the universe is extinguished; the empire has lost its head; the whole world has perished in a single city.'[3] The sack of the

---

[1] *Ep.* 60. 16; cf. 123. 16–17.   [2] Gibbon, op. cit., ch. xxx, p. 269.
[3] Jerome, *Ep.* 127. 12 and 128. 4.

capital revealed, as nothing else could have done, the grim truth that *Romanitas* had reached the end of the road.

Less spectacular, perhaps, but no less impressive evidence of this truth may be found in the dry records of the Theodosian Code. These records show that, coincident with the irruption of the barbarians and with the barbarization of the services, the social structure of antiquity was everywhere breaking down. It has been declared that a thousand years of vigorous civic life was Rome's real contribution to Western civilization. If this be so, there could not be a more ironic commentary upon the process of *Romanitas* than is to be seen in the fate of the municipalities during the Theodosian age.

Of this fate, premonitions were already evident in the intensified financial stringency which began with Theodosius' reign. Thus, in 380, the government forbade magistrates to spend on the construction of new public buildings money needed for the repair of old ones.[1] Ten years later, it threatened to exact from them personally the cost of such buildings as they had the temerity to erect.[2] Five years more and it was forced to come to the rescue of distressed communities, by undertaking to defray from the imperial treasury one-third of the expense involved in necessary renovations, 'lest the splendour of the municipalities should decay with age'.[3]

These measures betray the fact that the municipalities, for so long the bone and sinew of the republic, were at last confronted with the spectre of bankruptcy. The result was to produce a sense of exasperation mingled with despair. These impulses presently overcame the habit of obedience, and there appeared on all sides indications of what was presently to resolve itself into a veritable flight from the state. Evidence of this may be found in legislation providing that two-thirds of the members of a *curia* should thenceforth constitute a quorum, their decisions to be binding on the whole;[4] in the institution of a system of fines designed to check the practice of sheltering runaway curials;[5] and, finally, in an enactment by virtue of which the estates of runaways were to be confiscated after the lapse of five years.[6] A law of 396 specifically forbade *curiales* to seek refuge from their obligations by fleeing to the country.[7] Four years

---

[1] *Cod. Theod.* xv. 1. 21.   [2] xv. 1. 28 (390).   [3] xv. 1. 32 (395).
[4] xii. 1. 142 (395).   [5] xii. 1. 146 (395).
[6] xii. 1. 143 and 144 (395).   [7] xii. 18. 2.

later the government publicly admits that this is precisely what has, in large measure, taken place.[1] As with the local aristocracies, so also with the members of local guilds. An edict of 400[2] declares that the municipalities, deprived of their services, have lost their pristine glory, the majority of the *collegiati* having forsaken urban life to bury themselves in secret and inaccessible places; while, at the same time, it decrees that such of them as may be unearthed are to be relegated without exception to their original duties.

The bankruptcy of the municipalities was the bankruptcy of an empire based upon them. Whatever the form to be assumed by the society of the future, it was clearly not to be that of Antonine or even of Constantinian times. Meanwhile, the conditions which so adversely affected municipal life were operating to modify the life of other classes within imperial society as well. It was, indeed, still possible in the middle of the fifth century for members of the senatorial aristocracy (such as Sidonius Apollinaris) to maintain themselves in something like their customary grandeur upon their vast and largely self-contained estates throughout the provinces. This they could do, however, only by dissociating themselves from their traditional relationships and by repudiating their obligations to the central power. An edict of Valentinian, Theodosius, and Arcadius[3] declares that, in view of complaints on the part of senators that they could no longer support the *onera glebalia*, the senate had resolved that those unable to discharge their liabilities should compound for them by an annual payment of seven *solidi, pro sua portione*, to the treasury. 'This we ratify', add the emperors, 'with the qualification that they may be free to choose whether they should not rather resign from the senate.'

Apart from the multitudes who lost their lives in the turmoil and confusion of the times, it is difficult to know what became of those who obeyed the impulse to cast off burdens long since become intolerable. Some, no doubt, found their way into the ranks of the clergy. Others put themselves under the domination of men still powerful enough to guarantee them protection. Still others went over, body and soul, to the barbarians, among whom they discovered opportunities for freedom and happiness denied them in the moth-eaten society of the declining empire; the history of such renegades provided interesting variants on

[1] xii. 19. 2 and 3.   [2] xii. 19. 1.   [3] vi. 2. 15 (393).

the traditional theme of the advantages of barbarism as compared with those of civilization.[1] But the vast majority, if they did not perish, must have taken refuge in the woods and mountains, to eke out a precarious existence by rapine and murder.

A sharp increase in the number of such public enemies towards the end of the fourth century gave rise to a heightened sense of insecurity among the civilian population, a sense of insecurity which the government could do little or nothing to allay. Legislation of 383 or 391 provided that any one giving aid or comfort to brigands should be liable to punishments ranging from fines to the lash, while the agent or foreman of an estate who, without knowledge of the proprietor, concealed such vagabonds or neglected to give them up to justice, was threatened with burning alive.[2] By another edict, householders were permitted to resist with arms the clandestine entry of robbers into their homes by night, as well as open attacks during the day.[3] Still another edict decreed that all deserters from the army should be rounded up and placed in custody, there to await the decision of the emperor.[4] But the final paralysis of government was revealed in a law which authorized all persons *pro quiete communi* 'to exercise with impunity the right of public vengeance against the common enemy' by exterminating malefactors, brigands, or deserters, wherever they could be found.[5] With this humiliating confession of impotence *Romanitas* virtually abdicated her secular task. The imperial power which, in words ascribed to an enemy, had made a desert and called it peace, had encountered its ultimate nemesis; as the Roman wolf, which for centuries had waxed fat on the carcasses of its victims, at last perished not of surfeit but of anaemia. And, when the great beast finally expired, there was once more resumed the warfare of each against all, the interminable strife

'wherein men live without other security than what their own strength and their own invention shall furnish them withall. In such condition, there is no place for Industry, because the fruit thereof is uncertain; and consequently no Culture of the Earth; no Navigation, nor use of the commodities that may be imported by Sea; no commodious Building; no Instruments of moving and removing such

[1] See the story of one such individual retailed by Gibbon, op. cit., ch. xxxiv, p. 429; see also Salvian, *De Gubernatione Dei* (*circa* 455).   [2] *Cod. Theod.* ix. 29. 2.   [3] ix. 14. 2 (391).   [4] vii. 1. 16 (398).   [5] vii. 18. 14 (403).

things as require much force; no knowledge of the face of the Earth; no account of Time; no Arts; no Letters; no Society; and, which is worst of all, continuall feare, and the danger of violent death; And the life of man, solitary, poore, nasty, brutish and short.'

Translated from terms of analysis into those of history, this means that Europe now made ready for her dramatic plunge into the Dark Ages.

In this way the city, which had shown the world how the political community could be organized, was in the end to provide a spectacular illustration of how that community is dissolved. And, as the heavy hand of autocracy was suddenly relaxed, the ghosts of dead ideas came floating out of the distant past to haunt the troubled present. The emperor Honorius vainly sought to evoke the spirit of patriotism and local self-help, to be achieved through the creation of municipal militia. In Britain and Armorica, after their final evacuation by the legions, the embers of that spirit appear for a moment to have flickered into life in formal 'declarations of independence' made by the co-operating *civitates* and confirmed by the emperor who 'thus permanently abdicated his sovereignty over them'.[1] Meanwhile, in Egypt, the fighting bishop Synesius indulged in the dream of 'a nation in arms' as the only possible hope of salvaging the wreckage of an empire.[2]

In general, however, such visions of freedom and of co-operative effort were condemned in advance to futility. They were, indeed, but the pale reflection of notions wholly alien to the mentality and circumstances of the Theodosian age. And this fact may serve to emphasize a truth upon which we have elsewhere insisted and which, indeed, is the underlying theme of this work. The fall of Rome was the fall of an idea, or rather of a system of life based upon a complex of ideas which may be described broadly as those of Classicism; and the deficiencies of Classicism, already exposed in the third century, were destined sooner or later to involve the system in ruin. Recognizing this fact, the object of the renovationist emperors had been to come to terms with Christianity as a force calculated to invigorate the state. In this respect, the difference between Constantine and Theodosius lay in the distance to which each was prepared to go in conforming to its demands. From this point of view, the inclination of Constantine was, as we have seen, to burke the

---

[1] Gibbon, op. cit., ch. xxxi, pp. 351-6.   [2] *De Regno,* 21 foll. (*circa* 398).

logical consequences of his action in 'recognizing' Christianity; but Theodosius went to the ultimate limit possible for a Roman emperor by instituting the forms and order of the Catholic state. Despite this difference, however, both emperors were alike in one fundamental respect: what they required of Christianity was that it should subscrve a dcfinitcly social and economic function, i.e. they still thought 'politically'. In this fact, perhaps, may be found an explanation for the failure of their efforts, the net result of which was simply to hasten the end.

If this be so, it raises a question of profound interest and importance. That question is whether there was, at bottom, any real possibility of effecting a reconciliation between Classicism and Christianity, between the claims of a system which was directed to the achievement of temporal peace and one which aimed at the realization of a peace not of this world. To this question no final answer is perhaps possible. It should, however, be observed that, while Christianity contained elements which might be employed to reinforce the established order, at the same time it embodied ingredients of a highly explosive character, sufficient indeed to shatter the already weakened faith in classical ideals and thus to empty the system of whatever meaning it still possessed. Hence, without denying to both emperors and churchmen of the fourth century credit for sincerity and good will in their efforts to compromise or at least to conceal their differences, we are bound to insist that they failed to arrive at anything like a permanent solution of the problem of the two societies. It might, indeed, be asserted that, by bringing to a focus the issue between them, they precipitated the downfall of the ancient world.

To speak in terms of 'downfall' is, in a way, indecent: it is to put oneself in a false position and to abandon all real sense of historical perspective. To a Julian or a Symmachus, the events of the fourth century must certainly have appeared to portend the end of civilization and, with it, everything which gave value and significance to human life. For the modern, however, these momentous developments were the necessary preparation for a new and radically different future; and, in order that this future should materialize, it was inevitable that *Romanitas*, despite her pretension to eternity, should perish from the earth.

In conclusion it should be noted that, in the process of dismantling the empire, Christianity and barbarism were associated rather than allied powers. What the barbarians coveted was a place in the sun; and, in some degree, their ambitions were realized in the form of those short-lived Gothic and Vandal kingdoms which, in the period from Alaric to Clovis, rose and fell throughout the Western provinces. Christianity, on the other hand, concerned itself with the problems of economic and cultural life only in a secondary sense; despite the fumbling and uncertain character of its efforts, its real object was still to build the Kingdom of God. From this point of view it becomes possible to estimate the role of the Church in the period succeeding the eclipse of the empire. The Church did, indeed, help to civilize the barbarians, partly by assuming custody of the literature which, throughout classical times, had contained the spiritual nourishment of men, partly by communicating to the invaders something of the spirit of order and discipline which it had acquired from its association with the fallen empire.[1] Infinitely more important than this, however, its problem was to offer them a faith less inadequate to human needs than that which they had brought with them from the forests of Germany. The question thus arises: how far was it equipped to do so? To answer this question, it becomes necessary to retrace our steps and, within the necessary limitations of this work, to examine, in certain of its more significant aspects, the development of Christian thinking in the period subsequent to Nicaea.

[1] Gibbon, op. cit., ch. xxxviii, p. 142, on Visigothic Spain.

PART III
REGENERATION
X
THE CHURCH AND THE KINGDOM OF GOD

Thus far, we have traced the declining fortunes of *Romanitas* through the vicissitudes of four hundred years. In the programme of conservation inaugurated by Augustus Caesar we have seen an attempt to salvage all that was of permanent value in the thought and aspiration of classical antiquity and to give it effective expression under the aegis of Eternal Rome. But the apparent fulfilment of the Augustan programme in the second century was merely the prelude to its breakdown in the third; and, with the collapse of the classical commonwealth, various princes devoted themselves to projects of reform, culminating in that undertaken by Constantine and his successors, the emperors of the fourth century. Our examination of that effort has revealed, in some degree, the reasons for its failure; but, for a fuller comprehension of those reasons, it is necessary to consider the implications of Nicene Christianity as they were developed by certain of the great contemporary churchmen. This study will serve to emphasize the futility of the hopes entertained by renovationist emperors from Constantine to Theodosius, the impossibility of achieving, within the forms of the New Republic, the spirit of the Christian Commonwealth. At the same time, it will make more intelligible the attitude of the fourth-century Church to what, in the language traditional to Christianity, was known as the Kingdom of God.

To the fourth-century Church the vision of the Kingdom was the vision of a spiritual aristocracy, a society regenerated by the acceptance of Christian truth; and, for it, the heart and centre of this truth was contained in the Nicene formula. To develop the implications of that formula was to be the achievement of the fourth-century exponents of Christianity. This 'revaluation of values' served to complete the moral and intellectual revolution which, in the words of a recent writer, has created the psychological gulf between antiquity and modern times.[1] In undertaking their task fourth-century apologists had,

[1] Lot, *La fin du monde antique*, ad fin.

of course, the benefit of guidance from scriptural and apostolic, as well as from earlier ecclesiastical authority. But they gained fresh confidence to attack it because of the fact that the fundamentals of Trinitarianism were now precisely indicated in the Creed. Unlike their predecessors of the pre-Nicene period, they had therefore nothing to fear from pagan 'science'. As a consequence they were emboldened to advance the theory that 'all truth is Christian truth'; and from this proposition, by an easy inference, they derived the practical maxim, 'spoil the Egyptians'. In the process of spoiling the Egyptians they did much to close the gap between Christianity and Classicism without, however, compromising the essentials of the faith.

Thus envisaged, the work of the fourth-century ecclesiastics marks an attempt at a synthesis of human experience for which there had been no parallel since the time of Plato. Thus far, indeed, in the history of speculation, Plato had been the only thinker to essay what, from this point of view, may be called a 'Catholic' philosophy; and so nearly did he approach to success that, for centuries, his system continued to provide the most formidable elements of opposition to evolving Christianity.[1] But, as the history of Platonism shows, Plato had failed in certain essential respects to effect the synthesis at which he aimed and thus to build an enduring home for the spirit. The nature and consequence of this failure will, we hope, become apparent as Platonism is seen in contrast with the alternative system proposed by Christianity. At this point it will be sufficient to observe that the cause for Plato's failure lay in his inability to overcome the radical deficiencies of the classical approach to experience. From this standpoint it may indeed be suggested that the function of fourth-century Christianity was to heal the wounds inflicted by man on himself in classical times and, by transcending while still doing justice to the elements of truth contained in philosophic paganism, to revive and give direction to the expiring spiritual ideals of classical antiquity. In considering this development it must be remembered that the present work is in no sense a history of dogma: our object is simply to bring out certain salient points of Christian thinking in relation to the classical background, as the central feature of the historical revolution which we are attempting to describe. For this purpose it will be enough to examine cross-sections, so

[1] Augustine, *Retract.* i. 1. 4.

to speak, of that thought which will serve to illustrate its distinctive characteristics. This we shall now try to do.

Of such cross-sections the first and not the least significant may be found in the work of St. Athanasius. We have already encountered Athanasius as a man of action, the steadfast opponent of heretical tendencies sponsored by the imperial court, the gallant and stubborn defender of Christian liberty against the machinations of Constantius. We have also received some indication of his beliefs, so far as these are suggested in the *Life of St. Anthony*, considered as illustrating at once the redemptive power of Christ and the power of the redeemed soul. And, in this connexion, it is important to notice that, for Athanasius and those who shared his faith, the actions and sufferings of Anthony are not just 'poetry', but a record of spiritual truth, exemplifying the gift of illumination and power implicit in the revelation of Christ and manifested by His followers.

It was, however, as the protagonist and exponent of Trinitarian doctrine that Athanasius attained his chief importance in the history of his age. As such, his attitude is fully and decisively expressed both in the Nicene Creed and in the creed which bears his own name.[1] But these documents are mere declarations of faith, bearing in Christian thought much the same relation to reasoned discussion as, in another context, the *Communist Manifesto* bears to *Das Kapital*. Accordingly, in order to comprehend their full significance, it is necessary to recall the argument by which they are supported. This argument is contained in the controversial works of Athanasius, especially his *Comments on the Decisions of the Nicene Synod*, the four essays *Against the Arians* and that *Against the Gentiles*, all of which are devoted to the one end of expounding and advocating the Trinitarian position.

To say this is to indicate, in general, the contribution of Athanasius to Christian thought. Athanasius was, indeed, a man of one idea, but that idea was of profound and far-reaching consequence. To him it was evident that, if Graeco-Roman speculation had issued in insoluble puzzles, this was the inevitable result of its having accepted a vicious or defective starting-point. And, in Trinitarianism, he found a basic principal broad and inclusive enough to bear the weight of the conclusions

---

[1] The so-called Athanasian Creed is generally regarded as a work of the sixth century.

derived from it and to sustain, rather than stifle, the life of religion and philosophy. In this connexion it should be noticed that, in referring to the Trinity, the term he regularly employs is *arché* (ἀρχή), a word consecrated by immemorial usage among the Greeks; and, by adopting it, Athanasius associates himself with the spirit of Greek thought from its beginnings with Thales and the naturalists. But in the character which he ascribes to or rather discovers in it, Athanasius departs radically from the Greek philosophic tradition. For, while the Greeks sought for this *arché* in 'nature', Athanasius perceived that it was not to be found either 'within' or 'without' the frontiers of the physical world. And, while they conceived of it as a 'cause' or rather as the 'cause of causes', he contended that what is presupposed in the nexus of events within the order of time and space could not be causally related to them. Knowledge of such a principle, therefore, differed *toto caelo* from knowledge of nature; and it was not to be attained by pursuing the chain of natural causation to its limit. In other words it was a matter of direct and immediate apprehension to be recognized by 'its working and power'. As such, the consciousness of it was part of the original spiritual legacy of mankind. But, as this consciousness had, for various reasons, become obscured, it needed to be revealed afresh; and this revelation it was the function of Christ and the Scriptures to supply. From this standpoint, however, it claimed a validity not less absolute, and infinitely more comprehensive, than that possessed, for example, by the first principles of mathematical and physical science.

With respect to the Trinity, it has been observed that the notion is 'intellectually incomprehensible'. 'Either the word Trinity denotes a mere abstraction or the word Unity does.'[1] The writer adds that it is 'incompatible with certain of our axioms of thought, indisputable in themselves but foreign and inapplicable to a sphere of existences of which we have no experience whatever'. He is thus prompted to the conclusion that 'those high truths have (we may conceive) been revealed to us for devotion; and, for devotion, the mystery presents no difficulty'.

But it is one thing to affirm that mystery lies at the heart of the universe and quite another to suggest that human beings should hug that mystery in and for itself. What Newman does

[1] J. H. Newman, *St. Athanasius*, vol. ii. p. 317.

is virtually to set up a cult of unintelligibility which, we may be sure, was alien to the mind and thought of Athanasius. The audience to which Athanasius addressed himself was made up of men who found it difficult or impossible to emancipate themselves from classical ways of thought. Upon these men he was concerned to urge a view of ultimate reality which, as he insisted, so far from giving countenance to obscurantism, was the necessary presupposition to a wider intelligibility, if not to all intelligibility whatsoever. In other words, what he offered them was an intellectual, no less than a moral and spiritual, release. This release was from the perplexities involved in pagan *scientia* and from the backwash of pagan obscurantism to which it inevitably led. It represented the fourth-century version of the promise: *the truth shall make you free.*

In attempting to communicate this truth, however, Athanasius was confronted by a difficulty which was not unnatural, since it was precisely the difficulty of the 'natural' man. In the new *arché* or starting-point, he claimed recognition for a principle which, because of its unique character, transcended the normal processes of apprehension. To grasp it, therefore, required a vigorous effort of thought and imagination and, in particular, it was necessary to expel from the mind the anthropomorphisms of pagan science. From this standpoint, distinctions fundamental to the scientific outlook simply disappeared. For, as the source of Being, this principle was not to be apprehended 'objectively'; it eluded analysis in terms of substance, quantity, quality, and relation, all the categories in short which yield a knowledge of the phenomenal world. But, although not cognizable as an object, it was not therefore reducible to terms merely of subjective feeling, for its reality was presupposed in all the various manifestations of conscious life, of speculative as well as practical activity.

In defending the claims of such a principle, it should be remembered that Athanasius was mainly interested in the revelation of the Trinity in its first and second 'persons'; it remained largely for the Western theologians to develop the implications of the third *hypostasis* in the doctrine of the Holy Spirit. The reason for this may perhaps be found in the contemporary historical situation. At the time when Athanasius wrote, the chief opposition to Nicene Christianity came from the Arians, backed by the power and prestige of the Constantinian court; and, for the Arian opponents of Trinitarianism, the difficulties which it presented were intellectual rather than moral; although, of course, the two aspects of the problem could not ultimately be separated. These intellectual difficulties Athanasius sought with all the force of a powerful and subtle dialectic to overcome; and, in the effort to confute his opponents, he spoke in terms which they might understand and in the language peculiar to his day. But his intention is none the less evident, as may perhaps be gathered from his own words. 'God', he declares, 'is not nature, all the constituents of which are mutually interdependent. Nor is He the totality of its parts; for He is not compounded of parts on which He depends, but is Himself the source of existence to all.'[1] 'To think of God as composing and putting together the universe out of matter is a Greek notion, and it is to represent Him as a workman ($\tau\epsilon\chi\nu\acute{\iota}\tau\eta s$) rather than as a creator ($\pi o\iota\eta\tau\acute{\eta}s$).'[2]

In these and analogous passages Athanasius traces the genealogy of Arianism to its roots in classical science. They are incidental to his effort to establish, in a positive fashion, the elements of Nicene theology. To do this, Athanasius seeks to convey a sense of the divine principle, apprehended on the one hand as the source of Being or Existence, on the other as its manifestation in the Word or Order of the universe; in the language of religion, of 'God the Father' and 'God the Son'. Because of the nature of his problem, the description must largely be in terms of negations; by trying to show what the principle is not, he reveals by implication what it is:

'From the Holy Scriptures, we learn that the word "Son" is used in two senses (figuratively and literally). . . . If they (the Eusebians) apply the name to the Word in the first sense, in which sense it belongs also to those who have earned it because of an improvement in their character, and have received the power to become Sons of God; if they will have it this way, then it is evident that the Word differs in no respect from us, nor will it be necessary to describe Him as only-begotten, inasmuch as He too, because of His qualities ($\dot{\epsilon}\xi$ $\dot{a}\rho\epsilon\tau\hat{\eta}s$), has obtained the name of Son.[3] . . .

'If pressed, they will blush and reply: we understand the Son to excel all other creatures and therefore to be called "only begotten", because He alone was made by God alone, and all other things were created by God through the Son as His agent or deputy ($\dot{\upsilon}\pi o\upsilon\rho\gamma\acute{o}s$).'[4]

[1] *Contra Gentes*, 28c.
[2] *Orat.* ii. 22.   [3] *De Decretis*, 6.   [4] 7.

But this, argues Athanasius, is blasphemy, since:

'the Word is Son in the literal sense, not by grace or adoption. For nature (φύσις) and nothing short of nature is involved in the idea of sonship, generation, or derivation; while likeness does not imply identity . . .'.[1]

'God indeed creates, and the word creation (τὸ κτίζειν) is used with reference to men; and God is the principle of existence (ὤν ἐστι), but men also are said to exist, deriving their being from God. Are we then to say that God creates as men create or that His existence is similar to that of men? Perish the thought! These terms we apply in one sense to God, and we understand them in quite another sense as applied to men. For God creates by calling the non-existent into being, requiring nothing in addition. But men work upon pre-existing material (ὑποκειμένη ὕλη), deriving their knowledge of what to do from Him who is the architect of all things through His own Word. Moreover, men, who are unable to call themselves into being, discover themselves as confined in space and existing in the Word of God. But God is, by Himself, the principle of existence, containing everything and contained by nothing; He is in everything by virtue of His goodness and power, but outside of everything by virtue of the being which is proper to Him. Human growth is by emission and assimilation, and the generation of men, like that of animals, is in time. But God, being devoid of parts, is without division or affection Father to His Son. For there is no emission from that which is incorporeal, nor does it require any assimilation to itself, as is the case with men. Simple by nature, God is Father to but one Son, who for this reason is described as the only-begotten and rests alone in the bosom of the Father.'[2]

'In this sense, also, the genesis of the Son surpasses and transcends the conceptions of men. For as we ourselves emerge in time from not-being to being, so also we become the fathers of successive children in time. But God, being eternal, is the eternal Father to the Son.'[3]

Thus in view of the perfection and unchangeableness of the divine nature and, once more, by contrast with anthropomorphic ideas, it is proper to speak of the 'perpetual generation' of the Son.

'For', as he argues,[4] 'the essence of the Father was never "imperfect", so that what belonged to it could afterwards come to it, nor is the generation of the Son similar to that of men, following subsequent upon the being of the Father. But He is the offspring of the Father and, as the only-begotten of the eternally existing God, the

---

[1] 10.   [2] 11.   [3] 12.   [4] *Orat.* i. 14.

Son is eternally begotten. It is peculiar to men that they should beget issue in time because of the imperfection of their nature, but the begotten of God is timeless because of the eternal perfection of His nature.'

By thus disposing of scientific anthropomorphisms, Athanasius paves the way for a revolutionary view of the *operatio Dei* on the universe.

'The created universe is not to be regarded as existing either casually or spontaneously (εἰκῇ καὶ ἐκ ταὐτομάτου) nor as having originated by accident (κατὰ τύχην), according to the views of the atomists; nor yet is it, as certain of the heretics assert, the product of a second "demiurgic" god, nor again, as others declare, the construction of certain angels. But, inasmuch as everything derives its existence from God, the principle of existence, by Himself, through His Word, therefore it is declared to be, and is, of God. . . . But the Word, because It is not anything created, is alone said to be and is in truth of the Father, and this is what is meant when it is asserted that the Son is of the substance of the Father.'[1]

The argument proceeds:

'If then anyone considers God to be composite, possessing anything of the accidental in His being with which He is, so to speak, enveloped as by a garment, or supposes that there is anything round about Him completing His existence, thus implying that, when we speak of God or address him as Father, we do not refer to His invisible and incomprehensible essence, but to the things which are round about Him; such men may blame the Council for having written that the Son is of the substance of God, but they must realize that, in holding such opinions, they are guilty of the following blasphemies (a) of introducing a corporeal deity and (b) of falsely alleging that the Son is not of the Father Himself but of those things which are round about Him.'[2]

'The madness of the Arians is in falsely describing the offspring of the Father as analogous to their own.[3] . . . His nature is one with that of the Father; since the begotten is not unlike the begetter: for He is His image, and the attributes of the Father all belong to the Son. Therefore the Son is not another God, to be conceived (anthropomorphically) as external to the Father.'[4]

In these passages Athanasius seeks to expose the source of Arian error, and to urge, in its stead, a recognition of the purely spiritual character of ultimate reality. And, from the way in which he handles the issue, it is evident that with him the

[1] *De Decretis*, 19.   [2] 22.   [3] *Orat.* i. 15.   [4] *Orat.* iii. 4.

statement of Christian principles has lost nothing of its characteristically paradoxical character. Thus, while retaining the
traditional religious imagery as perhaps best suited to express
the relationship between the universe and its creator, he nevertheless makes it fully apparent that what is called the 'act of
creation' bears no analogy whatsoever to the processes of nature
with which mankind is familiar. The 'Word', indeed, 'by which
all things were made' is such that It embodies the whole substance, life, and power of the Father. That is to say, the universe
is to be understood as a product of the free, creative activity of
God, rather than as an 'emanation' from the Monad subject to
natural necessity.

'Again,' as he elsewhere puts it,[1] 'if the Son once was not, then the
Triad is not from eternity (i.e. really "absolute"), but was a Monad
first, and afterwards a Triad. . . . Then again, if the Son has come
out of nothing, I suppose the whole Triad came out of nothing too;
or, what is still more serious, being divine, it included in its essence
a created thing.'

To deny this is to detract from the sovereignty of God by
making Him subject to time[2] as well as to the 'laws of nature'.[3]
Or, stated otherwise, it is to involve oneself in Neoplatonic
pantheism. Finally, as against the Arian doctrine that 'the
essences do not mix with one another' ($\dot{\alpha}\nu\epsilon\pi\dot{\iota}\mu\iota\kappa\tau o\iota$ $\dot{\epsilon}\alpha\upsilon\tau\alpha\hat{\iota}\varsigma$ $\alpha\dot{\iota}$
$\dot{\upsilon}\pi o\sigma\tau\dot{\alpha}\sigma\epsilon\iota\varsigma$), the Athanasian position is further emphasized in
the doctrine of co-inherence ($\pi\epsilon\rho\iota\chi\dot{\omega}\rho\eta\sigma\iota\varsigma$) among the 'persons'
of the Trinity; but, while the Word is described as Son, the
idea of the divine sonship specifically excludes the notion of
physical generation as well as that of a beginning in time; time
thus being denied the character of an *hypostasis* or substantial
principle of nature.

With the acceptance of a starting-point such as that just
indicated, it becomes possible to envisage the divine principle
as both transcendent and immanent, 'prior' to nature, the
world of time and space in which we live, and yet operative
within it. For, while the properties of matter are such that two
bodies cannot occupy the same space at the same time, the
special characteristic of spirit lies in its permeability. And
therein, it may be suggested, lies the significance, practically
speaking, of the new starting-point. For, from this point of
view, the panorama of human history may be conceived as a

[1] *Orat.* i. 17.   [2] 5 and 13.   [3] 14; 22; 27.

record of the divine economy, the working of the Spirit in and through mankind, from the creation of the first conscious human being to its full and final revelation in the Incarnate Word.

But if this be history, it is history in a sense wholly without parallel in secular literature. For it is neither economic nor cultural nor political, local and particularist or general and cosmopolitan; it deals neither with problems of war and peace nor with those of competition and co-operation; and it does not concern itself in the least with the 'search for causes'. What it offers is an account of human freedom, its original loss through the first Adam and its ultimate recovery through the second. This it presents in the form of a cosmic drama; but the drama is not Promethean, it tells no story of 'virtue' in conflict with 'chance' or 'necessity'. For, with the disappearance from Christian thought of the classical antithesis between 'man' and the 'environment', there disappears also the possibility of such a conflict. The destiny of man is, indeed, determined, but neither by a soulless mechanism nor by the *fiat* of an arbitrary or capricious power external to himself. For the laws which govern physical, like those which govern human, nature are equally the laws of God.

From this point of view, human history may be regarded as the history of conscious life, the life of beings created free and with a potentiality for happiness, this freedom and this happiness depending upon their capacity for deliberate choice.[1] To express this idea the word employed is προαίρεσις, and its use in this connexion links Athanasius once more with the speculative tradition of Classicism. It may be remembered that Aristotle, in proposing his scheme of political emancipation, had declared that the state is not for slaves and other animals, because these have no share in happiness or in the life according to choice.[2] For Athanasius, however, felicity is not the peculiar privilege of the citizen, nor is liberty confined to civilized men; but, as these blessings depend upon the power of choice, and as this, in turn, is a function of conscious life, it is inherent in the native endowment of mankind. As such, it is inalienable; in the sense, at least, that it can be impaired by no power from

---

[1] *De Incarnatione Verbi*, 3.
[2] *Pol.* iii. 9. 1280ᵃ, 33–4: οὐκ ἔστι (δούλων καὶ τῶν ἄλλων ζῴων πόλις) διὰ τὸ μὴ μετέχειν εὐδαιμονίας μηδὲ τοῦ ζῆν κατὰ προαίρεσιν.

outside, but only by its own perversion or abuse. This, however, is exactly what occurred in the Fall of Man.[1]

With regard to the deeper, moral implications of this doctrine, Athanasius says little or nothing; these were to be developed later by Augustine in what he had to say about original sin. Athanasius himself is content to identify the Fall with the acceptance of a false ideology. Such an ideology may take any one of several different forms. It may, for example, find expression in Epicureanism, which undertakes the problem of explaining the universe in terms of matter and motion, and which denies that there is any principle of discrimination in nature beyond that of physical pleasure and pain. Or it may appear as Platonism which, with its admission of a pre-existent matter, yields an inadequate idea of God by reducing Him to the status of a mere mechanic. Or again, it may emerge as one of the various types of Gnosticism which, because of their underlying dualism, deny the unity of the cosmos. But, whatever form it assumes, the results of departing from the Word are alike intellectually and morally disastrous. Intellectually, men lose the principle of understanding, and undergo a progressive blindness of perception. Morally, they lose the principle of life, and suffer a spiritual *phthisis* or wasting away.[2]

It was, indeed, possible for the Creator, in His omnipotence, to intervene in order to prevent such degradation; but such intervention would have involved an arbitrary interference with the integrity of human nature, which requires to be healed, renewed, and recreated, rather than destroyed. Accordingly, for the fulfilment of the divine purpose, it was essential that man, having lapsed into sin and error through the abuse of his faculties, should be restored through the recovery of their proper use. Such restoration, however, could not be brought about by fallen man through his own efforts, but only by the incarnation of the Word.[3]

Thus Athanasius arrives at the central idea of the divine economy, the notion of the redemption of mankind through the assumption of manhood by the Word. For him, the purpose of this event was to serve as a revelation of the invisible through the visible, and thus to indicate the true relationship between life and death, the ascendancy of the one over the other.[4] Its reality, besides being implied in the very nature of the Word

[1] *De Incarnat. Verbi*, 4.   [2] 4–10.   [3] 17–20.   [4] 31.

Incarnate, was attested by experience and confirmed by subsequent historical developments.[1] As such, it was offered as a challenge alike to the inveterate obstinacy of the Jew and to the frivolous cynicism of the Greek. From the Jews Athanasius demanded belief on the double ground of principles admitted by themselves and of prophecies fulfilled. For the Greeks he pointed to the decay of popular and philosophic paganism as evidence of its barrenness. Upon both he urged, as a reason for accepting the faith, the fact of its salutary influence upon the life of individuals and societies, claiming that it embodied the sole hope of creative peace, since it alone imbued human beings with a really pacific disposition and, by transmuting the strife of man with nature and his fellows into a conflict against evil, made possible a realization of the promise: *they shall beat their swords into ploughshares and there shall be no more war.*[2]

The validity of these claims depended, of course, upon a recognition of the historic Christ as the very embodiment of cosmic order, and on this Athanasius insists as the whole burden of the Evangel. 'It is', he declares, 'the distinctive purpose and characteristic of Holy Scripture that it makes two things clear about the Saviour, first that He was always God and Son, the Word, the Splendour and the Wisdom of the Father and, secondly, that for us He assumed flesh from the Virgin Mary, mother of God, and became man.'[3] As such, the Messiah exhibited in their fullness the two natures, divine and human, which in Him were fused but not confused: He was wholly man and wholly God (ὅλος θεός, ὅλος ἄνθρωπος). 'Thus, on the one hand, while being God, He had a body of His own and became man, using this body as an instrument for our sake. And therefore the specific affections of this body were His while He was in it, such as hunger, thirst, suffering . . . even death.' . . . And these He suffered voluntarily, because He willed to do so. But, while submitting to the affections of the flesh, He at the same time performed actions proper to the Word; such, for example, as raising the dead, making the blind to see, and curing the woman with a haemorrhage . . . and, while the Word endured the infirmities of the body because of its weakness, since the body was His, nevertheless the body subserved the works of divinity, because He was in it, for it was the body of a God.[4]

[1] 29–32.
[2] 52.
[3] *Orat.* iii. 29: ἐκ παρθένου τῆς θεοτόκου Μαρίας.
[4] 31.

Hence the θεανδρικὴ ἐνέργεια, the two distinct but inseparable energies manifested in Christ: 'Because when the body suffered, the Word was not outside it, therefore the suffering is said to be His. Again, when with divine power He accomplished the works of the Father, the body was not outside Him, but He did these things while in it.'[1] So far, therefore, as concerns the person of the Saviour, the meaning of the incarnation might be summarized in the statement that 'he did not suffer limitation from being confined within the body; but, on the contrary, the body was divinized and rendered immortal',[2] thus providing a full and perfect illustration of divine power and justifying the claim: *he that hath seen me, hath seen the Father.*[3]

As for mankind, the consequences of this revelation were no less startling than its character; they are indicated in the assertion that 'the incredible and wonder-working Word of God, bringing light and life . . . imparts to all His own energy'.[4] What this amounts to is nothing less than the prospect of deification for every man. Athanasius recalls the promises recorded by St. Peter and St. John: *that you may become partakers of the divine nature;* and, *to as many as received him, he gave authority to become children of God.*[5] He recalls also the query of the Apostle: *do you not know that you are temples of the living God?* The passages in which Athanasius adverts to this assurance are too numerous to mention.[6] To him it constitutes the real significance of the incarnation. As such, its implications may be stated briefly as follows: (1) οὐ φυσικὴν εἶναι τὴν ἁμαρτίαν—to sin is not a necessity of nature; (2) ἐλεύθερον τὸ φρόνημα—the spirit is free. In the acceptance of these propositions lies the possibility that our human nature may be redeemed from animality, 'that we, not being merely clay, may not revert to clay, but that, being joined with the Word from heaven, we may through Him be brought to heaven'; or, otherwise, that 'we may transcend and divinize our humanity, using it as an instrument for the energizing and illumination of the divine within'.[7] We are thus to think of ourselves no longer either as mechanisms or organisms, but as persons, endued with latent spiritual powers to be activated through the indwelling Word, by virtue of which we may share

[1] 32. [2] *De Decretis*, 14. [3] *Orat.* i. 16.
[4] *Contra Gentes*, 44. [5] *Orat.* i. 16 and 43.
[6] See esp. ibid. i. 51; ii. 10, 47, 55; iii. 19, 25, 33, 34, 40, 53.
[7] iii. 33 and 53.

the divine nature. In this way we are rendered immortal or, as Athanasius prefers to say, immune from destruction (ἄφθαρτοι), the intellectual and moral phthisis of the natural man.

In this brief and imperfect sketch we have sought to comprehend the elements of a position which was developed in great detail during many years of stormy controversy. But enough has been said to indicate that, in all essential respects, it marks a radical departure from classical ways of thought. To the classical precept 'remember to think of yourself as a mere man' (ἀνθρώπινα φρονεῖν) it opposed the promise of deification for humanity. And, while Classicism rejected the possibility of apotheosis, except for the hero or superman, this possibility was now extended to all who believed in Christ. For the one, such apotheosis depended upon the possession of inherent virtue. For the other, it was to be accomplished, not through the development of intrinsic qualities of surpassing excellence, but by submission to a law superior to that of nature. How vast was the difference represented by these conflicting claims may perhaps be illustrated by reference to a well-known utterance on the part of one who still, in the fourth century after Christ, ranked as among the most reputable of the 'ancient theologians'.[1]

'One is the race of men and Gods, from a single mother Earth we both derive the breath of life. Yet a power wholly sundered divides us, so that the one is nothing while, for the other, the brazen heaven endures as an abiding place secure for ever. And yet we mortals have some affinity either in mind or nature with the immortals; albeit we know not to what goal, by day or night, fate hath ordained our course.'

Profound, however, as was the gulf which separated the thought of Athanasius from that of Classicism, or from any of the various types of Christianity which sought to compromise with the classical spirit, it was, nevertheless, in the form advocated by him that the Christian faith was destined to ultimate triumph, more particularly in the West.

To say this is not to imply that the West itself had nothing to add to Christian theology; for, as has already been suggested, it was destined to make a characteristic contribution with regard to the third *hypostasis* of the Trinity by deepening and enriching the doctrine of the Spirit. Nevertheless, the lines on which its thought was to develop were, in the Athanasian sense, strictly

Catholic; and for evidence of the truth of this statement it is only necessary to consult the works of Ambrose of Milan. In these works may be seen the fruits of the victory secured for orthodoxy at Nicaea as well as of the elaboration of orthodox doctrine accomplished by Athanasius himself.

In considering Ambrose as a representative Western churchman it is necessary to remember that he possessed the defects of his qualities. A typical product of the secular order, schooled in the ancient disciplines of *Romanitas*, he had been snatched in middle life from the duties of civil administration to be transformed, suddenly and with apparent reluctance, into a bishop. It is not surprising, therefore, that he carried with him into his new vocation something of the attitude and outlook characteristic of the imperial aristocrat and public official. Moreover, as bishop, he was by force of circumstances occupied largely with the burning issues of Church and State canvassed during the Theodosian age; and this fact, coupled with the pressure of routine episcopal duties, served to confirm in him the habits of a man of action rather than those of a profound or original thinker. Accordingly, his service was not so much perhaps to the intellectual, as to the communal and institutional, life of the Church. To this he made a twofold contribution through the development of a hymnology in which the majesty of Latin verse was invoked to bring *ordo* and *plebs* together in praise of the Creator,[1] and by leadership which, if not invariably wise, was at any rate bold, effective, and transparently honest.

It is in strict accordance with such a temperament that, in the field of theory, the chief distinction of Ambrose should have been as an exponent of Christian ethics: a subject to which he gave his attention, not merely in the *De Officiis*, but also in shorter studies such as the *De Virginitate*, as well as in many of the *Letters*. Space unfortunately forbids any detailed examination of these works; but, with regard to them, one or two general observations may be pertinent. The *De Officiis* has been described as a curious blend of Stoic and Christian principles; although, in some respects such, for instance, as the attitude to rent and interest, its spirit is reminiscent of Hebrew wisdom rather than classical science and most, if not all, the illustrations employed are drawn from Biblical sources. On this level, however, the work is characterized not less by an impassioned

[1] Aug. *Confess.* ix. vii. 15.

puritanism than by a sturdy common sense, in which a reasoned view of the good to be achieved holds in leash the vagrant sentiments and emotions. From this point of view it represents a marked departure from the temper of Lactantian or Constantinian ethical theory. In form, the *De Officiis* is consciously and deliberately Ciceronian; yet it differs in two essential respects from the ethics of humanism. The first is that, in the Catholic *arché*, it has a fixed and definite starting-point; thus, for it, piety, devotion to, and reverence for God, rather than self-realization or adjustment to social demands, constitutes the spring of conduct and the source of duty. In the second place, it involves a recognition of the part played by divine grace in determining the will of believers. It is this fact, rather than any disposition to compromise with secularism, which accounts for the existence of a so-called 'double standard' of morality in Ambrosian ethics. In this connexion it may be observed that the double standard is not final; for, throughout, grace is depicted, not as a denial of nature, but as its fulfilment. With respect to this point, the attitude of Ambrose may, perhaps, be illustrated by reference to the *De Virginitate*. In this work chastity is described as a triumph over the lusts of the flesh, signalizing utter emancipation from physical desire; as such, it is a 'gift of grace' to which none but the very few may aspire. But this, he goes on to declare, implies no disparagement of marriage, to condemn which (as the heretics do) is to condemn the birth of children and the fellowship of the human race, prolonged through a series of successive generations. Moreover, though on a less exalted plane than chastity, matrimony involves a discipline of its own: marry, he says, and weep.[1]

As a moralist, Ambrose was profoundly impressed with the evils to be apprehended from apostasy;[2] and, because of the perils to which the faithful were exposed through contact with the world, he was convinced of the necessity for keeping them, so to speak, a race apart. This he saw as one of the main duties of leadership within the organized Church. A letter addressed to Vigilius, who had just been elevated to the episcopate, in response to a request from the latter for advice, may be accepted as embodying the principles which governed his own policy as bishop. In this letter[3] he urges upon Vigilius the duty of hos-

---

[1] Op. cit. 6 ; see also *Ep.* lxiii. 107.
[2] *Ep.* lxiii to the church at Vercellae.   [3] *Ep.* xix.

pitality, at the same time warning him not to allow the faithful to enter upon marriages with unbelievers and, so far as possible, to keep the people from fraud and usury. But the most serious of these warnings is that which concerns mixed marriages. Citing the story of Samson and Delilah, he asks how it is possible to speak of marriage where there exists no community of belief. In the attitude thus expressed by Ambrose may be seen something of the protective spirit which has become traditional in the Roman Church.

It would be unjust, however, to describe the attitude of Ambrose towards his flock as merely protective; for, throughout his ethical teachings, he insists upon the necessity of a proper intention on the part of the subject. 'It is not enough', he declares, 'to wish well, we must also do well; and it is not enough to do well, unless from the source of a good will.'[1] In other words, there is ultimately but one standard in terms of which conduct can be appraised and that is its spiritual value.

It was an acute awareness of this fact which inspired Ambrose both as ecclesiastical statesman and religious leader. For he saw the organized Church as, in at least two senses, a distinctive embodiment of the spiritual order: it was trustee for the 'oracles of God', and it was custodian of the sacraments. From this standpoint Ambrose pressed its claims upon the emperor Gratian in the essay entitled *De Fide*. The essay begins with a definition of the faith according to the Nicene formula, together with certain observations on the unity of the Godhead.[2] This is followed by a long statement of various Arian heresies with respect to the second *hypostasis* of the Trinity.[3] These heresies raise questions which, according to Ambrose, are to be settled not by argument or disputation, but by reference to the Scriptures, the apostles, the prophets, and Christ.[4] After this introduction the writer proceeds with a positive statement of the Nicene position, in which he repeats the now conventional Catholic doctrine supported by the conventional arguments, without comment or criticism that may be identified as his own. But if this be true with regard to the first and second persons of the Trinity, the same can hardly be said of his treatment of the third. For, in the brief essay, *De Spiritu Sancto*, Ambrose develops a theory of the Holy Spirit as the principle whereby

---

[1] *De Officiis*, i. 30.   [2] i. 1–4.   [3] i. 5.   [4] i. 6.

human life is sanctified, a theory which, as compared for instance with Tertullian's views of the Paraclete, is distinctively Catholic. As such, this essay stands in intimate relationship with a third, the *De Mysteriis*, in which he discusses the sacraments as the means of grace, emphasizing the function of the organized church and priesthood in ministering, through them, to the spiritual needs of men. In so doing, he looks back once more to Athanasius; but, in an even more significant sense, he points forward to Augustine.

For if it be true to say that, with Ambrose, we see the social ideals of *Romanitas* reconsecrated to a new end, it may with equal truth be asserted that the task of Augustine was to reconsecrate its philosophy. Augustine has commonly been regarded as a Neoplatonist, who advocated, in the name of Christianity, a form of Plotinian doctrine vulgarized and watered down for popular consumption. This view, which is to all intents and purposes that of W. R. Inge,[1] has been elaborated by Alfaric, who contends that, for Augustine, Christ was the Plato of the masses and concludes that, if Plato came to life with Plotinus, Plotinus in turn came to life in Augustine.[2] It is to be noted that, according to Alfaric, this applies more particularly to the second period of his intellectual development. In the third, he arrived at a peculiar form of Catholicism which can only be described as Augustinian.[3]

The basis for this opinion lies in the undoubted affinities between Christianity and Platonism, affinities of which Augustine himself was fully aware. In this connexion we may call attention to the generous terms in which he speaks of Plato; although this may well be merely the compliment which he pays to an old schoolmaster. Both in the *Confessions* and elsewhere, he carefully acknowledges the help which he has received from Platonic sources in his quest for truth; as, for instance, where he credits Plato with discovering the immateriality of God.[4] Moreover, in the essay on *True Religion*, he observes that, in order to convert the Platonists, all that was needed was the modification of a few words and formulae.[5]

Few as they were, however, the points at issue between

---

[1] Op. cit.   [2] Alfaric, *L'Évolution intellectuelle de St. Augustin*, vol. i, p. 525.
[3] Preface, p. viii.
[4] *Conf.* vii. xx. 26; *De Civ. Dei*, viii. 6: 'nullum corpus esse deum'.
[5] *De Vera Relig.* iv. 7.

Christianity and Platonism were fundamental; otherwise they could hardly have served to create the difference between the Plotinian *Platonopolis* or Julian's hellenized republic on the one hand and, on the other, the Augustinian *Civitas Dei*. But, in order to understand the reason for this difference, it is necessary to examine, however inadequately, the work of Augustine. To do so should make it apparent that, so far from neutralizing Christianity with Platonism, Augustine appropriated such elements of this and other existing philosophies as suited his purpose, in order to build them into the system which bears his name.

In seeking to describe the 'greatness' of Augustine, the author of the biography in Hastings, *Encyclopedia of Religion and Ethics*, ascribes to him a significant contribution to Catholic theology, pre-eminently as the 'doctor of grace'; while, at the same time, he regards him as the spiritual ancestor of Protestantism, considered, on its dogmatic side, as a triumph for the doctrine that grace is 'free'. To Augustine, also, he attributes the origin of Platonic Christianity, which embodies a mysticism derived from Plato as opposed to Aristotelian rationalism. Besides this, Augustine is credited with having inspired, through the *De Civitate Dei*, conceptions underlying the Medieval Church and empire; in confirmation of which it is recorded that Charlemagne habitually slept with a copy of this work beneath his pillow. As though this were not enough, it is supposed also that he influenced the development of Cartesianism, with its basis in 'clear and distinct ideas'; while, through his 'romanticism', his 'self-assured subjectivity', and his 'penetrating psychological insight', he anticipated certain distinctive aspects of what is called modernism. Finally, he is said to have been the first thinker to undertake a philosophy of history.

By thus revealing something of what posterity has discovered in Augustine, this statement excites attention as to the source of such extraordinary influence. Interest in this question has, of course, been immensely greater on the Continent than in Great Britain or America; but, among English references to Augustine, the following may be accepted as representative. Gibbon, who regards him as typical of the forces making for the subversion of antiquity, declares in a characteristic footnote[1] that his learning was too often borrowed, his arguments too often his own;

[1] Ch. xxviii, p. 211, n. 86.

and, while admitting an imperfect acquaintance with his work, assesses it as follows:[1]

'according to the judgment of the most impartial critics, the superficial learning of Augustin was confined to the Latin language; and his style, though sometimes animated by the eloquence of passion, is usually clouded by false and affected rhetoric. But he possessed a strong, capacious, argumentative mind; he boldly sounded the dark abyss of grace, predestination, free will, and original sin; and the rigid system of Christianity which he framed or restored, has been entertained with public applause and secret reluctance by the Latin Church';

to which he adds,[2] 'the church of Rome has canonized Augustine and reprobated Calvin. Yet the *real* difference between them is invisible even to a theological microscope.' This may be taken as the verdict of neo-classical naturalism upon one who had done his best to slay the hydra of naturalism in its original classical form. On the other hand, Warde Fowler, speaking as a student of Roman paganism, quotes with approval the opinion of Westcott, who sees in Augustine the conquest of the Christian by the Latin spirit.[3]

'He looked . . . at everything from the side of law and not of freedom; from the side of God, as an irresponsible sovereign, and not of man, as a loving servant. In spite of his admiration for Plato, he was driven by a passion for system (how this reminds us of the old Roman religious lawyers!) to fix, to externalize, to freeze every idea into a rigid shape. In spite of his genius, he could not shake off the influence of a legal and rhetorical training, which controversy called into active exercise.'

In America, modern liberal theology apparently finds Augustine almost wholly unintelligible.

'In his doctrine of God and man and sin and grace, the curious combination of mystic piety, Neoplatonic philosophy, Manichean dualism, Christian tradition, strained exegesis, rigorous logic and glaring inconsistencies born of religious instincts and moral needs, can hardly be matched in the history of human thought.'[4]

On the other hand, American humanism has no hesitation in denouncing him for what, to it, is a very obvious reason.

'The intellect was not only put in its proper subordinate place but

[1] Ch. xxxiii, p. 407 and n. 33.   [2] Footnote 31.
[3] *The Religious Experience of the Roman People*, p. 458.
[4] A. C. MacGiffert, *A History of Christian Thought*, vol. ii, pp. 98–9.

brought under positive suspicion. The way was opened for obscurantism. Man was humbled and his will regenerated, but more
or less at the expense of the critical spirit.'[1]

Finally, by those who, in reaction from the pragmatic and
positivist tendencies of contemporary American thinking, reassert the claims of reason, the Augustinian vision of historical
process is found inadmissible.

'The attempt to derive theologico-ethical values from history
begins with Augustine . . . but, without doing injustice to his powerful intellect, we may safely say that the attempt to make the facts of
history prove the truth or validity of Christian ethics is convincing
only to those who are determined to be convinced beforehand.'[2]

The diversity of these opinions may serve, perhaps, to emphasize the many-sided and elusive character of Augustinianism,
but it also suggests a problem of understanding. To this problem modern psychology has come forward with a characteristic solution. Thus, for William James, Augustine represents
the classical example of discordant personality.[3]

'You all remember', he declares, 'his half-pagan, half-Christian
bringing-up at Carthage, his emigration to Rome and Milan, his
adoption of Manicheism and subsequent scepticism, and his restless
search for truth and purity of life; and finally how, distracted by his
own weakness of will when so many others whom he knew and
knew of had thrown off the shackles of sensuality and dedicated
themselves to chastity and the higher life, he heard a voice in the
garden say, *sume, lege*; and, opening the Bible at random, he saw the
text, "not in chambering and wantonness, etc.," which seemed
directly sent to his address, and laid the inner storm to rest forever.
Augustine's psychological genius has given an account of the trouble
of having a divided self which has never been surpassed . . . "the new
will which I began to have" etc., . . . There could be no more perfect
description of the divided will, when the higher wishes lack just that
last acuteness, that touch of explosive intensity, that dynamo-genic
quality (to use the slang of the psychologists) that enables them to
burst their shell and to make the inruption efficaciously into life and
quell the lower tendencies forever.'

This method of interpretation tends to become more and
more purely subjective and esoteric until, in its more recent
manifestations, Augustine is depicted as the victim of a diseased

---

[1] Babbitt, *Democracy and Leadership*, p. 177.
[2] M. Cohen, *Reason and Nature*, p. 377.
[3] *The Varieties of Religious Experience*, p. 171–3.

psyche, finding, in his devotion to mother Church, compensation for a passion morbidly fixed upon the memory of Monica,
his mother. But, in a less extravagant form, Augustine's vision
of the two cities, formerly understood as the projection of contemporary political and ecclesiastical issues, becomes in fact a
reflection of unresolved tensions within his own soul, the inner
history of which is represented as one of incessant turmoil and
strife.

Now Augustine would be the last to deny the element of truth
contained in these assertions, the genesis of which may, indeed,
be traced remotely to his own way of thought; since he himself
was among the first to insist upon the vital importance of experience in determining the attitude and outlook of men and,
in the constitution of experience, he stressed the role played by
the instinctive and unconscious, the *irrationabiles motus* of the
turbulent human spirit.[1] The difficulty, then, lies not so much
in the method as in its abuse. It has been applied in an arbitrary
and unscientific fashion, with the result that certain incidents
of Augustine's life have been magnified and distorted, to the
exclusion or neglect of others which possess a much more evident significance. For to study that life as a whole is to perceive
that the one insatiable passion of Augustine was a passion for
truth; that this should have been so and that it should have
been, ultimately, the determining factor in his career, becomes
obvious the moment one considers him in relation to the time of
crisis in which he lived.

Augustine was born into a world the perplexities of which
have probably never been exceeded by any period, before or
since, in human history. Behind him lay more than a millennium of sustained endeavour, during which men had laboured
to realize the classical idea of the commonwealth; and almost
four centuries had elapsed since Vergil had declared that the
problem had finally been solved by the genius of Rome. But
for over a century prior to the birth of Augustine, *Romanitas* had
been suffering from a chronic debility, and nothing which
political activity could achieve seemed capable of restoring its
original vigour. It thus became possible for Ambrose, in a letter
of condolence modelled on that addressed by Servius Sulpicius
to Cicero, to copy the phraseology used by him in portraying
the desolation of Hellas and, with the mere substitution of local

---

[1] *De Civ. Dei,* ii. 1.

place-names, to apply it *verbatim* to Vergil's Italy. Meanwhile, as the evidences of internal decay multiplied on every hand, a succession of overwhelming military disasters proclaimed the fact that the strength of the Colossus was undermined, his power of resistance all but extinguished.

In this atmosphere Augustine passed his youth and early manhood. Born in 354, under Constantius, a few months after his costly victory over Magnentius at Mursa and before the appointment of Julian as Caesar in Gaul, he was ten years old at the time of Julian's defeat and death in Mesopotamia, and the fatal battle of Adrianople occurred when he was twenty-one. To a boy reared in the remote and relatively secure province of Africa, these far-off incidents upon the Northern and Eastern frontiers doubtless meant little, except for the intensified financial pressure which they occasioned throughout the empire; but this must have been felt within the household of Augustine, since his father was one of those impoverished *curiales* on whose shoulders the economic burden chiefly fell, and it was only by the generous assistance of a wealthy neighbour that he found the sums necessary for his son's education. However, by 382, early in the reign of Gratian, Valentinian II, and Theodosius, Augustine, having passed successfully through the schools of Thagaste, Madaura, and Carthage, was established as a teacher of rhetoric in the provincial metropolis when, conscious of his superior abilities and wearying of the local atmosphere, he risked the experiment of emigrating to Italy. There, after a few months spent in the ancient capital, he was appointed to the chair of rhetoric in the Imperial city of Milan (383).

Academic distinction such as this was not to be achieved without painstaking effort. Already as a boy of nineteen, Augustine was immersed in the philosophic dialogues of Cicero, whom he was later to describe as a mere *philosophaster*;[1] but, the speculative faculty once aroused, nothing could quench the ardour of his search for truth, beauty, and goodness. He thus read widely in the accessible authors and, as a critical examination of his sources indicates, acquired a thorough knowledge of Latin, as well as some acquaintance with Greek literature, the latter gleaned mainly through the medium of translations.[2] In this connexion it should be noted that the quest of Augustine

---

[1] Ibid. 27. Welldon (*ad loc.*) accepts this as 'undoubtedly the true reading'.
[2] Alfaric, op. cit.; Combès, *St. Augustin et la culture classique*.

was inspired by no mere scholarly *curiositas* but by a sense of the urgent need for a personal rule of life. That he was profoundly conscious of such a need is suggested by the fact that, while still in Carthage, he was attracted to Manicheism, the tenets of which he did not finally renounce until his thirty-first year; just as, during his stay at Rome and Milan, he energetically explored the various current forms of Platonism until, ultimately, he came under the influence of Catholicism as represented by Ambrose. The increasingly acute mental and spiritual activity marked by these interests culminated in 386 in the crisis of his conversion. This event served to reverse the whole course of his career. Devoting himself to the life of religion, Augustine resigned his academic post to return to his native province, with which his fortunes were thenceforth to be associated as monk (386), priest (390), and bishop (395); his elevation to the see of Hippo coinciding with the death of Theodosius and the accession of Arcadius and Honorius. Augustine thus entered upon his life-work just as twilight descended upon the Western Empire.

The year of Augustine's conversion marks the beginning of an immense literary productivity which continued without interruption as long as he lived and which, apart from voluminous correspondence and more than five hundred (extant) sermons, consisted mainly of philosophic studies and polemics. The former exhibit the mental processes by which he overcame difficulties such as those presented by Manicheism, Academic scepticism, and Neoplatonism, and thus succeeded in defining his own position. In the latter he sets himself with indefatigable energy to defend that position by a refutation of current heresies in the light of an expanding vision of Christian truth. These documents thus constitute the best possible evidence for his intellectual history. As such, they reach a fitting conclusion in the *Retractations*, a work composed within a few months of his death (430).

In the autobiography of Augustine the *Retractations* must be accepted as a necessary complement to the *Confessions*, the record of his thought and activity as a mature man thus following upon that of his earlier years, the period of his formation. To those who regard that life as one of violent repressions and bitter theological strife, the tone of this work must come as a surprise. For, with it, the intoxication of discovery, the fury and heat of controversy have been succeeded by unruffled calm. With a curious and disarming candour, the product of a detachment amounting almost to selflessness, Augustine surveys the development of his mind as he sees it mirrored in the works of forty-two years. And what he therein discerns is a progressive emancipation from pagan ideology, the *pessima consuetudo* of thought and expression in which he had grown up.[1] Such emancipation could not but have been gradual, and it was marked on occasion by lapses into Classicism, especially in his less mature work. But, so far from attempting to conceal such lapses or to 'reconcile' earlier positions with those assumed later, Augustine, with strict fidelity to truth, does his utmost to expose them to the light. Exact to the point of meticulousness, he regrets the admission to certain of his essays of terms such as *fortuna, casus, naturae necessitas*, as implying a denial of absolute providence; just as, in repudiating the use even in jest of a word like *omen*, he urges the need of a purged and purified language to clothe the new way of thought.[2]

But while, by his own admission, Augustine was slow to perceive the more remote implications of his conversion, it is none the less evident that the experience at Cassiciacum constituted a real turning-point in his life. What it gave him was the light necessary to perceive the deficiencies of Classicism. By the same light, however, he was enabled to recognize the element of truth which it contained. He was thus in a position to resume, in the spirit of Plato but from a fresh standpoint and with fresh resources, the long-neglected attempt at a synthesis of experience; and, quite apart from the question of its finality, there can be little doubt that his work resulted in a fuller and more adequate knowledge of man and of his universe than anything of which Classicism had proved capable. From this point of view, the progress of his thinking may well be described in the words of Alfaric: 'sa vie intellectuelle se présente comme une lente ascension vers des sommets qui toujours se dérobent.' Thus, if his findings have assumed the character of a rigid and inflexible system, in this respect he has suffered a fate common to all seminal thinkers, his mere authority having resulted in a substitution of the letter for the spirit of his doctrine. In his case, however, this fate is the more cruel since, as opposed to other systems, it was precisely the character of the new

[1] *Retract. Prologue.* [2] i. 1. 2.

arché that it made possible the growth and development of thought.

It is in this, rather than in any narrowly 'theological' sense, that the famous *fides quaerens intellectum* must be understood as the guiding maxim of his life. In a world, the moral and intellectual foundations of which appeared to have been shattered, he clung doggedly to a faith that, however 'vicious' or defective in principle, the secular effort of mankind had not been wholly in vain; and he was determined not to resign himself, like so many of his contemporaries, to the cult of futility. But, as such futility seemed to be the logical outcome of Classicism, this fact inspired a revolt, not merely from the nihilism of the Academics, but from the spirit of Graeco-Roman *scientia* as a whole. In the case of Augustine, however, the revolt was not from scepticism to animal faith, a primitivism sustained by an arbitrary 'will to believe'. Despite superficial resemblances, the *De Utilitate Credendi* represents in no sense an anticipation of modern pragmatism. For, in the Trinity, he discovered a principle capable of saving the reason as well as the will, and thus redeeming human personality as a whole. It saved the reason because, while denying its pretensions to omniscience and infallibility, it nevertheless affirmed the existence of an order of truth and value which, being *in* the world as well as beyond it, was within the power of man to apprehend. And, in saving the reason, at the same time it saved the will, by imparting to it that element of rationality without which it must degenerate into mere subjective wilfulness. By so doing it provided desperately needed grounds of reassurance to the sense of selfhood, defeated by its failure to meet the Socratic challenge, together with a fresh vindication of the ideals and aspirations of the classical peoples. This, however, was to present the faith in a light which, to judge from Julian's identification of Christianity with barbarism, must have been relatively unfamiliar to the fourth century. It was to reassert the Pauline attitude and, by offering it as a gospel addressed to the wise no less than to the simple, to recommend it as a specific for the needs of civilized man.

Herein we may perceive the affiliations of Augustine with the classical and especially with the Latin spirit. For, in tracing the flaws of *Romanitas* to the acceptance of a defective *arché*, he implied that what was needed to rehabilitate the system was a radical revision of first principles; and this he proposed to his countrymen as the real fulfilment of the Roman promise. From this point of view, he was as Latin as old Cato himself; and his work was beyond question intended as a tract for the times.

'It is here', he declares, 'that the safety of an admirable state resides; for a society can neither be ideally founded nor maintained unless upon the basis and by the bond of faith and strong concord, when the object of love is the universal good which in its highest and truest character is God Himself, and when men love one another with complete sincerity in Him, and the ground of their love for one another is the love of Him from whose eyes they cannot conceal the spirit of their love.'[1]

In thus urging a recognition of Christian principles as the one true foundation for a new science of politics, Augustine revealed a faith that, notwithstanding all appearances, those principles were supreme in the physical world.

But to assert the supremacy of the Christian law cannot properly be represented as 'an attempt to derive theologico-ethical values from history'. For this would have been to reduce that law to the level of mere scientific induction, i.e. to the terms of a discarded ideology. And it cannot be too strongly insisted that, with respect to the fundamentals of faith and morals, the approach of Christianity was not inductive. Of this fact Augustine was fully cognizant. Thus, in undertaking to celebrate the glories of the celestial city, he declares that he writes primarily for the encouragement of sympathetic and understanding readers. For the rest, no amount of argument would suffice to ensure conviction; since this is at bottom a matter of insight rather than of knowledge, and such insight is denied to those who remain wilfully blind to the truth.[2] It is, indeed, possible to envisage the universe in either of two ways, with or without the eyes of a Christian; the results in each case being apparent.[3] But, to the Christian mystic no such alternatives present themselves; for him there can be no more doubt about the existence and nature of God than there is of his own. It thus becomes inevitable that, as his spiritual perceptions are sharpened, he should come to perceive the *operatio Dei* in every phase of his own life. It is equally inevitable that, as he contemplates the world, he should catch in it a vision

---

[1] *Ep.* 137. 17 *ad Volusianum.*
[2] *De Civ. Dei*, ii. 1: 'nimia caecitas, obstinatissima pervicacia'.
[3] xxii. 22 and 24.

of the Divine Society which, though destined to ultimate triumph, subsists as yet by faith and like a foreign element, so to speak, in a community of unbelievers.[1] Such was the experience of Augustine, as it was to find expression in two of his greatest works, the *Confessions* (*circa* 397) and the *City of God* (413–26).

It has been asserted that the *Confessions* represent no more than a conclusion from the Augustinian doctrine of original sin, falsely presented in the form of a personal experience.[2] But it is one thing to say that Augustine saw his past in the light of a fully matured theory of human nature; it is quite another to suggest that, in so doing, he consciously or unconsciously falsified the record. To suppose that this was the case is to overlook the fact that, already in this work, Augustine exhibits to a marked degree those qualities of detachment, of close and accurate observation which have been noted as characteristic of the *Retractations*. It is also to forget that, whatever its defects, the picture which he offers of evolving experience sets a wholly new standard in autobiography.

It is indeed a suggestive truth that, in more than a thousand years of literary history, the Graeco-Roman world had failed to produce anything which might justly be called a personal record; in this sense, Augustine was perhaps anticipated only by the emperor Marcus Aurelius.[3] But the differences between the *Confessions* and the *Meditations* are not less remarkable than the resemblance between them. They are epitomized in the fact that, while the work of Augustine was addressed to God, that of Aurelius was addressed to himself. In the *Meditations* the shadow of the great man lies for ever across the page. A scion of the imperial household, favoured by every circumstance of heredity and environment, he studies by the constant exercise of Stoic virtue to realize the qualities of temperance, courage, prudence, and justice which will fit him for the role of citizen-prince; and, in that capacity, he exhibits the herculean energy expected of one whose duty is to guard the trust reposed in him, striving to maintain the order prescribed by classical reason against the turbulent forces of change. The *Confessions*, on the

---

[1] i, *praefatio*: 'gloriosissima civitas Dei . . . in hoc temporum cursu . . . inter impios peregrinatur ex fide vivens.'   [2] Alfaric, op. cit. p. 57.
[3] And, in his own day, by Julian the Apostate. See Bidez, *L'Empereur Julien*, Introduction and p. 60. Cicero, of course, never intended to give himself away as he did in the *Letters*.

other hand, are marked by a naive simplicity; they betray not the most remote suggestion of pretension or priggishness. The story they tell is that of a boy born, not to the purple, but to a relatively humble station in life, the offspring of an unequal marriage between a hard-working citizen of an African municipality and a presumably better-class woman, whose well-meaning but ineffective efforts at maternal guidance were redeemed only by the tenderness of her concern for her son.[1] Unlike the emperor again, the saint was cast for no fixed and clearly-defined role. Given the conventional literary education, he was launched upon the moving sea of life, there to lose all sense of direction until, 'by the pity, mercy, and help of God', he finally came to anchor in religion. Aurelius, as well as Augustine, combines passages of description and analysis with those of devotion. The one, in a spirit of generous recognition for favours received, offers dutiful, if somewhat perfunctory, acknowledgement to the gods who, together with his parents, have helped to make him what he is; the other pauses at frequent intervals in the process of self-examination, that he may render heartfelt thanks to the power which has revealed him to himself, or that he may utter burning invocations for continued guidance and support. Such differences are far from accidental; they point to the gulf which separates the mentality of the classical from that of the Christian humanist. The former is concerned never to expose a weakness, remembering that it is his business to exemplify so far as possible the conventional type of excellence enshrined in the heroic ideal. The latter is content to defy every canon of Classicism in order merely to bear witness to the truth. Accordingly, the one produces a text-book of virtue, to be admired and imitated by a Julian;[2] while the other achieves a record so fresh and vivid as to have moved William James to describe him as the 'first modern man'; the picture of a concrete human being in whose presence the barriers of time and space drop away to reveal him as one in all respects akin to ourselves; a being so far unique in history, yet clothed with the common graces and disgraces of mankind.

To have done no more than write the *Confessions* would be to prove that what came to life in Augustine was neither Plato nor Plotinus but Augustine himself. It would also be to suggest that his philosophy was quite as much an expression of that self as

[1] Op. cit. iii. xii. 21.   [2] See Ch. VII, above, p. 264.

any other aspect of his experience. The incidents which he recounts are, perhaps, sufficiently familiar. But it may be noted that, in recording them, the author makes a discovery of fundamental importance, viz. that experience is both continuous and cumulative. It is continuous in the sense that, from the most primitive and rudimentary indications of consciousness to its highest and fullest manifestations, it involves a progressive unfolding of the so-called faculties without *saltus* or break. It thus begins, in the new-born infant, with elementary motions such as reaction to light, followed by a gradual establishment of location in space and contact with the immediate environment; and this the infant accomplishes in a fashion peculiarly his own: 'iactabam et membra et voces, signa similia voluntatibus meis'.[1] From such beginnings, he presently develops the less generalized and more specific characteristics of the human ego; especially as there dawns upon him a sense that 'in ordered and coherent utterance' effective communication becomes possible with the outside world: *puer loquens eram*.[2] With the discovery and perfection of this means of self-expression, the child is 'launched more deeply into the stormy intercourse of human life'. But, if such development is continuous, it is also cumulative; for it is marked by a constant carry-over of impressions and feelings from the past into the present, as the mere process of living calls into play the mysterious forces of imagination, memory, and recollection.[3] Thus it is that, however transitory and fleeting, each 'moment' of experience somehow enters into and remains, if obscurely, within the constitution of the whole. It is likewise to be noted that every single one of these moments has a certain emotional content, a 'value' of pleasure or pain, of satisfaction or distress. These also, the *affectiones animi* as Augustine calls them, are retained within 'the spacious palace of memory', to be evoked on occasion 'not as the mind felt them at the moment of experience but otherwise, according to a power of its own'. 'For without rejoicing I remember myself to have joyed; without sorrow I recollect bygone sorrows. That I was once afraid I recall without fear; and without desire am reminded of desires past.'[4] Nevertheless, since 'that which all men will is happiness, and there is none who altogether wills it not',[5] the values thus established play their part in fixing the

---

[1] *Conf.* i. vii. 11; cf. *De Civ. Dei*, xi. 2.   [2] *Conf.* i. viii. 13.
[3] x. viii. 12 foll.   [4] x. xiv. 21.   [5] x. xx. 29.

norms of appetition and aversion which go to make up a characteristic mode or pattern of behaviour.

Thus with Augustine each individual human being is envisaged as a centre of radiant energy. Born into a world of contacts, he presently develops a whole tissue of external relationships, but the 'subject' is not on that account to be resolved into any or all of the relationships thus established. On the contrary, it accepts the raw material of sense-perception streaming in through the various channels; recording, sorting, and assessing it in the light of standards which mature with maturing experience, only to make it the basis of further demands upon what appear to be the available sources of satisfaction. From this standpoint, the different so-called faculties may all be considered as functions of will. Thus regarded, the apparently spasmodic and mechanical reactions of the infant, tossing himself about and giving vent to incoherent sounds, may be accepted as evidence of incipient volition, destined as such to find expression in the consolidated dispositions and aptitudes of the adult man. As he elsewhere puts it, *quid sumus nisi voluntates?*

It thus becomes apparent that, so far as concerns the human animal, the problem of life is a problem of consciousness. But, if so, the question arises: in what is consciousness to discover the fullest measure of satisfaction? This question is not gratuitous; but, in view of the multifarious possibilities offered by life and of the consequent necessity for discrimination, it presents itself as inescapable. It is, indeed, true that, in some degree, the spirit of man finds gratification on what may be called the lower planes of acceptance. Life itself has a natural sweetness, as Augustine observes in agreement with Aristotle; and the mere exercise of the vital functions such as eating and sleeping, if unimpeded, is attended by a relatively innocuous, though hardly exalted, pleasure. But it is none the less evident that, for the normally constituted human being, the demands of consciousness are not completely fulfilled on those levels of life which he shares with brute creation; and it is equally certain that those demands cannot permanently be denied. This being so, there remains the insistent problem of how, in the last analysis, they are to be met. To this problem Augustine proposes three possible solutions, the merits of which he canvasses in turn.

The first and perhaps the most obvious of these solutions is that life itself is the answer to its own problems; and to this theory Augustine, in his adolescence and early manhood, appears to have subscribed. Judged by modern standards, this part of his career is hardly to be described as flaming youth. Nevertheless, it would be a mistake to underestimate the possibilities for self-indulgence afforded by life in Roman Africa. According to the *Confessions*, the period was characterized by a passion for experimentation, in flat defiance of all external guidance and restraint; the desire, as he puts it, to be scraped by the touch of objects of sense.[1] To this desire he gave free rein in the conventional misdemeanours of student life at Carthage, when he 'walked the streets of Babylon and wallowed in the mire thereof'. It found expression chiefly in a 'miserable madness' for stage-plays, as well as in a series of vagrant and ephemeral loves; in pursuit of which he cast off the inhibitions of childhood, deliberately adopting the principle of living dangerously. 'Safety I hated and a way without snares.'

It goes without saying that Augustine's subsequent repudiation of this principle was complete and unequivocal. But it must not be supposed that, in rejecting it, he rejected in its entirety the life of sense. For, as against the Manicheans, he held tenaciously to the doctrine that there was no intrinsic evil in what is called 'matter'. And, with equal vigour, he denied the idealist contention that material existence is involved in necessary ambiguities and contradictions, from which escape becomes possible only in the life of pure 'form'. He does, indeed, argue that materialism accepted as a philosophic principle leads to a disastrous confusion of values as 'out of the muddy concupiscence of the flesh mists rise up to becloud and benight the heart'.[2] But, from the Trinitarian standpoint, the reason is that this implies a 'heresy', the heresy of accepting the mere intensity or duration of an experience as the sole gauge of its value. This is by no means to exclude these factors as criteria; Augustine was, indeed, to discover that, measured thereby, the love of God, which is the love of truth, beauty, and goodness, far exceeds that of any other possible source of satisfaction. It does, however, suggest that, taken by themselves and in abstraction from quality, they provide a wholly inadequate basis for discrimination. They thus tend to promote a programme of behaviour which, so far from embodying the spon-

[1] *Conf.* iii. i. 1.   [2] iii. ii. 2.

taneity and charm attributed to it by modern romanticism, is merely artificial and, in the end, involves the utter waste of precious human energy.[1] The liberty which it affords is likewise imperfect and precarious; it is a *fugitiva libertas*, the liberty of a runaway slave. For ultimately there is no satisfaction to be discovered merely in motion, apart from an intelligible and worthy goal. It was a conviction of this truth, rather than any morbidly exaggerated sense of guilt, which underlay the remorse of Augustine when he recalled incidents of his boyhood such as the famous theft of the apples. What concerned him was, not so much the enormity, as the utter wantonness and futility of the deed.

It is from this standpoint that we must understand the criticisms levelled by Augustine against specific aspects of his youthful experience; what he has to say, for instance, regarding the theatricals which, in the Carthaginian period, so completely absorbed him.[2] Classical reason, he notes, had sought to rationalize the peculiar form of excitement stimulated by the Graeco-Roman stage and, at the same time, to give it a functional significance in the communal life, by pronouncing it cathartic. But such catharsis, if indeed it exists, is, he argues, of more than dubious value. 'Shall pity', he asks, 'be put away?' To do so is to let off much-needed steam.[3] In his experience, however, the stage-play operated as an irritant rather than as a cathartic; its result, like that of scratching a wound, was a poisonous infection. The same was true, but to an even greater degree, of the *spectacula gladiatoria* which maintained such a hold upon the population of the empire, in which the deep roar of the brutalized multitude, suddenly called forth by the sight of blood, inspired even in the uninitiate a kind of reluctant fascination, so that he gazed with savage and intoxicated glee upon the horrors of the gory pastime.[4] In the *gladiatoria*, the element of tragedy was only too real; but, with respect to the stage-play, what Augustine deplores is its inherent falsity. This falsity depends upon its character as *mimesis* or imitation. The basis of imitation lies in an artificial dissociation of thought and emotion from action, as a result of which 'the auditor is called upon not to relieve, but only to grieve' and 'his pleasure is enhanced by the measure of his grief'.[5] It thus promotes in a

[1] ii. i. 1.   [2] iii. ii. 2, 3, 4.   [3] iii. 3. 3.
[4] vi. viii. 13.   [5] iii. ii. 2.

subtle way the forces of demoralization by stimulating the tragic emotions only to drain them away into the barren sands of inactivity. The same is true, but in a still more damaging sense, of irresponsible amatory adventure, which gives rise merely to a fluctuating heat barren of foresight, *vagus ardor inops prudentiae*, thus prostituting a natural function to an ignoble end.[1] And generally, as regards the satisfactions to be obtained on this level, the conclusion is that they fail to disclose any principle of integration capable of giving to them permanent value and significance. Their indulgence, therefore, offends the deep-seated and insistent demand of men for 'wholeness', the relation of means to ends in an ordered life. Accordingly, so long as it exists, there will be need for some kind of external 'law' to impose its restrictions upon the vagaries of the unruly ego.[2]

But if this be so, is it then true to say that the meaning and possibilities of life are fully revealed in the social discipline which is a product of the schools and which embodies, in its highest and noblest manifestation, the spirit of the universal empire? Such discipline was, indeed, far-reaching and pervasive. It had already begun with the spontaneous effort of the infant to communicate with those about him, indicated in 'the motions of the body, the natural language, so to speak, of all mankind'.[3] From this, by an equally natural development, the child proceeded to learn his mother tongue. This he accomplished with comparative ease, not less through the native urge to self-expression than by the kindly encouragement of parents and friends; since, in learning, a 'free curiosity has more force than enforced compulsion'.[4] But, with the attainment of school age, education assumed a formal character, beginning with the elements of reading, writing, and arithmetic, 'that hateful sing-song, two times two makes four', and culminating in the so-called liberal arts, the acquisition of which marked full admission to the community of culture; a whole body of traditional subjects and techniques elaborated, as he says, 'in order to multiply toil and grief upon the sons of Adam'.[5] And, since *Romanitas* was, as we have elsewhere noted, bilingual, these subjects included as an almost essential feature some acquaintance with the sister classical language, 'in which the difficulty of a foreign tongue dashed with gall the sweetness of Grecian fable'.

[1] iv. ii. 2. [2] ii. ii. 3. [3] i. viii. 13.
[4] i. xiv. 23. [5] i. ix. 14.

Consecrated by the usage of centuries, this discipline was recommended to Augustine as the one certain avenue to success in life, *ut in hoc saeculo florerem.*[1] As such, it appeared to him that, while it ought to mean much, it meant in fact very little. Already in the initial stages of his education he was divided between a boyish hatred of study and fear of the master's cane;[2] and since, in the acquisition of knowledge, he placed so high a value upon the operation of spontaneous curiosity, he never quite abandoned his distrust of corporal punishment as an aid to understanding. But of the need for compulsion he was fully conscious; this he attributed largely to a sense of the vanity and boredom of studies in which the schoolboy was 'called upon to weep the death of Dido for love of Aeneas' and, in emphasizing the unreality of such studies, he warned the 'hawkers of grammar-learning to make no outcry' against him.[3] This unreality he ascribed to the power of custom and tradition, an 'almost irresistible torrent' which, in educational practice, meant a disposition to cling to dead subjects and dead ideas.[4] As a consequence, the pages of Vergil were ransacked to provide themes for recitation, declamation, and elocution; such drill being held essential to the development of rhetorical ability. Rhetoric, while loudly advocated for its alleged value in the law-courts and elsewhere, was in reality cherished by its practitioners because of 'their intoxication with the wine of error'; proficiency therein being, in a sense, symbolic of the pride and vainglory of unregenerate man. Yet, such as it was, the training afforded by the schools was not ineffective; for, gradually, the pupil imbibed the false ideals of civilization, the strict conventions of elocution whereby 'to murder the word *human being* became a crime more heinous than murdering a human being himself'; preciosity such as this leading in turn to a contempt for Scripture, on the ground that it was filled with solecisms likely to corrupt the thought and expression of the cultivated citizen of the world. But, while thus successfully promoting the ideal of adjustment, the discipline did little or nothing to root out the incipient vices of pride, vanity, and deceit in which the boy revealed himself as father to the man.[5] In Augustine's own case it was to carry him to the Milanese chair of rhetoric, in the tenure of which, as he says, 'I was to utter many a lie and, lying,

---

[1] i. ix. 14.   [2] i. ix. 15 and xii. 19.
[3] i. xiii, 21, 22.   [4] i. xvi. 25.   [5] i. xviii. 28, 29, 30.

was to be applauded by those who knew I lied'.[1] Less emphatically, perhaps, its ideal was elsewhere stated as 'the desire to please myself and to be pleasing in the eyes of men'.[2]

It may thus be inferred that, regarded as an instrument of liberation, Augustine found the secular education worse than useless; by itself it was like salt water which, so far from slaking, aggravates thirst. But, in his mature judgement, it was not on that account utterly devoid of value. Part of this value was moral; it lay in the habits of obedience and industry inculcated by the course; 'from the master's cane', he says, 'to the martyr's trials'. But, in the main, its value was intellectual and this was twofold. In the first place it helped him to adopt a critical attitude towards much of the pretentious nonsense current in his time and, in particular, to dispose of certain fallacies of Manichean 'science' which, among the credulous, passed for wisdom.[3] But, still more important, it provided him with the solid linguistic foundation indispensable to an intelligent study of truth where this could really be found. Thus, however incidentally and indirectly, it served to promote the knowledge of God.

To say this is to suggest that, for Augustine, the ultimate meaning of experience was to be disclosed on the plane of religion; in the last analysis, he was to understand himself only in terms of Christian truth. But if this be so, it raises a problem of the greatest magnitude; since, for the apprehension of this truth, the prerequisite was Christian insight or *sapientia*, and, in his efforts to attain such insight, the seeker was confronted by an apparently unsurmountable obstacle; he was debarred from it by an *originale vitium*, an inherent deficiency of his nature. This deficiency was already apparent in infancy, in the sins of envy and malice; it was confirmed in childhood, as work and play excited the evils of the competitive spirit and the vainglorious love of praise; finally to become ingrained when, with maturing years, the victim steeped himself in the invisible but heady wine of self-will.[4]

To Augustine, such manifestations were evidence of an expanding egotism which accepts the empirical or contingent self as independent and cherishes it to the exclusion of all else; when the mind, as he puts it, 'deserts that to which it should

[1] vi. vi. 9.   [2] ii. i. 1.
[3] v. iii. 3.   [4] i. vii. 11 and x. 16; ii. iii. 6 and 7.

cleave as its first principle, seeking to become and to be, so to speak, a first principle to itself'.[1] As such they portended utter moral ruin, from which redemption was possible only through the *vestigia Dei* surviving in the human heart.[2] These, in his own case, consisted mainly in a love of truth and some capacity for expression, a vigorous memory, a boyish sense of equity, and the love of friends. For the possession of such powers he claimed no credit; for their perversion or misuse he held himself to blame. As elements of the native endowment they were apportioned among men by divine grace; their abuse was due, not so much to any inherent love of villainy, as to intellectual and moral limitations on the part of the beneficiary, whereby he became incapable of seeing and desiring the ultimate source of good. From this standpoint Catiline himself was not a 'natural killer'; since no one who preserves a shred of sanity wills sheer destruction. His criminality was thus merely an illustration, in an extreme form, of the defective values of secularism.[3] But, asks Augustine, in view of these limitations, what man has the face to ascribe the purity and innocence of his life to the strength of his own powers?[4]

Of such limitations Augustine was deeply and acutely sensible, not least of all in his own case. As an individual he was conscious that his very being was circumscribed by definite bounds of time and space, and that his capacity both for intellectual and moral achievement was not less rigidly conditioned by the circumstances of his birth and upbringing. Nor was he able to discover in the long record of Graeco-Roman experience any solid ground for believing that these limitations might be overcome; secular philosophy was moribund, discredited by its persistent failure to exhibit a good accessible to men, and what passed for religion was a tissue of sham and imposture.[5] From this impasse deliverance was, indeed, possible; but it was to be accomplished, not so much by any effort of his own, as by an act of acceptance. Ultimately he was to find it in a recognition of the God of Athanasius and Ambrose.

With Augustine, however, this consummation was long delayed, for reasons which in retrospect he tries to reveal. Tracing the development of his religious experience he declares that, as a boy, he had learned to think of God (according to his powers)

---

[1] *De Civ. Dei*, xiv. 13.   [2] *Conf.* i. xviii. 31.
[3] ii. v. 11.   [4] ii. vii. 15.   [5] esp. iv, v, vi.

as of some Great One who, though hidden from our senses, could nevertheless hear and help us, and who thus became the object of his infantile petition that he might escape beatings at school; a prayer which served merely to excite the contemptuous amusement of his parents.[1] But when, with maturing years, he discarded this puerility, it was only to plunge into the seething whirlpool of secularism, therein to be 'torn piecemeal while, turning from Thee, the one true Good, I lost myself among a multiplicity of things'.[2] Thus, as he says, 'for the space of nine years, from my nineteenth year to my twenty-eighth, we lived seducing and seduced, deceived and deceiving, in manifold lusts; openly, by sciences deemed liberal, secretly with a religion falsely so-called; here proud, there superstitious, altogether vain'.[3] Throughout this period Augustine was intractable and God maintained an enigmatic silence;[4] but, amid the snares and delusions of this life, he felt himself none the less the unconscious object of divine providence, his footsteps having thus been guided to Rome and Milan.[5] There, still doggedly pursuing his quest for certainty, determined not to be put off either with a bogy to fear and propitiate or with a delusion to hug, his search was at last to be rewarded by a vision of the Christian Trinity.[6] But for some time still the vision was withheld, while he wrestled with baffling aesthetic, moral, and intellectual questions, those of beauty and its conditions,[7] of freedom and necessity,[8] of unity and multiplicity, the One as the Good, division as the source of irrationality and evil;[9] pondering, among other things, the problems of substance, quantity, quality, and relation raised by Aristotle's *Categories*, with its implicit assumption that 'whatever was, was comprehended by the ten predicaments'.[10] In attacking these questions, he was confronted with the difficulty of conceiving substance as spiritual, but with the discovery that this was possible, the greatest of his intellectual problems was solved.[11] For he was thus enabled to perceive that, so far from being ultimate, 'form' and 'matter' alike were merely figments of the human mind; they were the spectacles through which men saw the corporeal or object world. His subsequent emancipation

[1] i. ix. 14. [2] ii. i. 1. [3] iv. i. 1.
[4] ii. ii. 2; iii. xii. 21. [5] v. viii. 14 and xiii. 23.
[6] vii foll., esp. xiii. v. 6; xi. 12; xvi. 19. [7] iv. xiii. 20. [8] vii. iii. 4 foll.
[9] iv. xv. 24–7. For a characteristic sample of this type of discussion, see Plut. *De Defectu Oraculorum*, chs. xxxiv and xxxvii. [10] *Conf*, iv. xvi. 28, 29. [11] v. xiv. 25.

from the delusions of materialism and idealism followed as a matter of course and, with this, the revolution was complete.

This revolution, which was of so much consequence to Augustine personally, was hardly less significant in the history of the Church. For, by his acceptance of Trinitarian Christianity, he identified himself with the effort of thought initiated by Athanasius. To that effort he made a contribution, the measure of which is indicated by the difference between the slight and sketchy *De Incarnatione* on the one hand and, on the other, the massive proportions of the *City of God*.

It is hardly necessary to recall the occasion and scope of a work which, apart perhaps from the *Confessions*, ranks as most familiar among those of Augustine. Its object, as indicated by the author himself, was twofold.[1] Begun in 413, three years after the sack of the Eternal City by Alaric, it was designed in the first instance 'to refute those who, contending that the Christian religion was responsible for the overthrow of Rome, began to blaspheme the true God with even more than their habitual bitterness and virulence'. From this standpoint it expanded into a general assault upon the philosophic foundations of *Romanitas*, in other words upon the claims of Vergil's City of Men. But, out of the polemic against secularism, emerged a second and more fundamental purpose, that of offering encouragement to those whose faith had been shaken and who had yielded to the superstitious fears of the time, for whom, as ground of reassurance, he enunciated a body of positive moral, social, and philosophic doctrine. With Augustine as with Athanasius, this takes the form of a running commentary on the scriptural narrative, with special reference to the creation, fall, and redemption of humanity, together with the rise, progress, and destiny of the Church in the world; and into it he pours the full resources of his mature thought upon the universe, nature, and man. It thus resolves itself into a descriptive analysis of the *operatio Dei*, the working of the Spirit in human history.

As such, according to Gibbon, the *City of God* claims the merit of 'a magnificent design, boldly and not unskilfully executed'. With great elaboration of detail, the author expounds what have come to be regarded as the characteristic

---

[1] *Retract.* ii. 43. 1 and 2, quoted in translation by Welldon, *De Civitate Dei*, introd., pp. vii and viii.

features of Augustinianism. These embrace the doctrine of
original sin and its consequences, including the damnation of
unbaptized infants; of redemption through grace according to
a law which, as it predestines some to eternal salvation, predestines others to eternal torment; of history as an account, not
of causes, but of prophecies fulfilled and to come and thus of
divine preparation for (a) the incarnation, and (b) the atone-
ment and its results, especially as they find expression in the
constitution and authority of the Church; not to speak of an
eschatology which, among other elements, includes the end of
the *Saeculum*, the bodily resurrection of the dead, the second
coming of Christ and the last judgement, conceived as a final
manifestation of divine justice and love. And, while proclaiming these doctrines, Augustine takes occasion to affirm his
implicit belief in the authority of Scripture, asserting even the
verbal inspiration of the Septuagint. On the strength of that
authority, he rejects the possibility of life at the Antipodes, but
confirms the legends regarding the gigantic stature and extreme
longevity of antediluvian man. He believes implicitly in the
existence of angels and demons and declares his faith in miracle,
especially as it clusters about the figure of the Redeemer: 'whoever', he says, 'denies the authenticity of biblical miracle, denies
the providence of God.' Moreover, he specifically accepts the
contemporary miraculous phenomena at Milan and Hippo
Regius as evidence that divine activity analogous to that described in the Scriptures continues to his own time. And yet,
paradoxically, he claims throughout to be writing not fable
but, in the deepest and truest sense of the word, fact. The
question thus presents itself: what does he really mean? To
this question we shall attempt an answer in the concluding
chapters of this work.

XI

NOSTRA PHILOSOPHIA: THE DISCOVERY OF PERSONALITY

IN the sketch thus offered of Trinitarian Christianity we are conscious of certain omissions. No reference, for instance, has been made to Basil who, as has been said,[1] 'succeeded Athanasius in the management of the Trinitarian cause' to which, by his prudent and statesmanlike leadership, he ensured general, if not universal, acceptance.[2] But our purpose will be served if we have succeeded in indicating the relation of Augustine to his predecessors, the Christian thinkers of the fourth century. To see him in this relationship is to recognize that his spiritual affiliations were with Athanasius and Ambrose rather than with Plotinus or Porphyry. It is also to attain the proper perspective for an appreciation of his work. From this standpoint that work may be described as one of fulfilment. For, by pressing to a logical conclusion the implications of the new starting-point, he completed the effort of thought initiated by the Fathers and laid the foundations of what he claimed to be 'ours, the one true philosophy'.[3] In Augustine we may thus perceive the full meaning of the Evangel as it presented itself to the mind of the fourth century and, therewith, the measure of the revolution in attitude and outlook which resulted from the impact of Christianity upon the Graeco-Roman world.

As thus envisaged, the work of Augustine possesses a twofold significance. To begin with, it offers a way of escape from the insoluble riddles of Classicism, as well as from those of the marginal systems of thought which succeeded the extinction of the purely classical spirit. Seen in the light of the new *arché*, *principium* or first principle, problems inherent in the discarded ideology either recede into the background or, in another context, assume a wholly different complexion. At the same time, Augustinianism emerges, not as a conglomerate of indiscriminate borrowings, but as a mature philosophy which seeks

---

[1] Gibbon, op. cit., ch. xxv, p. 26.

[2] For the work of Basil, see Duchesne, op. cit. ii[4], ch. xi, p. 387 foll. For that of Hilary of Poitiers, ibid., p. 523. Duchesne describes Hilary as the man who, of all the western bishops, had throughout the last struggles with Arianism played the most active role, not merely in Gaul but in the East and in Italy.

[3] Ch. VI, above, p. 231.

to do justice to all aspects of experience and, in particular, to overcome the apparent discrepancy between the demands of order and those of process; i.e. between the so-called Apolline and Dionysiac elements in life.[1] It thus provides the basis for a synthesis which, whatever may be thought of its claim to finality, serves at least to meet the legitimate aspiration of Classicism for a principle of order; while, in its vision of process and of the goal to which it moves, it discloses worlds to which Classicism, from the limitations of its outlook, remains inevitably blind.

In this respect the limitations of Classicism were those of 'reason'. Accordingly, in rejecting its pretensions, Augustine associates himself with the revolt against 'reason' which we have elsewhere noted as typical of Christianity.[2] *Ex fide vivimus, ambulamus per fidem*; we live and walk by faith, he reiterates with no less insistence than Tertullian himself. For Augustine, however, the revolt from 'reason' does not mean a return to the instinctive, nor does it imply that the intellect is radically corrupt. On the contrary it points the way to an attitude from which, if faith precedes understanding, understanding in turn becomes the reward of faith.[3] In this understanding Augustine discovers at once the answer to his quest for certitude and the recovery of his birthright as a rational animal. For it enables him to perceive that, so far from being antithetic, 'faith' and 'reason' are in reality correlative and complementary aspects of experience. It thus provides a vindication of what may be called the primitive and original values of selfhood, the sense of existence, of awareness, and of autonomous yet orderly activity which constitute the native endowment of mankind. At the same time it imparts fresh significance to those values by exhibiting their dependence upon a principle which being at once beyond them and in them, cosmic and personal, is put forward as genuinely 'creative'; i.e. as fulfilling the requirements of the unmoved mover (τὸ κινοῦν ἀκίνητον) desiderated by Aristotle. In the acceptance of this principle he finds an

---

[1] *Conf.* i. vi. 9: 'apud te rerum omnium instabilium stant causae, et rerum omnium mutabilium inmutabiles manent origines, et omnium inrationalium et temporalium sempiternae vivunt rationes.' For an analysis of the psychic phenomena classified as Dionysiac in classical antiquity see Rohde, op. cit., chs. ix and x. Nothing in Christianity is more instructive than the fresh interpretation which it puts on such phenomena.   [2] Ch. VI, above.

[3] *In Joan. Evang., Tract.* xxix. 6: 'intellectus merces est fidei.'

answer to problems arising from the classical distinctions (a) between subject and object, and (b) between the life of sense and that of thought; thereby making possible a philosophy of dynamic personality.

The point will bear emphasis; it is, indeed, crucial for the appreciation of Trinitarianism as a doctrine of salvation from the shortcomings (vitia) of the classical and post-classical world. 'Far be it from us', declares Augustine, 'to suppose that God abhors in us that by virtue of which He has made us superior to other animals. Far be it, I say, that we should believe in such a way as to exclude the necessity either of accepting or requiring reason; since we could not even believe unless we possessed rational souls.'[1] For Augustine, therefore, it was no cure for the vices of thinking to abjure thought; to lapse back into a kind of intellectual somnambulism in which the will moves 'in darkness, without sight or understanding', that it may 'act straight from the dark source of life, outwards, which is creative life'.[2] Nor could he have been satisfied with a mode of acceptance in which faith is content to remain blind, i.e. to stop short with the credo quia absurdum of Tertullian. There is, he urges, a world of difference between belief and credulity; and it is only because they confuse faith with a shameful or rash assent to opinion that, according to many people, we ought to believe in nothing which we cannot with certainty know.[3] For if knowledge be defined as that which is apprehended certissima ratione, it at once becomes evident that, of the sum-total of possible experience, only certain elements may be regarded as known or, indeed, knowable in this sense, while the vast bulk of what men accept as truth is dependent upon some kind of authority.[4] Furthermore, if confidence in this authority be undermined, the whole structure of human relationships must inevitably collapse.[5] To recognize this fact is simple honesty; but it affords no comfort to the religious obscurantist.[6] For if authority demands faith, it also

---

[1] Ep. 120. 3: ad Consentium.

[2] The point of view thus indicated is common in modern times. It is reflected, e.g., in the remark of J. A. Stewart, Myths of Plato, p. 45, that 'feeling stands nearer than thought does to that basal self or personality which is at once the living problem of the universe and its living solution'. He quotes Plotinus, Enn. iii. 8. 4.

[3] De Util. Cred. §. 22: 'inter credentem et credulum plurimum interest'; 23: 'aliud est credere, aliud credulum esse.'   [4] Ibid. 25.

[5] Ibid. 27; De Fide Rerum, 2, 4: 'si auferatur haec fides de rebus humanis, quis non attendat quanta earum perturbatio et quam horrenda confusio subsequatur'.

[6] Conf. vi. v. 7.

prepares mankind for reason, while reason in its turn guides him to understanding and knowledge.[1] While, therefore, authority is prior in time to reason, reason is prior to authority in fact.[2] Such is the constitution of human nature that, when we undertake to learn anything, authority must precede reason.[3] But this authority is accepted only as a means to understanding. 'Believe', he says, 'in order that you may understand.'

By thus recommending faith, not as a substitute for, but as a condition of understanding, Augustine formulates, in terms which recall and reinforce the language of Athanasius, the true issue between Classicism and Christianity. To the enemies of the faith that issue had presented itself as a conflict between science and superstition, in which the blind acceptance of an alien and incredible tradition was proposed as an alternative to the secular effort of *Romanitas* to discover in nature and reason a rule for the conduct of human life. From this standpoint Christianity assumed the character of an escape-religion, which sought to provide in a self-created world of the imagination a refuge from the stern demands of the natural order, as that order was revealed to the eye of classical science. The *crede ut intellegas*[4] meets and disposes once and for all of this crude and erroneous notion. The claim of the heretics was that they could dispense with faith, teaching nothing except what was clear and evident to reason, and giving an account in terms of reason of the most obscure things.[5] In this claim, as Augustine perceived, was concealed the great illusion of Classicism, an illusion common to all the heresies which derived from the classical spirit. This was the supposition that while opinion (roughly equivalent to 'faith') was subjective, reason contained within itself the power to transcend the limitations of mere subjectivity and to apprehend 'objective' truth. Classical reason was thus committed to an ideal of scientific objectivity, as well as to the discovery of a dialectic or technique of transcendence whereby that ideal might be realized; and, from this standpoint,

[1] *De Vera Relig.* 24. 45: 'auctoritas fidem flagitat et rationi praeparat hominem. ratio ad intellectum cognitionemque perducit.'

[2] *De Ordine*, ii. 9. 26: 'tempore auctoritas, re autem ratio prior.'

[3] *De Mor. Eccl.* i. 2. 3,

[4] This famous phrase originates in the Septuagint, Isaiah vii. 9.

[5] *De Util. Cred.* i. 2: 'se dicebant, terribili auctoritate separata, mera et simplici ratione eos qui se audire vellent ... errore omni liberaturos.' ix. 21 : 'profitentur omnes haeretici . . . rationem se de obscurissimis rebus reddituros.'

Pyrrho, the most radical of the sceptics, asserted for his *logos* a validity not less absolute than that postulated by the dogmatists whose errors he denounced.[1] To this claim Augustine replies with a challenge that reason itself present the credentials by virtue of which it presumes to operate. In other words he calls for a phenomenology of the human mind, as the preliminary to any real understanding of the thought and activity of men. The question which thus confronts him is: What must I accept as the fundamental elements of consciousness, the recognition of which is imposed upon me as an inescapable necessity of my existence as a rational animal?

To this question Augustine answers that consciousness, reduced to its lowest terms, implies in some sense (1) existence, (2) knowledge, and (3) will.

'I would', he says, 'that men would consider these three, that are in themselves. . . . For I am and know and will; I am knowing and willing; I know myself to be and to will; I will to be and to know. In these three, then, let him discern who can how inseparable a life there is, one life, one mind, and one essence; how inseparable a distinction and yet a distinction.'[2]

To this assertion of the triune character of selfhood he returns in other passages:

'We both exist, and know that we exist, and rejoice in this existence and this knowledge.[3] In these three, when the mind knows and loves itself, there may be seen a trinity, mind, love, knowledge; not to be confounded by any intermixture, although each exists in itself, and all mutually in all, or each in the other two, or the other two in each.'[4]

To this awareness of selfhood as a triad of being, intelligence, and purpose, Augustine ascribes the character of infallible knowledge; it has this character, because it is the knowledge by the experient of himself. As such, he argues, it cannot possibly be an illusion, since he does not attain it by any bodily sense, but as a direct deliverance of consciousness, independent of all mediation through sense and imagination and thus exempt from

---

[1] See Diog. Laert. *Vitae* (Loeb), ix. 76 foll.: ὁ Πυρρώνειος λόγος and the ten modes of its application.

[2] *Conf.* xiii. xi. 12: 'esse, nosse, velle. Sum enim et scio et volo; sum sciens et volens; et scio esse me et velle; et volo esse et scire . . . quam inseparabilis vita et una vita et una mens et una essentia, quam inseparabilis distinctio et tamen distinctio.'

[3] *De Civ. Dei*, xi. 26: 'et sumus et nos esse novimus et id esse et nosse diligimus.

[4] *De Trin.* ix. 5. 8.

the possibility of error implicit in his knowledge of nature or the environmental world.

'It is beyond question', he declares, 'that I exist, and that I know and love that existence. In these truths there is nothing to fear from the argument of the Academics: what if you are mistaken? Since if I am mistaken, I am. One who does not exist cannot possibly be mistaken. Thus if I am mistaken, this very fact proves that I am. Because, therefore, if I am mistaken, I am, how can I be mistaken as to my existence, for it is certain that I exist, if I am mistaken? Accordingly, since I must exist in order to be mistaken, even if I should be mistaken, it is beyond doubt that I am not mistaken in this, that I know myself as knowing. It follows, then, that I could not be mistaken as to the fact that I know myself as knowing. For, as I know myself to exist, so, also, I know this, that I know. And to these two, since I love them, I join that love as a third element of equal value to those things which I know.'[1]

Virtually the same argument is repeated elsewhere:

'If, then, we take away those things which come into the mind from the bodily senses, how much remains, of which we have knowledge as certain as that we are alive? Regarding which, moreover, we have no fear lest perhaps we may be deceived by any specious probability, because it is certain that even the man who is deceived is alive. Nor does this knowledge depend on those visual images, which are presented to us from outside, so that in it the eye may be deceived as when, for example, an oar immersed in water appears to be broken and castles to be in motion for those sailing by, or in a thousand other cases where things are other than they seem; inasmuch as the truth of which I am speaking is not perceived through the eye of the flesh. It is by virtue of an inner knowledge that we know we are alive . . . accordingly, the man who asserts that he knows he is alive, cannot possibly be mistaken or deceived. A thousand illusions of sense may be presented to his vision; he will fear none of them, since even the man who is deceived must be alive in order to be deceived.'[2]

Augustine then proceeds to assert the 'substantiality' of this consciousness of selfhood. By this he means that it is not rendered in the slightest degree more intelligible by being translated into terms other than itself, especially into terms of physiology; to do this indeed is merely to add one mystery to another.[3]

'The question being the nature of the mind, we must dismiss from

[1] *De Civ. Dei*, xi. 26.　　　[2] *De Trin.* xv. 12. 21.　　　[3] x. 10. 14.

consideration all notions acquired from outside through the bodily senses and pay the most careful attention to those facts of which we have said all minds have knowledge concerning themselves and which are indubitable. Men have expressed doubt as to whether the power of life, memory, intelligence, volition, thought, knowledge and judgement is a function of air, fire, brain, blood or atoms, or of some unknown body over and above the four familiar elements, and as to whether it is within the power of some concretion or arrangement (*compago vel temperamentum*) of our flesh itself to perform these operations; and some have ventured to assert one theory, some another. But who is there to doubt that he is alive, remembers, understands, wishes, thinks, knows and judges? Since even if he has such doubt, he lives; if he doubts, he thinks. Whatever doubts he has, therefore, regarding other things, he ought not to have doubts regarding all these; for if he did not exist, he could not have doubt regarding anything.'[1]

He goes on to contrast this self-knowledge with knowledge of the external world.[2]

'It is wholly incorrect to speak of a thing as known, while its substance remains unknown. Accordingly, when the mind knows itself, it knows itself as substance and when it is certain regarding itself, it is certain regarding its substantiality. It could not possibly be thus assured that it was either air or fire or any body or any element of body. It is not, therefore, any of those things, and all of which it can possibly be certain resolves itself into this, that it is not any of those things regarding which it is uncertain, but that only which it is certain that it is. . . . For all those things, whether fire, air, this or that kind of body, element or concretion and arrangement of body, it apprehends through visual images, but it apprehends itself with direct and immediate awareness . . . as it apprehends that it lives, remembers, knows and wishes.'

Finally, he asserts that in these functions is to be discovered a substantial unity, independent of and distinguishable from any relations which it may possess.[3]

'These three, therefore, memory (i.e. the sense of being or personal identity), intelligence and will, since they are not three lives but one life, nor three minds but one mind, must accordingly constitute not three substances but one substance. For the term memory, as used with respect to life, mind and substance, implies nothing but itself; as used with respect to anything else, it implies relations. I might say the same thing also regarding intelligence and will; . . . Con-

---

[1] Cf. *De Civ. Dei*, viii. 5, for a general criticism of materialist theories of cognition.
[2] *De Trin.* x. 10. 15-6.   [3] x. 11. 18.

sequently, these three are one, embracing one life, one mind and one essence.'

The unity of substance thus described is, accordingly, not to be resolved into a tissue of external relationships, but may be said to 'transcend' the world of time and space in which it finds itself and which, as he says, it apprehends through 'the eye of the flesh'.[1]

But to assert the existence of the self as a substantial and transcendent unity is, at the same time, to assert its limitations; it is limited in its being, as well as in its capacity for knowledge and movement. It must not, therefore, be regarded as 'independent', in the sense that it is or can become a law unto itself. On the contrary it is subject to restrictions which effectively condition each and every manifestation of its activity. Such restrictions are evident, e.g. in the effort of poetic composition, which thus exhibits a principle of orderly movement analogous to that of life itself; so that the ideal of an absolutely free verse becomes at once intellectually absurd and aesthetically reprehensible.[2] They are evident, also, in the science of mathematics, considered as a revelation of structure; structure being, no less than process, *ex rerum natura*, involved in the very nature of things. In these restrictions, therefore, we may perceive the true principle (*arché* or *principium*) of its being, any attempt to ignore or evade which is simply to repeat the sin of Adam. But, as he goes on to point out, such an assertion of selfhood involves the danger of fatal misapprehension. The presumption of mankind may, indeed, lead him to suppose that, in his consciousness of existence and of activity, there is evidence that he embodies a scintilla of the divine essence, the mere possession of which constitutes a prima-facie claim to divinity, lifting him above the natural order of which he forms a part. On the other hand, his folly may suggest that the limitations of which he is sensible are, in effect, physical, i.e. 'external' to the experient. This is to indicate an ideal of independence, to be realized through the accumulation and exploitation of material resources. In the indulgence of such specious fancies, however, lies the cause of sin and error from which, so long as he entertains them, there is no possibility of escape. The alternative is to recognize himself as 'created'; his consciousness of selfhood

[1] *De Gen. ad Litt.* vii. 21. 28.
[2] *De Musica*, vi. 14. 48: 'subditur legibus qui non amat leges.'

as, in some mysterious sense, forever dependent upon an inexhaustible and unconditioned source of Being, Wisdom, and Power in whose 'image' he is made. This is to proclaim a mystery of which, Augustine feels, no rational explanation is either possible or necessary. Reflection upon it serves merely to prompt him to two conclusions, both of significance for his philosophy. 'How many ages (*saecula*) may have passed before the human race was instituted I confess I do not know; but of this I have no doubt, that there exists nothing in the created universe which is co-eternal with the Creator.'[1] Furthermore, there is involved in the problem of genesis what he describes as 'the extremely difficult question how, in view of his eternity, God could produce genuine novelty without any innovation of will'.[2] It must thus be regarded as a fact to be accepted rather than as a question to be solved. The difference, then, between Creator and Creature emerges as radical. Accordingly, it is not to be bridged by any merely human process of reason and imagination or by any merely human act of will. From this it follows that, in order to achieve felicity, man should abandon as chimerical his aspirations whether to apotheosis or to escape, and that he should rather study to fulfil the law of his Creator which is, at the same time, the law of his own being as an embodied soul.

Thus, in the sense of his dependence and imperfection, Augustine finds reason for recognizing God as the *arché* or *principium* of his being, thought, and purpose; and belief in God assumes the character of *intima scientia*, a kind of 'inner knowledge' akin to belief in the self; it is presumed or presupposed in the consciousness of his own existence and activity. This belief neither requires nor admits of 'external' verification; scientifically speaking, it is both undemonstrated and undemonstrable. Nevertheless, it yields a knowledge of the Divine Being, the *intellectualis visio Dei*, sufficiently clear and precise to make it possible for him to say that, 'next to myself, I know God'. It thus underlies the paradoxical *crede ut intellegas*, 'believe in order that you may understand'. But, for the attainment of such understanding, it is essential to overcome the congenital ten-

---

[1] *De Civ. Dei*, xii. 17.
[2] Ch. 22: 'hac quaestione difficillima propter aeternitatem Dei nova creantis sine novitate aliqua voluntatis.' Cf. 21: 'possunt fieri nova, quae neque antea facta sint nec tamen a rerum ordine aliena sint.'

dency of man to think in terms of bodily images—a tendency which gives rise to anthropomorphisms ranging all the way from the crude and childish picture of the Deity as a titanic figure 'God the colossus', the 'God with the red hair' (*deus colosseus, rutilus deus*) to those refinements of the scientific intelligence by which He is represented as a kind of world-soul (*anima mundi*). For Augustine it was easy enough to dismiss the notion of God as a being defined by human form; it was much more difficult to shake off the feeling that He was 'something bodily', 'either infused through space into the universe or, even beyond it, diffused through infinity'.[1] The alternative to such errors of the conceptualizing imagination was to recognize the creative principle as pure spirit. This once accomplished it became possible for him to declare.[2]

'We worship God, not heaven and earth, the two parts of which this world is constructed; nor yet 'soul' or 'souls', however diffused through living creatures, but God, the maker of heaven and earth and of all things which are in them, the maker of all souls, whether those that merely live and are devoid of sense and reason, or those also which possess sense, or those also which possess intelligence.'

This is to suggest a point of view from which, properly speaking, the creative principle ceases to be an 'object' of thought, as it ceases to be an 'object' of sense-perception. Moses, indeed, according to tradition, had seen God in the burning bush. To Augustine, however, it was evident that, in this vision, the prophet had perceived merely the *vestigia Dei* or traces of the divine being; and, for him, this fact serves to emphasize the truth that no man can see God face to face. From this standpoint, it becomes possible to understand the paradox, *scitur Deus melius nesciendo*,[3] or, as he goes on to add: 'there is in the mind no knowledge of God except the knowledge of how it does not know Him.'[4] By this he means that God as the principle of self-conscious life is not to be apprehended in terms of any category of the discursive reason. 'Whence', he declares, 'it is evident that, as applied to God, even the category of substance is used improperly (*abusive*), in order that, by a more familiar term, we may understand what is truly and accurately described as "essence" or "being". Perhaps, therefore, we ought to use the term "essence" with reference to God alone.'[5] Accordingly,

---

[1] *Conf.* vii. i. 1.   [2] *De Civ. Dei.* vii. 29.
[3] *De Ord.* ii. 16. 44.   [4] 18. 47.   [5] *De Trin.* vii. 10.

'it becomes our duty to envisage God, if we can and so far as we can, as good without quality, great without quantity, creator without necessity, foremost without relations, comprehending all things but possessing no mode of existence, everywhere present but without location, eternal without subjection to time, capable of action without submitting to the changes of mutable things and of feeling without passion. Whoever thus thinks of God, although he is by no means able to discover Him, nevertheless takes such precautions as are possible against entertaining false notions regarding Him.'[1]

In this series of striking paradoxes Augustine endeavours to give point to his contention that the creative principle eludes all categorization. In this fact, however, he sees no reason for regarding it as inaccessible to the consciousness of mankind. On the contrary, he asserts, 'you will now be able to apprehend God more clearly than a brother; more clearly because more directly, more immediately and more certainly.'[2] But, in order to do so, 'don't go outside yourself, return into yourself. The dwelling-place of truth is in the inner man. And if you discover your own nature as subject to change, then go beyond that nature. But remember that, when you thus go beyond it, it is the reasoning soul which you go beyond. Press on, therefore, toward the source from which the light of reason itself is kindled.'[3]

Thus apprehended, the creative principle presents itself as the eternal, the immutable and the self-sufficient, the source of all being, of all wisdom and of all perfection. As such its operation is evident, dubiously and indirectly, in those *vestigia* which are manifest to the eye of the flesh; directly and indubitably to the inner man as the basis of his existence, the light of his intelligence, and the mainspring of his activity.[4] It is thus recognized as 'the good by which all goods or values are created . . .

[1] *De Trin.* v. 1. 3: 'alia quae dicuntur essentiae sive substantiae capiunt accidentia, quibus in eis fiat vel magna vel quantacumque mutatio; Deo autem aliquid huiusmodi accidere non potest, ideo sola est incommunicabilis substantia'; cf. *Ep.* 187. iv. 14: 'sic est Deus per cuncta diffusus ut non sit qualitas mundi sed substantia creatrix mundi, sine labore regens et sine onere continens mundum. Non tamen per spatia locorum quasi mole diffusa . . . sed in solo caelo totus, et in sola terra totus et in caelo et in terra totus et nullo contentus loco sed in se ipso ubique totus.'

[2] *Soliloq.* i. 6. 12 and 13.

[3] *De Vera Relig.* 39. 72.

[4] *De Civ. Dei*, viii. 4: 'causa subsistendi, ratio intellegendi, ordo vivendi.'

created, I say, and not begotten. For these values are complex and, therefore, mutable. . . . But whatever is begotten of a simple good is likewise simple and the same in kind as that of which it is begotten'.[1] Furthermore, the creative or moving principle is apprehended as a single essence, the nature of which is fully expressed in its order and activity; in the language of religion, as one God in three *hypostases* or *persons*, the Father uncreated, the Son uncreated, the Spirit uncreated. In this formula the first *hypostasis*, *Being*, the creative principle properly so called is, strictly speaking, unknown and unknowable, except in so far as it manifests itself in the second and third; the second *hypostasis*, the principle of intelligence, reveals itself as the *logos*, *ratio*, or order of the universe; while the third, the *hypostasis* of spirit, is the principle of motion therein. To assert that these *hypostases* are uncreated is simply to assert their existence as principles. As such they are not to be 'confused' in person; being is not to be resolved into order, nor is order to be resolved into process. At the same time, as a substantial unity or unity of substance, they do not admit of 'separation', i.e. they are not mutually exclusive or antithetic. In other words the opposition between them is purely and simply one of internal, necessary relations. Accordingly, they present themselves as a Trinity which may be described as that which IS unchangeably and KNOWS unchangeably and WILLS unchangeably.

'And Thy essence knoweth and willeth unchangeably and Thy knowledge is and willeth unchangeably and Thy will is and knoweth unchangeably.'[2]

'And under the name of God, I comprehend the Father who made these things; and under the name of Beginning (*in principii nomine*) the Son, in whom He made these things; and, believing, as I did, my God to be a Trinity, I searched further in His holy words and lo! Thy Spirit moved upon the waters. Behold, then, the Trinity, my God, Father, Son and Holy Spirit, Creator of all creation!'[3]

Augustine thus discovers in the Trinity a fresh foundation for what we have called the values of personality. And here the breach with Classicism was radical; what it involved was nothing less than a question of first principles. But, in this connexion, it should be noted that Augustine's revolt was not from nature; it was from the picture of nature proposed by classical science;

[1] *De Civ. Dei*, xi. 10.   [2] *Conf*. xiii. xi. 12 and xvi. 19.   [3] xiii. v. 6.

i.e. from a cosmology and an anthropology constructed in terms of form and matter as the basis for a 'formal' ethic and a 'formal' logic. This was to smash the kingdom of Jove and to unbind Prometheus, who was thus revealed as the victim of nothing but his own obsessions, the obsessions of the 'scientific' understanding. It was also to dissipate the nightmare involved in the concept of nature as a closed system, determined by its own exclusive laws and, therewith, of the antithesis between human liberty and natural necessity which rendered mankind a stranger in his own household.

In thus reorienting himself toward traditional problems, Augustine was no doubt assisted by the breakdown of classical ideology which, by his day, was in a state of evident collapse. But, over and above this, it means that he acknowledged as authoritative the formulation of Christian principles made at Nicaea. For, he declares, the new starting-point, not being given *ratiocinando*, is inaccessible even to the most acute intelligence and must, therefore, be accepted on 'faith'. To the lack of such a starting-point he attributes the deficiencies of classical speculation in its effort to investigate the problems of nature.[1] In this statement we may find the clue to its meaning and value for Augustine. For him, as for Athanasius, it was to constitute the preface to a new and valid philosophy. In this respect its character is emphasized by contrast with that of the undifferentiated and all-inclusive *One* of Plotinus. With Plotinus the vision of the One had occurred only in ecstasy and its content was wholly incommunicable. Augustine, however, is never more himself than when he contemplates the Trinity; and, while this experience excites in him the most profound emotion, at the same time it heightens his perceptions, thus serving to stimulate and provoke thought.[2] It is thus recognized as the light by virtue of which he sees himself in relation to his universe.

'Can you', he demands of the Manichean Faustus, 'describe this intellectual light, which gives us a clear perception of the distinction between itself and other things, as well as of the distinction between those things themselves? And yet even this is not the sense in which it can be said that God is light. For this light is created, whereas God is the creator; this light is made, He is the maker; this light is changeable, for the intellect changes from dislike to desire, from ignorance to knowledge, from forgetfulness to recollection, whereas

---

[1] *De Civ. Dei*, ii. 7. [2] See *Conf*. x–xiii.

God remains the same in will, in truth, and in eternity. From God we derive the beginning of existence, the principle of knowledge, the law of affection. From God all animals, rational and irrational, derive the nature of their life, the capacity of sensation, the faculty of emotion. From God all bodies derive their subsistence in extension, their beauty in number, their order in weight.'[1]

Thus envisaged, the Trinitarian principle presents itself, not as a refinement of the scientific intelligence, a tissue of metaphysical abstractions having no existence except in the imagination of theologians, but rather as an attempt to formulate what is 'imposed' upon the intelligence as the precondition of science; and its acceptance as such marks a rejection of the claim that the discursive reason can authenticate the presumptions which determine the nature and scope of its activity otherwise than in terms of their 'working and power'. Accordingly, the choice for man, as Augustine sees it, does not so much lie between science and superstition as between two kinds of faith, the one salutary, the other destructive, the one making for fulfilment, the other for frustration. Of these alternative faiths, the former saves by illumining experience and giving it value in terms of an absolute standard of truth, beauty, and goodness. To pledge allegiance to this faith is thus to experience no sense of limitation, but only a feeling of enhanced freedom and power. The latter may well be described as Promethean. Based as it is on a distorted or partial apprehension of ultimate reality, its character is necessarily felt as oppressive; and the sense of oppression bears its inevitable fruits in defiance and revolt to be followed by confusion, defeat, and despair.

To say this is to indicate the immensity of the demands implied in the Trinitarian formula. To begin with, it must embody a truth which is genuinely 'creative', in the sense that it constitutes the ground or basis of experience apart from which experience loses much of its meaning. In order to serve this purpose it must possess certain definite characteristics. It must, for instance, be 'independent', for only thus will it yield the 'law for man', canons or norms to which, in the very nature of things, the human mind is bound to subscribe. But, while thus transcending the thought and imagination of the experient, it must not prove to be either beyond reach, i.e. a 'pattern laid up in heaven', nor yet esoteric, accessible only to the moral and

[1] *Contra Faustum*, xx. 7.

intellectual superman. In other words it must be immanent or, as Augustine puts it, present and available to man as man; since otherwise it cannot possibly accomplish its salutary task. Then, too, it must be comprehensive, and this from two points of view. In the first place it must meet the requirements of the 'total man', of the head as well as the heart, thus satisfying the legitimate demand for 'wholeness'. But, since the demand for 'wholeness' is a demand, not of sense, but of reason, its fulfilment implies that the life of sense must be brought into intelligible relationship with the life of reason. It thus points to an effective technique of redemption for the flesh as an alternative to the conclusion of Platonism, *omne corpus fugiendum est*. Finally, it must meet the requirements of all men, by supplying a basis for community less fragile and precarious than that proposed by the philosophers of the *polis*, whether conceived as city-state or world-empire.[1]

Merely to state these conditions is to perceive the vanity of the effort made by Classicism to attain to such a formula by means of 'scientia'. For science, argues Augustine, does not create; it constructs, using for this purpose the material of sense-perception. Thus the *ratio scientiae*, as he calls it, comes into play only when the mind directs its attention 'outwards', addressing itself to the task of organizing this material.[2] Its working is therefore contingent upon the assumption that the material in question will present itself in 'patterns' capable of apprehension by the mind; and this assumption it can by no means verify. Furthermore, the patterns as they emerge are in all cases relative to the capacities of the observer—a condition which must be accepted, disturbing as are the possibilities involved in its recognition. For, in this respect, his limitations are not merely those of his faculties, the organs of sense-perception whose deliverances, however feeble and dubious, he nevertheless rejects at his peril.[3] They are those also of a creature immersed in the flux of time and space, and thus himself swept along by the current whose velocity and direction he endeavours to chart. From these limitations there is not the remotest possi-

---

[1] *De Civ. Dei*, x. 32: '. . . religio quae universalem continet viam animae liberandae . . . regalis via . . . quae non suae cuique genti propria, sed universis gentibus communis divinitus impertita est. . . . haec via totum hominem mundat et immortalitati mortalem ex omnibus quibus constat partibus praeparat.'

[2] *De Trin*. xi. 1: 'foras se nostra proicit intentio.'

[3] *De Civ. Dei*, xix. 4 and 18.

bility of escape. Plato, indeed, had made a strenuous effort to transcend them; but, in so doing, he merely exposed himself to the jibe of Tertullian, *nondum mortuus philosophabatur*, 'before undertaking to philosophize, he ought to have waited till he was dead'. The scientist, *qua* scientist, is thus inevitably confronted with the fate of Prometheus; a fate which he can avoid only if he transfers his allegiance from the tyrant Zeus to the God whose service is perfect freedom.

Translated into terms of logic, the appeal of Augustine is from the *ratio scientiae* to the *ratio sapientiae*, from what he calls the method of science to that of insight or wisdom. For to *sapientia*, he declares, 'belongs the intellectual apprehension of the eternal' as distinguished from 'the rational apprehension of the temporal' which is the work of science.[1] The *ratio sapientiae* may thus with perfect justice be described as a function of reason (*actio rationalis*); indeed, in view of the service which it renders, the most exalted of such functions, since what it provides is nothing less than an apprehension of the creative principle upon which the very possibility of reasoning depends. Accordingly, to grasp this principle is, he feels, to grasp the 'rules of wisdom' which, for him as for Athanasius, are true and immutable in precisely the same way as those of mathematics.[2] In this sense it consti- tutes what we have called the 'law for man', equipping him with a principle of discrimination by virtue of which he becomes capable of positive science in the modern sense.[3] But, in this connexion, an emphatic warning may be salutary. The mere existence of a body of mathematical principles does not absolve the mathematician from the necessity of working out his pro- blems as they arise, nor does it protect him from the risk of error in trying to do so. So also with the *regulae sapientiae*, the true service of which is purely as an instrument for accurate thinking, in no sense as a substitute for correct thought.

Such an instrument is, however, indispensable and Augustine looks to insight or wisdom to supply it. From this standpoint 'if faith seeks, understanding finds'. In this it succeeds, because the truth for which it is looking is, as has been said, available

---

[1] *De Trin*.xii. 15, 25: 'ad sapientiam pertinet aeternarum rerum cognitio intel- lectualis, ad scientiam vero temporalium rerum cognitio rationalis.'

[2] *De Lib. Arbit*. ii. 10. 29: 'quam ergo verae atque incommutabiles regulae numerorum. . . . tam sunt verae atque incommutabiles regulae sapientiae.'

[3] ii. 12. 34: 'interiores regulae sapientiae quibus . . . de corporibus iudicamus.'

for the asking to every man. Or, as he elsewhere puts it: 'Thy truth is neither mine nor that of any other individual; it belongs to all of us whom Thou dost summon publicly to share it.'[1] Accordingly, by contrast with the pagan sage, Christian philosophers may be defined 'not as men of talent or genius, but as those in whom exists, so far as may be in a man, the clearest possible knowledge of man himself and of God, together with a mode of life consistent with such knowledge'.[2]

In this definition we may perceive the Augustinian version of the *anima naturaliter Christiana* to which, as will be remembered, Tertullian had made his appeal.[3] But, with Augustine, that appeal is no longer from knowledge to ignorance, from experience to inexperience. It is rather from a kind of knowledge which inflates to one which chastens, from that which befogs to that which clarifies the mind. The knowledge in question is elsewhere described as that of the 'spiritual' man;[4] that is to say, of the man who sees his universe, not 'through the eye of the flesh' but in the light of a principle whereby he is enabled 'to judge everything, without himself being judged by any man'. Such knowledge may be said to represent a departure from 'the abstract and theoretical to the concrete and practical; insight, wisdom, understanding—call it what you will—being a practical rather than a theoretical gift, born and developed more in living and sympathetic contacts than in the detachments of technical study'. On this account it manages to avoid certain pitfalls of the scientific intelligence which, proceeding as it does by way of analysis, breaks up the concrete whole of experience into what it conceives to be its original elements ($\sigma\tauο\iota\chi\varepsilon\hat{\iota}\alpha$), only to find itself confronted with the problem of reassembling the scattered fragments and of galvanizing them into life. But if Christian *sapientia* evades these difficulties, is it not merely to fall into others not less serious? Has not the Christian sage abandoned the ideal of scientific objectivity merely to replace it by his own private intuitions? And does not this substitution of the 'inner' for the 'outer' light mean, in effect, that the operations of Christian *sapientia* are wholly erratic; to be ascribed with Tertullian, to a mythical *paraclete*, the counterpart to the *daemon* of Socrates? To suggest such conclusions would be to

---

[1] *Conf.* xii. xxv, 34.   [2] *De Util. Cred.* xii, 27.   [3] Ch. VI, above, p. 223.
[4] *De Civ. Dei*, xx. 14, and many other passages. Augustine is evidently thinking of the distinction made by St. Paul in 1 Cor. ii. 14.

misrepresent the attitude of Augustine. It would be to forget
that he thought of himself, not as the founder of just another
speculative system, but as a member of the Church and thus
possessed of a truth which was in no sense 'private'; the task
imposed upon him being one merely of exposition and advocacy
as his share in the *militia* of Christ.

Accordingly, the appeal of Augustine was not, as it had been
with Tertullian, purely and simply to the individual, conceived
as an 'independent' vessel of the Spirit. It was rather from one
kind of authority to another. What it thus involved was the
substitution of a new standard of objectivity for that proposed
by classical *scientia*; this objectivity was that of history, envisaged as a progressive disclosure of the creative and moving
principle. To accept this standard was, of course, to suppose,
in the words of St. Paul, that God had not left Himself without
witness in any nation. Specifically, however, it was to recognize
the witness of the Hebrews as, in a peculiar sense, significant;
that is to say, to see in the Scriptures the authentic vehicle of the
Word. From this standpoint, the true meaning of experience
was thought to have been foreshadowed in the Law and the
Prophets, whose utterances were thus regarded, not as the out-
pourings of God-drunken ecstasy, the result of some mysterious
and divine *afflatus*, but as the sane and deliberate judgements
of men who had submitted themselves to the discipline of the
Spirit. Ultimately, however, it depended upon an acknowledgement of the claim of the historic Christ to embody in His person
a full and final revelation of the divine nature and activity.
Accordingly, the promise of the *pneuma* was to be understood,
not as the promise of a power to create 'new' truth, but rather
as a gift of insight into truth which was, in fact, as old as
creation itself. In this sense, it pointed to what was described
as a programme of 'fulfilment' for mankind.

In saying this, we are not unmindful of the difficulty which
Augustine, in common with others, experienced in trying to
formulate his convictions with regard to the service and sacrifice
of Christ. This he describes as fundamentally a work of mediation ('mediator Dei et hominum, homo Christus Jesus'). This
term, like so many of those adopted by the Christians to indicate
their beliefs, simply reeked of associations derived from the most
primitive and degraded levels of pagan superstition. But, so far
from rendering it inappropriate for their purpose, this circum-

stance served merely to enhance its value and significance as applied to the Redeemer. This it did by emphasizing the fact that the days of the *hostia*, victim or scapegoat, were thenceforth at an end; hereby proclaiming the salutary truth of the future as against the deadly error of the past.[1] At the same time, the mediation of Christ possessed an application no less vital to errors equally deadly, though by no means primitive or degraded, i.e. to those of the philosophers. In this connexion its service was to provide an answer to the secular quest for a *logos* through the revelation of God as the one supreme substance (*summa substantia*) underlying and sustaining all things visible and invisible; hence the source of actuality, truth, and value; capable, as has been said, of producing novelty without innovation of will, and with potentialities which were simply inexhaustible.[2] This vision of the Godhead served to dispose of many erroneous philosophic fancies. To begin with, it excluded the possibility of an independent, contrary principle;[3] and, from this standpoint, the devil himself was not independent; his very devilishness, indeed, lay in a false claim to be so.[4] In the second place, it constituted the foundation for a new theory of the relationship between body and soul, based on the doctrine of the Spirit as the unmoved mover;[5] a point of view from which evil could no longer be ascribed to the 'substance or nature of the flesh'.[6] Finally, in the acceptance of Christ as the Incarnated Word there were contained important implications for the theory of knowledge. For, if it denied the hope of a technique of transcendence such as the Platonists had dreamed of, on the other hand it provided an assurance that the concepts of human science, so far from representing a distortion of cosmic order, depended for their very existence upon it. Hence the oft-repeated description of Christ as the 'rock' or 'foundation' for a new physics, a new ethic, and a new logic.

---

[1] *De Civ. Dei*, x. 20: 'in forma servi sacrificium maluit esse quam sumere, ne vel hac occasione quisquam existimaret cuilibet sacrificandum esse creaturae . . . huic summo vero sacrificio cuncta sacrificia falsa cesserunt.' Cf. xix. 23: 'cessaturas victimas'. For pagan theory, see Rohde, *Psyche*, ch. ix, p. 296: 'the famous scapegoats were nothing but sacrifices offered to appease the anger of the unseen and thereby release a whole city from "pollution" . . . a superstitious fear of uncanny forces surrounding men and stretching out after them a thousand threatening hands in the darkness. It was the monstrous fantasies of their own imagination that made men call upon the priests of purification and expiation for much-needed aid and protection.'   [2] *De Civ. Dei*, xi. 10, and 24 foll.   [3] xii. 2.   [4] xix. 13.
[5] x. 12: 'temporalia movens, temporaliter non movetur.'   [6] x. 24.

From this standpoint, the Trinitarian principle is hardly to be explained as 'an hypostasization of what is in fact merely a sensation at the pit of the stomach'; a highly sophisticated version of the 'God-hypothesis' which, inspired by the dread of malign and sinister forces in nature, seeks either to 'work' or to propitiate those forces by techniques of magic or appeasement. Nor, on the other hand, can it be understood merely as a fresh philosophic 'set-up'; a point of view from which it has been denounced as 'the ideology of a vanished epoch', a 'reflex in terms of spiritual values of a complex of material realities' which, by our day, have disappeared as completely as the Roman empire itself. For an ideology, in this sense, is simply a rationalization invented by the discursive reason in order to bridge a chasm which its own activity creates; its value for this purpose being in no sense dependent upon its inherent truth but wholly upon its capacity to stimulate 'action'. This it does 'by evoking hopes and fears, love and hate, desire, passion, the driving urge of egoism, the *me*'; and, 'in this process, the imagination has no other role to play than to give an impulse to these motive forces, succeeding therein as it presents them with "objects" sufficiently powerful to excite them'.[1]

For such perversions of intellectual activity Augustine has a name and it is a strong one; he calls them *fantastica fornicatio*, the prostitution of mind to its own fancies. To him, therefore, they represented, in its grossest and ugliest aspect, the betrayal of understanding. As such, they were errors of the scientific intelligence in its effort to become an instrument of control. That is to say, they originated from the temptation to eat of the tree of knowledge rather than of the tree of life. Recognition of this fact does not, however, move Augustine to turn his back on science; for it is not by a reversion to the primitive, by the denial of that which specifically constitutes their manhood, that the sons of Adam are to recover their lost Eden. On the contrary, it prompts him to ask whether, if such be the conclusions from their reasoning, they do not point to some radical defect or flaw in the apprehension of the first principle from which all valid deduction and inference must proceed. From this standpoint he regarded the Trinitarian principle as useful from two points of view. Negatively, it was to serve as the basis for a radical criticism of classical error; positively, as the point of

[1] Georges Sorel, *Réflexions sur la Violence* (1912), p. 45, footnote.

departure for a fresh attack on old problems, exempt from the defects which had vitiated the thought of classical antiquity.[1]

Classical error, as the classicists themselves fully appreciated, was hydra-headed; to demolish it seemed to them a task reserved only for supermen and thus not unworthy the labours of Hercules himself. To Augustine, however, the problem did not appear in any sense hopeless; for, widespread as were the ramifications of that error, and various as were the fruits which it produced, they all originated from a single root, to cut which was to destroy the whole luxuriant tangle by denying it the nutriment from which it drew its strength. From this standpoint, he drew the indictment of Classicism in one comprehensive formula, discovering the source of its difficulties in the fact that it acknowledged the claim of science to be architectonic and, therefore, entitled to legislate with sovereign authority for the guidance of human life.[2]

The error of Classicism was in this respect original; it could, indeed, be traced to the world of naïve experience revealed by Homer and the poets.[3] The world to which Homer introduces his reader is a world of movement, in which impressions succeed one another with lightning rapidity. Against this background emerges the figure of man, face to face with a mysterious universe which his riotous imagination peoples with demonic forces; while, at the same time, his reason struggles vigorously to reduce those forces to some kind of order. To this endeavour he is impelled by a conviction that on his power to overcome the obstacles which confront him depends his lot or destiny ($\mu o \hat{\iota} \rho a$) and, therewith, the possibility of achieving the heroic ideal, the conquest by virtue of chance or necessity. His difficulties are indeed prodigious, since the forces with which he is in contact are no less powerful than erratic. They are, moreover, a prolific growth, some of which are envisaged as personal and thus capable either of benevolence or malignancy, others as impersonal and so remorseless and inexorable in their operation, there being no clear or obvious line of demarcation between the two. In these circumstances life is felt as eminently precarious,

[1] De Civ. Dei, vii, praef.: 'diligentius me pravas et veteres opiniones veritati pietatis inimicas, quas tenebrosis animis altius et tenacius diuturnus humani generis error infixit, evellere adque exstirpare conantem,' etc. . . .

[2] Plato, in the Phaedo, had, of course, criticized this claim. His difficulty, as Augustine saw it, was that he could not suggest a possible alternative.

[3] De Civ. Dei, iv. 26, 30; v. 8; ix. 1.

charged to the full with possibilities of peril and hazard. Nevertheless, success (ὄλβος) is by no means out of the question, at least for those who are endowed by fortune (τύχη εὐδαιμονίη τε[1]) with the requisite qualities of manly excellence (ἀρετή) and of confidence or faith (θάρσος, the faith of the warrior), and who are thus ready and willing to accept the challenge to live dangerously. For such exceptional and outstanding spirits, the 'god-like' heroes, the world of the *Iliad* and the *Odyssey* is, on the whole, a bright world and life a proud adventure, the glory and exhilaration of which are tempered only by the ever-present fear of death and of the prospect which awaits even an Achilles among the shades.

The work of Homer as a poet points directly to his work as a theologian. As poet it is his business to 'construct'; as theologian, to explain. The task of construction he performs with consummate skill, drawing the elements of his cosmology from the stream of common life and thus from a source much closer to reality than were the subsequent abstractions of science and philosophy. The elements so derived serve as material for his *myth* (ἔπος καὶ μῦθος) which thus presents itself at once as a story told for the entertainment of his hearers and as a plausible or 'convincing' account of the facts as the poet and his audience see them. And since, for the Greeks of the Homeric as for those of later ages, 'all things are full of gods', plausibility in this case means that the poet has, at the same time, succeeded in discharging the second part of his task, by 'creating' a world fit for heroes to live in. In so doing, he provides an early but none the less definitive expression of the classical genius, in one of the most significant of its many aspects. The world of heroes, however, continues to be recognized as the real world only by those who are themselves cast in the heroic mould and who thus, in some degree, share the heroic spirit. For the rest, the triumphs and satisfactions which that world offers are merely apples of Sodom. Already in the *Odyssey*, the optimism which the *Iliad* appears to justify becomes somewhat remote; and, as the vision of triumph to be achieved through wit and endurance (μῆτις or πραπίδες and ἀνδρεία), the main ingredients of virtue, fades from the screen, there arises a further, more energetic and, at the same time, more conscious and deliberate search for a principle of understanding. This was the heritage which Homer be-

[1] H. Hymn. xi. 5; cf. Pindar, *Ol.* 8, 67; *Pyth.* 8. 53; *Nem.* 6. 24, etc.

queathed to his successors in the craft of poetic composition. As such, it was to bear its own ripe fruits in the work of Hesiod, Pindar, and the Athenian dramatists.

We cannot afford to linger over the efforts of these men to succeed where Homer failed.[1] Their apparatus and methods were, like his, dramatic, i.e. the *logos* or account which they had to give emerged as an integral element of the moving pattern of action which they constructed as a setting for it; the 'set' as thus arranged yielding them their *data*, the constituents of a world in miniature.[2] Like Homer also they looked for a solution along the lines of aesthetic rather than of intellectual satisfaction; although, of course, there could be no absolute divorce between the two. What they thus offered was a higher criticism of Homeric ideas; conducted, however, from within the limits of an ideology which was, in essence, that of Homer himself.[3] The effort thus undertaken was to culminate in the work of the Athenian playwrights, who were destined to wrestle valiantly with the insoluble problem of man at grips with necessity ($\dot{a}\nu\dot{a}\gamma\kappa\eta$) until with Euripides, her strength flagging, tragedy dissolved into a flood of tears. But not until long after philosophy had arisen to pursue the same quest along lines which were distinctively its own.

The inspiration of philosophy was identical with that of poetry. By the discovery of a principle of understanding, which should embody the true *logos* or explanation of action and reaction, of doing and suffering in this world, it aimed at once to satisfy the spirit of classical curiosity and, at the same time, to possess itself of an instrument by which to control the environment ($\tau\dot{o}$ $\pi\epsilon\rho\iota\acute{\epsilon}\chi o\nu$). In its quest for such a principle, however, philosophy laid claim to a certain autonomy. The basis of this claim was twofold; it rested upon (*a*) a fresh and original attitude towards the data, and (*b*) a new sense of propriety regarding the interpretation which might justly be put upon them. Thus, with respect to the data, it denied itself the indulgence which poetry had shown itself so ready to exploit, i.e.

---

[1] Needless to say, the 'failure' of Homer as a theologian does not in the slightest detract from his success as a poet!

[2] See, e.g., Aristotle, *Poetics*, vi, on the six elements of tragedy; three external, viz. spectacular presentation ($\dot{o}$ $\tau\hat{\eta}s$ $\ddot{o}\psi\epsilon\omega s$ $\kappa\dot{o}\sigma\mu os$ or $\ddot{o}\psi\iota s$), lyrical song ($\mu\epsilon\lambda o\pi o\iota\acute{a}$), diction ($\lambda\acute{\epsilon}\xi\iota s$); three internal, viz. plot ($\mu\hat{v}\theta os$), character ($\mathring{\eta}\theta os$), and thought ($\delta\iota\acute{a}\nu o\iota a$), together with his observations on the relative importance of the various elements.

[3] Ibid. xxvi, on the question of 'whether the epic or the tragic mode of imitation ($\mu\acute{\iota}\mu\eta\sigma\iota s$) is the better'.

that of constructing its *cosmos* freely and without let or hindrance. On the contrary, it professed the utmost regard for phenomena, the 'observed facts'; and from this standpoint its chief concern was to 'save the appearances' even if this was to magnify out of all proportion the difficulties of its task. Then, with respect to the *logos* or explanation, it boldly transferred the court of final appeal from the heart to the head; thereby committing itself to the pursuit of intelligible connexions rather than of aesthetic satisfaction. These self-imposed decencies constituted the *differentia* of philosophy. By accepting them she was to attain significance in her own right as the supreme effort of Classicism to interpret the riddle of the Sphinx.

Historically the process of philosophy developed as an inescapable consequence of the preconceptions with which it embarked upon its mission. It thus began with an attempt to 'determine' the frontiers of nature, by representing it as a closed system of orderly relationships. It then proceeded to disengage the 'elements' (στοιχεῖα, *elementa mundi*) of this system; as, in the first instance, with the so-called hylozoists, fire, air, water, earth; or subsequently, when methods of investigation had become refined, either as 'the limited and the unlimited', as 'atoms and the void' or, finally, as 'form and matter'.[1] In so doing its purpose was to lay bare the principle (ἀρχή) underlying phenomena, and this principle it identified with ultimate being or reality. This being, whether conceived as water (Thales), air (Anaximenes), fire (Heraclitus), or some element undefined (Anaximander) or on the other hand as the limit, form (τὸ πέρας— Pythagoras), was recognized as the first *arché* or creator (*causa subsistendi* or substantial cause, *causa principiumque rerum*). But, with the recognition of such a principle, it became apparent that there was needed also a second principle, to relate the world of pure 'being' to that of 'becoming' (τὸ ὄν and τὸ γιγνόμενον). And thus philosophy found itself committed to the recognition of a second *arché* or creator, which it designated as the principle of movement (*ordo vivendi* or *finis omnium actionum*). The 'search for causes' was completed by the recognition of still a third principle which was intended to exhibit the connexion between the principles of being and of movement. As such, it took rank as a third *arché* or creator, which might be described as the principle

[1] See Burnet, *Early Greek Philosophy*, 3rd ed. 1920, pp. 287, 333, and *Greek Philosophy from Thales to Plato*, Pt. I, 1920, pp. 44–6.

of intelligibility (*ordo* or *ratio intellegendi, lumen omnium rationum*).[1] Thus, by a process which was at once logical and chronological, philosophy woke up to discover that she had on her hands no less than three independent *archae* or first principles, each of which meant in fact an independent problem; she had to offer an account of being, of movement, and of the order or relationship between them. In these circumstances it is not surprising that she should have faltered somewhat in her stride.[2]

The increasing sense of difficulties to be surmounted left its impress on both thought and action in the latter part of the sixth and throughout the fifth centuries, during which it found expression in a widely diversified crop of philosophic heresies. Of these, not the least significant was the fully matured system of dialectical materialism worked out by Heraclitus on the basis of Ionian philosophic monism.[3] Over against this we may set the emergence, in Magna Graecia, of what was to blossom forth as the mystical idealism of the Pythagorean school. A third development of importance was the critique of opinion instituted by Parmenides and Zeno, the result of which was to demonstrate either the impossibility or the unintelligibility of motion. It was, no doubt, a realization of the impasse created by this and analogous problems which presently suggested the possibility of evading the tyrannical dictates of the new mistress of human thought. This took effect in one of two ways: (1) an assertion of the claims of 'positive' science, (2) a drift into subjectivism and sophistry. 'Positivism,' the claims of which were powerfully urged by Hippocrates in his treatise *Ancient Medicine*, depended upon the acceptance of a distinction between primary

[1] Rohde, op. cit., p. 388, observes that it was only with Anaxagoras that philosophy arrived at 'the first distinct separation of the intellectual thinking principle from the material substance with which it was—not fused, much less identified but—contrasted in sovereignty and independence'. Anax. περὶ φύσεως,—πάντα χρήματα ἦν ὁμοῦ, εἶτα νοῦς ἐλθὼν αὐτὰ διεκόσμησε.

[2] For his summary account of the development of Greek thinking, Aug. *De Civ. Dei*, viii. 1–8 and 10. For his view regarding the relation of the Trinity to the so-called tripartite division of philosophy, ibid. xi. 24 and 25. He thinks that this division contains an 'intimation' of truths to be explicitly formulated in the Trinitarian principle.

[3] Lest it should be supposed that this is mere romancing, attention may be directed to the statement of Hegel (*Geschichte der Philosophie*, i, p. 328), quoted by Burnet (*Early Greek Philosophy*, p. 144, footnote), that there was not a single proposition of Heraclitus which he had not taken up into his own logic. It is generally supposed that the achievement of Marx was 'to stand Hegel on his head'. The truth is that he merely saw through him to his original in Heraclitus. The bearing of this will be evident from what we have to say in the concluding chapter.

and secondary causes, and upon concentration on the latter to the exclusion of the former as the duty of true science. Subjectivism, on the other hand, received its mandate at the hands of Protagoras in the famous maxim, 'man is the measure of all things; of those that are that they are, and of those that are not that they are not'. Coincident with these developments occurred a widespread recrudescence of obscurantism, which owed its direct inspiration to the popular mystery cults but, at the same time, received a certain support and encouragement from Pythagoreanism. In this combination of factors we may perceive the situation which was to excite the anxious concern of Plato.

Both in his diagnosis of the sickness of philosophy and in the remedy which he proposed, the work of Plato was of crucial significance for the future of human thought. Plato began by accepting the three traditional problems as he had inherited them from his predecessors, viz. the problem of being, of movement, and of order. But, with regard to these problems, his acute intelligence enabled him to perceive two facts of supreme importance. These were:

(*a*) That none of the *archae* so far put forward transcended the limitations of mere opinion (δόξα); they were thus merely 'hypothetical', the result of a gallant but none the less empirical and arbitrary effort of scientific simplification.

(*b*) That no intelligible, i.e. necessary, relationship had as yet been established between the *arché* of being and that of movement; for this, he supposed, the responsibility must rest upon some defect in the apprehension of the third *arché*, that of order. This being so, it pointed inevitably to concentration upon the third problem as the ultimate problem of philosophy. It was in this connexion that, according to the Christians, Plato made the blunder of his career, a blunder which was the more tragic because he had come within a hair's breadth of stumbling upon the truth.[1] For, instead of pausing to ask himself whether, if the conclusions thus far reached were so disheartening, the

---

[1] See Augustine, *De Civ. Dei*, the passages in which he offers an appraisal of Platonism, esp. viii. 5: 'nulli nobis quam isti propius accesserunt.' Cf. chs. 6, 7, 8 and *De Vera Relig.* 4. 7: 'si hanc vitam illi viri nobiscum rursum agere potuissent . . . paucis mutatis verbis adque sententiis Christiani fierent, sicut plerique recentiorum nostrorumque temporum Platonici fecerunt.' *Sermo* 141. 1: they see the truth like Moses from afar, but have achieved no effective plan of saving themselves from error: 'ad tam magnam, ineffabilem, et beatificam possessionem qua via perveniretur non invenerunt.' For Augustine's final and conclusive repudiation of Platonism and the reasons for it see *Retract*. i. But it must here be pointed out that

reason for this might not lie in some radical misapprehension of the problem as originally proposed, Plato took precisely the opposite course. Assuming that the deficiencies of opinion were those of sense-perception, he identified reality with the pattern or 'idea', illusion and error with the deliverances of sense. From this it was concluded that 'ideas' were 'independent', possessing an existence in their own right and without relation to their applicability to sensible data. Their validity was thus to be tested only in terms of an ideal principle which might be accepted as absolute. Accordingly, with respect to the three problems of contemporary philosophy, Plato inferred that what was needed was a principle of unification and verification, an idea of ideas, the Form of the Good, the One. To the vain effort of discovering such a principle he devoted much of his working life, sublimely unconscious of the fact that, in so doing, he was making himself the prisoner in his own cave.

The acceptance by Plato of this erroneous logic was, in the opinion of Augustine, the reason for his errors in physics and ethics. Not that, as has been argued, it 'introduced a reason fashioned after human models' to replace the materialist explanation of natural phenomena in terms 'of immutable necessary laws' and therewith a system of teleological rather than of mechanical 'causation'.[1] For, as must surely be evident, and as indeed the earlier history of materialism had gone to prove, the attempt to delimit 'nature' in either of these ways was not so much to close the frontiers of the *cosmos* as it was to close one's own eyes. The real difficulty was that, as materialism had failed to do justice to the problem of mind, so idealism failed to do justice to the problem of matter, which it sought to define as the 'all-but-nothing'. This was to immobilize reality, reducing it purely to terms of structure, so that time was represented as a 'moving image of eternity'[2] and process, as such, was identified with 'irrationality' and 'evil'. The counterpart to this in human nature was the picture of the multiple soul, a composite (σύνθετον) of discrete elements confronting one another in a struggle to be

he regarded the Platonists as far and away superior in all three departments of philosophy. So his criticism of Plato boils down to this: that, although he had discovered God as *principium nostrum, lumen nostrum, bonum nostrum* ('causa constitutae universitatis et lux percipiendae veritatis et fons bibendae felicitatis'), this God is strictly transcendental. Accordingly, Plato cannot display his immanence while, at the same time, doing justice to the *vitia* of the material world.

[1] Lange, *History of Materialism*, i p. 52.   [2] *Tim.* 37 D: εἰκὼν κινητός τις αἰῶνος.

concluded only by the final release of mind from its prison-house in matter and by its return to the source of its being, the 'life' of pure form. The fallacies involved in such a theory of human nature were endless, but they were epitomized in the fact that it represented individuality, the existence of man in the flesh, not as a vehicle for the expression of personality but as an obstacle to its realization, an obstacle to be surmounted only by an utter repudiation of the life of sense. To embrace this ideal was, however, suicidal; it was not merely to misunderstand the significance of sense-experience but to rob the soul of its dynamic. These deficiencies were to become apparent as Platonism entered the stream of history, when they were to manifest themselves in doctrines like those of Porphyry and Julian. And, however wild and fanciful, such doctrines were the legitimate offspring of Platonic science.

It is instructive to consider the teaching of these men, as representing the last important effort of classical idealism to vindicate the claims of intelligence and life and, at the same time, to reconcile those claims with one another. For, by their failure to do so, they exposed the utter paralysis of the *ratio scientiae*, thus helping to create the situation which resulted in the conversion of Augustine and other Platonists to Christianity. By the Platonists, as they called themselves, the sum and substance of reality was described, in a manner which indicates the fusion of Pythagorean with genuinely Academic elements, as the *Monad* or the *One*. They thus began by identifying the creative principle, in the first instance, with *Unity* (τὸ ἕν) as the origin of numerical series, from whence all subsequent numbers were 'derived', while the beginning of division was found to lie in the *Dyad*, duality being thus envisaged as a 'second', though dependent principle, and as such the source of such further differentiation as might in turn 'generate' multiplicity. But if this was the intention, it was not to succeed, since all that the creative principle served to engender was a complex of wholly unreal and insoluble problems where none, in fact, existed.[1] As an incidental consequence of its activity, however, it gave rise to a prolific growth of scientific myth, which was thus designed,

[1] On this 'primal differentiation', see Plot. *Enn.* vi. 9. 5, where the 'intellectual principle' is described as having 'sundered itself from the One by an act of self-assertion (τόλμα)'. This is to suggest that original sin is to be ascribed to the Godhead. Yet, in *Enn.* ii. 9. 4, Plotinus declares that the soul did *not fall* in order to create the world of body.

by filling the interstices, to conceal the cracks in the edifice. To begin with, by a wholly artificial construction, the Platonists managed to associate duality with the origin of the subject-object relationship. Then, conscious of the disturbing possibilities involved in this relationship and as a measure of reassurance, they declared that the demiurge (the subject), as the Divine Intelligence, First Born of the One, contained 'within himself' the eternal forms or archetypes of Being. The question was, then, how to relate this second creator with the visible and palpable world. To answer this question the Platonists assumed the existence of a third *hypostasis* or order of being, the Universal Soul, the function of which was to establish effective contact between the world of Ideas and that of sense. For this purpose this Soul was conceived as having its residence, so to speak, outside both worlds; it 'looked upward' in order to contemplate the eternal archetypes, 'downward' in order to impose those archetypes on matter, which was thus 'informed' or given body. This it accomplished by means of its 'generative' power. From which the inference may be drawn that, for Platonism, body derives its character as such, if anywhere, from the Ideal world. And since body may be defined as that which involves displacement, it follows, either that space has been smuggled illegitimately into the picture or that the Ideal world itself is spatial; in which case space attains a *locus standi* in ultimate reality. From this point of view, Platonic idealism is exposed in its nakedness as nothing but a crypto-materialism, in which the idea plays the role of Homeric ghost to matter. At the same time it is exposed as rotten with anthropomorphism and myth. Its character as an anthropomorphism is betrayed by the constant use of terms such as 'beget', 'generate', 'derive', 'upward', 'downward', 'emanation', 'emergence', the 'One' and the 'Many', which it invokes as a means of describing cosmic process. Surreptitiously borrowed for this purpose, terms such as these belong in fact to human activity, for the description of which they were originally invented, and their application to the problem of *genesis* is sheer metaphor. The mythologizing tendency of Platonism, on the other hand, begins with its attempt to envisage the creative principle as an all-inclusive *One*. It is further revealed when Platonism hypostasizes the number *Two* and ascribes to it the generative power of a second god. Finally, the Universal Soul, depicted as a *Third Creator*, was in fact nothing but a pure hypothesis intended to supply a link between the two worlds of sense and intelligence (κόσμος αἰσθητός and κόσμος νοητός); as such, it constitutes a typical rationalization of the human mind.[1] It is not surprising, therefore, that in the shadow of such a cosmology there lurked a host of demons, ready and waiting to spring to life.

So much for description, the 'cosmos' as envisaged by the Neoplatonists; now for the *logos*, *ratio*, or reason in terms of which that system was to become intelligible. The problem of Platonism, as indicated by the master himself, was to build a bridge from the *Many* to the *One*; that is, to lay hold of a principle by virtue of which it would be possible to 'unify' and 'verify' the findings of experience. The method by which it proposed to achieve this end was that of 'dialectic'; dialectic being conceived as the instrument by which the reason elevates itself from the illusory world of sense to that of the forms or patterns, the 'archetypes of reality' and, from thence, to the 'Absolute' which lies behind and beyond them.[2] That is to say, the problem of Platonism was one of transcendence; it had somehow to find a means of passing to a 'heavenly place' (τόπος ὑπερουράνιος) beyond the point at which the subject-object relationship, inherent in the operations of the discursive reason (διάνοια), still remained to trouble the activity of pure thought (νοῦς). To the successors of Plato in the New Academy that problem presented itself as ultimately insoluble. Accordingly, they took refuge in the so-called 'law of probability', as a sufficient guide for the ordinary purposes of life. The Neoplatonists, however, refused to content themselves with this purely pragmatic settlement. Perceiving, as they did, that to accept the Academic rule 'suspension of judgement' was virtually to convict oneself of radical scepticism, they resumed with all possible energy the attempt to reach a solution of the problem along the lines originally proposed by Plato. The result, however, was simply to expose the essential futility of the Platonic programme, together with the elements of obscurantism which it contained. In this connexion we may note as especially significant the work of Plotinus, whose mission it was to demon-

---

[1] Augustine, commenting on the Neoplatonic triad, remarks (*De Civ. Dei*, x. 24) that the character and function of the Third Creator (*Spiritus*) is necessarily ambiguous.

[2] *Tim.* 28 A: νοήσει μετὰ λόγου περιληπτόν; see *Phaedo* 79 A: τῶν δὲ κατὰ ταὐτὰ ἐχόντων οὐκ ἔστιν ὅτῳ ποτ᾽ ἂν ἄλλῳ ἐπιλάβοιο ἢ τῷ τῆς διανοίας λογισμῷ.

strate, among other things, that objects exist only for subjects. By so doing he arrived at a *reductio ad absurdum* of the classical ideal of scientific objectivity, thus bringing the process of strictly classical speculation to an ignominious end. For in this conclusion was involved an admission that, as between the scientific and the super-scientific intelligence (classical διάνοια and classical νοῦς), there yawned an impassable gulf.

But if Plotinus did this it was with evident reluctance. For it was one thing to show that the subject-object relationship constituted a squirrel-cage of the scientific intelligence; it was quite another to concede that, if such were the case, the 'really real' lay beyond the range of rational apprehension. It was thus that Plotinus clung doggedly to the aspiration of *scientia*, even after its method had broken in his hands; and that, as the One had ceased to be a possible object of thought, he embraced it as an object of adoration. With this in view he undertook to exercise himself by moral and spiritual gymnastic for the apprehension of a supreme reality which was still, as he supposed, 'out yonder'.[1] This involved a rigorous programme of *ascesis*, variously described as a progressive 'evacuation' by the soul of all elements of complexity, i.e. of sense-perception and positive knowledge, otherwise as a process of unification (ἕνωσις) and simplification (ἅπλωσις), which was undertaken as a necessary preliminary to the communion of 'like with like'.[2] This peculiar form of self-torture was, however, to fail miserably of its purpose and Plotinus succeeded merely in plunging himself into a morass in which his successor, Porphyry, was to wallow helplessly, in a vain endeavour to reach solid ground. The efforts of Porphyry to save himself were those of desperation. He devised an elaborate scheme of purgations as a means of purifying his mind (*anima intellectualis*); while, in order to cleanse his spirit (*anima spiritalis*) of what Augustine scornfully calls 'the falsities of imagination and the deceitful play of vain phantoms', he even had recourse to the dubious art of theurgy, which thus

---

[1] The basis for such 'purification' is, of course, already to be found in Plato. See *Phaedo*, 67 c: κάθαρσις εἶναι τοῦτο ξυμβαίνει . . . . τὸ χωρίζειν ὅτι μάλιστα ἀπὸ τοῦ σώματος τὴν ψυχὴν καὶ ἐθίσαι αὐτὴν καθ' αὑτὴν πανταχόθεν ἐκ τοῦ σώματος συναγείρεσθαί τε καὶ ἀθροίζεσθαι . . . ἐκλυομένην ὥσπερ [ἐκ] δεσμῶν ἐκ τοῦ σώματος.—This should be contrasted with the Christian ideal of 'regeneration' of the flesh.

[2] For this return of the soul see Plot. *Enn.* vi. 8. 3: 'We ascribe free will only to him who, enfranchised from the passions of the body, performs actions determined solely by intelligence', i.e. the 'evil will' is not 'free'.

appears, in purpose if not in method, as the ancient equivalent of modern psycho-analysis. But, strenuous though they were, the net result of his endeavours was merely 'to blind him to a recognition of the true wisdom which is in Christ'.[1] Meanwhile, to Augustine, the explanation of Porphyry's failure was obvious; it was simply that, as he put it, the latter was 'wrongly placed' for the apprehension of truth. It was equally obvious that, if Porphyry was ever to overcome his difficulties, he must approach them from a radically different point of view. That is to say; in his search for a principle of intelligibility, he must abandon the *logos* of Plato in favour of the *logos* of Christ.

For Augustine the failure of Platonism was the failure of what he generously acknowledged to be by far the most vital and tenacious of the philosophic heresies. In his eyes, therefore, that failure was catastrophic, as marking the utter bankruptcy of classical reason; and the tragedy was heightened by the fact that it arose, not from any inherent deficiency of the instrument, but from its abuse. As such, however, it was from the beginning implicit in Classicism, the inevitable consequence of (*a*) the spirit and purpose with which it approached its problems, and (*b*) its attempt to solve them by means of the *ratio scientiae*. From this standpoint the apparent independence of philosophy was, he undertook to show, wholly illusory; classical philosophy was, indeed, simply classical poetry in cap and gown. For philosophy, like poetry, began by envisaging the 'subject' as in some sense 'opposed' to the 'object' world.[2] It then proceeded to tell itself a story, the purpose of which was to establish an intelligible relationship between the two. But, from the very nature of the case, the relationship thus established could not possibly rise above the level of plausibility and attain to the character of necessary truth. In other words it remained inevitably mythical or hypothetical; and, from this point of view,

---

[1] *De Civ. Dei*, x. 9 foll., 23, 27, 28, 32. In this connexion there is a certain significance in Augustine's remarks about the Christian Eucharist. For the believer to partake of the elements is not, he says, to contaminate himself with matter. Ch. 24: 'Non enim caro principium est aut anima humana, sed Verbum per quod facta sunt omnia. Non ergo caro per se ipsam mundat, sed per Verbum a quo suscepta est.—Nam de carne sua manducanda mystice loquens, cum hi qui non intellexerunt offensi recederent . . . respondit: *spiritus est qui vivificat, caro autem non prodest quicquam.*'

[2] It might be argued that this opposition makes its appearance with Heraclitus when he predicates λόγος and φρήν of τὸ περιέχον ἡμᾶς. See Diels, *Fragmente der Vorsokratiker* ed. 5, vol. i, p. 148, ll. 37–8.

there was little or nothing to choose between the work of Pindar or Aeschylus and that of Plato and Aristotle.[1] It may here be observed that, as employed in such a context, myth or hypothesis serves the purpose of a fuse which is introduced into an electrical series in order to complete the circuit of intelligibility but which is in danger of blowing out whenever the load becomes too heavy for the system to bear. By using it in this way Classicism foreshadows certain modern attempts to solve what is essentially the same problem by methods which are at bottom analogous. In such cases, however, the *logos* or demiurge is normally subjected to a second baptism according to the prevailing fashion of the hour. But, despite the Protean capacity with which it thus disguises itself, it represents in fact nothing but an obfuscation of the discursive reason, powerfully though perhaps unwittingly supported by a 'will to believe'.

This being the case it is not surprising that in its quest of the *logos* Classicism was foredoomed to failure, condemned *ab initio* to an interminable conflict between scepticism and dogmatism.[2] From this impasse there was no escape, whether upwards by way of transcendence, or downwards into positivism. The former, the way of Plato, found an unsatisfactory issue in the subjectivism of Plotinus and Porphyry. As for the latter, it depended upon the acceptance of a wholly arbitrary distinction between 'primary' and 'secondary' causes; and, thereafter, upon the possibility of making, from the totality of existent fact, an equally arbitrary selection of such factors as it might choose to dignify with the name of 'cause'.

Augustine rejected scepticism with complete assurance: 'Academic doubt,' he says, 'is academic madness'.[3] The grounds of this assurance were at once intellectual and moral. It thus depended, in part, upon the conviction that there could be no significant doubt except upon the presumption of actual knowledge. But, in his case, this conviction was reinforced by a fear that the acceptance of probabilism as a rule of life would engender in many minds an utter despair of any truth to be discovered; a consideration which, on its own level, was not less valid or cogent than the first.[4]

---

[1] In this connexion Aristotle recognizes that, however different are myth and hypothesis, there is nevertheless a quite definite relationship between them. *Metaph.* 982b18: ὁ φιλόμυθος φιλόσοφός πως ἐστιν.

[2] See Ch. IV, above, p. 164.   [3] *De Civ. Dei*, xix. 18.   [4] *Retract.* i. 1.

But if Augustine thus emphatically repudiated the solution of the sceptics, it was not to fall into the opposite pitfall of dogmatism. Indeed, when considered in relation to the philosophic background, Trinitarian Christianity presents itself, not as dogma, but as the rejection of dogma, not as the assertion but rather as the denial of anthropomorphism and myth; and it calls for a final and conclusive expulsion of these elements from the description of ultimate reality as the preliminary to a starkly realistic account of nature and of man. In so doing it pointed to a fulfilment of the desideratum of Classicism, μόνον ὁ μῦθος ἀπέστω—a promise made in turn by each significant figure in the long history of classical speculation. But it insisted that, for the accomplishment of this undertaking, it was necessary to begin with the findings of *sapientia* rather than with those of *scientia*, i.e. with 'creative' rather than 'poetic' or 'scientific' truth. With this reorientation of attitude there at once emerged consequences of the utmost importance. Negatively, it made possible a drastic revision of the valuations of Classicism; positively, it offered a revelation in consciousness of the essential constituents of selfhood, together with a recognition of their dependence upon the creative principle—in the language of religion, of 'personality in God'. The clue to which, as has already been indicated,[1] might be found in asking and answering the question: What do I really know?

The elements of Augustinian epistemology are, as is now fully recognized, drawn from Platonic sources, especially from Plotinus; and, so far as concerns the terminology employed, it is possible to establish an almost exact coincidence between the two.[2] The real problem, however, is not so much to find verbal parallels, as to examine the use to which Augustine puts the Plotinian terminology, with a view to discovering, if possible, what elements of novelty it contains. In this connexion it is important to observe that, for Augustine, the operation of consciousness is a continuous and uninterrupted process, in which no hiatus develops at any point.[3] The truth of this may be illustrated by what he has to say regarding the knowledge of what he calls the *exterior* man. This knowledge begins with sense-perception and culminates in science. On the former

---

[1] Above, pp. 403 foll.
[2] See Alfaric, op. cit.; Gilson, *Introduction à la Philosophie de St Augustin.*
[3] See Ch. X, above, p. 388.

level, its rudiments are already present in the life of sense (*sensualis vita*) which mankind has in common with the higher animals. These include memory, recollection, desire, and aversion, leading to the pursuit of physical satisfaction and the avoidance of physical pain. Moreover, by a law of compensation, certain animals are endowed with senses more acute than the corresponding senses in man, as some of them also excel him in bodily strength and stamina. On the other hand, domestic animals, such as the dog, exhibit characteristics which identify them closely with human beings; they can even play and smile (*iocari et ridere*).[1] Science, however, envisaged as a capacity for ordered knowledge, involves mental processes which are peculiar to and distinctive of mankind, the *actio rationalis*. It thus presupposes the existence of a reasoning mind.[2] But this fact constitutes no title to divinity; it represents merely the fulfilment of his nature as a human being.[3] It thus remains dependent upon the creative principle; man has it, indeed, because he is 'made' in the 'image' of God. A similar continuity is evident in the relationship between what Augustine calls the knowledge of the *exterior* and that of the *interior* man; i.e. between the awareness of objects and the awareness of being aware; since, as we have already seen, the one is unthinkable except in relation to the other. It is, indeed, precisely this fact which gives to man his character and enables him to fulfil his destiny as a human being. Thus, for Augustine, there is no break whatever between the lower and the higher manifestations of conscious life. Throughout, the distinctions are simply those of descriptive analysis; to make them is not to imply that there is any real discontinuity in the series.

The absence of such discontinuity is emphasized by the fact that the mind does not operate *in vacuo*; in all of the various phases of its activity, it is moved by desire, which may thus be described as the spur of dynamic personality. From this standpoint sense-perception emerges as a complex process, the elements of which are hardly to be separated even in thought; a 'unity in trinity' which embraces (*a*) *corpus*, the 'body' which is seen, presenting itself as *res visibilis*, *species corporis*, or *impressa imago sensui*; (*b*) *anima*, the vision (*ipsa visio*) of the percipient

---

[1] *De Lib. Arbit.* i. 8. 18 foll.; *De Vera Relig.* 29. 53; *De Trin.* xii. 2.
[2] *De Trin.* xii. 3. 3: 'illa rationalis nostrae mentis substantia'.
[3] *De Lib. Arbit.* ii. 6. 13: 'ratio . . . mens rationalis . . . in quibus natura nostra completur ut homines simus'.

soul; (c) *voluntas* or *intentio animi*, a conscious and deliberate effort of apprehension, uniting (*copulans*) the two in a manner so violent that it can only be described as desire, passion, or lust (*amor, cupiditas, libido*).[1] In this connexion Augustine pauses to observe that he has no complaint to make regarding the senses; they are faithful and competent reporters, if only their messages are rightly understood. To understand them aright is the task of scientific reason.[2]

Scientific reason accepts as its data objects which are revealed through sense-perception as *phantasiae imaginationis* or *imaginalia figmenta*, depending upon whether they are actually present or have to be recalled to mind.[3] It then undertakes to discriminate between fact and fancy, by checking the evidence of the senses and inferring therefrom the true 'nature' of the object revealed *imaginaliter*.[4] To do so, it applies to this evidence 'norms' such as equality, likeness, &c., which, while meaningless except in relation to sense-data, are nevertheless not provided by them.[5] This fact reveals the dependence of the scientific intelligence upon the creative principle.[6] But, here again, there is the most intimate relationship between the mental activity and its practical consequences (*intellectus et actio vel consilium et exsecutio*); so much so that the process of reason may otherwise be described as reasonable appetite or desire (*ratio et appetitus rationalis*). Or, as he elsewhere puts it, 'desire is the neighbour of scientific reason' and 'mental parturition is invariably attended by desire'; the desire in question being nothing more or less than the desire to know which had been consecrated by Classicism as an end in itself under the name of *curiositas*. For Augustine, however, its character is merely economic or functional. In human life it fulfils a role precisely analogous to that of sense-perception on those levels of apprehension which are common to man and animal. This it does by providing him with a body of systematic knowledge, the 'knowledge of temporal and mutable things', adequate to the conduct of his affairs.[7]

---

[1] *De Trin.* xi. 2 foll.
[2] *Contra Acad.* iii. 11. 26; *De Gen. ad Litt.* iii. 5.
[3] *De Trin.* x. 6.　　　　[4] 10.　　　　[5] *De Vera Relig.* 30.
[6] *De Trin.* xii. 2. 2: 'sublimioris rationis est iudicare de ipsis corporalibus secundum rationes incorporales et sempiternas, quae ⟨rationes⟩ nisi supra mentem humanam essent, incommutabiles profecto non essent.'
[7] 12. 17: 'cognitio rerum temporalium et mutabilium navandis vitae huius actionibus necessaria'.

In this formula there is involved a radical departure from the classical view of science as a 'search for causes', and a recognition of its true character as 'descriptive' of nature. As such, its ideal is fulfilled in the 'necessary' truths of mathematics, e.g. the proposition $7+3 = 10$; a proposition which, as it is vindicated by the certainty of reason, may be accepted as always and everywhere valid.[1] But the vast bulk of what is called science never attains to this level of universality; it possesses merely the character of experiential truth; i.e. of truth which rests upon generalizations of experience.[2] Such generalizations are inevitably *ex post facto*, and subject to exceptions, as, e.g., with the rule 'buy cheap and sell dear', and their validity depends upon whether all parties to the transaction cherish the same standard of value.[3]

This analysis reveals at once the scope and limitations of scientific or 'man-made' truth. For it thus becomes apparent that, as the study and systematization of empirical fact, science enables mankind to rise above the level of animal creation and to behave in a manner distinctively human, by relating means to ends in an ordered scheme of life. As such, it unquestionably has 'its own good'.[4] The good of science, however, is limited by the fact that it fails to disclose an end other than that of mere adjustment, *ut conformemur huic saeculo*. It is thus incapable of satisfying the appetite for felicity to which mankind, by the very conditions of his being, necessarily aspires. Accordingly, it reveals its dependence upon *sapientia* as the source of valuations in the light of which alone the sovereign good may be achieved.

This view of *sapientia* or Christian wisdom as a basis for the judgement of value marks a final revolt from the spirit and method of Platonic science. Verbally, Augustinian *sapientia* is the exact equivalent of Plotinian νοῦς. For Plotinus, however, the function of νοῦς was to communicate with the One which is beyond knowledge and beyond being, and which is thus revealed, as has been already noted, only in ecstasy. Augustinian *sapientia*, on the other hand, is emphatically not ecstatic and it presupposes no such detachment from this material world. As the judgement of value, it is, indeed, 'independent' of science

---

[1] *De Lib. Arbit.* ii. 8. 21.

[2] *De Trin.* xiii. 1. 2: 'et ad scientiam pertinet quae historica cognitione continetur.'   [3] 3. 6: 'vili emere, caro vendere'.

[4] xii. 14. 21-2, and elsewhere.

and of the scientific discipline. That independence, however, serves merely to establish its right to supplement the deficiencies of science, by providing a fresh vision of the cosmos and of man's place in it. In the light of *sapientia*, man no longer sees himself over against a 'nature', conceived anthropomorphically whether as 'thought' or 'mechanism'. On the contrary, he sees himself and his universe together as an expression of beneficent activity, the activity of the creative and moving principle—in the language of religion, as a 'creature', whose origin, nature, and destiny are determined by the will of God.

Accordingly, the creative principle is recognized as the *summa substantia* which manifests itself in the orderly movement of the cosmos and the source of truth, beauty, and goodness, as these are progressively disclosed to the consciousness of mankind. Thus, for the Christian, there can be no question regarding either the validity or the significance of experience. The world in which he finds himself is, indeed, as Classicism had supposed, the world of nature (φύσις), but it is a 'nature' transfigured by the fact that he sees it as the theatre of divine activity.[1] And this he is enabled to do, only by virtue of powers with which he has been providentially endowed. Thus, says Augustine:

'I laboured to discern and to appraise everything according to its worth, taking some things on the evidence of my senses, inquiring about others which I felt were mingled with myself, numbering and distinguishing the reporters ⟨the senses⟩ themselves and, in the treasure-house of memory, revolving some things, storing up others, drawing out others. . . . Thou art the abiding light which I consulted regarding all these, whether they were, what they were, and how they were to be evaluated. . . '.[2]

Needless to say, this is not to assert a theory of 'innate ideas', a theory which, together with that of reminiscence, properly belongs to Platonic science. It is merely to declare that the possibility of knowledge must remain for ever an insoluble mystery, to be ascribed to the activity of the creative and moving principle, as revealed by Christ. In this sense it becomes true to say that Christ the 'Word' is present as an inward teacher in every act of apprehension.[3]

The revelation of Christ was the revelation of the Divine Nature as a Trinity. Accordingly, in the Trinity, Christian

---

[1] *De Civ. Dei*, xxii. 22 and 24.   [2] *Conf.* x. xl. 65.
[3] *De Magist.* 12: 'Christus veritas intus docet.'

wisdom discovers that for which Classicism had so long vainly sought, viz. the *logos* or explanation of being and motion, in other words, a metaphysic of ordered process. In so doing, it does justice to the element of truth contained alike in the claims of classical materialism and classical idealism; while, at the same time, it avoids the errors and absurdities of both. Thus, for example, with regard to being, this is involved in the consciousness of orderly movement which, unless utterly illusory, as the sceptics maintained, certainly implies existence. To the question: What sort of existence? the answer readily suggests itself: The existence of 'body'.

But in this answer lies the danger of serious misapprehension. For, on the one hand, it is possible to regard this body as ultimate, i.e. the real principle of our existence as human beings. This, indeed, is the way in which body presents itself to the naïve intelligence, and to have accepted it as such had been the error of Tertullian, who was thus driven to account for consciousness as a kind of epiphenomenon.[1] On the other hand, body might be resolved, as it was by the Platonists, into mere 'appearance', deriving such reality as it possessed from a world of self-subsistent forms beyond itself—a view which, if accepted, would suggest the false ideal of Plotinus and Porphyry. To Augustine, however, these alternatives are equally unsatisfactory; body is neither absolute reality nor absolute appearance; it is the organ by which mankind establishes contact with the objective world. And, vice versa, it is the mode in which that world discloses itself when regarded 'objectively', i.e. through the eye of the flesh. As such, it is wholly dependent upon sense-perception, in the analysis of which its true character is revealed.

Augustine thus reasserts the Heraclitean sense of a 'flux', but only to put a fresh interpretation upon it. From this point of view 'everything', he declares, 'which the bodily sense touches and which is thus called sensible, is subject to change without intermission, and this goes on constantly and continuously without out the slightest pause'. Of the multitude of stimuli which thus inflict themselves (*infligo*) upon consciousness, an indefinite number are too 'slight' and too 'brief' to register as bodies at all; since, in order to do so, they must have some degree of permanence.[2] Body thus manifests itself as 'protraction'; it is

---

[1] *De Mor. Eccl.* i. 21. 38; *De Gen. ad Litt.* x. 25 and 26, 'Tertulliani error de anima'.
[2] *De Div. Quaest.* lxxxvii, qu. 9: 'quod autem non manet percipi non potest.'

simply that which appears to us to 'occupy' space and to 'take' time; accordingly, it may be defined as extension.[1] As thus conceived, it assumes the form of an *imaginale figmentum*, an image which the mind frames for itself to serve, so to speak, as a ticket of recognition. This process yields the world of moving patterns visible to the carnal eye.[2]

This analysis indicates that the apprehension of bodies is not a merely passive process, but that it involves an effort of attention on the part of the percipient which may be described as a *distentio animi*, a tension or 'stretching of the mind'.[3] The nature of this effort may be illustrated by the fact that, even in reading a sentence, there is a suspension of meaning until the period is reached.

It may thus be inferred that there is no such thing as absolute body, but that what we call 'size' is relative to ourselves as observers: 'the world itself is great, not absolutely, but only as compared with the smallness of ourselves as one of the animals of which it is full'.[4] The same is true of what we call time, the intervals of which, as e.g. in the case of music, differ for every animal endowed with the sense of hearing.[5] In other words, if all parts of the universe should become proportionately smaller or proportionately greater at one and the same moment, there would be no appreciable difference: 'nihil in spatiis locorum et temporum per se ipsum magnum est sed ad aliquid breve, et nihil rursus in his per se ipsum breve est sed ad aliquid maius'.

With this assertion of a general relativity of size, Augustine arrives at conclusions of considerable interest. In the first place, it suggests that time, apart from the motions of body, is unthinkable;[6] in the second, that any attempt to identify time with the motion of particular bodies is wholly arbitrary. 'I once heard a learned man say', declares Augustine, 'that the motions

[1] *De Natura et Origine Animae*, iv. 21. 35: 'corpora . . . id est quae per distantiam longitudinis, latitudinis, altitudinis locorum occupant spatia'.

[2] *De Civ. Dei*, viii. 6: 'ordinatus motus et elementa disposita a caelo usque ad terram et quaecunque corpora in eis sunt'; xi. 4: 'mundus ipse ordinatissima sua mutabilitate et mobilitate et visibilium omnium pulcherrima specie'; *De Trin.* iii. 2. 7: 'ordo naturalis in conversione et mutabilitate corporum'.

[3] *Conf.* xi. xxvi. 33.

[4] *De Vera Relig.* 43. 80: 'mundus ipse magnus non pro sua quantitate sed pro brevitate nostra'.   [5] *De Musica*, vi. 7.

[6] *De Civ. Dei*, xii. 16: 'ubi nulla creatura est, cuius mutabilibus motibus tempora peragantur, tempora omnino esse non possunt'; *De Gen. ad Litt.* v. 5: 'motus si nullus esset nec spiritalis vel corporalis creaturae, quo per praesens praeteritis futura succederent, nullum esset tempus omnino.'

of sun, moon and stars are times themselves, but I did not agree. For why should not rather the motions of all bodies be times?'[1] The conclusion follows: 'it is in thee, my mind, that I measure times. . . . I measure the impression (*affectionem*) which things as they pass by make upon thee, and which, when they have passed, remains; it is this which is still present that I measure, not the things which pass by to make this impression'.[2] From this the inference may be drawn that each and every one has his own 'times', past, present, and future; and that these are not the same for any other man. 'There are three times; a present of things past, a present of things present, a present of things to come. . . . These three exist, in some sense, in the soul, but otherwise I do not see them: present of things past, memory; present of things present, sight; present of things to come, expectation.'[3] Thus, what we loosely describe as a 'long future' is in fact 'a long expectation of the future'; a long past, 'a long memory of the past'.[4]

But if Augustine thus appears to shake the firmament about our heads, it is with no intention of offering any endorsement to philosophic doubt. What he wants to establish is simply this: that time is not a *principium*. Accordingly, to recognize ourselves as creatures in time is to recognize ourselves as in relation to other creatures. These relationships constitute our 'nature'. Our 'bodies' are thus, in the Latin sense of the word, our 'natures'. This being the case, it becomes superfluous to invoke a 'principle of individuation' from outside; since these natures are what they are by virtue of an inner principle, the law of their own being; in the language of religion, they are 'made' or 'created', not 'begotten' or 'derived'. From this point of view we may see ourselves as possessing the *inseparabilis distinctio* and *distincta coniunctio* of a quasi-trinity; being, nature, and consciousness. The nature is not to be confused with the essence of our being; since the relationships in question are meaningless except, as we say, to us. On the other hand, the essence has no significance apart from the nature through which and in which it finds expression; so far as it is revealed, it is revealed only in its activity. Finally, while neither 'essence' nor 'nature' is to be identified with awareness of them, they are, on the other hand, meaningless abstractions except in relation to it. Accordingly.

---

[1] *Conf.* xi. xxiii. 29.　　　　[2] xxvii. 36.　　　　[3] xx. 26.
[4] xxviii. 37; for the application of this theory of time, see Ch. XII, below.

it is just as absurd to conceive of ourselves 'subjectively' as beings (entities) apart from bodies (relationships) as it is to conceive of ourselves 'objectively' as body apart from being. To ask for either is to demand the impossible. To which we may add that the reality, whether of being or of nature, does not in the least stand in need of vindication. And as for the question: What would happen if either were different from what it is? this question may be dismissed as purely gratuitous, since no man by thought or otherwise adds a cubit to his stature; nor is he an engine with replaceable parts. In other words, we are what we are by virtue of the inner law of our own being. As such, we are endowed with powers of perception and discrimination such as are necessary for the conduct of life. These powers are developed with habit (*consuetudo*) and they require constant exercise, without which they are in danger of atrophy.[1] This is a truth of fundamental importance, for on it depends our place in the sun.

In these considerations Augustine finds the 'law' which governs human thought and activity. For man to recognize this law is to perceive that it is impossible for him, by any effort of knowledge or imagination, to escape from the limitations of his nature and to view things as they 'really' are, *sub specie aeternitatis*. It is thus to relinquish the aspiration to omniscience, recognizing that his powers of apprehension are determined by the conditions of his existence as a creature in time and space and, as such, irrevocably subject to what Augustine calls the *vicissitudo spatiorum temporalium*.[2] This being so, his problem is, in the vernacular, 'to beat the clock', and in this fact lies for him the real significance of time. From this standpoint it becomes apparent that time is anything but otiose.[3] But to say that time works wonders is really to say that men work wonders in time. It is, indeed, through their consciousness of spatio-temporal movement that they are enabled to see themselves (*a*) directly and actually, as lords of creation, and (*b*) indirectly and potentially, as heirs to immortality.

From this point of view nature reveals itself as a hierarchy of concrete existences or beings, each and every one of which

---

[1] *De Musica*, vi. 7; *De Gen. ad Litt.* v. 12.

[2] *De Civ. Dei*, xi. 5 and 6, esp.: 'quod enim fit in tempore et post aliquod fit et ante aliquod tempus; post id quod praeteritum est, ante id quod futurum est.'

[3] *Conf.* iv. viii. 13: 'non vacant tempora nec otiose volvuntur; per sensus nostros faciunt in animo mira opera.'

moves according to its own specific principle. To man, as observer, the principle remains unknown; what he perceives is merely the movement.[1] Thus, as we say, a stone moves downward 'by force of gravity', but that is merely a scientific myth. Furthermore, the rationale (*ratio*) of such motion is in no sense external to or imposed upon the beings in question but, in the words of Augustine, 'intrinsic' to them.[2] Accordingly, it may be said that the 'tree is hidden in the seed; but such is the principle of its being that there is no seed from seed without the intervention of a tree'.[3]

Accordingly, the process of nature as a whole may be described as follows:[4]

'The whole process of nature, to which we are accommodated, involves certain natural laws of its own, according to which the spirit of life, which is a creature,[5] gives expression to its own definite urges, determined in a certain way, so that they cannot be contravened even by a bad will. And the elements of this corporeal world have each their specific power and quality, determining what each may or may not do, and what each may or may not become. From these original principles, everything which comes into existence, each in its own season, derives its origin and process, and on them depend the end and extinction of each several kind. Thus it happens that beans are not produced from grains of wheat, nor grains of wheat from beans, nor men from animals, nor animals from men.'

What Augustine here means to assert is that ants, as such, do not breed elephants; that nature, as we see it, presents itself as orderly movement. This movement is determined by a law which operates directly to 'create' and 'sustain' the natures in question; they are what they are by reason of its unremitting activity: *omnia ordine complectitur; temeraria nequaquam natura*.

To assert the operation of such a law was to dispose of certain characteristic problems of the Greeks. It was, for example, to perceive that 'chance', 'contingency', or 'accident', so far from being a principle either of 'creation' or 'limitation', was a mere illusion of classical idealism; nothing, in fact, but the apotheosis of the unintelligible. At the same time it was to recognize the impossibility of establishing any necessary connexion between the motion of bodies and the moving principle, since that

[1] *De Gen. ad Litt.* v. 20. 'movet (Deus) occulta potentia universam creaturam.'
[2] vii. 16.   [3] v. 23.   [4] ix. 17.
[5] Not, as the Platonists had supposed, a 'Third Creator' independent of the beings whose motion it occasions.

principle was known only in and through its manifestation in bodily motion: *invisibiliter visibilia operatur*. Finally, inasmuch as the working of that principle was direct and immediate, 'intrinsic' to the natures in which it operated, there could not possibly arise any antinomy between Creator and Creation. Thus the notion of a demiurge, or principle of *liaison*, producing multiplicity as a magician produces rabbits from a hat, was exposed as a gratuitous assumption of the scientific understanding. In the language of religion the will of God was the necessity of things: *Dei voluntas rerum necessitas*.[1]

Accordingly, in the spectacle of evolving nature, Augustine finds ground for recognizing the universal sovereignty and providence of God. But in so doing, he is well aware that he has passed beyond the point of which science can tell anything, since science sees the work but not the worker. Thus any attempt to describe the *operatio Dei* involves the use of symbols which, strictly speaking, are metaphorical. In using such symbols, Augustine does so with the full consciousness that they are metaphor.[2] Moreover, he endeavours to avoid misleading implications such as that involved in the thought of nature as the 'living mantle of God', since this would be to suggest Platonic pantheism. In his effort to suggest the Christian idea of this relationship, the first point which he seeks to emphasize is that of dependence. This he does in the notion of sovereignty. But the sovereignty in question differs in two essential respects from that of Caesar: (1) it is not physical (visible and palpable), (2) it is not based on any jealous monopoly of material power.[3]

Secondly, and in a manner truly Roman, Augustine represents the divine sovereignty as constitutional rather than arbitrary, an *imperium* rather than a sultanate. To illustrate this he invokes the Stoic and Neoplatonic seminal reasons (λόγοι σπερματικοί or *seminales rationes*) as an appropriate means of illustrating the orderly process of nature. In this connexion he encounters the problem of miracle, with which he deals in

---

[1] *De Gen. ad Litt.* vi. 15. 26.

[2] e.g. *De Civ. Dei*, xii. 24: 'manus Dei potentia Dei est . . .'.

[3] Ibid., ch. 26: 'ipsas omnino naturas, quae sic vel sic in suo genere afficiantur, non facit nisi summus Deus, cuius occulta potentia cuncta penetrans incontaminabili praesentia facit esse quidquid aliquo modo est, in quantumcumque est.' Ibid. vii. 30: 'ipsis etiam inferis dominationem suam potestatemque non subtrahit . . . itaque administrat omnia quae creavit ut etiam ipsa proprios exercere et agere motus sinat.'

characteristic fashion. Among the pagans, miracle or portent had been understood as the sudden and violent interruption of what was otherwise a regular order, occasioned by the intervention of supernatural powers desirous of signalizing pleasure or annoyance. For Augustine, on the other hand, miracle, so far from representing a violation of nature, is simply the (humanly speaking) obscure and incomprehensible in nature. 'Nature', he says, 'is all order and all miracle, but the miracle is the order, and greater than any miracle performed by man is man himself.'[1]

To say this was to deny the opposition which Classicism had set up between man and nature and, therewith, the heroic ideal, the conquest of chance or necessity by human virtue. It was to see nature as a whole, in which, from the lowest to the highest forms, there was absolutely no *saltus* or break; since all, without exception, were equally dependent upon the creative principle. These forms might be classified in an ascending scale as inorganic, organic, and conscious, the basis of distinction being respectively mere existence (*esse*) as of a stone, life (*vivere*) as of an animal, and intelligence (*intellegere*) as of a man;[2] and of these, intelligence, as the fullest and most perfect expression of organic life, might be taken to mark the highest development of terrestrial existence. From this standpoint the emergence of man was that of an *animal rationale mortale*[3] or, more exactly, as an *anima rationalis mortali atque terreno utens corpore*;[4] in other words, as an embodied soul. This meant that he existed as an individual, born into a certain period of time and space and subject to the general conditions of organic life, especially to that of mortality.[5] It meant also that his perceptions were individual and 'private': 'singulos nos habemus sensus; tuum sensum non nisi tuum et meum non nisi meum'. And what was true of his senses was no less true of his mind: 'manifestum est etiam rationales mentes singulos quosque nostrum singulas habere'. The mind, then, was no scintilla of the divine essence, enjoying an immortality foreign to the life of sense. But, such as it was, it nevertheless played a vital part in the human economy; since, by making possible a vision of his nature and

---

[1] *De Civ. Dei*, x. 12; *De Gen. ad Litt.* ix. 17.   [2] *De Lib. Arbit.* ii. 17. 46.
[3] *De Civ. Dei*, xvi. 8.   [4] *De Mor. Eccl.* i. 27. 52.
[5] i.e. since the 'Fall', which is the starting-point of human history, properly so called.

capacities denied to other creatures, it pointed to a programme of conscious and deliberate activity as the law for man.

But in order to envisage mankind in this light, it was necessary, as Augustine perceived, to transcend the strictly scientific attitude. Thus, he declares, 'when a living body, whether of animal or man, presents itself as a moving object, there is no way open to our eyes by which they may discern its mind, since mind, indeed, is invisible to the eye. Nevertheless, we realize (*sentimus*) that in this mass (*illi moli*) there is something akin to that which is in our own mass, i.e. life and soul.'[1] This recognition of soul as the activating principle in human life does not represent an appeal from the authority of Democritus and Epicurus to that of Hippocrates, Aristotle, or Galen, i.e. from what we should call a mechanistic to a vitalistic 'science'. On the contrary, it marks a complete departure from scientific method since, in fact, it rests upon a recognition of the third *hypostasis* of the Trinity as the principle of cosmic motion.[2]

From this point of view Augustine sees the life-process of human beings in terms of a body-soul complex in which body fulfils the requirements of an organ or instrument to soul, and this he applies no less to the elementary vital functions than to the highest manifestations of conscious and deliberate activity. Thus, as he says, 'soul is that by which I vivify my flesh' (*qua vivifico carnem meam*); it is this mysterious substance which 'unifies the body, resists disintegration, regulates the distribution of nutriment, and presides over generation and growth'.[3] Such processes are, as he recognizes, subconscious; but in attempting to describe those which fall within the margin of consciousness, he uses language which indicates that, for him, their character is precisely analogous. Thus it is soul which makes possible sense-perception, 'by which I sensitize my flesh' (*qua sensifico carnem meam*). Sensation may therefore be defined as a 'passio corporis per se ipsam non latens animam', 'a stimulation of the sense-organs sufficiently powerful to register in consciousness'.[4] As such, it is immediately translated into an emotion (*perturbatio animi*), in which form it gives rise to movements of appetition or aversion, the so-called *sensuales animae motus*.[5] Such movements

[1] *De Trin.* viii. 6. 9.
[2] Aristotle, no doubt, approximates to this in his doctrine of soul as the 'entelechy' of body. Nevertheless, he regards νοῦς (the higher intelligence) as distinct from the organic *psyche*.
[3] *De Quant. Animae*, xxxiii. 70.   [4] xxx. 58.   [5] *De Trin.* xii. 12. 17.

may be classified as those of desire, pleasure, fear, and pain; but they are all subsumed beneath the one category of love, 'the love', as he says, 'by which I love my own existence'.

From this analysis two points of fundamental importance emerge. The first is that 'the motions of the soul are not alien to us'.[1] With all the vigour at his command Augustine insists upon the continuity of experience, and denies the existence of any real hiatus between the life of sense and that of thought.[2] 'From the soul and from the body, which are the parts of a man, we arrive at the totality which is man: accordingly, the life of the soul is not one thing, and that of the body another: but both are one and the same, i.e. the life of man as man'.[3] That is to say, the roots of our nature as human beings strike deep into the physical world but they are not on that account any the less spiritual; nor do the manifestations to which they give rise become different simply because psychologists choose to give them different names; there is, indeed, little or no point in rebaptizing the fundamental affections as 'rational states'.[4] In other words it is precisely the same divine *hormé* which, on the lowest plane of instinctive life, impels the animal to fight for bare existence and which, on the highest, provides the saint with power to triumph over such obstacles as may interfere with a realization of felicity through the knowledge and love of God.

The second point follows as a corollary to the first, and it is this; that love is to the mind what weight is to a body.[5]

'The body, by its own weight, strives towards its own place. The pull of weight is not downward only, but to its own place. Fire tends upward, a stone downward. They are urged by their own weight, they seek their own places. Oil poured below water rises above the water; water poured upon oil sinks below the oil. They are urged by their own weights to seek their own places. When out of order, they are restless; restored to order, they are at rest. My weight is my love; thereby I am borne whithersoever I am borne.'

It is thus inevitable that we should pursue that course of action

[1] *De Civ. Dei*, xiv. 19, 23 and 24.
[2] See *Retract*. i. iv. 2 for an important emendation to what he regards as a careless statement made in the *Soliloquia*.
[3] *De Civ. Dei*, xiv. 4: 'et ab anima namque et a carne, quae sunt partes hominis, potest totum significari quod est homo; adque ita non est aliud animalis homo, aliud carnalis, sed idem ipsum est utrumque, id est secundum hominem vivens homo.' [4] Ibid., ch. 8; Stoic εὐπάθειαι.
[5] *Conf.* xiii. ix. 10: 'pondus meum amor meus; eo feror quocumque feror.' Cf. *De Civ. Dei*, xi. 28; *Ep.* 157. ii. 9, &c.

which pleases us best: 'quod amplius nos delectat, secundum id operemur necesse est'. In this fact lies the immeasurable significance of the human affections, whether for good or evil; they are so to speak the feet of the soul: *quasi pedes sunt.* Accordingly, if our loves are evil, they will most certainly lead us to perdition; if good, they will with equal certainty save us from it: 'The flesh is the nag on which we make the journey to Jerusalem.'[1]

From this analysis of movement or the *hormé* it follows that the destiny to which mankind is subject is one to which he subjects himself. 'Every living soul,' declares Augustine, 'not merely the rational or human soul, but also the irrational souls of cattle, birds, and fish, is moved by representations (*visis movetur*). But whereas, with irrational beings, these representations at once give rise to movement to which each creature is impelled in accordance with its specific nature, the rational soul is at liberty either to consent to these representations or to withhold consent.'[2] The motivation of the rational soul may thus be analysed as follows:

(1) *suggestio*: suggestion, derived either from thought or sense-perception (*sive per cogitationem sive per sensus corporis*).

(2) *cupiditas*: desire, the natural urge prompting to the satisfaction of the motive suggested.

(3) *consensio rationis*: the assent (or refusal) of reason, dictated by a consideration of ends and means.

The freedom of the rational soul is thus part and parcel of its rationality. 'The stone', declares Augustine, 'has no power to restrain its downward motion, but the mind is not moved until it wills to be moved.'[3] Accordingly, will may be defined as an 'uncoerced motion of the mind, making for the attainment of an object or for the prevention of its loss'.[4] As such, it constitutes an original element of the human endowment, the possession of which distinguishes the behaviour of man from that of other animals and translates it into conduct.

To this conception of will, as an autonomous determination of the total self, Augustine adheres tenaciously at all stages of his career.

'There is nothing which I feel with such solid and intimate assurance as that I have a will, and that it is by this will that I am moved

---

[1] Sermon (very probably apocryphal) *De Cantico Novo* 3: 'caro nostra iumentum nostrum est: iter agimus in Ierusalem.'   [2] *De Gen. ad Litt.* ix. 14. 25.
[3] *De Lib. Arbit.* iii. 1. 2.   [4] *De Duabus Animis*, x. 14.

to all forms of satisfaction. I do not, indeed, find anything which I can call my own, if the will by which I will and nill is not my own.'[1]

'Will is certainly in all men; nay, we are all nothing else but wills. For what are desire and pleasure other than will in consenting to those things which we want; and what are fear and distress other than will in dissenting from those things which we do not want?'[2]

'You could not imagine anything so much in our power as that when we will to act, we act. Accordingly, there is nothing so much in our power as will itself.'[3]

This is to go much farther than to assert that 'our wills are included among the efficient causes' and to argue that 'effort is efficacious'. It is to brush aside this and other equivocations of science in order to proclaim a revolutionary view of will as the one efficient cause of human activity. To Augustine it was evident that to stop short of this was to impair the unity and integrity of conscious life. Accordingly, he places himself squarely in opposition to those who, from whatever standpoint, admit a 'cause of will' independent of the willing subject. Conspicuous among such persons were the Manicheans who, by recognizing a 'principle of evil', frankly acknowledged the existence of such a 'natural' or 'essential' cause of evil will.[4] But Augustine was no less concerned to expose the error of the Platonists which, as he insisted, rested upon a false antithesis between body and soul.

'Platonism', he declares, 'manages to avoid the cosmic dualism of the Manichaeans by attributing all the elements of this visible and palpable world to God as architect. Nevertheless, the Platonists suppose that souls are so affected by their earthly joints and moribund members that they attribute to these the diseases of desire, fear, joy, and pain, the four perturbations or passions in which is contained all the vitiation of human conduct.'[5]

But to assert that the will is uncoerced is not to suggest that it is undetermined. It is merely to insist that its determinations are governed, not by what Athanasius had called 'things outside' ($\tau\grave{a}$ $\check{\epsilon}\xi\omega\theta\epsilon\nu$), but by a principle of inner control. In so doing, it removes the ambiguity which classical naturalism had attached to the word 'cause'. Accordingly, what Classicism had described as 'physical' causes, Augustine understands as factors which may condition but in no sense dictate the determinations

---

[1] De Lib. Arbit. iii. 1. 3 (circa 389).   [2] De Civ. Dei, xiv. 6 (circa 400–13).
[3] Retract. i. 8. 3 (circa 427).   [4] De Civ. Dei, xii. 9.   [5] xiv. 5.

of the will. 'Physical or corporeal causes', he declares, 'are negative rather than positive, and they are in no sense to be included among the efficient causes.'[1] In order to take effect as such, they must first be translated into terms of appetition or aversion; and it is only as this occurs that they serve to move the wills of men.[2] Accordingly, it appears that what is called a 'good will' is nothing more or less than a 'good love' and vice versa.[3]

In this analysis we may perceive a fresh approach to the classical problem of sin and error, as well as to that of incontinence;[4] the origin of which Augustine ascribes to a bad will, rooted in a bad love. This bad will he defines as the 'will to power' when, as he says, 'the soul, loving its own power, relapses from the desire for a common and universal good to one which is individual and private'.[5] As such, it gives rise to phenomena such as a passion to explore the secrets of nature (Faustian *curiositas*) or a thirst for domination over one's fellow men (*tumidus fastus*) or, simply, the filthy whirl of sensual pleasure (*caenosus gurges carnalis voluptatis*), but, whatever its particular manifestations, it involves the subordination of spiritual to material goods, i.e. to some form of what he calls the *cupiditas mundi*.[6] It may thus be traced, in the first instance, to pride (*superbia*), the desire 'to try out one's own power' and so 'to become like gods'; otherwise, to the pursuit of an ideal of self-sufficiency, in utter disregard for the fact that human nature has not received the capacity to achieve felicity without acknowledging its dependence upon the principle of its life and being.[7]

Intellectually, this bad will finds expression in an effort

[1] *De Civ. Dei*, v. 9: '. . . quoniam hoc possunt quod ex ipsis faciunt spirituum voluntates'.
[2] Ibid. xiv. 6: 'et omnino pro varietate rerum quae adpetuntur atque fugiuntur, sicut adlicitur vel offenditur voluntas hominis, ita in hos vel illos affectus mutatur vel vertitur.'   [3] Ibid., ch. 7.
[4] The ἁμαρτία as revealed in tragedy together with classical ἀκρασία, *Arist. N. E.* vii. 1–4.   [5] *De Trin.* xii. 9. 14.   [6] Ibid. xi. 3. 6; *De Patientia*, 14.
[7] *De Trin.* xii. 11. 16; *De Gen. contra Manich.* ii. 21 and 22. This, the doctrine of 'original' sin, may be regarded as the crux of Augustinianism and, indeed, of Christianity. It was directed, in the first instance, against the maxim of classical naturalism, *lex est perire*. As against this, the Christians asserted that the soul of man, though naturally immortal, was subject to death by reason of sin (*De Civ. Dei*, xiii. 2: 'anima humana veraciter immortalis'. By death they meant physical death, the 'separation of body and soul'. Ibid. 3: 're vera mors, qua separantur anima et corpus'). On this paradox rested the whole of Christian theology.

'to make one's own truth', i.e. to justify one's conduct by rationalizations which are blindly and stubbornly adhered to for the very reason that they cannot stand the light of day. Such rationalizations are the involuntary tribute which vice pays to virtue. They are pernicious precisely because they normally embody an element of truth, since absolute falsehood is absolute nonsense and thus incapable of deceiving any but the veriest dupes. From this standpoint, pride is the devil's own sin, and the devil himself is first in the field as an ideologist.

From this Augustine concludes that sin is due originally to a corruption, not of body but of soul.[1] As such, it begins with a wrong determination of the will and develops as the result of physical satisfactions derived therefrom, until it is finally confirmed by the bond of habit.[2] Its consequences are thus insidious, far-reaching, and cumulative; the ultimate nemesis being frustration or self-defeat through the loss of genuine freedom and power. The atrophy of native capacity manifests itself in a progressive weakening or enfeeblement both of mind and character (*infirmitas, imbecillitas*). It thus finds expression in (a) ignorance or blindness (*ignorantia, caecitas*), the 'error' which permits one's own shadow to interfere with one's vision, and (b) in *difficultas* or *necessitas*, an increasing inability to resist the seductions of sense. Accordingly, he says, 'the man who, knowing the right, fails to do it, loses the power to know what is right; and the man who, having the power to do right, is unwilling, loses the power to do what he wills'.[3] Thus, strictly speaking, the definition of will as 'an uncoerced movement of the mind' applies only to the will of Adam before the fall; i.e. before he deliberately transgressed the divine command.[4] As for the will of the natural man, it cannot properly be described as free, since its determinations are throughout vitiated by his refusal to acknowledge his dependence upon the creative and moving principle. He may thus be described as a slave to sin, that is, to his own aberrations of mind and heart.

From this condition deliverance is indeed possible, but it is not to be achieved either by taking refuge in illusion or by kicking against the pricks. It thus depends, in the first instance,

[1] *De Civ. Dei.* xiv. 2 and 3.　　　[2] *De Patient.* 14; *De Lib. Arbit.* iii. 19. 53.
[3] loc. cit.; *De Vera Relig.* 20; *Retract.* i. 15. 3.　　　[4] *Retract.* i. 15. 5.

upon an accurate diagnosis of the situation. This involves a recognition by man of the fact that there is no 'essential' cause for his shortcomings; that it is by reason of his own pride and wilfulness that he has become an outcast from his Eden.[1] To apprehend this truth is to perceive that 'there could have been no error in religion, had not the human spirit chosen to take as its god either soul (the Platonic world-soul) or body (the matter of the physicists) or fancies of its own creation (*phantasmata sua*), whether singly or in conjunction'.[2] Thus, observes Augustine, the word *anima* is never used in the Scriptures except to denote 'that by which mortal animals, including man, live, so long as they are mortal'.[3] So much for the notion of a 'world-soul,' entertained by the Stoics and others.[4] On the other hand, he dismisses as equally fallacious the supposition that nature is composed exclusively of 'body' or of 'images derived from body'.[5] But, in even greater degree, the possibility and the hope of redemption rest upon a conviction that, since man, in his inmost heart, craves for nothing so much as true felicity, he will not for ever be content with spurious imitations, but will, in the end, be prepared to submit to the conditions whereby alone his desire may be realized.

Trinitarianism thus points to a new and effective technique of salvation. This salvation consists, in the first place, of emancipation from *ignorantia* and *caecitas*, the ignorance or blindness which results from a misapprehension of the possibilities contained in the instrument of apprehension and from its consequent misuse. To experience such emancipation is to perceive that, alike in 'form' and in 'matter', mankind worships nothing but rarefied abstractions of his own fancy. *A fortiori*, it is to recognize that his problem is one neither of transcendence nor of submersion; he is not required to identify himself with a disembodied, impersonal, and, therefore, wholly supposititious One, nor yet to merge himself in a world conceived as purely quantitative, but simply to open his eyes to the existence and activity of the *logos* within his own breast. To do so is to eliminate the errors characteristic of scientific ideology, errors of reification and word-fetishism which flow from the

---

[1] *De Vera Relig.* 36, 66: 'falsitas non ex rebus sed ex peccatis'; *Retract.* i. 15. 4: 'cupiditas non alienae naturae additamentum sed nostrae vitium'.
[2] *De Vera Relig.* 10.   [3] *Retract.* i. 15.
[4] e.g. Verg. *Georg.* iv. 221–2.   [5] *De Mor. Eccl.* i. 21. 38.

acceptance of a distorted or partial view of reality. But, difficult as it may be to rid the mind of the stubborn obsessions of
science, this in itself is not enough. For, as we have seen, these
errors have their roots in a passion for independence and self-
sufficiency. This means that the conditions of wisdom are, at
bottom, not so much intellectual as moral. Accordingly, for the
attainment of wisdom, what is needed is a radical reorientation
of the affections, whereby the love of self (*amor sui*) may be
subordinated to the love of God (*amor Dei*). This is the 'regeneration' by virtue of which alone 'difficulty' can finally be
overcome.

But, for the purpose of such regeneration, there is need for
what Augustine calls the gift of divine grace. This need he
asserts in the most comprehensive and unequivocal terms, as
essential both to the possibility of and the will for salvation.[1]
For, as he shrewdly observes, to stop short with a body of pro-
hibitions is not to destroy but merely to intensify the desire to
sin; while, in order that true justice may triumph, it must be
embraced with a consuming and overmastering passion.[2] But,
on the other hand, what is the actual condition of the human
heart? 'Of itself, it is devoid of light; of itself, devoid of strength.
All that is beautiful—virtue and wisdom—has its residence in
the heart. Yet it is not wise of itself nor strong of itself; it is
neither its own light nor its own strength.'[3]

The doctrine of sin and grace marks, in its most acute form,
the breach between Classicism and Christianity. It had been
the considered judgement of Aristotle that 'virtue and vice are
both alike in our own power'.

'For where', he says, 'it is in our power to act, it is also in our power
to refrain from acting, and where it is in our power to refrain from
acting, it is also in our power to act. . . . But if it is in our power to
do and, likewise, not to do what is noble and shameful, and if so to
act is, as we have seen, to be good or bad, it follows that it is in our
power to be virtuous or vicious.'[4]

To Augustine, however, there was no such folly among the
many follies of philosophy as to suppose that mankind, by
reason of any capacity inherent in himself, possessed the ability
to discover a good independent of that which was intrinsic to
him as a created being, much less to generate within himself the

---

[1] *De Grat. Christi*, &c. [2] *De Civ. Dei*, xiii. 5.
[3] *Enarr. in Psalm*. lviii. 18. [4] *N.E.* iii. 5. 2 (Welldon's translation).

impulse needed for its realization. Thus, for him, the classical ideal of perfectibility through knowledge or enlightenment was wholly illusory; and, for the aberrations of humanity, he saw no remedy through education, whether conceived as intellectual discipline or moral habituation or both, *apart from* a recognition of the creative truth in the light of which alone these processes might properly be understood. It was, indeed, on this very question that he took issue with Pelagius.

The intention of Pelagius was evidently to combat tendencies towards an attitude of mere passivity on the part of Christians; to this end he insisted upon the necessity of a strenuous individual effort for salvation. But, in advocating the doctrine of personal responsibility, he stated his position in such a way as to betray what seemed to Augustine the gravest misconceptions regarding the character and operation of the creative principle and, therewith, of the human nature which he desired to save. To Pelagius, the necessity of sin (*necessitas peccandi*) was the consequence of a failure to see the light; error was thus to be imputed merely to the bond of habit (*consuetudo, usus*). On the other hand, the revelation of Christ was essentially a revelation of 'doctrine'. Its significance was thus as a gift of knowledge (*donum scientiae*) rather than as a gift of love (*donum caritatis*). What it therefore provided was the possibility of, rather than the will for, salvation; while perfectibility, in the sense of a desire to achieve the good, rested with man 'according to his merits'.[1] In this sense mankind remained the architect of his own destiny.

To state the issue in this way is to perceive that what Pelagius had done was virtually to proclaim once more an idealism of the classical type.[2] In so doing, he had divorced 'mind' from 'interest' and 'affection', thus undermining the Augustinian doctrine of the will and subverting the very foundations of dynamic personality. At the same time he had introduced afresh a dualism between creature and Creator, by ascribing to God the work of illumination, while reserving for man the task of initiating movement. It was with a vivid appreciation of these facts that Augustine undertook to give him his answer.

---

[1] *Retract.* i. 9. 3: *secundum merita*; cf. *Epist.* 186. xi. 37: 'sibi beatam vitam virtute propriae voluntatis efficere'.

[2] For the salient points of Pelagianism see Duchesne, op. cit. iii, p. 211.

That answer will serve to epitomize all that is peculiar to and distinctive of what is called Augustinianism.

'For we', declares Augustine in opposition to Pelagius, 'assert that the human will is so far assisted by divine aid in the accomplishment of justice that, over and above the fact that man is created with the power of voluntary self-determination, over and above the teaching from which he derives precepts as to how he ought to live, he also receives the Holy Spirit, whereby there is engendered (*fiat*) in his mind the love for and delight in that supreme and immutable good which is God, even now while he still walks by faith and not yet by sight; that, this being given to him as a free offering (*munus gratuitum*), he may be inflamed with desire to approach to participation in that true light.'[1]

In other words, mankind does not create his own 'values' from experience. On the contrary he derives from the Creator not merely his standards of truth, beauty, and goodness, but also his capacity to transform them into living fact. In this sense, *bona voluntas*, a 'good will' is proclaimed to be the greatest gift of God to man and grace is 'prevenient', supplying energy to the will which is good.[2] It is from a conviction of this truth that Augustine denounces as paganism the sentiment that 'God helps those who help themselves; the fact being that He also helps those who do not help themselves in order that they may help themselves'.[3]

Translated into terms of psychology, the doctrine of grace resolves itself into the doctrine that 'my love is my weight' and that the greater love is ultimately irresistible. As such, the working of the Spirit emerges, not as magic but, in the deepest and truest sense of the word, as 'natural law'.[4] Accordingly, it may be described as *ardor caritatis*, or *ignis voluntatis*, the 'heat of love', the 'flame of the will'. Its efficacy as a means of salvation thus depends upon the assumption that the image of God, i.e. of the creative and moving principle, has not been wholly effaced from the hearts even of unbelievers.[5] This being so, the process of salvation may be understood as one of sublimation in which the same human love discovers a new centre of fixa-

---

[1] *De Spiritu et Littera*, v. Cf. *De Gen. ad Litt.* v. 20. He thus censures the Pelagians 'qui arbitrantur tantummodo mundum ipsum factum a Deo, cetera iam fieri ab ipso mundo, deum ipsum nihil operari; contra quos profertur illa sententia Domini: *Pater meus usque modo operatur*, &c.'

[2] *Retract.* i. 9 and 10. [3] i. 13. 4 and 5.

[4] Ibid. ii. 42; commentary on *De Natura et Gratia*:"gratia non contra naturam, sed per quam natura liberatur et regitur'. [5] *De Spiritu et Litt.* xxviii.

tion; concupiscence, which is self-love, being thus transmuted into dilection, which is the love of God.[1] From this standpoint Augustine argues that, so far from there being any inconsistency between the notions of free will and grace, the perfection of grace is the perfection of freedom.[2] At the same time he urges that difficulties of understanding are to be ascribed to a 'hang-over' from scientific ideology in which 'grace' is confused with 'fate', as though the *operatio Dei* were merely external and mechanical and men were marionettes.[3]

From this analysis we may perceive the meaning of 'justification by faith', i.e. the acceptance of Trinitarian Christianity as a condition for the eradication of intellectual and moral short-comings as well as for the realization of those positive values to which mankind aspires.[4] Negatively it gives a point and value to asceticism, without which chastity itself emerges as nothing better than the spiritual pride of old maids.[5] Positively, it serves to overcome weakness and to provide a release of creative energy (*l'élan vers le bien*) by the disclosure of a goal which is at once intelligible and, in the highest degree, worth while.

That goal is the integration of personality. Approximation to it means, in the first place, emancipation from erroneous and muddled conclusions such as must inevitably result from the acceptance of a vicious starting-point. It thus levels ideological stone walls which, so long as they stand, constitute an insur-mountable obstacle to truth. At the same time it offers a fresh vision of the possibilities of science, exempt from the error which produces a flatulence not unnaturally mistaken for growth.[6] That is to say, it makes possible, but in a significantly new sense, the classical ideals of freedom and detachment.[7] In the second place it provides the technique necessary for the casting out of devils, the expunging of congenital and habitual complexes which serve merely to inhibit constructive activity.[8] In so doing it points to a realization of the classical ideal of

---

[1] *De Nat. et Grat.* lvii foll.; cf. *De Fide et Operibus.*   [2] *De Spir. et Litt.* xxx.
[3] *Contra Duas Epist. Pelag.* ii. 9 and 12.
[4] Note that this doctrine flatly contradicts that of Classicism, viz. the doctrine of perfectibility through 'virtue' (*De Civ. Dei,* xix. 25).
[5] *De Sanct. Virg.* 33.
[6] *Scientia inflat,* the metaphor is Augustine's, *De Trin.* xii. 11. 16.
[7] *De Lib. Arbit.* ii. 13. 37; *De Civ. Dei,* xxii. 30; *Retract.* i. 2. especially from the hallucination of dependence upon *Fortuna.*
[8] *De Civ. Dei,* xiii. 20; xiv. 15 and 16 (*libido*).

peace, not through the mortification but through the regeneration of the flesh. And finally, in the achievement of freedom and peace, it discovers the meaning of true felicity, the sovereign good, so far at least as this may be attained under the conditions of mortality. This it does by revealing a vision of personality which is not truncated at any point and in which self-consciousness has at last ceased to be the blight of life.

XII

DIVINE NECESSITY AND HUMAN HISTORY

THE discovery of personality was, at the same time, the discovery of history. For, by giving significance to individual experience, it gave significance also to the experience of the race, thereby providing a clue to the meaning and direction of historical process. To the Christians, however, this clue was to be found, not in any figment of the human mind, but in the revelation of Christ, accepted as a full and final revelation of the working of the Spirit and, therefore, the true *logos* or account of being and movement in the universe. Trinitarian Christianity thus pointed to an interpretation of history purely and simply in terms of the will of God. Such an interpretation, already foreshadowed in the *De Incarnatione* of Athanasius, received fulfilment with Augustine's *De Civitate Dei*.

To say this is not to suggest that Athanasius and Augustine, between them, 'created' the philosophy of history. In this, as in other branches of speculative activity, their contribution was merely to offer, in terms of Christian principles, a solution to problems long since envisaged by the thought of classical antiquity. But the divergence between Christianity and Classicism was in no respect more conspicuously or emphatically displayed than with regard to history; in a very real sense indeed it marked the crux of the issue between the two. This being so, it becomes instructive to examine the nature and claims of Christian historiography in relation to those of its Graeco-Roman counterpart. For this purpose we may begin with the work of Herodotus.

Herodotus deserves to be called the 'father of history', not merely as the most ancient of surviving authorities, but also because of his intrinsic importance. This may be ascribed in some degree to the interest of his theme, the crisis of Hellenism provoked by the rise and expansion of the Persian Empire and culminating in its defeat at the hands of the free Greek states. Ultimately, however, it depends upon the spirit with which he embarks upon his task. To that spirit the author himself bears witness in his opening lines:[1] 'This is the record of an investigation (ἱστορία) undertaken by Herodotus of Halicarnassus, now

[1] Hdt. i. 1.

set forth in order that the achievements of men may not be obliterated by the lapse of time; that the great and wonderful deeds performed alike by Greeks and barbarians may not be left uncelebrated; and, finally, to discover the reason why they fought one another.'

In this statement the word *historia* is profoundly significant. Already employed by Heraclitus with reference to Pythagoras to denote the practice of philosophic inquiry,[1] its use in this connexion by Herodotus invites special attention; it points, indeed, to what has rightly been called a literary revolution.[2] By adopting it to indicate the nature of his work, Herodotus dissociates himself from the tradition of logography in general and, in particular, from that of Hecataeus.[3] At the same time he identifies himself with the contemporary effort of investigation, in a sense which corresponds both to the etymology of the term and to the connotation which it was to have for Plato, Aristotle, and Theophrastus.[4] The *logos* of Herodotus thus professes to be the *logos* not of poetry but of philosophy. In its application to problems arising out of the great Persian war, it raises that inquiry from the level of mere narrative or chronicle, and justifies the description of the author as the 'most philosophic' of classical historians.

Specifically the purpose of Herodotus was, as he himself declares, threefold; it embraced the study (*a*) of fact (τὰ γενόμενα), (*b*) of value (ἔργα μεγάλα καὶ θωμαστά), and (*c*) of causation (ἡ αἰτίη). As thus conceived, his 'plan' offers scope for the utmost range and variety of interest. It allows for the discussion of questions such as the shape, size, and limits of the *orbis terrarum*, unique or unusual physical phenomena, the distribution of flora and fauna over the earth's surface. It raises problems of anthropology, ethnology, sociology, and politics, of primitive or localized custom and belief; of the genealogy, migration, and settlement of races; of the forms of economy distinctive of peoples dwelling under radically different conditions in widely separated parts of the habitable world; of the

---

[1] Diels, op. cit. *Heracl.*, *fr.* 129.

[2] Croiset, *Histoire de la Littérature Grecque*, ii. 613.

[3] Hdt. ii. 45 (on Heracles): λέγουσι δὲ πολλὰ καὶ ἄλλα ἀνεπισκέπτως οἱ Ἕλληνες· εὐήθης δὲ αὐτῶν καὶ ὅδε ὁ μῦθός ἐστι τὸν περὶ τοῦ Ἡρακλέος λέγουσι. . . . Hecataeus had opened his book, *The Circuit of Earth*, with the words, Ἑκαταῖος Μιλήσιος ὧδε μυθεῖται, 'Hecataeus of Miletus has this tale to tell'.

[4] See Liddell and Scott, *sub voc.*

origin, character, and purpose of government. In a word it presents a vivid panorama of thought and action which illustrates as nothing else could do the eager inquisitiveness of the age for which the author writes. But, while thus ministering to what has been called 'a vagabond and garrulous curiosity', Herodotus is by no means to be dismissed as a mere gossip-writer, interested only in assembling a miscellaneous body of information designed to provide amusement for the idle moments of a reader. On the contrary his object is to lay down the elements of a cosmology, in the light of which to elucidate the clash between Persia and Hellas. From this standpoint the material thus accumulated acquires a relevance which is not, perhaps, at first sight apparent. For it comprises a moving pattern of life which, whether considered as a whole or in the slightest and most insignificant of its details, serves equally to illustrate and support a specific theory of cosmic law. The work of Herodotus thus points directly to a study of causes, the *arché* or *principium*, as he sees it, of action and reaction in nature and in man. To this, the ultimate purpose of the inquiry, it owes its abiding significance.

By thus envisaging history as a 'search for causes', Herodotus reveals his affiliation with the spirit and tradition of Ionian physical science. It has been justly observed that his 'peculiar position in Greek culture' arises from the fact that 'he is the crown of the intellectual greatness of the Asiatic-Greek sea-board'.[1] In him we may therefore expect to find, as a matter of course, a record of the thoughts and preoccupations which distinguished the life of the frontier between Europe and Asia. This in itself is, perhaps, enough to account for the synoptic character of his work. But Herodotus went much farther than this. In his quest for a principle of intelligibility he alined himself with the effort of thought initiated by Thales and pursued with uninterrupted zeal by his successors of the philosophic *diadoché* to its culmination in the work of Heraclitus. To the latter, in particular, it may be suggested that the inspiration of the historian was due.

It is unnecessary to dilate upon the widespread influence exerted by Heraclitus upon the attitude and outlook of fifth-century Hellas. So far as concerns Herodotus, that influence manifests itself in the demand for a *logos*, to apprehend which,

[1] J. Wells, *Studies in Herodotus*, x, p. 184.

in the words of the philosopher, is to apprehend the eternal wisdom which governs all things.[1] To Heraclitus, the *logos* in question is everlasting and universal; for it knowledge, however encyclopaedic, constitutes no adequate substitute.[2] It may thus be described as 'natural justice', according to which 'not even the sun may overstep his bounds, since otherwise the furies, servants of justice, will find him out'.[3] As such, it is wholly independent of human conventions regarding beauty, goodness, and truth, of the merely subjective fancies and hopes of mankind.[4] Recognition of its real character leads to distrust of the theological poets, especially of Homer, whose imagination has filled the universe with anthropomorphic gods which intervene spasmodically in human affairs, and are amenable to prayer or propitiation, and capable of love as well as hate.[5] It likewise inspires contempt for contemporary mysticism, with its message of 'escape' from the wheel of destiny through *ascesis* or purification.[6] To the victims of such illusion Heraclitus offers but cold comfort; his 'deity' is the impersonal law of natural or physical necessity and the task of wisdom is simply to find how that law works.[7]

In his effort to promote this knowledge Heraclitus, indeed, occasionally employs poetic diction as when, for instance, he speaks of the eternal wisdom 'governing' all things, or of the furies which 'keep' the sun on his course. Notwithstanding such language, however, it is clear that, for him, as for his precursors in the Ionian tradition, the 'process' of nature is determined by its 'matter'. Of this matter he distinguishes four constituent elements, fire, air, water, and earth, of which fire is in one sense ultimate, the others being 'an exchange for fire'[8]. As such they are destined to follow 'an upward and downward path' (i.e. motion in time and space) according to a law by which the 'death' of one becomes the 'life' of another.[9] From this standpoint the cosmos presents itself as an uncreated and perpetual flux, 'the ever-living fire, with measures kindling and measures going out'.[10] Bodies in nature are, therefore, not simple but

---

[1] Diels, *Heracl.*, *fr.* 41.

[2] *Fr.* 1: τοῦ δὲ λόγου τοῦδ' ἐόντος ἀεί; *fr.* 1: γινομένων πάντων κατὰ τὸν λόγον τόνδε; *fr.* 40, on the futility of Pythagorean πολυμαθία.

[3] *Fr.* 94.   [4] *Frs.* 23, 28, 102.   [5] *Fr.* 42.

[6] *Frs.* 14, 15.   [7] *Fr.* 67.   [8] *Fr.* 90.   [9] *Frs.* 60, 62, 76.

[10] *Fr.* 30: κόσμον τόνδε τὸν αὐτὸν ἁπάντων οὔτε τις θεῶν οὔτε ἀνθρώπων ἐποίησεν, ἀλλ' ἦν ἀεὶ καὶ ἔστι καὶ ἔσται πῦρ ἀείζωον, ἁπτόμενον μέτρα καὶ ἀποσβεννύμενον μέτρα.

composite, a 'harmony', 'fitting-together', or 'balance' of different elements in which, it may be added, 'those which are most different most agree'.[1] Such 'differences' are everywhere apparent; they are evident in the antithesis between day and night, winter and summer, tall and short, broad and narrow, sharp and flat, black and white, cold and hot, moist and dry. The 'harmony' to which they give rise is the result of 'conflict'; a point of view from which it may be said that 'everything is generated by strife', 'strife is justice', and 'war is father and king of all'. Moreover, the life which thus materializes *consists in* the strife; for, though all differences may be destined to ultimate resolution, the resolution of those differences is not life but death.[2]

Seen in the light of Heraclitean principles, the characteristic features of Herodotus' cosmology assume fresh significance. In the first place it may be noted that his *cosmos* is spatial. It thus includes the whole extent of the habitable world together with its natural divisions considered both in relation to one another and to a general scheme of orientation, for the issue to be discussed is envisaged as merely the culminating phase of a perpetual conflict between 'East' and 'West'. In the second place it is temporal, the impulses of the present having their origin in those of the past, since for Herodotus as for Heraclitus time, like space, is a thing and thus, in itself, a cause of motion. Finally, it is 'material'. As such it generates its own motive forces, the ebb and flow of which takes place according to a law which operates mechanically to maintain a natural balance or equilibrium. This law, which may be described as one of compensation (τίσις), constitutes for Herodotus the true *logos* or account of cosmic movement. In describing its operation he sometimes follows Heraclitus in using the language of the theological poets; it is 'nemesis' or 'the nemesis of the god'. Ordinarily, however, in referring to the divine power, he employs the neuter (τὸ θεῖον) which serves more accurately to indicate its spontaneous and automatic character; and from this standpoint it makes little difference whether, e.g., the conditions observable at Tempe 'are to be attributed to Poseidon or to an earthquake'.[3]

To Herodotus the law of balance or compensation is the law

---

[1] *Fr.* 8: ἐκ τῶν διαφερόντων καλλίστη ἁρμονία.
[2] *Fr.* 65, on the final conflagration (ἐκπύρωσις) of the universe.
[3] Hdt. vii. 129.

to which all physical processes are ultimately subject; and its tendency is to restrict or check the growth of those things which tend to exceed the norm.[1] It may thus be invoked to explain phenomena such as that of the periodic Nile flood; 'concerning which', he declares, 'I was able to obtain no information from the Egyptians, although I enquired of them what power the Nile has to exhibit characteristics directly opposed to those of other rivers'.[2] Conventional Greek explanations of this phenomenon were three in number. First, the Etesian winds, blowing from the north, 'back up' the water which is thereafter released to flood the valley. To this Herodotus offers the sound objections (a) that the winds do not always blow, and (b) that other rivers similarly affected do not behave in the same way. Second, it depends somehow upon the 'stream of ocean' which, according to the poets, surrounds the habitable world. This, says Herodotus, is more marvellous but more ignorant; it is 'a mere fable of Homer'. Third, the Nile stream is derived from melted snow. To this the retort is that it flows from a hot to a cold country. Accordingly, he rejects all three theories to propound his own.[3] This is that, in winter, when all rivers are normally in flood, the sun being over Libya 'draws' water from the Nile, thereby reducing the size of the stream. During the summer, when other rivers fail, this water is 'discharged' to create the Nile flood.

The *logos* of physics is, at the same time, the *logos* of physiology. Heraclitus had observed that the *genesis* and *phthora* of organic life proceeds in accordance with the ordinance of the god.[4] To this doctrine, Herodotus offers confirmation when he declares that 'divine providence' (τοῦ θείου ἡ προνοίη) has dictated that animals which are cowardly and edible should be prolific, in order that the supply may not fail; while those which are fierce and destructive are the reverse. Thus the hare is prolific, while the lioness breeds but once in a lifetime. The vipers and winged serpents of Arabia are subject to a similar mechanical limitation; since, if they multiplied as rapidly as their nature admits, there would be no possibility of life on earth for man.[5]

We have noticed that the law which governs cosmic movement is both eternal and comprehensive; from it, therefore, mankind himself is not exempt. As an historian, the problem of

[1] Hdt. vii. 10 e: φιλέει ὁ θεὸς τὰ ὑπερέχοντα κολούειν.
[2] ii. 19–27.   [3] ii. 24 foll.   [4] Diels, *fr.* 11.   [5] Hdt. iii. 108–9.

Herodotus is to apply this law to the elucidation of human behaviour, the 'activity of man in pursuit of his ends'. For this the ground had already been prepared by the work of the Ionian physicists in psychology, the problems of which they had attacked from a materialist standpoint with interesting results, particularly as regards the theory of sense-perception.[1] To the Ionian physicists 'souls' were nothing more or less than combinations of cosmic matter, destined as such to follow the upward and downward path ordained for nature as a whole. From this standpoint their 'motion' could be explained as the result of what Herodotus calls a divine urge (δαιμονίη ὁρμή). This urge he identifies with desire (θυμός, ἐπιθυμία) which thus, envisaged as the human counterpart to physical 'attraction', becomes the dynamic of life. Desire demands fulfilment and this, appropriately enough, is designated by the word εὐδαιμονία or *happiness*. But the self-same law which dictates the urge to εὐδαιμονία also puts a limit upon it. In the language of theology the god seldom grants to men more than a 'taste' of happiness and then only to snatch it from their grasp. The whole course of history, he argues, goes to attest the validity of this law, evidence for which may be found alike in the annihilation of Troy and in that of Persia.[2]

In this connexion it has been argued that Herodotus is devoid of anything which can properly be described as an 'ethical interest' and that what he offers the reader is 'an older and more vulgar conception of divine jealousy (φθόνος) which is envious of human greatness in itself, quite apart from any moral fault'.[3] To us the conception is neither old nor vulgar; it arises from the attempt to interpret human life and conduct in terms of a *Weltanschauung* constructed on the basis of Ionian philosophic materialism. Two problems emerge, the first of which is psychological. What, it may be asked, is the relationship between the cosmic urge on the one hand and, on the other, the phenomenon of conscious and deliberate choice? This latter Herodotus understands and describes with perfect accuracy in different passages; his difficulty is to demonstrate the connexion between it and the actual outcome or event. And, from this standpoint, the merely psychological gives rise also to an ethical problem;

---

[1] See the so-called treatise of Hippocrates, *De Victu*, i, printed by Diels as an appendix to the fragments of Heraclitus.

[2] Hdt. ii. 120 and vii–ix. [3] J. Wells, op. cit., p. 194.

for, unless this connexion can be made intelligible, the sense of human freedom and responsibility resolves itself into a simple illusion of consciousness. Aware of the problem, Herodotus undertakes to solve it by establishing a correspondence between the (subjective) order of values and the (objective) order of material fact. This he asserts in the general proposition that 'the penalties which men are doomed to suffer are in every case the consequence of their own wrong-doing',[1] and this proposition he illustrates by reference to numerous individual instances.[2] He thus agrees with his contemporaries, the Athenian dramatists, that, in order to account for and justify the divine visitation, there must be a fault or defect ($\dot{a}\mu a\rho\tau\dot{\iota}a$) in the human actor sufficient to render him responsible ($a\ddot{\iota}\tau\iota os$) for it. But, when he seeks to identify this fault, Herodotus is only partially successful. For the question he propounds is like that recorded in another connexion: Who hath sinned, this man or his ancestors, that he should have been born blind?[3] And, to this question, all that he can provide is a series of *ex post facto* rationalizations of questionable validity. The difficulty is intensified by the necessity under which he labours of translating what appear (subjectively) as qualities of virtue and vice into terms of quantity in the objective order. For, as in nature it is the tallest trees which are smitten with the lightning bolt, so also the fortunes of men are determined in such a way that their 'fall' is in direct proportion to their 'rise'. And, from this standpoint, it may be doubted whether the penalty they suffer can have any ethical significance beyond that of mere punishment. That is to say, $\tau\dot{\iota}\sigma\iota s$, conceived as a principle of equilibrium or compensation, chastens but does not purify.

To Herodotus the struggle between Greece and Persia presents itself as a supreme example of the working of this principle. Accordingly, as an incident in human history, it is not unique or abnormal; it is merely one of an endless succession of events which may be taken to illustrate the eternal dialectic of time, space, and matter. From this standpoint, the first six books of

---

[1] Hdt. v. 56: $o\dot{\upsilon}\delta\epsilon\dot{\iota}s$ $\dot{a}\nu\theta\rho\dot{\omega}\pi\omega\nu$ $\dot{a}\delta\iota\kappa\hat{\omega}\nu$ $\tau\dot{\iota}\sigma\iota\nu$ $o\dot{\upsilon}\kappa$ $\dot{a}\pi o\tau\dot{\iota}\sigma\epsilon\iota$.

[2] vi. 72, Leotychides; vi. 84, Cleomenes; iii. 126, 128, Polycrates; viii. 109, Xerxes; where the king is represented as subject to divine jealousy because he is $\dot{a}\nu\dot{o}\sigma\iota os$ and $\dot{a}\tau\dot{a}\sigma\theta a\lambda os$, having burned temples and beaten the sea. I owe this point and the appropriate illustrations to the courtesy of Professor J. L. Myres.

[3] John ix. 1–5, the question and the reply given to it indicate a wholly different approach to the problem.

the history, so far from being an excrescence, constitute an essential preparation for the concluding triad; they serve to reveal the operation of the *logos*, the elements (στοιχεῖα) of which are set forth in the opening chapters of the first book. Following immediately upon the statement in which he indicates the nature and purpose of his work, Herodotus proceeds to assert that 'the beginning of contention' is to be traced to a series of retaliatory raids, to and fro, across the Aegean sea. These he designates as (1) that of Io by the Phoenicians from Argos to their own land or (alternatively) to Egypt; (2) that of Europa by the Cretans from Tyre; (3) that of Medea from Colchis by the Greeks; (4) that of Helen by Alexander from Sparta to Ilium, the event which first brought Europe and Asia face to face in combat on the ringing plains of windy Troy. In this connexion we may note the role played by space and time. Generally speaking, movement is from East to West and from West to East, the antithesis between which is thus established as fundamental to the situation. Time, as a factor, plays a part no less significant than that of space; the rape of Helen, for instance, occurring in the 'second generation' after that of Medea. But, while time and space thus have their importance, they operate as causes of movement only in conjunction with physical 'desire'. This desire, which according to Persian tradition is personified in the form of a woman, constitutes the primary impulse to activity.[1] To it must be added, as a secondary motive, the thirst for compensation (ἴσα πρὸς ἴσα) which is stimulated, e.g., by the Greek refusal to make amends for the rape of Medea. It was their unwillingness to do so which, once more according to the native tradition, brought the Persians, as Asiatics, into the quarrel, leading them to hold the Europeans blameworthy for their subsequent attempt forcibly to recover the ravished Helen from Troy.

For Herodotus the fact that these early conflicts were marked by constant vicissitudes serves to demonstrate that the law of τίσις is one of 'ups' and 'downs'.[2] Of such vicissitudes there

[1] Herodotus himself is dubious regarding the propriety of this personification. In ii. 120 he adheres to the account given by the Egyptian priests but later repudiates it, stating emphatically that it was not any sentiment about Helen but rather divine retribution which really brought about the fall of Troy. I owe this note also to Professor Myres.

[2] i. 5: τὴν ἀνθρωπηΐην κτλ. the process is normally from weakness to strength and vice versa.

could be no more spectacular illustration than that provided by the career of Croesus, king of Lydia. With this apparently abrupt transition, Herodotus passes from prehistory to the more or less solid ground of verifiable fact. But the abruptness is more apparent than real. For (a), in the conflict between Asia and Europe, East and West, Lydia, the buffer-land between them, inevitably becomes focal. And (b), as regards Croesus, the *logos* or principle of understanding is identical with that which served to elucidate the movements of primitive times. For these reasons the Lydian history constitutes a natural link between the account of prehistoric and that of contemporary events.

Examined from this point of view, the story of Croesus reveals to perfection the salient features of Herodotean technique. For the historian, Croesus, fifth and ultimate representative of his house, fulfils in his person the destiny marked out for him by the sin of his ancestor Gyges, the latter having destroyed Candaules, last of the Heraclid dynasty, to seize the throne. This Candaules had himself been 'doomed to an evil fate' by reason of immoderate passion (θυμός), the object of which is in this case represented as the queen; while, in a precisely analogous way, the law of compensation is invoked to account for the domestic and political tragedy.[1]

The spectacle of Croesus, in his turn, confronted by a nemesis from which there is no escape, naturally gives rise to the general problem of human happiness. This problem is canvassed in the dramatic dialogue between the king and Solon. But, for one who is fated as is Croesus, discussion of this kind would appear to be futile; and, as the conventional methods of aversion fail, the monarch presently falls victim to his destiny. In so doing he provides a further vindication of the 'theological principle', a demonstration of the truth that the process of human life is inevitably cyclical and that 'it is impossible for the same man to enjoy happiness for ever'.[2]

We may here pause to observe that the explanation of Croesus' fate is that also of Polycrates', which has been noted as one of the best examples in Herodotus of the doctrine of nemesis.[3] Throughout Hellas the 'luck of Polycrates' had become proverbial, but it was not enough to save him from catastrophe which thus, in the end, overtook him, as it was subsequently to overtake his murderer.[4] And, in general, it is worth remarking

---

[1] i. 8 foll.   [2] 207. 2.   [3] iii. 39 foll., 120 foll.   [4] Ibid. 126.

that, of the various protagonists in the great Persian war, not a single one succeeds in evading ultimate disaster. This is true of Greeks as well as barbarians and, one and all, their ruin is the result of 'immoderate' desire.

Passion or desire ($\theta\upsilon\mu\acute{o}\varsigma$, $\grave{\epsilon}\pi\iota\theta\upsilon\mu\acute{\iota}\alpha$), being purely quantitative, may be said to find its logical expression in expansion. While, therefore, it is in some degree manifested by the Lydian kingdom, 'the first imperialism', it attains its final development only with the world-empire of Persia. The origins of that empire may be traced all the way back to Deioces the Mede, first among his countrymen to exemplify the *libido dominandi*.[1] Its real beginning, however, is attributable to Cyrus, who, having wrested ascendancy from the Medes, embarked upon an aggressive programme of conquest and acquisition in all directions until he met his death in combat with an obscure tribe of trans-Caspia.[2] The effort of expansion thus initiated was, however, continued by his successor Cambyses, who added Syria and Egypt to his dominions, though at the cost of his reason and his life.[3] To Darius, second founder and so-called Augustus Caesar of the empire, was reserved the glory of carrying Persian arms north-westward across the Bosphorus to a frontier on the Danube. To him Herodotus ascribes a formulation of the *logos* of imperialism in the following terms: a conquering race is bound to go forward till it meets with a reverse, and inactivity means decay. In this connexion it is interesting to note the explanation offered by the author for Darius' invasion of Scythia.[4] 'Since Asia was teeming with man-power and immense material resources were being accumulated, Darius was moved by an impulse ($\grave{\epsilon}\pi\epsilon\theta\acute{\upsilon}\mu\eta\sigma\epsilon$) to repay ($\tau\epsilon\acute{\iota}\sigma\alpha\sigma\theta\alpha\iota$) the Scythians . . . for their wrong-doing', the wrong-doing in question being the so-called Cimmerian raid of nearly two centuries earlier, an event which, according to tradition, had occasioned profound disturbance in Asia!

It is in the light of notions such as these that we must seek to understand the passage[5] in which the author undertakes to analyse and explain the enterprise of Xerxes. To begin with he represents Mardonius as actively exciting the passion of the monarch. The idea, he says, was one of retaliation for injuries suffered by the Great King, his father, at the hands of the free

---

[1] Hdt. i. 96: $\grave{\epsilon}\rho\alpha\sigma\theta\epsilon\grave{\iota}\varsigma$ $\tau\upsilon\rho\alpha\nu\nu\acute{\iota}\delta o\varsigma$.   [2] i, *ad fin.*   [3] iii. 65 foll.
[4] iv. 1; cf. 4 *ad fin.*   [5] vii. 1 foll.

Greek states.[1] At the same time it was aggressive and acquisitive, since the one thing needed to complete the mastery of the world was the subjugation of Hellas. On these grounds the conflict is represented as inevitable. This sense of inevitability is emphasized (a) by the failure of prudential considerations, exemplified in the speeches of Artabanus, to serve as a deterrent, and (b), when the king hesitates, by the appearance of an apparition to propound, in terms which recall the formula of Darius, the *logos* of expansionist imperialism.[2] With this manifestation the issue ceases to be a matter of debate, and final instructions are issued by which the might of Asia is hurled against Greece.

The ensuing clash may be taken to illustrate, in the fullest and most complete sense, that 'conflict of opposites' which, for Ionian materialism, is the law of life. From this standpoint it is envisaged in at least four modes: (1) spatially, as a struggle between East and West, a point of view from which 'extremes meet';[3] (2) temporally, as a turning-point in the ceaseless ebb and flow of forces which have operated throughout the whole course of recorded history; (3) racially, as the strife of 'Europeans' with 'Asiatics'; (4) ideologically, as a contest between 'freedom' and 'despotism'. Within this framework Herodotus is able to offer at least a partial rationalization of the 'glorious deliverance' at Salamis and Plataea. But, since the issue is humanly speaking irrational or, as we should rather say, suprarational, its solution must ultimately be in analogous terms. Accordingly, the 'theological principle' previously illustrated in the fate of Croesus and Polycrates is once more invoked to account for the disaster which overwhelmed Xerxes. To Herodotus, the *nemesis* which overtook the great king serves to restore an equilibrium which had been threatened as never before by the accumulation of such vast human and material resources in the hands of a single man.

Beyond this we may observe that the historian has no moral to point and no cause to urge. By contrast with the logical incoherence of its modern analogue, classical materialism is sternly and relentlessly 'scientific'. It thus excludes the prospect of an earthly millennium to be achieved whether through the 'progressive' amelioration of human life or catastrophically, by

---

[1] ὁ λόγος ἦν τιμωρός.
[2] vii. 18. 3.
[3] See the Persian army list, bk. vii. 61–99.

'revolution'. Therewith it excludes also the evangelical motive
of modern communism. With the extrusion of these elements
the picture of the cosmos reduces itself to one of matter in
motion. This motion is perpetual and incessant; and in it the
only order to be discerned is a monotonous upward and downward curve, the fall of the index being on each occasion equivalent to its previous rise. Translated into terms of human
behaviour, this means that the *psyché* is so constituted that, like
fire, it 'tends upward'. Now and then, here and there, it
succeeds in overcoming the resistance of those elements which
make for depression and, when it does so, it exhibits the phenomena of accumulation and acquisition on a more than ordinary
scale. But nowhere is there evidence of any real 'organic'
growth. Moreover, the principle of expansion operates at the
same time as a principle of limitation. For, as an inevitable
consequence of its activity, it generates opposition, the intensity
and duration of which are proportionate to the pressure exerted.
And out of this opposition arises conflict in which successive
agglomerations of potential *eudaemonia* are shattered and destroyed. The process to which mankind is subject is therefore
self-defeating; it is like the oscillation of a pendulum. To this
truth point and emphasis are given by what Herodotus has to
say with regard to the role of mind in the historic process. This
role is simply that of a passive spectator, utterly without power
to influence the course of events. Self-consciousness thus resolves
itself into a consciousness of impotence in the grip of material
necessity. In the words of a modern, 'brief and powerless is
man's life; on him and on all his race the slow, sure doom falls
pitiless and dark'.

The acceptance of this conclusion must necessarily breed a
profound and ineradicable pessimism. In Herodotus such
pessimism is everywhere apparent, but it finds no more dramatic
or apposite expression than in words which he puts into the
mouth of a Persian grandee at the Theban dinner-party given
on the eve of Plataea. 'That which is destined to come to pass
as a consequence of divine activity', he declares, 'it is impossible
for man to avert. Many of us are aware of this truth, yet we
follow because we cannot do otherwise. Of all the sorrows
which afflict mankind, the bitterest is this, that one should have
consciousness of much, but control over nothing.'[1]

---

[1] ix. 16: ἐχθίστη δὲ ὀδύνη τῶν ἐν ἀνθρώποισι αὕτη, πολλὰ φρονέοντα μηδενὸς κρατέειν.

Subsequent efforts of classical historiography may be regarded as attempts to escape from the conclusions reached by Herodotus. Of these, undoubtedly the most significant was that of Thucydides.[1] Here the barest summary must suffice. To Thucydides the weakness in the work of his predecessor was that, despite its pretensions to philosophic objectivity, it nevertheless remained impregnated with myth. This weakness he ascribed to a recognition by Herodotus of the 'general hypothesis', a cosmic principle of being and motion which, in his opinion, was wholly supposititious. For him, therefore, the way of emancipation was to distinguish between 'primary' and 'secondary' causes, rejecting the former and admitting the latter as alone susceptible of observation and verification, i.e. as 'scientific' in a sense given to the word by the contemporary Hippocratic treatise, *Ancient Medicine*. From this standpoint history ceases to be an exercise in virtuosity, a 'prize-essay' to delight the ear, in order to assume the character of a search for truth conducted on positive lines and with due regard to specified canons of method; an inquiry into the behaviour of men as individuals and in the mass which, by yielding a body of useful generalizations, was to constitute a 'possession for ever'.[2]

Accordingly, with Thucydides, attention is no longer distracted by any mythological *logos*, the mere creation of philosophic fancy; it is focused upon the things which men, in their relations with one another, actually say and do (λόγοι καὶ ἔργα). Recognition is thus accorded to a plurality of causes, rather than to the single principle postulated by philosophic and historical monism. From this standpoint the factors involved are at least twofold; they may be described as men × circumstances.

In accepting man as in some sense a 'cause' of his own activity, Thucydides appears to have reverted to the poetic tradition so emphatically repudiated by Ionian science. But if this be so, his attitude was confirmed and reinforced by the findings of contemporary medicine. It thus rested on presuppositions to be shared by Hippocrates, Aristotle, and Galen. To Galen we owe the clearest and most emphatic statement of what these presuppositions were and what they involved.[3]

---

[1] For a detailed discussion of the latter from this point of view we may refer the reader to an earlier study, *Thucydides and the Science of History*, Oxford, 1929.

[2] Thuc. i. 21–2.

[3] Galen, *The Natural Faculties*, bk. I. xii. 27–30 (Loeb), pp. 42–9.

'Broadly speaking', he says, 'there have arisen the following two sects in medicine and philosophy among those who have had anything definite to say with regard to nature. I refer of course only to those who know what they are talking about, and who perceive the logical consequence of their hypotheses and are prepared to defend them. . . . The one supposes that all substance which is subject to genesis and destruction is both continuous and capable of alteration. The other assumes that substance is unchangeable, unalterable and divided into minute particles separated from one another by empty space.

'Now everyone who can appreciate the implications of an hypothesis recognizes that, according to the latter school, there exists no substance or faculty peculiar to ⟨organic⟩ nature or the soul, but that these owe their development to the way in which the primary particles, which are unaffected by change, group themselves together; while, according to the former, "nature" is not dependent upon these primary particles, but is emphatically prior to them. According to this school, therefore, it is "nature" which constructs the bodies both of plants and animals, endowing them with power to attract and assimilate that which is appropriate, and to expel that which is foreign. Furthermore, she skilfully moulds them as embryos; while after birth she also provides for them by employing still other faculties, such as love of and care for their offspring, or sociability and friendship with their kin. According to the other school, none of these characteristics pertains to them by nature, nor is there in the soul any congenital and original idea whether of agreement or difference, separation or synthesis, justice or injustice, beauty or ugliness; but, they declare, all these arise in us from and through sensation, and animals are steered by certain images and memories.

'Some of these people actually go so far as to assert that the soul possesses no capacity for reason, but that we are propelled like cattle by our sense-impressions and that we have no power to refuse or dissent from anything. With them, obviously, courage, wisdom, temperance and self-control are so much nonsense and we neither love one another or our offspring, nor do the gods care anything about us.[1]

'Granting that bodies are steered only by material forces (ταῖς τῶν ὑλῶν οἰακιζόμενα ῥοπαῖς) . . . we should make ourselves ridiculous by discussing physical, not to speak of psychical, power or indeed life as a whole.[2]

'If anyone takes the trouble to familiarize himself with the writings of Aristotle and Theophrastus, he will see that they consist of commentaries on the *physiology* of Hippocrates.'[3]

---

[1] §§ 27–9 f.   [2] II. iii. 81.   [3] II. iv. 89.

To accept the Hippocratic view of human nature as organic is to recognize that it possesses a real, if limited, capacity for creative thought and activity. It thus gives new validity to the ancient poetic concept of natural excellence (ἀρετή). In Thucydides this concept is subjected to a fresh analysis, according to which it reveals two aspects, the one intellectual (σύνεσις or γνώμη), the other moral (ἀνδρεία); as it likewise appears in two phases, the one congenital, the other acquired (φύσις and τέχνη or μελέτη). It is by virtue of intelligence and manliness, whether innate or the result of training, that human beings are equipped for life.

To the historian this life presents itself as a continuous and unending struggle. For man, as a cause, is confronted always by circumstances or the environment (τὰ ἔξω, τὰ ἔξωθεν, the Heraclitean περιέχον). This environment is partly physical, partly psychical and moral. It thus includes geographical elements such as land and sea, the varied possibilities of which he must learn to exploit. But it is also customary and institutional, the 'atmosphere', e.g., of Athens or Sparta created and maintained by their respective ways of life (ἐπιτέχνησις, ἐπιτήδευσις, νόμιμα, τρόποι); the 'conditions' produced whether by peace or war. In this connexion we may recall the observation that 'war is a harsh master which, by withdrawing the easy provision of daily wants, assimilates the disposition of men to their necessities'. Accordingly, the movement (κίνησις) of human life consists of doing and suffering (ποιεῖν καὶ πάσχειν), of response to stimuli which it seeks to understand and control. And, since the probability is (κατὰ τὸ εἰκός) that men will respond to similar stimuli in a similar way, there arise uniformities or sequences of behaviour which may be discerned alike in individuals and in groups.

Belief in the existence of such uniformities is contingent upon the assumption that, as the constitution of human nature is on the whole stable, the characteristic reactions of mankind will normally remain what past experience has shown them to be.[1] Among the most fundamental of such reactions, Thucydides recognizes that of fear (φόβος), the dread of poverty (ἀχρηματία), weakness (ἀσθένεια), and distress (ἀπορία) which involves a corresponding demand for peace, security, and well-being or

[1] Thuc. i. 22. 4: ὅσοι δὲ βουλήσονται τῶν τε γενομένων τὸ σαφὲς σκοπεῖν καὶ τῶν μελλόντων ποτὲ αὖθις κατὰ τὸ ἀνθρώπινον τοιούτων καὶ παραπλησίων ἔσεσθαι . . .

prosperity (ἡσυχία, ἄδεια, ἀσφάλεια, εὐτυχία). Man is thus represented as an acquisitive animal who, in his desire for gain, will
submit even to enslavement at the hands of the powerful, while
the more powerful (men and communities) employ their resources to reduce the lesser to a condition of subjection.[1] But,
while the economic motive thus bulks large in his thinking, its
satisfaction is made to depend upon another factor, viz. that of
political power; and, from this standpoint, his work constitutes
a monumental chapter in the ideology of *Machtpolitik*. For him
the state, based on a division of functions and upon the accumulation and prudent expenditure of capital (περιουσία χρημάτων)
is a creation of wisdom coupled with power.[2] As such it rests
upon certain conventions as to the elements of good order
(εὐνομία), conventions which are supported by religion, by the
various forms of social discipline and, if necessary, by force. As
for this last sanction, we may pause to note his account of the
'blood-bath' which followed the profanation of the mysteries,
the so-called 'conspiracy' of 415 B.C. Concerning this matter his
comment is significant. 'It is doubtful', he says, 'whether the
victims were justly punished, but the rest of the city at any rate
was for the time being visibly helped.'[3] It thus illustrates the
situation for which Aristotle was to propose a remedy in the
tragic *catharsis*; tragedy in this way was to serve an important
purpose in the political order.

Thus envisaged, organized society presents itself as a sustained endeavour to secure by political methods the economic
and moral foundations for human happiness. But, as such, it is
liable at all times to shocks which may serve to throw it off
balance. And, whatever their ultimate psychological repercussions, it is noteworthy that, in general, these shocks originate
from 'outside'. An excellent example is provided by the plague
at Athens.[4] It descended upon the city without warning (ἐξαπι-
ναίως ἐσέπεσε), suddenly attacking individuals who were otherwise perfectly healthy (ἐξαίφνης ὑγιεῖς ἐλάμβανε) in an otherwise
healthy year. And, while the symptoms were easy enough to
describe, the epidemic did not conform to any type (εἶδος)
known to contemporary medicine. It thus defied existing tech-

---

[1] i. 8. 3: ἐφιέμενοι γὰρ τῶν κερδῶν οἵ τε ἥσσους ὑπέμενον τὴν τῶν κρεισσόνων δουλείαν,
κ.τ.λ.
[2] i. 1–18, the evolution of Hellenic polity, and ii. 15. 2, the work of Theseus:
ἀνήρ γενόμενος μετὰ τοῦ ξυνετοῦ καὶ δυνατός.
[3] vi. 60.   [4] ii. 47–54, esp. 50 and 51.

niques of medical treatment (τέχνη ἀνθρωπεία), not to speak of
the methods of aversion familiar to religion. In other words, it
was utterly beyond reason and calculation (παρὰ λόγον), a
matter of sheer contingency, chance, or luck (τύχη). The result
was to shatter the conventions of public order. Fear of the gods
and respect for law lost their power as restraints, and Athens
experienced the first stage of her descent into moral and social
anarchy.[1]

The plague was by no means an isolated incident in the life
of a single city. On the contrary it was but one of a series of
violent shocks to which the Hellenic world was subjected in the
course of twenty-seven years of almost uninterrupted warfare.
And, to a degree unusual in times of peace, the tendency of
war is to produce such shocks. This it does by giving rise to
unprecedented or abnormal situations which nothing but the
most remarkable insight can possibly anticipate and control.
The effect of these shocks is cumulative for, with every slip or
miscalculation (σφάλμα), there is a weakening of morale until
society finally breaks under the strain.

From this point of view the 'inquiry' of Thucydides assumes
a character hardly less disconcerting than that of Herodotus.
For the story he has to tell is that of human reason defeated and
crushed by the forces of irrationality. These forces manifest
themselves in war-time Athens when the democracy, freed from
control by its natural leaders, oscillates to the wildest impulses
of pity and terror, hatred and greed, and plunges from the
excesses of blind hope to those of equally blind despair. They
are evident also in states like Corcyra where, with the dissolution of communal spirit, they vent themselves in class-conflict
and internecine strife. And, in either case, they find their chief
embodiment in individuals who, inspired by no motives higher
than those of self-aggrandizement, avarice, and ambition, set
themselves to lead the dance of death. They are thus apparent
in the demagogism of a Cleon who, in his effort to whip up war-
psychosis, does not hesitate to appeal to the basest sentiments of
the mob; or in the diabolism of an Alcibiades who, with the
bitterness of a renegade, denied the liberalism traditionally
associated with the Alcmaeonid house.[2] And, in these as in other
examples, it is to be noted that the forces of disruption owe their

---

[1] ii. 53. 1 : πρῶτόν τε ἦρξε καὶ ἐς τἆλλα τῇ πόλει ἐπὶ πλέον ἀνομίας τὸ νόσημα.
[2] vi. 89–92.

release to the 'hazards' of war which thus, for Thucydides, exhibits the extreme of incalculability (τοῦ πολέμου τὸ παράλογον).

But if τύχη, the incalculable, intervenes in human affairs to destroy, it serves also to create. For Thucydides, as a positivist, the meaning attached to this word was limited strictly by the terms of his scientific faith and it remained simply the 'contingent' or 'accidental'. To his successor Polybius such limita- tion did not exist. Loudly proclaiming himself a 'pragmatic' historian and thus able to recognize 'fact' when he saw it, regard- less of preconceived ideas, Polybius showed himself ready to identify the conception with 'providence', and to treat it as the 'missing link' in an otherwise imperfect chain of causation, a *deus ex machina* of history to be invoked when 'natural' explana- tions failed.[1] This was to revert once more to popular and poetic ideology and it presupposed a corresponding attitude of mind and heart. The 'fortune' of Polybius was the self-same 'fortune' to which the unhappy Melians had looked in vain for succour when they were threatened with destruction at the hands of the Athenians.[2] It was identical with the 'divine event' preached by the theologian Pindar, the appropriate response to which was a sense of holy awe.[3] It is but a short step from the worship of 'fortune' to that of 'fortune's favourites', and the identification of the two is a mere matter of empirical judge- ment, depending upon the association of ideas. Once re- habilitated as a positive force in human affairs, the concept served to account for the most stupendous development of the centuries, the rise of Rome to world-power. Having thus been identified with the 'manifest destiny' of the Eternal City, it was by an easy process transferred to that of the Caesars and, with this dismal conclusion, the quest for a principle of historical intelligibility came to an ignominious end.[4]

To the Christians the failure of classical historiography was the result of its inability to discover the true 'cause' of human being and motivation. Accordingly, it pointed to a substitution of the *logos* of Christ for that of Classicism as a principle of understanding; in other words, to the abandonment of secular literature in favour of the Bible as the repository of historical truth. But to proclaim the historicity of the Bible was not in itself, as Augustine perceived, to provide oneself with a ready-

---

[1] Polyb. xxxvii. 4 and xxxviii. 18. 8.   [2] Thuc. v. 104: τύχη ἐκ τοῦ θείου.
[3] ὁσιότης, αἰσχύνη, αἰδώς.   [4] See Ch. III, above.

made solution for all possible difficulties. For, while the authority of Scripture was admittedly absolute, its meaning was not always clear. On the contrary it was veiled in enigma, the nature of which was twofold. The first and most obvious source of difficulty was verbal, since words, as symbols or signs of meaning, occasionally bore a double significance and, in such cases, there was always the danger of getting one's signals mixed. But to the verbal, was added a material ambiguity, arising from the fact that teaching even with regard to fundamentals appeared to differ in different books, especially of the Old and New Testament; and, in some respects, the divergence was so vast as to suggest an absolute relativity of doctrine. It was, indeed, this fact which, already in the second century, had provoked the heresy of Marcion, whose distinction between the god of Justice[1] and the god of Love[2] was so sharp that it virtually nullified the value of the Bible as a continuous revelation of the divine will. In Augustine's day problems of interpretation found expression in puzzles such as that propounded by Manichean rationalism: What was God doing in the time before creation? It was easy enough to reply with the jibe: He was preparing hell for those who pry into mysteries.[3] Nevertheless, the barb stuck and Augustine was not content until he had found a way of answering such questions seriously.

In so doing he developed a new and distinctive basis for interpretation. To begin with, he recognized that words, as instruments of expression, could operate no less effectively to embalm, than to enshrine, truth. It was thus apparent that he could not accept and defend in a literal sense every statement of Scripture. For the rejection of literalism Augustine invoked the authority of St. Paul: *the letter killeth*; and, in throwing it overboard, he doubtless owed something to the example of Ambrose. But he did not escape from the pitfalls of literalism in order to lose himself in the banalities of allegory.[4] For he perceived that, however obscure and difficult to comprehend, the purpose of words was none the less to convey meaning; and, in order to arrive at this meaning, it was necessary to understand the true significance of the text. This presupposed a knowledge of Greek and Hebrew, the languages in which it had originally been composed. Then, for the solution of merely verbal questions, it was possible to derive help from different

[1] O.T.   [2] N.T.   [3] *Conf.* xi. xii. 14.   [4] *Retract.* ii. 24. 1.

branches of secular scholarship, thus 'spoiling the Egyptians' of
the fruit of their inquiries in mathematics, the natural sciences,
including astronomy, the mechanical arts, history and institutions, rhetoric and dialectic.[1] Of these rhetoric and dialectic
might be used to resolve ambiguities of interpretation arising
from the double significance of words, either by reference to the
context or in terms of one or another of the various figures of
speech.[2] This was not so much to prostitute science to religion
as to recognize that, while Scripture contained the elements of
dogma, it was, as literature, subject to the rules of criticism
current in the school of liberal arts. Nevertheless, for its full
comprehension, the *liberales disciplinae* were of limited value. In
the first place it was obvious that vast erudition was perfectly
compatible with moral obliquity.[3] Secondly, as with the crucial
question of the *In Principio*, it sometimes happened that the
merely verbal passed into a material difficulty, for the solution
of which the methods applicable to literary criticism were
wholly inadequate. To Augustine it was evident that, if such
questions were to be answered at all, it could only be *spiritaliter*,
i.e. in the light of the Spirit.[4]

At this point, however, an emphatic warning becomes necessary. By the light of the Spirit Augustine does not mean the
ecstatic illumination professed by Tertullian on the basis of
Montanist notions regarding the *Paraclete*.[5] Nor does he give
the slightest countenance to millennialism of the kind illustrated
in Commodian. The Augustinian view of inspiration thus
constitutes no ground whatever for regarding the Scriptures as
a cosmic almanac, by the aid of which to prognosticate specific
historical developments such, e.g., as the fall of the Roman
empire. This, declares Augustine, is to read them, not in the

---

[1] *De Doct. Christ.* ii. 7–25. For an important statement regarding the relationship of scriptural and profane literature see *De Gen. ad Litt.* i. 18. 37: 'In rebus
obscuris atque a nostris oculis remotissimis si qua inde scripta etiam divina legeri-
mus, quae possunt, salva fide qua imbuimur, alias atque alias parere sententias, in
nullam earum nos praecipiti affirmatione ita proiciamus ut, si forte diligentius dis-
cussa veritas eam recte labefactaverit, corruamus; non pro sententia divinarum
scriptarum sed pro nostra ita dimicantes ut eam velimus scripturarum esse, quae
nostra est, cum potius eam quae scripturarum est, nostram esse velle debeamus.'
Cf. ibid. i. 19. 39 and Aquinas, *Summa Theologica*, 1a, qu. 68, art. 1.

[2] *De Doct. Christ.* iii. 1 foll.

[3] *Retract.* i. 3. 2: 'liberales disciplinas quas multi sancti multum nesciunt; quidam
etiam qui sciunt eas sancti non sunt'.

[4] For the 'spiritual man' see above, Ch. VII, p. 241.

[5] See above, Ch. XI.

spirit of prophecy but with human eyes, and the conjectures to which it gives rise are in no sense different from the exploded pagan superstition that Christianity was to endure for precisely 365 years.[1] 'What amazes me', he says, 'is the presumption of those who hazard such opinions.'[2]

To Augustine the real purpose of Scripture is to reveal the means whereby we may attain to a just and happy life (*quo recte beateque vivamus*). In this sense it is indubitably apocalyptic. It thus points unerringly to a future which includes 'the conversion of the Jews, the reign of Antichrist, the second coming of Christ, the last judgement, separation of the good from the evil, the conflagration and renewal of the world'.[3] 'All of which', he affirms, 'we are bound to believe will certainly come to pass.' 'But how and in what order', he goes on to add, 'is a matter for experience at the time rather than for the mind of man to apprehend fully at the present.'[4] These, indeed, are not events to be forecast by any sort of scientific prevision; they are value-judgements, to appreciate which presupposes a kind of authority analogous to that which is requisite for the proper interpretation of the poets.[5] The Scriptures are replete with such value-judgements, the nature of which may be illustrated by reference to texts like that of John i. 1–14: 'In the beginning was the Word; there was a man, sent from God, whose name was John.' In the latter pronouncement, the words 'there was a man . . . whose name was John' constitute a statement of fact (*temporaliter gestum*). As such, they are subject to the methods of verification conventional to science. But science, though it may serve to verify the fact, can in no way establish the value. 'Those who hold it do so as a consequence of faith; for those who do not hold it by faith, it remains a matter either of doubt or of contemptuous disbelief'.[6] It thus becomes evident that, for Augustine, history as prophecy is the exposition of values, the values in question being those of Christian insight or *sapientia*.[7]

[1] *De Civ. Dei*, xviii. 52; cf. 54: 'non prophetico spiritu, sed coniectura mentis humanae'.　　　　[2] xx. 19.

[3] The idea of an ἐκπύρωσις, originally Heraclitean, thus finally re-emerges with Christianity. In the meanwhile it had appeared in Mithraism where, according to Cumont, it was associated with the return of Mithra from heaven to earth, the resurrection of the dead, and a last judgement, which included the gift of immortality to the good and the annihilation of the evil, together with Ahriman the evil principle. See Cumont, R.O.[4] pp. 147–8.

[4] *De Civ. Dei*, xx. 30.　　　　[5] *De Util. Cred.* vi. 13.

[6] *De Trin.* xiii. 1.　　　　[7] See above, Ch. XI, p. 435.

The recognition of *sapientia* as an instrument for historical interpretation involves implications of the utmost importance. To begin with, it is equally opposed to the conception of history whether as art or as science. Christian historiography thus denies as purely supposititious the artistic and philosophic assumption that 'nature' consists of a closed system of 'necessary' physical laws. In so doing it repudiates the cruder form of determinism postulated by astrology.[1] 'The stars', it asserts, 'are not the fate of Christ, but Christ is the fate of the stars': 'Our souls, therefore, are by nature subject to no part of physical creation, even to that of the heavens.'[2] But it also rejects what may be called the humanist compromise, the notion that man shares with 'circumstance' the determination of his destiny; and, from this standpoint, the denial of fate is at the same time a denial of fortune.

Throughout this work there have been numerous indications of the role played by the concept of fortune in pagan thought. Its importance cannot better be suggested than by the fact that the very word for happiness or felicity is εὐδαιμονία or εὐτυχία (τύχη ἐκ τοῦ θείου); in which sense it is first accorded recognition by the poets. From poetry it passes into science, there to become a stumbling-block to historians and philosophers alike. We have already alluded to the effort of Thucydides to rationalize the notion, an effort which was to be continued by Aristotle.[3] We have noted also the failure of that effort as indicated in the work of Polybius. The result of this failure was calamitous. For the ideal of intelligibility thus betrayed took speedy vengeance upon its betrayers as τύχη or *fortuna* assumed the character of a 'principle', to be invoked as the 'explanation' of otherwise unaccountable developments according to the merely subjective whim of the observer. As such, it illustrates in a most sinister form the artistic and philosophic vice of *fantastica fornicatio*.

At Rome the idea of fortune first manifests itself in the *Fors Fortuna* of Servius Tullius.[4] And, though 'she does not appear in the calendar, has no flamen and must have been introduced

---

[1] *De Civ. Dei*, v. 1: 'caelestis necessitas'; cf. *Conf.* iv. iii. 4.

[2] *De Gen. ad Litt.* ii. 17. 35.

[3] *Politics*, 1323ᵇ27: τῶν μὲν γὰρ ἐκτὸς ἀγαθῶν τῆς ψυχῆς αἴτιον ταὐτόματον καὶ ἡ τύχη; cf. 1295ᵃ28: χορηγία τυχηρά; *Rhet.* 1361ᵇ39: εὐτυχία (not εὐδαιμονία) δ᾽ ἐστιν ὧν ἡ τύχη ἀγαθῶν αἰτία; *Metaph.* E 2, 1027ᵃ13: ὥστε ἡ ὕλη ἔσται αἰτία ἡ ἐνδεχομένη παρὰ τὸ ὡς ἐπὶ τὸ πολὺ (regularity) ἄλλως τοῦ συμβεβηκότος.

[4] Warde Fowler, *The Religious Experience of the Roman People*, p. 235.

from outside', her presence in the city at this early stage marks a recognition by the Romans of a quite illusory belief in luck. But, whatever the significance of the primitive conception, it was overlaid in the later republic by notions which, while perhaps owing their origin to Polybius,[1] assumed ever-increasing prominence until, in the early empire, they found expression in a regular cult of Fortune.[2] In this connexion we may observe that nothing so clearly exposes the break-down of classical *scientia* as the deification of chance itself. To make the course of history turn on such a principle is fatal to intellectual integrity and moral responsibility alike.

In the light of these considerations Augustine's repudiation of fortune emerges, not as an arbitrary theological preference but as a matter of sheer intellectual and moral necessity. That repudiation is both explicit and comprehensive: *omnia revocanda ad divinam prudentiam*; 'everything', he says, 'must be referred to divine providence'.[3] It thus includes the notion of chance, whether conceived as mere fortuity (*fortuitus rerum eventus*) or as a pagan providence, the *deus ex machina* of poets and historians. In opposition to the latter his assertion of 'divine necessity' serves at once to counter the pagan charge that Christianity was an escape-religion and to turn that charge against paganism itself.[4] As to the former, he remarks that the apparent independence of the so-called accidental or contingent event merely reflects our inability to perceive the connexions which it involves. But since this may be attributed to a defect of the scientific intelligence, it is by no means conclusive as to the facts of the case. 'What we call the fortuitous (*casum*) is nothing but that, the reason and cause of which is concealed from our view'.[5] This fresh analysis of fortuity enables him to do justice to the element of truth contained in pagan conceptions of τύχη or *fortuna*. This is that the individual historical event is *ipso facto* unique and unpredictable. For us, as observers, it is impossible to recognize its relationships until after it has occurred and then only imperfectly. This, however, provides no valid reason for supposing that it marks the intervention of an arbitrary and erratic cosmic force. Indeed, as a manifestation

---

[1] p. 474 above.
[2] *Cl. Rev.* xvii. 153, 445, *Fortuna* in the writings of Caesar and Polybius; cf. Pliny, *N.H.* ii. 7. 22 and Plutarch, *De Fortuna Romana.*   [3] *De Civ. Dei*, v. 9, 10, 11.
[4] See above, Ch. VII, p. 264.   [5] *Retract.* i. 1 and 2.

of divine providence it constitutes an essential part of the necessity of things (*necessitas rerum*). Accordingly, that which Classicism designates as the irrational factor in history (τὸ παράλογον) becomes for Christianity merely the 'paradoxical', which is none the less real; and, from this standpoint, Augustine asserts that each and every occurrence in the manifold of events bears witness to the activity of God.

By thus discarding characteristic prejudices of classical mentality, Augustine opens the way for a philosophy of history in terms of the *logos* of Christ; i.e. in terms of the Trinity, recognized as the creative and moving principle. Fully to understand what this implies it is necessary to recall the detailed argument of *nostra philosophia*.[1] At this point it will be sufficient to observe that, in substituting the embodied for the disembodied *logos*, Christian historiography claims to establish a concrete principle of interpretation in lieu of the barren ideologies of Classicism. Accordingly, to describe this principle[2] as 'the arbitrary will an extra-cosmic person' is to betray a complete misapprehension of its nature and operation. It is equally fallacious to regard it as a possible alternative to any or all of these—'the class-war, of moral law, of climate, of the caprices and physiological peculiarities of those in power, of economic struggle, of race, of pure reason making judicious choice of the pleasurable, of blind animal instinct'.[3] For this is to envisage it in terms of just those categories of the discursive reason which Augustine has been at such pains to repudiate. It is thus to rob it of its intrinsic, dynamic and, if we may use a term to which Augustine appears to have given currency, its 'progressive' character.

History in terms of the embodied *logos* means history in terms of personality. As such, it makes possible a fulfilment of the great *desideratum* of Classicism, viz. an adequate philosophic basis for humanism. But, as distinct from its classical prototype, Christian humanism is emphatically neither anthropocentric nor anthropomorphic. On the contrary, it accuses Classicism of that very vice.

'If an ignorant man', says Augustine,[4] 'enters the workshop of a craftsman, he will there encounter many instruments the reason for which he does not comprehend, and, if he is a fool, he will pronounce them superfluous. In the same way, having stepped into a

---

[1] Ch. XI, above. [2] With Bury, *Selected Essays*, p. 24.
[3] Aldous Huxley, *Proper Studies*, No. XV. [4] *De Gen. contra Manich.* i. 16. 25.

forge, or wounded himself by the maladroit handling of a sharp tool, he will imagine that he is surrounded by many deadly and injurious things. Human beings are such fools that, even though, in the presence of an artisan, they dare not abuse what they do not understand, yet they have the impudence to vilify many things in this universe whose founder and governor is God, only because they fail to perceive the reasons for them.[1] To confess the truth, I myself do not see why mice and frogs, flies and worms, have been created. Nevertheless I recognize that each, in its own way, is beautiful. For when I consider the body and members of any living creature, where shall I not find measure, number and order exhibiting the unity of concord? Wherever you see measure, number and order, look for the craftsman.'

From this standpoint the problem of the Christian is not so much to read into nature the values of truth, beauty, and goodness as to detect those values in it. Still less is it to perpetrate the farce of attempting to 'conserve' them as purely human ideals in the face of a soulless universe. For this deliverance he is indebted to the *logos* of Christ.

At this point the question arises whether the Christian *logos* does not rescue mankind from the tyranny of nature only to make him the puppet of God; in other words, whether predestination does not, as has been suggested, 'take all meaning out of history'. The problem is one with which Augustine deals on many occasions and at great length but, apparently, without having succeeded in making himself wholly clear. Into the details of the controversy we cannot go further than to suggest that the origin of the difficulty may be found in the congenital anthropomorphism of mankind.[2] To this may be ascribed a disposition to 'objectify' God, i.e. to envisage Him in terms of body, a point of view from which predestination resolves itself into the theological counterpart of philosophic determinism while, on the other hand, the notion of spiritual freedom is identified with a philosophic principle of indeterminacy. For Christian *sapientia*, however, this dilemma of the scientific intelligence does not exist. Accordingly, in opposition to classicists like Cicero, Augustine contends that, so far from being incompatible with autonomous self-determination, the prescience of the Almighty is its sole and sufficient guarantee.[3] 'The religious mind will therefore choose and profess both, affirming them

---

[1] § 26.   [2] *De Civ. Dei*, xi. 21.
[3] *De Lib. Arbit.* iii. 3 and 4.

both in a spirit of faithful devotion.'[1] This statement will rank
as a paradox only for those to whom the effort of philosophy is
unfamiliar; who are ignorant of the difficulties it encountered
in attempting to defend the possibility of human freedom and
responsibility while, at the same time, vindicating the omnipotence of a Creator who is both wise and good.[2]

To accept the Trinity as the principle of order and motion
is to accept the *ordo conditionis nostrae*, the inescapable conditions
of human thought and activity, the law for man. Included
among these conditions are time, space, and matter, the
elements, so to speak, of all mutable natures. But, with
respect to these conceptions, the *logos* of Christ once more intervenes to prevent misapprehensions which had troubled the
classical mind and, by so doing, to throw a fresh light upon
historical necessity. To Christianity time is neither a 'thing' nor
is it an illusion. As the 'order of becoming', it is indeed as real
as human life itself and, in precisely the same way, quite as
irreversible. What is true of time is no less true of space. For
if time is the sequence, then space is the pattern in which events
present themselves to consciousness. That is to say, time and
space are intrinsic to our perceptions of body. But to recognize
this fact is by no means to admit that time, space, and matter
or body are independent, i.e., in any real sense, 'principles' of
movement; since movement, like everything else in the created
universe, depends entirely upon the will of the Creator. In the
language of religion, God created the material world not 'in
time' but 'with time'.

In these considerations we may find a warning against certain
popular fallacies which philosophy had done little or nothing to
dispel. One such fallacy is contained in the maxim, *veritas filia
temporis*, 'truth is the daughter of time'. But what of error? Is
she not likewise one of time's progeny, cherished with a solicitude no less eager and persistent than that bestowed on truth?
Another similar fallacy is that of the *Zeitgeist*, the 'time-spirit'
against which none but quixotic idiots are rash enough to con-
tend. Behind these notions lurks a sense that the rhythm of
human history depends on forces which, whether friendly or

---

[1] *De Civ. Dei*, v. 9.
[2] With these difficulties Plato struggles valiantly in the *Timaeus* and elsewhere.
In the *Republic* he solves them by taking refuge in myth: *Rep*. 617 E, αἰτία ἑλο-
μένου, θεὸς ἀναίτιος.

hostile, are at any rate alien to mankind. In modern times these 'forces' have generally been regarded as 'progressive', although recent events have tended to shatter this naïve belief. Antiquity thought of them as, on the whole, circuitous; representing them accordingly either as an 'upward and downward path' or as a 'wheel'.

In this connexion we may call attention to the vigorous attack launched by Augustine against the theory of cycles, the *circuitus temporum*, as he calls it; 'those argumentations whereby the infidel seeks to undermine our simple faith, dragging us from the straight road and compelling us to walk with him on the wheel; argumentations which, if reason could not refute, faith could afford to laugh at'.[1] According to him the real basis of this theory may be traced to the inability of the scientific intelligence to grasp the notion of 'infinity' and to its consequent insistence upon 'closing the circle'. But this, he goes on to point out, is a demand of the human reason which, not unlike the human stomach, is disposed to reject what it cannot assimilate. It is therefore to be deprecated as an attempt to measure 'by the narrow standards of a mutable human mentality the divine mind, wholly immutable, capable of apprehending whatever degree of infinity and of numbering the innumerable without alteration of thought'.[2]

To the Christians, of course, nothing could be more abhorrent than the theory of cycles. For it flatly contradicts the Scriptural view of the *saeculum* as, from beginning to end, a continuous and progressive disclosure of the creative and moving principle. It likewise denies by implication the Christian message of salvation for mankind. In the form which it assumes with classical materialism, it represents motion as dependent on forces beyond control; as a modern writer puts it: *l'irrationnel conduit l'histoire*. For classical idealism it takes shape as a belief in the endless reiteration of 'typical' situations, a belief which does the grossest injustice to the unique character and significance of the individual historical event. Augustine's repugnance for the *circuitus* finds expression in an impassioned outburst.[3]

[1] *De Civ. Dei*, xii. 18; cf. 21 for the 'wheel' of Porphyry. For earlier Christian criticism of the theory of cycles see above, Ch. VI, p. 245.

[2] Ibid.: 'argumenta philosophorum quorum acutissimum illud putatur quod dicunt nulla infinita ulla scientia posse comprehendi; ac per hoc deus, inquiunt, rerum quas facit omnium finitarum omnes finitas apud se rationes habet.'

[3] *De Civ. Dei*, xii. 14,

'Far be it from the true faith', he declares, 'that by these words of Solomon[1] we should believe are meant those cycles by which they (i.e. *philosophi mundi huius*) suppose that the same revolutions of times and of temporal things are repeated so that, as one might say, just as in this age the philosopher Plato sat in the city of Athens and in the school called Academy teaching his pupils, so also through countless ages of the past at intervals which, however great are nevertheless certain, both the same Plato and the same city and the same school and the same pupils have been repeated, as they are destined to be repeated through countless ages of the future. God forbid, I say, that we should swallow such nonsense! Christ died, once and for all, for our sins: *semel mortuus est Christus pro nostris peccatis.*'

In this bold assertion he bears witness to the faith of Christians that, notwithstanding all appearances, human history does not consist of a series of repetitive patterns, but marks a sure, if unsteady, advance to an ultimate goal. As such, it has a beginning, a middle, and an end, *exortus, processus, et finis*. In this conviction he finds the marching orders, so to speak, of the *militia* of Christ.

For Augustine, therefore, the order of human life is not the order of 'matter', blindly and aimlessly working out the 'logic' of its own process, nor yet is it any mere reproduction of a pattern or idea which may be apprehended *a priori* by the human mind. To think of it as either is to commit the scientific sin of fornicating with one's own fancies; in other words, of disembodying the *logos* in such a way as to rob the *saeculum* of all possible significance. For the Christian, time, space, matter, and form are all alike, in the words of St. Ambrose, 'not gods but gifts'. They thus present themselves, not as causes but as opportunity. As such they may be said both to 'unite' and to 'divide'. This they do by giving us our status as individuals in the *saeculum*. But this status involves its specific limitations, not the least of which is the difficulty of communicating with our fellows. This difficulty is intensified by the confusion of tongues (*diversitas linguarum*) which results from the effort of men to surround themselves with economic and cultural barriers of their own creation; and from it not even the saint can claim to be exempt. 'Moses said this and passed on,' remarks Augustine, 'what did he really mean?' The difficulty in question is that of creatures whose limitations of *mind* and *sense* compel them to

---

[1] Really *Ecclesiastes*, 'There is nothing new under the sun'.

adopt such expedients as that of 'making noises in the air'.[1] Yet he accepts these limitations as inescapable, and sharply denounces all attempts to establish a mystical bridge either between one individual and another or between the generations as promptings of the devil.

From this standpoint human history presents itself as 'a tissue of births and deaths', in which the generations succeed one another in regular order.[2] In this context of generations, each and every individual has his own times and spaces, so that the notion of a man 'out of his age' is a vicious and irrelevant abstraction. 'As for his origin, how it comes to pass that he is in the flesh, whether from that one man who was first to be created when man became a living soul, or whether one human being is born similar to another, I neither knew then (when I wrote the *De Academicis*) nor do I yet know'.[3] In other words, our consciousness of individuality is not so much a problem as a fact, for which no scientific explanation is or can be forthcoming.[4] To accept it is to recognize that our nature and destiny are those of individuals, both here and hereafter. On this conviction, rather than on any pagan fancy of a ghost world, rests the Christian belief in a bodily resurrection. But as for the characteristics of the resurrection-body, the position of Augustine is once more a *non scio*. That is to say, it remains for him a question, not of knowledge but of faith.[5] As such, however, it is a belief of supreme importance, for it means that there is nothing inherently 'fatal' in matter, whether the matter of the individual human body or of what we call 'material' civilization; the real and tragic fatality lies in the illusion that there is, since this implies that it is impossible to 'subdue the flesh'. But to make this assumption is to ignore the status in nature to which Providence has assigned mankind.

As part and parcel of the natural order, mankind is indeed, like all creatures organic and inorganic, subject to the fundamental *appetitus* or urge of things. His likings may thus be described as the weight or pull of the soul.[6] 'The loves of the body are like weights which either depress it or raise it up. As a body is moved by its weight, so the soul is drawn by its love

---

[1] *De Trin.* xiii. 1. 4; see Ch. X, p. 388, above.
[2] *De Civ. Dei*, xvi. 10: 'series *or* contextio generationum'; xv. 1: 'saeculum in quo cedunt morientes succeduntque nascentes'.   [3] *Retract.* i. 1. 3.
[4] *De Anima et eius origine*, iv. 7, 8.   [5] *De Civ. Dei*, xx. 20, 21, 22.
[6] *Conf.* xiii. ix. 1; *De Musica*, vi. 11. 29: 'delectatio quippe quasi pondus est animae.'

whithersoever it is drawn.' But the dynamic urge which thus finds expression in the human soul is not blind. On the contrary, it is illumined by intelligence. Accordingly, it attains satisfaction (*requies adpetitionum*) only as it discovers its 'place', i.e. learns to conform to the true order of its being. In this fact we may perceive the superiority of man to brute creation. 'Why', asks Augustine, 'am I better than the swallow or the bee? They too realize the order of their being, unwittingly indeed and without instruction, yet they do it by the operation of nature.' With these creatures as with man, it must be recognized that they do not 'make' the order by which and in which they live; but in living it they manifest the glory of the Creator. 'I am therefore better than they, not because I make but simply because I perceive number and proportion.'[1] That is to say, the business of man as such is to glorify, by knowing and loving, God.

Augustine thus discovers the clue to human history, not in any fine-spun philosophic abstraction (particles of matter ceaselessly grouping and regrouping themselves; the type monotonously repeating itself in countless individuals); but purely and simply in the congenital impulse of human beings to attain happiness. And this happiness they find in order; that is to say, in 'a disposition or arrangement of equal and unequal things in such a way as to allocate each to its own place';[2] apart from which the consequence is *perturbatio* and *miseria*, 'disturbance' and 'distress'. Life is thus conceived as inherently and intrinsically order. With unintelligent creatures the 'arrangement' by which this order becomes possible is merely organic; it is a *pax corporis*, that is to say, 'an ordered disposition of the parts of the body resulting in a cessation of desire'. But, with rational spirits, the demands of order go further; they are to be fulfilled only in a *pax rationalis*, that is, 'agreement between knowledge and activity' (*cognitionis actionisque consensio*). And, since man is an embodied soul, a truly human order must be at once organic and spiritual, i.e. 'an ordered life and salvation of the living being' ('pax corporis et animae ordinata vita et salus animantis').

In the effort to achieve such an order, success or failure will

---

[1] *De Ordine*, ii. 19. 49.
[2] *De Civ. Dei*, xix. 13 (cf. 14): 'parium dispariumque rerum sua cuique loca tribuens dispositio'.

depend upon (*a*) an accurate estimate of the things in which true felicity may be found, and (*b*) the subordination of all other values to those which are found to be ultimate. In other words it depends upon a combination of intellectual insight and moral power. In this sense it becomes true to say that 'to think correctly is the condition of behaving well'. But, however salutary the admonition to correct thinking, it is by no means easy to observe. For, in the first place, it presupposes a grasp of first principles, in default of which thought must inevitably run wild. And, in the second, it involves processes which are no less moral than mental, the gravest danger confronting the thinker being that of permitting his own shadow to fall between himself and the truth. 'It is obvious', observes Augustine, 'that error could never have arisen in religion, had the mind not chosen to worship either itself or body or its own vain imaginings.'[1] That it should have succumbed to this temptation is, of course, to be attributed to pride (*superbia*) which thus for him, as for Tertullian, is the devil's own sin and, peculiarly, the sin of philosophers. As such it is the manifestation of a deep-seated 'vice', the passion, that is, to 'try out one's own power'.[2] This passion finds expression in an effort 'to make one's own truth'; so that the devil, the prince of rogues, is at the same time prince of liars and impostors.[3]

The *logos* of Christ thus serves to introduce a new principle of unity and of division into human life and human history. The unity in question is not merely physical, a unity of the 'flesh' whether conceived as the 'matter' which enters into our constitution or as the 'processes' to which that matter is subjected in what is called organic life. Nor yet, on the other hand, is it merely mental, depending upon a world of timeless and immaterial patterns. It is in fact a unity of 'nature', the nature of a being created in the divine image and predestined to fulfil the divine will. Human values, therefore, are values not for Greek, Roman or Jew, for German or Celt, for European or for Asiatic, but for man as man. In this conclusion Christianity reinforces and gives fresh meaning to the classical Stoic intimation of human brotherhood. At the same time it provides a new sanction for it in the *logos* of Christ.

The new principle of unity serves at the same time as a prin-

---

[1] *Retract.* i. 13. 2.
[2] See above, Ch. XI, p. 448.
[3] *Mendacii pater*; cf. St. John viii. 44.

ciple of division among men.[1] For if the true basis of unity lies in nature, the nature of the old Adam before the fall, or of the new Adam in whom the demands of the flesh are subordinated to those of the spirit, it then follows that division must be ascribed to some defect or perversion of nature. Unity rests on the assumption that there is one world, one nature, and one destiny for mankind. To deny that assumption is to introduce into human life a fatal cleavage or heresy from which, apart from divine grace, there is no possibility of escape. This, however, is precisely what occurs when, as he says, 'the will turns aside from a good which is incommutable and common in order to pursue a good which is private or external or inferior'.[2] That is to say, it develops in consequence of what is called the effort of self-realization, where the self to be realized is envisaged as in opposition to God and His universe.[3]

In human history the new principle of unity and division finds expression in two societies, which may be described mystically (*mystice*) as two cities.[4] These societies are at every point in sharp contrast: 'The one is the city of Christ, the other of the devil; the one of the good, the other of the evil; both composed of angels as well as men.'[5] This vast generalization serves to comprehend the whole human race, 'all the numerous peoples scattered throughout the earth, living by diverse rites and customs, distinguished by the utmost variety of languages, arms, and clothing'.[6] It comprehends also the whole of human history: the life of these two societies extends 'from the beginning of the race to the end of the *saeculum*, during which they are mixed physically but separated morally (*voluntate*), on the day of judgement to be separated physically as well'.[7] They are secular society and the society of God.

The point of divergence between these two forms of association is to be found in their respective desires.

[1] *De Civ. Dei*, xix. 17.   [2] *De Lib. Arbit*. ii. 19. 53.

[3] To the classical doctrine of the ἁμαρτία or vice in human nature Christianity opposes that of 'original' (as opposed to 'actual') sin. Original sin is ascribed to pride or the desire for independence. Its consequence is to introduce the warfare of the members which results in moral and physical disintegration or 'death'. For the application of this doctrine to the question whether unbaptized infants are 'damned' see *inter alia* the statement of Augustine, *De Civ. Dei*, xxi. 16.

[4] *De Civ. Dei*, xv. 1.   [5] *Enchirid*. xxix.   [6] *De Civ. Dei*, xiv. 1.

[7] *De Catech. Rud*. 19. 31; cf. *De Gen. ad. Litt* xi. 15. 20; *De Civ. Dei*, xviii. 54: 'duarum civitatum, caelestis atque terrenae, ab initio usque in finem permixtarum mortalis excursus.'

'That which animates secular society (*civitas terrena*) is the love of self to the point of contempt for God; that which animates divine society (*civitas caelestis*) is the love of God to the point of contempt for self. The one prides itself on itself; the pride of the other is in the Lord; the one seeks for glory from men, the other counts its consciousness of God as its greatest glory.'[1]

These desires may therefore be described respectively as greed (*avaritia*) and love (*caritas*). 'The one is holy, the other foul; the one social, the other selfish; the one thinks of the common advantage for the sake of the higher association, the other reduces even the common good to a possession of its own for the sake of selfish ascendancy; the one is subject to, the other a rival to God; the one is peaceful, the other turbulent; the one pacific, the other factious; the one prefers truth to the praises of the foolish, the other is greedy of praise on any terms; the one is friendly, the other envious; the one desires the same for his neighbour as for himself; the other to subject his neighbour to himself; the one governs his neighbour in his neighbour's interest, the other in his own.'[2]

From this standpoint the *civitas terrena* presents itself as a reflection of values which have their roots in self-assertive egotism (*amor sui*). As such, its genesis depends upon the fact that sheer antagonism is suicidal; as within the individual life, so also for the relations between men, some degree of order is indispensable. Accordingly, *amor sui*, accepted as a principle of order, begins with an assertion of the animal right to live which resolves itself basically into a satisfaction of the demands of belly and loins. In this sense it gives rise to the kind of concord exhibited, e.g. by a gang of pirates, which may thus be taken to represent the lowest limit of co-operative endeavour. But this by no means exhausts its possibilities as a basis for cohesion; since indeed it serves to embrace the whole vast array of secular values. These include, to begin with,

'the body and its goods, i.e. sound health, keen senses, physical strength and beauty, part of them essential to a good life and therefore more eligible, part of less account. In the second place, freedom, in the sense in which one imagines he is free when he is his own master, i.e. the sense in which it is coveted by slaves. Thirdly, parents, mothers, a wife and children, neighbours, relatives, friends and, for those who in any way share our (Graeco-Roman) outlook, membership in a state which is venerated as a parent, together with honours, rewards, and what is called popular esteem. Finally,

---

[1] *De Civ. Dei*, xiv. 28. [2] *De Gen. ad Litt.* xi. 15. 20.

money, the term being taken to comprehend everything which we legally possess and are empowered to sell or otherwise dispose of.'[1]

The values of secularism find expression in characteristic mechanisms wherein form and function are more or less perfectly reconciled, and these mechanisms constitute the secular order. This order, the *pax terrena*, manifests itself in at least three phases. The first is that of the *pax domestica*, the order which determines life in the household.[2] This order depends ultimately upon the union of male and female (*copulatio maris et feminae*). But this union, as the source of offspring 'according to the flesh', may at the same time be regarded as the seed-bed of the city (*seminarium civitatis*). Accordingly, the order of the household gives rise to a second and more comprehensive order, the *pax civica*.[3] A third phase of human association emerges as household and city expand on a world-wide scale (*a domo et ab urbe ad orbem*) to blossom forth as the imperial state.[4] Differing as they do both in constitution and objectives, these three forms of secular society have this much at least in common, that their existence depends upon will.[5] The will in question, however, is not that of an 'oversoul', nor may it be described as 'general' except in so far as it marks 'a composition or fitting together of individual human wills with respect to such objects as pertain to mortal life'.[6] This being so, such order as is evolved within secular society can hardly be more than imperfect.

'Associations of mortals, scattered as they are throughout the earth and confronted by the greatest possible diversity of local conditions, are nevertheless impelled by the bond of a common nature to pursue their respective advantages and interests. So long therefore as the object of appetition is insufficient for any or for all, since it does not possess that character (or, "since its character lacks permanence"— *quia non est id ipsum*)—the association is normally divided against itself and the stronger element oppresses the weaker ('adversus se ipsam plerumque dividitur et pars partem, quae praevalet, obprimit'). The vanquished submits to the victor, because he prefers peace and safety on whatever terms to mastery or even to freedom, so that

---

[1] *De Lib. Arbit.* i. 15. 32.
[2] *De Civ. Dei*, xix. 14: 'pax domestica, id est ordinata imperandi oboediundique concordia cohabitantium'.
[3] xv. 16.   [4] xix. 7: 'imperiosa civitas'.
[5] *De Lib. Arbit.* i. 12 and 13.
[6] *De Civ. Dei*, xix. 17 *b*: 'concordia civium, ut sit eis de rebus ad mortalem vitam pertinentibus humanarum quaedam compositio voluntatum.'

those who have chosen to die rather than be slaves have always excited the greatest wonder.'[1]

By thus rewriting Thucydides in a no less realistic spirit, Augustine denies the pretensions of philosophic idealism as enunciated by the Ciceronian Scipio who, in the *De re publica*, had defined the commonwealth 'as the interest of the people, the people being a group *(coetus multitudinis)* associated together by the tie of common advantage *(utilitatis communione)* and by a common sense of right *(iuris consensu)*'. 'For how', he asks, 'can there be right where there is no justice?'[2] As he elsewhere puts it,[3] 'in the absence of justice, what are realms except great robber-bands? And what are robber-bands except little realms?' From this standpoint there is no essential difference between the empire of Alexander and that of the pirate whom he had arrested. 'The one infests the sea, the other the whole earth.' Accordingly, he rejects the idealist contention in order to re-define the state as 'a group of rational beings, associated on the basis of a common tie in respect of those things which they love'.[4] From this standpoint the quality of any community may be measured in terms of the objects of its desire.

We may here pause to insist that according to Augustine the objects in question are not to be classified as either material or ideal; that is to say, the line of demarcation is not between ponderables and imponderables. They are accurately described as temporal; and the *pax terrena* represents a consolidation of temporal goods.[5] Divine providence, says Augustine, has furnished mankind with the physical basis for an adequate human order by providing him with goods which are congruous to mortal life. These goods comprehend certain 'ideal' values such as 'safety and the society of his kind, whatever indeed is necessary for maintaining and repairing this order—light, a voice, air to breathe, water to drink, and all that goes to nourish, cover, care for, and adorn the body'.

To Augustine the point of real significance is not so much the goods of secular life as the attitude which secularism adopts towards them. This attitude he designates as one of 'possessiveness'; and, from this standpoint, the distinctive mark of the *civitas terrena* is greed or the lust for possession *(libido dominandi)*. That is to say it treats those goods as 'private' *(privatum)*, claim-

[1] xviii. 2. [2] xix. 17–19. [3] iv. 4.
[4] xix. 24. [5] xix. 14. [6] xix. 13.

ing a right to make them 'its own' for distribution within the group (*sua cuique distribuere*); a claim which presumes at the same time the right of exploitation (*uti abutique*, in the phraseology of Roman law.) In the secular order, the claim thus indicated finds expression in 'property' which thus, whatever form it may assume, becomes the 'immovable foundation of human relationships', destined as such to warp and pervert conceptions like that of personality, marriage, and the family. But to 'appropriate' in this sense is also to 'divide'; its ideal of independence is at the same time an ideal of isolation, the isolation of economic and moral self-sufficiency. Furthermore, the greed for property in temporal goods is inevitably exclusive and monopolistic. 'For he who desires the glory of possession would feel that his power was diminished, if he were obliged to share it with any living associate.' Secular society may thus discover its prototype in Babylon, 'the city of confusion', hopelessly rent by schism and dissension which, by reason of self-imposed limitations, it cannot overcome.[1] And, since 'Cain signifies possession', it may look to the fratricide as its founder and first citizen.[2]

Such limitations are those of a society whose ideal of concord never rises above that of composing individual interests in relation to the demands of temporal life.[3] Accordingly, the dominant passion must find a vicarious fulfilment 'in the persons of its leading members or in those of the nations which it subdues. . . . Accordingly, it cherishes its own manhood in its own powerful men (*in suis potentibus diligit virtutem suam*).'[4] The result is that it becomes the theatre of a struggle for survival, the law of which is 'fish eat fish'. 'This world', says Augustine, 'is a sea wherein men devour one another in turn like fish'. By thus reducing secular life to purely biological terms he does ample justice to the Herodotean concept of conflict in society. Such conflict is an inherent and ineradicable feature of secularism from which, on its own principles, there is no conceivable escape. 'For if the household, the common refuge from the evils of human life, affords but imperfect security, how much more so the state which, the larger it is, is the more full of civil

---

[1] xvi. 11: 'de poena venit illa multiplicatio mutatioque linguarum'; xix. 7: 'linguarum diversitas hominem alienat ab homine.' [2] xv. 5, 7, 17.
[3] xix. 14: 'omnis igitur usus rerum temporalium refertur ad fructum pacis terrenae in terrena civitate.'
[4] xiv. 28.

suits and crime, even when for the moment it earns a respite from turbulent, often bloody, seditions and civil wars, from the occurrence of which states are rarely free, from the apprehension of them never.'[1] From this standpoint the maintenance of the *pax civica* depends in the last analysis upon fear, i.e. upon the power to coerce the recalcitrant (*metus quo coerceat*). Or, in the words of a modern: 'l'armée est la manifestation la plus claire, la plus tangible, et la plus solidement attachée aux origines que l'on puisse avoir de l'état'.[2]

Thus envisaged, the *polis*, so far from being a cure for heresy, is itself the greatest and most shameless of heresies; and this is equally true whether it assumes the form of kingdom or commonwealth, realm or republic (*regnum vel civitas, res publica*). This truth applies in the first instance to Assyria, the prototype of Oriental achievement in statecraft, exemplar of brutal conquest and exploitation, 'to be described only as brigandage on a colossal scale'.[3] But it is no less evident in the case of European than of Asiatic political experiment; of Athens, 'mother and nurse of liberal learning, home of so many great philosophers, the glory and distinction of Hellas';[4] of Rome which, by reconciling the civic claim to 'a good life' with the demands of imperial security, had epitomized and completed the political endeavour of the West, triumphantly realizing the secular ideals of stability, prosperity, military glory and untroubled peace.[5]

The advice of Augustine is therefore not to put your trust either in princes or in peoples, in kingdoms or in commonwealths. Of kingdoms and kings he observes that they estimate their achievement in terms, not of the righteousness but of the servility, of their subjects.[6] The vice of the commonwealth, on the other hand, lies in its ideal of merely economic and political (utilitarian) justice with which is bound up the equally vicious ideal of conformity or, as we should say, social adjustment. 'Like the Athenian woman', he says, 'you can by a series of small doses accustom yourself to poison.'[7] Yet such is the pressure to con-

---

[1] xix. 5.   [2] Sorel, *Réflexions sur la Violence*, p. 162.
[3] *De Civ. Dei*, iv. 6: 'quid aliud quam grande latrocinium nominandum est?'
[4] xviii. 9.
[5] xviii. 2; cf. ii. 20: 'tantum stet, inquiunt, tantum floreat copiis referta, victoriis gloriosa vel, quod est felicius, pace secura sit.' The reference is possibly to Cicero, *Ep. ad Attic*. viii. 11. 1 and 2.
[6] *De Civ. Dei*, ii. 20.   [7] *De Mor. Manich.* 8. 12.

form that recusancy means nothing less than social ostracism
and 'he is a public enemy to whom this ideal of happiness does
not appeal'.[1] But it is an illusion to suppose that there can be
any escape from the evils of organized society through a return
to primitivism, since this involves the fallacy that 'nature' is
intrinsically virtuous and 'law' the mark of degeneracy. This,
however, is a heresy, for it presumes that corruption is somehow
inherent in the political fabric, independently of the wills which
create and sustain it. In primitive Rome this notion led to a
revolution against the kings; but 'republican liberty' was no
sooner achieved than it gave rise to oppression, by exposing the
weak to the 'injuries of the strong', whose excesses presently
resulted in a secession of the plebs.[2] To those excesses there was
but one effective check, the fear of danger from abroad; the
sense of the Romans that, if they did not hang together, they
would hang separately. This fear induced a kind of cohesion,
but one merely of a negative character. It thus fell short of a
sound basis for creative peace.

Subsequent events of Roman history served merely to emphasize the original deficiencies of the secular ideal. The economic
motive being dominant, it found expression in 'the exploitation
of plebeians by patricians as though they were slaves', through
the greedy monopolization of land and a barbarous administration of the law relating to interest and debts. Yet, so far from
attempting to correct their shortcomings, the Romans proceeded
to aggravate them by embarking upon an extensive programme
of conquest and acquisition, in which 'they pleaded the necessity of defending security and freedom, as an excuse for satisfying their greed for human glory'.[3] Yet the national passion for
prestige was not without its value; as 'the one vice for the sake
of which they suppressed all other vices',[4] it served to bring
them an unprecedented measure of material prosperity (*res
prosperae*). But material prosperity was to carry with it no real
prospect of relief from the maladies which afflict the competitive
state; and the successes of Rome in Italy and abroad simply
provided increased opportunity 'for making and spending
money'. In this way they promoted the growth of economic
dynasties 'as the more powerful employed their wealth to subject the weaker to their sway'.[5] At the same time they gave rise

[1] *De Civ. Dei*, ii. 20.   [2] ii. 18.
[3] iii. 10.   [4] v. 13.   [5] ii. 20.

to a veritable flood of social evils, a scramble for wealth which
threatened the principle of private property itself, 'as a generation grew up which could neither keep its own estates nor suffer
others to do so'.[1] Coupled with this was a novel form of parasitism
in which, while the poor battened on the rich in order to enjoy an
'inert quiet', the rich preyed upon the poor as a means of ministering to their sense of pride.[2] The upshot was that 'concord was
disrupted and destroyed, at first by savage and murderous seditions, subsequently by a long series of iniquitous civil wars'.
Accordingly, 'the lust for possession, thus exhibited in its purer
form among the Romans, triumphed in the persons of a few
men of exceptional power, only to reduce and exhaust the
remainder and, ultimately, to impose upon them the yoke of
servitude'.[3] Yet, in attempting to fix responsibility for these
developments, it should be remembered that 'ambition would
have had no chance whatever, except among a people corrupted by avarice and luxury'.[4] In these circumstances, how
feeble the argument of Scipio that Rome was or ever had been
a true commonwealth.[5]

Finally, the acquisition of empire serves merely to increase
the perils to which competitive politics are exposed, by producing 'a happiness dazzling as crystal but equally fragile, and
a still more terrible fear lest it should suddenly be shattered'.[6]
For the dangers of a body of water are proportionate to its size.
Conscious of these dangers the imperial state

'seeks to neutralize them by imposing upon its subjects not merely
its yoke but its culture (*linguam*). But at what cost in the effusion of
human blood! Nevertheless there still remain foreign nations to
subdue! And, with the increase of dominion, there increases also the
possibility of intestinal strife, more pernicious even than foreign war.
And yet, they declare, the wise man will be ready to wage just wars!
As though, if he remembered his humanity, he should not rather
deplore the necessity of wars which, if they were not just, he would
not have to wage. Accordingly, for the wise man there would be
no wars.'[7]

It thus appears that, for Augustine, conflict is an inevitable
function of organized secular society. To this fact he attributes

---

[1] ii. 18; cf. iii. 10: He quotes *Aeneid*, viii. 326–7:
        Deterior donec paulatim ac decolor aetas
        et belli rabies et amor successit habendi.
[2] *De Civ. Dei*, ii. 20.   [3] i. 30.
[4] i. 31.   [5] xix. 21.   [6] iv. 3.   [7] xix. 7.

the illusory character of secular achievement. For, in the conflicts to which secularism is committed, even 'its victories are deadly or at any rate deathly';[1] so that the doom with which it is ultimately confronted is that of Assyria and of Rome. In these terms Augustine does justice to facts of social history to which Classicism had vainly endeavoured to give intelligibility, whether through the Herodotean 'principle of decline' or through the humanist myth of corruption, the corruption of *virtù*. At the same time he gives to secular history a moral such as none but the Hebrew prophets had as yet perceived, when he declares that, 'by devoting themselves to the things of this world, the Romans did not go without their reward'.

'God the author and giver of felicity, because He is the one true God, Himself grants earthly kingdoms both to the good and to the evil, yet not at haphazard and, so to speak, fortuitously, inasmuch as He is God; nor yet by fortune, but in accordance with the order of times and seasons, an order which, though hidden from us, is fully known to Him. This order He observes though Himself in no sense subject to it, but governing and disposing of it as lord and master. Felicity, however, He does not grant except to the good.'[2]

'The greatness of the Roman empire is not therefore to be ascribed either to chance or fate. Human empires are constituted by the providence of God.'[3]

God thus 'disposes the times and issues of battles',[4] permitting those to win whose martial qualities enable them to do so. To suppose, however, that the martial qualities are, on that account, necessarily exalted is a fallacy; since there is no way of consecrating egotism, and power, whether material or moral, if taken in abstraction from charity, is a 'vice', the exercise of which cannot but have deleterious consequences. In this law Augustine perceives, not the operation of an Herodotean *nemesis*, but the hand of God working in history to visit the sins of the fathers upon their children from generation to generation. Those visitations they may indeed escape, but upon one condition only; viz. that they cease to dope themselves with illusion and make up their minds to face the facts. This, however, was precisely what Classicism stubbornly and persistently refused to do.

We have seen that, in order to be truly human, an order must be intelligible, i.e. it must succeed in some degree in reconciling

[1] *De Civ. Dei*, xv. 4.   [2] iv. 33.   [3] v. 1.   [4] v. 22.

practice with theory, action with thought.[1] Secularism thus gives rise to a characteristic effort of understanding which, as an attempt (a) to rationalize, and (b) to justify its activity, may properly be described as the ideology of power. As such its origins are lost in the mists which obscure the dawn of human history. But primitive ideology survives in numerous and varied forms of fetishism and taboo, in the reification of fancies, fears, and hopes, not to speak of elaborate techniques of propitiation and sacrifice. The existence of such phenomena testifies in the most emphatic manner to the strength of *amor sui*, the human desire for an effective means of self-preservation amidst the dangers of an obscure and mysterious environment. To the persistence of this impulse into Graeco-Roman times is due the birth of the gods. These gods may be classified, following the conventional Varronian scheme as (1) those of the poets (*ad theatrum*), (2) those of the philosophers (*ad mundum*), and (3) those of the peoples (*cives, maximi sacerdotes*); or, to accept the modification proposed by Augustine, as (1) civic and poetic, and (2) 'natural' or philosophical.[2]

As such, the first to be considered are the civic or, as we should say, 'official' deities, the gods of household and of state; the genesis and history of which corresponds with that of society itself. For, with the collapse of the heroic social structure and the rise of the *polis*, these gods, as Augustine points out, come to be selected for economic and political reasons, i.e. with a view to the promotion of civic virtue; the selection so made going to form what, following Cicero, he designates the 'constitution of religions'.[3] This develops on a purely empirical or pragmatic basis but, once established, it acquires a conventional character which is felt to be eminently conservative and safe (τὰ νόμιμα, *pax deorum*). The sense of security is, however, illusory; since the *constitutio religionum* evolves with the evolution of political life, so that the 'superstition' of to-day becomes the licensed cult of to-morrow. In this sense there can be no graver threat to political stability than what Cicero had called a 'confusion of religions'.[4] It is for this reason that the priesthoods count for so much within the civic order and that their control so often becomes the supreme object of political ambition, to be coveted even by those who privately doubt or deny the gods. For, while

---

[1] See p. 486, above. [2] *De Civ. Dei*, iv. 27 and vi, vii, viii, *passim*.
[3] vii. 2: 'Di selecti (constitutio religionum)'. [4] *De Legg*. ii. 10. 25.

the right and duty of maintaining the *pax deorum* is justly regarded as a department of public interest for which the magistrate is ultimately responsible, nevertheless the priestly colleges are entrusted with special functions of a comprehensive character. These include (*a*) the augurate and *haruspicina*, operating according to conventional methods to discover and interpret the 'will of the gods'; (*b*) the discharge of ritual observances, mainly sacrificial, connected with the licensed state-cults; and (*c*) the regulation and control of *religio*, outbursts of which are liable to occur at critical junctures with dire consequences to the established order. For centuries the Roman pontificate had been conspicuous for the skill with which it succeeded in neutralizing and, if necessary, embalming subversive religious impulses; but the need for political intervention on the occasion of the Bacchanalian conspiracy was a sure indication that its ability to do so was on the wane. That is to say, the efficacy of *religio* as an instrument for social discipline (the narcotic or stimulant of the people) was, at least in the traditional forms, a thing of the past. That this should have been so was, as Augustine perceived, inevitable. For to identify virtue with economic or political utility was to undermine its very foundations. It was thus to admit such obscenities as those connected with the cult of *Magna Mater*. On this account it was absurd to imagine that the pagan gods ever did or ever could provide a sanction for right living.[1] As Tertullian had already put it: 'Romani non ob religiositatem magni sed ob magnitudinem religiosi.' To suppose otherwise was to put the cart before the horse.

The second aspect of Graeco-Roman ideology is that of fiction,[2] i.e. the effort of the poets, working with mythological concepts drawn from the vast reservoir of popular imagination, to offer a convincing account of power and justice. The social significance of such activity could not for long escape notice; it is commemorated, among other traditions, by that of Tyrtaeus inciting his countrymen to victory in the Messenian wars. It is no less evident in the Ionian lyricists who, by propagating their message of individual self-indulgence, contributed mightily to the notorious demoralization of Ionian life. Accordingly 'art', at first spontaneous and unfettered, presently comes under state supervision and control. In Rome, as Augustine notes,

---

[1] *De Civ. Dei*, ii. esp. 4, 5, 6.
[2] Ibid. ii. 8 and 14, *fabulae, figmenta poetarum*, or *poetica*.

this control finds expression as early as the XII Tables which 'among the very few offences for which capital punishment was provided, included that of publishing libellous and defamatory verses';[1] a statute which was subsequently to be reinforced by the establishment of a censorship of dramatics.[2] The attitude thus assumed by the practical Romans found theoretical justification in Plato, who proposed a rigid state control over freedom of speech. This control Augustine endorses as at least a mitigation of the evils for which secular art is responsible; at the same time he regards it as indicative of moral and social vices for which mere prohibition is in no sense a real cure.[3] The Platonic attitude to art was, however, far from being universally accepted. For, on the other hand, it was claimed, e.g. by Aristotle, that, properly understood as 'imitation', art could fulfil a positive, cathartic function in the *polis*. That function was homoeopathic; by exciting and appeasing the emotions of pity and terror, any excess of which rendered political life impossible, it offered a harmless alternative to the savage blood-purge. What Augustine thought of this theory we have already tried to indicate.[4]

Popular ideology, whether embodied in civic life or in the life of art (*fabulosa vel civilia, theatrica vel urbana*), passes by an easy metamorphosis into that of philosophy. This occurs as there is substituted for the concept of superhuman forces operating sporadically through nature that of God regarded as cosmic energy or the world-soul.[5] By entertaining this notion, philosophy condemns itself *ab initio* to failure in its effort to resolve the confusions and perplexities of popular thought. At the same time she is no mean antagonist and there is need of vastly increased caution in undertaking to examine and expose her claims.[6] Yet, for all the finesse with which she develops and supports her positions, she cannot conceal the fact that, like the more popular forms of secular ideology, they represent nothing but the consecration of selfishness; and are thus of the earth, earthy (*civitas terrigenarum*).

'It is the peculiarity of secularism that it worships a god or gods, by whose aid it may reign victorious in temporal peace, animated

---

[1] ii. 9.   [2] ii. 13.   [3] ii. 14; cf. xiii. 5.   [4] Ch. X, p. 391, above.
[5] *De Civ. Dei*, vi. 8; vii. 6: 'deum se arbitrari esse animam mundi, quem Graeci vocant κόσμον, et hunc ipsum mundum esse deum.'
[6] viii. 1: 'intentiore nobis opus est animo.'

not with the love of wise counsel but with the lust for possession. For the good use this world in order that they may enjoy God; but the evil use God in order that they may enjoy this world.'[1]

We cannot follow Augustine in his long and painful effort to uproot the various forms of illusion embodied in popular ideology; the illusions of peoples, poets, and philosophers. Upon this task he embarks in a veritably Lucretian spirit,[2] but with infinitely heavier artillery than Epicureanism could command. One and all, he asserts, these are not gods but words, exposing them as devices of *scientia* to conceal ignorance rather than of *sapientia* to disclose truth. Accordingly, regarded as gods, they are fraudulent; all that is necessary is to expose them and they will disappear into thin air. Nevertheless, as words, they point to some kind of reality, however dimly apprehended, distorted, and misconstrued. Thus, though in fact delusion, they are terribly and disastrously real to those who believe in them. From this standpoint it may be suggested that, however tenuous the bodies of demons, they have substance enough to burn.[3]

In this respect the error of Classicism may be summarily described as a failure to identify the true source of power and, therewith, its true character and conditions. The error thus indicated is original, and to it may be ascribed the whole tissue

---

[1] xv. 7.   [2] See Ch. II, above.

[3] *De Civ. Dei*, xxi. 10. In this paragraph I have tried to indicate the substance of Augustine's demonology. Belief in the existence of *aëriae potestates* was deeply rooted both in the Hebrew tradition and in that of Graeco-Roman antiquity. The notion that they were capable of doing good or evil to mankind was equally widespread in popular thought. Thus Julian, himself a firm believer in demons, says of the Christians that their theology boils down to two things: (1) whistling to keep the demons off, and (2) making the sign of the cross upon the forehead, p. 268 n. 3, above.

Augustine fully accepts the existence of demons but denies them any capacity for independent action, the possibility of which is excluded by the Christian doctrine that God's action upon the world is immediate and direct. Demons, therefore, have power to do only what they are permitted to do; and they are permitted to subject and afflict only those whom, in the judgement of God, it is just that they should afflict and deceive. In this sense the (authentic) phenomena of spiritualism may be traced to their activity (*De Civ. Dei*, vii. 35). But it is important to remember that, according to Augustine, they have no influence except over the sinful mind (ibid. x. 21 and 22): 'non enim ⟨aëria potestas⟩ vincit aut subiugat nisi societate peccati'; that is to say, there is an element of subjectivity involved in every case. From this standpoint he vigorously denies the pagan contention that they are in any real sense 'intermediaries' between a pure god and a world contaminated by matter.

The result is to immobilize rather than to eradicate Lucifer and his crew; so that popular demonology, together with the mechanical methods of exorcism mentioned above, survives through the Middle Ages and into modern times.

of fallacies which frustrate the secular aspirations of men. These fallacies Christianity explodes in a sentence: *all power cometh from on high.* In so doing, it does not subscribe to the antithesis which sets 'power' in opposition to 'benevolence' after the manner of those flabby sentimentalists whom Aristotle so sharply criticizes in a famous chapter of the *Politics.*[1] Nor is it condemned to labour with Aristotle himself in a vain endeavour to effect a partial reconciliation between the two. For it perceives that, however vicious in principle, the secular desire of man to apprehend and possess himself of power is but the perversion of a wholly natural and proper impulse to save himself from danger and destruction; and that it may be explained as a consequence of his inability to recognize his own highest and greatest good. Accordingly, for the Christians, the antithesis is not between 'benevolence' and 'power'; it is rather between the love of power and the power of love. From this standpoint the *pax caelestis*, the order of the divine society, constitutes at the same time the order of love.[2] This may well be mysterious, but it is not mythical or hypothetical. For it means simply that the self-same human wills have attached themselves, not to transcendental objects (that they leave to Platonism) but to a principle which gives to the 'object' world a wholly fresh complexion, thus 'making all things new'.[3] That is to say, what it prescribes is *adhaerere Deo*, adhesion to God, the source of truth, beauty, and goodness, the supreme reality, as the one fundamental principle for individual regeneration and for social reformation, the point of departure for a fresh experiment in human relationships, on the acceptance of which rests the only real hope of fulfilling the promise of secular life. This is the Christian alternative to the pagan proposition that correct action presupposes correct thinking; and it may accurately be described as 'justification by faith'.

Accordingly, the appeal of Christianity is directed first and foremost to the individual envisaged, not as a speck of cosmic matter, 'shooting like a meteor through space and for a brief moment lighting up the sky, before the darkness once more closes around it', nor yet as ἄνθρωπός τις, a mere specimen in a biological, racial, occupational, cultural or political group but,

---

[1] Ch. III, above, p. 76.
[2] *De Civ. Dei*, xv. 22: 'ordo amoris, dilectionis, caritatis'.
[3] See the magnificent chapters *De Civ. Dei*, xxii. 22, 23, 24.

in Tertullian's words, as the *vas spiritus*, the one real subject of volition (*voluntarius motus*), i.e. of intelligent and deliberate activity. To this appeal the individual responds by an act of will, 'the reaction of the soul to the tug or pull of its love'; in other words by conversion which thus, in the Christian scheme of salvation, assumes a significance among the compulsions of nature wholly unsuspected by the classical world. The phenomenon of conversion had been ignored by Aristotle, whose discipline was based upon habituation (ἐθισμός), as well as by Plotinus, who relied upon 'the intensive cultivation of the speculative faculty'. Its existence had, indeed, been acknowledged by Plato, especially in the *Republic* and the *Symposium*; where it is described as a 'revolution of the soul toward the light' and identified with the working of an impulse designated Ἔρως or Love.[1] But, on examination, the analogy between Platonic and Christian love is revealed as nothing more than superficial. For the 'passion' of Plato is a passion for transcendence; behind it lurks the assumption of an hiatus or discontinuity between the sensible and the intelligible worlds which this concept is intended to bridge; and its use for this purpose provides an excellent illustration of the way in which science resorts to the mythical or hypothetical in order to give plausibility to its artificial constructions; the 'vice' against which Christian realism so vigorously protests and which it claims to have eliminated. In this case the fallacy lies in the original assumption; and, from this standpoint, Plato's invention turns out to be entirely gratuitous, since the connexion which he labours so industriously to establish already exists. Accordingly, it serves merely to direct attention to a genuine need, the need for a connexion, not between sense and intelligence but between man as a whole, the subject of *voluntarius motus*, and the object world in which 'he lives and moves and has his being'. This connexion, however, does not any more than the other have to be 'established'; it needs only to be recognized, since it also exists, as it has from the beginning and will to the end of the *saeculum*. To recognize its existence is to recognize the existence of divine grace.[2]

[1] *Rep.* 518 B foll.; *Symp.* 202.
[2] See above, Ch. X, p. 395 for Augustine as 'pre-eminently the doctor of grace'. His account and defence of grace is developed especially in the anti-Pelagian treatises (ed. Bright).

The need for grace is the need of perceiving a relationship, the reality of which is or rather would be self-evident, except for the wilful and perverse blindness of mankind. And, by contrast with the fictitious 'connexions' set up by the discursive reason, this perception is absolutely devoid of all elements of hypothesis or myth. As a matter of direct immediate experience (*intima scientia*), it belongs to precisely the same order of psychological fac' s that to which every human being bears witness when he first becomes aware of himself as endowed with capacities of sense-perception and discrimination which it is his duty and privilege to enjoy. It may, indeed, be regarded simply as the renewal in a sharply intensified form of that self-same experience of childhood.[1] For experience of this kind no 'explanation' is either possible or necessary. To direct attention to it is merely to direct attention to an indubitable fact of conscious life, the existence of which had been dimly apprehended by Classicism, although its significance had been gravely misconstrued.

Thus envisaged, 'grace' emerges as the answer to a perfectly normal and legitimate human demand, the demand for illumination and power; and it points to an ideal, not of mental or spiritual vacuity,[2] but of Christian wisdom or insight (*sapientia*). For, as Augustine never ceases to insist, the demand of faith is a demand for understanding; a demand which is not to be satisfied by any kind of intellectual or moral hugger-mugger, but only by the clearest and most certain knowledge regarding the true character of the human endowment and the manner in which it may best be enjoyed.[3] This knowledge is not to be understood as anything magical, the sudden, inexplicable, and final gift of an 'inner light', but as the culmination of a long and arduous process of self-discipline by which the natural is gradually transformed into the spiritual man.[4] As such it is accurately described, not as the transcendence but as the fulfilment of nature, not as reconstruction but as regeneration and renewal. To say this is to raise the question of how grace works.

[1] Ch. X, p. 395, above.

[2] That again it leaves to Platonism; see Ch. IV, p. 172, above, on Plotinus, and Ch. XI, p. 429, the ἕνωσις, 'simplification' of the soul to be attained by a process of 'evacuation'.

[3] See *De Civ. Dei*, xxi. 19 foll. on the use and abuse of prayer and sacrament.

[4] *De Vera Relig*. 26 indicates successive stages in the evolution of the spiritual man. Cf. *De Doct. Christ*. ii. 7, the *gradus ad sapientiam* as outlined by Isaiah (1) *timor*, (2) *pietas*, (3) *scientia*, (4) *fortitudo*, (5) *consilium*, (6) *purgatio cordis*.

As a mystery which defies scientific analysis, the operation of grace can only be described metaphorically; 'it is', says Augustine, 'the medicine of the soul, working internally as drugs work externally upon the body'.[1] As such it involves a relationship to the spiritual, analogous to that of exercise to the physical constitution; it is mental and moral gymnastic. The possession of bone and sinew is part of the physical endowment, of which some men enjoy more and others less; but even a Samson may forfeit his strength for lack of practice or from abuse. The same truth is otherwise illustrated in the parable of the talents. In this consideration may be found the answer of Augustine to the question whether grace is free or conditioned. As an essential part of the constitution of things it is as free and unconditioned as the atmosphere or the sunlight. But it is theoretically possible for men to exclude the air and light from their bodies, though the penalty they pay for such folly is certain physical death. Similarly, they are at liberty, if they so choose, to deny and repudiate grace, but with consequences no less disastrous to the spirit. On the other hand, the vast majority of men, however unconsciously, accept the gifts of grace to this extent that they at least refrain from committing deliberate suicide. But of those who so accept it, there are few indeed who appreciate its full significance as a means to the realization of their true potentialities as human beings. In this connexion Augustine denounces as rank paganism the sentiment that 'God helps those who help themselves'. 'God', he declares, 'also helps those who do not help themselves in order that they may help themselves.'[2] This He does by providing them with the elements necessary to the attainment of a good will. That is to say, He so 'diffuses love through their hearts that the soul, being healed, does good not from fear of punishment but for love of justice'.[3] This being so, it becomes instructive to consider the stages whereby it accomplishes its salutary work.

Starting from the conception of natural or intrinsic virtue, classical (Pindaric) theology had worked out a scheme to mark the descent of the soul from prosperity through satiety and arrogance to destruction. It remained for Christianity, whose

[1] *De Civ. Dei*, xv. 6.
[2] *Retract.* i. 9; *Ep.* ccxvii (a) ch. v; *De Dono Persev.* xxiv. 60.
[3] *De Corrept. et Grat.* ii and iii.

original assumptions were precisely the reverse, to offer an intelligible account of the process and technique of salvation. This it undertakes to do somewhat as follows. The operation of grace begins by producing in the soul a conviction of 'sin', i.e. of the truth that the *malaise* (*perturbatio et miseria*) from which it suffers is due, not to anything external to itself, but to its own congenital and acquired deficiencies. Coincident with this, however, there dawns a sense that these deficiencies are not incurable, but may be overcome through a recognition of the salutary principle and of its capacity to minister to a mind diseased. This means 'forgiveness', i.e. a realization of the possibility of a clean sheet and a new deal to follow automatically as a consequence of accepting the Christian starting-point.[1] But to say that forgiveness depends upon the acceptance of Christian principles is to say that it points to humility, i.e. 'sticking to God' (*adhaerere Deo*), as the condition of renewal. Christian humility, however, so far from implying self-abasement before the world, is the one assurance of independence from the world. That is to say, it brings with it strength rather than weakness, not the vain dream of Herculean or superhuman strength, but the substantial strength which flows from dependence upon the true source of illumination and power. It thus makes possible the effort required to overcome internal discord and dissension, and ultimately to establish that co-ordination of flesh and spirit which is described as the 'peace of God'. In other words it indicates a specifically Christian discipline as the avenue to felicity.

The discipline thus indicated is, indeed, painful and exacting; as Augustine observes, there will be revulsions (*reluctationes*) of the flesh against the spirit so long as life endures. Accordingly it presupposes such further 'gifts of grace' as that of perseverance,[2] the perseverance needed for the development of whatever moral and mental muscle a man may possess. It thus includes frequent and rigorous self-examination, the rule of which is, in all doubtful and difficult problems of thought and action, to be suspicious of nothing or nobody so much as of oneself. It includes also the practice of virtues such as con-

---

[1] Ch. VII, p. 264, above. Julian's failure to apprehend the meaning of forgiveness is illustrated by his remarks about Constantine and by his reaffirmation of the 'iron law of retributive justice'.

[2] *De Dono Perseverantiae*, i. 1: 'asserimus ergo donum Dei esse perseverantiam qua usque in finem perseveratur in Christo.'

tinence and mercy.[1] Finally, it includes endurance (*patientia*) together with all that this implies in the way of suffering and sacrifice. With respect to these latter, it may be observed that their value is not to be gauged merely in terms of intensity and duration without regard to the end which they subserve. As Augustine puts it: 'It is the cause for which he suffers rather than the fact of his suffering that makes the martyr.' That is to say, suffering, in order to have a moral value, must be intelligible. This it is only when the end to which it points is, in the highest degree, worth while. For Augustine that end is the suppression of disorderly heat (*turbidus calor*) and the development of spontaneous power (*spontanea potestas*). It is this which explains and justifies the Christian effort of self-discipline, at the same time distinguishing it from all the multifarious forms of asceticism current in the pagan world. This discipline is described as the subjugation of the flesh, the sovereign good, eternal life.[2]

The attainment of this life is the attainment of an ideal of wisdom to which paganism vainly aspired, the wisdom of Christian insight. Christian insight finds expression in what may be called two modes (*a*) as substantial (rather than 'formal') truth, and (*b*) as substantial (rather than 'formal') morality. As truth it may be described as reason irradiated by love; as morality, love irradiated by reason. It is thus at one and the same time the value of truth and the truth of value. Envisaged as value-truth, it marks an abrupt departure from the ideal of truth postulated by classical science. That ideal had been accurately stated by Julius Caesar as truth apprehended in the cold light of reason, free from hatred and love, anger and pity, the passions which obfuscate the mind'.[3] In the light of Christian wisdom, however, the classical ideal of truth is revealed for what it is, viz. as heretical. This it is from two points of view, equally important. For, to begin with, it is, as the very word heresy (αἵρεσις) implies, the result of an arbitrary preference or choice and thus, in Christian terminology, 'man-made'. The fact that this is so does not mean that it is useless. On the contrary it justifies its claim to a certain limited validity. This claim it can, however, defend only in terms of coherence, consistency, etc.;

---

[1] *De Mor. Eccl.* 19. 35: 'in coercendis sedandisque cupiditatibus quibus inhiamus in ea quae nos avertunt a legibus Dei et a fructu bonitatis eius'; *Retract.* ii. 33, the importance of remembering the prayer: Forgive us as we forgive our debtors.
[2] *De Civ. Dei*, xix. 4, *aeterna vita*.　　　　　　[3] Sall. *Cat.* 51. 1–2.

i.e. in relation to a 'system' of thought which, being devised for human purposes by human minds, is to that extent artificial or fictitious. As truth, therefore, its value is merely utilitarian or pragmatic, tainted with a relativity which, being *original*, it can by no means escape. And, secondly, to say that classical truth is man-made truth is to direct attention to the maker and to the conditions under which it is made. But, unhappily, this affords little or no ground for reassurance as to its character. For, as we have seen, the ideal of classical *scientia* is that of a 'pure' reason operating *in vacuo*. As an ideal of knowledge, this is humanly speaking impossible and absurd; since, as Augustine insists, there can be no knowledge without feeling and no feeling without knowledge. Granting, however, for the sake of argument that such an ideal could be achieved, it would be only at the cost of a frightful mutilation of the knowing subject. Accordingly, from the standpoint both of subject and object, the knower and the known, classical *scientia* is heresy. As such it may attain a conventional value; but it cannot claim the value of essential and creative, i.e. of divine truth.

The criticism of classical truth is, at the same time, a criticism of classical ethics. To Classicism morality is a matter *either* of emotion *or* of reason. The former it regards as subjective, particularist, barbarian; the other as objective, universal, the morality of civilized man.[1] Christian *sapientia*, however, cuts across these heresies of the scientific intelligence in order to base the moral judgement on *bona voluntas*, thereby giving to it a validity to which no system of formal ethics can properly lay claim.[2] For the judgement of *bona voluntas* is a judgement neither of blind instinctive emotion on the one hand nor, on the other, of calculated individual or social utility. It is a judgement of the man as a whole. Accordingly, it discards the ideals whether of barbarism (thinking with the blood) or of civilization (classical *ataraxia, apatheia*) to insist that 'the passions are to be so governed and held in leash that they may be turned to the service of justice'. 'The question for us', declares Augustine, 'is not if the mind is angry but why it is angry; not if it is sad, but why it is sad; not if it is afraid, but why it is afraid.'[3] In this fresh attitude Augustine discovers the basis, not of a formal but

[1] See Ch. VII, p. 270, above: the strictures of Julian upon Christian ethics as revealed (*a*) in Constantine, and (*b*) among the Antiochians.
[2] *De Lib. Arbit.* i. 13. 27.　　　　[3] *De Civ. Dei*, ix. 4 and 5.

of a substantial ethic; the sum-total of which is comprehended by the law of love (*lex caritatis*).

'The law of love', he declares, 'comprehends all the discussions and writings of all the philosophers, all the laws of all states. It is embodied in two precepts upon which, in the words of Christ, hang all the law and the prophets: *Thou shalt love the Lord thy God with all thy heart and with all thy soul and with all thy mind; and thy neighbour as thyself.*'

'Here', he concludes, 'is your physics, here your ethic, here your logic; here also is salvation for the state which deserves to be praised.'[1]

For what it provides is the basis of a fresh co-ordination of mind and sense, of thought and activity, moving forward in conjunction and, so to speak, under a full head of steam. As such, it is offered as a doctrine of salvation for the individual and, through him, to 'a rotting and disintegrating world'.[2]

Thus envisaged, its first service is to deflate the idols of the market-place and the academy, i.e. the mythology of secularism. As we have seen, this mythology falls into two general divisions, (1) that of classical materialism, and (2) that of classical idealism; the former of which envisages the cosmos as one big machine, the latter as one big soul. To Augustine the machine-cosmology is so grotesque that it hardly merits the attention of a serious thinker.[3] Regarded as a picture of the universe it is the grossest of all possible abstractions; while the philosophy of mind and motion which it involves is such that it could hardly have been invented except by those who fancy themselves as automata, a role which, in the nature of things, the human being cannot consistently or for long sustain. The other, the one-big-soul cosmology, was in classical antiquity much the more prevalent and, at the same time, much more seductive and dangerous, inasmuch as it appealed to the spirit of devotion and self-sacrifice which is one of the fundamental and most deep-seated instincts of the race. Yet it evoked this spirit only to degrade, pervert, and ultimately to destroy it. For, as it implied an impossible ideal of unity, so also it pointed to an effort of unification through identification or submergence, the consequence of which could only be morally and physically disastrous to whoever undertook it. What it demanded was, in

[1] *Ep.* cxxxvii. ch. v. 17.
[2] *De Civ. Dei*, ii. 18: 'doctrina saluberrima tabescenti et labenti mundo'.
[3] viii. 5 and 7; xi. 5.

effect, that the individual should abnegate his God-given status, in order to prostrate himself before, not a reality but a figment of his own imagination, the so-called 'group-spirit' as exemplified in family, class, or state. Of such personifications perhaps the most obvious was that which found expression as 'the spirit of the family', whose supposed 'immortality' stood in marked contrast with what was presumed to be the ephemeral character of its transient 'representatives', of those who, in the language of jurisprudence, 'carried the person' of this hypothetical entity. The error here was at once intellectual and moral. For, as it involved the logical fallacy that the 'type' alone was real, so also it provoked a vain effort to dramatize oneself in the role of one's dead ancestors, an effort which precluded all possibility of genuine ethical development on the part of the living individual. And what was true of the family was no less true of any other group, even though its claims to comprehensiveness and finality were those of Eternal Rome.

To subvert the ideology of secularism was not to destroy the actual structure of secular society; it was merely to envisage it in a new light. Yet this was of immense importance. For it was to see the state, no longer as the ultimate form of community, but merely as an instrument for regulating the relations of what Augustine calls the 'exterior' man (*exterior homo*). This function it fulfilled by the application of methods the value of which depended upon their efficacy as a 'means of intimidating the evil and enabling the good to live more quietly among them'; and, from this standpoint, the institutions of the secular order 'had not been designed in vain', but might claim the justification of a 'certain reason and utility'.[1] The advantage thus realized was, however, purely negative, since 'the effect of law is to condemn the act, without removing the evil disposition'. It was, moreover, attained by damming back psychological forces, the explosiveness of which is proportionate to the pressure which the state finds necessary to exert. 'For prohibition serves merely to aggravate the longing for what is forbidden, when justice is not so loved that the love of it overcomes the desire to do wrong.'[2] That is to say, the role of the state is purely formal;

[1] *Ep.* cliii. 16: 'non sane frustra instituta sunt potestas regis, ius gladii cognitoris, ungulae carnificis, arma militis, disciplina dominantis, severitas etiam boni patris. habent ista omnia modos suos, causas, rationes, utilitates. haec cum timentur, et coercentur mali et quietius inter malos vivunt boni.'

[2] *De Civ. Dei*, xiii. 5.

as such, it can 'reconstruct' or 'renovate', but it cannot possibly 'regenerate'. In these terms Augustine marks a sense of the limitation of political action which dissociates him, not merely from the claims of classical idealism, but also from much of the ill-conceived legislative activity undertaken by the nominally Christian empire.[1]

But if Augustine thus emphatically rejects the pretensions of creative politics, it is not with a view to setting up a new heresy, comparable with any of the anti-political heresies current in the classical and post-classical world. He is not a Christian cynic, claiming the right to isolate himself either physically or morally or intellectually from the society of his kind. And, if he asserts a right to freedom, it is not the freedom 'to say what you think, and think what you like', but the freedom which consists in subjection to truth. This is not to ignore the empirical values of *liberté, égalité,* and *fraternité.* It is however to perceive that whatever genuine meaning these values may possess is dependent upon the maintenance of spiritual or 'personal' freedom, and that to permit the evilly-disposed to enslave one's mind is to offer him the best possible opportunity of enslaving one's body. But if Augustine is no isolationist neither is he a secessionist of the type represented by Tertullian.[2] To him it is evident that, ultimately, there can be no compromise between the claims of Caesar and those of Christ. Caesar must therefore abandon his pretension to independence and submit to Christian principles, or he must be prepared for the doom which awaits sin and error in its secular conflict with justice and truth. For Christ, as he points out, did not say, *my kingdom is not of* THE *world,* but *my kingdom is not of* THIS *world.* His meaning is best conveyed in the prayer, *Thy kingdom come.*[3] Accordingly, to admit as final any dualism between 'moral man' and 'immoral society' is to perpetrate the most vicious of heresies; it is to deny the Christian promise and to subvert the foundation of the Christian hope.

On the other hand, to accept that promise as valid is to recognize the possibility of a fresh integration of human life in terms of which the manifold forms of secular heresy may at last be overcome. This integration is possible because its basis is a good which, unlike the goods of secularism, is common, comprehensive, inexhaustible, in no wise susceptible of expropria-

[1] See above, Chs. V–IX.   [2] See above, Ch. VI.   [3] *Retract.* i. 3. 2.

tion or monopolization, nothing less indeed than God Himself. Accordingly, in its application to the individual, it does not confine him within the narrow limits of the *polis* (a territorial, racial, and cultural 'unity'), nor does it confront him with the necessity of a choice between alternatives which are equally arbitrary and artificial, viz. the life of 'activity' or that of 'reason', of 'society' or 'contemplation', heresies within a heresy; but, on the contrary, it offers him a 'life' which subsumes them all, the life of 'good will'. And, while thus overcoming the heresies and schisms of individual life, it overcomes those also which vitiate the life of society. For, as it recognizes no element in individual experience which cannot be explained in terms of individual will, so also it denies that there exists any unknown quantity in the 'life' of society which is not to be resolved into terms of association, the deliberate association of individuals in pursuit of such ends as they deem good. By so doing it reveals its power to exorcize demons, dissipating once and for all the bogies (gods or ghosts) which haunt the political mind. At the same time it proclaims the solidarity of mankind, not as a vague aspiration of the remote future but as a present and living fact, in the light of which all obstacles to human brotherhood are exposed as merely artificial. As we have already noted, this solidarity is based upon a unity of nature.[1] That is to say, it is the unity of beings endowed with the capacity to feel and to think.[2] As such, it transcends all distinctions of race, class, culture, and sex.[3] Thus 'Adam is everyman'; not, however, as a 'type' but as 'prefiguring' in his individual experience the experience of all his descendants. And, for the same reason, 'everyman is my neighbour'.

To admit the truth of these propositions is to perceive that, in order to give effect to this fact of human neighbourhood, what is really needed is a concerted effort of good will. That is to say, it points to a fresh vision of society based on 'the unity of faith and the bond of concord'. This unity is absolute; the society so constituted is 'one body in Christ'. At the same time it is universal in a sense undreamed of even by the so-called universal empire; potentially it is as broad and inclusive as the

[1] p. 487, above.
[2] *De Gen. ad Litt.* iii. 20 and *De Gen. ad Manich.* i. 17. 27.
[3] *De Trin.* xii. 7. 12: 'hic factus est homo ad imaginem Dei, ubi sexus nullus est, hoc est in spiritu mentis suae'; cf. *De Civ. Dei*, xxii. 17: 'creatura est ergo Dei femina sicut vir'.

human race itself. Furthermore, it is unique among societies, for in it alone 'the life of the whole' is not secured at the expense of the parts; but, so far from doing violence to, it exists to promote the fullest possible development of individual personality. This means that it rejects the secular ideal of totalitarianism, whatever guise it may assume; its ideal is not one of communism or fascism but of community, the 'communion of saints'. It means also that it is profoundly democratic, and that from several points of view. For (1) as Augustine says, 'it recruits its citizens from all races and from all cultures, without the slightest regard for differences of custom, law, and institutions'.[1] And (2) it imposes upon all alike precisely the same obligations and duties; the obligations and duties prescribed in the Law of Love. Finally, (3) because it assumes that all alike are sinners, it absolutely rejects the claims of the superman-saviour, an earthly providence to whose *virtù* and *fortuna* mankind is invited to commit his destiny. Accordingly, it postulates a radically new kind of leadership, differing both in purpose and technique from any of the various types of leadership current in the secular world. This is the episcopate, a name, as he says, 'not of distinction but of work'.[2] For these reasons the Christian society claims to be a 'perfect society' (*societas perfecta*). Instead of the 'semblance and shadow of peace' precariously ensured by secularism, it embodies the substance of a peace exhibiting the fullest measure of order and concord possible to human beings, the peace of an association whose members 'enjoy God and enjoy one another in God'.[3] To this peace they pledge themselves in a new oath or sacrament (*sacramentum, sacrum signum*); a sacrament conceived, not as an act of self-surrender analogous to that whereby the citizen of this world resigns his will into the keeping of a temporal sovereign, but rather as a covenant of emancipation from temporality, mutually undertaken by men who thus profess themselves aliens from secularism (*peregrini*). It is a testament, not of subjection to, but of salvation from, the divinity of Caesar, mystically proclaimed through baptism in the name of the Father, the Son, and the Holy Spirit.[4] At the same time it

---

[1] *De Civ. Dei*, xix. 17.   [2] xix. 19.   [3] xix. 13.

[4] The so-called baptismal formula given in Matt. xxviii. 19. Mithraism had borrowed the term *sacramentum* from the Roman army. Cumont, *R.O.*[4], pref., p. x and p. 207, n. 5. For the *sacramentum* to Caesar taken by the civil population, see Dessau, *I.L.S.* 8781 (province of Paphlagonia, 3 B.C.).

is a vow of unyielding opposition to all who deny or reject the claims of the Evangel. In this opposition Christianity finds the true logic of the *saeculum*, the hand of God in human history.

Thus envisaged, human history emerges as indeed a 'conflict of opposites', but the elements of opposition are not what Classicism had supposed. For they constitute no reflection of contending physical forces, in the clash of which mankind plays a dubious and uncertain role as 'the subjective factor of an objective process'. Nor do they mark a revulsion of man from nature, the subject from its object, a conflict for the realization of material or ideal, i.e. merely human and subjective, goods which recede forever from the grasp. Properly understood, history is the record of a struggle, not for the realization of material or ideal values but for the materialization, embodiment, the registration in consciousness of real values, the values of truth, beauty, and goodness which are thus so to speak thrust upon it as the very condition of its life and being. In these terms and in these terms alone can the secular effort of the human spirit be explained and justified, for only thus does it become intelligible.

To describe these values as real is to say that they are essential, substantial, inherent in the very constitution of the universe. As such they have always existed: *In the beginning was the Word*. There can thus be no such thing as essential or substantial evil; what is called evil must, in the nature of things, be a deficiency or perversion of good, but there exists nothing, the corruption of which has so far vitiated its nature as to destroy the last vestiges thereof.[1] In other words the nature even of the devil, in so far as it is a nature, is good; even his lies, in order to serve their purpose as lies, must have verisimilitude, i.e. they must be interspersed with elements of truth. The goodness and truth which are thus original in nature are, moreover, final to it. In the secular conflict with sin and error they are substance confronting shadow, unity division, the whole a distorted and partial image, a mere parody of itself. In such a conflict who can doubt to which side final victory must belong? Accordingly, the apparently irreconcilable antitheses which present themselves everywhere in nature are not to be accepted as ultimate. Their destiny, indeed, is to be utterly consumed in that final

[1] *De Civ. Dei*. xix. 12.

conflagration or burning up of sin and error which is to signalize the renewal of the world.

'The coming of Christ in the flesh together with all the magnificent works which have been accomplished in him and performed in his name, the repentance of men and the turning of their wills to God, remission of sins, the gift of righteousness, the faith of the devout . . . subversion of the worship of images and demons, the testing of faith by trials, the purification of those who have persevered and their deliverance from all evil, the day of judgement, resurrection of the dead, eternal damnation of those who are associated in infidelity, eternal supremacy of the most glorious society of God and its enjoyment forever of the vision of God, all these events have been predicted and promised in the Scriptures—predictions of which we clearly see so many fulfilled that we are entitled by a proper spirit of devotion to anticipate the fulfilment of the rest.'[1]

To anticipate such a future is to believe that the values which are metaphysically and physically real are, at the same time, historically real. Inherent in the creative principle, they reveal themselves in history as the values of creative experience, as such to be progressively embodied in the consciousness of the race. That experience may, therefore, be described as the disciplining of human beings to the knowledge and love of their proper good. In this process God is the teacher, man the pupil; the prize of victory is eternal life, the penalty for failure is death, the second death or death not of the body but of the soul. That is to say, this world is a school-house, not a treadmill (*ergastulum*). And, if the trials and tribulations to which mankind is subjected appear to be harsh, their harshness is mitigated by the fact that they are imposed for no other reason than to rescue him from the abyss of inveterate sin and error, thus preparing him for the future which is in store.[2] The future thus indicated is a future of abundant life, the life of the fully integrated will; the assurance of which is contained in the promise of a better 'world to come'.

Accordingly, the millennial vision is not a myth, the unsub-

---

[1] *De Civ. Dei*, x. 32 (s).

[2] Ibid., xxi. 15. In this connexion Christianity distinguishes between physical and moral evil. On physical evil, see *Enchirid*. iii: 'Deus omnipotens . . . nullo modo sineret mali aliquid esse in operibus suis, nisi usque adeo esset omnipotens et bonus, ut bene faceret et de malo'. In the meanwhile the duty of the Christian is to follow the precept implied in John ix. 1–6. On moral evil, *De Trin.* xiii. 16. 20: it is either a call for the emendation of sin, or exercise and probation, or (finally) an indication that true felicity is not to be achieved here below.

stantial dream of a Golden Age, a lotus-land of ease and idleness which represents, at bottom, nothing but a heresy of the
conceptualizing imagination. Nor is its attainment contingent
upon the presumed activity of demonic forces, the superhuman
power of a Promethean intelligence or of a muscularity like that
of Hercules. On the contrary it is a prospect held out to human
beings, a prospect for which they are called upon to work and
fight because it constitutes the fulfilment of their humanity.

As for the validity of that promise it can hardly be questioned.
Cosmically it is, as we have seen, implied in the nature of the
creative and moving principle; historically, it has been demonstrated (1) in the life of Christ, the 'man without sin', the
mediator between God and man, and (2) in the lives of those
who, through the mediation of Christ, have apprehended the
way of salvation. In this connexion it may be noted that the
Christian doctrine of mediation is developed in sharp contrast
to pagan notions which connected it, not with a genuine incarnation of the Word, but with the existence of 'intermediate
beings', in the light of which the possibility of salvation becomes
as hypothetical as is the existence of the beings upon whom it
is made to depend.[1] We have already observed that behind
these notions there lurks the most vicious of heresies, the heresy
of two worlds, the discontinuity between which paganism seeks
by this feeble expedient to bridge. For the Christian, however,
with his faith in the existence of but one world of genuine reality
and that not archetypal but the actual world of concrete experience, it becomes true to say that the kingdom is already present
among men, if only they have the wit and the desire to see it.
That kingdom is nothing more or less than the divine society,
the congregation of the faithful, the Church in the world ('ergo
et nunc ecclesia regnum Christi regnumque sanctorum'). In
human history, therefore, the hand of God is the power of God,
and the power of God is the power of the good, i.e. of the fully
integrated will.

To see history is this light is to see the point of departure
between the two societies 'both alike enjoying temporal goods
and suffering temporal evils, but with a faith that is different,
a hope that is different, a love that is different.'[2] It is to see that
the 'disparity and contrariety' between them is one, not of

---

[1] Plato, *Symp.* 202 D: πᾶν τὸ δαιμόνιον μεταξύ ἐστι θεοῦ τε καὶ θνητοῦ.
[2] *De Civ. Dei*, xviii. 54.

nature but of will.[1] It is, moreover, to perceive that in the final and complete ascendancy of the good over the bad will is to be found the true issue of the *saeculum*. This is not a struggle to be settled by mere blows, as though the contending forces were nothing more than masses in motion. Nor is it a mere battle of abstract ideas, to be conducted in the rarefied atmosphere of the academies. What it demands is a united effort of hand and heart and head, in order to expose the fictitious character of secular valuations and to vindicate the reality of Christiàn claims. On the other hand, since it is a conflict with error and delusion, it is to be waged without rancour or bitterness, but only with pity and love. To this task the Christian militiaman is impelled by the conviction that, as Christian truth alone is genuinely salutary, its immediate acceptance is of the highest possible moment to the welfare of the race. For him, therefore, history is prophecy; i.e. its true significance lies not in the past, nor in the present, but in the future, the life of 'the world to come'. That this future should thus far have been retarded is due, not to any fault on the part of the divine schoolmaster, but solely to the blind and obstinate resistance of mankind.

[1] xi. 33.

INDEX

Academics (New Academy), 41, 164, 431.

Actium, 15.

adaptability of Roman genius, 95, 102.

Aeneid, 28, 64, 65 ff.

Alexander the Great, 8, 15; rise, 86; character, 87; aims, 88; cosmopolitanism, 89; effect of conquests, 89 f., 278.

Alexandria, 190, 258, 271, 280, 332, 340.

alimentaria, 140, 199, 220.

Ambrose of Milan, career, 347–50; belief in church's authority, 349 f.; typical Western churchman, 373; ethical teaching, 374 f.; cited or mentioned, 187, 190, 201, 325, 332, 380.

Ammianus Marcellinus: philosophy of, 311 f.; as historian, 314 ff.; limitations, 316 f.; 256, 271, 284, 288, 290, 344.

Anthony, St., *Life* of, 339 ff., 361.

Antonines, state of empire under, 137 ff., 144 f.; 'slogans' coined by, 140 f.

Antoninus Pius, 137, 139, 141.

Antony, Marc, 11 f., 13.

Apollo, 66, 68, 70, 84, 161, 274.

apotheosis: of Caesars, 25, 110; for Christians, 371 f.

Ardashir of Persia, 153.

Arian controversy, Arianism, 209 f., 233 f., 257 f., 332, 335, 340, 363.

aristocracy: republican, under Caesars, 123 ff.; imperial, 144; local, oppression of, 202, 252; frivolity of, 314 f.; 331, 353.

Aristotle: his idea of justice, 76; theory of human nature, 80 ff.; concept of the *polis*, 82 f.; defence of slavery, 84; cited, 31, 49, 74, 75, 86, 87, 103, 105, 111, 122, 141, 144, 234, 243, 368, 400, 451, 469, 478, 499, 501, 502.

Arius, 210, 218, 232 ff.; Constantine and, 249.

army: and emperor, 109, 116 f.; *curiales* in, 252 f.; Christians discouraged from, 285; recruiting in 4th cent., 297 ff., 319 f.

Arnobius Afer, 191.

astrology, 2 f., 102, 132, 158, 478; forbidden, 255, 295.

Athanasius: contra mundum, 257 f.; methods, 258 f.; Julian and 271, 284; Trinitarianism of, 361 f.; and Arians, 364 ff.; 187, 190, 339, 447.

Athens, 82 f., 472 f., 493; in Peloponnesian war, 85 f.

auctoritas, 17; of Emperor, 116 ff.

Augustan History, 173.

Augustine: tribute to Cicero, 39, to Plato, 376; Vergilian antitype of *Civitas Dei*, 71, 397; *De Moribus Ecclesiae*, 342; *De Civitate Dei*, 397 ff.
   modern estimates, 377 ff.; career, 381 f., 390; attitude to Classicism, 383 f., 400, 419, 430; *Confessions*, 386 ff.
   on stage-plays, 391; education, 392 ff.; religious development, 395 ff.; faith and reason in, 400 ff.; philosophy of, ch. xi *passim*; Trinitarianism of, 410 ff.; Christology, 416 f.; epistemology, 432 ff.; view of *sapientia*, 435 f.; on space and time, 438 f.; human will, 446 ff.; interpretation of Scripture, 474 ff.; philosophy of history, 480 f., 486, 496; disbelief in historical cycles, 483; theory of two societies, 488 f.; classification of gods, 497; on grace, 504.
   realizes limits of state action, 510; cited or mentioned, 71, 73, 150, 163, 165, 214, 218, 241, 242, 248, 344, 503.

Augustus: aims, 1, 3; success, 16 f.; constitutional position, 19 f., 108 f.; policy, 22 ff.; apotheosis, 25, 110; Vergil and, 28; and Cicero, 38, 61; permanence of his work, 74; methods, 93 f.; Livy and, 108; peace policy, 115 f.; use of censorial power, 121; problems confronting, 122 ff.; currency reform, 143; 71, 102, 201, 278.

Aurelian, 3, 152, 179.

Ausonius, 313.

'autarky', *see* self-sufficiency.

Barbarians, northern, 116, 138; invasions, 153, 297, 319, 351; conversion of, 210, 217; intermarriage with, 311, 346; Theodosius and, 344 f.; Church and, 357. *See also* Constantine, frontiers, Goths.

Basil, St., and monasticism, 341, 399.

bourgeoisie, Constantine and, 182, 202, 205.

brigandage in 4th cent., 354.

Caesarism, 115; its failure, 157.

Caesaropapism, 187, 207, 268.

Caesars, literary tradition on, 126, 129.

calendar reformed by Theodosius, 330 f.

Capitol as seat of university, 310.

Carthage, 33 f., 67, 91.

Catholicism, accepted as principle of citizenship, 328 f., 332, 334.